CW01511034

# Postmodernist and Post-Structuralist Theories of Crime

# The Library of Essays in Theoretical Criminology
*Series Editor: Stuart Henry*

**Titles in the Series:**

**Anomie, Strain and Subcultural Theories of Crime**
*Robert Agnew and Joanne M. Kaufman*

**Social Learning Theories of Crime**
*Ronald L. Akers, Christine S. Sellers and L. Thomas Winfree, Jr*

**Postmodernist and Post-Structuralist Theories of Crime**
*Bruce A. Arrigo and Dragan Milovanovic*

**Biosocial Theories of Crime**
*Kevin M. Beaver and Anthony Walsh*

**Feminist Theories of Crime**
*Meda Chesney-Lind and Merry Morash*

**Cultural Criminology**
*Jeff Ferrell and Keith Hayward*

**Psychological, Developmental and Lifecourse Theories of Crime**
*Paul Mazerolle and Tara Renae McGee*

**Rational Choice, Situational Choice and Routine Activities Theories of Crime**
*Mangai Natarajan*

**Theories of Social Control and Self-Control**
*Joseph H. Rankin and L. Edward Wells*

**Social, Ecological and Environmental Theories of Crime**
*Jeffery T. Walker*

# Postmodernist and Post-Structuralist Theories of Crime

*Edited by*

## Bruce A. Arrigo
*University of North Carolina at Charlotte, USA*

and

## Dragan Milovanovic
*Northeastern Illinois University, USA*

ASHGATE

Published by
Ashgate Publishing Limited
Wey Court East
Union Road
Farnham
Surrey GU9 7PT
England

Ashgate Publishing Company
Suite 420
101 Cherry Street
Burlington
VT 05401-4405
USA

www.ashgate.com

**British Library Cataloguing in Publication Data**
Postmodernist and post-structuralist theories of crime. –
   (The library of essays in theoretical criminology)
   1. Criminology. 2. Criminal behavior. 3. Criminal
   psychology.
   I. Series II. Arrigo, Bruce A. III. Milovanovic, Dragan,
   1948-
   364-dc22

**Library of Congress Control Number**: 2010921163


ISBN 9780754629276

**Mixed Sources**
Product group from well-managed
forests and other controlled sources
www.fsc.org Cert no. SGS-COC-2482
© 1996 Forest Stewardship Council
FSC

Printed and bound in Great Britain by
TJ International Ltd, Padstow, Cornwall

# Contents

*Acknowledgements*                                                                                    *vii*

*Series Preface*                                                                                        *ix*

*Introduction*                                                                                          *xi*

## PART I  THEORETICAL DEVELOPMENTS AND INTEGRATIONS

1  Stuart Henry and Dragan Milovanovic (1991), 'Constitutive Criminology: The
   Maturation of Critical Theory', *Criminology*, **29**, pp. 293–316.                                   3
2  Bruce A. Arrigo (1995), 'The Peripheral Core of Law and Criminology: On
   Postmodern Social Theory and Conceptual Integration', *Justice Quarterly*, **12**,
   pp. 447–72.                                                                                          27
3  Dragan Milovanovic (1996), 'Postmodern Criminology: Mapping the Terrain',
   *Justice Quarterly*, **13**, pp. 567–610.                                                            53
4  Bruce A. Arrigo, Dragan Milovanovic and Robert C. Schehr (2000), 'The French
   Connection: Implications for Law, Crime, and Social Justice', *Humanity and Society*,
   **24**, pp. 162–203.                                                                                 97

## PART II  CRITICAL APPLICATIONS IN LAW, CRIME, JUSTICE AND SOCIAL CHANGE

5  Jamie Murray (2006), 'Nome Law: Deleuze and Guattari on the Emergence of
   Law', *International Journal for the Semiotics of Law*, **19**, pp. 127–51.                          141
6  Jeffery T. Walker (2007), 'Advancing Science and Research in Criminal Justice/
   Criminology: Complex Systems Theory and Non-Linear Analyses',
   *Justice Quarterly*, **24**, pp. 555–81.                                                            167
7  George Pavlich (1996), 'The Power of Community Mediation: Government and
   Formation of Self-Identity', *Law and Society Review*, **30**, pp. 707–33.                          195
8  T.R. Young (1992), 'Chaos Theory and Human Agency: Humanist Sociology in a
   Postmodern Era', *Humanity and Society*, **16**, pp. 441–60.                                        223

## PART III  TRANSFORMATIONAL ANALYSES AND MARGINALIZED IDENTITIES

9  Robert Carl Schehr (2000), 'From Restoration to Transformation: Victim–
   Offender Mediation as Transformative Justice', *Mediation Quarterly*, **18**,
   pp. 151–69.                                                                                         245
10  Nancy A. Wonders (1997), 'Determinate Sentencing: A Feminist and Postmodern
   Story', *Justice Quarterly,* **13**, pp. 611–48.                                                    265

11  Christopher R. Williams (1998), 'The Abrogation of Subjectivity in the
    Psychiatric Courtroom: Toward a Psychoanalytic Semiotic Analysis',
    *International Journal for the Semitics of Law*, **11**, pp. 181–92.                    303

12  Mary Bosworth (2007), 'Creating the Responsible Prisoner: Federal Admission
    and Orientation Packs', *Punishment and Society*, **9**, pp. 67–85.                     315

13  Mark Halsey (2004), 'Against "Green" Criminology', *British Journal of
    Criminology*, **44**, pp. 833–53.                                                      335

**PART IV  INTERNATIONAL, TRANSNATIONAL AND POST-NATIONAL
          DIRECTIONS**

14  Susan S. Silbey (1996), '"Let Them Eat Cake": Globalization, Postmodern
    Colonialism, and the Possibilites of Justice', *Law and Society Review*, **31**,
    pp. 207–35.                                                                            359

15  Ronnie Lippens (1998), 'Alternatives to What Kind of Suffering? Towards a
    Border-crossing Criminology', *Theoretical Criminology*, **2**, pp. 311–43.            389

16  Gregg Barak (2007), 'Doing Newsmaking Criminology from within the
    Academy', *Theoretical Criminology*, **11**, pp. 191–207.                              423

**PART V  POSTMODERN AND POST-STRUCTURAL CRIMINOLOGY AND ITS
         INTERLOCUTORS**

17  Joel F. Handler (1992), 'Postmodernism, Protest, and the New Social Movement',
    *Law and Society Review*, **26**, pp. 697–731.                                         443

18  Martin D. Schwartz and David O. Friedrichs (1994), 'Postmodern Thought
    and Criminological Discontent: New Metaphors for Understanding Violence',
    *Criminology*, **32**, pp. 221–46.                                                     479

*Name Index*                                                                               505

# Acknowledgements

The editor and publishers wish to thank the following for permission to use copyright material.

American Society of Criminology for the essays: Stuart Henry and Dragan Milovanovic (1991), 'Constitutive Criminology: The Maturation of Critical Theory', *Criminology*, **29**, pp. 293–316. Copyright © 1991 American Society of Criminology; Martin D. Schwartz and David O. Friedrichs (1994), 'Postmodern Thought and Criminological Discontent: New Metaphors for Understanding Violence', *Criminology*, **32**, pp. 221–46. Copyright © 1994 American Society of Criminology.

Humanity and Society for the essays: Bruce A. Arrigo, Dragan Milovanovic and Robert C. Schehr (2000), 'The French Connection: Implications for Law, Crime, and Social Justice', *Humanity and Society*, **24**, pp. 163–203; T.R. Young (1992), 'Chaos Theory and Human Agency: Humanist Sociology in a Postmodern Era', *Humanity and Society*, **16**, pp. 441–60.

John Wiley and Sons for the essays: George Pavlich (1996), 'The Power of Community Mediation: Government and Formation of Self-Identity', *Law and Society Review*, **30**, pp. 707–33. Copyright © 1996 The Law and Society Association; Robert Carl Schehr (2000), 'From Restoration to Transformation: Victim Offender Mediation as Transformative Justice', *Mediation Quarterly*, **18**, pp. 151–69. Copyright © 2000 Josse-Bass; Susan S. Silbey (1996), '"Let Them Eat Cake": Globalization, Postmodern Colonialism, and the Possibilites of Justice', *Law and Society Review*, **31**, pp. 207–35. Copyright © 1997 The Law and Society Association; Joel F. Handler (1992), 'Postmodernism, Protest, and the New Social Movement', *Law and Society Review*, **26**, pp. 697–731. Copyright © 1992 The Law and Society Association.

Oxford University Press for the essay: Mark Halsey (2004), 'Against "Green" Criminology', *British Journal of Criminology*, **44**, pp. 833–53. Copyright © 2004 the Centre for Crime and Justice Studies.

Sage Publications for the essays: Mary Bosworth (2007), 'Creating the Responsible Prisoner: Federal Admission and Orientation Packs', *Punishment and Society*, **9**, pp. 67–85. Copyright © 2007 Sage Publications; Ronnie Lippens (1998), 'Alternatives to What Kind of Suffering? Towards a Border-crossing Criminology', *Theoretical Criminology*, **2**, pp. 311–43. Copyright © 1998 Sage Publications; Gregg Barak (2007), 'Doing Newsmaking Criminology from within the Academy', *Theoretical Criminology*, **11**, pp. 191–207. Copyright © 2007 Sage Publications.

Springer Science and Business Media for the essays: Jamie Murray (2006), 'Nome Law: Deleuze and Guattari on the Emergence of Law', *International Journal for the Semiotics of Law*, **19**, pp. 127–51. Copyright © 2006 Springer Science and Business Media; Christopher

# Series Preface

Because of its pervasive nature in our mass mediated culture, many believe they are experts in understanding the reasons why offenders violate the law. Parents and schools come high on the public's list of who to blame for crime. Not far behind are governments and legal systems that are believed to be ineffective at deterring offenders – too many legal protections and too few serious sentences. Some learn how to behave inappropriately as children, while others are said to choose crime because of its apparent high reward/low cost opportunity structure. Yet others hang out with the wrong crowd, or live in the wrong neighborhood, or work for the wrong corporation, and may get their kicks from disobeying rules in the company of like-minded others. A few are seen as evil, insane or just plain stupid. While such popular representations of the causes of crime contain glimpses of the criminological reality, understanding why people commit crime is a much more complex matter. Indeed, for this reason the quest to establish the causes of crime has been one of the most elusive searches confronting humankind.

Since the mid-19th century, following the advent of Charles Darwin's *The Origin of Species*, those who sought scientific knowledge to understand crime abandoned philosophical speculation and economic reductionism. In its place they founded the multifaceted interdisciplinary field of criminology. Unlike criminal law and legal theory that explored the logic of prohibitions against offensive behavior, and in contrast to criminal justice that examined the nature and extent of societies' responses to crime through systems of courts, police and penology, criminology's central focus is the systematic examination of the nature, extent and causes of crime. Criminological theory as a subset of criminology, comprises the cluster of explanation seeking to identify the causes or etiology of crime. This *Library of Essays in Theoretical Criminology* is designed to capture the range and depth of the key theoretical perspectives on crime causation.

While there are numerous criminological theories, most can be clustered into 10 or 12 theoretical perspectives. Moreover, each of these broad theoretical frameworks is, itself, rooted in a major academic discipline. The most predominant disciplines influencing criminological theory include: economics, anthropology, biology, psychology, geography, sociology, politics, history, philosophy, as well as the more recent multi-disciplinary fields such as gender studies, critical race studies and postmodernist social theory.

Criminological theories are rarely discrete. Although they often emphasize a particular disciplinary field, they also draw on aspects of other disciplines to strengthen their explanatory power. Indeed, since 1989 a major development in criminological theory has been the emergence of explicitly integrative theoretical approaches (See Gregg Barak, *Integrative Criminology*; Ashgate, 1998). Integrative/interdisciplinary approaches bring together several theories into a comprehensive explanation, usually to address different levels of analysis; these range from the micro-individual and relational approaches common in biology and psychology, to the meso-level institutional explanations that feature in sociological analysis, to the macro-level geographical, political, cultural and historical approaches that deal with societal and global structures and patterns. Recent developments in criminological theory have seen an acceleration of this trend compared with that of single disciplinary explanations of crime (See Stuart Henry and Scott Lukas, *Recent Developments in Criminological Theory*; Ashgate, 2009).

Although there are now over 20 English-language criminological theory textbooks and numerous edited compilations, there is a need to make available to an international audience a series of books that brings together the best of the available theoretical contributions. The advantage of doing this as a series, rather than a single volume, is that the editors are able to mine the field for the most relevant essays that have influenced the present state of knowledge. Each contribution to the series thus contains many chapters, each on a different aspect of the same theoretical approach to crime causation.

In creating this series I have selected outstanding criminologists whose own theories are discussed as part of the literature and I have asked each of them to select a set of the best journal essays to represent the various facets of their theoretical framework. In doing so, I believe that you will receive the best selection of essays available together with an insightful and comparative overview placing each essay in the context of the history of ideas that comprises our search to better understand and explain crime and those who commit it.

STUART HENRY
*Series Editor*
*School of Public Affairs*
*San Diego State University, USA*

# Introduction*

## Overview

This volume highlights a representative sampling of postmodernist-inspired theoretical advances, emphasizing their relevance for and application to criminology. We classify the previously published essays assembled in this volume into five major sections, reflecting some shared but nevertheless evocative themes. At the outset, we acknowledge the significant contribution each essay has made in furthering the 'discursive turn' in crime, law and justice studies. However, unlike more conventional introductions, we want to be consistent with 'critical criminology' and offer a schema for a critical ('writerly') reading (Barthes, 1968) of the texts found in this collection.[1]

---

\* This introduction intends to draw the reader's attention to the seminal ideas, struggles and luminaries that have formed (and continue to form) the heterodoxy of postmodernism and post-structuralism. As such, the introduction represents a flash of light, a poetic spark and a molecular line of flight. The volume's contributing essays reflect this experimental and innovative orientation but through targeted criminological investigations in law, punishment, community and social change. The introduction, as an incomplete and mutating force/flow, proposes how (criminological) rigidities, singularities, categories and axiomatics emerge, take up residence in a socius and can be overcome. This is a nomadic journey, a will to power, for a people yet to come. The works that we consult provide the intellectual wherewithal for undertaking this permanent revolution and they are listed at the end of the introduction for the reader's consideration. Throughout the prose, we strategically (and modestly) insert in-text citations, indicating the works from which we draw intellectual support and pragmatic guidance. Our purpose here is twofold: (1) to allow the introduction's narrative to speak, resonate and evolve as a departure (rather than arrival) in meaning; (2) to clearly indicate our indebtedness to those authors whose path-breaking insights have inspired our own journey, our own becoming, as researchers, teachers, mentors and activists.

[1] Canvassing the intellectual history of postmodernist and post-structuralist thought – including their respective relevances for criminology – is decidedly beyond the scope of this volume's brief introduction. However, three 'waves' of influential research are discernible in the extant literature. The first of these includes key luminaries such as Jacques Lacan, Gilles Deleuze, Felix Guattari, Julia Kristeva, Michel Foucault, Jean-François Lyotard, Luce Irigaray, Roland Barthes, Helene Cixous, Jacques Derrida and Jean Baudrillard. Their individual and collective insights ushered in a novel agenda for re-conceiving the human agency – social structure mutuality. These critics demonstrated where and how the modernist project often unwittingly advanced an oppressive and alienating teleology, especially within the realms of culture, science, consumerism and politics. The second wave of postmodernist and post-structuralist thought sustained this philosophical foray in rethinking the discursive dimensions of the self/society duality. Initially, this included a more sceptical and pessimistic strain of discontent in which relativism, fatalism and nihilism prevailed. Building on Hegel's reaction–negation dynamic and his master–slave dialectic, the more conservative postmodernist assessment maintained that 'the absence of any grounded reality or agreed upon social contract impli[ed] that progress, change, and justice [were] merely a part of an illusory nonreality that signifi[ed] our fragile and fictionalized existences' (Arrigo, Milovanovic

Accordingly, in order to identify some commonalities and propose a number of directions for future analyses, this introduction is divided into three parts. First, we present our classificatory schema with five interrelated sets of foci. The operation of this schema as a 'cut' of *réalité* (Lacan, 1977) is then outlined.[2] Next, we summarily indicate how the constituents of our schema may be productively employed to 'read' this volume's compilation of essays. Finally, we conclude by briefly recommending the development of a multidimensional schema composed of three interacting planes: (1) the primordial, (2) the *réalité*, and (3) the transcendental (PRT). As we provisionally demonstrate, the suggested multidimensional schema raises several innovative, though certainly pragmatic, questions about the ontological, epistemological, ethical and aesthetical grounding of criminology's dynamic potential and corresponding molecular revolution.[3]

### Critical ('Writerly') Schema

Our critical writerly schema for reading the assembled essays as texts evolves from our book *Revolution in Penology: Rethinking the Society of Captives* (Arrigo and Milovanovic, 2009). Its central argument functions at both the level of mediation and the level of metaphor. As meditation, we critiqued the prison as a concept, structure and institutional form, and examined the harm that it recursively enacts through extant correctional philosophies, principles and practices. This is harm that reduces/represses the human agency/social structure dialectic in ways that are consistent with the culture of control, the normalization of violence and the

---

and Schehr, 2005, p. 36). In response, an affirmative and transformative perspective was (and still is) emerging. This perspective, traceable in part to Nietzsche's view of the master–slave dialectic, indicated how alienated and oppressed individuals or collectives could affirmatively and actively speak about and act upon their needs, beliefs and desires without instantiating the values of the master. When articulated as such, this 'overcoming' contains within it visions of the possible that help to liberate the self/society mutuality from (rather than condemn it to) its dislocated, fragmented and undecidable condition. The works of Ernesto Laclau, Chantal Mouffe, Judith Butler, Pierre Bourdieu, Anthony Giddens, Henri Giroux, Drucilla Cornell and Roberto Unger are especially noteworthy. The third wave continues the tradition of affirmative postmodernist thought. The essays assembled in this volume represent important criminological contributions that demonstrate how to undertake affirmative postmodern analyses as well as how to generate conceptual integrations of the same. These ongoing efforts at 'border crossing' (from the physical sciences to the social sciences, from the life sciences to the humanities) reflect the breadth and depth of the first wave's continued relevance, and suggest innovative and experimental research directions in law, crime and justice studies.

    [2]    By *réalité* we refer to a phenomenology of the present; the taken-for-granted perceived world 'as is'. This is a multifaceted sphere of sociopolitical comprehension that is historically situated and linguistically derived (see Lacan, 1977).

    [3]    As we subsequently indicate, the 'molecular' is the realm of potentialities, mutation, change and transformation. The molecular is the locus of overcoming axiomatics, categories and singularities that would otherwise reduce/repress the individual to fixed, static and rigid identities. These identities (especially including race, gender and class dynamics and their intersectionalities) are more 'molar' in composition as they set limits to one's being and impose constraints on one's becoming. The molecular, then, is the domain of transpraxis where the human subject's will to power, as an emergent, transcends in non-hierarchical, historically specific though manifest form such predictable and stable regularities (Deleuze and Guattari, 1983, 1987; Nietzsche, 1966, 1968).

'criminological shadow'. This shadow generates and sustains harm that sets limits to one's being (the recovering subject) and imposes barriers to one's becoming (the transforming subject). The criminological shadow extends its harm from the kept to their keepers, from their managers to their watchers. All are held captive by the imagery, language and logic that essentializes prison. This captivity as violence is unwittingly deemed healthy, normal and inevitable, as *réalité*.

As metaphor, however, *Revolution in Penology* draws attention to those co-productive and interdependent spheres of influence that form the socius (society + I + us)[4] engulfing the self/society mutuality such that the culture of control endures panoptically. This is a culture in which the 'digital self' (Baudrillard, 1983), the simulation of surveillance (Foucault, 1973), the sedimentation of system-reinforcing narratives (Derrida, 1977, 1978) and the psycho-dynamically derived political-economic forces that nurture and sustain them all (Fromm, 1994) are reciprocally and simultaneously reified and, through this process, legitimized. This is a culture wherein citizenship is reconstituted politically, sociologically and psychologically. And it is here, within this realm of re-ontologizing the self and re-epistemologizing the social, that the dark ethic of the criminological shadow is given birth (Arrigo and Milovanovic, 2009).[5]

Our 'cut' of *réalité* integrates disparate postmodern and post-structural approaches within a temporary and incomplete commonality. We term this a critical writerly schema, a Poincaré section or cut of sorts that reveals an underlying, though incomplete and temporary, structure (Poincaré, 2002). By *réalité* we suggest, following Jacques Lacan (1977), a phenomenology of the present, a political-economic and cultural-historical representation of perceived reality. Moreover, following Foucault (1970), *réalité* is a normalized and disciplinary power/ knowledge construction that is constitutive of everyday existence; the world lived *as is* without critical examination of its wherewithal and its potential mutational possibilities. Many cuts can be usefully employed, each shedding some light on the material under examination. It goes without saying that the strengths of our schematized *réalité* also convey some limitations in that with each cut some nuanced analysis may not be sufficiently incorporated. Nevertheless, Poincaré cuts provide a multitude of schemas with which to critically orient our reading. As outlined below, our initial cut is rooted more in a Hegelian (1955, 1998) *réalité* constituted by lack. However, in this introduction's final section, we resituate our cut within a more

---

[4] Our neologism borrows from Deleuze and Guattari's notion of the 'socius' (1983, 1987) rather than the idea of a social formation. Thus, the interdependent and interrelated facets of the socius are porus, ambulant and mutating rather than fixed, static and permanent. This rendition is consistent with Bauman's notion of liquid identity/sociality (2000), and it is a mutating process through which stasis, repetition and 'capture' can be overcome.

[5] The ethic of the criminological shadow (and its counterpart, the ethic of the criminological stranger) refers to the dialectics of the self/society mutuality and the interdependent and co-productive forces that sustain it. These forces extend from the symbolic to the linguistic, from the material to the cultural. The conditions under which these forces are mobilized and activated (for example as 'lack' or as overcoming lack, as negative or as positive freedom) yield a certain moral philosophy about the nature of knowing (in law, crime and/or justice). This ethic either reduces/represses the human agency– social structure duality (the shadow) – or liberates this mutuality from such limit-setting always already in provisional, positional and relational contexts (the stranger).

**Figure 1 The critical writerly schema as *réalité*: the socius and its five interrelated sets of foci**

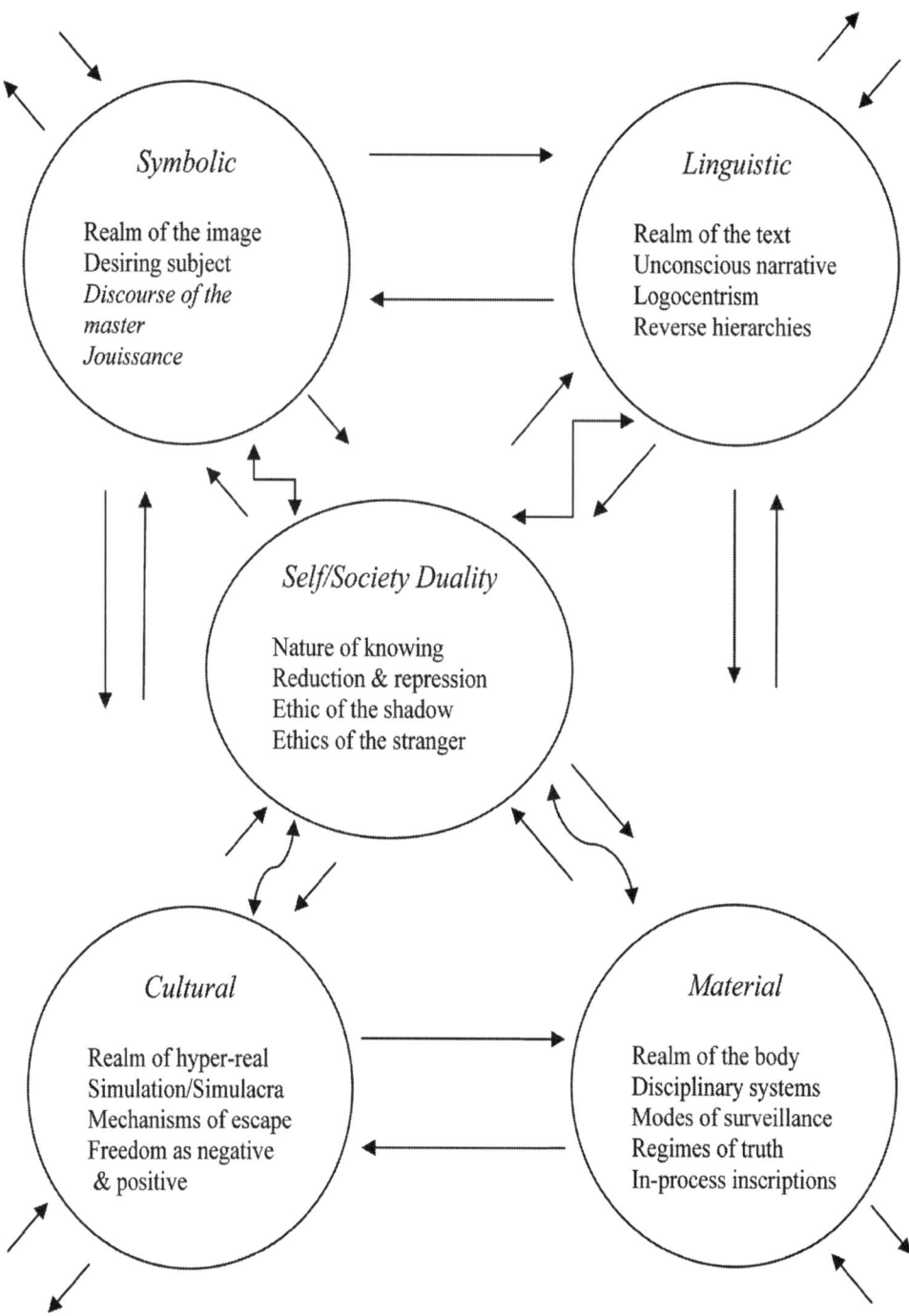

*Symbolic*

Realm of the image
Desiring subject
*Discourse of the master*
*Jouissance*

*Linguistic*

Realm of the text
Unconscious narrative
Logocentrism
Reverse hierarchies

*Self/Society Duality*

Nature of knowing
Reduction & repression
Ethic of the shadow
Ethics of the stranger

*Cultural*

Realm of hyper-real
Simulation/Simulacra
Mechanisms of escape
Freedom as negative
& positive

*Material*

Realm of the body
Disciplinary systems
Modes of surveillance
Regimes of truth
In-process inscriptions

Nietzschean (1966, 1968) framework constituted by the overcoming of lack that seeds and nurtures a transpraxis.

Our critical schema in this book is composed of five contiguous spheres that form the relations of co-production (see Figure 1). Co-production refers to the self/society constitutive mutuality that is reciprocally and simultaneously replicated (for example the nature and method of knowing in crime and justice; the character of truth and the quality of ethic such knowing endorses) (Giddens, 1984; Henry and Milovanovic, 1996). Moving in a clockwise direction and beginning with the upper left-hand corner, these spheres include (1) the symbolic (what images abound in the unconscious?), (2) the linguistic (what narratives do these images construct and for whom do these texts speak?), (3) the material (what 'bodies' of knowledge are manufactured and inscribed within and throughout the self/society constitutive mutuality?), and (4) the cultural (which inscriptions are replicated/propagated?). Situated within each sphere are several pivotal dimensions that help to specify the culture of control and the ethic of the shadow it therefore spawns.

We note further that each sphere extends through, and is affected by a fifth, namely, the self/society constitutive mutuality. This is the realm from which desire as lack (Lacan, 1977) seeks recognition notwithstanding the culture of control, and to which the boundedness of subjectivity and discourse (desire) is mobilized as an incomplete text given the extant relations that interactively co-produce the socius. Each of the four spheres interacts with the others, and with a fifth. This movement conveys the constitutive and porous nature of the postmodern condition, expressed through the mutuality of the human agency–social structure nexus.

Additionally, the spheres in each of the four regions (that is upper-left, upper-right, lower-right and lower-left) contribute to the composition of the others, and likewise each is co-shaped by the others. This is what it means to speak of the mutually constitutive nature of the culture of control. As a reactive and molar line of flight (Deleuze and Guattari, 1983, 1987), this movement produces linear, predictable and static values or equilibrium conditions. As an active and molecular line of flight, this movement recognizes that minor inputs (for example in images, texts, inscriptions or replications) can produce disproportionate and disruptive effects consistent with non-linear, unpredictable and fluid values or far-from-equilibrium conditions (for example Briggs and Peat, 1989; Prigogine and Stengers, 1984).

Prospects for an active energy flow (Deleuze and Guattari, 1983, 1987) (for example a radicalized version of justice; the ethic of the stranger), rather than a reactive energy flow (for example system-sustaining logic and rhetoric; the ethic of the shadow), depend on the frequency, duration, intensity and critical timing of the socius, forces impinging on and affected by the self/society duality. Thus, the dialectical nature of the human agency–social structure mutuality emerges as a synthesis from these interactive and constitutive energy flows. Specifying the emergent ethic of the stranger, then, entails the identification of symbolic, linguistic, material and cultural constituents, to and from which the self/society constituted mutuality can be dialectically re-established. The strategies of deterritorialization and reterritorialization facilitate this undertaking (Deleuze and Guattari 1983, 1987).[6]

---

[6] We see *réalité*, the socius, as being constituted by the continuous clash of static forces (reactive, molar) and dynamic change (active, molecular). Informing this perspective is the inspirational theoretical work of Nietzsche (1966, 1968), Spinoza (1991), Deleuze and Guattari (1983, 1987) and Foucault (1973, 1977). Additionally, more recent and stimulating applications by Dyer-Witheford (1999) and Hardt and Negri (2009) extend and deepen the conceptual analyses.

Deterritorialization (the undoing of political economic and historically situated forces) involves dismantling the vanquishing of difference. Examples of more reactive, molar forces constituting stasis, repetition and equilibrium conditions, include the sanitization of speech vis-à-vis the *discourse of the master* (Lacan, 1977), the normalization of identity by way of logocentrism (Derrida, 1977)[7] and panopticism (Foucault, 1973), the stabilization of knowledge through disciplinary systems (Foucault, 1977), the pathologization of self-organization anchored in regimes of truth (Foucault, 1970) and the homogenization of community through the simulations/simulacra of hyper-reality (that is, a virtual non-reality) (Baudrillard, 1983a). Reterritorialization (developing new articulation of forces in more active directions) entails cultivating dynamic, rhizomatic and non-linear lines of flight. Examples of these emergent co-productions include replacement forms of consciousness that retrieve the subject from its status of lack or not-all as *jouissance* (that is, the excess) and the development of innovative, more dynamic and processual master signifiers that resist closure (Lacan, 1977); new vistas of meaning in which hierarchies are reversed temporarily so that binary terms/values can thrive interdependently rather than oppositionally (Derrida, 1977, 1978); novel, in-process inscriptions that transcend and transform the body's simulated surveillance (Kristeva, 1984); actualization of the many potentialities that a body possesses (Cornell, 1991, 1998); desire not based on lack, but more in keeping with continuous, active transformations of forces (Cornell, 1993), along with an ethic of the Other constituted in a reciprocal ongoing relationship (Levinas, 2004); and alternative multimedia-based cultural re-presentations that displace the digital self, carnival capitalism, mechanisms of escape, social/systemic pathology and negative freedom (Arrigo and Milovanovic, 2009; Arrigo, Milovanovic and Schehr, 2005).

These efforts at disassembling and reassembling the human agency–social structure mutuality inform and are shaped by an evolving socius, a particular form of society, along with its organizing spheres of influence. This is how reason, method and truth are constituted within the postmodern and post-structural perspectives. This is how the ethic of the stranger as transpraxis mutates, positionally, relationally and provisionally. This *is* the molecular revolution for a people yet to come!

**Postmodern and Post-structural Criminology: Applications**

Part I of this volume focuses on the intellectual history of postmodern and post-structural criminology (PPC). This includes several seminal essays that demonstrate the scope of novel theorizing and integrative analyses encompassing the evolving PPC landscape. Of particular focus are prominent themes emanating from (1) constitutive theory; (2) chaos, complexity and topology theory; (3) psychoanalytic semiotics; (4) deconstructionism; (5) discourse analysis and dialogical pedagogy; and (6) rhizomatics and schizoanalysis (for the latter, see Deleuze and Guattari, 1987).

---

[7]    Derrida (1977, 1978) critiques the history of Western thought, arguing that it celebrates (knowingly or otherwise) logocentrism. Logocentrism refers to terms in binary opposition in which the first value (for example white, male, young, objective) is privileged and made present while the second value (for example black, female, old, subjective) is postponed and made absent. He argues that both terms/values mutually depend on one another to more completely communicate meaning and to establish new or alternative sense-making possibilities (in crime, law and justice).

In Chapter 1 Stuart Henry and Dragan Milovanovic draw attention to the self/society constitutive duality and the molar, reactive forces that sustain crime through an ideology that ignores the importance of non-reflexive control discourse in co-producing that which it seeks to negate. Through their excessive investments in the logic and language of crime (that is, ideology), human agents co-produce crime-based philosophies, principles, practices and behaviour as concrete realities. Our critical writerly schema amplifies how these static lines of flight, as harms of reduction/repression, are repetitively and cyclically re-enacted in the socius for all those who participate in this reification process that essentializes crime. Intersecting and overlapping symbolic, linguistic, material and cultural sets of foci act upon and are shaped by the human agency–social structure dialectic, thereby contributing to the culture of control, the normalization of violence and the ethic of the shadow.

Chapter 2, by Bruce Arrigo, problematizes several reified and taken-for-granted modernist social constructions (for example role formation, the structure of society, knowledge acquisition and causality and change) as appropriated in law and criminology. Several fluid, non-linear and dynamic reconceptualizations for each are proposed based on selected insights derived from postmodern, post-structural and semiotic theory. These insights suggest the possibility of realizing provisional, positional and relational manifestations of justice in keeping with legal and criminological transpraxis. Our critical writerly schema, our cut of *réalité*, further specifies how the modernist framework of lack, repetition, stasis and closure, reciprocally and simultaneously repeats itself through sedimented images, texts, inscriptions and reproductions. These molar, homeostatic and reactive intensities/flows reduce/repress the transformational potentials of law and criminology.

Dragan Milovanovic, in Chapter 3, develops an affirmative postmodern criminology based principally on the methodological and conceptual tools of chaology, catastrophe theory and topological mathematics. A number of suggestions for furthering transformational and rhizomatic lines of flight are proposed, informed by Lacanian psychoanalytic semiotics. Our cut of *réalité* indicates both the sources and the effects from and to which possible emergents may take up residence in the socius, consistent with a reciprocal ethic of the Other. This is a will to power that resists axiomatics, overcomes lack and embraces the liberating potential of alterity, ambiguity, contradiction and spontaneity. The stranger's (criminological) journey is to molecularly re-conceive, re-tell, re-inscribe and re-propagate the self/society constitutive dialectic and its interrelated sets of foci.

In Chapter 4 Bruce Arrigo, Dragan Milovanovic and Robert Schehr integrate several affirmative postmodern theoretical, methodological and analytical insights that advance criminology's dynamic potential for humanistic change. Contributions from Lacan, Derrida, Barthes, Kristeva, Irigaray, Baudrillard, Foucault, Deleuze and Guattari, Cixous, and Lyotard inform the analysis. Our critical writerly schema builds on these observations demonstrating how the reactive and molar forces constituting the criminological shadow conceal and forestall the evolving rediscovery of crime, law and social justice.

Part II applies the conceptual and methodological insights of postmodern and post-structural criminology to topical concerns in law, crime, justice and social change. This includes both stand-alone and synthetic analyses. Specific issues explored include (1) law and a Deleuzian-inspired transformative justice; (2) criminal justice/criminological research informed by non-linear analyses and complexity theory; (3) community mediation, governmentality and the Foucauldian construction of the human subject (that is the subject of legal decision-making);

and (4) the relevance of chaos theory for liberating human agency and promoting social change.

In Chapter 5 Jamie Murray proposes an integration of Deleuze and Guattari's pragmatic semiotics with a theory of emergence and complexity as applied to law. This integration is suggestive for developing a noological (the study of images of thought) legal theory at far-from-equilibrium conditions that re-conceives law's origins, genealogy and ontological/ epistemological grounding. Our critical writerly schema sensitizes the reader to law's manufactured images and convenient fictions (for example the juridic subject, the reasonable man/women standard, interest-balancing), and the bodies of knowledge that the law therefore instantiates and replicates. Within this over-arching framework, the self/society dialectic and its interrelated sets of foci always already are engulfed in limit (and point) attractors whose disciplinary normalization provides choices for legal theorizing and decision-making. However, these choices are circumscribed by the noology out of which these illusions are conceived and given genealogical signification.

Jeffery Walker, in Chapter 6, utilizes complex systems science as a basis to engage in criminological analysis, especially in the context of recasting criminology's approach to, or modelling of, neighbourhood crime research. Termed 'ecodynamic' theory, error data otherwise discarded in linear cause–effect modes of positivist inquiry are recognized for their potential to further explain fluctuations in crime at the neighbourhood level. Thus Walker proposes that in ecodynamic theory the same factors producing non-criminal behaviour at one point in the system can produce criminal behaviour at other points (p. 167). Our cut of *réalité* indicates how positivist science, as a rigid, fixed and closed system of communication, is consistent with Lacan's concept of the *discourse of the master* and the narrative of logocentrism. As a disciplinary system, the regime of reductionistic truth that science reiterates proliferates through hyper-real significations (for example actuarial modelling, simulation studies and evidence-based analyses). As such, the self/society mutuality reproduces *ad infinitum* crime ideology that cannot account for, and does not make a space for, 'noise in the system' (for example statistical anomalies, outliers, alternative renditions of criminological *verstehen*). This is how the culture of control, the normalization of violence and the ethic of the shadow endure panoptically in a molar socius.

In Chapter 7 George Pavlich demonstrates how conflict mediation and dispute resolution programmes 'domesticate' self-identities much like the power of a confessional dialogue. This occurs when the state's system-reinforcing language and totalizing logic of responsibility, recovery, reconciliation and restitution is advanced. However, governmentally conceived (and static) notions of 'offenders', 'victims', 'community', 'harm' and 'healing' impose limits to one's being (recovery) and foster denials of one's becoming (transformation). Our critical writerly schema indicates how the process of normalizing (reducing/repressing) identity construction is sustained for the kept, their keepers, their managers and their watchers. Docility, negative freedom and the subject as lack abound for one and all through the images, texts, inscriptions and replications the state manufactures within and throughout the homogenized mediation exchange.

A vision of postmodern humanism informed by the insights of chaos theory and complex systems science is put forward by T. R. Young in Chapter 8. Social change and the possibilities of justice emerge at far-from-equilibrium conditions, through dissipative structures and with strange (rather than limit/point) attractors. Our cut of *réalité* shows how the duality that is the self/society constitutive dialectic cannot realize its transformative potential through a molecular revolution, given the construction of the socius as steeped in molar, reactive forces or linear lines of flight. In order to more fully realize this liberating potential, the intersecting and overlapping sets of foci – from the symbolic to the linguistic, from the material to the cultural – must be noological, reconceived, always and already in provisional, positional and relational ways. This is a socius for a people yet to come.

In Part III the focus is on postmodern and post-structural criminological applications to law, crime, justice and social change with an emphasis on transformational analyses as well as a concern for marginalized identities. One of the central features of PPC is its intention to develop strategies for inclusiveness that acknowledge and celebrate excluded voices without fostering reversal of hierarchies or hate politics (for example extreme forms of political correctness). Specific themes delineated through the essays in this section include (1) victim–offender mediation as transformative justice; (2) the integration of feminist and postmodern inquiry as a basis to re-conceive the determinate sentencing of women; (3) the construction of the human subject in the psychiatric courtroom based on psychoanalytic semiotics; (4) prisonization discourse that reduces/represses the identities of incarcerates; and (5) heterodox reasoning in environmental crime and its regulation.

In Chapter 9 Robert Schehr extends the analysis of victim–offender mediation from the governmentally controlled, limit-setting narrative of restorative justice to the participant-centred emancipatory potential of transformative justice. Our critical writerly schema amplifies how the former approach advances the ethic of the criminological shadow, and the latter strategy furthers the ethic of the criminological stranger. The socius is composed of static forces (reactive, molar) and dynamic change (active, molecular). However, the various co-productive and interactive spheres of influence that constitute it are in perpetual struggle. Victim–offender mediation is but one social formation within which these forces are at play. The schizoanalytics of deterritorialization and reterritorialization help to resist static singularities (in identity construction, meaning-making and reconciliation) and to usher in nomadic emergents (becomings, potentialities, mutations) for all participants.

Nancy Wonders, in Chapter 10, integrates feminist and postmodern theorizing as a basis to reconceptualize the determinate sentencing of women. By focusing on several dimensions of narrativity (the deconstruction of objectivity, the celebration of process, the ambulant construction of identity and the mutuality of power), determinate sentencing (for women) is interpreted as a crisis of the imagination. Our critical writerly schema extends and deepens this reasoning. Women exist as lack (*pas toute*) or 'not-all' in the phallocentric Symbolic Order. This desire, when spoken as an unconscious (though embodied) text promotes a regime of truth. When these truths are recursively replicated and panoptically reified – especially by way of the metaphysics of presence – the masculine over the feminine prevails (for example objectivity defers subjectivity, homeostatic identities displace dynamic identities, power as consumption/accumulation postpones power as production/transformation). Given these molar and reactive energy flows/forces, the self/society constitutive duality cannot conceive of women except in their absences.

In Chapter 11 Christopher Williams explores the dialectics of linguistic struggle for users of mental health services channelled to and from the psychiatric courtroom. Drawing from psychoanalytic semiotics, the human subject's standing as 'lack' is problematized. Our cut of *réalité* embodying our configuration of the socius indicates how the interdependent spheres of the symbolic, linguistic, material and cultural sustain and legitimize this struggle through the self/society constitutive duality. To speak in the psychiatric courtroom is to insert one's self and/or to be situated within a bounded space where master signifiers, such as 'mental illness', 'knowing', 'responsibility' and 'dangerousness', are pre-thematically encoded with the logic of medico-legal science. As a logocentric text, a disciplinary body of knowledge is inscribed on the kept, their keepers, their managers and their watchers. This body of knowledge is reproduced as a hyper-reality, wherein images of 'disease', 'risk' and 'dangerousness' pervade the socius. The psychiatric citizen's subjectivity is not merely postponed; rather, it is cleansed and made consistent with the normalizing language and logic of the medico-legal edifice, assuring smooth categorization, processing, confinement and order.

The federal admission management documents (manuals and handbooks) that US prisoners receive when placed in custody are examined by Mary Bosworth in Chapter 12. The language of these penal documents shifts full responsibility to offenders for recovery (self-improvement, making good, restitution), indicating that risk-avoidance through governmentality informs the prison industrial assemblage/flow. This is correctional management that monitors offenders as merely a 'client group' or a 'customer base'. Our critical writerly schema proposes how this orientation towards controlling, managing and monitoring prisoners is sustained in a socius whose lines of flight are reactive rather than active; molar rather than molecular. Through these penal documents, the incarcerate is reduced/repressed to a mere shadow of his/her becoming self, spoken (and quashed) through such regulatory pronouncements, disciplined when failing to demonstrate steadfast compliance to such penal truths and re-made (over and over again) in the static, fixed, linear image of the prison industrial assemblage/flow.

In Chapter 13 Mark Halsey challenges the orthodox rhetoric of environmental crime and regulation. This is a rhetoric that theoretically and pragmatically erodes the possible horizon of meanings for the nature of environmental harm and its regulatory amelioration. As but one dimension of the socius, as a social form, 'green criminology' can foster revenge/hate politics from the Left (as a rigid form of political correctness or 'rightness'). The five intersecting sets of foci that constitute our critical writerly schema suggest that limits to one's being and denials to one's becoming originate in images of thought that are themselves the source of (often unintended) harm. This is harm that must be noologically transcended if the self/society constitutive dialectic is to be more fully emancipating.

In Part IV several global themes and controversies that are relevant to postmodern and post-structural criminology are considered. The attention to international, transnational and post-national themes furthers the volume's focus on cutting-edge theorizing, integrative analyses and transpraxis. Essays address such issues as (1) colonialism and the possibility of justice; (2) re-imaging suffering, radicalizing democracy, the hyper-modern age and reflexive critical criminology; and (3) news-making criminology, social constructionism and emancipatory praxis.

Susan Silbey examines the dominant narratives of globalization (by way of law, markets and science) in Chapter 14, arguing that these morality tales mask the dynamics of power to construct (and control) social relations/exchanges and, in their wake, limit articulations of justice. In the realm of law and society, this is understood as postmodern colonialism. In Chapter 15 Ronnie Lippens calls for a 'border-crossing criminology' (a radicalized democratic politics) as a basis to address the ambivalence, fragmentation and dislocation spawned by the hyper-modern age. Overcoming this harm/suffering/oppression – from the local to the global levels – necessitates experimental and reflexive images, vocabularies, inscriptions and reproductions. Gregg Barak, in Chapter 16, provocatively suggests that one facet of this hypermodern 'overcoming' is news-making criminology. This is a strategy of re-engagement in which the socially constructed narratives that reify crime ideology are resisted, deterritorialized and reterritorialized. Our cut of *réalité* (and its five intersecting sets of foci) provides the wherewithal for interpreting the processes through which law and criminology's molar rigidities are cyclically re-enacted. Postmodern colonialism, dislocated identities and legal/criminal ideology are three reactive energy flows whose overcoming in the socius awaits the molecular revolution.

Part V identifies notable challenges to postmodern and post-structural research, especially in relation to theory construction, methodological orientation, social practice/activism and political subtext. In Chapter 17 Joel Handler focuses on the postmodern enterprise as a likely (and viable) movement for societal change. Martin Schwartz and David Friedrichs, in Chapter 18, consider the practicality of deconstructing and reconstructing images of violence, questioning the material grounding of this enterprise. Our critical writerly schema demonstrates that these concerns, while understandable, are but part of an ongoing productive dialogue, the resolution of which leads to continuous molecular developments.

In summary, the socius is composed of five intersecting sets of foci that affect and are affected by each other. This is the locus through which lived struggle in images, texts, bodies and replications unfolds. It is a struggle constituted by active/reactive forces; it is a struggle where dynamic change can occur, temporarily and incompletely, in non-hierarchical though manifest form(s); it is a permanent revolution and a people yet to come!

## Concluding Remarks

As we have argued, our critical writerly schema highlights the wide-ranging, provocative, and novel insights generated by authors whose selected essays have been assembled in this volume. However, in the spirit of ongoing critical development, we want to briefly suggest not one plane where 'lack' in a socius plays itself out in a more static form; rather, we want to suggest three intersecting and mutually constituting planes: the primordial (the play of bio-political power on the plane of immanence), *réalité* (the more static, molar socius) and the transcendental (a plane informed by the previous two, but more in the direction of concretely manifesting possibilities that inhere within the other two) (PRT). Thus, instead of 'postmodern', we suggest an 'altermodernity' (Hardt and Negri, 2009); instead of 'identity politics', we suggest the 'people yet to come' (Deleuze and Guattari, 1987).

We previously argued that the current socius cut from which *réalité* is constructed privileges the molar and a ubiquitous and omnipotent 'lack' as the basis of desire. It is the realm within which subjectivity/discourse is captured in axiomatic logic (see, for example, Deleuze and Guattari, 1983, 1987; Derrida, 1977, 1978; Foucault, 1970, 1973). Once desire is captured within a historically situated linguistic coordinate system as a founding principle, it leads, via deductive logic, to restrictive meanings and conclusions. This process is most conspicuously seen in law's commitment to formal rationality (Arrigo, Milovanovic and Schehr, 2005). But, unlike Lacan's (1977) more descriptive schematizations accepting lack and oedipalization as a given,[8] we also want to suggest how fruitful investigation can conceive of a more primordial level which undergoes various 'captures' in a historically situated political economy.

In this analysis, the suggestive inquiries of Nietzsche (1966, 1968), Bergson (1998), Deleuze and Guattari (1983, 1987), Derrida (1977, 1978) and Foucault (1970, 1973, 1977) are synthesized. This is the plane of quantum, far-from-equilibrium conditions; it is the 'plane of immanence'. Within this realm, active and reactive forces compete for manifestation in a *réalité*. It is the body that is the locus, a 'body without organs' (Deleuze and Guattari, 1987), a 'presemiotic chora' (Kristeva, 1984) that is amenable to various possibilities of capture and normalization. This is Spinoza's critique (1991) in which he explores what the body is capable of doing. From the quantum level of Schroedinger's wave function, where its collapse produces a high probability of an 'event', we see a primordial clash of images (see Aczel, 2003). Some of these images become momentary configurations with degrees of intensity. Delanda (1997), borrowing from dynamic systems theory, quite succinctly notes how far-from-equilibrium conditions witness emergent configurations. Some of these emergents momentarily undergo stasis; more often, however, they undergo further splitting, producing cascades of possibilities. These possibilities can be subsequently captured within various historically situated and contingent articulations of complex iterative loops, or COREL sets (Henry and Milovanovic, 1996). Often, the primordial is connected to the extant molar formation; but it can also be connected to potential possibilities on a new, transcendental plane within which a transforming orderly disorder may be the basis of an alternative *réalité*.

This third plane, a transcendental plane, has been verbalized as a 'permanent revolution' (Deleuze and Guattari, 1983, 1987; see also Holland, 1999), an 'altermodernism' (Hardt and Negri, 2009), a 'common wealth' (Dyer-Witheford, 1999), even as a post-postmodernism. Within this plane, novel emergents may take up residence, but always in contingent form; always dissipative structures; always resisting closure, stasis and molar ossification. What is privileged here is the molecular: becomings, mutations and radical jazz players.

We see this permanent revolution in historically and politically-economically informed understandings of legal fetishism. Consider, for example, the construction of the juridic subject and the favouring of its emergent, phenomenal forms. As Derrida (1991) further tells us, law even becomes connected with justice where both find their essential relation in terms of economic rationality. However, this tendency must give way to an ethic of the Other (Levinas, 2004). Still, more is needed. Indeed, the insights of Levinas, Derrida and Lyotard (1984) warrant further examination, especially on the privileging of the Other's orientation as a basis to construct a novel and transforming principle of justice. This altermodern, kaleidoscopic vision of justice would be rooted more in historical and political economic conditions; it would be reflexively analysed through our critical writerly schema; and it would be situated within our three intersecting planes – a molecular form, a dissipative structure, if you will, that awaits further refinement, critical reflection and continuous restatement. Our criminology of the stranger begins to address these latent possibilities (Arrigo and Milovanovic, 2009).

Our three planes, PRT, must be envisioned as intersecting, with various flows of forces, lines of flight that are rhizomatic, initiating various singularities and consequent cascades of possibilities, This is not a linear movement as in P→ R→T; rather, lines of flight may move

---

[8]     We note that Lacan (1991) did offer suggestions for a prescriptive as developed in his '*discourse of the analyst*' and, with more amplification, in his Schema I.

from T, such as an epiphany, backward to have an effect on plane R and even again, forward, to T. We do not discount even similitude, such as in Carl Jung's notion of synchronicity, or in what Albert Einstein noted in his polemic against quantum mechanics as the possibility of 'spooky action at a distance'. Our transpraxis (Nietzsche, 1968), our everyday struggles for a better society, must consider the play of these intersecting planes and the possibilities each presents. We must resist capture in molar forms. Our transpraxis must be vigilant against reactive forces taking hold. Accordingly, the proceeding essays take us into exciting directions for liberating thought. Each, in unique ways, more often implicitly addresses this larger picture of three interacting planes. Our goal is to make explicit many of these emergents by employing our critical writerly schema. It paves the way for a more holistic examination of the socius and its constitutive forces.

# References

Aczel, A. (2003), *Entanglement*, New York: Penguin Books.

Arrigo, B.A. and Milovanovic, D. (2009), *Revolution in Penology: Rethinking the Society of Captives*, Lanham, MD: Rowman & Littlefield.

Arrigo, B.A., Milovanovic, D. and Schehr, R.C. (2005), *The French Connection in Criminology: Rediscovering Crime, Law, and Social Change*, Albany, NY: SUNY Press.

Barthes, R. (1968), *Writing Degree Zero*, New York: Hill and Wang.

Baudrillard, J. (1983), *Simulations*, New York: Semiotext(e).

Baudrillard, J. (1983a). In the Shadow of the Silent Majority. New York: Semiotext(e).

Baumann, Z. (2000), *Liquid Modernity*, Cambridge: Polity Press.

Bergson, H. (1998), *Creative Evolution*, trans. A. Mitchell, Mineola, NY: Dover.

Briggs, J. and Peat, D. (1989), *Turbulent Mirror*, New York: Harper and Row.

Cornell, D. (1991), *Beyond Accommodation: Ethical Feminism, Deconstruction, and the Law*, New York: Routledge and Kegan Paul.

Cornell, D. (1993), *Transformations*, New York: Routledge and Kegan Paul.

Cornell, D. (1998), *At the Heart of Freedom*, Princeton, NJ: Princeton University Press.

DeLanda, M. (1997), *A Thousand Years of Nonlinear History*, New York: Zone Books.

Deleuze, G. and Guattari, F. (1983), *Anti-Oedipus: Capitalism and Schizophrenia*, Minneapolis: University of Minnesota Press.

Deleuze, G. and Guattari, F. (1987), *A Thousand Plateaus: Capitalism and Schizophrenia*, Minneapolis: University of Minnesota Press.

Derrida, J. (1977), *Of Grammatology*, Baltimore, MD: Johns Hopkins University Press.

Derrida, J. (1978), *Writing and Difference*, Chicago: University of Chicago Press.

Derrida, J. (1991), *The Force of Law: The Mystical Foundations of Authority*, Paris: Galilee.

Dyer-Witheford, N. (1999), *Cyber-Marx*, Chicago: University of Illinois Press.

Foucault, M. (1970), *The Order of Things: An Archeology of the Human Sciences*, New York: Pantheon.

Foucault, M. (1973), *Archeology of Knowledge*, New York: W.W. Norton.

Foucault, M. (1977), *Discipline and Punish*, New York: Pantheon.

Fromm, E. (1994), *Escape from Freedom*, New York: Henry Holt & Company.

Giddens, A. (1984), *The Constitution of Society: Outline of a Theory of Structuration*, Stanford, CA: Stanford University Press.

Hardt, M. and Negri, A. (2009), *Commonwealth*, Boston, MA: Belknap Press.

Hegel, G.W.F. (1955), *Philosophy of Right*, trans. T.M. Knox, New York: Oxford University Press.

Hegel, G.W.F. (1998), *Phenomenology of Spirit*, trans. A.V. Miller, New York: Oxford University Press.

Henry, S. and Milovanovic, D. (1996), *Constitutive Criminology: Beyond Postmodernism*, London: Sage.

Holland, E. (1999), *Deleuze and Guattari's Anti-Oedipus*, New York: Routledge.

Kristeva, J. (1984), *Revolution in Poetic Language*, New York: Columbia University Press.

Lacan, J. (1977), *Ecrits: A Selection*, New York: W.W. Norton

Lacan, J. (1991), *L'Envers de a psychanalyse*, Paris: Editions du Seuil.

Levinas, E. (2004), *Otherwise Than Being*, Pittsburgh, PA: Duquesne University Press.

Lyotard, J.F. (1984), *The Postmodern Condition*, Minneapolis: University of Minnesota Press.

Nietzsche, F.W. (1966), *Beyond Good and Evil: Prelude to a Philosophy of the Future*, ed. Walter Kaufmann, New York: Vintage.

Nietzsche, F.W. (1968), *The Will to Power*, ed. Walter Kaufmann, New York: Vintage.

Poincaré, H. (2002), *The Value of Science: The Essential Writings of Henri Poincaré*, New York: Library Press.

Prigogine, I. and Stengers, I. (1984), *Order Out of Chaos*, New York: Bantam.

Spinoza, B. (1991), *The Ethics: Treatise on the Emendation of the Intellect; Selected Writings*, Indianapolis, IN: Hackett.

# Part I
# Theoretical Developments
# and Integrations

# [1]

# CONSTITUTIVE CRIMINOLOGY: THE MATURATION OF CRITICAL THEORY*

STUART HENRY
Eastern Michigan University

DRAGAN MILOVANOVIC
Northeastern Illinois University

*This paper synthesizes recent trends in the development of critical criminology into a new theoretical direction in thinking about crime. It rejects approaches to criminological theory that reduce crime to an outcome of micro causes or macro contexts. It suggests instead that thinking about crime should be reconsidered as the coterminous discursive production by human agents of an ideology of crime that sustains it as a concrete reality. It argues that this coproduction occurs when agents act out criminal patterns, when others seek to control criminal behavior, and when yet others attempt to research, philosophize about, and explain crime. The paper argues that reducing crime will only come about with a reduction of investment by human agents in the ideology of crime production. Such a reflexive re-conceptualization requires the development of a replacement discourse, rather than an oppositional one, a peacemaking discourse rather than a conflicting one. We call this new theoretical direction* constitutive criminology.

Critical criminology has recently seen the delineation of several new and competing perspectives (Schwartz, 1989; Thomas and O'Maochatha, 1989). These include left realist criminology, socialist-feminist criminology, peacemaking criminology, and post-structuralist criminology.[1] Each of these perspectives is undergoing internal critique, while variously engaging each of the

---

* We would like to thank Gregg Barak, Byron Groves, Peter Fitzpatrick, Christine Harrington, David Nelken, Nigel South, and the anonymous outside reviewers for their very helpful comments and suggestions.

1. On realist criminology, see especially, Dekeseredy and MacLean, (1990), (in press); Jones et al., (1986); Kinsey et al., (1986); MacLean, (1991); Matthews, (1987); Matthews and Young, (1986); Young, (1987, 1988, 1989); and the special issues on left realism of *Contemporary Crises*, Vol. 11, (1987), and *The Critical Criminologist*, Vol. 2, Summer (1990). On socialist-feminist criminology, see Cain, (1989); Chesney-Lynd, (1986); Currie, (1986, 1989, in press); Daly, (1987); Daly and Chesney-Lynd, (1988); Danner, (1989); Gelsthorpe and Morris, (1988); Harris, (1987); Klein, 1973; Messerschmidt, (1986); Schwendinger and Schwendinger, (1983). On peacemaking criminology, see Braswell, (1990); Bianchi and van Swaaningen, (1986); Christie, (1981); Dennis, (1989); de Haan, (1986); Pepinsky, (1986, 1989); Quinney, (1988); Pepinsky and Quinney, 1991). For post-structuralist criminology, see Manning, (1986, 1987, 1988, 1990); Milovanovic, (1988b:125–140; 1989, 1991a, 1991b); Pfohl, (1985).

other perspectives. Such developments might raise the specter of a Kuhnian paradigm crisis, with fragmentation taken as indicative of a failure of the existing critical criminological paradigm to resolve the mounting anomalies with which it is confronted (Greenberg, 1981; Klockars, 1980). Indeed, a not dissimilar crisis has been identified in critical legal studies (Boyle, 1985; Coombe, 1989; Friedrichs, 1986, 1989; Hunt, 1987; Milovanovic, 1988c).

An alternative interpretation of these transformations might be that the current divergence of perspectives is the foundation of a new critical para-digm, whose character will depend on one of the emerging positions becom-ing victorious. The problem here is that such divisions might also lead to the all-too-familiar radical factionalism in which internecine wars among critical thinkers sap new life from each other's potential growth. Put simply, the recent developments are subject to the dialectic of enlightenment and con-straint. In constructing distinctions between different theoretical positions, criminologists must be cautious not to overlook the connections that exist between them. Thus, rather than address these issues through criticism, we sketch an approach that draws on developments in social construction, left realism, socialist feminism, and post-structuralism. We also borrow heavily from social and critical legal theory, from the rich intellectual history of con-stitutive thinking, and from discourse analysis.[2]

Our aim here is not to add another shot to the paradigmatic cross fire, but to examine reflexively the paradigmatic umbrella under which these saplings of critical growth can gain strength. It is this umbrella that we term *constitu-tive criminology* (Henry, 1989a). In the following sections, we address core themes that will lead to the establishment of the necessary and logically ordered elements of a constitutive criminology. These themes are (1) the codetermination of crime and human subjects through crime control ideology and how this ideology has the capacity to reproduce and to transform; (2) dis-cursive practices as the medium for the structuring of crime and its control institutions; (3) symbolic violence as the hidden ideological dimension of legal domination; and (4) the use, by control agencies, of sense data to construct meaning that claims space and displaces the intersubjective construction of

---

2. We are especially indebted to the post-Foucauldian critical legal theory of Boyle (1985), Coombe (1989), Fitzpatrick (1984), and Hunt (1987); the critical approach to legal ideology found in the work of Brigham (1987), Harrington and Merry (1988), and Klare (1979); Cohen's (1985) vision of social control; Bourdieu's (1977, 1989) sociology of knowl-edge; Giddens' (1984) structuration theory; and the variations of macro-micro integrative theorizing found in the work of Knorr-Centina and Cicourel (1981). Key links, we argue, must also begin to integrate discourse analysis as formulated by Baudrillard (1981), Benveniste (1971), Deleuze and Guattari (1987), Derrida (1981), Foucault (1977), Lacan (1977), Lecercle (1985), and others from the more pragmatic orientation, such as, Bakhtin (1981) and Volosinov (1986).

## CONSTITUTIVE CRIMINOLOGY 295

meaning and, through this process sustains control institutions as relatively autonomous structures.

# THE CODETERMINATION OF CRIME AS IDEOLOGY

A core theme of constitutive criminology is its rejection of reductionism. Advocates decline the seduction that either human agents, through choice or predisposition, or structural arrangements at institutional and societal levels, have priority in shaping crime, victims, and control. Rather, following Giddens (1984), they see social structure and its constituent control institutions as the emerging outcome of human interaction that both constrains and enables criminal action and recognizes that those structures are simultaneously shaped by the crime and crime control talk that is part of their reproduction. Constitutive criminology is not an exercise in polemics, in which human agency is separated from the structures that it makes. Thus, we share Coombe's (1989:70) view that

> To characterize structure and subjectivity as two poles of an ineluctable dichotomy is problematical and that . . . we need to radically reconsider our understandings of structure and subjectivity if we are to appreciate the complexity of the relationship between the structures of the socially constructed "languages" like liberal legal discourse and the subjective consciousness of social actors and if we are to avoid reproducing the conceptual poles that characterize liberalism in our efforts to deconstruct it.

## THE MAKING OF HUMAN SUBJECTS: TRANSPRAXIS

Constitutive criminology, then, is concerned with identifying the ways in which the interrelationships among human agents constitute crime, victims, and control as realities. Simultaneously, it is concerned with how these emergent realities themselves constitute human agents. It follows from this that the current notion of praxis needs to be replaced. If praxis is taken to be purposive social activity born of human agents' consciousness of their world, mediated through the social groups to which they belong, then this must be supplanted by the richer notion of transpraxis. Transpraxis assumes that critical opposition must be aware of the reconstitutive effects—the reproductions of relations of production—in the very attempts to neutralize or challenge them. The dialectic of control is such that praxis assumes dualistic forms—negation/affirmation, denial/expression. In the process of negation, relations of production are often reconstituted along with the human subjects that are their supports. But often neglected is that with affirmation, relations of production are also deconstructed, along with those same human subjects. Thus, its very dynamic reveals the tenuous nature of the ideological structure on which it is based. Critical theorists have been particularly myopic as to the potential for change afforded by this insight.

Labeling theory tried to cover some of this ground, particularly in its notions of role engulfment and deviancy amplification. But labeling separated meaning from the agents generating it. It posited a dualism between agency and structure rather than a duality (Giddens, 1984). Ignored was any sense of an interconnected whole. Although early symbolic interactionism elaborated the ways that the human actor became that which the audience constructed, it said little about the way audiences—their imageries, symbolic repertoire, and *verstehen*—are constructed, constituted, and undermined by historically situated human agents in the context of a historically specific political economy. The construction process tacitly acknowledged and uncritically accepted that the power relationship flowed one way, monolithically and asymmetrically. While those who were officially designated deviant actively participated in their own identity transformation, little construction was done of the control agents, by themselves. Actors designed as deviant or criminal ultimately became passive acceptors of audiences' degradation and fulfillers of their prophecies. Audiences made victims. But little was said of the making of audiences during their attempt to construct labels for others; absent was the dialectic of control. Coombe (1989:117) notes that "one of the most promising areas of research suggested by a practice theory is the consideration of the ways in which legal discourse and practice actively participate in the making of human subjects and thus reproduce social relations of power." The danger here, however, is reifying human subjects by giving priority to their discourse as though discourse somehow operated independently of those using it. Even more problematic is losing sight of the potential for transformation inherent in the reproduction process, since it is precisely here, in the remaking of subjects through the ideology of control, that they are revealed as vulnerable to unmaking.

Constitutive criminology, then, recognizes human agents' power to undermine the structures that confront them and asserts that agents both use and are used in the generation of knowledge and truth about what they do. Agents' ability to undermine and invert structures of control, to episodically render them edifices of subordination, is one of the major missing dimensions of conventional and critical criminology.

Occasional glimpses of the dual nature of this process are exposed in examples of prisoners' power over prison guards through trade in contraband, of police committing or facilitating the commission of property crime, and of police provocation of the very riots they are supposed to prevent (Jefferson, 1990). The notion of "confinement by consent" found in the accounts by Milovanovic (1988a) and Milovanovic and Thomas (1989) of the inmate, turned jailhouse lawyer, who inadvertently maintains legitimation and conventional understandings of capitalist legality, is as constitutive of the hegemony of overarching capitalist relations as is the workplace trade unionist defending employee disciplinary cases in settings of private justice (Henry, 1983). But both are also undermining of that which had previously been constructed. Or consider Goffman's (1961) early work in *Asylums*, in which he showed that some inmates in their "secondary adjustments" internalized and verbalized psychiatric jargon as a way of leveling hierarchical power relations; while negating, they also affirmed, implicitly or explicitly, the very hierarchical structures that they attempted to neutralize. Again, consider the work of Bannister and Milovanovic (1990), in which they showed that the activist lawyer attempting to politicize the trial begins to make use of the constraining categories and legal discourse that are the very supports of the rule-of-law ideology. Indeed, Karl Marx (1984:115) recognized this duality facing practitioners of radical change when he observed that

> the tradition of countless dead generations is an incubus to the mind of the living. At the very times when they seem to be engaged in revolutionizing themselves and their circumstances, in creating something previously non-existent, at just such epochs of revolutionary crisis they anxiously summon up the spirits of the past to their aid, borrowing from them names, rallying cries, costumes, in order to stage the new world historical drama in this time-honored disguise and borrowed speech.

For Marx, the crucial issue for revolutionary change was whether the concepts of the past could be used selectively to enable the liberation of the future. Until the spirit of revolutionary change could be captured and used without reference to the past, automatically and spontaneously, it was but a bourgeois revolution, short lived, soon reaching its climax. No more vivid an illustration of this process exists than Henry's (1985, 1988b, 1989b) accounts of the way those oppositional collectives, cooperatives, and communes, whose commitment was to an alternative socialist order, typically resorted to capitalist control forms and state law in their ironic attempts to defend their own internal order, thereby reproducing the very structures that undermined and overwhelmed them. Similarly, in presenting the polemic between Nietzsche and Hegel, Milovanovic (1991a) has indicated that would-be reformers often react and negate rather than act and affirm positive values. In fact, transpraxis, an oppositional agenda, actively negates and produces, affirmatively, new values. Socialism, for example, as envisioned by Marx, is a transitional phase to the "higher forms." Here there still exists a predominant reactive and negative orientation, and that still reconstitutes the very *forms* of domination found in capitalism, be it now by the victorious proletariat. The state apparatus becomes but an instrument of the victorious proletariat to be used to repress the former repressors, and thus is the cycle react-negate-reconstitute perpetuated.

298　　　　　　　HENRY AND MILOVANOVIC

TWO SIDES OF TRANSPRAXIS

These contradictions are not temporary aberrations of the structure of control but fundamental pillars of its constitution. In Bourdieu's (1977) terms, they are instances of the way in which the discourse of control in society is in harmony, even when in apparent opposition. This dialectic of control must be addressed. That criminologists and practitioners ignore it is part of the constitutive silence that sustains crime and control as object-like entities. A transpraxis must envision oppositional practices themselves as inadvertently reaffirming instruments of hierarchy and control.

Transpraxis should not, however, ignore the reverse side of this dialectic of control. The affirmative reproduction of social control by human purposeful action also undermines that which is being constituted. For example, it has been shown (Henry, 1988a) that when state agencies seek to control economic relations that fall outside national tax accounting, they attach derogatory labels to such activity and attribute to it motives carrying negative connotations. Terms such as the "black," "hidden," "underground," "shadow," "secret," "subterranean," "submerged" economy are used to suggest that the economic relations of those working "off-the-books" are perpetrated by nefarious creatures of the night who are interested unilaterally in pecuniary rewards incommensurate with effort, who are dishonest, and who cannot be trusted. Although such attempts at control may initially dissuade some from participation, they also show many of those who participate, and others who subsequently do so, that these accounts are inaccurate descriptions of the meaning of their relations. Those whose actual experience of irregular work is enjoyable, communal, and socially nutritious stand in contrast to the cutthroat black market dealing that control-labeling suggests. Another well-documented example of the same process occurs in drug education in regard to the discredit that can be brought on the "moral, clean living" messages found in the scare of shock talk of health educators. When directed at young people whose actual experimentation and peer knowledge reveal that drug use does not produce instant addiction, necessary escalation, or death, the effects can be counterproductive.

Thus, the more state agencies elaborate their control talk, and the more people experience the different reality of relations subject to control, the more contempt accrues to the controllers and their control institutions. As a result, people begin to question other distinctions, such as those between theft and the legitimate acquisition of property, between honesty and dishonesty, between street crime and white-collar crime, and between hard and soft drugs. Such questioning, stemming from the attempts of control institutions to control, actually undermines that which the controls were designed to protect: the existing relations of production and the moral and social order.

We now turn to three additional foci (discursive practices, symbolic violence, and sense data and meaning construction) that are integral to the process of codetermination, as seen by constitutive criminology.

## DISCURSIVE PRACTICES AS THE MEDIUM OF CODETERMINATION

A central issue in constitutive criminology is the role of human agents' discursive practices. The use of particular ways of talking, as in Cohen's (1985) "control talk," Manning's (1988) "organizational talk," or Milovanovic's (1986, 1988a, in press) and Thomas's (1988) "law talk," both reflects and constitutes narratives that provide the continuity to reproduce social structures of crime and its control, in time and space. As Knorr-Cetina and Cicourel (1981) have argued, human agents transform events that they see or experience as micro-events into summary representations, or mind patterns, by relying on routine practices through which they convince themselves of having achieved the appropriate representation of these events; these are then objectified in coherent narrative constructions.[3] The well-documented media synthesis of harmful incidents into crime waves is allied with Fitzpatrick's notion of the "synoptic process," whereby disparate patterns of regulation are synthesized into formalized law (Fitzpatrick, 1988). But no clearer example exists than the very categorization of the diversity of human conflicts and transgressions into crime, or of the multitude of variously motivated acts of personal injury into violent crime or types of violent crime, such as when various disputes between family members are described under the unifying term "domestic violence" or "spouse abuse."

In the constitutive criminological vision, social structures are the categories used to classify the events that they allegedly represent. As such, they are strengthened by routine construction in everyday life and by activity organized in relation to them, as though they were concrete entities. The principal means through which social structures are constituted is language and discursive practices that make conceptual distinctions through the play of differences (Derrida, 1973, 1981; Lacan, 1977).

At the organizational level of analysis, the complexity of the human condition is given a static, decontextualized meaning to enable controllers to better negotiate routine cases (Cicourel, 1968; Manning, 1988; Sudnow, 1965; Thomas, 1988). Discourse, indeed, is the "disciplinary mechanism" by which "docile bodies" are created and "bodies of utility" stabilized (Foucault, 1977).

At the societal level of analysis, capital logic and the integrally related

---

3.   In other contexts, see also, Cressey's (1953) discussion of embezzlers' "verbalizations" and Schwendinger and Schwendinger's (1985:128–160) discussion of "moral rhetorics" of delinquent youths.

processes of rationalization are constitutive of categories that capture essential relations, be it often in fetishistic forms. Not the least are rhetorical structures, figurative expressions, and verbal mannerisms that are used as primary signifiers of meaning. Consider, for example, those signifiers used to give material form to capital logic (e.g., commodities, market forces, producers and consumers, the juridic subject), to technological imageries (e.g., "she's a dynamo," "coiled for action"), and to the phallocentric order itself in which male signifiers occupy a privileged position (e.g., the power "to penetrate," as opposed to the weakness of "seduction"). Hence, at the levels of intersubjective communication, organizational processing, and capital logic, discursive practices are given anchorings, a "pinning down" (Lacan, 1977; Manning, 1988; Milovanovic, in press). In other words, discursive practices produce texts (narrative constructions), imaginary constructions, that anchor signifiers to particular signifieds, producing a particular image claiming to be the reality. These texts become the semiotic coordinates of action, which agents recursively use and, in so doing, provide a reconstruction of the original form.

Once social structures are constituted as summary representations, their ongoing existence depends on their continued and often unwitting reconstruction in everyday discourse, a discourse replete with tacit understandings whose basis lies outside the realm of intrinsic intersubjective communication and intersubjectively established meaning. Core meanings are typically preconstructed elsewhere as part of a common "stock of knowledge" (Schutz, 1967; see also, Manning, 1988). Agents in organizational settings tend to reduce feedback that represents contaminating and disruptive "noise." The fluidity of organizational processing in criminal justice contexts demands a high degree of rationality and formalism, which is both the product and the effect of crime control practices. In part, this is due to the increasing complexity in the social formation, which demands more abstract categorization encompassing more and more variants—a "surplus of possibilities" (Luhmann, 1985), but which produces, in the process, symbolizations that are steps removed from the "real" (e.g., concrete reality). For example, process justice is held to require equality of treatment, that is claimed to be enabled by general rules of procedure that reduce people to like individuals, decontextualized of their different cosmologies of meaning, and substituted by a universal individual intent tied to units of material reward. In order to sustain abstractly constructed distinctions, these representations are made applicable to events, despite the contradictory evidence that comes from renewed micro-interaction. Contradictory evidence and potential disruptions are engendered by the internal transfer of messages, a basis of instability that is best negotiated by framing it into already understood narrative constructs (Goffman, 1974, 1981; Manning 1988; Thomas, 1988).

It is often not enough, however, simply to repeat distinctions in order that

## CONSTITUTIVE CRIMINOLOGY 301

such representations be sustained as apparent realities. Part of the reality-constituting process involves routinely investing faith and interest in them; fighting over them, manipulating them, and above all defending them (Knorr–Cetina and Cicourel, 1981). These morality plays often take place in symbolic form in publicized trials, political and business scandals, "moral panics," and other boundary-policing structures. In more subtle forms, they take place by the use of prevailing discursive practices, even in the use of the oppositional form. As Foucault (1977) and others (e.g., Morrissey, 1985) have reminded us, oppositional discourse is as constitutive of existing reality as is supportive discourse, since each addresses and thereby reproduces the prevailing distinctions while disputing their content rather than deconstructing them or discrediting them through the construction of a new, replacement discourse. For example, Selva and Bohm (1987) have emphasized that, in many respects, an oppositional legal discourse, which utilizes the existing structure of legal discourse, may prove more productive and liberating than a replacement discourse, but this downplays the significance of the constitutive effects of "liberating" practices in law. A graphic example of this process is the oppositional adolescent reaction to the school by working-class kids. Although they "resist" and reject the system that rejects them, it is their very reaction that subsequently consigns them to the bottom of the very hierarchy they despise (Willis, 1977).

Organizing action to defend representations—framed and objectified in narrative texts—is one of the principal means of defending and conferring object-like reality on them, providing life, form, energy, sustenance, and a high degree of permanence. The institutions of capitalist legality (involving formal police, courts, and prisons) represent the visible manifestation of human agents organized to defend the overarching social form of capitalist society from internal deconstruction. Capital logic is a ubiquitous rationalizing form; the more investment that is made in it, the more difficult it is to sustain that which it is not. This is not to imply conspiracy but to specify formal function, for while defending the wider totality, agents and agencies also compete to defend their own integrity within the framework of capital logic, as Jessop's (1982) work forcibly reminds us.[4] Compare, for example, the mobilization of opposition to racism and sexism that manifested itself, within the legal frame, in the form of affirmative action programs, formal equality doctrines, and comparable worth legislation. The latter two essentially maintain capital logic—subjects are still measured by some external

---

4. We need not unilaterally accept a pure capital logic formulation, for, as critics have shown, it is replete with an economic reductionism. We do, however, acknowledge its continued pervasive and ubiquitous force. It would be reasonable to point out, also, that bureaucratic logic, regardless of the capitalist mode, is just as pervasive and ubiquitous, as Weber showed.

standard of equality and are still compared to an abstract criteria that is constitutive of capitalistic social relations. Consider, also, Daly and Chesney-Lind's (1988) insightful analysis advocating a socialist-feminist perspective and critiquing "first-wave feminism," which often advertently or inadvertently (1) situated itself in legal discourse with its reliance on notions of formal "justice" and "equality" and hence celebrated the fetishistic notion of the juridic subject, (2) used male standards as the criteria of correctness and an ideal end, (3) laid the groundwork for greater and more pervasive forms of state and informal control in women's lives, and (4) grasped too quickly the get-tough approach, thereby rejuvenating deterrence and retributivist theory.

Alternatively, human agents can be envisioned as unique, with a multiplicity of needs, drives, desires, and abilities, and as intersubjectively constituted. Any subsuming of these qualities to some "equal" measure must be read as an imposition, a reification by submission to macro-constituted forms of capital logic, an idealization of relations constitutive of the capitalistic mode of production. Affirmative action, indeed, is the more radical in so far as the use of substantive rational criteria militates against a universalism and points to a recognition of built-in biases of the sociopolitical and legal order. The imagery of affirmative action is system destabilizing, and it is now evident that the sociopolitical order is being brought around from this recognition (e.g., the mobilization of the ideology of "reverse discrimination"). Socialist feminism, however, is on the cutting edge in redirecting analyses of hierarchical and exploitative relations often objectified in seemingly value-neutral criteria and standards.

From the perspective of constitutive criminology, then, control institutions are the relations among human agents acting to police the conceptual distinctions among discursively constructed social structures. Those relations are mediated by the availability, through intersubjective relations, of a sedimented, differentiated symbolic system, a repository of value-laden signs that are politically anchored. Once constituted, those relations, expressed in symbolic form, themselves become structures, and, as agencies and institutions, appear to have relative autonomy from both wider structure and human agency. In turn, they too are policed by further "private" or internal relations of control. Thus, signifying chains, narrative constructions, and objectified bits and pieces of everyday actively float within specific discourses, within which distinctive, discursive subject-positions exist that structure what can be framed, thought, and said. Tacit understanding is rooted in these subterranean semiotic systems that continuously receive support through their use (Manning, 1988).

## SYMBOLIC VIOLENCE AS IDEOLOGICAL DOMINATION

According to Bourdieu (1977:192) "symbolic violence" is a form of domination that is exerted through the very medium in which it is disguised, wherein it is the "gentle, invisible form of violence, which is never recognized as such, and is not so much undergone as chosen, the violence of credit, confidence, obligation, personal loyalty, hospitality, gifts, gratitude, piety. . . ." But criminologists have forgotten this dimension of domination. The silence of the present and the celebration of that aspect that is likened to be law constitute the forms of control that appear as reality. Suppressed by silence, this pervasive domination is itself frozen in the past as "custom" (the informal law of nonindustrial societies), "pre-law," and the "law" of multiplex relations (Black, 1976, 1989), as if multiplex relations can exist without simplex relations or simplex without multiplex! But, in so far as we accept that they exist independently, we are actively, though unreflexively, creating and maintaining the illusion that is the reality of law. The omission of informal, nonstate social control from consideration as part of criminal justice is how "criminal justice" is constituted. Buying into dominant definitions of what counts as law, crime policing, and justice by excluding rules, deviance, informal social control, and private justice is part of the way these concepts, as entities, are made and remade as realities. Take as an example again, a constitutive view of law (Fitzpatrick, 1984; Harrington and Merry, 1988; Hunt, 1987; Klare, 1979). Rather than treating law as an autonomous field of inquiry linked only by external relations to the rest of society, or investigating the way law and society, as concrete entities, influence or affect each other, as is typically done in nonconstitutive approaches, constitutive criminology takes law as its subject of inquiry, but as Hunt (1987) and Harrington and Yngvesson (1990), have argued, constitutive theory pursues the study of law by exploring the interrelations between legal relations and other social relations. As Harrington and Yngvesson (1990:143) say,

> To speak of the constitutive dimension of ideology is to examine legal ideology as a form of power that also creates a particular kind of world, specifically, a liberal-legal world constituted as separate spheres of "law" and "community," with "practice" or "process" located uneasily between the two. In such a world actors impose ideologies or persuade others to take them on as "voluntary."

From the constitutive perspective, the notion of the "juridic subject" (i.e., the reasonable man/woman in law), for example, can only be understood in its inherent dualistic relation of being both a constitutive element and a recursive outcome of capital logic. As Henry (1983) argues, with such an approach one begins to see the possibility of transcending the view that law is either a product of structure or the outcome of interaction. One begins to see how informal social control is not so much an alternative form of law but a necessary part of the ideological process whereby the crystallized, formalized, object-like qualities of law are created and sustained in an ongoing manner, be it within a different arena. Thus, constitutive criminology directs attention to the way law, crime, and criminal justice are conceptualized and implied as objective realities having real consequences, consequences attributed to their claim.

Seen in this way, institutions of law are the organized acting out of discursively produced "control thoughts," whose very action reflects on the reality of that which they are organized to defend. There are parallels here with John Brigham's (1987:306) research on social movements, in which he found that the social movement was integral with the law that it used, such that ". . .Legal forms are evident in the language, purposes, and strategies of movement activity as practice." As such, legal forms and their control institutions are rooted in control discourse and in their own parent social structures and cannot be divorced from them, but nor can the structures exist without their control forms since each implies the other.

No better an example of symbolic violence exists than in "fighting crime" rhetoric. In a microcosmic form, undercover work of policing in the 1980s, such as those Gary Marx (1988) and Bob Weiss (1987) so poignantly document, produced the new "maximum-security society." Here, there is an increasing emphasis by control agents on developing dossiers in computerized form; an increasing use of predictive and actuarial instruments that focus on producing statements about persons in particular created categories; and an obsession to find the "predisposed" criminal. This has led to an extreme manipulation of the environment, with the continued acceptance by the courts, to induce the very criminality that is the controller's own creation. It is concluded by Gary Marx that the resultant new transparent society has seen the erosion of traditional notions of privacy such that even the citizenry has been recruited to monitor others as well as themselves for deviance or deviance proclivities (G. Marx, 1988:219).

At the same time, however, the constitutive nature of the dialectic of control is apparent in its oppositional form. When Gary Marx and others oppose the affront of privacy, they actually take part in perpetuating the elaboration of privatized relations of production, since they unwittingly defend this bastion of capitalist society while discrediting and displacing notions of commonality. Indeed, it is ironic that in seeking to defend people against the invasion of their lives by control agents, critical criminologists have acceded to supporting the ideological protection of privacy while being silent on the theft of that which was traditionally held in common. Protecting privacy is nothing less than ideological legitimation for theft of the common (Einstadter, 1989).

## SENSE DATA AND MEANING CONSTRUCTION

All this leads to recognizing the high premium on collecting, filtering, categorizing, and disseminating increasingly complex information framed in coherent narrative constructions (Jackson, 1988; Manning, 1988; Thomas, 1988). The process of constructing meaning intersubjectively is increasingly being both abdicated and usurped by agents of organizations who use these constructions as the criteria by which to survey, control, and act on subjects, particularly those in predicted high-risk categories in the existing social arrangements. Simultaneously, these constructions are inadvertently given ideological support through oppositional attacks on the autonomization of social control instruments. Oppositional attacks by some critical theorists and reformers take as a given many of the concepts, presuppositions, or working hypothesis of these same agents of control, thereby in the end, reproducing the self-perpetuating machine. We are reminded of how escape from reproduction is constrained, even in the most radical perspectives, by the actions of others who read criticism as simply more of the same; for example, booksellers who categorize works like Cohen's (1988) *Against Criminology* in the section of their bookstore dealing with criminology and publishers who reject proposals that they are unable to fit into the needs of a preexisting market. Indeed, there is some danger of the "realist" criminological perspective having this tendency toward reproduction, which has been recognized in the private soul-searching of various of its members. The challenge for a transpraxis here is substantial. How does one build an alternative "framing" of narrative texts to the exclusion of system-sustaining elements (e.g., imageries, signifier-signified anchorings, and so on)?

Institutions of social control are framed within the mediating effects of symbolic systems. Symbolic systems are constituted by sign systems, which in turn, make use of the dyad of (1) signifiers—acoustic images, psychic imprints, or simply expressions—and (2) the signified—the concept referred to, the content.[5] Organizational agents, including control agents, must produce stable meaning in the very process of controlling deviance. Hence,

---

5. Meaning, as Greimas (1987), Jackson (1988), Jakobson (1971), and Lacan (1977) have pointed out, is constructed at the intersection of the two main axes in semiotics, the paradigmatic and the syntagmatic. The syntagmatic represents discursive constructions, that is, narrative constructions in linear sequence held together by grammatical, syntactical, and morphological rules. The vertical axis, the paradigmatic represents the play of differences in signs (the semantical dimension). It is the repository of dissimilar signs. Consider a prosecutor uttering the following: "The defendant willingly inflicted gross and unprovoked bodily harm on the victim." Each word is chosen from a storehouse of possible words (paradigm), each existing with specific legal meanings (signifieds), and each

human agents' semiotic work stabilizes the endless drift of signifieds under those signifiers, giving a particular meaning that is formalistic, rationalistic, and logical, and producing a stable and static semiotic grid that henceforth anchors the multiplicity of forces in movement (Milovanovic, in press). Meaning construction based on "purposive rational action," as opposed to shared intersubjectively constituted meaning (Habermas, 1984, 1987), increasingly underlies the constitutive process within the semiotic grid producing narrative coherence. This becomes the narrative structure (text) that conveys images of deviant behavior and simultaneously produces agents that are its supports. Those who, in their nonreflexive practices, oppose images of deviance, more often inadvertently affirm the reality of their existence. Organizational imperatives, which reflect human agents' deference to concepts of rationalization and capital logic, rely on signifying practices by those agents. The agents in turn rely on a tacit understanding in constructing meaning (Manning, 1988).

The outcome of this constitutive work is the organizational supports, deviant cases, correctors, and rebels who unwittingly purify these structural distinctions in their critical attack on its assumed operating principles. Oppositional narratives (texts), for example, are most often replete with the very core imageries, metaphors, and signifiers that are the supports of a hierarchical and dominating apparatus. But activating system-supportive imageries and then attempting to react and negate does not in itself produce alternative imageries of what could be. The "at best"—react and negate—turns often to be "at worst," for the canceling of a negation by a negation in the Hegelian sense does not produce transcendence. At best it produces, instead, destruction on one level, but a reconfirmation of system-generated elements on another.

Social control agents both produce and sustain deviant categories, and they tacitly frame coherent narratives of "what happened," hence objectifying primordial sense data. These objectifications become increasingly the anchoring points for every day constructions by those in the social formation, which in turn, sustain the organizationally framed narrative. Routine investment of time and energy make this constitutive process recursive and self-referential, cyclically generating a more refined and purified version of the substance of their actions as object.

To refer to control institutions as relatively autonomous, then, is not to say they are separate from the wider social structure since they are part of its

---

placed in a definite linear order (syntagm) to produce meaning. Additionally, the metaphoric can be assimilated to the paradigmatic and the metonymic to the syntagmatic (Lacan, 1977; Milovanovic, in press). The former produces rhetorical effects; the latter, displacements. Thus, meaning falls along this intersection of the paradigmatic-metaphoric and the syntagmatic-metonymic. But meaning is inherently unstable, or to put it in Lacanian language, signifieds perpetually slide, or drift, under the signifier.

constitution. It is to say, rather, that recursivity reinforces conventional notions by giving permanence and stability to them. Nor do control institutions support the wider structure simply because that is their assigned social function. Such a vision is rabidly reifying because it ignores the integral role of human agency in this process. Rather, as Fitzpatrick (1984) reminds us, control institutions support the relations of reproduction within the totality of society because they *are* some of those relations of reproduction. Therefore as we have argued elsewhere (Henry, 1985, 1987, Milovanovic, in press), these social relations do not exist independently of human agents who repeatedly bring them into being.

Likewise the "internal" relations that monitor control institutions *are* some of the relations of the control institutions that they police. A police agency would not be what it is without the relations that police it, informal or otherwise, and those relations would not be what they are without the action of human agents. As a result, any examination of control institutions that analyzes them outside of the structural context that they police, that ignores the internal relations that police them, or that ignores human agents' recursive action, produces a partial account that itself becomes part of the constitutive discourse that sustains their reproduction. Concomitantly, any challenging practices used by agents not sensitive to the reconstituting effects of their very practices, further reproduce, elaborate, and stabilize the existent structural arrangements. Thus, although relations of control are most visible in their institutional form, that should not lead one to neglect their pervasive presence in informal and alternative modes of control or even in Foucault's sense of a dispersed disciplinary technology pervasive throughout our society. Neither should it lead one to gloss over the human agent's renditions and intersubjective creative work that daily makes these relations into organizations and structures. So what is to be done? As implied in our preceding argument, there are a number of ways that a constitutive approach to criminology can be transformative. In the concluding section we suggest a direction that this might take, but a more elaborated treatment must await further analysis.

## CONCLUSION

In short then, constitutive criminology, in the tradition of dialectical theory, is the framework for reconnecting crime and its control with the society from which it is conceptually and institutionally constructed by human agents. Through it criminologists are able to recognize, as a fundamental assumption, that crime is both *in* and *of* society. Our position calls for an abandoning of the futile search for causes of crime because that simply elaborates the distinctions that maintain crime as a separate reality while failing to address how it is that crime is constituted as a part of society. We are concerned, instead, with the ways in which human agents actively coproduce that which they take to be crime. As a signifier, this perspective directs attention to the way that crime is constituted as an expansive and permeating mode of discourse, a continuously growing script—a text, narrative—whose writers are human agents, obsessed with that which we produce, amazed that *it* is produced, denying that *it* is created by us, claiming that *it* grows independently before us, but yet worshipping the very alienating, hierarchical creations that are our own. A direct consequence of such an approach is that any "rehabilitation" from crime requires that criminologists and practitioners alike deconstruct crime as a separate entity, cease recording it, stop dramatizing it, withdraw energy from it, deny its status as an independent entity. Through this vision, we are suggesting that criminologists write a new script, a replacement discourse that connects human agents and our product back to the whole of which we are a part. "Control talk" (Cohen, 1985), "organizational talk" (Manning, 1988), and "law talk" (Milovanovic, 1986, 1988a; Thomas, 1988) must be replaced by a reflexive discourse that allows for change, chance, being, becoming, multiplicity, and irony, and that reflects a sensitivity to the nuances of being human. Criminologists must explore "alternative logics" in criminology, as Nelken calls them. We must cease to invest in the myth that human agents are either individuals with free choices driven by a utilitarian calculus or biologically and psychologically programmed, when all that is known shows that human agents are inextricably social beings whose total script is the medium of birth to our differences and whose differences continuously, but cumulatively, shape our total script.

Control concepts, such as the juridic subject and hierarchically organized dualisms—rational/irrational, subject/object, actor/action, center/periphery, agent/structure, with their privileging of the former term over the latter, and other logocentric, reconstituting discursive practices must give way to an "affirmative action" of discursive practices that privileges the interconnectedness, the interrelatedness, of phenomena in the social formation rather than any privileged hierarchical division. One of the few criminological scholars to recognize the importance of developing an agenda of replacement discourse is Gregg Barak (1988) with his "newsmaking criminology." He says (Barak, 1991:5) that "in the post-modern era, social problems such as homelessness, sexual assault, or drug abuse are politically constructed, ideologically articulated, and media produced events." He advocates that criminologists become credible spokespeople and that they make criminological news and participate in the popular construction of images of crime and crime control, that is, produce crime themes "as a means of bringing about social change and social justice" (Barak, 1988:585; see also, Barak and Bohm, 1989).

Constitutive criminology, then, is a step in the deconstitution of crime, a peacemaking movement (Pepinsky and Quinney, 1991) toward an alternative vision of what is and what might be. Transpraxis must be the guide for those

## CONSTITUTIVE CRIMINOLOGY 309

challenging hierarchical structures of domination. Anything less, advertently or inadvertently, contributes to hegemonic practices that sustain human agents' subordination to that which we construct. Accepting this does not mean that criminology should be blind to the human suffering that is the reality of crime for those who are its victims. Indeed, their suffering is not aided by the public celebration of their pain, nor by the glorification, sensationalization, and vilification of their offenders. Constitutive criminology is also peaceful criminology. It recognizes the harm and suffering and seeks to examine how criminology might reduce it through transforming the totality of relations of which it is a part. It does not imagine that some structural transformation will eventually rescue society from the harm of murder, rape, and corporate fraud. Rather, it seeks to affirm those aspects of intersubjective experience that are capable, if invoked, of displacing the excess crime that comes from giving in to those energizing its continuity. Of course, it is true that even in a society of saints there will be sinners, but the task of constitutive criminology is to suck life from their discursive enterprise.

## REFERENCES

Bakhtin, Mikhail
  1981    The Dialogical Imagination. Austin: University of Texas Press.

Bannister, Shelley and Dragan Milovanovic
  1990    The necessity defense, substantive justice and oppositional linguistic praxis. International Journal of the Sociology of Law 18:179–198.

Barak, Gregg
  1988    Newsmaking criminology: Reflections on the media, intellectuals, and crime. Justice Quarterly 5:565–587.
  1991    Homelessness and the case for community-based initiatives: The emergence of a model shelter as a short term response to the deepening crisis in housing. In Harold Pepinsky and Richard Quinney (eds.), Criminology as Peacemaking. Bloomington: Indiana University Press.

Barak, Gregg and Bob Bohm
  1989    The crimes of the homeless or the crime of homelessness. Contemporary Crisis 13:275–288.

Baudrillard, Jean
  1981    For a Critique of the Political Economy of the Sign. St. Louis: Telos Press.

Benveniste, Emile
  1971    Problems in General Linguistics. Coral Gables, Fla.: University of Miami Press.

Bianchi, H. and R. van Swaaningen, eds.
  1986    Abolitionism: Towards a Non-Repressive Approach to Crime. Amsterdam: Free Press.

Black, Donald J.
  1976    The Behavior of Law. New York: Academic Press.
  1989    Sociological Justice. New York: Oxford University Press.

310                    HENRY AND MILOVANOVIC

Bourdieu, Pierre
    1977    Outline of a Theory of Practice. New York: Cambridge University Press.
    1989    Social space and symbolic power. Social Theory 7:14–25.

Boyle, James
    1985    The politics of reason: Critical legal theory and local social thought.
            University of Pennsylvania Law Review 133:685–780.

Braswell, Michael
    1990    Peacemaking: A missing link in criminology. The Criminologist 15(1):3–5.

Brigham, John
    1987    Right, rage and remedy: Forms of law in political discourse. Studies in
            American Political Development 2:303–316.

Brigham, John and Christine Harrington
    1989    Realism and its consequences: An inquiry into contemporary sociolegal
            research. International Journal of the Sociology of Law 17:41–62.

Cain, Maureen
    1989    Growing Up Good: Policing Behaviour of Girls in Europe. London: Sage.

Chesney-Lind, Meda
    1986    Women and crime: The female offender. Signs: Journal of Women in
            Culture and Society 121:78–96.

Christie, Nils
    1981    Limits to Pain. Oxford: Martin Robertson.

Cicourel, Aaron
    1968    The Social Organization of Juvenile Justice. New York: John Wiley &
            Sons.

Cohen, Stanley
    1985    Visions of Social Control. Oxford: Polity Press.
    1988    Against Criminology. New Brunswick, N.J.: Transaction Books.

Coombe, Rosmary J.
    1989    Room for manoeuver: Toward a theory of practice in critical legal studies.
            Law and Social Inquiry 14:69–121.

Cressey, Donald
    1953    Other People's Money. Glencoe, Ill.: Free Press.

Currie, Dawn
    1986    Female criminality: A crisis in feminist theory. In Brian MacLean (ed.),
            The Political Economy of Crime. Scarborough, Ontario: Prentice-Hall.
    1989    Women and the state: A statement on feminist theory. The Critical
            Criminologist 1 (Spring):4–5.
    1990    Battered women and the state: From the failure of theory to a theory of
            failure. Journal of Human Justice 1:77–96.

Currie, Dawn, Brian MacLean, and Dragan Milovanovic
    In press Three traditions of critical justice inquiry: Class gender and discourse. In
            Dawn Currie and Brian MacLean (eds.), Struggle for equality: Re-Thinking
            the Administration of Justice. Toronto: Garamond Press.

Daly, Kathleen
    1987    Discrimination in the criminal courts: Family, gender, and the problem of
            equal treatment. Social Forces 66:152–175.

# CONSTITUTIVE CRIMINOLOGY 311

Daly, Kathleen and Meda Chesney-Lind
1988    Feminism and criminology. Justice Quarterly 5:497–438.

Danner, Mona J.E.
1989    Socialist feminism: A brief introduction. Critical Criminologist 1 (Summer):1–2.

Dekeseredy, Walter and Brian MacLean
1990    Researching women abuse in Canada: A realistic critique of the conflict tactics scale. Canadian Review of Social Policy 25 May:19–27.
In Press Exploring the gender, class, and race dimension of victimization: A realist critique of the Canadian urban victimization survey. International Journal of Offender Therapy and Comparative Criminology.

Deleuze, Gilles and Felix Guattari
1987    A Thousand Plateaus. Minneapolis: University of Minnesota Press.

Dennis, Dion
1989    Richard Quinney: An interview, 8/1/89. Critical Criminologist 1 (Summer):11–14.

Derrida, Jacques
1973    Speech and Phenomena. Evanston, Ill.: Northwestern University Press.
1981    Positions. Chicago: The University of Chicago Press.

Einstadter, Werner
1989    Asymmetries of Control: Technologies of Surveillance in the Theft of Privacy. Paper presented to Society for the Study of Social Problems, San Francisco, August.

Fitzpatrick, Peter
1984    Law and societies. Osgood Hall Law Journal 22:115–138.
1988    The rise and rise of informalism. In Roger Matthews (ed.), Informal Justice. London: Sage.

Foucault, Michel
1977    Discipline and Punish. New York: Pantheon.

Friedrichs, David
1986    Critical legal studies and the critique of criminal justice. Criminal Justice Review 112:15–11.
1989    Critical criminology and critical legal studies. The Critical Criminologist 1 (Summer):7.

Gelsthorpe, Loraine and Alison Morris
1988    Feminism and criminology in Britain. British Journal of Criminology 28:93–110.

Giddens, Anthony
1984    The Constitution of Society. Oxford: Polity Press.

Goodrich, Peter
1984    Law and language: An Historical and Critical Introduction. Journal of Law and Society 11:173–206.

Goffman, Erving
1961    Asylums: Essays in the Social Situation of Mental Patients and Other inmates. Garden City, N.Y.: Anchor.
1974    Frame Analysis. New York: Harper & Row.

312          HENRY AND MILOVANOVIC

1981      Forms of Talk. Oxford: Basil Blackwell.

Greenberg, David F., ed.
1981      Crime and Capitalism. Palo Alto, Calif.: Mayfield Publishing.

Greimas, Algirdas
1987      On Meaning. Minneapolis: University of Minnesota Press.

de Haan, Willem
1986      Abolitionism and the politics of bad conscience. In H. Bianchi and R. van
          Swaaningen (eds.), Abolitionism: Towards a Non-Repressive Approach to
          Crime. Amsterdam: Free Press.

Habermas, Jurgen
1984      The Theory of Communicative Action. Vol. 1: Reason and the Rationaliza-
          tion of Society. Boston: Beacon Press.
1987      The Theory of Communicative Action. Vol. 2: Lifeworld and System: A
          Critique of Functionalist Reason. Boston: Beacon Press.

Harrington, Christine
1988      Moving from integrative to constitutive theories of law. Law and Society
          Review 22:963–967.

Harrington, Christine and Sally Merry
1988      Ideological production: The making of community mediation. Law and
          Society Review 22:709–735.

Harrington, Christine and Barbara Yngvesson
1990      Interpretive sociolegal research. Law and Social Inquiry 15:135–148.

Harris, M. Kay
1987      Moving into the new millenium: Toward a feminist vision of justice. The
          Prison Journal 67:27–38.

Henry, Stuart
1983      Private Justice. London: Routledge & Kegan Paul.
1985      Community justice, capitalist society and human agency: The Dialectics of
          collective law in the cooperative. Law and Society Review 19:301–325.
1987      Private justice and the policing of labor: The dialectics of industrial
          discipline. In Clifford Shearing and Philip Stenning (eds.), Private Policing.
          Beverly Hills, Calif.: Sage.
1988a     Can the hidden economy be revolutionary? Toward a dialectic analysis of
          the relations between formal and informal economies. Social Justice
          15:29–60.
1988b     Rules, rulers and ruled in egalitarian collectives: Deviance and social
          control in cooperatives. In James G. Flanagan and Steve Rayner, Rules.
          Decisions, and Egalitarian Societies. Aldershot, United Kingdom: Avebury.
1989a     Constitutive criminology: The missing link. The Critical Criminologist 1
          (Summer):9, 12.
1989b     Justice on the margin: Can alternative justice be different. The Howard
          Journal of Criminal Justice 28:255–271.

Hunt, Alan
1987      The critique of law: What is "critical" about critical legal theory? Journal
          of Law and Society 14:5–19.

Jackson, Bernard
1985      Semiotics and Legal Theory. New York: Routledge and Kegan Paul.

# CONSTITUTIVE CRIMINOLOGY 313

1988     Law, Fact and Narrative Coherence. Merseyside, United Kingdom: Deborah Charles Publications.

Jakobson, Roman
1971     Two aspects of language and two types of aphasic disorders. In Roman Jakobson and Morris Halle, Fundamentals of Language. Paris: Mouton.

Jefferson, Tony
1990     The Case for Paramilitary Policing. Milton Keynes, United Kingdom: Open University Press.

Jessop, Bob
1982     The Capitalist State. New York: New York University Press.

Jones, Trevor, Brian MacLean, and Jock Young
1986     The Islington Crime Survey: Crime, Victimization, and Policing in Inner-City London. Aldershot, United Kingdom: Gower Press.

Kinsey, Richard, John Lea, and Jock Young
1986     Losing the Fight Against Crime. London: Basil Blackwell.

Klare, Karl
1979     Law making as praxis. TELOS 40:123–135.

Klein, Dorie
1973     The etiology of female crime: A review of the literature. Issues in Criminology 8:3–30.

Klockars, Carl
1980     The contemporary crisis of Marxist criminology. In James A. Inciardi (ed.), Radical Criminology. Beverly Hills, Calif.: Sage.

Knorr-Cetina, Karen and Aaron Cicourel
1981     Advances in Social Theory and Methodology: Toward an Integration of Macro- and Micro-Sociologies. London: Routledge & Kegan Paul.

Lacan, Jacque
1977     Ecrits, trans. Alan Sheridan. New York: W.W. Norton.

Lecercle, Jean-Jacque
1985     Philosophy Through the Looking Glass: Language, Nonsense, Desire. London: Hutchinson.

Luhmann, Niklas
1985     A Sociological Theory of Law. Boston: Routledge & Kegan Paul.

MacLean, Brian
1991     In partial defense of socialist realism. Crime, Law and Social Change: An International Journal 15(3).

Manning, Peter
1986     Signwork. Human Relations 39:283–308.
1987     Semiotics and Fieldwork. Newbury Park, Calif.: Sage.
1988     Symbolic Communication: Signifying Calls and the Police Response. Cambridge, Mass.: The MIT Press.
1990     Semiotics and postmodernism. In David Dickens and Andrea Fontana (eds.), Post Modernism and Sociology. Chicago: University of Chicago Press.

314                    HENRY AND MILOVANOVIC

Marx, Gary
    1988      Undercover: Policy Surveillance in America. Berkeley, University of
              California Press.
Marx, Karl
    1984      The eighteenth brumaire of Louis Bonaparte, 1852. K. Marx and F. Engels,
              Werke, in Eugene Kamenka (ed.), The Portable Marx. New York: Penguin.
Matthews, Roger
    1987      Taking realist criminology seriously. Contemporary Crisis 11:371–401.
Matthews, Roger and Jock Young, eds.
    1986      Confronting Crime. London: Sage.
Messerschmidt, James D.
    1986      Capitalism, Patriarchy and Crime: Toward a Socialist Feminist Criminol-
              ogy. Lanham, Md.: Rowman and Littlefield.
Milovanovic, Dragan
    1986      Juridico-linguistic communicative markets: Towards a semiotic analysis.
              Contemporary Crises 10:281–304.
    1988a     Jailhouse lawyers and jailhouse lawyering. International Journal of the
              Sociology of Law 16:455–475.
    1988b     Primer in the Sociology of Law. Albany: Harrow and Heston.
    1988c     Review essay: Critical legal studies and the assault on the bastion. Social
              Justice 15:161–172.
    1989      Critical criminology and the challenge of post modernism. The Critical
              Criminologist 1 (Winter):9–10, 17.
    1991a     Images of unity and disunity in the juridic subject and the movement to the
              peacemaking community. In Harold Pepinsky and Richard Quinney (eds.),
              Criminology as Peacemaking, Bloomington: Indiana University Press.
    1991b     Law, Semiotics and Reality Construction, unpublished manuscript, North-
              eastern Illinois University.
    In press  Rethinking subjectivity in law and ideology. In Dawn Currie and Brian
              Maclean (eds.), Struggle for Equality: Rethinking the Administration of
              Justice. Toronto: Garamond Press.
Milovanovic, Dragan and Jim Thomas
    1989      Overcoming the absurd: Prisoner litigation as primitive rebellion. Social
              Problems 36:48–60.
Morrissey, Elizabeth R.
    1985      Power and control through discourse: The case of drinking and drinking
              problems among women. Contemporary Crisis 10:57–79.
Pepinsky, Harold
    1986      This can't be peace: A pessimist looks at punishment. In W. Byron Groves
              and Graeme Newman (eds.), Punishment and Privilege. New York: Harrow
              and Heston.
    1989      Peacemaking in criminology. Critical Criminologist 1 (Summer):6–10.
Pepinsky, Harold and Richard Quinney, eds.
    1991      Criminology as Peacemaking. Bloomington: Indiana University Press.
Pfohl, Stephen J.
    1985      Toward a sociological deconstruction of social problems. Social Problems
              32:228–232.

CONSTITUTIVE CRIMINOLOGY 315

Quinney, Richard
    1988    The Theory and Practice of Peacemaking in the Development of Radical
            Criminology. Paper presented to American Society of Criminology, Chicago,
            November.

Schutz, Alfred
    1967    The Phenomenology of the Social World. Evanston, Ill.: Northwestern
            University Press.

Schwartz, Martin
    1989    The Undercutting edge of criminology. The Critical Criminologist 1
            (Spring):1–2, 5–6.

Schwendinger, Julia and Herman Schwendinger
    1983    Rape and Inequality. Newbury Park, Calif.: Sage.
    1985    Adolescent Subcultures and Delinquency. New York: Praeger.

Selva, Lance and Bob Bohm
    1987    Law and liberation: Toward an oppositional legal discourse. Legal Studies
            Forum 113:243–266.

Sudnow, David
    1965    Normal crimes: Sociological features of the penal code in a public defender
            office. Social Problems 12:255–276.

Thomas, Jim
    1988    Prisoner Litigation: The Paradox of the Jailhouse Lawyer. Totowa, N.J.:
            Rowman and Littlefield.

Thomas, Jim and Aogan O'Maochatha
    1989    Reassessing the critical metaphor: An optimistic revisionism view. Justice
            Quarterly 6:143–172.

Volosinov, Valentin
    1986    Marxism and the Philosophy of Language. Cambridge, Mass.: Harvard
            University Press.

Weiss, Robert P.
    1987    From "slugging detectives" to "labor relations". In Clifford D. Shearing and
            Philip C. Stenning (eds.), Private Policing. Beverly Hills, Calif.: Sage.

Willis, Paul
    1977    Learning to Labor. Farnborough, United Kingdom: Saxon House.

Young, Jock
    1987    The tasks facing a realist criminology. Contemporary Crisis 11:337–356.
    1988    Radical criminology in Britain: The emergence of a competing paradigm.
            British Journal of Criminology 28:159–183.
    1989    Realist Criminology. London: Sage.

316                    HENRY AND MILOVANOVIC

Stuart Henry is Associate Professor in the Department of Sociology, Anthropology and Criminology at Eastern Michigan University, where he teaches criminology, law and society, and white collar and corporate crime. His research has explored the constitutive relationship between informal networks of crime and justice and formal structures of society and law.

Dragan Milovanovic is Associate Professor of Criminal Justice at Northeastern Illinois University. He graduated from the School of Criminal Justice, State University of New York at Albany. His current research efforts are focused on post-modernism and semiotics and their impact on critical theory in ideology and law.

# [2]

# THE PERIPHERAL CORE OF LAW AND CRIMINOLOGY: ON POSTMODERN SOCIAL THEORY AND CONCEPTUAL INTEGRATION*

BRUCE A. ARRIGO
Duquesne University

Despite significant challenges to some of the ideological underpinnings of the postmodern critique, critical theory building in law and criminology increasingly is subjected to the wholesale advances of this growing, albeit heterodox, school of thought. One greatly underexamined component of postmodern research is a provisional treatment of how its various formulations might suggest alternative approaches to understanding criminal justicians, their research, and their practice. Accordingly this essay assesses core themes (both sociological and epistemological) informing the regard of this perspective for theory construction in law and criminology. Several topics are considered: the social structure of society, role formation, human agency, discourse construction, knowledge or sense making, and social change. Building on Milovanovic's conceptual distinctions between the modernist and the postmodernist projects, the author concludes by speculating on what a model of postmodern conceptual synthesis might encompass, and on how this vision of reality promotes a more humanistic justice than the conventional forms of theoretical integration.

The postmodern perspective gained prominence in law and criminology during the late 1980s. Some observers suggest that this perspective belongs at the more radical fringe of critical criminology (Schwartz and Friedrichs 1994:221-22). Others question whether critical criminology itself is not an expression or an extension of the postmodern condition (Cohen 1990:22). As an ideological framework, postmodernism signals an epistemological break from the more traditional understandings of scientific knowledge, reason and rationality, and social phenomena. Accordingly this alternative perspective rejects all conventional cause-effect relationships,

* A previous version of this paper was presented at the 46th annual meetings of the American Society of Criminology, held November 9-12, 1994 in Miami. The author wishes to acknowledge his indebtedness to Gregg Barak, Jim Thomas, Thomas Bernard, and Douglas Harper for support and advice on earlier drafts of this manuscript, and to two anonymous *Justice Quarterly* referees. Correspondence concerning this article should be addressed to Bruce A. Arrigo, Department of Sociology, Duquesne University, Pittsburgh, PA. 15282.

linear processes in thought, sense, and logic, and absolutist strategies for empirical, knowable investigation. For postmodernists, the path to solving human problems entails the use of a different set of scholastic tools.

Efforts to define the appropriate role of the postmodern critique as linked to contemporary issues in law and criminology continue to receive growing academic attention. Selected works have addressed relevant themes such as mental illness and punishment (Arrigo 1993a), feminism and law (Cornell 1991, 1993; Smart 1989), psychoanalysis and legal semiotics (Milovanovic 1992), rape and social violence (Arrigo 1993b), critical criminology and social justice (MacLean and Milovanovic 1991), policing and organizational behavior (Manning 1992), psychology and criminal justice (Arrigo forthcoming a), and legal discourse and legal reasoning (Goodrich 1987, 1990). This critical analysis continues to flourish, despite significant challenges to some of the ideological underpinnings of this "sense of theory" or school of thought (Hunt 1990:539).

Many divergent criticisms have been leveled against postmodernism. Opponents are divided into three major camps. Some view the theory as an anarchic science promoting an antithetical form of knowledge. Others perceive it as a pseudoscience promoting an antifoundational form of knowledge. Still others allege that it is difficult to specify the relationship, if any, of postmodernism to science and knowledge because of its abstruse language.

In support of the first challenge, critics dismiss postmodernism altogether. They contend that it is nothing more than subjectivism, relativism, fatalism, nihilism (Hunt 1990, 1991, 1993; Teubner 1992). As these scholars point out, if it is ultimately impossible to define notions such as truth, knowledge, progress, order, and the like, what, if anything, can be said about society, events in society, the human condition, or our encounters with the social order?

In support of the second challenge, critics are skeptical about postmodernism. They caution that in seeking to expose and "deconstruct" (i.e., trash) the inherent contradictions, inconsistencies, and other so-called irregularities in the construction of phenomena, postmodernism offers no recipe for improvement, tenders no forward-thinking advice, identifies no alternative script or text (Cohen 1990, 1991, 1993; Handler 1992; Rosenau 1992).

In support of the third challenge, critics are unsure of postmodernism. They struggle with the esoteric writing style of typical postmodern treatises and claim that such tracts suffer from a solipsistic, and self-aggrandizing discontent (Palmer 1990; Ritzer 1990). Schwartz and Friedrichs (1994:228), commenting on the dense and cryptic style of the writing, warn that postmodern analyses can be viewed as "gratuitously obscure, incoherent, and undisciplined." Alternatively, they suggest that these analyses may contain a political agenda, necessitating some serious consideration. For several critics, this very ambiguity in the prose fosters uncertainty about the role of postmodernism as praxis.

Despite these (and other) collective criticisms, a more deliberately focused investigation of the postmodern in criminal justice is conceptually and methodologically wanting. Accordingly, in this paper I explore how the postmodern agenda can provide some different ways of understanding law and criminology. Further, I consider how postmodern studies can tell us something more or something other about how jurists, criminologists, and criminal justicians view themselves in relation to their respective research and/ or practice roles. Both of these matters are potentially significant because they offer alternative approaches to reflective social criticism. As I will demonstrate, such an investigation is especially useful because the postmodern enterprise alerts us to what we do not know and subverts the comfortable structures of thought, images of reality, and certainty of thinking that underlie conventional criminal justice science.

This investigation extends Milovanovic's (1995) provisional assessment of several core sociological and epistemological forces underpinning both conventional (i.e., modernist) and nonconventional (i.e., postmodernist) theory construction and applies them to law and criminology. These themes of import include the social structure of society, role formation, human agency, discourse construction, knowledge or sense making, and social change. I believe that this conceptual approach offers great potential for appreciating postmodernism and its likely contributions to criminal and legal thought. Along the way, I use various justice-based illustrations to help ground the otherwise abstract and philosophical material. I conclude by speculating on the importance of theoretical synthesis in the study of modernist and postmodernist law, crime, and deviance. This supplemental commentary will extend and apply the previous analysis to an identifiable topic of criminal justice concern. Further, this analysis will provide a provisional, speculative backdrop from which to respond directly to the criticisms leveled against the postmodern perspective.

## UNDERSTANDING THE POSTMODERN PERSPECTIVE

There is delicious irony in presenting a postmodernist version of criminal justice while relying on a more traditional, shared (i.e., logocentric) system of communication. If postmodernism signifies a perspective outside or apart from standard methods of knowing, experiencing, and living, how can one nevertheless invoke that traditional discourse, which itself is anathema to the postmodern enterprise in law and criminology, to explain that enterprise? Although philosophically I concede the contradiction, methodologically my aim is to make a provisional case for the conceptual project; for now, this can be accomplished only from within the conventional reader's frame of reference. Accordingly I use traditional categories of logic (e.g., consistency in thought, syllogistic reasoning, principles of coherence) to interpret the meaning of postmodern theory for purposes of criminology and law. This approach does not detract from my argument; it simply acknowledges one area where analysis beyond the scope of this article is required. Thus the objective here is to teach the reader about the relevance of the postmodern perspective for criminological and legal theory construction by writing (i.e., discoursing) in its unique grammar and system of communication.

The theoretical constituents and/or antecedents of postmodernism rely heavily on the philosophy of poststructuralism, the science of semiotics, and the method of deconstructionism (Arrigo 1993a:27-75; also see Benson 1989:158-61; Einstadter and Henry 1995, ch. 12). The brief definitional statements that follow are vast over simplifications and are intended to convey only useful, though limited, introductory distinctions.

*Poststructuralism* is primarily a French and German orientation to the sociology of knowledge in which the unveiling of "deep" structures in language systems (such as law and criminology) is understood never to be entirely possible. Poststructuralists maintain that the meaning of "texts"—whether spoken or written, or whether visual images such as film or nonverbal images such as communication by gesture—always explodes and scatters, defying the certainty of any one particular truth or any ultimate Truths.

*Semiotics* is the study of language understood as a collection of *signs*. There are many languages (e.g., sports, medicine, computers, engineering, law); therefore there are many sign systems. Semioticians maintain that all words, phrases, gestures, and the like within a language system represent something more or something other than the things themselves. Accordingly they examine the multiple and evolving meaning(s) communicated in and through discourse.

*Deconstructionism* is a literary and discursive method of analysis that shows how all human affairs and all social phenomena are assembled, and how they can be disassembled and eventually reassembled to incorporate excluded "voices" or multiple and sometimes

contradictory images of reality. Deconstructionism, as the preferred form of postmodern inquiry, accomplishes this goal by teasing out the significant warring factions (i.e., implicit and explicit
messages representing values) communicated in the discourse of
any text.

   Collectively, poststructuralism, semiotics, and deconstructionism reflect a unique view of language and intersubjective communication. For the postmodernist, meaning and intent are *always*
conveyed from within a particular language system. An example
from the legal sphere illustrates this point. To do "good law," the
litigator must invoke a particular grammar. This grammar represents the discourse of the legal community. Thus attorneys who
have any hope for a successful practice must situate themselves
and be inserted in the "language (and rules) of the game" (Lyotard
1984:10; also see Wittgenstein 1953). The expressions *legalese* and
*lawspeak* are invoked to convey this point. The discourse itself,
then, is a specialized code or language system (Milovanovic
1986:281-96) most appropriately known to practitioners or others
uniquely informed. Those of us who have deliberated over the interpretive details of a copyright contract, a lease agreement, a will,
an appellate transcript, and the like can appreciate how legal intent and meaning are conveyed from within a particular communicative market.

   The postmodern perspective presents the same invitation to
discourse as does any language system. The listener or reader must
enter and be situated within the specialized coordinates of
postmodernism. Thus, customary thought processes are challenged—if not altogether repudiated—as reflected in the form and
content of many postmodern critiques. As Milovanovic suggests
when considering the application of Lacanian psychoanalytic semiotics to law,

> To read Lacan one must undo the conventional ties and
> psychological commitments to discourse and develop more
> intuitive ideas generated by a new vocabulary that at-
> tempts to provide the unconscious . . . with a somewhat
> recognizable voice (1993a:314).

Schwartz and Friedrichs ponder the potential of postmodern
thought to provide new metaphors by which to understand criminological theory on violence:

> Is the obstacle the fact that the rest of us are unable to
> liberate ourselves from the constraints of interpreting the
> world in the familiar idiom of rational, contemporary social
> science? If we reoriented ourselves, would we find modes
> and styles of understanding that are ultimately more valid
> and more revealing in a changing, endlessly complex
> world? (1994:228)

Following this reading of the postmodern perspective, we take the position that a theoretical project as outlined (i.e., in relation to the foregoing themes) is not an arrival at truth but a *departure* from truth (Barthes 1988:263-65). That is, the explication that follows is intended to sensitize: raising provisional questions about the peripheral core of law and criminology leads to further provisional questions. Thus the text presented here must be viewed as layered or tissued; it merely identifies "ruptures" or digressions in conventional meaning and invites the reader to assume greater responsibility for discovering or interpreting the identified themes as they unfold.

## (POST) MODERN THEORY BUILDING IN LAW AND CRIMINOLOGY

*The Social Structure of Society*

Currently in vogue are conceptions of law and criminology that borrow heavily from structural-functional ideology. The legacy of Durkheim, Weber, Parsons, and Merton finds expression in Luhmann's (1985, 1992; also see Teubner 1988, 1993) systems theory of autopoiesis, Dworkin's (1986) coherence principle of juridical reasoning, Posner's (1986, 1992) economic efficiency rationale privileging social accord, Hirschi's (1969) control theory assessing crime and deviance (also see Gottfredson and Hirschi 1990; Nettler 1984). Underlying these and other consensus-oriented approaches are notions of order, stasis, predictability, normativity, positivity, homogeneity. These forces are understood to be at the center of our existence. Society is said to be governed by global organizing principles that seek discovery and articulation. Causal explanations of law and crime begin by invoking linear, predictable (stimulus-response) forces or heretofore concealed but anchored realities, which the deviant repeatedly and certifiably transgresses.[1]

The postmodern agenda, however, is situated within an altogether different logic. Its centerpiece is a resistance to linear foundations—that is, a debunking of predictability and permanence— not simply as a gesture of political opposition but more particularly as an acknowledgment of the indeterminate structuration of the lifeworld (Giddens 1984, 1990). Predictable unpredictability (i.e.,

---

[1] Admittedly, various strains of conflict criminology have endeavored to expose several of the structural conditions in society which promote status quo practices in law, crime, and deviance (e.g., Black 1976; Collins 1975; Quinney 1970). They have largely failed, however, to address the commodity of discourse which privileges certain modes of linguistic production while invalidating others (Rossi-Landi 1977; for Marxist-based applications in law and criminology, see Arrigo 1993c:16-20; Milovanovic 1986:294-96). In this regard, then, typical modernist conceptions of conflict ideology unwittingly adopt the consensus position that language is neutral.

chaos theory or orderly disorder) is said to condition social interaction. Indeed, postmodernists, relying on the advances of quantum physics and mechanics (Bohm 1951, 1981; Wolf 1981, 1984), catastrophe theory, Heisenberg's *uncertainty principle* (that reality is created by the observer even at the level of subatomic events), and Gödel's (1962) theorem on the impossibility of formal closure (i.e., the absence of finiteness or bounded realities), identify and embrace a perceived paradigmatic rupture within the origins of social formations.

The natural science community, informed by the works of Briggs and Peat (1989), Feigenbaum (1980), Gleick (1987), Mandelbrot (1983), Porter and Gleick (1990), Prigogine and Stengers (1984), and Stewart (1989), initiated this foray into the realm of essential structural instabilities. They challenged Aristotelian logic, Euclidian geometry, Newtonian physics, and all other overarching principles of order contained in the positivistic, deterministic naturalistic sciences. The theory has it that order lurks within apparent randomness. This randomness itself represents a set range of results, an underlying but not predictable order—that is, chaos. To illustrate, a few years ago a group of researchers at Harvard Medical School created a stir when they demonstrated how the human heart operates as a *chaotic system.* Contrary to conventional medicine, these scientists pointed out how an erratic heart is healthier than one showing a perfect EKG. As they suggested, "Counterintuitively, increasingly regular behavior sometimes accompanies aging and disease. Irregularity and unpredictability, then, are important features of health" (Marino 1994:11).[2]

This logic of natural instabilities or *far-from-equilibrium* conditions as structuring the social order was first applied in literature (Hayles 1990, 1991; Serres 1982a, 1982b) and then in psychoanalysis and psychology respectively (Abraham, Abraham, and Shaw 1990; Butz 1991, 1992; Deleuze and Guattari 1987; Milovanovic 1992; Wolinsky 1991, 1993). More recently, the insights of chaos theory developed in the physical sciences have found some legitimacy in the social scientific community as well. In particular, studies in criminology (Arrigo forthcoming a; Young 1991) and law (Arrigo 1994a, 1994b, forthcoming b; Brion 1991; Young 1991; Milovanovic 1993a, 1993b) are beginning to explore the significance of practices based on orderly disorder in justice-related research.

---

2 Following this line of inquiry, a similar analysis could help explain the figuration of other natural phenomena thought to be accidental and anomalous, such as the pattern of waves washing up against a coastal shoreline, the sundry designs of windblown snowscapes, or the symmetry of brainwave activity during bouts of dissociation.

454   LAW, CRIMINOLOGY, AND POSTMODERN THEORY

Theory construction in law and criminology often begins with global assumptions (rationales about situational crime notwithstanding). Yet these totalizing assumptions about individual actors, specific events in the social order, precise definitions of a deviant's behavior, and such are positioned in a normatively contrived and homeostatically articulated arrangement of reality. *The nature of law and crime is such that it is retrievable, reducible, and therefore essentially knowable.* This equilibrium model itself is illusory, and ultimately is rejected. In other words, chaologists regard such absolutist characterizations as lacking the subtleties, the contradictions, and the incompletenesses that symbolize the more organically based dynamics of the lifeworld (e.g., its serendipity, irony, incommensurability, spontaneity).

Nonlinear conditions of flux are viewed more appropriately as ordering the universe, according to chaos theorists. Consider the disturbing aftermath of the first trial of Los Angeles County officers prosecuted for using force against Rodney King. When the jury rendered its verdict, *several* major cities were besieged by riots, bloodshed, and violence. The outbursts in jurisdictions such as Philadelphia, Detroit, Seattle, and New York could not be linked causally or linearly to the acquittals of officers in Los Angeles. A definite relationship existed, however. As chaologists would remind us, the example of the jury verdict is comparable to the flapping of wings by a butterfly in southeast Asia eventually causing a hurricane in Florida. In both cases, structuration (predictability) stems from initial conditions of chaos (indeterminability). In other words, order emerges from chaos or apparent randomness.

*Role Formation*

The postmodern regard for position or status departs significantly from the modernist approach. The modernist schema celebrates the socially prescribed responsibilities and privileges coordinating the role. The effect is a reduction— that is, a closure to possibilities of greater being or becoming. Thus individuals assume and live out stable and predictable characterizations that tend to promote "either/or" identifications. People are interpreted as deviants or conformists; law violators or law abiders; villains or heroes; liberals or conservatives; straights or gays. In the words of one virulent critic of the positivist approach,

> Modern science . . . has separated subject and object, mind and body, self and other, human and animal, man and woman and earth. All objects in the modern world, even the human subject and human body, are treated as lifeless, as cadavers (Malhotra Bentz 1993:122).

In the postmodern sciences, roles are open-ended and effusive. In accordance with the contributions of chaology, identity is a constant source of negotiation.[3] The example, in law, of the "hard case" is instructive here. The judge is presented with at least two possible resolutions. In that instance, when a jurist deliberates and ponders the decision, tension between validating legal heritage and endorsing legal heresy fosters a situation of resolute undecidability (Brion 1991:64-75). After several rulings on difficult cases, however, a decision-making pattern (a juridical identity) is recognizable.

Postmodern or "second wave" feminist commentators add to the question of role formation in their critique of the gendered subject in discourse. The psycholinguistics of Luce Irigaray (1985, 1990), the literary criticism of Julia Kristeva (1977, 1980, 1984), and the educational psychology of Carol Gilligan (1982; also see Brown and Gilligan 1993; Gilligan, Lyons, and Hanmer 1990) have been significant to the postmodern feminist movement, each in their own way. More recently, these insights have been applied to studies on law (Arrigo, 1992; Cornell 1991, 1993; MacKinnon 1987, 1989; Smart 1989, 1992) and criminology (Arrigo 1993b; Gelsthorpe and Morris 1990; Smart 1990). Standpoint epistemology identifies where and how women and minorities with their differential statuses in society, continue to experience exclusion in criminal and legal practices (e.g., Cain 1992; Currie 1993:15-19; Daly and Chesney-Lind 1988). Postmodern feminism, however, makes sense of these differences and validates these multiplicities (i.e. gender, race, and class) *within the discourse of theory building*.

The essential challenge of second-wave feminism is to articulate a grammar (an *écriture féminine*) freed from the misogynous trappings of the phallocentric culture and language (Arrigo 1992:21-24, 1994c). This privileged "malestream" code possesses the capacity to define women and minorities (i.e., to assign role-appropriate formations) only in masculine terms. According to these terms, *phallogocentric* interests (i.e., gender-based conventional

---

3 The issue of negotiating identity does not lack verification. Here negotiation stands for the proposition that the constitution of one's self has meaning only in relation to one's projects over time. Existential-phenomenological thought first developed this theme in connection with intuiting, through a *directed glance of attention* (i.e., the eidetic reduction via intentionality), one's *transcendental ego* (essential identity formation) (Husserl 1983:199-201), or intersubjectively experiencing one's bodily and perspectival *being-in-the-world* (Heidegger 1962; Merleau-Ponty 1962). Ethnomethodologists refined this notion further in their critique of the social construction of reality as constituting the *stock of knowledge* (Berger and Luckman 1966; Garfinkle 1956, 1967; Schutz 1967). Interactionists contributed their dramaturgically informed regard for the *presentation of the self* (Goffman 1959, 1966, 1967). Constructivists participated through their investigation of social problems as typifications (Best 1989; Spector and Kitsuse 1987).

logic) (Arrigo 1992:19; Irigaray 1985:70-72; Lahey 1985:538; Smart 1989) are advanced and esteemed. Thus, by extension, "uniaccentuated" power is embedded in notions such as law, crime, victimization, and control—that is, power anchored by a specialized discourse in which individual identity is always and already a reduction enveloped in masculine meanings.

*Human Agency*

The modernist regard for the subject's pivotal role in communicating meaning, being, identity, freedom, discourse, and embodiment was celebrated most fully during the Renaissance era. The prominent intellectual movement was Enlightenment philosophy; its preeminent representative was René Descartes. Cartesian epistemology presupposed the existence of a knowing, acting, unified subject. The thinking being was understood to be rational, stable, purposive. This centered and ubiquitous subject (or "I") was at the core of all human affairs. The modernist's appreciation for subjectivity was best exemplified in Descartes's renowned maxim: *Cogito, ergo sum.*

Unlike the rationalistic, mechanistic, and individualistic prescription of Cartesian logic, postmodernity offers an alternative reading of role formation. Several proponents of the latter perspective are persuaded by the contributions of Jacques Lacan (1975, 1977, 1985, 1991) and his psychoanalytic semiotics on intrapsychic (internal) and intersubjective (interpersonal) communication.[4]

The Lacanian version of subjectivity presents a vastly different understanding of the self-actualizing and self-governing individual. For Lacan, the unconscious is structured much like a language in which the speaking being (*l'être parlant*) is more determined than determining; that is, regulated more by unconscious workings, which themselves are situated in competitive grammars (discourses) communicating multiple and sometimes contradictory meanings. Ultimately, however, the mellifluous voices of the primary-process region (i.e., the unconscious, or *Autre*) are harnessed and anchored by one language system, in keeping with materialistically based and system-maintaining discourse (Arrigo 1994a, forthcoming a,b,c). In other words, our unconscious thoughts already are *accented* (i.e., systemically encoded) with desire, representing

---

4 The emphasis on Lacan (and his epigones) is not surprising when we consider that many well-known and highly regarded postmodern ideologues (e.g., Julia Kristeva, Michel Foucault, Roland Barthes, Luce Irigaray, Jacques Derrida, and Jean Baudrillard) were known to have attended Lacan's famous Parisian lectures, delivered from the 1950s through the 1970s.

the logic of capital and saturated in a phallocratic economy (Althusser 1971; Lacan 1977:193, 303-16. For a feminist critique of Lacanian *phallic desire,* see Irigaray 1985; Ragland-Sullivan 1986; Sellers 1991. For an application to law and criminology, see Arrigo 1993b, 1994c). Thus the subject in speech is not centered, unified, self-actualized; rather, the individual is more appropriately *decentered,* divided, determined. Descartes's famous aphorism is recast as "I think where I am not, therefore I am where I do not think" (Lacan 1977:166). In other words, rather than the plenary, unified "I," Lacan proposes a version of the subject determined *both* by conscious states and by the effects of unconscious processes (Arrigo forthcoming c).

Intimately linked to the idea of human agency is the place of desire. The understanding and regard of modernity for desire is expressed perhaps most vividly in some of Freud's (1927, 1949) works. Desire symbolizes that which must be regulated, held in check, or placed in abeyance. It is a conservative force that one must reckon with if order and predictability are to prevail. One's unconscious longings, if neglected, will result in psychic disorganization and social disequilibrium.

The desiring subject also figures prominently in the postmodern conception of human agency. Once again we must turn to Lacan for guidance. In the Lacanian conception, desire represents the excess or that which is beyond existential fulfillment awaiting articulation. Lacan termed this desire *jouissance* or *jouissense.* The subject is denied his or her need to convey personalized meaning (and being) in the act of speech precisely because ideologically repressive state apparatuses (Althusser 1971:143) (e.g., faith communities, the corporate sector, the educational sphere, the criminal justice apparatus) superimpose their discursive communicative structures (their linguistically accented reality) on the discourse of others. Thus desiring subjects, endeavoring to communicate their interiorized longing, seeking to articulate their intrinsic meaning and being, are imprisoned in the prevailing language system.[5]

---

[5] Lacan (1991) has described this process in greater detail, demonstrating how the decentered subject functions as the unwitting participant in the *discourse of the master* (also see Arrigo 1994a, forthcoming, c; Bracher 1988). The *discourse of the master* is one of four specialized discourses developed by Lacan along with the *discourse of the university, the hysteric, and the analyst.* The relationship and the complexity of these communication modalities have been examined by others (e.g., Arrigo 1994b, forthcoming a, c; Bracher 1993; Lee 1990; Milovanovic 1992). For our purposes, following the *discourse of the master,* subjects constitute and are constituted by that unique grammar which advances only system-supporting declarations (i.e., the logic of capital as phallocratically conceived). Lost in the discourse is the possibility for establishing genuine, more authentic forms of interaction and intersubjective communication.

458     LAW, CRIMINOLOGY, AND POSTMODERN THEORY

Both law and criminology provide many occasions for exposing the juridic subject to the state's practices of linguistic hegemony. In the courtroom, for example, jailhouse lawyers find that they must *re-present* the inmate's story in ways that are consistent only with the system-endorsing and -normalizing speech contained in the legal sphere (Milovanovic 1988). If the jailhouse lawyer resists, opposing counsel will state objections and the bench may declare the inmate's case nonjusticiable. To illustrate further, individuals petitioning to be released from involuntary civil confinement must demonstrate to a psychiatric tribunal that they are no longer a danger to themselves and/or to others. To achieve this result, petitioners must rely on discourse which suggests that they are *depathologized* (Arrigo 1993a, 1994a, forthcoming a,c). In other words, they must comport themselves linguistically in such ways that their desire, as expressed to the court, is consistent with language signifying psychological wellness. If the petitioners adopt any other pattern of communication, it can precipitate a return to institutional confinement. These examples demonstrate that desire, anchored by speech consistent only with system-maintaining declarations, may deny individuals their linguistic and concomitant social reality. The manifestation of this problem is the essence of linguistic oppression.

In postmodernity, desire symbolizes a liberating, freeing, positive presence (Dews 1987:132). Modernity seeks the *territorialization of desire* (Deleuze and Guattari 1987); postmodernity endeavors to emancipate it. The latter perspective accomplishes its goal by legitimating previously excluded voices and by revalidating those language systems which communicate the marginalized citizen's unencumbered meaning *and* essential being (Lacan 1977:275; Lee 1990:95-99, 168-70).

*Discourse*

Unlike the modern sciences, the postmodern perspective views language as value-laden, nonneutral, and politically charged. Discourse represents the interests and goals of oppressive power elites or other collectives. This understanding in criminological and legal theory construction has roots in legal realism and includes notables such as Holmes (1897), Pound (1908), Frank ([1930]1963), Llewellyn (1930, 1931), Llewellyn and Hoebel (1941), and Rumble (1968). Today the realist tradition has resurfaced in the form of the critical legal studies (CLS) movement and is infused with the more acerbic expressions of postmodern discontent. CLS writers endeavor to unmask the layered dimensions of subjectivity and indeterminacy inherent in traditional understandings of law and crime, victimization and control, justice and punishment (Arrigo 1993a:51-55; Benson 1989; 161-65; Kelman 1987; Peller 1985). As one commentator remarked when exploring the junctures and disjunctures between legal realism and critical legal studies,

> [W]hile the realists too believed law was politics, right down to the partisan politics of individual judges, the politics CLS has in mind is the deeper political ideology of liberal individualism, which privileges the individual over community, hierarchy over equality, the private sphere over the public, free will over social cause explanations. These privileged norms—and the classist, racist, sexist, and domineering arrangements which result from them— are systematically cemented into our culture by legal discourse; *departures from the norms are repressed, treated as exceptions* (Benson 1989:164; emphasis added).

More recently, however, the CLS agenda and its emphasis on discourse construction has been supplanted by criminological and legal ideology embracing Michel Foucault's work on *disciplinary institutions* and Jurgen Habermas's treatment of *steering mechanisms* (Arrigo 1992, 1993a, 1993b; also see Lecercle 1985 on the *violence of language*). In brief, these investigations show how certain forms of technology or discoveries in science promote new modes of surveillance (e.g., advances in forensics, criminology, epidemiology) and inform our response to crime control, such that certain discourses are privileged as discursive formations of knowledge or truth. These normalizing practices are linked to power, and affirm only those knowledge assertions which advance the prevailing truth regime. Any resistance, such as the invocation of alternative grammars (e.g., oppositional speech patterns or codes), although it challenges the legitimacy of the prevailing language system, is thwarted by sociolinguistic hegemony and reification. Through these disciplinary mechanisms (hegemony and reification) a certain discourse, a specialized grammar, maintains its privileged status. This esteemed discourse, as a system of communication (i.e., as a system of meaning), embodies desire that invalidates the difference which constitutes resistant or oppositional citizens.[6]

---

6 Lacan's rich psychoanalytics are instructive here as well, particularly when they signal how much semiotic activity occurs before the spoken word (paradigm) is coupled with the actual speech chains (syntagm). Desire in language begins at a more nonreflexive, unconscious level. What we say and how we say it (Lacan's paradigm-syntagm semiotic axis) depends on the effects of other pre-uttered forces, including the condensation-displacement axis and the metaphor-metonymic axis. According to Lacan, these three tropes constitute a semiotic grid (Milovanovic, 1992; also see Arrigo forthcoming b, c for criminological application). Their combinatory impact is what is meant by intrapsychic and intersubjective communication. Exploring these overlapping axes is beyond the scope of the present study, although they are the source of rich theoretical insight pertinent to law and criminology. For our

460   LAW, CRIMINOLOGY, AND POSTMODERN THEORY

Several postmodernists have offered suggestions for overcoming the dictatorial hold of language. In addition to decentering activities such as Lecercle's insistence on the disruptive language of the body (*délire*), Deleuze and Guattari's (1986, 1987) suggestion of *minor literatures*, and Serres's (1982a:65-70) notion of *noise*, Lacan (1985:145) makes an excursion into alternative forms of *jouissance*—for example, an *écriture féminine* or a supplementary discourse grounded in an uncultivated, nonmisogynized female sexuality.[7]

Related to these suggestions is constitutive theory. As developed in criminology (Henry and Milovanovic 1991) and law (Hunt 1993), constitutive thought examines the dialectics of linguistic control. Proponents of this ideology maintain that the complicity of the subjects (e.g., judges, defense advocates, police agents, victims, lay professionals, the media) in acquiescing to language and its dictatorial constraints needs to be investigated. In brief, constitutive theorists argue that crime reduction and justice rendering are *coterminous* and will come about only when subjects abandon their co-constitutive investment in the established doctrine (the ossified language) of criminal justice.

*Knowledge*

Much of the preceding discussion points to the question of knowledge and the conditions in which it is constituted. For the modernist, knowledge as truth embodies an attainable, certifiable object awaiting discovery. The epistemology of Enlightenment science endeavored to quantify and posit the world and social phenomena, embracing a tension-reduction dynamic always in search of *ultimate truths* or *totalizing realities*. The modern episteme is committed to certainty, closure, finiteness, determinacy, completeness. Much of that period's legacy lives on today in many empirical works exploring topical issues related to law and criminology.

---

purposes, however, we wish to point out that the interactive effects of the grid produce the spoken word and *re-present* the first level of semiotic production. The first sphere is the structural axis (i.e., the unconscious, systemic encoding of desire) discussed previously in relation to subjectivity.

   [7] Another strategy developed by Lacan includes the joint effects of the *discourse of the hysteric and the analyst*. He developed these two additional communication modalities. Within the combinatory operation of these discourses, different forms of *jouissance* are embodied in the structure of alternative, nonauthoritarian grammars. In the clinicolegal apparatus, for example, where defendants are seeking psychiatric justice, replacement speech patterns embodying the jargon of inconsistency, absurdity, indeterminacy, incompleteness, and flux need to be valorized. Of course, this newly embraced language system must be affirmed insofar as it, too, does not function as a privileged and therefore oppressive code (Arrigo 1994a, forthcoming a, b, c). I maintain that such a system of communication would offer transformative possibilities for denoting alternative, more complete expressions of articulated *jouissance* within criminal justice praxis.

The postmodern sciences interpret sense making differently. Unlike "scientific" knowledge, which is privileged as the dominant discourse in modernist thinking, postmodern analysis seeks the discovery of "narrative" knowledge (Sarup 1989:120-21; also see Arrigo 1992:24-27; 1993b:33-37 on *imaginative discourse*; Cornell 1991:168-96 on the *imagination and utopian possibility*; Lacan 1985:143-47 on *mythic knowledge*). Truth, justice, reason, progress, and other similar abstractions are based on myths, symbols, and metaphors representing the historicity of a given culture as an incomplete and unfolding life story. Postmodern thought seeks the discovery, articulation, and affirmation of repressed voices (excluded stories) and the codes of speech that constitute their logos. In this regard, then, knowledge is provisional and relational; that is, logic is local, not global (Dews 1987); meaning is contingent, not certain (Sarup 1989); understanding is fragmented, not complete (Lyotard 1984); truth is a departure, not an arrival (Barthes 1988).

Contributions from feminist ideology further support the postmodern agenda. In part, the maxim "The personal is empirical" (McDermott 1992:237-45) signals how liberal feminists interpret knowledge. That which is personal, however, may also be the site of power and therefore may also advance the subordination of those who experience differently. Accordingly, postmodern feminist thought is equipped with the insights of Foucault, Irigaray, Marx, Kristeva, Habermas, and Lacan. Selected works in law and criminology have been especially careful to point out that any systematic constitution, as a doctrinal approach, possesses the capacity to function as an oppressive methodology (Arrigo 1993a:45-51; 1993b:32, 38-43; 1994c). Therefore, that which is offered as knowledge must be debunked flexibly: "What is posited must also be reversed, only to loop around again as a supplement to the reversal" (Arrigo 1992:20-21).

The application of postmodern principles of sense making to law and criminology challenges and disrupts the icons of modernist justice. Embedded in the language of expressions such as "burdens of *proof*," "a demand for *factual evidence*," "*actual* legal intent," "*expert* testimony," "*causes* of crime," and "the *reasonable* wo/man standard" are notions of power, conveying only certain truths and representing the ideology of the male-centered *master discourse*. A blend of Lacan's *discourses of the hysteric and analyst* (see notes 6-7 and the accompanying text), postmodern feminist ideology, and constitutive theory points to a more liberating process in which alternative or new knowledge claims can be embodied in intersubjective communication.

*Social Change*

The modern sciences embrace a linear understanding of historical change. Evidence is found in Darwin's ([1959]1968) biosocial *theory of evolution*, Weber's (1978) critique of *formal rationality* (also see Habermas 1984 on *purposive rational action*), and Hegel's ([1807] 1977) phenomenology of the *Absolute Spirit*. In short, the modernist tradition harbors a lingering suspicion that "a backstage mechanism, an outside reality [exists], affecting the human drama" (Benson 1989:159). Thus the search for objective mechanisms (e.g., basic structural mechanisms that anchor the law and criminology) not only contributes meaningfully to our understanding of human affairs but also provides reassurance of an underlying, permanent stability to the social order.

Change in the modernist framework therefore entails reducing the undifferentiated possibilities to discernible linear outcomes through institutional responses. In other words, social transformation begins when ossified systems react functionally to differentiation in the environment. In law, for example, we see this linear regard for social change in Hart's (1961) assessment of the penumbra of uncertainty structuring legal rules. Essential or "settled" meanings are situated at the "core" of this uncertainty. More recently, Dworkin's (1986:216) analysis of legal reasoning shows how judges search for the single best answer to a legal issue by "finding the interpretation which brings all the relevant legal materials together into the most coherent scheme" (as cited in Benson 1989:164; also see Luhmann 1985:237 on the *surplus of possibilities* and law). The result is a tension-reduction dynamic, yielding predictability in social planning.

The postmodern perspective on social change is attuned more closely to the nonlinear features of the lifeworld. The pivotal thinker is Nietzsche (1980) with his notion of *transpraxis* (also see Deleuze 1983; Henry and Milovanovic 1991:305-309). Unlike Hegel's ([1807]1977) reaction-negation dynamics regarding the master-slave relationship, Nietzsche's perspective points to a more active phenomenon of change which includes deconstructionism and reconstructionism. Following Hegel, when one reacts to perceived hierarchical power relations and seeks to repudiate them, the act of negating creates new forms of domination (i.e., the reproduction of relations to production); these also exert their marginalizing effects on human subjects. Conversely, in Nietzschean transpraxis, critical attention is directed toward the reconstitutive effects inherent in any attempt to neutralize or challenge that which is negated.

In regard to our Lacanian analysis of subjectivity, discourse, and desire, postmodernists endeavor to transcend the imposed parameters and imagery of conventional truth claims. They embrace that version of historical change in which flux, chance, indeterminacy, and irony prevail. Social planning requires a *double negation* or *negative dialectics* (Adorno 1973). Thus the marginalized subject (e.g., the disempowered citizen in law) must break free from the constraining linguistic categories of traditional reason and rationality imposed by the *discourse of the master*. Moreover, the subject in discourse must become a divided self embodying that difference which constitutes his or her logos (see Pecheux 1982 on *dis-identification* and Cixous 1990 on *le dépense*).

In justice-related pursuits, some movement toward such change can be traced to the peacemaking agenda (e.g., Pepinsky 1993; Pepinsky and Quinney 1991). Accordingly, postmodernists recognize the harm, suffering, and pain caused by acts of violence and "seek to examine [what legal and criminological pursuits] might reduce [them] through transforming the totality of relations of which [the harm, suffering, and pain] [are] a part" (Henry and Milovanovic 1991:309). Much of this transformation relates to our embracing alternative conceptions of society's social structure, role formation, human agency, discourse construction, knowledge, or sense making, along with other important themes not examined here. Therefore social change and social justice require a responsible and active debunking (i.e., deconstruction) by criminal justice scholars and practitioners addressing the politically constructed, ideologically articulated, media-driven dimensions of social problems (Barak 1988:585).

The task here is not to construct "new and different" versions of truth, justice, law, crime, and the like in ways that typify systematic reconstitutions. This exercise would foster nothing more than the reaction-negation problem implicit in Hegelian thought. Rather, the peacemaking agenda envisioned here considers the *duality* (or mutuality) implicit in our understanding of victimization, control, punishment, law, and order. Further, this agenda endeavors to change our *linguistic* (and therefore social) relationship to such phenomena in ways that foster a more liberating experience of human subjects, the social order, and their interconnectedness.

## (POST)MODERN CONCEPTUAL INTEGRATION IN LAW AND CRIMINOLOGY: RETHINKING THE DEBATE AND RECONSIDERING (CRIMINAL) JUSTICE

In this section I extend and apply my conceptual analysis to theoretical synthesis in law, crime, and deviance. In particular, I speculate on how postmodern theoretical integration is distinct from modernist forms of synthesis (i.e., classical integration or theory competition). I conclude by explaining how a postmodern reading of conceptual synthesis represents an alternative vision of reality construction—that is, a more inclusive replacement logic in justice-oriented endeavors. I maintain that this type of conceptual application helps to deepen out appreciation for the vagaries of postmodernism and their likely contributions to law, criminology, and humanistic justice.

In recent years, traditional theories of crime, deviance, and law have argued for the necessity of conceptual integration (e.g., Messner, Krohn, and Liska 1989:2-5; also see Bernard 1989; Colvin and Pauly 1983; Elliot 1985; Luhmann 1985; Pearson and Weiner 1985). These advocates, who largely embrace Collins's (1986:1345) position on the central role of theory in scientific endeavors, maintain that "the essence of science is precisely theory." Thus, in the conventional context, the aim of theoretical synthesis is to point out the linkages among different conceptual arguments as a way of advancing theoretical scientific growth because synthetic analyses offer a more cogent explanation for promoting objective science than do other strategies (Messner et al. 1989:2; also see Wagner and Berger 1985).

Accordingly, for example, we can speak of *up-and-down* (deductive), *side-by-side* (parallel), or *end-to-end* (sequential) types of integration in criminology (Hirschi 1979) when applied to micro-, macro-, or cross-level integration. These tell us more about the nature of crime and delinquency than does the conventional strategy of theory competition. In the latter instance, a criminological approach such as social learning may be positioned against social control, labeling against deterrence, role strain against conflict. The more successfully a given theory survives *crucial tests* of verification (i.e., an evaluation of a tested theory's implications against empirical observations), the greater its perceived credibility and the greater the skepticism regarding its competitors (Stinchcombe 1968:27-28).

The difference between classical integration and competition by an alternative theory can be defined summarily. The former constructs a causal model by identifying similar themes contained in different criminological and/or legal perspectives; the latter privileges its own model as the single best causal explanation in the study of justice-related concerns. In other words, classical integration practices totalizing analyses by emphasizing *sameness* (connections), whereas theory competition supports globalizing assessments by stressing *uniqueness* (i.e., that theory X, not theory Y or Z, is the best conceptual model).

Because both approaches value overarching principles of logic when accounting for criminological and/or legal problems, they must be viewed much like two sides of the same coin. They represent different ways of expressing a *shared* reality: rigorous scientific investigation of social phenomena yields a world that is objectifiable, reducible, knowable, and predictable. Postmodernists resist this equilibrium, *modernist* agenda of grand theory construction (whether through the lens of an integrative or a specialized perspective), and in this resistance the essence of postmodern theoretical integration can be defined provisionally.

Postmodern conceptual synthesis is not concerned with the scope and magnitude with which it accounts for *the* conditions or *the* causes of social problems. It seeks, however, to understand the manifold and ever-changing ways in which disparate groups communicate and give meaning to local sites of crime, justice, law, and community. Thus the idea of postmodern integration refers to its relational, positional, and provisional function to interpret, reinterpret, validate, and repudiate *multiple discourses* and their expressions of reality construction in divergent social arrangements. In this regard we can speak of *standpoint epistemologies* (i.e., knowledge embedded in divergent ideological frameworks), in which each epistemology shapes its own circumscribed method, images, and discourse. Therefore postmodern theoretical integration does not presume to understand *the* conditions or *the* causes of criminal or legal controversies by offering either a homeostatically based integrative model or a rigidly specialized theory.

According to postmodern theoretical integration, such absolutist truth claims would be illusory; in addition, such approaches themselves would oppress different ways of knowing and different ways of communicating meaning. The synthesis envisioned here is in flux with and sensitive to the ever-present perturbations, ironies, contingencies, absurdities, coincidences, discontinuities, and incompletenesses of living and being human. Integration, then, is not a systematic, reconstitutive closure to possibilities; rather, it is an opening-up to multiple, discordant, and different expressions by which meaning and being are articulated and lived.

466   LAW, CRIMINOLOGY, AND POSTMODERN THEORY

Earlier I stated that the postmodern perspective suffers from three general criticisms. These challenges are: 1) a construction of knowledge regarded as nihilistic, relativistic, and nonvisionary, 2) a method of inquiry regarded as cynical, pseudoscientific, and antifoundational, and 3) a use of language regarded as solipsistic, elitist, and idiosyncratic. The application of postmodern conceptual synthesis to theory construction in law and criminology demonstrates how these criticisms are essentially flawed or lacking in substance.

The integrative themes signify how knowledge is local, temporary, and relational. This is not the same as anarchical or antithetical sensemaking. The subject-in-process encounters provisional decidability or a *contingent universality* in the social world (Milovanovic 1995:39-40). The integrative themes demonstrate how method *is* language understood as reflective social criticism. This is not the same as a false science or a conspiring attitude. Reflexivity of thought, which is central to transpraxis, is the cornerstone of a deconstructive/reconstructive agenda. This method decodes rather than reifies established institutions and their ossified expressions of reality (Freire 1985; Unger 1987). The integrative themes signify how discourse embodies desire, is politically charged, and excludes certain voices. This is not the same as playing language games or succumbing to Hegelian reaction-negation dynamics. The unfinished project of postmodernism, through the cultivation of speech and replacement grammars, is to foster new and different cultural styles of awareness—those which incorporate the full spectrum of subjects and constituencies into the larger social fabric without privileging one aesthetic of living at the expense of others.

In justice-related pursuits the questions to be asked therefore must go beyond the normative and the positivistic—for example, What is crime? Who makes the law? What are the conditions under which crime and law are created? Instead we must question *the conditions under which we come to say what conditions the constitution of law and crime, and how our communication differs from that of others.* This more reflective activity not only questions the values embedded in one's selection of language in relation to the values embedded in the languaged standpoints of others. It also examines how these collective ways of knowing—despite their plurality—often are reduced to certain patterns of speech, certain expressions of logic-in-justice. Further, it invites others—scholars, practitioners, students, the public, the media—to do the same. This self-interrogating process challenges all of us to be increasingly sensitive to the desperation of marginalized voices. Further, it asks us to consider how we may be contributing, knowingly or not, to that very marginalization we seek to renounce. Finally, the postmodern agenda reminds us of the importance of provisional and relational understanding in interpreting social problems. Therefore that version of legitimated reality and the discourse used to encode it with one's meaning and being must not be viewed as an ultimate Truth or even as the final word on a particular truth.

The significance of postmodern thought for the future of criminal justice enterprises centers on the ethical dimension of the conceptual and integrative project in its alternative vision of, and relationship to, law and criminology. That is, we are confronted with an understanding of the life drama and the social order which returns dignity to passion and legitimacy to the inexplicable. Freed from the illusions of grand theory, false consciousness, unrealistic aspirations, and unattainable ends, we are called not merely to celebrate the "decentering" of traditional explanatory rationales through celebrating individual and collective differences, but to face up to ethical accountability and capacity in foundational, yet deracinated, ways. Instead of substituting the ethical dimension of our existence for an aesthetic of daily living, the postmodern agenda endeavors to make us all a bit more honest in relation to others and to our communities. Accordingly the legacy of postmodern justice, through its sociological and ontological themes, invites us to experience the incommensurable fullness of all human actors (e.g., victims, criminals, police agents, correctional officials, courtroom administrators, judges, attorneys) in their contradictory being and becoming, especially as they participate in the irony and the serendipity of the social order. The contribution of postmodernism to law and criminology presents a morality without an ethical code, an awareness absent the familiar, and antifoundational perspective from which we may proceed and begin once again.

## REFERENCES

Abraham, F., R. Abraham, and C. Shaw (1990) *A Visual Introduction to Dynamical Systems Theory for Psychology.* Santa Cruz: Aerial Press.
Adorno, T. (1973) *Negative Dialectics.* New York: Continuum.
Althusser, L. (1971) *Lenin and Philosophy and Other Essays.* New York: New Left Books.
Arrigo, B. (1992) "Deconstructing Jurisprudence: An Experiential Feminist Critique." *Journal of Human Justice* 4(1):13-30.
_____ (1993a) *Madness, language and the Law.* New York: Harrow and Heston.
_____ (1993b) "An Experientially-Informed Feminist Jurisprudence: Rape and the Move toward Praxis." *Humanity and Society* 17(1):28-47.
_____ (1993c) "Civil Commitment, Semiotics and Discourse on Difference: A Historical Critique of the Sign of Paternalism." In R. Kevelson (ed.), *Flux, Complexity, and Illusion,* pp. 5-32. New York: Lang.

468    LAW, CRIMINOLOGY, AND POSTMODERN THEORY

____ (1994a) "Legal Discourse and the Disordered Criminal Defendant: Contributions from Psychoanalytic Semiotics and Chaos Theory." *Legal Studies Forum* 18(1):93-112.

____ (1994b) "The Insanity Defense: A Study in Psychoanalytic Semiotics and Chaos Theory." In R. Kevelson (ed.), *The Eyes of Justice*, pp. 57-83. New York: Lang.

____ (1994c) "Rethinking the Language of Law and Justice: Postmodern Feminist Jurisprudence." In D. Caudill and S. Gold (eds.), *Radical Philosophy of Law*, pp. 88-107 New Jersey: Humanities Press.

____ (forthcoming a) *The Contours of Psychiatric Justice: A Postmodern Critique of Mental Illness, Criminal Insanity and the Law.* New York: Garland.

____ (forthcoming b) "Toward a Theory of Punishment in the Psychiatric Courtroom: On Language, Law and Lacan." *Journal of Crime and Justice.*

____ (forthcoming c) "Desire in the Psychiatric Courtroom: On Lacan and the Dialectics of Linguistic Oppression." *Current Perspectives in Social Theory.*

Barak, G. (1988) "Newsmaking Criminology: Reflections of the Media, Intellectuals, and Crime." *Justice Quarterly* 5:565-587.

Barthes, R. (1988) *The Semiotic Challenge.* New York: Hill and Wang.

Benson, R.W. (1989) "Semiotics, Modernism and the Law." *Semiotica* 73½:157-75.

Berger, P. and T. Luckmann (1966) *The Social Construction of Reality.* New York: Doubleday.

Bernard, T. (1989) "A Theoretical Approach to Integration." In F. Messner, D. Krohn, and A. Liska (eds.), *Theoretical Integration on the Study of Deviance and Crime: Problems and Prospects*, pp. 137-60. New York: SUNY Press.

Best, J. (1989) *Images of Issues: Typifying Contemporary Social Problems.* New York: Aldine.

Black, D. (1976) *The Behavior of Law.* new York: Academic Press.

Bohm, D. (1951) *Quantum Theory.* London: Constable.

____ (1981) *Wholeness and the Implicate Order.* London: Ark.

Bracher, M. (1988) "Lacan's Theory in the Four Discourses." *Prose Studies* 11:32-49.

____ (1993) *Lacan, Discourse, and Social Change: A Psychoanalytic Cultural Criticism.* Ithaca: Cornell University Press.

Briggs, J. and F.D. Peat (1989) *Turbulent Mirror: An Illustration Guide to Chaos Theory and the Science of Wholeness.* New York: Harper and Row.

Brion, D. (1991) "The Chaotic Law of Tort: Legal Formalism and the Problem of Indeterminacy." In R. Kevelson (ed.), *Peirce and Law*, pp. 45-77. New York: Lang.

Brown, L. and C. Gilligan (1993) *Meeting at the Crossroads.* Cambridge, MA: Harvard University Press.

Butz, M. (1991) "Fractal Dimensionality and Paradigms." *The Social Dynamicist* 2(4):4-7.

____ (1992) "Chaos, an Omen of Transcendence in the Psychotherapeutic Process." *Psychological Reports* 71:827-43.

Cain, M. (1992) "Realist Philosophy and Standpoint Epistemologies, or Feminist Criminology as a Successor Science." In L. Gelsthorpe and A. Morris (ed.), *Feminist Perspectives in Criminology*, pp. 124-40. Philadelphia: Open University Press.

Cixous, H. (1990) *Reading with Clarice Lispector.* Minneapolis: University of Minnesota Press.

Cohen, S. (1990) "Intellectual Skepticism and Political Commitment: The Case of Radical Criminology." Bonger Memorial Lecture, University of Amsterdam, May 14.

____ (1991) "Talking about Torture in Israel." *Tikkun* 6(6):23-30, 89-90.

____ (1993) "Human Rights and Crimes of the State: The Culture of Denial." *Australian and New Zealand Journal of Criminology* 26:97-115.

Collins, R. (1975) *Conflict Criminology: Toward an Explanatory Science.* New York: Academic Books.

____ (1986) "Is 1980 Sociology in the Doldrums?" *American Journal of Sociology* 91:1336-55.

Colvin, M. and J. Pauly (1983) "A Critique of Criminology: Toward an Integrated Structural-Marxist Theory of Delinquency Production." *American Journal of Sociology* 89:513-51.

Cornell, D. (1991) *Beyond Accommodation: Ethical Feminism, Deconstruction and the Law.* New York: Routledge.

_____ (1993) *Transformations: Recollective Imagination and Sexual Difference*. New York: Routledge.

Currie, D. (1993) "Unhiding the Hidden: Race, Class and Gender in the Construction of Knowledge." *Humanity and Society* 17(1):3-27.

Daly, K. and M. Chesney-Lind (1988) "Feminism and Criminology." *Justice Quarterly* 5:495-535.

Darwin, C. [1859] 1968 *On the Origin of Species*, New York: Penguin.

Deleuze, G. (1983). *Nietzsche and Philosophy*. New York: Columbia University Press.

Deleuze, G. and F. Guattari (1986) *Kafka: Toward a Minor Literature*. Minneapolis: University of Minnesota Press.

_____ (1987) *A Thousand Plateaus*. Minneapolis: University of Minnesota Press.

Dews, P. (1987) *Logics of Disintegration: Post-Structuralist Thought and the Claims of Critical Theory*. London: Verso.

Dworkin, R. (1986). *Law's Empire*. Cambridge, Mass: Belknap Press.

Einstadter, W.J. and S. Henry (1995) *Criminological Theory: An Analysis of Its Underlying Assumptions*. Fort Worth: Harcourt, Brace.

Elliot, D. (1985) "The Assumption That Theories Can Be Combined with Increased Explanatory Power: Theoretical Integrations." In R.F. Meier (ed.), *Theoretical Methods in Criminology*, pp. 123-49. Beverly Hills: Sage.

Feigenbaum, M. (1980) "Universal Behavior in Nonlinear Systems." *Los Alamos Science* 1:4-27.

Frank, J. ([1930]1963) *Law and the Modern Mind*. New York: Doubleday.

Freire, R. (1985) *The Politics of Education*. South Hadley, MA: Bergin and Garvey.

Freud, S. (1927) *The Ego and the Id*. London: Hogarth.

Freud, S. (1949) "Three Essays on the Theory of Sexuality." In J. Strachey (ed.), *The Standard Edition*, pp. 23-46. London: Hogarth.

Garfinkel, H. (1956) "Conditions of Successful Degradation Ceremonies." *American Journal of Sociology* 61:420-24.

_____ (1967) *Studies in Ethnomethodology*. Englewood Cliffs, NJ: Prentice-Hall.

Gelsthorpe, L. and A. Morris eds. (1990) *Feminist Perspectives in Criminology*. Milton Keynes, —: Open University Press.

Giddens, A. (1984) *The Constitution of Society*. oxford: Polity.

_____ (1990) *The Consequences of Modernity*. Stanford: Stanford University Press.

Gilligan C. (1982) *In a Different Voice*. Cambridge, MA: Harvard University Press.

Gilligan, C., N.P. Lyons, and T.J. Hanmer (1990) *Making Connections*. Cambridge, MA: Harvard University Press.

Gleick, J. (1987) *Chaos: Making a New Science*. New York: Penguin.

Gödel, K. (1962) "On Formally Undecidable Propositions." In R.B. Braithewaite (ed.), *"Principia Mathematica" and Related Systems*, pp. 173-98. New York: Basic Books.

Goffman, E. (1959) *The Presentation of the Self in Everyday Life*. New York: Doubleday.

_____ (1966) *Encounters*. Indianapolis: Bobbs-Merrill.

_____ (1967) *Interaction Ritual: Essays on Face-to-Face Behavior*. New York: Doubleday.

Goodrich P. (1987) *Legal Discourse*. New York: St. Martin's.

_____ (1990) *Languages of Law*. London: Weidenfeld and Nicolson.

Gottfredson, M. and T. Hirschi (1990) *A General Theory of Crime*. Stanford: Stanford University Press.

Habermas, J. (1984) *The Theory of Communicative Action*. Vol. 1: *Reason and the Rationalization of Society*, trans. by T. McCarthy. Boston: Beacon.

Handler, J. (1992) "The Presidential Address, 1992, Law and Society: 'Postmodernism, Protest and the New Social Movement.'" *Law and Society Review* 26:697-731.

Hart, H.L.A. (1961). *The Concept of Law*. Clarendon Press.

Hayles, N.K. (1990) *Chaos Bound: Orderly Disorder in Contemporary Literature and Science*. Ithaca: Cornell University Press.

Hayles, N.K. (1991) *Chaos and Order: Complex Dynamics in Literature and Science*. Chicago: University of Chicago Press.

Hegel, F.W. [1807] 1977. *Hegel's Phenomenology of Spirit*. A.V. Miller (Trans.). Oxford: Oxford University Press.

Heidegger, M. (1962) *Being and Time*. New York: Harper and Row.

470     LAW, CRIMINOLOGY, AND POSTMODERN THEORY

Henry, S. and D. Milovanovic (1991) "Constitutive Criminology: The Maturation of Critical Theory." *Criminology* 29:293-315.
Hirschi, T. (1979) *Causes of Delinquency*. Berkeley: University of California Press.
____ Hirschi, T. (1979) "Separate and Unequal Is Better." *Journal of Research in Crime and Delinquency* 16:34-37.
Holmes, O.W. (1897) "The Path of the Law." *Harvard Law Review* 10:457-78.
Hunt, A. (1990) "The Big Fear: law Confronts Postmodernism." *McGill law Journal* 35:507-40.
____ (1991) "Postmodernism and Critical Criminology." In B. MacLean and D. Milovanovic (eds.), *New Directions in Critical Criminology*, pp. 79-85. Vancouver: Collective Press.
____ (1993) *A Constitutive Theory of Law*. London: Routledge.
Husserl, E. (1983) *Ideas Pertaining to a Pure Phenomenology and to a Phenomenological Philosophy*, trans. by F. Kersten. The Hague: Nijhoff.
Irigaray, L. (1985) *This Sex Which Is Not One*, trans. by C. Porter and C. Burke. Ithaca: Cornell University Press.
____ (1990) *The Ethics of Sexual Difference*, trans. by C. Burke. Oxford: Blackwell.
Jessop, B. (1990) *State Theory: Putting the Capitalist State in Its Place*. Cambridge, UK: Polity.
Kelman, M. (1987) *A Guide to Critical Legal Studies*. Cambridge, MA: Harvard University Press.
Kristeva, J. (1977) *Polylogue*. Paris: Seuil.
____ (1980) *Desire in Language*. New York: Columbia University Press.
____ (1984) *Revolution in Poetic Language*. New York: Columbia University Press.
Lacan, J. (1975) *Encore*. Paris: Editions du Seuil.
____ (1977) *Écrits: A Selection*, trans. by A. Sheridan. New York: Norton.
____ (1985) *Feminine Sexuality*. New York: Norton.
____ (1991) *L'Envers de la Psychanalyse*. Paris: Editions du Seuil.
Lahey, K. (1985) "Until Women Themselves Have Told All That They Have to Tell. . . ." *Osgoode Hall Law Journal* 23:519-41.
Lecercle, J.J. (1985) *Philosophy through the Looking Glass: Language, Nonsense, Desire*. London: Hutchinson.
Lee, J.S. (1990) *Jacques Lacan*. Amherst: University of Massachusetts Press.
Llewellyn, K. (1930) "A Realistic Jurisprudence—The Next Step." *Columbia Law Review* 30:431-65.
____ (1931) "Some Realism about Realism." *Harvard Law Review* 44:1222-64.
Llewellyn, K. and A. Hoebel (1941) *The Cheyenne Way: Conflict and Case Law in Primitive Jurisprudence*. Norman: University of Oklahoma Press.
Luhmann, N.A. (1985). *A Sociological Theory of Law*. Boston: Routledge and Kegan Paul.
Luhmann, N.A. (1992) "Operational Closure and Structural Coupling: The Differentiation of the Legal System." *Cardozo Law Review* 13:1419-41.
Lyotard, J.F. (1984) *The Postmodern Condition: A Report on Knowledge*. Minneapolis: University of Minnesota Press.
MacLean, B. and D. Milovanovic eds. (1991) *New Directions in Critical Criminology*. Vancouver: Collective Press.
MacKinnon, C. (1987) *Feminism Unmodified: Discourses on Life and Law*. Cambridge, MA: Harvard University Press.
____ (1989) *Towards a Feminist Theory of the State*. Cambridge, MA: Harvard University Press.
Malhotra Bentz, V. (1993) "Review of James M. Ostrow's *Social Sensitivity*." *Humanity and Society* 17(1):121-23.
Mandelbrot, B. (1983) *The Fractal Geometry of Nature*. New York: Freeman.
Manning. P. (1992) *Organizational Communication*. New York: Aldine.
Marino, G. (1994) "Chaos: An Overview." *Penn State Liberal Arts Alumni Newsletter* 5(2):10-11.
McDermott, M.J. (1992) "The Personal Is Empirical: Research Methods and Criminal Justice Education." *Journal of Criminal Justice Education* 3:237-49.
Merleau-Ponty, M. (1962) *Phenomenology of Perception*, trans. by Colin Smith. New York: Humanities Press.
Messner, S.F., M.D. Krohn, and A. Liska (1989) *Theoretical Integration in the Study of Deviance and Crime: Problems and Prospects*. Albany: SUNY Press.
Milovanovic, D. (1986) "Juridico-Linguistic Communicative Markets: Toward a Semiotic Analysis." *Contemporary Crises* 10:281-304.

_____ (1988) "Jailhouse Lawyers and Jailhouse Lawyering." *International Journal of the Sociology of Law* 16:455-75.

_____ (1992) *Postmodern Law and Disorder: Psychoanalytic Semiotics and Juridic Exegesis.* Liverpool: Deborah Charles.

_____ (1993a) "Lacan, Chaos, and Practical Discourse in Law." In R. Kevelson (ed.), *Flux, Complexity, Illusion*, pp. 311-37. New York: Lang.

_____ (1993b) "Lacan's Four Discourses: Cahos and Cultural Criticism in Law." *Studies in Psychoanalytic Theory* 2(1):3-23.

_____ (1995) "Dueling Paradigms: Modernist versus Postmodernist Thought." *Humanity and Society* (19):1, 19-44.

Nettler, G. (1984) *Explaining Crime.* New York: McGraw-Hill.

Nietzsche, F. (1980) *On the Advantage and Disadvantage of History for Life.* Cambridge, MA: Hackett.

Palmer, B.D. (1990) *Descent into Discourse: The Reification of Language and the Writing of Social History.* Philadelphia: Temple University Press.

Pearson, F.S. and N.A. Weiner (1985) "Towards an Integration of Criminological Theories." *Journal of Criminal Law and Criminology* 76:116-50.

Pecheux, M. (1982) *Language, Semantics and Ideology.* New York: St. Martin's.

Peller, G. (1985) "The Metaphysics of American Law." *California Law Review* 73:1151-1290.

Pepinsky, H. (1993) "What Is Crime? What Is Peace?: A Commentary." *Journal of Criminal Justice Education* 4:391-94.

Pepinsky, H. and R. Quinney eds. (1991) *Peacemaking in Criminology.* Bloomington: Indiana University Press.

Porter, E. and J. Gleick (1990) *Nature's Chaos.* New York: Penguin.

Posner, R.A. (1986) *Economic Analysis of Law*, 3rd ed. Boston: Little, Brown.

Posner, R.A. (1992) *Sex and Reason.* Cambridge, MA: Harvard University Press.

Pound, R. (1908) "Mechanical Jurisprudence." *Columbia Law Review* 8:605-23.

Prigogine, I. and I. Stengers (1984) *Order out of chaos.* New York: Bantam.

_____ (1986) *Economic Analysis of Law.* 3d ed. Boston: Little, Brown.

Quinney, R. (1970) *The Social Reality of Crime.* Boston: Little, Brown.

Ragland-Sullivan E. (1986) *Jacques Lacan and the Philosophy of Psychoanalysis.* Chicago: University of Illinois Press.

Ritzer, G. (1990) *Frontiers of Social Theory: The New Synthesis.* New York: Columbia University Press.

Rosenau, P.A. (1992) *Postmodernism and the Social Sciences: Insights, Inroads, and Intrusions.* Princeton: Princeton University Press.

Rossi-Landi, F. (1977) *Linguistics and Economics.* City: The Hague: Mouton.

Rumble, W., Jr. (1968) *American Legal Realism.* Ithaca: Cornell University Press.

Sarup, M. (1989) *Post-Structuralism and Postmodernism.* Athens: University of Georgia Press.

Schutz, A. (1964) *The Phenomenology of the Social World.* Evanston, IL: Northwestern University Press.

Schwartz, M. and D. Friedrichs (1994) "Postmodern Thought and Criminological Discontent: New Metaphors for Understanding Violence." *Criminology* 32:221-46.

Sellers, S., ed. (1991) *Feminist Criticism, Theory and Practice.* London: Routledge.

Serres, M. (1982a) *Hermes: Literature, Science and Philosophy.* Baltimore: Johns Hopkins University Press.

_____ (1982b) *The Parasite.* Baltimore: Johns Hopkins University Press.

Smart, C. (1989) *Feminism and the Power of the Law.* London and New York: Routledge.

_____ (1990) "Feminist Approaches to Criminology, or Postmodern Woman Meets Atavistic Man." In L. Gelsthorpe and A. Morris (eds.), *Feminist Perspectives in Criminology*, pp. 70-84. Milton Keynes, PA: Open University Press.

_____ (1992) "The Women of Legal Discourse." *Social and Legal Studies: An International Journal* 1:29-44.

Spector, M. and J.I. Kitsuse (1987) *Constructing Social Problems.* New York: Aldine.

Stewart, I. (1989) *Does God Play Dice?* New York: Blackwell.

Stinchcombe, A. (1968) *Constructing Social Theories.* New York: Harcourt, Brace and World.

Teubner, G. (1988) *Autopoetic Law: A New Approach to Law and Society.* New York: Walter de Druyter.

472    LAW, CRIMINOLOGY, AND POSTMODERN THEORY

____ (1992) "The Two Faces of Janus: Rethinking Legal Pluralism." *Cardozo Law Review* 13:1443-62.

____ (1993) *Law as an Autopoetic System*. Oxford: Blackwell.

Unger, R. (1987) *False Necessity*. New York: Cambridge University Press.

Wagner, D. and J. Berger (1985) "Do Sociological Theories Grow?" *American Journal of Sociology* 90:697-728.

Weber, M. (1978) *Economy and Society*, G. Roth and C. Wittich (eds. Berkeley: University of California Press.

Wittgenstein, L. (1953). *Philosophical Investigations*. Oxford: Basil Blackwell.

Wolf, F.A. (1981) *Taking the Quantum Leap: The New Physics for Nonscientists*. New York: Harper & Row.

____ (1984) *Star Wave: Mind, Consciousness, and Quantum Physics*. New York: Macmillan.

Wolinsky, S.H. (1991) *Trances People Live With: Healing Approaches to Quantum Psychology*. Norfolk, CT: Bramble.

Wolinsky, S.H. (1993) *Quantum Consciousness: The Guide to Experiencing Quantum Psychology*. Norwalk, CT: Bramble.

Young, T.R. (1991) "Chaos and Crime: Nonlinear and Fractal Forms of Crime." *The Critical Criminologist* 3(2):3-4, 10-11.

# [3]

# POSTMODERN CRIMINOLOGY: MAPPING THE TERRAIN

## DRAGAN MILOVANOVIC
### Northeastern Illinois University

An affirmative postmodern criminology is in its developing stages. This article provides some examples of some of the methodological and conceptual tools for inquiry. Accordingly it draws from chaos theory, catastrophe theory, and topology theory, focusing on psychoanalytic semiotics and three exemplary topological constructions: the Mobius band, the cross-cap, and Borromean knots. The relevance to doing critical criminology is indicated by focusing attention on some selected criminological theories that have affinities for an integrative approach, particularly those on "edgework," "invitational edge," and the "foreground factors." This emergent state is more in tune with modeling and with explaining dynamic, nonlinear, transformational states (complexity theory).

Affirmative postmodern criminology has emerged in the 1990s as a paradigm not only for deconstructing oppressive forms, but also for affirmatively reconstructing the new order. Whereas the emergence of postmodernism is accounted for in literary theory, criminology has been less than enthusiastic, even hostile, to its central concepts.[1] Here we provide some examples of alternative methodologies in doing critical criminology. We focus on chaos, catastrophe, and topology theory; these approaches are qualitative, although the quantitative is not discounted. Rather than privileging linear effects and homeostasis (order), postmodern analysis is more likely to assume nonlinear effects and far-from-equilibrium conditions (orderly disorder). With alternative conceptual tools, a

---

[1] Elsewhere we have compared the modernists with the postmodernists on eight dimensions: nature of society and social structure, social roles, subjectivity/agency, discourse, knowledge, space/time, causality, and social change (Milovanovic 1995). Our vision is situated in the more recent development of an affirmative postmodernism as opposed to the earlier nihilistic forms advocating the "death of the subject" and fatalism (see Henry and Milovanovic 1996; Milovanovic, forthcoming a; forthcoming b; for a critique of the nihilistic forms, see Schwartz and Friedrichs 1994). The use of a "math-based metaphor" (as some call it) arises, first, because much of the early developmental work in chaos theory was mathematical, and, second, because it attempts to show that indeterminacy prevails even in those systems which have been seen as most deterministic and subject to the rigors of mathematics. Our use of "fanciful" iterative polynomials, qualitative mathematics (topology), and various algorithms of Lacan, therefore, are in the tradition of a "cross-fertilization" (see note 3) and in no way discount ethnographies; on the contrary, our work is consistent with the ethnographic emphasis on explanation, not prediction.

new discourse is implicated; the use of more conventional discourses often includes embedded assumptions and metanarratives
(also see Arrigo, 1995a, 1995b). For possible applications we have
chosen several studies that are especially relevant for postmodern
criminology (Ferrell 1995; Katz 1988; Matza 1964, 1969; O'Malley
and Mugford 1994).[2]

## POSTMODERN METHODOLOGIES

Postmodern criminology is faced with the dilemma of how to
better model or map complex dynamics, those which predominantly
exhibit nonlinearity (complexity) over time. Lyotard's (1984) call is
worthy: He calls for a postmodern methodology that uncovers instabilities through quantum mechanics, catastrophe theory, chaos
theory, Gödel's theorem, and discursive analysis. We discuss three
of these perspectives here. (1) Chaos theorists have provided the
notion of phase maps or phase portraits, along with such notions as
attractors, bifurcation diagrams, and Mandelbrot sets (hereafter M-
sets); (2) catastrophe theorists offer the notion of the fold and the
"cusp catastrophe model"; and (3) Jacques Lacan proposes other topological structures such as the cross-cap, the Mobius band, and
Borromean knots. We will develop each perspective briefly and provide applications to a postmodern criminology. The use of ethnographic studies is also an important methodology, but space
limitations prohibit discussion here (also see Ferrell 1995; Lyng
1990).

The use of concepts often developed from the physical sciences
raises some legitimate concerns about their applicability in the social sciences. Loye and Eisler (1987; also see Baker 1993; Kaplan
and Kaplan 1991; Smith and Comer 1994) have made a good case
for the "crossover," as have Gregersen and Sailer (1993) in an article that we cite below.[3] Abraham (1992) has provided three goals in

---

2 We make no claim to provide completely new theories; the various applications merely suggest lines of inquiry, which would entail much more development.

3 Loye and Eisler (1987), for example, indicated that leading chaos theorists
such as Prigogine cited the works of Comte, Durkheim, and Spencer. In cosmology
and nuclear physics, we note that when Einstein was developing his theory of relativity he was reading much philosophy by thinkers such as Ernst Mach, Immanuel
Kant, and David Hume (Peat 1988:335). Heisenberg, one of the main developers of
quantum mechanics, was led by Pauli to think philosophically in order to understand observer effects more clearly (Peat 1988:335). Georg B. Riemann, a key devel-
oper of non-Euclidean geometry and higher dimensionality, was influenced heavily
by philosopher Herbart (Nasio 1996:42; Russell 1956:13-15). Michio Kaku (1994:
104) makes a case for "cross-pollination" from Riemann to the arts and sciences and
then through mathematicians such as Theodor Kaluza back to the sciences. The
new cosmologists developing "string theory" have resorted more and more to philosophical thinking (Peat 1988). Fritjof Capra's (1988) early demonstrates how quantum mechanics has similarities to Eastern religion, and David Bohm's (1980)
investigations have led him to look at the structure of language and how it hinders
thought by instilling static conceptualizations. One of the major crises here is the

the application of dynamical systems theory (chaos). It can be used (1) as a metaphorical tool, (2) in "the adoption of previously developed models to new empirical domains," and (3) for the active development of new models (1992:111-1). Topology theory also is being used in postmodern analysis for at least two reasons: for exposition, and as a means of discovery (Milovanovic 1993b). Dor (1996) and Nasio (1987) argue, for example, that Lacan uses topology for illustrative metaphors. The usage is "revelatory and imaginary"; perhaps the term *topologery* is more suitable (Dor 1996; Nasio 1987). Alternatively, a stronger "fit" is found in the idea of homology, a similarity in development. Complexity theory offers new ways of envisioning transformations in complex, dynamic systems.

How to conceptualize space has become a central question. Multidimensional space is applied increasingly in indicating the narrowness of simple two-dimensional (Euclidean) constructs. Consider, for example, how regression analysis assumes the x, y coordinate system, linear or curvilinear relations, and integer dimensions. Chaos theory provides the idea of "fractals." Contrary to the Euclidean geometry of no-, one-, two-, and three-dimensional space, there exist "in-between" dimensions, or fractions of dimensions (fractal geometry). This literally and figuratively opens up an infinite space. The complex plane, making use of imaginary numbers, has also been employed (see, for example, the construction of the M-set below). Higher-dimensional space also provides greater room for analysis, understanding, and social change. All of this indicates that the time has come to reconsider contemporary core assumptions in doing criminology.

---

inability of physics to explain physical phenomena with merely probability-based methods. In the other direction, we note only Whorf's (1956) work on the "linguistic relativity principle," which draws heavily on the central ideas of quantum mechanics and relativity theory.

This situation has led some to argue that "isomorphisms" exist and can be the basis for bona fide investigations. (See Loye and Eisler [1987:59], who add that these are "cross-fertilizations.") Thus we see the importance of being able to transcend the narrow disciplinary boundaries. We should engage in clarifying homologies, metaphors, correspondences, analogies, and the appropriateness of usage. Wasn't it Marx who made use of the "superstructure metaphor" as a "guiding principle" in his investigations? Haven't we gone far with Marx's commodification thesis? Consider the homology between commodity, juridic, and linguistic forms (Pashukanis 1978; Rossi-Landi 1983). Similarly, Freud made use of an optic metaphor in his construction of the psychic apparatus, especially in *The Interpretation of Dreams* (1965). Perhaps worthy of further inquiry is Hayles's (1990:176, 185-86) attention to the importance of an "ecology of ideas," a "closed topological space" that has cultural specificities. (Also see Lem 1981 and Ragland-Sullivan's discussion, following physicist Gerald Holton on the notion of a "propositional space"; 1990b:56-57.)

## CHAOS AND CRIMINOLOGY

*Phase Map (Portraits)*

Linear systems, as often portrayed by path analysis, have been dominant in criminological thought. They consistently overlook feedback mechanisms, cumulative and disproportional effects of "minor" factors, and nonlinear dynamics. Chaos theory offers non-linear models and ways of mapping them. Nonlinear systems tend to settle down to some pattern over time. This settling-down phenomenon results in four major patterns that can be located on "phase maps," sometimes called phase portraits. A moment in phase space sums up what the entire dynamic system in movement is doing at any moment. Consider how this compares with the more static models prevalent in criminological investigation, which merely take snapshot views without sensitivity to dynamic change over time.

Various attractors exist. Point attractors are those in which phenomena settle down to some region approximating a point. Cyclic attractors (or limit attractors) are those which converge to an oscillating cycle. In torus attractors (which resemble inflated inner tubes), one witnesses quasiperiodicity. Chaotic attractors, of which the butterfly attractor is the most prominent, are bounded (have global stability), but internally the trajectories are unpredictable (they display local indeterminacy). Here a very small change in some crucial control parameter, even a difference of .0001, will produce unexpected results after a number of iterations. This, of course, is the much-stated notion of "sensitive dependence on initial conditions." These attractors can be located on phase maps.

The simplest instructive phase map presented in the literature is that of a pendulum (Briggs and Peat 1989:34-37; see appendix). This simple phase portrait depicts two coupled and interacting variables (momentum and location) in a dynamic system. Consider again the more prevalent modeling in criminology, in which movement over time is lacking. Linear notions, too, most often underlie these modernist models. The contributions of feedback loops and disproportional outcomes are not accounted for. In pointing out the "variance explained" many "minor" contributions are discounted (often two, three, or four variables are said to suffice), and rounding takes care of the rest. "Noise" is systematically dismissed as having no important contributory effects. Most often, the search for point attractors is celebrated; the search for periodic, torus, and strange attractors is methodologically voided. Chaos theory attempts to correct this deficiency. Young (forthcoming), for example, offers five foci:

1. To locate the attractors hidden in complex data sets;
2. To determine how many attractors exist in that data set;
3. To find the change point(s) at which new attractors are produced.
4. For purposes of social control, to identify the key parameters that drive the system into ever more uncertainty.
5. For purposes of social policy, to determine which setting of those key parameters is acceptable to the whole society.

We wish now to consider more complex phase maps, the bifurcation diagram and the M-set, each of which indicates nonlinearity and the occurrence of various attractors.

### Bifurcation Diagram and Attractors

Nonlinear dynamics make use of nonlinear equations (see Cunningham 1958; McLachlan 1958). Results of the computation process are fed back into the equations for recomputation (iteration), the answer to which is fed back once again into the equation, and so forth.[4] These equations show extreme sensitivity to initial conditions, and, because of feedback, display nonproportional effects. Without going into the details of the mathematical computations (see Briggs and Peat 1989:53-65; also see Peak and Frame 1994:161-86; Peitgen, Jurgens, and Saupe 1992:195-267), diagramming various iterations as $b$, the parameter value, ranges from 1 to 4 shows that "bifurcations" or splittings occur at several key points (see Figure 1). Modernist criminology generally assumes that with a proportional increase in some parameter value, a proportional effect develops, and that one outcome results for any control parameter value (point attractor). Chaos theory fundamentally challenges these assertions; it demonstrates disproportional effects (the "butterfly effect") and shows that even for the *same* parameter value, various periodicities may arise.

*Construction.* We must first run a number of iterations to see the pattern that will emerge. At different parameters ($b$-values) we

---

4 One classic example (the "logistic map" or the Verhulst formula) is found in the growth of gypsy moth populations from year to year (Barton 1994; Briggs and Peat 1989:53-65, 66-71; Peak and Frame 1994:161-86). The formula is given by $x' = x + bx(1-x)$, where $x' = x_n+1$ and $n = 0,1,2,3...$; in other words, the steps in an iterative sequence; or when rewritten with subscripts to indicate iteration from one time to another, this formula is $x_n+1=bx_n(1-x_n)$. Again, stated differently to indicate iteration from one time to another, this formula can be rewritten as $x_n+1 = (1+b) x_n-bx^2_n$ (where $x_n$ is multiplied by itself and produces feedback or the iterative effect). The left-hand side of the equation represents this year's population; the right-hand side, last year's. Where $x_t$ represents the first value (iterate) to be iterated, the vertical axis reflects normalization (a simplification device) as ranging between 0 and 1; $b$ is a constant expressing the rate of birth that potentially would occur if the food supply was continuous (in practice, it is really a contingent factor); it will vary from 1 to 4 along the horizontal axis. This factor therefore is called a parameter.

572    POSTMODERN CRIMINOLOGY

## Figure 1.  Bifurcation Diagram

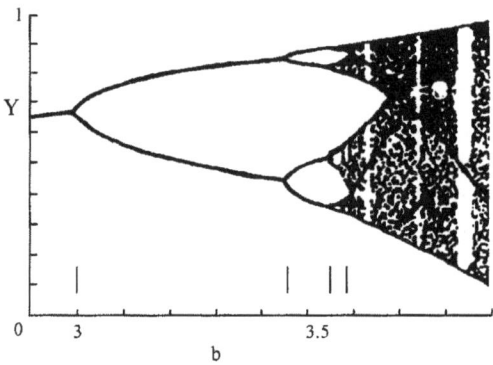

(Created by software provided by Wegner and Tyler 1993)

shall see that for even the same value, two or more outcome basins may arise at bifurcation points, or singularities. At values less than *b* = 3 we see in Figure 1 a somewhat horizontal line from the y-axis to a fork; up to the fork the results of iteration produce a steady state, or a point attractor. In other words, the population growth of (say) gypsy moths remains at a constant value. In modernist criminology, an assumed increase, even incremental, in some specified variable in the causation of crime is said to produce a certain amount of crime. The amount of crime is said to converge to a point. Consider, for example, the stated effects of population growth and delinquency (i.e., birth cohort studies).

At the value *b* = 3 we note the first bifurcation. This means that two possible outcome states (outcome basins) are now possible; that is, the results of the computation move back and forth between two values. (A normally law-abiding person, with declining income, may attempt to supplement that income illegally, hence oscillating between two states.) We should keep in mind that the control parameter has increased incrementally, but the outcome basin has changed from a point to a periodic or cyclic attractor. At the value of approximately *b* = 3.45 we see a second bifurcation and four outcome possibilities. (The person may add child/spousal abuse and excessive drinking as further outcome behaviors and may fluctuate among these states.) Here we see a torus attractor develop. At *b* = 3.56, eight periods or outcome basins are present; at *b* = 3.59, sixteen, and so forth. This is known as "period doubling." A strange attractor begins to emerge as we approach the limit of the bifurcation sequence. A limit is reached at approximately *b* = 3.6, where the outcome basins become infinite; no prediction is possible here.

Most important, our control parameter has increased proportionally, but the outcome has not; tori and strange attractors have formed.

In Figure 1 we then note vertical white bands, which indicate that "intermittency" or periodicity, or order out of disorder, is once again emerging. In other words, "self-organization" occurs: For example, consider Matza's (1964) deviant juvenile, who undergoes "maturational reform," or consider "spontaneous remission." This pattern is sensitive to initial conditions; thus, if our $x$ value is off by as little as .0001, divergences are expected after several iterations. This bifurcation diagram has appeared again and again in a variety of studies, leading chaologists to conclude that it may also be relevant to the social sciences, and (for our purposes) to criminology (Young 1991a, 1991b, 1992, forthcoming; also see Smith and Comer 1994). In order to demonstrate its applicability we shall make use of Matza's theory of delinquency and "drift." (For applications in criminology, see Forker forthcoming; Young 1991a, forthcoming; in law, Schulman forthcoming; in psychology, Butz 1992; Cislo 1996; in management, Leifer 1989; for the development of replacement discourses, see Milovanovic forthcoming b.)

*Application.* The application of the bifurcation diagram, either as an illustrative metaphor or as a homology for the social sciences, can take more simple or more complex forms. The simplest forms are those depicted in two-dimensions (2D, Euclidean). More complex forms appear in three dimensions. In even more complex, non-Euclidean forms, four or more dimensions may be portrayed. We first present the three-dimensional (3D) model and then discuss the possibilities of models with four or more dimensions, especially when modeling what constitutive criminologists call constitutive interrelational sets (COREL sets; see Henry and Milovanovic 1996).

*Simple bifurcation diagrams.* In modeling behavior (phase portraits), Abraham (1992) indicated that we need to tease out the relevant variables of some theory. This process is known as "dimensional reduction." Although there are some qualifications regarding its precision (Mandel 1995), social scientists progress by operationalizing their terms. (For a useful discussion of collapsing multivariate into univariate indices, see Oliva, Day, and MacMillan 1988:375.) We identify the key "control parameter," the dominant factor in affecting some of the phenomena under investigation. (In the more complex forms of the bifurcation diagram, this variable develops unevenly.)

We then identify the interacting variables at play. In other words, we construct a series of frames (Figure 2); each frame contains a phase portrait indicating how the variables interact, given some control parameter, and what results. Thus, in this phase portrait of a complex system, a series of vectors reflects different effects; these are seen as trajectories. Trajectories may be viewed as the integration of the vectors.

A third interacting variable, the rate of change, indicates that the other influencing factors change at different rates; hence trajectories may arrive at some region in their respective frames at different rates. Thus we have a 3D model. Other "intervening" variables and other influencing factors also might affect the vector field, thus necessitating more dimensions in the basic model being developed here. Each of the factors can be described by a differential equation; at least one is nonlinear (Abraham 1992:45; for a useful discussion of nonlinear equations and their applicability, see McLachlan 1958:1-8).

This is merely a model. One of its limitations is that pointlike states (as in the point attractors in Figure 2) are better conceptualized as regions, patches, or moments, consistent with what quantum mechanics tells us about indeterminacy when trying to specify location and momentum at the same time. In combination with the central idea of chaos concerning "sensitive dependence on initial conditions," then, we can never predict results precisely. A more complex bifurcation phase portrait (see below) is more responsive to this initial indeterminacy and to the question of directionality. Let us provide an example in which the more simple bifurcation diagrams are applied.

Matza's (1964) theory of delinquency indicates that the juvenile normally "drifts" between convention and crime. The juvenile, because of her or his status, finds at times that s/he is "pushed around," and experiences this as a "mood of fatalism." Episodically, in the "situation of company" (peers) and in a context containing discursive "neutralizations" for releasing oneself from the moral bonds of the law, the juvenile is free to commit delinquent acts. These key parameters can be located on our bifurcation diagram in Figure 2. Our control parameter is "being pushed around," and is assumed here to be increasing evenly (in linear fashion) from left to right. The x-axis represents neutralizations; the y-axis, the situation of company; the z-axis, the rate of change between the two interacting factors. (We could provide other examples, as well, such as Cressey's embezzler in *Other People's Money*, where the control parameter would be nonshareable financial problems and where $x =$

neutralizations, $y$ = opportunities and skills, and $z$ = rate of change.)

**Figure 2. Bifurcation Diagram and Matza's *Delinquency and Drift***

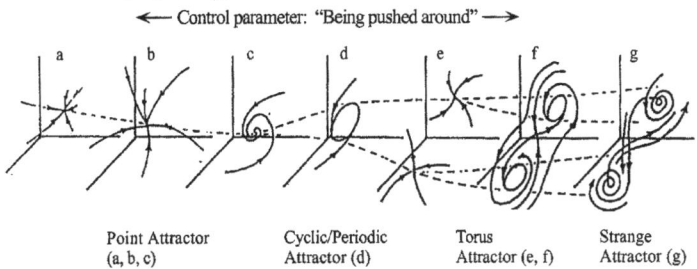

&larr; Control parameter: "Being pushed around" &rarr;

| Point Attractor (a, b, c) | Cyclic/Periodic Attractor (d) | Torus Attractor (e, f) | Strange Attractor (g) |

(Adopted from Abraham 1992)

In Figure 2a we start with a hypothetical situation in which the juvenile experiences some modicum of "being pushed around." This person finds herself or himself in a vector field where the situation of company and neutralizations are not overbearingly suggestive of committing delinquency. Here we see vectors that spiral to a point (region, patch, or moment). This point attractor indicates that the juvenile is in a somewhat homeostatic balance between the "mood of fatalism" and the "mood of humanism." Although the effects of exposure to the situation of company and neutralizations sometimes locate the juvenile at a distance from this more likely moment (point attractor), they are not so consequential as to produce a delinquent act. Schwendinger and Schwendinger (1985), for example, indicate other offsetting "moral rhetorics" that may be at play in the juvenile's everyday life (p. 141).

In Figure 2b we note that the trajectories or vectors are longer, indicating that the control parameter, "being pushed around," is increasing in intensity. As a result the juvenile begins at a greater distance from her or his more normal or bounded state (region). Further investigation along the lines suggested by Schwendinger and Schwendinger (1985) can explain more fully how, even with the increase in being pushed around, the different magnitudes in the situation of company and in neutralizations produce certain trajectories.

In Figure 2c, "being pushed around" has increased in intensity. Now the juvenile takes longer—as shown in spiraling toward the point, or (better) the region—to return to her or his more normal disposition. The juvenile is coming under increasing influence of the "situation of company" where lawbreaking is encouraged, and of available neutralizations that release her or him from the moral bonds of the law. At this moment, the juvenile maintains predominantly law-abiding behavior. Figures 2a, 2b, and 2c represent "point attractors." The trajectories, however, have become increasingly greater.

In 2c the first bifurcation has begun to develop (the diverging dotted horizontal lines). Two outcome basins result: The juvenile, given the prevalent neutralizations and being in the situation of company, now is free to entertain law-abiding *as well as* law-breaking behavior. Two outcome basins (a periodicity of 2) have developed, even though the control parameter has increased only proportionally. In 2d we note a greater amplitude (variability) in behavior; the juvenile no longer returns to a point (or region) but exists within a greater range of possible activities; this is the "cyclic" or "limit attractor." In 2e, because the intensity of "being pushed around" has increased even more, the juvenile fluctuates between two states (two point attractors). In one, s/he experiences the freedom to commit an "infraction"; in the other, to maintain law-abiding behavior.

With yet a greater increase in the parameter (being pushed around) a new bifurcation begins to develop in 2e. The juvenile's behavior now fluctuates in a yet more unpredictable manner between two coupled states (deviance and nondeviance). Here the torus attractor develops (and more fully in 2f). With a greater increase in the parameter, the strange (chaotic) attractor develops at 2g. As Matza tells us, "The delinquent *transiently* exists in a limbo between convention and crime, responding in turn to the demands of each, flirting now with one, now the other, but postponing commitment, evading decision. . .he drifts between criminal and conventional action" (1964:28).

It would be difficult to predict which state the juvenile occupies at any particular moment, but this is not the end of the story. One of Matza's important contributions is showing that most juveniles do not go on to become committed to their delinquent acts; they grow out of it; they undergo "maturation reform" (1964:25). In our diagram, we could add the right-hand side of Figure 1 to the right-hand side of Figure 2 to further indicate the dynamic process taking place. We note vertical white bands which indicate, for chaologists, "intermittency" or "order out of disorder." A maturing out of the delinquent enterprise occurs spontaneously.

In this bifurcation sequence, 2a through 2d would be well within the modernist paradigm and would be explained accordingly; that is, much prediction and certainty exist. Beginning with 2e, certainty and prediction become more fuzzy. At 2f and to the right, we enter far-from-equilibrium conditions (Prigogine and

Stenger 1984), where the postmodernist framework explains better what takes place. Here, things are uncertain, not totally predictable, and in a state of flux (the area where we find the torus and the strange attractor). Indeed, as labeling theorists have indicated, attempts at arresting the process may inadvertently focus exclusively on one wing of the butterfly attractor (lawbreaking); hence they may produce the forces favoring the occurrence of the secondary deviant (the "committed" delinquent, in Matza's view) and amplification of deviance. Matza's critique of positivism is equally relevant to contemporary criminological investigations, and his view that free will *and* determinism are not incompatible has much in common with the chaos notion of orderly disorder. This model also suggests policy implications for intervention strategies—that is, social policies for empowering youths, such as summer programs and creative strategies in offsetting neutralizing discourses.

*More complex forms of the bifurcation diagram: COREL sets.* With greater degrees of freedom (i.e., more dimensions at play), a more complex model is needed. Elsewhere (Henry and Milovanovic 1996) we developed the idea of constitutive interrelational sets (COREL sets) which indicate how various factors may be parallel, intersecting, and interpenetrating, and may contribute to the coproduction of reality (for a possible operationalization, see Crenshaw's [1993] discussion explaining how gender and race biases intersect and are not merely cumulative in the production of social injury). Here, the notion of space and directionality is problematic.[5]

Rather than privileging straight lines, which imply causation, a complex space suggests the use of "iterative loops," or nonlinear feedback loops (discussed further below), found in evolving and dissipating constellations or configurations in historical settings. Deleuze and Guattari (1987), for example, suggest a "smooth space" that has fractional dimensions with continuous variation in direction. Stated differently, running perpendicular to any abstract "line" are indeterminate ranges of possibilities, even as a tubelike structure is traced through space. Here we have global stability

---

[5] An alternative conceptualization of space could be derived from Riemann's (Russell 1956) notion of space as a "manifold," a collection of magnitudes in an infinite space where a "curvature tensor" could describe various intersecting magnitudes at any point; from chaos theorists' offering of fractal geometry as opposed to Euclidean geometry, where space can be noninteger and infinite variation can exist; from Deleuze and Guattari's (1987) discussion of "smooth" versus "metric space," where the former is more akin to Bergson's notion of "duration," or varying intensities, rather than merely numerical magnitudes; and from quantum mechanics, which questions whether a "point" can even be localizable in a dynamic system (a patch, region, or moment may be more appropriate).

(the tubelike structure) and local indeterminacy. A "rhizome" best captures movement in this space (Deleuze and Guattari 1987:21).

Our COREL sets have many affinities with the rhizome. Here rhizomatic multiplicities are constellations of iterative loops in constant construction and deconstruction, much as in the notion of "dissipative structures" that chaos theory offers (also see Deleuze and Guattari 1987:33). These constantly reconfiguring structures produce effects as well as emergent singularities. Intersectionality and its effects are best portrayed by "trouser diagrams" (Figure 5) and constellations of iterative loops (Figures 3, 4). (Yet another way of topologically depicting this phenomenon is the M-set, which indicates the various constitutive "orbits" or trajectories or COREL sets in three- and higher-dimensional space; see below.)

Adequately operationalizing a "variable" or a "factor" is a challenge. As a preliminary statement (to be developed more fully in future research) we suggest that variables are neither discrete nor static, but relational and uneven; they vary in intensity, duration, and magnitude. At best we may temporarily freeze a circumscribed cross-section of constellations of iterative loops in "naming" operations.

The complex bifurcation diagram indicates how singularities are likely to develop at the point at which various outcome basins and attractors arise.[6] This model does not assume pure chance and randomness: "Statements clarifying the limits and likelihoods of future behaviors can still be made for a chaotic process" (Peak and Frame 1994:158). Here, inherent uncertainties of measurement inevitably expand. Patterns may emerge; after all, a strange attractor may take the form of butterfly wings indicating some global stability; nevertheless, local indeterminacy prevails in the more complex bifurcation diagrams. Each of the evolving frames or phase portraits depicted in Figure 2 would be composed of constellations of iterative loops or rhizomatic multiplicities—or, to employ a notion from chaos theory, dissipative structures, with various bifurcations, periodicities, and forms of attractors.

We would like to move this analysis one step forward in providing directions for applications of the more complex bifurcation diagrams. Returning to our simpler bifurcation diagram and its application to Matza's theory, a more complex rendering would indicate that factors such as being pushed around, neutralizations, and situation of company are uneven, are iterated continuously,

---

[6] Marx's dialectical materialism, for example, indicates how quantitative changes may produce a qualitative change; that is, feudalism changes into capitalism, which is predicted to change into socialism and then into communism. Notwithstanding his linear prediction, assumed from Hegel's Absolute Spirit, the manifestation of singularities is being indicated.

and produce uncertainties in the results. Whether the mood of humanism or the mood of fatalism is dominant, whether the juvenile perceives herself/himself more as subject or as object, and whether the juvenile engages in law-abiding or in lawbreaking behavior become more problematic as the effects of the various interpenetrating iterative loops work themselves out. Static snapshots of this dynamic process overlook uneven development: Sometimes the juvenile appears delinquent; at other times, quite restrained by the moral order.

Similarly, critical race theorist Crenshaw's (1993) discussion of subordination arising from three intersecting and parallel factors (structural, political/discursive, and representational/imaginary) can be augmented by indicating the uneven development of the various iterative aspects identified (also see Collins 1993). Collins, for example, indicates that race, class, and gender were iterated differently in the antebellum south, where race oppression was salient, than in Haiti, El Salvador, and Nicaragua, where social class is salient (1993:28-29). We suggest the hypothesis that singularities also would occur, producing various periodicities and forms of attractors even with incremental increases of the negative effects of the three intersecting factors.

Lacan's many topological constructions explaining the relationship between the subject and discourse also clearly indicate feedback loops, iterative processes, and singularities, as in his graphs of desire (1977), Borromean knots (1976-1977), and Schema R (1977). Lacan's subject-in-process always returns as a more-than-one; that is, it is reconstituted with each iteration. This has important implications for various narrative constructions in the criminal justice system by citizens, lawbreakers, police, lawyers, juries, social workers, psychiatrists, probation officers, and others. The ability to reconstitute an "objective" reality—the "what happened," for example—is undermined because, with the passage of time, the subject finds herself/himself in constantly changing configurations of iterative loops and singularities. A narrative constructed about some event at time $N_t$, for example, would find a proliferation of possible interpretations at $N_t + 1$. This idea also can be applied to the notion of the dialectics of struggle, which indicates how otherwise well-intended social activists sometimes reproduce forms of domination, or set the grounds for new forms of domination or other unintended consequences.

Our own discussion of the harms of repression and of reduction (Henry and Milovanovic 1996) also could identify these dynamics.

580    POSTMODERN CRIMINOLOGY

Manifest harms may arise at various moments and do not necessarily appear evenly, to justify a conclusion that they exist. Singularities come and go, accompanied by various attractors (and periodicities) producing various outcomes, even from similar configurations of iterative loops. We must move away from the idea that when two people are exposed to a set of similar factors, similar results must appear. This law of equivalence must wither away and be replaced by a "law" of heterogeneous development.

We see beginnings of this research in the works of Katz (1988), Ferrell (1995), and Mugford and O'Malley (1994) in the notion of the phenomenology of pleasure and crime. These works indicate how singularities arise and how various bifurcations emerge. Along with the traditional "background factors" incorporated in research, this alternative approach incorporates the "foreground factors" that are more nonlinear in development. Accordingly, a postmodern perspective would model emerging and dissipating constellations of iterative loops, incorporating both factors, and would be sensitive to the effects of historicity.

## METAMODELING AND THE MANDELBROT SET

Those interested in modeling complex, dynamic, and especially coupled nonlinear systems over time sense a need to present their findings visually. The bifurcation diagram is one visual aid; its mappings suggest further hypothesis building and testing. In this section we show how criminological phenomena can be portrayed by (1) configurations of interacting, coupled iterative loops and (2) the exemplary attractor, the Mandelbrot set (M-set; Figure 4).[7] This is only a suggestive exercise. Postmodern methodologies are still in their infancy, and new methodologies will certainly require time to build.

In this section we draw much inspiration from Gregersen and Sailer's (1993) recent article justifying the applicability of chaos theory to the social sciences. In that article they show how to develop metamodels and how the M-set illuminates chaotic phenomena (also see Pickover 1988; Sinanoglu 1981). We also draw an example from our book *Constitutive Criminology: Beyond Postmodernism* (Henry and Milovanovic 1996), where we developed the notion of COREL sets in mapping parallel, intersecting, and interlocking dissipative structures and their effects.

---

[7] The M-set is created by a rather simple-looking algorithm, $z = z^2 + u$, or $z_n+1 = z_n^2 + c$. Starting with some constant, a test point, $u$, or $c$, usually expressed in complex numbers, iteration proceeds; results are plotted, orbits are traced, and some cutoff point is established. Those values remaining within two units of the origin are called prisoner sets; those escaping to infinity are called escape sets. The totality of prisoner sets traces out the M-set (Mandelbrot 1977).

*Construction*

In mapping phenomena, Gregersen and Sailer (1993) have developed a useful modeling technique whereby complex, dynamic phenomena in movement can be presented visually. These representations move us away from the privileged straight line implying linearity[8] and suggest that we start with a very simple iterative loop (Figure 3).

**Figure 3.  Iterative Loop**

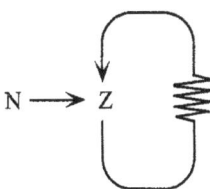

Note the "squiggle," which represents some nonlinear transformational law at work. Consider, for example, how words are continuously iterated in new contexts, producing ever new nuances of meaning; or think in terms of self-reflection, witnesses' recollections, or the mythical notion in law of some Founding Father's "original intent"; or consider generally how texts are continuously reinterpreted (also see Balkin 1987; Derrida 1976). This means that we start with some state vector, $z$, at time $t$, and then allow iteration to proceed (the computation of the transformational law said to be at work). This iteration then produces a new state, $Z_t + 1$.

---

8  Pickover's (1988) network models are useful. (See Figure 3.1.) Consider the representations:

**Figure 3.1.  Network Models**

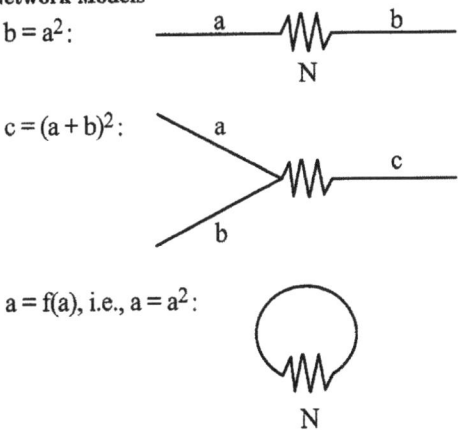

$$b = a^2:$$

$$c = (a + b)^2:$$

$$a = f(a), \text{ i.e., } a = a^2:$$

(Adopted from Pickover 1988)

With additional iteration, a new state results, and so on. This is a method of continuously taking the results of a computation and computing again. To capture the movement of the phenomena, however, in any of its states, as in modernist approaches, is merely to conduct cross-sectional analysis (that is, freezing dynamic systems), but at the price of losing an understanding of the overall dynamic movement over time, and of its various states. Complexity theory attempts to account for continuous and discontinuous change. This iterative loop can be expanded to include other influences, thus producing a configuration of coupled iterative loops (see Figure 4).

**Figure 4.   Modeling Chaos, the Mandelbrot Set, and Crime**

Phenomena   Metamodel    Mandelbrot Set      Mandelbrot Set
                         (Two-Dimensional)  (Three-Dimensional)

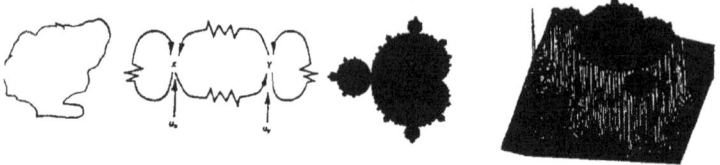

(Adopted from Gregersen and Sailer 1993; software provided by Wegner and Tyler 1993)

We could also identify another state vector, the environment within which the first is embedded as $u_t$. Thus the system's state at a particular time $(t + 1)$ reflects the environment state $u$ at time $t$ plus the system state, $Z_t$ (Gregersen and Sailer 1993:780). To indicate how two iterative loops interpenetrate each other (the structural coupling property), observe what appears under the heading "metamodel" in Figure 4.

*Application*

Take a modernist theory: Cressey's explanation of the embezzler in *Other People's Money*. Cressey's examination indicated that embezzlement takes place if three factors are present: a nonshareable financial problem, neutralizations present in the work environment that rationalize theft, and opportunities and skills. We imagine $x$ representing a nonshareable financial problem (an attitudinal variable) and $y$ the immediate work environment (opportunities to embezzle and prevalence of rationalizations). Perhaps $u_x$ and $u_y$ represent some external environmental conditions such as economic conditions and unemployment rates. Thus our

metamodel suggests that to understand the occurrence of embezzlement we must look at the interactions between $x$ and $y$ (and keep in
mind the squiggles between these two factors) and the effects of the
external environment $(u_x, u_y)$.

Gregersen and Sailer's suggestive study also indicates that we
should next consider the "law(s)" (or principles, formulations, algorithms) established for understanding the phenomena under
study—in other words, the transformations from one state to the
next. (See, for example, Lacan's use of the algorithm for metaphor
and metonymy, the two coordinating axes behind the "unconscious
structured like a language," note 12.) This is the authors' "fanciful
part"; it is merely suggestive. In their study they would suggest an
isomorphism between the chaos found in deterministic equations,
with their nondetermined results, and social science phenomena
undergoing iterations. They provide an example of polynomials
that hypothetically could summarize the interrelationships. In
their example they model the relationship between a worker's behavioral commitment $(x_t)$, his or her attitudinal commitment $(y_t)$,
and the supports in the work environment, where $u_x$ = coworker
relationships and $u_y$ = the formal reward system.

In their "fanciful part," Gregersen and Sailer make use of a polynomial: $x_t + 1 = x_t^2 - y_t^2 - u_x$ and $y_t + 1 = 2x_ty_t - u_y$ where $t =$
$0,1,2,3,\ldots$ and where the environmental state vectors, for simplification purposes, are held constant, $u_t = u$. Again, this would represent the transformational law said to account for the movement
from one state to the next. Thus if we start at some set of coordinates representing the state vector at time $t$ (equivalent to the constant value, $c$, in the algorithm for the M-set; see note 7) and then
proceed to iterate and observe the results, we can plot the outcome
on a phase map and end with a M-set in two dimensions (2D). We
also could portray it in 3D, where the vertical axis would represent
iterations (Figure 4).[9] In other words, by iteration we will find
some results that converge after a set number of iterations to the
black region (the M-set); other starting points, however, after the
same number of iterations, diverge to the white region.

In our example of the embezzler, we could similarly label the
three factors identified by Cressey as $x$, $y$ (with $y$ a collapsed variable), and environmental factors $u_x$, $u_y$. Then, by applying the logic
that an iterative polynomial is applicable (the "fanciful part"), we
could compute the results with various starting points. The points

---

9 Similarly, we could construct a 4D M-set expressed in hypercomplex numbers or in quaternions (Wegner and Tyler 1993). Quaternion mathematics has been
used for electricity and magnetism. 4D M-sets would have 4D orbits. The orbits can
be seen in 2D or 3D cross-sections.

that constitute the M-set (the black region) are the results of the iterated polynomial (representing the laws of transformation) and indicate those instances in which in fact embezzlement occurs. The "escape sets," or the divergent sets, are those white areas surrounding the M-set; in our example, they represent behaviors that are not embezzlement. (Keep in mind, too, that Cressey studied convicted embezzlers.)

Chaos theory suggests that if we start with two state vectors found in similar environments (i.e., the $c$ or constant value, representing the test points in the algorithm for the M-set; see note 7) and if both vectors end, after iteration, as prisoner sets (i.e., embezzlement), a third state vector found *between* these two initial points might, after iteration, have a result quite different than would be expected. In other words, we would have expected that the in-between starting values also should result in the convergent (prisoner) set. However, deterministic equations produce unpredictable results: The first two are in the convergent set, and the third is in the divergent set.

Another most interesting feature of the M-set is its boundary; note how jagged it is. Periodicity increases here. This boundary is *fractal*: it represents fractions of a dimension. Continuous zooms (magnifications) on the borders, up to 300 million, will show that these boundaries are infinitely varied (see Peitgen et al. 1992:453) and that no "best-fitting line," as in regression analysis, can possibly capture the phenomenon accurately. No prediction is possible at the boundary; at best the social scientist can have *explanation* as her or his goal (Gregersen and Sailer 1993). This is not necessarily to discount the usefulness of quantitative methodology; as Young (1991) and Gregersen and Sailer (1993) indicate, deciding what region of phase space one samples is critical. Near the boundaries, however, prediction by means of regression analysis becomes unproductive. Here, at best, understanding rather than prediction can be the goal, a case for ethnographic research. "Trouser diagrams" are more useful than path analysis for conceptualizing causal chains.

Trouser diagrams (or "world tubes") have been developed by cosmologists and nuclear physicists to better explain "particle" interactions more clearly (see Bohm 1980; Peat 1988), insofar as "particles" are problematic, and interacting "waves" or energies moving in space become more precise ways of thinking. As Bohm says, "This world tube represents an infinitely complex process of a structure in movement and development which is centered in a region indicated by the boundaries of the tube" (1980:10). Deleuze and

MILOVANOVIC 585

**Figure 5. Trouser Diagrams versus Path Analysis**

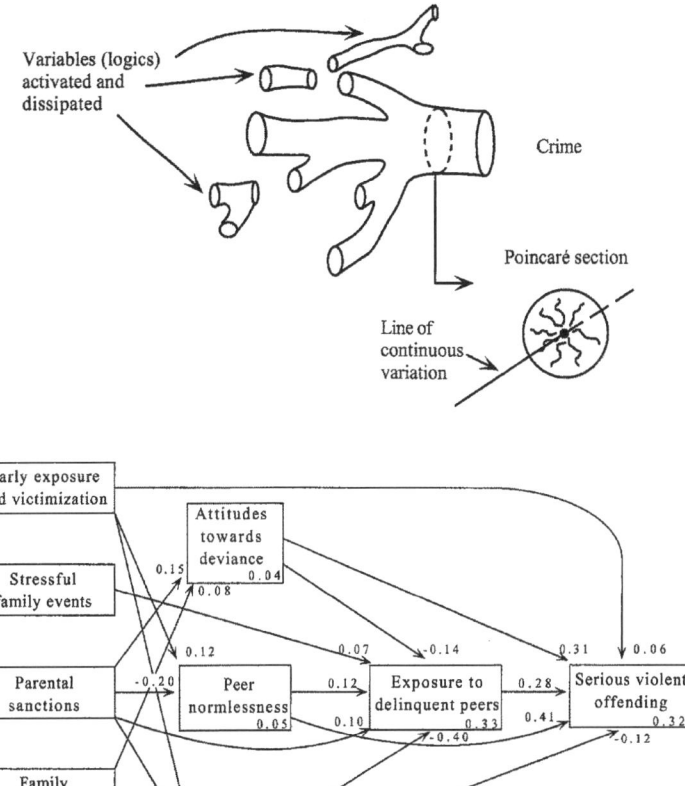

(Path Analysis from Elliot 1994:17)

Guattari (1987) offer a better conceptualization in terms of a "rhizome," a "continuous line of variation"; that is, along some "line" we have a perpendicular range of variation of some phenomenon, which cannot be given precise location at any moment in time (a snapshot). Or again, given some reasonably close approximation of location, it is impossible to specify the momentum variable, as quantum mechanics tells us. Here consider the torus attractor as a representation of global stability but local indeterminacy.

Let's return to our notion of the COREL sets. We could model these with a number of iterative loops that run parallel and intersect. (For the effects of the intersections of gender, race, and class in criminology, see Matsuda et al. 1993; Schwartz and Milovanovic 1996.) At least a 3D phase space would be needed here. Each iterative loop also is composed of others, which in turn are connected with a variety of others. Constitutive interrelational sets interpenetrate at different levels with effects, and every iterative loop contains many others that constitute it. Accordingly, in Figure 4, the metamodel would include many iterative loops that intersect, loop, feed back, and so on; each would have squiggles indicating nonlinear transformations.[10] The M-set reflecting the various iterations of the "laws" of transformation in the COREL sets would necessarily be in higher-dimensional space.

The significance of the jagged boundaries can be related to several approaches that have affinities with, or perhaps are the beginnings of, a postmodernist analysis, such as Matza's (1964, 1969) "drift" theory and the notion of the "invitational edge"; Lyng's (1990) "edgework"; O'Malley and Mugford's (1994) integration of Katz's and Lyng's work advocating a "phenomenology of pleasure"; Ferrell's (1995) political economy of criminal pleasure; and Giroux's (1992) "borderland," to name a few of the most prominent. In each case we find that the boundary region, the borderland, is the area of maximum indeterminacy, where subjects may easily find themselves in one basin of outcome rather than another. This is also the region in which the much-celebrated regression analysis fails us. It is the region of imaginary play, pleasure, excitement, and alternative embodiments of desire.

Contrary to the celebration of forces of rationalization, disciplinary mechanisms, and other centripetal forces that tend toward point or limit attractors, a postmodern perspective on the phenomenology of pleasure seeks to understand crimes at the border, the invitational edge, and edgework, the area of tori and strange attractors. Without in any way implying a *general* statement concerning crime, postmodern analysis would examine the many neglected foreground factors. Whether we take Katz's (1988) position concerning the purposefully contrived resignation of control, a contrived pacification or objectification of self; Lyng's (1990) position on edgework, a subjectivity confirmed in high-risk activity; or Matza's (1969; also see O'Malley and Mugford 1994) position that the subject is transformed from subject to object and then to a reclaimed

---

[10] These complex interconnections are best reflected in the hologram. Bohm (1980:145-47) argues that a hologram can reveal the undivided wholeness of phenomena in 3D, even if a laser light is directed only to part of a photographic plate. Bohm (like Lacan's topologies, as we shall see) indicates the importance of 4D space; he tells us that "the implicate order has to be considered as a process of enfoldment and unfoldment in a higher dimensional space. Only under certain conditions can this be simplified as a process of enfoldment and unfoldment in three dimensions" (1980:189).

subjectivity in its confrontation with the invitational edge, we see that the fractal experiences at the borders are a legitimate and fruitful focus of criminological inquiry. It may very well be, as pointed out by O'Malley and Mugford (1994:203; also see Ferrell 1995), that "As the crisis of self is accelerated by the process of commercializing human emotional labor and the real increasingly subverted by the hyperreal, a possible transcendent route for the individual lies in adopting pursuits that, by their excess and danger, stir powerful emotions that recreate and reassure oneself of oneself."

## CATASTROPHE THEORY

Discontinuities experienced in rather orderly systems are puzzling in criminology. Many of these occur in interpersonal conflicts that escalate until an abrupt, nonlinear change is experienced (Katz 1988). Accordingly the second area we would like to offer, which we believe is promising to the development of postmodern methodologies, has been linked by Lyotard (1984) to catastrophe theory as developed by Rene Thom (1975; also see Baack and Cullen 1992, 1994; Casti 1994; Oliva, Day, and MacMillan 1988; Oliva, Peters, and Murphy 1981; Zeeman 1976). Thom developed a mathematics which expressed the discontinuities that may arise in deterministic systems. Thom (1975) and Zeeman (1976) have identified seven forms of catastrophes that extend to 5D space (depending on how many variables are needed); with even more variables, however, higher-dimensional space is required.

*Construction*

A 3D model (Figure 6a, 6b) begins with two independent variables or control parameters. One is referred to as the "normal" control variable, the other as the "splitting factor." This latter factor can be seen as a "moderator" "that specifies the conditions under which the normal factor affects the dependent variable continuously or discontinuously" (Baack and Cullen 1994:214). Or, rather than a normal and splitting factor we could have two "normal factors," which are conflictual influences on the behavior parameter (Zeeman 1977:332-33). This is the "cusp catastrophe model" (for its recognition as such, see the five factors identified by Thom 1975 and Zeeman 1976, and lucidly presented by Oliva et al. 1988). We will provide an example already in the literature, and then will draw attention to a recent work of synthesis by O'Malley and Mugford (1994) which can be modeled.

Lyotard (1984) and Zeeman (1976) use an example of a dog's aggressiveness (this is the state variable). It is said to be directly

proportional to the dog's anger, which is defined as a control variable. When a certain level of anger is reached, it is predicted that an
attack will follow. The second possible control variable is fear.
Here, however, when a certain level is reached, flight will occur, the
reverse of the first response. We begin at a hypothetical point of
stability, where anger and fear are at a minimum. As the two control variables (anger and fear) increase, the two threshold levels
(for attack and flight) are approached at the same time. So far, linearity prevails; a deterministic equation can indicate this. At the
threshold, however, the dog oscillates between attack and flight
(i.e., two periods, attractor basins, or bimodality). Here we have a
bifurcation, or singularity, with two possible outcomes. The dog's
behavior is unpredictable; the system is unstable. This instability
exists even though the control variables (anger and fear) are continuous. The state variables are discontinuous.

In the cusp catastrophe model (see Figure 6a and 6b), the state
space or the dependent variable is the vertical axis and the wavy
plane with a smooth double fold that is generated. The horizontal
two-dimensional plane represents the control plane (x, y coordinates), reflecting two independent variables. Where the two independent variables intersect we may trace a perpendicular line
that extends upward toward the smooth doubly folded plane, which
represents behavior (the dependent variable). Note the "cusp" region (the folded plane) in the center and its projection (the "bifurcation set") on the bottom surface. This region is significant in
producing nonlinear effects. The middle pleat represents highly im-
probable behavior such as neutrality; fear and anger do not cancel
each other out; this unstable region will witness flight or attack.

"Folds" are involved where one control and one response parameter are present, and thus appear in two dimensions. Briggs
and Peat (1989) provide the example of blowing up a balloon: At a
certain point, it explodes. In other words, a catastrophe has
emerged. "Cusps," on the other hand, have two control parameters
and one response parameter, and can be modeled in three dimensions. Folds and cusps indicate where outcome values "jump" from
one value to another in a nonlinear manner. In other words, at the
edge of the fold the outcome will jump to the higher or the lower
plane; this jump reflects discontinuous (nonlinear) change. (Up to
that point, the change was continuous.) This is represented in Figure 6a and 6b as a jump from one plane to another, as in C to D and
D to E. This jump also can be conceptualized as a a bifurcation.

In Figure 6b the vertical line identifies two distinct point attractors. (Bimodality can be traced to the work of conflicting factors

**Figure 6. The Cusp Catastrophe Portrait and Postmodern Crime**

a. Three-Dimensional Portrait

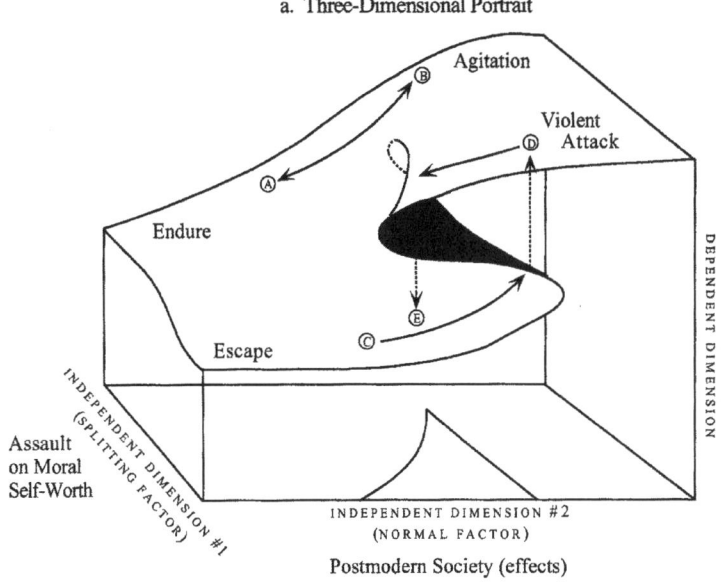

Postmodern Society (effects)

b. One-Dimensional Portrait

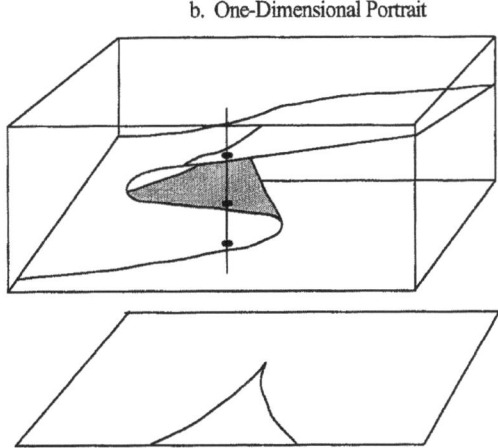

(Adopted from Abraham 1992; Casti 1994; Zeeman 1976)

or the splitting factor.) This one-dimensional line represents a portrait, or state space, in this 3D response diagram. Outside the cusp region there is only one attractor or outcome basin (Abraham 1992; Zeeman 1976). A catastrophe is defined as "a bifurcation where an attractor appears or disappears" (Abraham 1992:11-49; McRobie and Thompson 1994:155). McRobie and Thompson describe this situation well: "With gradual changes in [a] parameter, attractors generally evolve smoothly, but at certain critical points, called bifurcations, the attractor may split into different attractors or may simply disappear" (1994:155).

*Application*

As an example, an intriguing synthesis by O'Malley and Mugford (1994) builds on the work of Katz (1988) and on Lyng's (1990) analysis of "edgework." O'Malley and Mugford suggest that both Katz and Lyng provide answers to "explaining the dilemma of the modern self" (1994:200) and the effects of the coming of [post]modern society, where alienation and the hyperreal (Baudrillard), clock time, and commodification call forth, in response, experiences that arouse moral, sensual, and emotional states (the "foreground factors"). Thus a more Nietzschean vision is offered rather than merely a materialistic explanation of the onset of extreme forms of behavior. The difference between Katz's approach and Lyng's is that for Katz, the person welcomes the loss of control ("righteous slaughter"); for Lyng, however, the person attempts to maintain control under extreme conditions (as in skydiving). In both cases the person subjects herself/himself to extreme experiences in order to develop "mood changes as a form of resistance or escape from the mundane" (1994:193-94; also see Ferrell 1995).[11]

In our example, drawing from Katz's (1988) study of "righteous slaughter" and from O'Malley and Mugford's integration (1994), we first identify the dependent variable as behaviors that might result from the interacting effects of the two independent variables: endure, escape, agitation, and violent attack (see Figure 6a). The "normal factor" (the control variable or "independent dimension") is the emergence of postmodern society and some of its effects: here we collapse O'Malley and Mugford's (1994) three suggestive factors—an increase in alienation and the hyperreal, clock time, and commodification—into a single variable. Of course "collapsing" often entails the risk that the variables are not necessarily related or covarying, but for this example we follow the authors' suggestion that they are indeed. The other independent variable, the "splitting factor," would be a perceived assault on moral self-worth (Katz

---

[11] Perhaps what could be developed here is a triangle of crime: the offender/ tester of boundaries or the "invitational edge" (Ferrell 1995; Katz 1988 and Lyng 1990, but also see Halleck 1967; Matza 1964, 1969; Salecl 1993); the corrector (agents of social control or, generally, agents of the disciplining mechanisms as spelled out by Foucault); and the reporter (the journalist, cinema producer, criminologist). These three complete the cycle in these forms of arousal of the sensual.

1988). Thus the increasing effects of postmodern society in interaction with increasing perceptions of assaults on moral self-worth would produce an increasing intensity in the emotional state "humiliation." For Katz, this means that "the person is overcome with an intolerable discomfort. . . [it] takes over the soul by invading whole body" (1988:25). In a mild form, this situation would manifest itself by the subject enduring these degradations of self; at greater intensities it might translate into aggressive display, posturing, and the like; and in its most intense forms, humiliation might manifest itself in violent attack.

Figure 6a shows that as the normal factor (the effects of postmodern society) increases from left to right, various subjective states also vary in linear fashion (A to B). For example, behaviors indicating that the subject is enduring the interacting effects of postmodern society and attacks on moral self-worth (upper left-hand quadrant) could move in a linear way towards agitation (upper right-hand quadrant) whereby lesser harms are manifested in installments as well as in aggressive display, posturing, verbal "dozens," and so on. Here, continuities exist. The splitting factor, assault on moral self-worth, may be a factor in producing this continuity, or in its discontinuity. Lines CD and DE indicate discontinuous change (i.e., the jumps noted from one plane to another along a fold). Small differences in the initial conditions (i.e., the initial values) of the normal and the splitting variables may produce divergences.

The acceptance of increasing humiliation and the escape option may follow a linear path (following Katz, the subject may take comfort in feeling that at other times and places, s/he will be free from humiliation), but an unexpected, radical change will occur at the double fold. In other words, the acceptance of humiliation and the escape option might be maintained until one reaches the area of the double fold; there humiliation will be transformed into rage and violent attack (Katz 1988). In Figure 6a this is shown as the movement from C to D; note the "jump." Of course it could also work the other way: the line D to E indicates a situation in which violent attack is imminent but abruptly changes to escape. Thus we have either an "escape" (D to E) or a "violent attack" (C to D) catastrophe.

This model is useful in our understanding of escalating hostilities and violence in various interpersonal situations (also see Milovanovic forthcoming b, chap. 12). Intense arguments or differences (in which anger and fear are often latent constitutive elements) initially could take a more sober, more rational tone, but with an increase in reciprocating incremental assaults on the self, they may culminate in the cusp region, where a small additional increase in either control parameter may produce violent attack. In an increasingly diverse society it would seem that society-wide strategies need to be devised, wherein disputants can safely "walk away" or deescalate from spiraling emotional states (as presented in a current TV commercial), allowing cooler discussions of differences to be held later. Two limitations exist, however: the entrenched "frontier" ideology of holding one's ground, and the fact that "life chances" are distributed unevenly, so that many disenfranchised persons have no "escape" option (whereby one can fantasize another time and place in which one will not be subjected to degradation of self). In both situations the spiral may continue. Where hope, possibilities, and life chances in a political economy are greatly restricted, so too are the possibilities of defusing escalating hostilities.

Our more postmodern-oriented model, building on O'Malley and Mugford's recent integration, suggests the occurrence of certain kinds of crimes (and edgework) that do not follow linear logic. Rather, discontinuities would be likely to occur; an external observer would be unable to predict that a small increase in the control parameters would lead to crimes entailing "moral transcendence," such as those described by Katz. These would be hard to explain. As O'Malley and Mugford say, "Transcendence appears to involve crossing (or at the very least 'playing with') a threshold or limit between being in and out of rational control in order to experience the self in the grip of emotional or moral forces" (1994:191). We see much affinity between the above analysis and Matza's (1969) early work on the "invitational edge" and the necessity of a "leap" to do evil or to reestablish the "mood of humanism" (1964; also see Salecl's [1993] "mode of subjectivization").

Certain limitations, nevertheless, are present in the model and pose challenges for future research. Casti (1994), for example, argues that the model (1) applies only to a small class of dynamic systems, (2) assumes the dominance of the point attractor (as opposed to periodic, torus, and strange attractors), (3) identifies only a small number of input control parameters, and (4) assumes a relatively stable, homeostatic model until a singularity appears (as opposed to a model that is in a far-from-equilibrium condition, where small perturbations produce disproportional change and various forms of attractors). Moreover, the use of the cusp catastrophe model rests on the researcher's ability to clearly identify either the conflictual variables (i.e., anger, fear) or the splitting factor, which is said to contribute to continuity or discontinuity in the behavioral dimension. It may very well be that the model is best at explaining extreme conflictual emotional states. If this is so, it promises to be a helpful tool for understanding various interpersonal situations in which hostility escalates until a bifurcation is reached (sudden violence). The development of various testable hypotheses would certainly be an outcome of this line of investigation. This point underscores the idea that postmodern criminology entails developing various methodologies and being sensitive to their limitations.

## TOPOLOGY, LACAN, AND CRIMINOLOGY

Postmodern theory has focused on the nature of discourses and on their ability to adequately represent narratives of the disenfranchised, the oppressed, the marginalized, and the alienated. Rather than privileging global knowledge, postmodernists attempt to make the denied voices heard. In criminology we have been faced with the question of how narratives and stories are constructed, whether by citizens, witnesses, or police, or in reports and testimony, trial proceedings, court opinions, newspaper accounts, and scholarly research. A postmodern criminology wishes to explain the connection between subjectivity and discourse. A postmodern methodology, then, must provide some conceptual tools for viewing the nature of this interconnection. Jacques Lacan has been the critical figure in portraying the desiring subject's inseparability from discourse (Arrigo 1995a, 1995b; Milovanovic 1992, 1993a, 1993b). Sense production therefore must be explored. In this section we briefly outline the key topological constructs used by Lacan and their relevance for postmodern criminology. These include the Mobius band, the cross-cap, and the Borromean knots.

### The Mobius Band

*Construction.* The Mobius band (Figure 7) can be pictured as a rectangular strip that undergoes a modification whereby it produces a unilateral surface. This is Lacan's way of indicating how an "inside" (the unconscious) has continuity with an "outside" (the conscious). It is a constitutive element of the cross-cap, described below. Take a rectangle, make one twist, and then join the edges; the result is a Mobius band. An ant walking on one side will eventually return to its starting point without having crossed any borders. More accurately conceptualized, think of the band as soaked through both sides by an ink image (in our example, a drawing of a face with a hat); the image returns in inverted form. For Lacan, the Mobius band can represent various movements and transformations: how consistency is maintained via repetition by the psychic apparatus, a subject's internal dialogue; the workings of metaphor, the production of fantasy (perceptions of reality) as a basis for action (for the latter two items, see the cross-cap below); and legal obfuscations or reifications of phenomena.

**Figure 7. The Mobius Band**

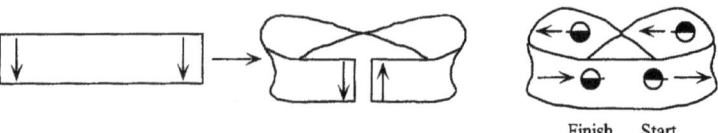

Finish    Start

*Application.* First, in regard to the internal dialogue, consider Lacan's (1977:312) notion that "the sender receives his [her] own message back from the receiver in an inverted form," that is, speakers often repeat the question posed to them: "Why do I do it?" "I do it because. . . ." "Why does Michael Jordan do it?" "*He* does it because. . . ." "What would I, or what would a reasonable man/woman, have done in such and such circumstance?" and the response, "Unlike the defendant, I would have. . . ." This internal dialogue by the subject can be also conceptualized as the subject's posing a question to the Other: "What do you want?" The answer begins "*I want. . .[objet petit a*, or *object of desire*]." In other words, an answer begins as an attempt to embody desire in a linguistically articulated demand. This is then translated into a drive and is followed by a movement toward recognition. Lacan's analysis of discourse implicates the performative (Lee 1990:75-79). The return of the message in inverted form indicates how internalized legal constructs and ideologies act as a backdrop for assessing matters such as culpability, rationality, and responsibility.

Second, the Mobius band has been presented in Lacan's (1977) algorithm for metaphor, one of two semiotic axes that are said to coordinate production of signifiers within the unconscious, within the Other, the "unconscious structured like a language" (Milovanovic 1992, 1993b).[12] It indicates how a primary signifier "crosses

---

12  Lacan makes heavy use of algorithms and symbols. They should not be used strictly mathematically, but more as intuitive devices or ideographs. He attempted to devise a way to overcome much of the baggage attached to conventional language. At times, he saw himself as a poet. His algorithm for metaphor is $f(S'/S) S \sim S(+)s$; or $S/S' \cdot S'/x \to S(1/s)$; or

$$\frac{\text{exchange value}}{\text{use value}} \cdot \frac{\text{use value}}{\text{unknown}} \to \text{exchange value} \cdot \frac{1}{\text{idea of use value}}.$$

When the two use values are crossed out, what remains is "exchange value" over "idea of use value," or the replacement of the unique by an abstraction. This is equivalent to Marx's idea of the fetishism of the commodity principle. Homologously, in the legal sphere, the juridic subject becomes equivalent to the exchange value (the "reasonable man" in law), and the uniqueness of the subject, or use value (e.g., abilities, needs), disappears (Milovanovic 1992:69-70, 98-100; 1994b:70-75, 147).

the bar" to the unconscious and is replaced with a substitute signifier (S' now stands for S). Consider metaphors such as "She is a dynamo." One signifier is replaced by another, which in turn, with a complete traversing of the Mobius band, reappears. Consider, too, how exchange value replaces use value in Marx's idea of fetishism of commodities. A homology exists within the commodity, juridic, and linguistic spheres (Rossi-Landi 1983). In the production of the juridic subject and in the homogenizing of signifiers, nuanced meanings are given more universal, more decontextualized, and more abstract meanings (Milovanovic 1994b:147; see note 12). Thus, and third, legal obfuscations or reifications are explained by the development of exchange values (i.e., abstractions such as juridic subjects, legal signifiers, empirical subjects, clinical categories, other bureaucratic identities of clients). Stated in another way, as Lacan tells it, a signifier represents the subject for another signifier (i.e., S' for S).

The "crossing" of the bar, the movement along the Mobius band, is the "spark" in the creation of meaning (Lacan 1977:157-58, 164, 166). It indicates how exchange values come to replace use values. Conceptualized differently, this crossing is an "operation" (Granon-Lafont 1990:47) isomorphic with our previous notion of the "squiggles" in transformational theory: It produces an effect. It is nonlinear insofar as other minute factors, such as the nuances of context, may produce different valuations. As Granon-Lafont said: "This arrow [a diagonal] which crosses the bar from one signifier to another can be read as the continuous side of the Mobius band" (1990:49; my translation).

*The Cross-Cap*

One of the most enigmatic topological constructs that Lacan employs is the cross-cap. For presentational purposes this can be shown in 3D space, but can be constructed without intersections in only 4D space. This construct indicates the intricate connections among discourse, fantasy, objects of desire, and subjectivity. It expresses how fantasy production—the variously framed perceptions of reality—takes place, and how performativity then results (social action). It moves beyond the empirical subject of many of the traditional positivistic approaches in criminology, and has great potential for exploring and understanding (1) nonmaterialistic factors such as the sensual, emotional, visceral elements, as well as desires, pleasures, excitement, entertainment, and adrenalin rushes in crime production (Ferrell 1995; Katz 1988; Matza 1969; O'Malley and Mugford 1994); (2) the effects of criminalizing words

596    POSTMODERN CRIMINOLOGY

and images (e.g., "fighting words," pornographic images with violent themes); (3) the interactive effects in the criminalization of appearance (i.e., "suspicious person," drug courier profiles, gang lists, hijacker profiles, and "crimes of style"); (4) "copycat" crimes (e.g., crimes emulated as a result of exposure in the media); (5) the relationship between subjectivity and discourse, and how certain voices are denied more genuine expression in the criminal justice system; and (6) the increasing emergence of the hyperreal as the coordinate of fantasy production. We first explain the construction of Schema R on the cross-cap and then provide some applications in postmodern criminology.

   *Construction.* The cross-cap, from projective geometry, inscribes Lacan's Schema R (Figure 9), the dynamic model of his decentered subject (the more static form is found in his Schema L). From this, numerous Mobius bands can be "cut." The cross-cap is a unilateral surface with no borders or edges; continuity exists between the "inside" and the "outside." The cross-cap begins with the seemingly impossible project of portraying a figure in which opposite points on the rim of a hemisphere are joined (Barr 1964:78-107; Frechet and Fan 1967:31, 42-44; Hilbert and Cohn-Vossen 1952:313-17; Weeks 1985:61-66). The construction of the cross-cap (Figure 8) can best be achieved with some effort in 3D.

**Figure 8.   The Cross-Cap (Derivation)**

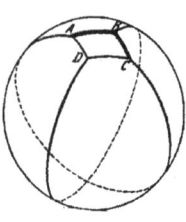 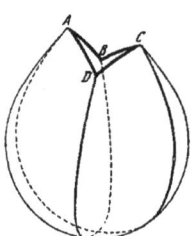 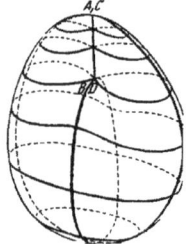

(Adopted from Hilbert and Cohn-Vossen 1952:314-317)

   The cross-cap depicts a deformed sphere on which, in the top portion, all points along the outside are connected to their opposites. It is constructed by taking a sphere, cutting out a quadrilateral ABCD, raising the corners of this quadrilateral, and then joining opposite edges AB with CD so that A and C now coincide, as do B and D. In 3D, a line of intersection necessarily will emerge, from AC to BD. In 4D space, no line of intersection exists.

   In Figure 9, Lacan's Schema R, depicting the relationship between the subject and her/his objects of desire in all of its complexities, is placed on the cross-cap. Here φ or small phi = the imaginary

**Figure 9. The Cross-Cap and Schema R**

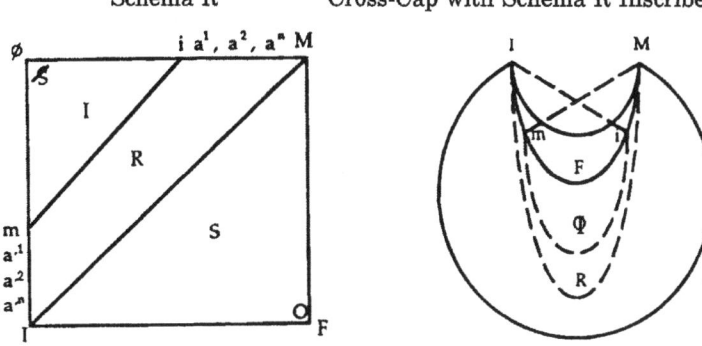

Schema R

Cross-Cap with Schema R Inscribed

(Adopted from Lacan 1977:197)    (Adopted from Granon-Lafont 1985:83)

phallus; i = specular image(s), imaginary; Φ or large phi = the symbolic phallus, signifier for *jouissance*, seen in the cross-cap as a singularity; m = ego (imaginary); a' = ideal ego(s); a = object(s) of desire, imaginary other; $ = divided subject; I = Imaginary Order (imagoes, sphere of imaginary constructions); S = Symbolic Order (culture, language); M = mother, primal object of desire; F = law of the father; I (lower left corner) = ego ideal; O = Other (the unconscious "structured like a language," the repository of signifiers); R = perceived field of reality, framed by the Symbolic and Imaginary Order, fantasy, $ <> a. (For a lucid explanation of terms, see Mueller and Richardson 1982:211-12, 245, 255, 259.)

Schema R portrays how word and narrative production implicate numerous processes, such as imaginary and symbolic constructions and their interplay, many of which remain unconscious (the sphere of the Other). The task is to join i to I, and m to M. In other words, we create the Mobius band (Granon-Lafont 1985; Milovanovic 1994a; Mueller and Richardson 1982; Nasio 1987; Vappereau 1988:303-26). The quadrilateral ABCD in Figure 8 corresponds to IFMϕ in Figure 9. If we cut the strip again from I to M and from i to m, we obtain the surface of the flat (2D) Schema R (region R in Figure 9). The complete 3D "cut" traces a Figure 8 (the Mobius band). "The subject is that cut itself, and what falls away through the action of cutting is the object" (Regnault 1995:71; also see Lacan 1977:197, 223, 333-34, 1981:271; Milovanovic 1994; Nasio 1987:160). The field of reality (R) is fantasy, represented by Lacan as $ <> a. It represents the variously framed perceptions of reality. The symbolic phallus, Φ, appearing at the singularity BD, and on the cross-cap replacing the imaginary phallus, $\phi$, although substitutable in an alternative sociocultural order, signifies power, potency, and the ability to overcome various "lacks" in being. This provides constancy for the psychic apparatus and is the basis of male gender dominance (phallocentric order).[13]

In other words, by this cutting operation (tracing a figure 8, *huit interieur*)—equivalent to the "squiggles" of chaos theory, indicating transformation, or the "crossing of the bar," as in Lacan's explanation of metaphor—we create the subject and the *objet petit a*, the unilateral surface of the Mobius band, and the bilateral surface of a disk (Lacan 1977:334; Nasio 1987), which includes the singularity, BD, for Lacan, $\Phi$. Lacan represents this "cut" as $S <> a$; or the subject ($S$), the cut ($<>$), and the *objet petit a* (Nasio 1987:160). This is Lacan's algorithm for fantasy. It reflects the connectedness between the subject and her/his objects of desire, which offer the illusory potential for overcoming the inherent gap or "lack" of being (*manque d'être*).

The cross-cap with Schema R inscribed is also the basis of Lacan's notion of "repetition," the subject's tendency to compulsively repeat and hence provide consistency and stability to its existence. Space limitations preclude a detailed discussion, but a figure 8 can be cut within the cross-cap by following the median of the Mobius band. This figure 8 represents the subject's repetition, but always returns as "more than one" (*un en plus*). In other words, iterability is involved; the new is built on the trace of the past. Therefore this function is not entirely homeostatic, because it assumes inherent instability.

*Applications.* Various applications are possible in postmodern analysis. First, many of the nonmaterialistic, emotional, and sensual crimes explained by Katz (1988) and developed further by O'Malley and Mugford (1994), as well as many of the crimes described by Halleck (1967), Matza (1964, 1969), and Salecl (1993), can be seen as entailing attempts at transcendence of repetition, a motivation centering on desire for alternative embodiment. Each crime entails responding to some unfavorably developing image of self, m(a'), which is at variance with the ego ideal (I). In Katz, one's self-worth is questioned; in Halleck, Matza, and Salecl, a sense of helplessness, fatalism, or disappearance of identity is experienced.

---

13 This singularity is the place where all lines converge and diverge, where the $S$ becomes the *objet petit a* and the *objet petit a* becomes $S$; it is the confluence of all forces acting all at once; it is the coloration of all by the male voice, the basis of gender inequality in a phallocentric symbolic order. The "disk," the residue of the "cut" in 2D, carries this singularity; in 3D we have what appears as a spiraling seashell, the place where the convergence point is reached, $\Phi$.

This is countered by imaginations of objects of desire, i(a), which offer the illusory potential for overcoming these assaults on self-worth or on the ability to be an active agent or an agent at all (fatalism). This is represented by the family of lines from m(a') to i(a) following a figure 8. The performative dimension then suggests that an infraction is a highly likely response.

To complete our triangle of crime, various agents of social control are also offered space and opportunities in which to engage in emotional highs, transcendence, and encounters with the invitational edge; so too are various reporters, including students of crime. Consider the often routine bureaucratic components of work, as opposed to the more unpredictable, more engaging elements at the boundary of activity, which often provide adrenalin rushes, highs, and breaks in the routine.

Second, consider that in the United States, "fighting words" are not legally protected by the Constitution. Here the *performative* dimension of discourse is acknowledged (in "speech act theory," defined as the ability to produce some effect on the attitudes and actions of others; Held 1995:265). These words cannot be protected objects of desire, or $ <> i(a), meaning the subject's identifications with various imaginary objects of desire (including an other). Here, too, critical race theory is likely to advocate more stringent regulating and sanctioning of hate speech (Matsuda et al. 1993).

In Canada, in *R. v. Butler* (1992), certain pornographic images (those coupled with violent themes) were said not to be protected. The court elaborated: "Images that people are exposed to bear a causal relationship to their behaviour" (p. 502). Here again, some couplings are being curtailed between a person's favorable view of himself/herself, or $ <> (a'),—meaning the subject's connectedness to her/his various imaginary, narcissistic conceptions of self, or the ideal ego—and some potential objects of desire, $ <> i(a), which offer the illusory potential of overcoming the *manque d'être*. Various strips, a "family of lines," can be traced between the i(a) and the m(a'); with a twist they trace a figure 8, representing movement along a Mobius band (e.g., the subject's idiosyncratically experienced reality, or R). That is, the subject's "choice" of objects of desire, i(a), always returns in inverted form as an answer to the question of a self (*moi*) that is an ideal, m(a'). For Butler, the very definition of the subject is given by a "regulated process of repetition" found in various discourses (1990:145).

Third, there are also interactive effects (coproduction) in the criminalization of appearance, which implicate Schema R. The very process of naming (i.e., various profiles and crimes of style,

such as wearing various insignia in public) provides a basis for repetition and hence creates consistency and stability for the subject.
Stated in another way, an outcome of the various constitutive forces
in the criminal justice system, the coproduction by offenders, controllers, and reporters, are various constructions of criminal conceptions (Barak 1988, 1994). These relatively stabilized ideological
constructions, or fantasies, offer stability and hence the (illusory)
hope of prediction and control. These aforementioned crimes, however, involve no "doer behind the deed" (an "individual") but only
the "deed" (Butler 1990:25, 142, 148; Nietzsche 1969). As Katz tells
us, "Typically, the person will not be able to help us with the analysis because he is taken in by his efforts to construct the dynamic. If
we ask, 'Why did you do it?' he is likely to respond with self-justify-
ing rhetoric" (1988:7; also see Matza's [1969] discussion of how the
subject, once objectified, becomes what the situation dictates). The
subject ("doer") must be seen as a set of relations in historically determined contexts with various, relatively stabilized discourses,
within which reality is constructed. In this sense, then, Butler's
suggestion for change, locating "strategies of subversive repetition"
(1990:147), offers the hope of providing the basis for alternative
forms of subjectivities.

Fourth, "copycat" crimes can be seen as involving a "pacified"
subject (Katz 1988:7-8; Matza 1969) fixated on a cycle of *repetition*
ending in a crime that emulates one which has been observed in the
media (Surette 1992). In Lacan's terminology, the subject's ideal
view of her/himself, m(a'), is connected to an object of desire, i(a),
the image that promises the (illusory) hope of overcoming *manque
d'être*. This is a source of pleasure (*jouissance*). The constructed
perception becomes the basis of a drive that is consummated in infraction. Some persons defend the media by arguing that fictional
criminals portrayed are merely copying crimes already in existence;
this fact may say more about how a hyperreality is given stability
and provides the coordinates within which "reality" is constructed.
Here Schema R is able to explain phenomena such as specular and
illusory images of self and others, objects of desire, phallocentric
biases, and the effects of more fully stabilized signifiers and discourses in their contributions to certain forms of crimes. Fantasy
production, the various "cuts" represented by the Mobius band, uncovers the internal dynamics at work in the psychic apparatus.

Fifth, the significance of Schema R is also relevant to the way
discursive production takes place, and especially to how the subject
is connected with various objects of desire, i(a), including words or
signifiers. Narrative constructions, storytelling, and decision making are internally operations in which signifiers are constructed,

and through appropriate linguistic codes are placed in correct linear order to produce grammatically correct sentences (Jackson 1988; also see Arrigo's [1993, 1995b] application to the insanity defense and to classroom instruction). Yet this process in most criminological treatises is not explained. Lacan's cross-cap indicates how the subject and his or her objects of desire (which include signifiers as offering an illusory hope for fulfilling demand, the linguistic attempt to embody desire) are constantly under construction. The subject (police officer, lawyer, judge, reporter, witness) places herself/himself within a particular discourse (e.g., legal, clinicolegal, police subcultural, journalistic) and within that sphere has a limited number of master signifiers that may be used in constructing "reality" in acceptable narrative forms. In other words, the embodying of desire, the variously framed perceptions of reality depicted in the Mobius band, is a circumscribed activity. The elements constructed are renditions of the "What happened?" that have been translated from the context of occurrence (i.e., the street scene) to the context of the courts and their particular legal discourse and available master signifiers.

Accordingly, not all voices are heard. Some constructions are more allowable than others and hence reconstitute dominant conceptions of reality. Other constructions are seen as nonjusticiable, grounds for an "objection" that is likely to be "sustained" by the judge. We have indicated this process in the context of jailhouse lawyers (Milovanovic 1988; Milovanovic and Thomas 1989), activist lawyers (Bannister and Milovanovic 1990), doing criminology (Henry and Milovanovic 1991), and decision making by a jury (Milovanovic 1994:107-108); also see Arrigo's application to the insanity defense (1993, 1994) and to pedagogy (1995b).

Finally, the various "cuts," the framing of "reality," also increasingly find coordinates in the emerging hyperreal. For example, Arrigo's (forthcoming) examination of the O.J. Simpson trial shows how signs, images, and cultural icons are in flux in the various media portrayals of Simpson. From our view, we can see how the Mobius band of Schema R represents this hyperreality and how initial fantasies of a cultural icon have undergone a contradictory development: Some still portray Simpson as a cultural hero and a victim of a racist criminal justice system; others, as a murderer and a spouse abuser.

### The Borromean Knot

The last topological construct that we present here is Lacan's (1972-1977) (see especially, Lacan 1976-1977) late work on the Borromean knots (Milovanovic 1993b; also see Fink 1996; Granon-

Lafont 1985, 1990; Skriabine 1989). Here, Lacan began to revise his view about what holds the psychic structure together—what gives it consistency, how subjectivity is connected with discourse, how sense production takes place, and how symptoms, based on repetition, are created and sustained. Knot theory provides conceptual tools for explaining how "semiotic fictions" in law and criminology are created; how "fillers" such as various legal concepts act to "knot" the various Orders, allowing coherent but circumscribed narrative constructions; and how "naming" of various phenomena in criminology can be traced to the functioning of Borromean knots.

*Construction.*  A Borromean knot in 3D can be presented as three interconnected circles (Figure 10) in which cutting one would release all three. Each circle represents one of the three Orders: Symbolic (culture and language), Imaginary (imaginary constructions, imagoes), and Real (primordial sense data). Within the intersection we find various phenomena. At the center of the three circles is *objet petit a*, the "cork" that holds back the rush of psychic material seeking expression. Objects of desire are those things which hold the potential for embodying the subject's unique desires; fulfillment, however, is only partial. Sense production is found at the intersection of the Imaginary and the Symbolic Order; that is, social constructions of reality in discourse are always constituted by imaginary and symbolic constructions. (In 4D space, let us add, that which is knotted becomes undone.)

**Figure 10.   The Borromean Knot**

Borromean Knot (Two-Dimensional)          Borromean Knot (Three-Dimensional)

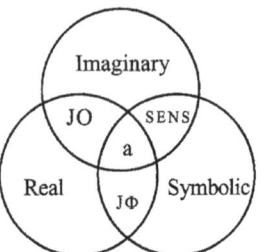
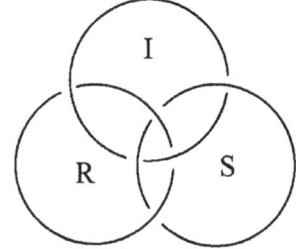

Here a = *le plus-de-jouir* (the "more than enjoyment," the left out; the "surplus-*jouissance*," Fink 1996); at the same time, the many illusory objects of desire that hold the potential for embodying the idiosyncratic desire of the speaking subject (*l'être parlant*). JO = *jouissance* of the Other; bodily *jouissance*; at the intersection of the Real and the Imaginary Order it finds no stable form of expression in a phallocentric symbolic order, rendering women and other disenfranchised voices *pas-toute* (not-all); but it offers the potential basis for an alternative form of expression and *jouissance* (i.e., *écriture féminine*, revolutionary discourse such as liberation theology, replacement discourses, "border pedagogy"). J$\Phi$ = phallic *jouissance*, attainable for those who assume the male discursive subject position. This is situated at the intersection of the Real and the Symbolic Order; it is traced back to the inauguration of the child into the Symbolic Order and the dialectics of mastery obtained at the cost of castration (separation) from the Real, which maintains a perpetual lack-in-being (*manque-à-être*). Sens = meaning unique to the speaking being. RSI = the three Orders: Real, Symbolic, and Imaginary.

We have developed the significance of the Borromean knots elsewhere (Milovanovic 1993b). We applied it to decision making in law and indicated how sense production takes place. In Lacan's more evolved theory of knots, begun in 1975, the symptom (*le sinthome*, $\Sigma$) became a dominant construction. It can be conceptualized as an attractor insofar as it accounts for recurring behavior. The quasi-periodic torus attractor is relevant in describing *le sinthome*, depicting the relationship among desire, demand, and objects of desire (also see Milovanovic forthcoming b: chap. 9). We see *repetition*, but with each iteration, we also see a return as a more-than-one. Self-similarity is punctuated by change, but always with a trace of the old; the old always asserts itself with effects. (The periodic torus may prevail in the more extreme cases.) We also could view *le sinthome* as a more stabilized configuration of iterative loops.

Lacan investigated how various "fillers" (substitutes provided by the political economy, the media, the advertising industry, and the legal sphere) held together the three Orders. Consider, for example, the notion of the juridic subject. Lacan also provided other examples: the "name-of-the-father," the basis of the phallocentric order; Freud's Oedipus complex; the fetishized construction of an ego, as in the writings of James Joyce; and, from Marx, phenomenal forms arising from the fetishism of commodities (see Figure 11).

The function of the fourth order is to repair, correct, mend, or restore a fault in the knot (Granon-Lafont 1990:141; Lacan 1975; Ragland 1995:49-50, 185; Skriabine 1989). According to Ragland-Sullivan, "the symptom may be a word. . ." (1990a:73). Occasionally the fillers may become undone, necessitating a repairing or a "doubling." Potentially, any signifier may function as "*le sinthome*" ($\Sigma$). For this reason, there is optimism about the development of new master signifiers (S1s), alternative embodiments of desire, and of

**Figure 11.** *Le Sinthome* **and Repairing the Knot**

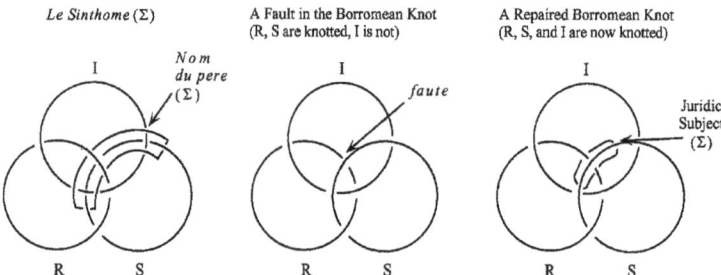

supports for new bodies of knowledge (S2; i.e., replacement discourses). Zeeman (1976:76), for example, explained how relatively stabilized attractors break down in neural brain dynamics and how new ones develop, which can be modeled by the elementary catastrophe models. (Also see the relevance of Lacan's four discourses; Henry and Milovanovic 1996.)

Lacan's model is a far-from-equilibrium model insofar as closure and stasis can never occur because of the inherent lack of being (*manque d'être*) that is the cost of inauguration into the Symbolic Order. Lacan's work has nonlinear dimensions (Ragland-Sullivan 1990b:58; Ragland 1995:158, 169), and his notion of "structure" is both "static and dynamic," "regulatory and disruptive," "anticipatory and retroactive" (Ragland-Sullivan 1990b:58). In the more equilibrium-based societal conditions portrayed by structural functionalists, the point and cyclic/periodic attractors would better reflect master signifiers, *le sinthome*, and *point de capiton* (the tentative anchoring of signifiers to signified). In far-from-equilibrium-based societal conditions, however, the quasi-periodic torus and strange attractors would be more prevalent and would assure the continued redevelopment of replacement discourses. In the latter, dissipative structures would be ubiquitous throughout the society and the psychic structure.

*Application.* The significance of the Borromean knot for a postmodern criminological methodology is that it indicates how the inherent "lack of being" (*manque d'être*) is (fictitiously) overcome by a political economy (Silverman 1982; Williamson 1987) and by the legal apparatus (i.e., the construction of various "semiotic fictions" such as the juridic subject and various clinicolegal classifications). It also shows how some persons are denied full expression in the Symbolic Order. Feminist postmodernists, for example, have taken seriously Lacan's analysis of *pas-toute* or "not-all." Women, argued Lacan, find that situating themselves in a phallocentric symbolic order does not provide them with the upper limit of *plenitude* (a sense of completeness), experienced as *jouissance* (J$\Phi$); in Lacan's use of puns, *jouis-sens*, "an enjoyment in sense," or *J'ouis sens*, "I hear sense"). The male's voice has a privileged position insofar as all key master signifiers in a phallocentric symbolic order are tainted with his voice ($\Phi$). He has access to the upper limit; she doesn't; she remains *pas-toute*.

The construction of the Borromean knot also indicates how various discursive constructions in the legal arena are based on some stabilized configuration of knots, as Laclau and Mouffe (1985) argue well in their provocative thesis *Hegemony and Socialist Strategy*. In the legal arena we could envision how key legal concepts have attained greater permanence (attractors) and how, then, narrative constructions are circumscribed so as to exclude many disenfranchised, disempowered, marginalized, and repressed subjects. Their voices are denied expression; grievances, differences, and appeals to the courts undergo translation into legalese, the dominant linguistic coordinate system, which inevitably sustains the dominant understanding (Yngvessen 1993).

Consider, too, Howe's (1994) provocative feminist analysis of penalty. Howe argues that disenfranchised persons are denied a useful "language for naming" (1994:171, 210-16; also see Butler 1993:208-22). In our use of Lacan's topological constructions of the Borromean knot we can see how restrictions are placed on "naming" (in Lacan's schema, *donner-nom*): Various dominant discourses (i.e., legal, clinicolegal, criminological, journalistic) have provided "fillers" by which dissent can be expressed, but which do not provide an adequate basis for critical narrative constructions. Howe, for example, indicates that the male's voice ("the law of the father" for Lacan) ultimately asserts itself in narrative constructions in penalty. Critical race theory is even more poignant:

> Too often victims of hate speech find themselves without the words to articulate what they see, feel, and know. In the absence of theory and analysis that give them a diagnosis and a name for the injury they have suffered, they internalize the injury done them and are rendered silent in the face of continuing injury. Critical race theory names the injury and identifies its origins, origins that are often well disguised in the rhetoric of shared values and neutral legal principles (Matsuda et al. 1993:13).

## CONCLUSION: VISIONS OF THE NEW (DIS)ORDER

In this article we have been concerned with sensitizing criminologists to postmodern methodologies. We offered various concepts and topological constructions in critical inquiry. Certainly, commitment to domain assumptions of various contemporary criminological paradigms would engender various polemics, but this debate is surely needed. We have suggested some directions for further inquiry. Most important for affirmative postmodernists is their desire for the development of a more humanistic world, one in which diverse desires may have room for embodiment in recognized discourses. Affirmative postmodern methodologies advocate an expansion in presenting "ways of describing possibilities," but this cannot take place by theorizing alone. Active struggle creates the "decidability" of the sign in the intersections of the Symbolic, the Imaginary, and the Real Order.

## REFERENCES

Abraham, F.D. 1992. *A Visual Introduction to Dynamical Systems Theory for Psychology.* Santa Cruz, CA: Aerial Press.

Aronowitz, S. and H. Giroux. 1992. *Postmodern Education.* Minneapolis: University of Minnesota Press.

Arrigo, B. 1992. "An Experientially Informed Feminist Jurisprudence: Rape and the Move Toward Praxis." *Humanity and Society* 17(1):28-47.

———. 1993. *Madness, Language and the Law.* Albany: Harrow and Heston.

———. 1994. "The Insanity Defense." Pp. 57-83 in *The Eyes of Justice*, edited by R. Kevelson. New York: Peter Lang.

———. 1995a. "The Peripheral Core of Law and Criminology: On Postmodern Social Theory and Conceptual Integration." *Justice Quarterly* 12:447-72.

———. 1995b. "Deconstructing Classroom Instruction: Theoretical and Methodological Contributions of the Postmodern Sciences for Crimino-Legal Education." *Social Pathology* 1(2):115-48.

———. Forthcoming. "Media Madness as Crime in the Making: On O.J. Simpson, Consumerism, and Hyperreality." In *Representing O.J.: Murder, Criminal Justice and Mass Culture*, edited by Gregg Barak. Albany, New York: Harrow & Heston.

Baack, D. and J.B. Cullen. 1992. "A Catastrophe Theory Model of Technological and Structural Change." *Journal of High Technology Management Research* 3:125-45.

———. 1994. "Decentralization in Growth and Decline: A Catastrophe Theory Approach." *Behavioral Science* 39:213-28.

Baker, P. 1993. "Chaos, Order and Sociological Theory." *Sociological Inquiry* 63:123-49.

Balkin, J.M. 1987. "Deconstructive Practice and Legal Theory." *Yale Law Journal* 96(4):743-86.

Bannister, S. and D. Milovanovic. 1990. "The Necessity Defense, Substantive Justice, and Oppositional Linguistic Praxis." *International Journal of the Sociology of Law* 18:179-98.

Barak, G. 1988. "Newsmaking Criminology: Reflections on the Media, Intellectuals, and Crime." *Justice Quarterly* 5:565-87.

Barak, G. 1994. *Media, Process and the Construction of Crime: Studies in Newsmaking Criminology.* New York: Garland Press.

Barr, S. 1964. *Experiments in Topology.* New York: Dover.

Barton, S. 1994. "Chaos, Self-Organization, and Psychology." *American Psychologist* 49(1):5-14.

Bohm, D. 1980. *Wholeness and the Implicate Order.* New York: ARK.

Briggs, J. and D. Peat. 1989. *Turbulent Mirror.* New York: Harper and Row.

Butler, J. 1990. *Gender Trouble.* New York: Routledge.

———. 1993. *Bodies That Matter.* New York: Routledge.

Butz, M. 1992. "Chaos, an Omen of Transcendence in the Psychotherapeutic Process." *Psychological Reports* 71:827-43.

Capra, F. 1982. *The Turning Point.* New York: Simon and Schuster.

Casti, J. 1994. *Complexification: Explaining a Paradoxial World through the Science of Surprise.* New York: HarperCollins.

Cislo, A. 1996. "Order out of Disorder: A Vision of Heraclitus." *Humanity and Society* 20(1):19-41.

Collins, P.H. 1993. "Toward a New Vision: Race, Class, and Gender as Categories of Analysis and Connection." *Race, Sex and Class* 1(1):25-45.

Crenshaw, K.W. 1993. "Beyond Racism & Misogyny: Black Feminism and 2 Live Crew." Pp. 111-132 in *Words That Wound,* edited by M. Matsuda, C. Lawrence, R. Delgado and K.W. Crenshaw. Oxford: Westview Press.

Cunningham, W.J. 1958. *Introduction to Nonlinear Analysis.* New York: McGraw-Hill.

Deleuze, G. and F. Guattari. 1987. *A Thousand Plateaus.* Minneapolis: University of Minnesota Press.

Derrida, J. 1976. *Of Grammatology.* Baltimore: Johns Hopkins University Press.

Dor, J. 1996. "The Epistemology Status of Lacan's Mathematical Paradigms." Pp. 109-21 in *Disseminating Lacan,* edited by D. Pettigrew and F. Raffoul. Albany: SUNY Press.

Ferrell, J. 1995. "Adrenalin, Pleasure, and Criminological *Verstehen.*" Delivered at the annual meetings of the American Society of Criminology, Boston.

Fink, B. 1996. "Rings of String." Unpublished manuscript.

Forker, A. Forthcoming. "Chaos and Modeling Crime: Quinney's Class, State and Crime." In *Chaos, Criminology and Social Justice: The New (Dis)Order,* edited by D. Milovanovic. Westport, CT: Greenwood.

Frechet, M. and K. Fan. 1967. *Initiation to Combinatorial Topology,* translated by H. Eves. Boston: Prindle, Weber and Schmidt.

Freud, S. 1965. *The Interpretation of Dreams.* New York: Avon.

Giroux, H. 1992. *Border Crossings.* New York: Routledge.

Granon-Lafont, J. 1985. *La Topologie Ordinaire de Jacques Lacan.* Paris: Point Hors Ligne.

———. 1990. *Topologie Lacanienne et Clinique Analytique.* Paris: Point Hors Ligne.

Gregersen, H. and L. Sailer. 1993. "Chaos Theory and Its Implications for Social Science Research." *Human Relations* 46:777-802.

Halleck, S. 1967. *Psychiatry and the Dilemmas of Crime.* Berkeley: University of California Press.

Hayles, K. 1990. *Chaos Bound.* Ithaca: Cornell University Press.

Held, B. 1995. *Back to Reality.* New York: Norton.

Henry, S. and D. Milovanovic. 1991. "Constitutive Criminology." *Criminology* 29:293-316.

Henry, S. and D. Milovanovic. 1996. *Constitutive Criminology.* London: Sage.

Hilbert, D. and S. Cohn-Vossen. 1952. *Geometry and the Imagination.* New York: Chelsea.

Howe, A. 1994. *Punish and Critique.* London: Routlege.

Jackson, B. 1988. *Law, Fact, and Narrative Coherence.* Merseyside, UK: Deborah Charles.

Kaku, M. 1994. *Hyperspace.* New York: Oxford University Press.

Kaplan, M. and N. Kaplan. 1991. "The Self-Organization of Human Psychological Functioning." *Behavioral Science* 36:161-78.

Katz, J. 1988. *Seductions of Crime.* New York: Basic Books.

Lacan, J. 1974-1975. *Seminar 22, RSI. Ornicar* 2, 3, 4, 5:15-110.

Lacan, J. 1977. "*Le Sinthome.*" Unpublished manuscript.

———. 1977. *Ecrits.* New York: Norton.

Lacan, J. 1981. *The Four Fundamental Concepts of Psychoanalysis.* New York: Norton.

Laclau, E. and C. Mouffe. 1985. *Hegemony and Socialist Strategy.* New York: Verso.

Lee, J. 1990. *Jacques Lacan.* Amherst: University of Massachusetts Press.

Leifer, R. 1989. "Understanding Organization Transformation Using a Dissipative Structure Model." *Human Relations* 42:899-916.

Lem, S. 1981. "Metafantasia: The Possibilities of Science Fiction," translated by E. de Laczay and I. Csicery-Ronary. *Science Fiction Studies* 8:54-71.

608    POSTMODERN CRIMINOLOGY

Loye, D. and R. Eisler. 1987. "Chaos and Transformation: Implications of Non-equilibrium Theory for Social Science and Society." *Behavioral Science* 32:53-65.

Lyng, S. 1990. "Edgework: A Social Psychological Analysis of Voluntary Risk Taking." *American Journal of Sociology* 95(4):851-86.

Lyotard, J. 1984. *The Postmodern Condition*. Minneapolis: University of Minnesota Press.

Mandel, D. 1995. "Chaos Theory, Sensitive Dependence, and the Logistic Equation." *American Psychologist* (February):106-107.

Mandelbrot, B. 1977. *The Fractal Geometry of Nature*. New York: Freeman.

Matsuda, M., C. Lawrence, R. Delgado, and K.W. Crenshaw. 1993. *Words That Wound: Critical Race Theory, Assaultive Speech, and the First Amendment*. Oxford: Westview.

Matza, D. 1964. *Delinquency and Drift*. New York: Wiley.

———. 1969. *Becoming Delinquent*. Englewood Cliffs, NJ: Prentice-Hall.

McLachlan, N.W. 1958. *Ordinary Non-Linear Differential Equations in Engineering and Physical Sciences*. Oxford: Clarendon.

McRobie, A. and M. Thompson. 1994. "Chaos, Catastrophes and Engineering." Pp. 149-61 in *Exploring Chaos*, edited by N. Hall. New York: Norton.

Milovanovic, D. 1988. "Jailhouse Lawyers and Jailhouse Lawyering." *International Journal of the Sociology of Law* 16:455-75.

———. 1992. *Postmodern Law and Disorder: Psychoanalytic Semiotics, Chaos and Juridic Exegeses*. Liverpool, UK: Deborah Charles.

———. 1993a. "Lacan's Four Discourses." *Studies in Psychoanalytic Theory* 2(1):3-23.

———. 1993b. "Borromean Knots and the Constitution of Sense in Juridico-Discursive Production." *Legal Studies Forum* 17(2):171-92.

———. 1994a. "The Decentered Subject in Law." *Studies in Psychoanalytic Theory* 3(1):93-127.

———. 1994b. *Sociology of Law*. Albany, New York: Harrow & Heston.

———. 1995. "Dueling Paradigms: Modernist v. Postmodernist." *Humanity and Society* 19(1):1-22.

———, ed. Forthcoming a. *Chaos, Criminology and Social Justice: The New (Dis)Order*. Westport, CT: Greenwood.

———. Forthcoming b. *Postmodern Criminology*. New York: Garland.

Milovanovic, D. and J. Thomas 1989. "Overcoming the Absurd: Legal Struggle as Primitive Rebellion." *Social Problems* 36(1):48-60.

Mueller, J. and W. Richardson. 1982. *Lacan and Language: A Reader's Guide to Ecrits*. New York: International Universities Press.

Nasio, J.-D. 1987. *Les Yeux de Laure*. Paris: Aubier.

———. 1996. "The Concept of the Subject of the Unconscious." Pp. 23-42 in *Disseminating Lacan*, edited by D. Pettigrew and F. Raffoul. Albany: SUNY Press.

Nietzsche, F. 1969, *The Genealogy of Morals*, translated by W. Kaufman. New York: Vintage.

Oliva, T., D. Day, and I. MacMillan. 1988. "A General Model of Competive Dynamics." *Academy of Management Review* 13:374-88.

Oliva, T., M. Peters, and H. Murphy. 1981. "A Preliminary Empirical Test of a Cusp Catastrophe Model in the Social Sciences." *Behavioral Science* 26:153-62.

O'Malley, P. and S. Mugford. 1994. "Crime, Excitement, and Modernity," Pp. 189-211 in *Varieties of Criminology*, edited by G. Barak, Westport, CT: Praeger.

Pashukanis, E. 1978: *Law and Marxism*, edited by C.J. Athur. London: Ink Links.

Peak, D. and M. Frame. 1994. *Chaos under Control*. New York: Freeman.

Peat, D. 1988. *Superstrings and the Search for the Theory of Everything*. Chicago: Contemporary Books.

Peitgen, H.O., H. Jurgens, and D. Saupe. 1992. *Fractals for the Classroom*. NY: Springer-Verlag.

Pickover, C. 1988. "Pattern Formation and Chaos in Networks." *Communications of the ACM* 31(2):136-51.

Prigogine, I. and I. Stenger. 1984. *Order out of Chaos*. New York: Bantam.

Ragland, E. 1995. *Essays on the Pleasures of Death*. New York: Routledge.

Ragland-Sullivan, E. 1990a. "Lacan's Seminars on James Joyce." Pp. 67-86 in *Psychoanalysis and . . .*, edited by R. Feldstein and H. Sussman. New York: Routledge.

———. 1990b. "Counting from 0 to 6: Lacan, Suture, and the Imaginary Order." Pp. 31-63 in *Criticism and Lacan*, edited by P. Hogan and L. Pandit. Athens: University of Georgia Press.

Regnault, F. 1995. "The Name-of-the-Father." Pp. 65-73 in *Reading Seminar XI*, edited by R. Feldstein, B. Fink, and M. Jaanus. Albany: SUNY Press.

Rossi-Landi, F. 1983. *Language as Work and Trade: A Semiotic Homology for Linguistics and Economics*. South Hadley, MA: Bergin and Garvey.

Russell, B. 1956. *An Essay on the Foundations of Geometry*. New York: Dover.

Salecl, R. 1993. "Crime as a Mode of Subjectivization: Lacan and the Law." *Law and Critique* 4(1):2-20.

Schulman, C. Forthcoming. "Chaos, Law and Critical Legal Studies: Mapping the Terrain" in *Chaos, Criminology & Social Justice: The New (Dis)Order*. Westport, CT: Greenwood.

Schwartz, M. and D. Friedrichs. 1994. "Postmodern Thought and Criminological Discontent: New Metaphors for Understanding Violence." *Criminology*: 32:221-46.

Schwartz, M. and D. Milovanovic, eds. 1996. Race, Gender, and Class in Criminology: The Intersection. New York: Garland.

Schwendinger, J. & H. Schwendinger. 1985. *Adolescent Subcultures and Delinquency*. New York: Praeger.

Silverman, K. 1982. *The Subject of Semiotics*. New York: Oxford University Press.

Sinanoglu, O. 1981. "1- and 2-Topology of Reaction Networks." *Journal of Mathematical Physics* 22:1504-12.

Skriabine, P. 1989. "Clinique et Topologie." Unpublished manuscript.

Smith, C. and D. Comer. 1994. "Self-Organization in Small Groups: A Study of Group Effectiveness within Non-Equilibrium Conditions." *Human Relations* 47:553-81.

Surette, R. 1992. *Media, Crime and Criminal Justice: Image and Realities*. Pacific Grove, CA: Brooks/Cole.

Thom, R. 1975. *Structural Stability and Morphogenesis*. Reading, MA: Benjamin.

Vappereau, J.-M. 1988. *Etoffe*. Paris: Duculot a Gembiousx.

Weeks, J. 1985. *The Shape of Space*. New York: Dekker.

Wegner, T. and B. Tyler. 1993. *Fractal Creations*. Corte Madera, CA: Waite Group Press.

Whorf, B. 1956. *Language, Thought and Reality*, edited by J. Carrol. New York: Wiley.

Williamson, J. 1987. *Decoding Advertisement*. New York: Boyars.

Yngvessen, B. 1993. *Virtuous Citizens*. New York: Routledge.

Young, T.R. 1991a. "Chaos and Crime: Nonlinear and Fractal Forms of Crime." *The Critical Criminologist* 3(4):3-4, 10-11, 13-14.

———. 1991b. "Change and Chaos Theory." *Social Science* 28(3):59-82.

———. 1992. "Chaos Theory and Human Agency." *Humanity and Society* 16:441-60.

———. Forthcoming. "The ABCs of Crime: Attractors, Bifurcations and Chaos." In *Chaos, Criminology and Social Justice: The New (Dis)Order*, edited by D. Milovanovic. Westport, CT: Greenwood.

Zeeman, E.C. 1976. "Catastrophe Theory." *Scientific American* 234:65-83.

———. 1977. *Catastrophe Theory: Selected Papers, 1972-1977*. London: Addison-Wesley.

## CASE CITED

*R. v. Butler*, I.S.C.R. 452 (1992).

610    POSTMODERN CRIMINOLOGY

## Appendix:  The Movement of a Pendulum

Consider the complexity involved. We start the swinging pendulum at some region in space (Figure A1). We note that it picks up speed and reaches a maximum at the bottom, after which it slows down, then stops, and returns in the other direction, again picking up speed until it stops once again to resume a new cycle. Correlated with the different speeds are the different distances covered by the pendulum.

Hypothetically we could have a pendulum with no frictional forces (and a small motor) in play, or with frictional forces in play. Now the task is how to map accurately this interaction between momentum and position. Our goal is to generate a picture of this dynamic interplay (here between two variables, momentum and distance/location) and to portray it as a moment in phase space. First, we create a phase map in which the horizontal axis reflects momentum and the vertical reflects position. Here the pendulum has two degrees of freedom: It moves from left to right and has various speeds. Second, we plot the trajectory of the pendulum's swing on the phase map (Figure A2). At B the momentum is zero and the displacement is the greatest (F corresponds to B at the other end of the arc); at D and G the maximum momentum exists.

| Figure A1.  Swinging Pendulum | Figure A2.  Phase Map of Swinging Pendulum |
|:---:|:---:|
| 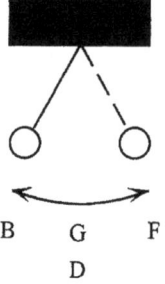 | 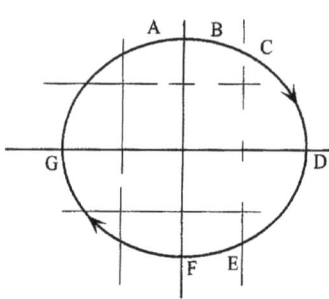 |

What is traced out is a trajectory in phase space that would be called the cyclic attractor (with no frictional forces and the aid of a small motor). (Also see Figure 2d.) With a greater initial push on the pendulum, a larger circle or amplitude would result. Without the motor and with frictional forces, the pendulum will slowly come to a halt, and thus will be represented by a point attractor (also see Figures 2a, 2b, and 2c). If we added another dimension (say, if the pendulum also vibrated while in its swinging motion, and if each of the vibrations were correlated precisely by a specific ratio with the left-right movement), we could trace out a periodic torus whereby the two movements are coupled as they move around the outside surface. If the vibrations were more erratic (involving no ratio), the result would be a quasiperiodic torus attractor (Figure 2f). Here we have a two-dimensional depiction of a 3D system.

# [4]

## THE FRENCH CONNECTION:
## IMPLICATIONS FOR LAW, CRIME, AND SOCIAL JUSTICE

*Bruce A. Arrigo*
*California School of Professional Psychology-Fresno*

*Dragan Milovanovic*
*Northeastern Illinois University*

*Robert C. Schehr*
*University of Illinois-Springfield*

### REFLEXIVE STATEMENT

Over the past twenty years, much has been made of the critical potential for French postmodern social theory to inform several noteworthy debates in law and criminology. This scholarship mostly has been applied, suggesting new and provocative in-roads for theory, practice, and policy. The extant research to date, however, is largely uncoordinated or under systematized, rendering its overall utility for advancing justice studies uneven and fragmented at best. The present article endeavors to fill the gap in this literature. Attention is paid to prominent French postmodern social theorists, including: Barthes, Baudrillard, Deleuze and Guattari, Derrida, Foucault, Irigaray, Kristeva, Lacan, and Lyotard. Their respective contributions, as developed in the applied research during the past twenty years, are succinctly described. Commentary on the significance of this scholarship for advancing affirmative and integrative postmodern analysis in law, crime, and justice is presented. Several postmodern synthetic linkages, as developed in the fields of confinement law, critical race theory, and alternative dispute resolution, are suggestively enumerated.

### INTRODUCTION

During the past twenty years, much has been made of French postmodern social theory and its capacity to inform cultural theory and contemporary media, art, and society.[1] Academic disciplines as broad ranging as politics, history, literary criticism, philosophy, architecture, gender studies, and anthropology have seized upon the insights of many postmodern concepts and have articulated new methods and strategies for understanding the social world and people in it. The disciplines of law and criminology are no exception to this trend. Indeed, during the 1980s and 1990s, many "second wave" sociolegal researchers appropriated the tools of the postmodern sciences in order to deepen our regard for crime and justice controversies.[2] Regrettably, however, little attention has been given to the consolidation and coordination of this scholarship in any systematic fashion. Thus, our appreciation for French postmodern social theory and its impact for sociolegal studies, remains uneven, fragmented, and disorganized at best.

163                    Bruce A. Arrigo, Dragan Milovanovic, and Robert C. Schehr

The present article represents a response to this dilemma.[3] We begin by succinctly describing the contributions of several prominent "first wave" thinkers whose work has contributed substantially to our understanding of postmodern thought.[4] These authors include Roland Barthes, Jean Baudrillard, Gilles Deleuze and Felix Guattari, Jacques Derrida, Michel Foucault, Luce Irigaray, Julia Kristeva, Jacques Lacan, and Jean-Francois Lyotard. In addition, this section summarizes where and how the in-roads of the respective social theorists have been utilized by various "second wave" authors, commenting on different facets of law, crime, and social justice. Next, we recognize that while adopting a postmodern attitude can produce a more nihilistic, fatalistic, pessimistic worldview, assuming such a stance can also lead to affirmative, transformative, and emancipatory praxis. We demonstrate the manner in which the more liberating dimensions of the perspective are possible, particularly in our efforts to integrate conceptually different theoretical strains of postmodernism, while simultaneously identifying scholars whose research in law, crime, and social justice accomplishes this affirmative and synthetic task. Finally, we explore how one can "do" an affirmative and integrative postmodern analysis in the sociolegal arena. We examine three noteworthy subjects presently receiving considerable attention in the relevant literature: confinement law and execution of the mentally ill; critical race theory; and alternative dispute resolution. Mindful of the contributions articulated by "first wave" French postmodern social theorists, we suggest possible strategies for affirmatively integrating many of these insights into a sustained analysis of the three sociolegal topics under consideration.

## THE FIRST WAVE: THE LINGUISTIC TURN IN SOCIAL THEORY

### Jacques Lacan

Jacques Lacan (1900-1981) arguably is the key figure in the development of French inspired postmodern analysis.[5] Lacan's (1977) main contribution was that the subject is intimately connected to discourse. This subject, or "speaking" (*"parlêtre"*) being, is a de-centered subject as opposed to the centered subject offered by Enlightenment epistemology.

Lacanian thought undermined the concept of the "individual," captured in the notion of the juridic subject in law or the "rational man" assumption contained in rational choice theory in criminology. Rather, the subject was depicted in a more static form in Schema L, and in a more dynamic, topological form in the Graphs of Desire, Schema R, Schema I, the Cross-Cap, and the Borromean Knots (Lacan, 1977, 1988). His topological constructions also included the Möbius Band and the Klein bottle. What he showed was that there were two planes to subjectivity: the subject of speech and the speaking subject (Lacan, 1981). The former included the deeper unconscious workings where desire was embodied in signifiers that came to "speak the subject;" the latter was the subject taking a position in various

Humanity and Society, Volume 24, Number 2, May 2000                164

discourses, identifying with an "I" as a stand-in for her/his subjectivity, and engaging in communication with the other. He was to show that three intersecting spheres existed in the production of subjectivity: the Symbolic, the Imaginary, and the Real Order. Since the Symbolic Order is phallocentric, all is tainted with the privileging of the male voice. According to Lacan (1985), women remain left out, *pas-toute*, not-all. However, they have access to an alternative *jouissance*, which remains inexpressible in a male dominated order (Lacan, 1985). Hence, the basis for the call for an *écriture féminine* (i.e, women's writing) to overcome *pas-toute*.[6]

Lacan's work has been influential with a number of second wave theorists. In law we note: Butler (gender construction, 1990, 1993, 1997a; injurious speech, 1997b); Cornell (critical feminist analysis, family law, sexual freedom, 1991, 1993, 1998); Caudill (subjectivity in law, 1997); Goodrich (legal speech production, 1990); Legendre (development of doctrines of the sacraments in the 12th and 13th centuries, 1996); Salecl (fantasy, repression, and justice, 1994); Stacy (aboriginal women's denial of voice in law, 1996); Arrigo (the insanity defense, 1997a; the guilty but mentally ill verdict, 1996a; desire in the psychiatric courtroom, 1996b); Halper (use of metaphor and metonymy in law, 1995); Slaughter (fantasy and the single mother in family law, 1995); Schroeder (property contract and subjectivity, 1997); and Milovanovic (integration of Lacan and chaos theory, 1992, 1996a). In criminology we see: Young (detective fiction, 1996); Salecl (crime as a mode of subjectivization, 1994); and Arrigo (criminal and civil confinement, 1996c, 1997b). In social justice we find: Bracher (culture and social change, 1993); Arrigo (liberatory pedagogy in the classroom, 1995a, 1998; ethics in crime and justice; 1995b); Arrigo and Schehr (victim offender mediation and restorative justice for juveniles, 1998); Butler (undermining traditional repetitive discursive production, 1993); Cornell (re-imagining of our world through myth, 1993; protecting the imaginary domain, 1998); Laclau and Mouffe (development of alternative discursive forms, 1985); Laclau (societal dislocations and the possibility of new liberatory articulations, 1996); and Milovanovic (critical legal practices informed by a Paulo Freire, Jacque Lacan, and chaos integration, 1996a).

## Roland Barthes

The contributions of Roland Barthes were exhaustively developed in his postmodern literary critiques of reading texts.[7] Barthes (1974: 35-41) recognized that all texts were constituted by a "galaxy of signifiers" that when minimally and provisionally decoded would "explode and scatter." Elsewhere, this approach to interpreting meaning led him to speak of enjoyment and pleasure (*jouissance*) as the object of textual analysis (Barthes, 1973b). Indeed, "the subject gains access to bliss by the cohabitation of languages [different modes of discourse] working side by side" (Barthes, 1973b: 4). In addition, Barthes (1988) maintained that the truth of a text was never an arrival in sense-making but was always a departure from it. Finally, the activity of ascertaining the message of a text included "forgetting meaning" [as an integral dimension] to reading" (Barthes, 1988: 264).

These later works and observations by Barthes emphasized the creative role of the reader (Berman, 1988: 147; see also Velan, 1972: 328, on Barthes and the mix of structure, language, and desire in literary interpretation). For Barthes, the person interpreting textual meaning was so profoundly significant to the process, that he was led to conclude that the reader could "make anything signify" (as cited in Culler, 1975: 138). As Berman puts it, "the reader naturalizes, seeks and, sure enough, finds meaning" (Berman, 1988: 148).

A key development in Barthes' literary criticism was the distinction between the "readerly" versus "writerly" text. The readerly approach reproduces the classic text's ideals. The organizing principles of this reading (and viewing) are primarily non-contradiction, coherency, and consistency. The reader/viewer is encouraged to accept "as truth" the words themselves. Thus, there is nothing behind or underneath the words. What the text means is direct, without question, on the surface. Missing from the readerly approach is the sphere of the text's production; that is, its connection to the political economy and to cultural inequalities which remain concealed. The reader/viewer experiences fulfillment. The text promises a coherent narrative and the reader/viewer interprets the text accordingly. Thus, in this reading, subjects reconstitute and re-validate the dominant understandings of reality embedded in the text. The readerly approach emphasizes the manifest content of the narrative. Missing from this rendition, however, is the deep structure of the text which often represents a more cloaked reality affirming certain power relationships and a certain understanding of the person in the social order.

Conversely, the writerly approach is a subversive and insurgent method of reading a text. It emphasizes a multitude of interpretations which validate an array of truths and knowledges. Unlike the readerly approach which tends toward closure or the text's finiteness, the writerly approach resists structure and a definable, singular product. In the writerly method the process is central. The underlying structures of signification, or meaning, are unearthed. The text is understood to contain an explosion and scattering of meaning. Rather than privileging one interpretation, one voice, through the text, the reader/viewer is encouraged to discover the multiple and repressed voices embedded in the words. Familiarity and coherence, cornerstones of the readerly approach, are resisted and supplanted with displacement and ambivalence. This is an active deconstruction (i.e., de-centering and destabilizing) of sedimented and privileged interpretations. It is also an active reconstruction of alternative truths and replacement ways of knowing.

Direct applications of Barthes' ideas in law, criminology, and social justice have been somewhat modest. This notwithstanding, his insights have been suggestive for several second wave theorists. Thus, in law we note: Tiefenbrun (exploring approaches to legal semiotics, 1986) and Arrigo (on narratives in mental health law, 1993). In criminology we see: Henry and Milovanovic (establishing a constitutive criminological praxis, 1996) and Arrigo (integrating postmodern theory, 1995c). In social justice we find: Deleuze and Guattari (describing the

Humanity and Society, Volume 24, Number 2, May 2000　　　　166

operation of "minor" literatures and rhizomatics as dimensions of social change, 1986) and Currie, MacLean, and Milovanovic (redefining the administration of critical social justice, 1992; see also Milovanovic, 1995).

## Jean Baudrillard

Baudrillard is recognized as a postmodern luminary *par excellence.*[8] The early work of Baudrillard (1968) examined mass consumption in advanced monopoly capitalism where objects or commodities "devoured" the consumer's "perception, thought, and behavior" (Best & Kellner, 1991: 113). This theme is renewed in Baudrillard's (1970) next work where he more closely studied the manner in which conspicuous goods, as sign objects, formed the basis of our everyday reality, organizing and constituting our existences into a mass-media consumer culture. In his subsequent work, Baudrillard (1981) attempted to integrate the political economy of Marxism with structuralism and semiotic theory, mindful of his previously articulated insights. As a trilogy, these tracts represent an outline for a developing neo-Marxian social theory in which semiotics and sign systems theory assume an important role in explaining the process of symbolic exchange in a consumer-oriented society (e.g., Poster, 1988; Best, 1989; Kellner, 1989).

It is not until Baudrillard's later works, however, that a social theory is posited considerably removed from the political economy of Marx. In these and other texts, Baudrillard claims that we live in a computerized and digitized world in which mass-media information and cybernetic control systems simulate reality and displace production as the organizing principle of society (Best & Kellner, 1991: 118). Simulation entails the use of models, signs, and codes in which a "semiurgic society" dominates social life (Baudrillard, 1981: 185). The semiurgic society Baudrillard has in mind symbolically produces mass media and conspicuously consumed images (e.g., the image of soap opera doctors receiving fan mail requesting medical consultation, the image of television lawyers inundated with petitions for legal advice). These simulations, as counterfeits of the real, as images of the factual, are more authentic than the "real" physicians and lawyers for whom such services might otherwise be solicited. Indeed, for Baudrillard (1983a:23), these simulations are "hallucinatory resemblances," that are more real-than-the-real. This is what Baudrillard means by the implosion of reality. These are moments in which the boundary separating form and substance, fact and fiction, reality and appearance, collapse and collide producing an implosion, "and with it the very experience and ground of 'the real' disappears" (Best & Kellner, 1991: 119).

The disappearance of the real, as a process of social entropy (Gane, 1991), makes possible the proliferation of increased symbolic exchanges and the circulation of multiple simulations, where codes of technology, sophisticated advertising, and computerized information produce a virtual authenticity, a hyper-reality, a world that is based on models of the real (e.g., the O.J. Simpson double-murder trial as simulated on "Entertainment Television").    According to Baudrillard, though, these representational, hyper-real forms become a determinant of the real; that is, the replica informs the authentic and the reality-appearance divide vanishes (Poster, 1988). In obliterating this boundary, however, not only does Baudrillard (1983a) remind us how the foundation of the real is undone (i.e., image and simulation displace it), he cautions that the foundation of the counterfeit is itself equally unstable. In other words, the counterfeit, although more real-than-the real, is nothing more than illusion and, thus, cannot signify factual existence. In short, simulation, implosion of reality, and hyper-reality leave nothing behind but a vacuous cybernetic state in which simulacra (i.e., words, extra-verbal cues, gestures) abound. These simulacra are floating, pseudo-sign images, without definite referents and are unable to be tangibly anchored, signifying (hyper)reality, disseminating simulated media messages, and conveying the illusory other worldliness of our postmodern condition (Kellner, 1989).

Applications of Baudrillard's work in the areas of law, crime, and social justice have been limited. In part, "second wave" scholars recognize that Baudrillard's critique arrestingly demonstrates that "we have no way to experience or conceptualize relationships between people except as these are defined by the exchange of [consumer sign image] commodities" (Willis, 1991: 162). The effect is a nihilistic, fatalistic, anti-foundational critique, lacking an identifiable substitute for progressive social change (Palmer, 1990: 199). This notwithstanding, several important efforts are discernible.  In law we note Arrigo (exploring the double murder trial of O. J. Simpson, 1996d). In criminology we find: Pfohl (investigating social problems in an ultramodern environment, 1993); and Ferrell, Milovanovic, and Lyng (indicating the ways ephemeral and ineffable emotional states are given meaning in situated contexts of media practices, 1998). In social justice we recognize: Barak and Henry (describing mass-mediated imagery and its relationship to developing an integrated, critical criminological understanding of social justice, 1999); Gottdiener (suggesting a strategy that reverses the one Baudrillard describes by reclaiming or restoring lost, repressed, and stripped signifieds in a cultural criticism that returns to "roots," 1995);[9] and Henry and Milovanovic (integrating the mass consumption of societal images, their symbolic meanings, and prospects for a radical pluralism, 1996).

### Gilles Deleuze and  Felix Guattari

Although Deleuze and Guattari[10] did not themselves position their work in the realm of the postmodern, their ideas represent a wholesale critique of the emblems of modernist thought.[11] Similar to Marx, Deleuze and Guattari identified the ultimate state of human oppression as a product of capitalism. Their prime objective was to free the realization of human desire from the artificial and subjugating constraints imposed upon it by capitalist social relations and normalizing techniques of domination. Deleuze and Guattari distinguished themselves from other social

Humanity and Society, Volume 24, Number 2, May 2000                    168

commentators (e.g., Hegel, Freud, and Lacan) who viewed the desiring subject as "lacking" wholeness or completeness. They articulated a theory of desire as "technology" that was a productive force (Best and Kellner, 1991: 86-87). It is the unpredictable, ambulant, chaotic, and unstable aspect of desire that stimulates cultural change and creativity.

Deleuze and Guattari (1983) promoted a new form of political activism referred to as "schizoanalysis." In order to establish smooth functioning social relations in the capitalist political economy, efforts are made to "territorialize" and "code" all behaviors as appropriate for or inconsistent with meritocracy and the preservation of commodity production. The purpose of the schizophrenic is to "deterritorialize" behavioral expectations, "destroying beliefs . . . representations, [and established] theatrical scenes" (Deleuze and Guattari, 1983: 314). Once the schizophrenic initiates deterritorialization, s/he becomes a "body-without-organs." This is a state of being that is fluid, fractured, and unbounded by the discursive constraints imposed by dominant cultural expectations. This ambulant and deterritorialized movement promotes the reconstitution of subject-positions in relatively new and previously unmanifested ways. While the emphasis is on the perpetual reconstruction of the individual based on the appropriation of political, economic, and cultural space, Deleuze and Guattari recognized that there were limits to this kind of activity. When schizoanalysis is effective in realizing deterritorialization, individuals experience a "breakthrough." However, when subjects encounter accidents and relapses that hinder breakthrough, they experience "breakdown" (Deleuze and Guattari, 1983:278). The latter condition is not in a position to reclaim desire for the body-without-organs.

What Deleuze and Guattari intimated was the need for a certain, methodical, and vigilant deterritorialization process. Radical transformations of culture and self may lead to breakdown. Consequently, as a matter of political praxis, Deleuze and Guattari championed social movements that combined micro and macro levels of analysis and action. For example, they believed that the core of fascism resided, not only in the manifestations of state inflicted oppression and violence, but also at the level of the unconscious. Thus, in order for any real political, economic, or cultural change to occur, subjects were encouraged to perpetually revisit their own oppressive and alienating tendencies. According to Deleuze and Guattari, social movement organizations need to remain reflexive, constantly challenging instances of marginalization within their ranks.

Deleuze and Guattari (1986) applied their schizoanalytic method to the literary work of Kafka and developed the concept of "minor literatures." They demonstrated how disruptions and departures from conventional interpretations of the written (or spoken) word produced opportunities for deterritorialization; that is, alterative and new forms of reading texts. Again, consistent with their critique of capitalism, minor literatures create an effusive and mobile space for alterity, multiplicity, and fluidity.

Deleuze and Guattari (1987) also argued for a rhizomatic politics of desire.[12]   Rhizomatics represent the dislodging of "root" or essentialist philosophical and political systems. Rather than moving on striated space, with carefully defined rules for engagement, Deleuze and Guattari envisioned a politics where space was smooth (i.e, plateaus) and movement was fractured and unpredictable. One of the most relevant aspects of their work on the rhizome was their contention that it simultaneously encourages segmentation *and* lines of escape. What this suggests, consistent with the science of chaos theory, is the presence of orderly and disorderly movement accounting for the behavior of complex systems.

A politics inspired by rhizomes anticipates the perpetual, though not necessarily overt, nature of "nomadic" struggle. Rhizomatic movements are like "weeds," impossible to completely eliminate. Deleuze and Guattari (1987:15) suggested that, "to be rhizomorphous is to produce stems and filaments that seem to be roots....We're tired of trees. We should stop believing in trees, roots, and radicals. They've made us suffer too much." Deleuze and Guattari maintained that American culture benefitted most from subterranean, rhizomatic, and nomadic activities that stimulated the realization of desire. In contemporary culture, we note that alternative and underground music, art, poetry, and film stand as ongoing examples of these theoretical observations.

The insights of Deleuze and Guattari recently have been applied to selected areas in law, crime, and social justice. The field of law includes: Lippens (nomadic subjective states and radical democracy, 1998a; legal thought and hybrid hopes for rhizologists, 1998b; postcolonial and feminist legal theory, 1999). In criminology we note: Lippens (critical criminology and utopia, 1995; rhizomatics and the establishment of a border-crossing criminology, 1998c; see also Giroux, 1992). In social justice we find: Young (hybridity in theory, race and culture, 1995); and Williams (the Self and Other in mental illness, 1998).

### Jacques Derrida

Derrida is often regarded as the leading exponent of French deconstructionist philosophy and social theory.[13]  A key proposition within Derrida's epistemology is the "metaphysics of presence" (Derrida, 1976). The metaphysics of presence exposes the hierarchical positions (e.g., "straight" over "gay", "white" over "black", "objective" over "subjective", "reality" over "appearance", man over woman) embedded in the words or phrases we use to communicate (shared) meaning. In each cited instance, the first term is privileged and rendered as presence. Conversely, the latter term is de-valued and rendered as absence. According to Derrida (1976), the concept that explains this notion of "privileging" the first term in the binary opposition is "logocentrism." Logocentrism indicates that the implied centrality of the first or dominant term masks and conceals the interdependence of both values. In Western thought, there is "a hidden premise that what is most apparent to our consciousness-- what is most simple, basic or immediate-- is most real, true, foundational, or important" (Balkin, 1987: 748). Thus, Derrida's

Humanity and Society, Volume 24, Number 2, May 2000          170

deconstruction entails a reflexive explication of those encoded hierarchical terms that conceal entrenched "value positions that need to be brought to light" (Agger, 1991: 121).

The metaphysics of presence and the critique of logocentrism are further delineated by Derrida's use of three interrelated principles. These precepts include: (1) the reversal of hierarchies; (2) the concepts *differance* and trace; and (3) arguments that undo themselves. Inverting privileged values allows us to consider what new or different insights might be contained within the words in binary opposition. In addition, the reversal demonstrates how the terms are mutually interdependent, displacing the notion that the first (or second) value is foundational.

The concept of *differance* (with an "a") conveys three interrelated meanings for Derrida. As Balkin (1987: 752) describes it:

> *Differance* simultaneously indicates that (1) the terms of an oppositional hierarchy are differentiated from each other (which is what determines them); (2) each term in the hierarchy defers the other (in the sense of making the other term wait for the first term); and (3) each term in the hierarchy defers to the other (in the sense of being fundamentally dependent upon the other).

*Differance*, however, is significant to Derrida's deconstructionist agenda for a related reason. The idea of trace implies that the two values in binary opposition rely for their clarity and cohesion on the differentiation between them. In other words, each term contains the vestige of the other within it, and it is this lingering trace which anchors *differance* making the deconstruction of hierarchical oppositions possible.

The related concepts of *differance* and trace give rise to Derrida's logic of justification that is ungrounded through deconstruction (see e.g., Derrida, 1976: 34-43 critiquing the privileging of speech over writing). In short, arguments supporting the privileging of the dominant term may be the reasons for endorsing the other value. The task of deconstructionist analysis, then, is to identify the play of differences and the mutual interdependencies between terms in a hierarchical opposition, as a way of demonstrating the positional, relational and provisional nature of all phenomena. In this context, meaning is "inexhaustible" (Sarup, 1989:36), and what is spoken or written is liberated from the author. We note, too, that the concepts of *differance* and trace are not essentialist terms in Derrida's epistemology. This thinking is antithetical to the deconstructionist project. Indeed, as Rorty (1978: 153) contends, such notions cannot be "divinized." *Differance* and trace fleetingly capture the "foundationless, provisional..., or reversibl(e)" nature of meaning in human affairs (Balkin, 1987: 752).

Applications of Derrida's epistemology to law, criminology, and social justice have been considerable. In law much of the Critical Legal Studies Movement was inspired by his philosophical and political insights (e.g., Kairys, 1982; Tushnet,

1986; Russell, 1986; Unger, 1986; Kelman, 1987; see also the special issue of the Stanford Law Review, 1984). More recent connections between Derrida's thought and law include: Cornell, Rosenfeld, and Carlson (legal decision making and feminist jurisprudence, 1992); Caputo (legal reasoning and the [im]possibility of justice, 1997; see also the Special Issue of the Cardozo Law Review, 1991); Cornell (feminist legal theory, the possibility of justice, and the feminine over the masculine voice, 1992); and Fuchs and Ward (an analysis of building cases in law, 1994). In criminology we note: Schwartz and Freidrichs (understanding metaphors of violence, 1994); Scheppele (definitions of rape, 1987); and Arrigo and Williams (execution of psychiatrically disordered prisoners, 1999a). In social justice we find: Wijeyeratne (exploring the linkages between semiotics and justice, 1998); Caputo (questioning the relationship between justice, law, and equality, 1997); and Arrigo (investigating the metaphors of war and peace in medical justice, 1999).

### Michel Foucault

It is difficult to locate with precision the place of Michel Foucault in the pantheon of postmodernism.[14]   Without question, however, Foucault's insights have substantially informed notable debates in the disciplines of history, sociology, political theory, feminism, linguistics, cultural studies, and psychoanalysis (e.g., Couzens, 1992). Foucault's most significant contribution was his relentless effort to understand and document the historically variable but, nonetheless, normalizing techniques of power, social control, and domination characteristic of European and North American culture. The breadth of Foucault's intellectual life was distinguished by three relevant periods pertinent to this theme: (1) the archeological; (2) the genealogical; and, as an aspect of his genealogical analyses, (3) techniques for constituting the self (Dreyfus & Rabinow, 1982; Best & Kellner, 1991).

      Foucault (1973) claimed that contemporary and inventive mechanisms of disciplinary control originated in discourse. Discursive techniques of power, activated by language, displaced the rational, reasonable, self-same subject of modernity. "Power [expressed through words] produces; it produces reality; it produces domains of objects and rituals of truth" (Foucault, 1977: 194). Foucault's archeology of knowledge manifested itself in hermeneutic interpretations of individual experiences. Directing attention to micrological manifestations of power and social control meant confronting modernity's totalizing essentialisms. According to Foucault, no "grand theory" of human nature could explain the "particularisms" that flourished at the level of the individual, the group, or the community.

      Foucault acknowledged the contributions of Marx and Freud; however, he found himself more closely aligned with Nietzsche and Heidegger. In opposition to a belief in a certain, but repressed, human essence, Foucault articulated an anti-foundational theory of agency constituted by and through discourse. As he

Humanity and Society, Volume 24, Number 2, May 2000     172

explained: "man is cut off from the origin that would make him contemporaneous with his own existence: amid all the things that are born in time and no doubt die in time, he, cut off from all origin, is already there" (cited in Dreyfus & Rabinow, 1982: 38). Elsewhere, for Foucault (1971), this move toward anti-essentialism and away from grand theory was described as the play of unpredictability, fissures, ruptures, and multiplicity. In these observations, Foucault (1971) advocated an analysis of discontinuity that focused more on ambulant patterns of behavior. In other words, he maintained that the seeds for change were located in the current epoch as reconceptualizations of pre-existing discursive stock.

Foucault initiated his genealogical attempt to provide specific institutional support for the historical transformation of modes of domination and control, conveyed through discourse, with the publication of *Discipline and Punish* (1977) and *The History of Sexuality* (1980). Institutions like the prison, the school, the hospital, and the military were noteworthy for their complicity in encouraging the production of docile bodies through inventive mechanisms of control. As established through technologically evolving facets of everyday life, the functioning of these structures demonstrated how power productively inserted itself into discourse. Indeed, the "power/knowledge" techniques used to probe the inner secrets of subjects' lives proved an invaluable source of information for institutions seeking to enhance the predictability and regulation of behavior. Clearly, as Foucault described, advances in the social and natural sciences were critical to the task of acquiring these data. He argued that the metamorphosis of disciplinary techniques was driven by the desire for better punishment and/or disciplinary control.[15]

In Foucault's (1986a, 1988) later works, he shifted his analysis toward the constitution of the self. Foucault sought an articulation of the person, particularly as a political entity, that celebrated the expression of desire. Moreover, since power was expressed through the effusive "carceral archipelago," Foucault called for the cultivation of multiple sites of political contestation. According to Foucault, given the diffusion of power, a single, monolithic political strategy was doomed to fail. Thus, as Foucault argued, "a plurality of autonomous struggles [was needed] waged throughout the microlevels of society: in the prisons, asylums, hospitals, and schools" (Best and Kellner, 1991: 56).

The application of Foucault's work in law, criminology, and social justice has been considerable. Thus, the field of law includes: Smart (feminism and the discursive power of legal thought, 1989); Litowitz (describing the inadequacy of the law to protect individual rights, 1997); Thorton (creating a feminist jurisprudence, 1986); and Hunt (exploring the sociology of law as governance, 1995). In criminology we note: Bell (describing the desexualization of rape, 1991; interrogating the practice of incest, 1993); Garland (examining subjugation and punishment in modern society, 1990); Woohull (exploring power, sexuality, and rape, 1988); and Howe (detailing a feminist, non-androcentric assessment of penality, 1994). In social justice we find: I. Young (interpreting the tension between

173                         Bruce A. Arrigo, Dragan Milovanovic, and Robert C. Schehr

individualism and community, 1990); Cobb (explaining how the discourse of violence in mediation is domesticated, 1997); Cohen (commenting on the phenomenon of "net widening" producing a disciplinary society in which subjects regulate themselves, 1979); and Pavlich (critiquing community mediation and self-identity, 1996).

## Luce Irigaray

Irigaray argues that women are other for the male in the Symbolic and Imaginary Order.[16] She is only defined secondarily in relation to the primacy of the male. The fixation of the libidinal economy, its territorializations, is such as to privilege male discourse and embodiments of desire, while de-privileging female voices. It is language, she argues, that maintains the patriarchal system. Following Lacan, woman is *pas-toute*, not-all, lack. Whereas the stabilized male discourse privileges possession, "singular meanings, hierarchical organization, polar oppositions, the division into subject-predicate form" (Grosz, 1990: 17), and subject-object relations in hierarchical and dualistic forms, the unarticulated forms of the female privilege enjoyment, unadulterated pleasure, fluidity, and relations that are without bounds or hierarchies. Women's identities remain outside of contemporary male-ordered representative schemas. Irigaray suggests the strategy of "mimesis" which involves production rather than passive imitation of imaginary and symbolic forms. Mimesis is a rhetorical tactic of converting subordination into affirmation. Specifically, Irigaray suggests that mysticism has come closest to offering an alternative articulatory practice. The basis of this orientation is a "surrendering of self," a "self-loss" whose language has yet to be developed. This orientation defies full capture in dominant discourse. It entails an overflowing of boundaries, an excess, a "feminine poetics," open ended possibilities, exploiting blanks and ambiguities in phallocentric discourse. In short, Irigaray argues for new spaces, an alterity, outside the male economy of representation, within which feminine desire may be articulated, producing new articulations without subjection of one sex by another.

Irigaray's influence has been substantial in law, less developed in criminology, and substantial in theorizing social change. Second wave theorists in law include: Cornell (developing an "ethical feminism," 1991; critiquing sex-discrimination law, formal equality, and laws of equivalence, 1992, 1993; rethinking family law, 1998); Butler (focusing on exclusionary and binary practices in the phallocentric order, 1993; suggesting strategies of subverting repetition as the basis for the development of new subjectivities, 1990); Spivak (developing a place from which to speak, 1991); and Grbich (describing the female body in taxation laws, 1996). In criminology we note: Naffine (developing a feminist histiography of criminology, 1996); and Spivak (developing strategies by which the "subaltern" can speak, 1991). In social change we find: Cornell (turning subordination into affirmation through mimetic practices, 1991; transcending "sameness ideology," 1993; cultivating the sanctity of the imaginary domain, 1998); and Naffine

Humanity and Society, Volume 24, Number 2, May 2000                    174

(delineating imaginative parody and mimicry, 1996).

### Julia Kristeva

Kristeva revised Lacan's analysis of the Imaginary and Symbolic Orders.[17] She argues that prior to the Oedipal phase of Freud and the development of the Imaginary and Symbolic Orders of Lacan, the child already has her/his drives organized in what is termed the semiotic sphere where the primary processes (i.e., unconscious thoughts, feelings, impulses) are ubiquitous. This sphere is more rhythmic, disordered, energy in movement, and a maternally structured space. For Kristeva, the imaginary domain goes beyond Lacan's focus on the visual, to include touch, taste, smell, and vocalizations that are preconditions for the acquisition of language and for discursive production. As Kristeva explains, the semiotic undergoes an oedipalized, territorialized structuration (akin to the work of secondary process described by Freud) by the *symbolic* transmitted through the mother: it is the discursive sphere responsible for the coherent, ordered, unified speaking subject governed by the law-of-the-father. The symbolic is always subject to the disruptions of the semiotic chora. These disruptions can be engendered by a "poetic language." The poetic transgresses the semiotic codes and allows the re-emergence of the semiotic, the sphere of the maternal. Kristeva cites authors who take full advantage of this disruptive style (i.e., Mallarme, Joyce, Artaud) (cf. the section of this article on Barthes for a description of the *writerly text*).

Kristeva's methodology of "semanalysis" is the study of the production of meaning and its disruptions, subversions, and dislocations of subjectivity in discourse. She recognizes two kinds of writers: the "realist writer" and the "poetic writer." The former produces the "phenotext" which, based on the primacy of the symbolic, represses polyvocality and the heterogeneous; the latter, produces the "genotext" which comes under the influence of the disruptions of the semiotic. She argues that motherhood offers love based on the development of growth and of the greatest realization of potential. Patriarchal forms are possessive or destructive of the other. Kristeva further suggests three kinds of oppositions: (1) the "rebel" who must still remain in the master-slave dialectic; (2) the "psychoanalyst" who searches for an alternative language to challenge patriarchal order; and (3) the "writer" who attempts further disruptions in language itself setting up alternative forms. So, too, the *avant-garde* (e.g., poets, artists), for Kristeva, provoke, disrupt, dislocate, and call forth the repressed, the excesses, the semiotic, the desire which is unspeakable. The poetic text provides an alternative construction of meaning, subjectivity, and pleasure than those constructions based in the patriarchal order.

Several examples of Kristeva's influence are discernible in law; however, more limited applications are found in criminology and social justice. The domain of law includes: Cornell (examining the repressed maternal as a basis of theorizing an ethical feminism, 1991; gender hierarchy being reproduced in law and how a critical reading of Kristeva provides alternative transformative vistas, 1993); and

175                    Bruce A. Arrigo, Dragan Milovanovic, and Robert C. Schehr

Ashe (introducing a psychoanalytic theory of subjectivity into feminist legal theory, 1990). In criminology we note: Arrigo (integrating feminist jurisprudence and criminology as the basis for a critical pedagogy, 1995a); and Moi (exploring the criminalized boundaries of sexual/textual politics, 1985). In social justice we find Butler (subversive practices which offer form to the feminine, 1990); and Moi (canvassing Kristeva's semiotical, psychoanalytical, and political excursions on the feminine, 1990).

### Jean-Francois Lyotard

Lyotard (1984) is best known for his search of instabilities rather than consensus as underlying modernist thought.[18] His "paralogy" considers quantum mechanics, chaos theory, catastrophe theory, Gödel's theorem, and the celebration of the small narrative (*petit recit*) over the grand narrative. His expressed emphasis and rallying cry was: "wage war on totality." Quantum mechanics questions linear, predictable, continuous pathways. Contrary to Einstein, it informs us that *"God does plays dice"* (Stewart, 1989). Chaos theory offers us the idea of fractal geometry, fractal spaces, attractors, bifurcations, and dissipative structures. Catastrophe theory provides the notion that discontinuities can exist in otherwise deterministic and continuous systems. Gödel's theorem represents the idea of "undecidability:" all cannot be subsumed under any generalized system of rules; exceptions shall *always* exist. *Petit* narratives cannot be subsumed under some consensus, nor is it desirable to do so. Thus, in Habermas's (1984, 1987) communication theory, the goal of dialogue (i.e., consensus for Lyotard) is not a desirable end for developing notions of justice. The linkage between consensus and justice is broken. Language games necessitate sensitivity to various truths. Consensus is only a momentary state in dialogue and cannot be an end in itself. It is paralogy that underlies the search for genuine dialogue.

      Much of Lyotard's work has had an indirect influence in law, crime, and social justice; however, postmodern theory has benefitted considerably from his ideas of paralogy. Thus, in law and chaos we note: Brion (legal reasoning, 1991); Conklin (legal discourse and how suffering is concealed through its specialized vocabulary and grammar, 1998); Schulman (critical legal studies, 1997); and Arrigo and Williams (civilly confining the mentally ill, 1999c). In criminology and chaos we find: T.R. Young (describing various attractor basins that arise from the political economy,1997); Forker (revising Quinney [1977] indicating the usefulness of non-linear dynamics, 1997); Pavlich (using Lyotard's idea of paralogy to sensitize critical criminology's need for expanding boundaries, 1999); and Henry and Milovanovic (developing a constitutive criminology, 1996). In justice studies and chaos theory we note: T.R. Young (outlining how justice may arise from non-linear dynamics, 1992, 1999); Schehr (devising an alternative model of social movement theory, 1997); Schehr and Milovanovic (critiquing mediation programs, 1999); and Williams and Arrigo ( integrating anarchist thought and chaology as an

Humanity and Society, Volume 24, Number 2, May 2000        176

alterative approach to social problems research, 2000). Relatedly, in the domain of catastrophe theory, Lyotard's postmodern epistemology, although minimally employed in the crime, law, and justice literature, has been useful. Thus, for example, in peace studies and catastrophe we note Milovanovic (developing a "third way" in de-escalating conflict situations, 1999).

## THE SECOND WAVE: INTERPRETING THE PAST, BUILDING THE PRESENT, AND FORECASTING THE FUTURE

In this section we draw attention to how postmodern lines of inquiry can be interpreted. While we recognize that several skeptical versions of the perspective have received considerable attention in the literature, we suggest how affirmative renderings of postmodernism are not only possible but are already in operation. Indeed, on this latter point, we specifically identify the contributions of several "second wave" scholars who have appropriated the interpretive tools of the postmodern sciences and have fashioned integrative strategies for engaging in law, crime, and social justice research. Several of these studies are cited above. However, in this section, we specifically emphasize how the cross-fertilization of affirmative postmodern ideas and strains of analyses represent the beginning of synthetic inroads awaiting refinement through future application studies.

### Doing Affirmative Postmodern Analysis

Early developments of postmodern analysis tended to be of the skeptical or nihilistic form. Derrida's notion of "anti-foundationalism," for example, tended to be interpreted in support of a conservative agenda. Since, according to the deconstructionist argument, any collection of criteria established to evaluate something could in turn be evaluated by another set of criteria, and that, in turn, by another (i.e., an infinite regress), why then bother? All is relative. Struggles are futile. Similarly, Baudrillard's thesis of an endless hyper-real devoid of grounding tended toward a nihilism, a denial of historical contingent foundation. Hegel's thesis, too, has been identified as inherently conservative along similar dimensions. Consider, for example, his master-slave dialectic. Following Marxist terminology, the master signifies the "bourgeois" and the slave the "proletariat." The master states values affirmatively; the slave develops values by first reacting to and then negating the master (i.e., a reaction-negation dynamics) (Deleuze, 1983; Bogue, 1989; Butler, 1999). In this arrangement, nothing inherently new is being offered. How, then, is the "subaltern" (Spivak, 1991) to speak? How, then, are the "true words" (Freire, 1972) of the slave to find expressive form?

Other negative implications can be derived from the Hegelian form. "Reversal of hierarchies," often attributed to Derrida, could mean just that: the subordinate group, after the revolution, now becomes the dominant, and the previous dominant group is subject to brutal repression. Cornell (1991), has applied this reasoning in her critique of Catherine MacKinnon. Cornell accuses MacKinnon of perpetuating "hate politics," "revenge politics." Elsewhere, we often see within over zealous activist groups a tendency toward "schmarxism," of "exorcism." The former is a neologism combining marxism and schmucky, indicating dogmatic, rigid forms of indoctrination; the latter, the tendency of constructing evil in the other and then attacking one's own construction. Of course, we have also experienced the more alienating forces of political correctness.

In order to stave off the tendencies of the Hegelian dialectic, nihilism, fatalism, schmarxism, and exorcism, an *affirmative* postmodern framework is needed. One response is the fluid and evolving intervention of a cultural politics of difference (Young, 1990). In this more liberatory vision, law, crime, and justice are rooted in *contingent universalities* (Butler, 1992; McLaren, 1994: 211). Provisional truths, positional knowledges, and relational meanings abound. New social relations, practices, and institutions materialize, producing a different, more inclusive context within which divergent and discordant sensibilities interact (Moufe, 1992: 380). In other words, the multiplicity of political, economic, and cultural identities that constitute our collective society interactively and mutually contribute to discourse on law, crime, justice, and social change.

One dimension to affirmative postmodern analysis is contained in the Nietzschean version of the master-slave dialectic (Deleuze, 1983). At issue is the establishment of an ethico-political context in which repressed voices might flourish (Spivak, 1991). In the Nietzschean paradigm, the slave states values actively and affirmatively; s/he is not inherently caught up in the Hegelian master-slave dialectic. The slave's affirmative action contains within it a beyond, a vision of the possible, a transpraxis. Transpraxis is the basis of the affirmative forms of postmodern analysis. It finds a nexus with interpreting Lacan's (1977) notion of desire not as inherently homeostatic, an overcoming of lack, but, rather, more in terms of a creative search with no clear end, a rhizomatic journey discovering other spaces, the in-betweens, the fractal spaces.

Butler's (1999) statement on the nature of desire is similarly depicted. After reviewing Lacan's notion of how desire finds and, at the same time, escapes expression in signifiers, and how his descriptive analysis specifies desire as constituted in relation to the law-of-the-father marking its limits,[19] she then critiques Hegel. Butler takes issue with Hegel's overly rational construction of desire, the notion of the self-transparent subject, the reactive-negative basis of desire for the subaltern, and the ultimate development of ressentiment and envy by the slave. She suggests that it is Deleuze to whom we must turn for guidance, particularly in his notion of a desire defined as productive and generative activity. This is expressed in the Nietzschean notion of a "will to power" ("will" not to be read as a conscious agency; "power" not to be read as domination).

Butler's reading of Deleuze is that desire is a "productive response to life in which the force...of it multiplies and intensifies in the course of an exchange with alterity" (1999: 213; see also Deleuze, 1983:49-72; Bogue, 1989: 20-34). The

Humanity and Society, Volume 24, Number 2, May 2000          178

notion of "will" is "responsive and malleable, assuming new and more complicated forms of organization through the exchange of force constitutive of desire....[D]esire is less a struggle to monopolize power than an exchange that intensifies and proliferates energy and power into a state of excess" (Butler, 1999: 213). Her use of the word "power" intends, therefore, multiple loci of affirmative and active forces.

According to Butler, productive forms of desire can also be found in Foucault's (1980) late work. For Foucault, desire finds itself captured in various historically contingent power relations crystallized in discursive practices. In Foucault's radicalized conception of the Hegelian dialectic Butler maintains that law reflects both rigidity and plasticity; the former creating desire as lack, but law's inherent plasticity creates "desire as a creative act, a locus of innovation, the production of new cultural meanings" (Butler, 1999: 231). In addition, Butler looks to Kristeva's (1986) work on the "semiotic" and "poetic language" as deterritorialized spaces abundant with possibilities and disruptive forces (see also Foucault's notion of the "heterotopic," 1986b). Our own affirmative postmodern approach finds a nexus with Butler's critique and understanding of desire as productive and life-affirming. We add, however, that chaos theory is implicit in Nietzsche's and Deleuze's work, and that desire, once mobilized, is much like the rhizome activating, putting into resonance, COREL sets (Henry & Milovanovic, 1996) that ultimately defy closure, linear expression, and predictability, while providing only momentary stabilized forms and "structures" (e.g., "dissipative structures").[20]

Thus, returning to the notion of transpraxis (i.e., the ambulant and conditional vision of what could be), we note that it resides in discourse. The production of alternative expressions of desire, of true words, requires that the voice(s) of alterity and multiplicity be embodied in civic life and human social behavior. Transpraxis involves the undecidability of interaction as a revelatory moment for potential and greater inclusiveness. As Derrida (1997: 107) notes, "the undecidable in discourse signifies "unstable identities...that...do not close over and form a seamless web of the selfsame." In short, the undecidability in discourse make possible the articulation of new and different vocabularies of meaning embodying the voices of and ways of knowing for excluded or marginalized citizens and/or collectives.

Consistent with this emancipatory agenda of transpraxis, an affirmative postmodern approach involves *border crossings* (Giroux, 1992: 19-36, 133-41, 170-176; see also JanMohamed, 1994; Lippens, 1997). Border crossings signify the deliberate displacement of established parameters of meaning, forms of consciousness, sites of knowledge, and loci of truth. Conventional boundaries are transgressed, resisted, debunked, and de-centered. Border crossings require one to embrace the confluence of multiple languages, experiences, and desires as folded into the polyvocal, multi-layered, and trans-historical narratives reflective of a society of difference (Giroux, 1992: 29; Irigaray, 1993). Thus, the desiring voice

179                          Bruce A. Arrigo, Dragan Milovanovic, and Robert C. Schehr

of marginalized subjects and of those others seeking recognition and legitimacy would be imbued with pluri-significant, contradictory, incomplete, effusive, fragmented, and multi-accentuated expressions of identity. These borderlands, as languages of possibility rather than as technologies of discipline (Henry and Milovanovic, 1996: 214-243), would be seen as "sites for both critical analysis and...a[s] potential source[s] of experimentation [and] creativity" (Giroux, 1992: 34).

Affirmative postmodern analysis therefore views the emerging postmodern society with its dislocations, logic of differences, undecidabilities, and boundary transgressions (Laclau, 1996; see also Lash and Urry, 1994) as an opportunity for new articulations of the Imaginary and Symbolic Orders, the occasions for new visions of the possible. In law, for example, Cornell (1991) indicates that within the constraints imposed by dominant discourse, metaphoric and metonymic slippages are at play, always suggestive of the new. In addition, Arrigo and Williams (1999b) contend that democratic justice and equality for minorities depend on the deconstructive and reconstructive activity of defining, on their own terms, identity freed from the trappings of majoritarian sensibilities. Similarly, critical race theory actively searches for new opportunities in "naming" injuries (Matsuda et al, 1983). In criminology, Howe (1994) offers a comparable analysis for the plight of incarcerated women. Barak (1988, 1994), too, has described the approach of "newsmaking criminology." He argues that criminal justicians need to be active, rather than passive, producers of knowledge when engaged with the media. In social justice literature, Schehr (1997) outlines a "fourth" social movement approach, "intentional communities," informed by the orderly-disorder perspective of chaos theory.

**Integrations**

Postmodernist thought is witnessing considerable integration in the contemporary scene, both between the physical and social sciences and within the social sciences. For example, by demonstrating the compatibility between chaos theory and the literary theory of postructuralism, Hayles (1990) suggests the formation of an "ecology of ideas." Stanislaw Lem (1981) even describes a topological space within which certain forms of integration are more likely (see Hayles, 1990: 185-86). Consider the notion of iteration. It is found in chaos theory, in literary analysis, and in legal textual analysis (see Derrida and Balkin in previous section). Others argue for cross-fertilization and point out that the disciplinary boundaries have always been transgressed (Giroux, 1992).

Within the social sciences, the integrative work of Barak (1998) and the "hyperintegrated" approach of Barak and Henry (1999) are exemplary (see also, e.g., Henry and Lanier, 1998; Farnsworth, 1989; Gibbons, 1994; Einstadter and Henry, 1995 chapter 12). These syntheses, however, as anarchists tell us, must be posited in non-static forms; hence, chaos's suggestion of "dissipative structures" is appropriate to all synthetic enterprises. In other words, global conceptualizing must ultimately proceed on a level of relative stability, but at the local level, instability and indeterminacy must prevail. Indeed, micro knowledge can never be completely subsumable within any "hyperintegrated" model.

Barak is particularly sensitive to this issue. He warns us that the modernist preoccupation is "aimed at the questionable objective of delivering some kind of positivist prediction of 'what causes criminal behavior'" (1998: 188). As Barak (*Ibid.*) contends, in postmodernist integrations "everything, at both the micro and macro levels, affects everything else, and...these effects are continuously changing over time." Barak and Henry (1999: 191-92) also suggest that future integrationist theories should be sensitive to at least five problematics: "[1] [the matter of] integrat[ing] theoretical concepts or propositions...[2] [the question of] how propositions are logically related...[3] [the issue of] the nature of causality... [4] [the issue of] the *level* of concepts and theories that are integrated...[5] [and the question of] what is to be explained, or  the *scope of integration*." In addition, efforts at theoretical synthesis must also consider the crucial role of social justice in any critical analysis. On this point, Barak and Henry (1999: 171) recommend the development of social justice ideas that both "deconstruct inequalities based on differences while celebrating differences."

Affirmative forms of postmodern integrative analyses are discernible. In law, for example, Cornell (1991) has developed an integrated approach drawing from Lacan, Irigaray, Derrida, Kristeva and Cixous, and indicates how an "ethical feminism" may begin to emerge. Butler's (1990) description of "contingent universalities" as a way of transcending the dichotomy of either relativism or essentialism, and her call for practices "subverting repetition" are similarly suggestive. These are lines of inquiry that integrate the works of Foucault, Kristeva, Irigaray, and Lacan. In addition, the idea of "contingent universalities" possesses a commonality with chaos theory's notion of  "dissipative structures." Both allow relatively stable political agendas to reach a tentative stability which becomes the basis of mobilization and opposition; however, these "universalities" are subject to refinement, qualification, deletion, and substitution as a function of historical contingency.

In criminology additional affirmative postmodern integrative efforts can be identified.  Henry and Milovanovic's (1996) notion of COREL sets represents a synthesis of ideas from several critical lines of thought, culminating in a theory of constitutive dialectics. Moreover, Arrigo and Young's (1998) integration of semiotics, chaos theory, and topology form the basis of a psychoanalytic critique of modernist criminological thought. They argue that the construction of theoretical criminology fails to include race, gender, and class differences as embedded within criminology's own conceptual language.

In social justice affirmative and integrative postmodern initiatives are discernible. Shehr (1996, 1997), for example, describes the development of the "third" and "even" fourth approach in social movement literature. This model

181                    Bruce A. Arrigo, Dragan Milovanovic, and Robert C. Schehr

combines selected insights from chaos theory and semiotic analysis. Additional syntheses include: Arrigo and Schehr (integrating chaos and semiotics as applied to an assessment of restorative justice programs, 1998); and Schehr and Milovanovic (integrating semiotics, chaos, and catastrophe theory as linked to a critique of mediation programs, 1999).

## NEW DIRECTIONS: DOING AFFIRMATIVE AND INTEGRATIVE POSTMODERN ANALYSIS

Affirmative and integrative postmodern analysis offers the researcher novel lines of investigating legal, criminological, and social justice phenomena. In this section we tentatively explore three such sociolegal topics; specifically: confinement law for psychiatrically disordered persons on death row; critical race theory; and alternative dispute resolution programs. We rely heavily on the insights of French postmodern social theorists as articulated in the first section of the article. In addition, though, we synthesize these observations suggestively demonstrating how each topic could be examined consistent with affirmative and transformative postmodern inquiry. Thus, we contend that the examples chosen in the pages that follow represent new and alternative directions for engaging in sophisticated sociolegal research and praxis.

### Confinement Law and Executing the Mentally Ill

The United State Supreme Court has determined that, under specific conditions, persons with psychiatric disorders can be subject to capital punishment. Execution of the mentally ill is problematic when questions are raised concerning the death row prisoner's right to refuse treatment, especially where competency restoration is the objective (Winick, 1997). There are a number of appellate cases that chart the development of the mental health law in this area; however, in recent years, three cases are particularly noteworthy: *Ford v. Wainwright*, (1986); *Washington v. Harper*, (1990); and *State v. Perry* (1992) (Winick, 1992). These cases are briefly summarized below.

The *Ford* case examined whether the Eighth Amendment's prohibition against cruel and unusual punishment prevented the state from executing an incompetent death row prisoner. The Court concluded that a prisoner must understand the death penalty and the reasons for the sentence before a state can carry out the execution (*Ford v. Wainwright*, 1986: 420-422). The *Harper* case assessed whether it was permissible to forcibly medicate a prisoner for eventual execution if the coercive treatment furthered the goal of prison safety and promoted the prisoner's medical needs. The Court determined that an incompetent death row inmate is subject to forced treatment if (1) the prisoner suffers from a mental disorder and/or is gravely disabled such that (2) the person poses a likelihood of serious harm to oneself, to others, and/or to another's property (*Washington v.*

Humanity and Society, Volume 24, Number 2, May 2000     182

*Harper*, 1990: 214). The *Perry* case considered whether the Eighth and Fourteenth Amendments prevented the state from forcibly injecting mind altering drugs into a condemned prisoner who was incompetent, when the medical intervention was administered *solely* for competency restoration resulting in execution. The Court found that when psychotropic drugs are used simply as a way to medicate and then execute, the medical intervention is unconstitutional: it neither improves prison safety nor is in the prisoner's best medical interest (*State v. Perry*, 1992: 751-752).

We note that while a conventional reading of the three cases and the Court's respective rulings yield useful sociolegal information, an affirmative and integrative postmodern analysis offers additional and alternative insight substantially advancing our knowledge of mental health confinement law, policy, and practice. For example, key words and phrases form the basis of the Court's decisions above. Collectively, these expressions communicate something more about the law's unconscious intent, hidden assumptions, and implicit values for psychiatrically ill prisoners and the process of executing them.[21] The words and phrases themselves signify an assembled "text" or narrative that can be evaluated or disassembled as such.

To elaborate, consistent with Barthes' (1973b) textual analysis, standard sociolegal interpretations emphasize the "readerly approach" to sense making: truth is a certain destination, a clear endpoint where meaning is exhaustible. Conversely, affirmative postmodern assessments emphasize the "writerly approach" to interpretation: truth is a departure where an array of knowledges and perspectives are valued signifying no definitive reading of the text.

Both Lyotard (1984) and Deleuze and Guattari (1986) offer similar analyses. The former's use of *petit récit* (i.e., small narratives) rather than grand narratives and the latter's comments on "minor literatures" are affirmative postmodern strategies that shatter and increase our understanding by disrupting and displacing conventional readings of a text. In short, they produce opportunities for locating instability rather than consensus in discourse (Lyotard, 1988a) and make possible the deterritorialization of that which is written (Deleuze and Guattari, 1987).

In mental health confinement law, key expressions such as "mental illness," "treatment," "competency," "dangerous," and "execution," are *signs*; that is, they are words and phrases that convey multiple, fluid, and evolving meanings in the law.[22] Barthes (1974: 35-41) observes that a "galaxy of signifiers" makes up any text and that such signifiers (i.e., words and phrases) can be decoded as sense-making explodes and scatters. Derrida's (1976) position on the "undecidability" of meaning resonates with this logic. The play of *différance* (e.g., "competency vs. incompetency," "mental health vs. mental illness") reveals how each term in the binary opposition relates to the other. In other words, notwithstanding the logocentrism of the first value position in the two hierarchies, each term in binary opposition: (1) is differentiated from the other (i.e., they are distinct); (2) defers the other term (i.e., makes it "wait"); and (3) defers to the other term (i.e., is dependent upon the other for meaning). These relationships reflect the undecidable in discourse; that is, the "foundationless, provisional.., or reversibl[e]" context within which sense-making takes place (Balkin, 1987: 752). In the extreme, following Baudrillard (1983a), *differance* and the writerly approach embody a "hypertext:" they signify a "hyper-reality" about our understanding of psychiatrically disordered prisoners on death row absent clear epistemological foundations or anchored sociolegal truths.[23]

Equally suggestive for purposes of an affirmative and integrative postmodern understanding of mental health confinement law is Foucault's (1972, 1977) power/knowledge construct, Lacan's (1977) notion of desire, and Lyotard's (1984) paralogy. Foucault insists that power, as knowledge-truth, assumes the form of a language in which thought and behavior are regulated through productive mechanisms of disciplinary control. The sign of mental illness must be "policed," (Foucault, 1965), and persons identified as such must be normalized, de-pathologized, and corrected. Capital punishment is *the* symbolic gesture, *the* ultimate act in which the prisoner's body, mind, and soul are territorialized. The trilogy of Court cases, representing the current state of mental health confinement law, legitimize the correctional system's use of execution as a productive mechanism for such territorialization. According to Foucault (1988), however, de-centering this manifestation of power/knowledge through multiple sites of contestation and diverse expressions of identity is crucial to liberating the alienating subject from disciplinary control.

Where Foucault calls for active resistance to the territorialization of desire (Deleuze and Guattari, 1987), Lacan (1991) psycho-semiotically explains how the subject is dismissed or silenced through discourse but can, nonetheless, be retrieved. The jargon of confinement law does not embody the experiences (i.e., the desire) of the mentally ill. Confinement law is a specialized system of communication (i.e., psycholegal discourse) privileging a (clinicolegal) narrative "producing a circumscribed knowledge understood [to be] psychiatric justice" (Arrigo, 1997b: 32). Lacan's (1991) notion of the *master discourse* conveys the alienating and repressive effects of certain coordinated language systems, including psycholegal discourse.[24] In addition, however, Lacan (1991) argues that alienated subjects (i.e., mentally disordered offenders) have access to an alternative system of communication that embodies the subject's sense of identity and way of knowing. This replacement *désir* (desire) is captured in Lacan's (1991) *discourse of the hysteric*[25] coupled with his *discourse of the analyst*.[26] The joint effects of these two discourses suggest a way in which psychiatrically disordered offenders can overcome their lack, their *pas- toute*, in repressive psycholegal discourse.

This theme of overcoming one's lack in discourse resonates with Lyotard (1984, 1988a), particularly in his concept of paralogy. In paralogy the search for instabilities and resistance to totalities is emphasized. The goal of dialogue is sensitivity to various truths, forms of identity, and expressions of knowledge. Relatedly, Lyotard's (1984) use of chaos theory's notion of far-from-equilibrium

Humanity and Society, Volume 24, Number 2, May 2000                    184

conditions suggests that the law's desire to arrive at a fixed, equilibrium resolution (i.e., a point attractor) regarding the execution of psychiatrically ill prisoners, dismisses the more natural and fluid behavior of the law. The law is a system of signs (Kevelson, 1988) and, as such, is more dynamic than static, more indeterminate than determinate, more unpredictable than predictable. Acknowledging the orderly disorder (i.e., chaos) of law opens up possibilities for exploring new vistas of sociolegal meaning and alternative interpretations for the signs of mental health confinement law, policy, and practice. Both are consistent with an affirmative and integrative postmodern textual analysis of execution for the mentally ill.

**Critical Race Theory**

Critical race theory in law is particularly well suited for incorporating and integrating postmodern concepts. Although somewhat provisionally accepted (Matsuda, 1996) by its key adherents in good part, we suppose, due to the limitations posed by the more skeptical forms of postmodern analysis (e.g., the death of the subject, anti-foundationalism, linguistic relativism, denial of law as a weapon to correct injustices, the evaporation of discursive subject-positions from which to speak, etc.), central concepts of critical race theory can nevertheless be further augmented by affirmative postmodern critical tools. Several of these foci will be discussed: multiple consciousness, intersectional analysis, deconstruction and reconstruction of categories, discourse analysis, "unconscious racism," and the dialectics of struggle.

Black feminist thought goes beyond essentialism in its recognition of diverse discursive subject positions. This is found in the notion of multiple consciousness (Harris, 1991; Williams, 1987; Matsuda, 1990, 1996; Cain, 1992) which also avoids the shortcomings of arguments that rely solely on the notion of "false consciousness" or on "standpoint epistemology" (see also Matsuda, 1990). The latter two are question begging. Rather, as Matsuda (1996) and Crenshaw (1993) tell us, multiple identities are more connected with the notion of intersectionality. Crenshaw's (1989: 149; 1993) observations are particularly poignant:

> "Black women sometimes experience discrimination in ways similar to white women's experience; sometimes they share very similar experiences with Black men. Yet often they experience double-discrimination – the combined effects of practices which discriminate on the basis of race, and on the basis of sex. And sometimes, they experience discrimination as Black women – not the sum of race and sex discrimination, but as Black women."

This is echoed by Collins (1993) who states we should move away from purely

185                         Bruce A. Arrigo, Dragan Milovanovic, and Robert C. Schehr

"additive analysis" to intersectional analysis – "How do race, class and gender function as parallel and interlocking systems that shape this basic relationship of domination and subordination?" (*Ibid.* 29). This is where critical race theory and postmodern analysis meet. According to Crenshaw, "I conceive of intersectionality as a provisional concept that links contemporary politics with postmodern theory" (1993: 114). This examination is pragmatic in orientation, is goal oriented, and is directed toward social change. In this view, the categorization 'women of color' "count[s] in naming the structure of 'racism' or 'patriarchy' and suggest[s] a category, 'women of color,' impacted by both" (Matsuda, 1990: 1773). The criterion of usefulness revolves around the degree to which "it helps us to know more than we would have known otherwise"(*Ibid.* 1774). Categories, therefore, are provisional. They are in constant need of construction, deconstruction, and reconstruction.

　　This is where affirmative postmodern analysis can be of further assistance. The categories gender, race, and class have been subject to deconstruction in the literature (see for example Bulter, 1990; Shepherdson, 1996; Laclau, 1996; Laclau and Mouffe, 1985). Structural dislocations and "radical undecidability" (Laclau, 1996) necessitate moving away from traditional understandings of these categories. New alliance formations (Mouffe, 1992) are often temporary, fleeting, singular in political focus, and dissipative once the primary issue has been addressed. Thus, rigid adherence to categories are fetters that must be shed. The work of Crenshaw, Matsuda, Harris and Williams clearly move in this direction.

　　Critical race theory notes the importance of speaking otherwise. Stories, particularly stories in law, are often consciously or unconsciously (Lawrence, 1987) reflective of a dominant ideology. The key, then, becomes attending to the voices of those excluded within and throughout the dominant (juridical) discourse in use. Thus, "naming" injuries by categories that can receive legal attention becomes important. In addition, though, one must also be cognizant of law's violence.

　　To illustrate, Sarat (1993) has shown how in capital trials various forms of narratives of violence are inflicted. Indeed, in the death of the victim a simple antiseptic legal construction of good and evil is created. Moreover, Sarat tells us, capital trials "are occasions for overcoming doubt and regaining stability... While the violence outside the law is unnecessary, irrational, indiscriminate, gruesome, and useless, law's violence, the violence of the death penalty, is described as rational, purposive, and controlled through values, norms, and procedures external to violence itself" (*Ibid.* 52). As he concludes "in capital trials the violence of law is inscribed in struggles to put violence into discourse and to control its discursive representation" (*Ibid.* 24-25). Along the same lines, Silbey (1997: 219) notes a form of "postmodern colonialism" that also follows a central idea of Baudrillard (hyper-reality): "where the worldwide distribution and consumption of cultural products removed from the context of their production and interpretation is organized through legal devices to constitute a form of domination;" in short, a form of juridic linguistic domination.

Humanity and Society, Volume 24, Number 2, May 2000          186

Hate speech is one area where an integration of critical race theory and affirmative postmodern analysis is useful. Crenshaw (1993), for example, argues that women of color often suffer double jeopardy because of their dual positioning in structural and intersectional arrangements. Thus, race and gender, and we add, class, appear in intersectional ways; that is, in fluid movement. In order to understand subordination, or harms of repression and reduction (Henry and Milovanovic, 1996), these articulations of instances must be addressed. Moreover, these intersections can be understood at different levels (e.g., Crenshaw, 1993, mentions structural, political and representational intersections).

For example, Russell (1998) has shown how subordination practices appear at the micro ("microaggressions") and macro ("macroaggressions") levels. At the microaggression level, perhaps the notion of "petit apartheid" is a case in point. Prior to official processing by the criminal justice system, many indignities are already being suffered by people of color, and these injustices are often cumulative. Postmodern analysis offers many conceptualizations of the subject (the interplay of imaginary and symbolic structures) and the relation of the subject to discourse which provide useful ways of discovering how forces of subordination are introjected, discovered, rejected, confronted, and changed.

At the macro level, consider Butler's (1996) analysis of hate speech in the "cross burning case" (*R.A.V. v. St. Paul*, 1992). In this instance, the Supreme Court was to engage in linguistic "reversals." Indeed, they cleansed the whole historical framework of cross burning from their decision and likened the proceedings to a freedom of speech case. Through metaphoric and metonymic discursive practices, the Court changed the inherent meaning of cross burning; however, by contrast, in the criminal case of the four police officers accused of beating Rodney King, the defendants were acquitted which, in turn, led to massive social unrest. Butler's (1996: 59) point is compelling: "the high Court might be understood in its decision of June 22, 1992, to be taking its revenge on Rodney King, protecting itself against the riots in Los Angeles and elsewhere which appeared to be attacking the system of justice itself." Matsuda and Lawrence (1993: 135) are in agreement: "the opinion [of the Court] proceeds as though we know nothing about the origins of the practice of cross burning or about the meaning that a burning cross carries both for those who use it and those whom it terrorizes." Thus, in this reversal, "The cross burners are portrayed as an unpopular minority that the Supreme Court must defend against the power of the state. The injury to the Jones family is appropriated and the cross burner is cast as the injured victim. The reality of ongoing racism and exclusion is erased and bigotry is redefined as majoritarian condemnation of racist views." In this reversal, "the Reagan-Bush judges are cast as the defenders for the down-trodden, the courageous upholders of the bill of rights" (*Ibid.:* 135). This reversal, this linguistic mockery of justice, can be made more visible by understanding the metaphoric and metonymic tropes at play. We submit that postmodern analysis offers much in this direction.

Critical race theory offers several suggestions for undoing the violence of legal language. Lawrence (1987), for example, has offered the idea of "unconscious racism" (relatedly, see Russell's notion of "microaggressions," 1996; and George-Abeyie's notion of "petit apartheid," 1990). He also recommends a "cultural meaning test" in law. First, reminiscent somewhat of the legal realists, he notes that the juridic notion of "intent" is insensitive to the "decision maker's beliefs, desires, and wishes" that often remain at the unconscious level (he makes use of the Freudian, not Lacanian form of psychoanalysis). He tells us: "certain actions, words, or signs may take on meaning within a particular culture as a result of the collective use of those actions, words, or signs to represent or express shared but repressed attitudes" (Lawrence, 1987: 356). Certainly the cross burning incident above is a case in point; however, it is one which the Court strategically avoided. Second, his "cultural meaning test" is offered as a way of bringing to heightened juridic scrutiny those symbolic messages embedded in governmental conduct. Thus, if the court, by a "preponderance of evidence" standard, determined "that a significant portion of the population thinks of the governmental action in racial terms, then it would presume that socially shared, unconscious racial attitudes made evident by the action's meaning had influenced the decision makers" (*Ibid.*). He also notes that "causal judgements" would not be central (i.e., where cause and effect relationships need to be "proven"); rather, an "interpretive judgement" would be critical because it "locates a particular phenomenon within a category of phenomena by specifying its meaning in the society within which it occurs" (*Ibid*: 361). According to Lawrence, cultural meaning entails this *interpretive* task, not causal ordering. He also provides some convincing case material to bring out this usage. This is echoed in Ewick and Silbey's notion of "subversive stories" (1995). Unlike "hegemonic tales" these narratives "recount particular experiences as *rooted* in and part of an encompassing cultural, material, and political world that extends beyond the local" (*Ibid*: 219).

Affirmative postmodern authors offer several supportive lines of inquiry: Barthes (how a writerly text disrupts hegemonic readings); Irigaray (how mimesis provides an elsewhere); Cornell (how subordination disrupted and changed into an affirmation; how the protection of the imaginary domain leads to beneficial utopian thinking; how an ethical feminism may develop); Lacan (how the notion of the Symbolic Order renders many "*pas-toute,*" not-all, and how it is overcome in myth, in *écriture féminine*; how the *discourse of the analyst* offers the development of new master signifiers which allow more critical narrative constructions); Deleuze and Guattari (how "minor literature," along with rhizomatic flows of desire undermine modernist linear reasoning and interpellation of the subject); and Henry and Milovanovic (how the "judo metaphor" reverses forces of domination; how replacement discourses might develop, 1996).

Finally, critical race theory also provides insights into the dilemma of the dialectics of struggle. As Matsuda tells us, "people of color cannot afford to indulge in deconstruction for its own sake" (1996: 24). Trashing law, for example, leaves the disenfranchised defenseless, without weapons with which to redress grievances.

Humanity and Society, Volume 24, Number 2, May 2000        188

It is here where critical race theory diverges from the early skeptical postmodern forms of analysis. In answering the question "how can the subaltern speak?" (Spivak, 1991), a critical analysis must take place on the notion of hegemony and reification in law. This is where affirmative postmodern analysis is very useful. Butler's (1991) notion of "contingent universalities" is instructive. Chaos' suggestion of "far-from-equilibrium conditions" (rather than static equilibrium societal conditions) where "dissipative structures" (rather than rigid bureaucracies are celebrated) prevail provides new insights, many of which seem to have been anticipated by Unger (1987). Cornell's (1991) warning against "hate politics" and "revenge politics," as well as the call against the early excesses of "reversal of hierarchies," are further cases in point.

In sum, critical race theory suggests that law can be used strategically as a weapon, but, at the same time, can be understood as an instrument of domination by powerful groups. Thus, it must be undermined and de-centered; stripped of its linguistically imbedded ideologies. Postmodern analysis brings to light how ideologies are indeed lodged in discourse, in linguistic coordinate systems (e.g., law), and how subjects are interpellated through the *discourse of the master* (Lacan). Finally, affirmative and integrative postmodern inquiry also offers possible directions by which new replacement discourses may begin to develop.

## Alternative Dispute Resolution

Similar to our critical sociolegal assessment of execution for the mentally ill and of critical race theory, the field of alternative dispute resolution (ADR) is equally well-suited for promoting affirmative and integrative postmodern praxis. We note that the existing ADR literature can be sub-divided into two divergent intellectual camps. Some observers advocate the dissemination of restorative justice programs that heal victims, communities, and offenders as a means of returning the nation (and the world) to a state of physical, emotional, and psychological health (e.g., Umbreit 1994, 1995; Galaway & Hudson 1996; Zehr 1990). Other commentators challenge the state's sophisticated techniques of disciplinary power and control legitimized through initiatives such as victim offender mediation (VOM) programs, "teen" courts, community justice boards, and the like. (e.g., Cohen 1988; Levrant, Cullen, Fulton, & Wozniak 1999; Harris 1989). The former perspective endorses more institutional or system-sustaining responses to the problems posed by crime and delinquency. The latter orientation questions the epistemological and criminological assumptions of any state-sponsored intervention.[27]

Regardless of intellectual approach, at the core of the ADR movement is a conviction that sustained *dialogue* between victims and offenders can be transformative and, ultimately, healing for mediation participants and the community of which both are a part. We agree. However, we also contend that an affirmative and integrative postmodern investigation demonstrates what the existing limits are to this anticipated emancipatory experience, while suggesting additional and discursive avenues for divergent expressions of agency and identity to be embodied in the overall VOM process.

Critics of alternative dispute resolution models draw attention to the disciplinary mechanisms at play in the social construction of speech situations (e.g., Pavilch, 1996; Cobb, 1997). Consistent with Barthes' (1973a, 1973b) literary analysis of reading texts, and Foucault's (e.g., 1971, 1973) archeological exploration of power as knowledge-truth, the discourse of VOM signifies an ossified text. It is characterized by key phenomenal forms or signs (e.g., "restoration," "reconciliation," and "restitution") that convey multiple meanings yet are reduced to certain, anchored representations regarding mediation, the mediation participants, and, thus, the discourse of crime and justice (Arrigo and Schehr, 1998: 636-639). This is what Barthes (1973a) intends when describing the "readerly approach" to sense making. For example, in his assessment of community mediation, Pavlich (1996: 728) demonstrates how the dialogical process is an extension of governmental authority designed to produce peaceful "individual selves." The discourse employed becomes an expression of state power endorsing and legitimizing only certain sign meanings about "legal rights" and "reconciliation" that, in effect, normalize individual identities (*Ibid*: 728-730).

While certainly suggestive of the power of discourse to "speak the subject" (Lacan, 1977), substantially missing from existing the ADR literature is a deeper exploration of unconscious linguistic forces activated and at work that define the parameters of acceptable speech, thought, and behavior in mediation sessions. In addition, questions remain about how the subject's unspoken identity and concealed being, relegated as an absence, lack, or *pas-toute* in discourse, can find expression and voice in the VOM process. In a larger context, consider also Collins (1999) who builds on Salecl's (1994) application of "surmise" in the Irish Peace Process, whereby fantasy (the Imaginary Order) plays an important role in the interpellation of the subject. According to Collins, political speech always is constituted by the intersections of the Imaginary and Symbolic with an excess, a lack, a remainder that escapes expression which may potentially undermine any lasting peace settlement.

A "writerly approach" (Barthes 1973a) to the text of VOM would resist the scripted and pre-configured sign meanings embedded in the activity of "settlement" and "reconciliation." This resistance is consistent with Deleuze and Guattari's (1983: 314) call for "deterritorialization [that] destroy[s prevailing] beliefs and [established] representations." It is also analogous to Foucault's (1986a, 1988) call for destabilizing strategies in which subjects cultivate multiple expressions of identity and sites of contestation.

One method of postmodern resistance that reveals the interplay of language in mediation practices is found in Derrida's (1976) deconstructive epistemology. Words and phrases such as "resolution," "reconciliation," "settlement," "restitution agreement," "healing," and "restorative justice" are constituted by and take on meaning through their binary oppositions. Thus, for example, the word "settlement" has meaning in relation to the term "disputation;" however, in the VOM process,

Humanity and Society, Volume 24, Number 2, May 2000                190

there is a "privileging" of the former value that masks, distorts, conceals, and/or otherwise dismisses the meaning of the latter value (Balkin, 1987: 748). This logocentrism (Derrida, 1976) silences the nuanced relationship the terms in binary opposition would otherwise share. Suppressing this relationship becomes the occasion for legitimizing, through speech, the currency of the first value position over and against the second value position within *multiple and divergent* contexts of human social interaction. What makes such silencing problematic is that all behavior and thought is then harnessed to be consistent with only hierarchical value terms. This unconscious process of (linguistic) coordination leads to the territorialization of desire (Deleuze and Guattari, 1987) and the homogenization of identity (Pavlich, 1996). Indeed, as Arrigo and Schehr (1998: 647) maintain in their analysis of juveniles processed through victim offender mediation programs,

> Th[e] choreography [of speech] is especially problematic for juveniles. They are made to conform to procedural and organizational strictures which *already* represent certain values about how to interact with others (i.e., their victims). Although not spoken, these rules are unconsciously organized to produce limited outcomes consistent with the linguistic coordinates of meaning representing the discourse of victim offender reconciliation. In other words, the flow of communication is pre-configured. It is designed to result in definable, self-referential outcomes. These outcomes are to be consistent with the language of restoration and reconciliation as ensured, as much as is possible, by the mediator who, by definition, only speaks to clarify, moderate, and reconcile.

Derrida's deconstructive methodology can also be integrated with Lacan's (1991) insights on the *discourse of the master*. The language of "restoration," "reconciliation,"and "restitution," as encoding the exchange of dialogue for mediation participants, constitutes the sphere of acceptable and appropriate VOM speech.[28] In other words, "the language that is invoked, when participants speak, becomes saturated with circumscribed parameters of meaning, consistent with the discourse of restoration" (Arrigo and Schehr, 1998: 648). Any communication falling outside this signifying sphere of meaning is reconstituted by the mediator whose essential task is to foster avenues for closure and consensus (Price, 1995:5).

   This move toward agreement and consensus in ADR strategies is also suggestive for affirmative and integrative postmodern praxis. What is lacking in VOM is the fluid space within which excluded and repressed voices can speak (Spivak, 1991). Lyotard's (1984) insistence on parology and *petit récit* (i.e., small narratives) Deleuze and Guattari's (1986) invocation of minor literatures, and Irigaray's (1985) notion of mimesis all indicate that closure, stasis, order, and predictability are not consistent with retrieving the *pas-toute* of the subject or

191                    Bruce A. Arrigo, Dragan Milovanovic, and Robert C. Schehr

cultivating transformative justice for society. Overcoming the discursive limits of VOM dialogue is possible and affirmative postmodern authors provide several provocative lines of analysis to substantiate this claim.

For example, chaos theory's position on dissipative structures, fractals, and far-from-equilibrium conditions (Baker, 1993) indicates that the natural flow of (mediation) dialogue necessarily includes inconsistencies, contradictions, absurdities, fuzzy logics, and other so-called anomalies of sense making. The orderly disorder (i.e., chaos) inherent in how participants speak "true words" (Freire, 1972) implies that mediation cannot proceed in a rigidly controlled, narrowly scripted, or tightly crafted context. To dismiss these occurrences is to deny mediation participants the fullness of their being and the richness of their humanity. Indeed, as Arrigo and Schehr (1998: 655) explain,

> During mediation sessions, youths and victims, in concert with the mediator, need to transcend the more formal strictures of restorative justice as expressed through the VOM dialogue. More than endorsing rigid parameters of meaning in which interaction is staged, discussion is stymied, resolution is forced, a fluid and dynamic process of reconciliation needs to unfold. It is within this spontaneous, unobtrusive experience that both the deconstructive and reconstructive effects of language and, therefore, of meaning possess their greatest likelihood for discovery and articulation. It is through this natural and unassuming enterprise, that new master signifiers can most likely be activated which more completely embody the de-centered subject's desire, thereby fostering alternative truths (knowledge-claims) about reconciliation and restorative justice.

In addition, however, we note several related themes of affirmative postmodern insight. Deleuze and Guattari's (1987) notion of the rhizome explains how ambulant, fragmented, and unpredictable lines of decision making can be encouraged such that nomadic struggle is affirmed and the realization of desire is stimulated. Barthes' (1973a) concept of the writerly text describes how undecidable readings can displace hegemonic meanings. Lacan's (1991) algorithm for the *discourse of the hysteric* linked to the *discourse of the analyst* depicts a process by which a replacement grammar about the self can be conceived and legitimized. Kristeva's (1984) semanalyis identifies how subversions, dislocations, and repressions of subjectivity can be called forth making possible alternative (poetic) texts of desire which heretofore were unspeakable. All of these strategies suggest novel investigatory approaches by which to understand the VOM process. Consistent with our interests in reclaiming the alienated subject and retrieving marginalized voices, these are constructive avenues that open up new pockets of opportunity for attending to conflict situations. These are provisional, positional, and relational interventions where "the feelings, [desires] and humanity of both victim and offender are respected" (Wright, 1991: 112). These are affirmative exemplars of postmodern transpraxis in which law, crime, and justice are transformed.

## CONCLUSIONS

More than being a heterodox and nihilistic intellectual fad, postmodern analysis significantly charts new directions for advancing law and society scholarship. The "first wave" French postmodern social theorists developed a robust collection of conceptual and methodological tools by which to ponder the nature of the universe, complex phenomena within it, and human social interaction. "Second wave" postmodern social theorists appropriated many of these insights, incorporating them into discipline-specific debates and/or applying them to content-based issues. Research in law, criminology, and social justice is replete with examples of this "second wave" tendency. Yet, there is still much more to do.

The next generation of postmodernists, building upon the legacy of the past, need to promote affirmative and integrative postmodern praxis. They need to demonstrate where and how sociolegal research can be transformative and emancipatory. They need to make possible the liberation of the subject in diverse institutional contexts. This is not a pessimistic, fatalistic, or nihilistic enterprise. Rather, it is a call to transcend the marginalizing limits of discourse and of coordinated language systems like the law. It is a challenge to insist that one's agency, identity, knowledge, and truth receive fuller, more complete legitimacy in state-sponsored criminal justice initiatives. It is an invitation to re-discover, through words, the emancipatory power that discursively resides within each of us. It is a commitment in principle that our existences, and all that it means to be with others through our life projects, always and already signify relationally, provisionally, and positionally.

### NOTES

[1]French postmodernism was fueled by many intersecting events: rapid economic modernization in the wake of World War II; new forms of mass culture, technology, consumerism, and urbanization that concealed psychological alienation and social oppression; the conceptual demise of Marxism, existentialism, and phenomenology and the intellectual birth of structuralism and post-structuralism; and several new theories about writing and discourse as developed by philosophers, psychoanalysts, and linguists of the infamous *Tel Quel* group. All of these events contributed to the riots of 1968, in which students and workers momentarily brought the political economy of France to a halt. Although short lived, the uproar of 1968 inaugurated a new historical epoch, a postmodern era, in which an epistemological shift was given life (Kellner and Best, 1991: 16-20).

[2]We recognize that not all the theoretical or applied research in law and criminology has been supportive of the postmodern enterprise. For example, Schwartz and Friedrichs (1994: 221-222) suggest that not only is this orientation outside the mainstream of legal and criminological thought but rests at the fringe of the critical tradition itself. In addition, Handler (1992) argues that discourse analysis, a component of postmodern conceptual inquiry, is not in any way theoretically based. "Rather, it is a method or process

193                    Bruce A. Arrigo, Dragan Milovanovic, and Robert C. Schehr

for raising questions and criticizing the presumptions of theory" (*Ibid.* 723). Our task in this article is not to directly challenge these and similar observations; rather, we wish to draw attention to where and how the more heterodox orientation of French postmodern social theory has been and can be significant for advancing our knowledge of law, crime, and justice.

[3]We realize that an appeal to language alone cannot overcome the forces of oppression and alienation that people confront. The limits of such an undertaking produce idealism and sentimentalism, absent an understanding of material conditions. We argue, however, that material conditions take on meaning through language and it is this language itself which is the source of considerable controversy. Indeed, as we demonstrate in a subsequent section exploring three pressing sociolegal topics, exposing the layered dimensions of marginalization is possible through an integrative and affirmative postmodern investigation. Thus, this article is designed to tease out the relationship between human agents and structural arrangements as they both shape and are shaped by language (Henry and Milovanovic, 1996: 185-243).

[4]We note that the ordering of the social theorists, accept for Jacques Lacan, is alphabetical. We explain our rationale for beginning with Lacan in note 5. Depending on one's scholarly orientation toward and intellectual proclivity for postmodern social theory, several ordering permutations could be suggested. Thus, for simplicity purposes, we adopted an alphabetical approach. Moreover, additional "first wave" French postmodernists contributing to our enterprise are certainly discernible (e.g., Moi, Bataille, Benveniste, Jakobson). Perhaps most significantly omitted in the pages that follow is the work of Helen Cixous (e.g., 1985, 1986, 1993). While Cixous' contributions considerably advance our knowledge of gender studies and human relationships (Sellers, 1994), there has yet to be any sustained sociolegal application of her work. This same logic regarding the selection process applies to other French postmodern social theorists whose insights might otherwise have been incorporated into this article.

[5] Many of the prominent social theorists of Lacan's era (including most of those described in this article) were known to have attended his lectures, to have been trained in the Lacanian tradition, and/or to have incorporated several of his formulations into their own conceptualizations. Lacan delivered a series of year-long Seminars in Paris in the 1950s until 1980. Lacan was to take the early Freud (1900-1920) and integrate and synthesize various theorists: Ferdinand de Saussure provided the theoretical statement for his non-referential semiotics; Kojeve offered the interpretations of Hegel's notion of desire; Benveniste specified the nature of the personal pronoun and how "I" is a shifter, a stand-in for the subject; Jakobson, through his studies on speech disorders, developed the idea that metaphor and metonymy are the two organizing principles of semiotic production; and Claude Levi-Strauss elaborated on the nature of the Symbolic Order. These integrations were the basis of his Seminars, most of which have yet to be translated into English; many still await even French publication (for a detailed application of Lacan's contributions in law, crime, and justice see, Milovanovic, 1997).

[6]As our subsequent assessment identifies, this insight can be extended to other disenfranchised people who, because they must engage in semiotic production in the dominant Symbolic Order, also remain *pas-toute*, not-all, incomplete (see sections on Irigaray and Kristeva for more).

[7]The early work of Barthes (e.g., 1973a, 1967, 1968a) was heavily influenced by existentialism. Thus, themes of autonomy, choice, and freedom-- all of which were anathema to the structuralist and post-structuralist enterprises– prevailed (Berman, 1988: 145). It was not until the publication of *On Racine* (1964), *Elements of Semiology* (1968b), and *S/Z* (1974) that Barthes substantially re-evaluated the form and structure of literary texts and the process of textual sense-making. He claimed that both author and the discourse of multiple readers fostered a "conflict" in interpretation. This insight was to form the basis for much of Barthes' subsequent literary criticism: an appraisal of classic books and novels that was to align him with much of the post-structural and semiotic thinking of his time.

[8]Best and Kellner (1991: 111) note that "Baudrillard's acolytes praise him as *the* 'talisman' of the new postmodern universe, as *the* commotion who theoretically energizes the postmodern scene, as *the* supertheorist of a new postmodernity." The trajectory of Jean Baudrillard's social theory has undergone several permutations significantly influencing cultural theory, media studies, and contemporary society

Humanity and Society, Volume 24, Number 2, May 2000 194

(Gane, 1991). These variations include: (1) a rejection of modernity's totalizing claims to truth, reason, and progress; (2) an effort to re-situate the categories of Marx within the consumerism of a postmodern society; (3) an unequivocal break from Marxist political economy rationales; and (4) a wholesale endorsement of such noted Baudrillardian concepts as "simulation", "hyper-reality", and "simulacrum." In this section we draw on Baudrillard's (1968, 1970, 1975, 1981, 1983a, 1983b) voluminous body of work to trace the evolution of his thought to date.

[9] Gottdiener (1995: 234) argues for the possibility of returning to "authentic cultural forms through the discovery of lost signifieds which counteract the superficial consumerist culture of postmodernism that privileges image, appearance, and disembodied signifiers." The concept of "lost signifieds" sounds question begging. This is similar in law to locating "original juridic positions" or the "original intent of the Constitution." Consistent with postmodernism, the question is from what contingent, local, and relational perspective do we engage in this search for original intent or lost signifieds? We contend that both notions seem to overlook the free play of the (legal) text. While our position is subject to debate, we suggest that Gottdiener's observations on lost signifieds might benefit from some additional conceptual refinement.

[10] Gilles Deleuze was trained as a philosopher and Felix Guattari was trained as a psychoanalyst in the Lacanian school. They began their joint projects in 1969, eventually publishing their first major collaboration: *Anti-Oedipus* (1983; orig. 1970). This was followed by *Kafka: Toward a Minor Literature* (1986; orig. 1975), and *A Thousand Plateaus* (1987; orig. 1980). Each is responsible for numerous independent works. In this section we specifically examine their collaborations only.

[11] As Best and Kellner (1991: 76) observe in their assessment of Deleuze and Guattari, "not only do [the theorists] not adopt the discourse of the postmodern.., [Guattari] even attacks it as a new wave of cynicism and conservatism...." Without question, however, the full force of Deleuze and Guattari's epistemology was a sustained rejection of order, unity, thesis, form, hierarchy, identity, and foundations. These are the cornerstones of modernist thought.

[12] As a cultural artifact, *A Thousand Plateaus* (1987) signifies a true postmodern presentation of deterritorialization. Chapters can be read in any order (with the exception of the Preface and Conclusion), and each draws on different time frames, topics, and points of emphasis. Unlike *Anti-Oedipus* (1983) where Deleuze and Guattari consistently apply the concept schizoanalysis, multiple metaphors are invoked to stimulate associations with ambulant, anti-essentialist, and fractured conceptualizations of a new politics of desire (i.e., rhizomatics, pragmatics, diagrammatism, cartography, micropolitics).

[13] More precisely, much of Derrida's (e.g., 1973, 1976, 1978, 1981, 1992) work represents a substantial critique of Western philosophy and thought (Culler, 1981: 92). This critique is linked to the convictions of post-structuralism (Berman, 1988) and the practice of deconstructionism (Culler, 1982). The former embraces incompleteness, fragmentation, uncertainty, different forms of consciousness, multiplicities of identities, and the instability of meaning (Best and Kellner: 20-1). The latter maintains that "the meaning of meaning is [of] infinite implication. [There is an] indefinite referral of signifier to signified....Its force is a certain pure and infinite equivocality which gives signified meaning no respite, no rest...it always signifies again and differs" (Derrida, 1973: 43).

[14] In an interview conducted in 1982 with Rux Martin, Foucault was asked how he identified himself. Was he a philosopher? A Marxist? Perhaps he was a structuralist? Or, maybe he was an historian? Foucault's response is illuminating. As he explains: "I don't feel that it is necessary to know exactly what I am. The main interest in life and work is to become someone else that you were not in the beginning. If you knew when you began a book what you would say at the end, do you think you would have the courage to write it? What is true for writing and for a love relationship is true also for life. The game is worthwhile insofar as we don't know what will be the end" (Martin, 1988: 9). From Foucault's (e.g., 1965, 1972, 1973, 1977) initial publications to those produced just prior to his death (e.g., 1980, 1986a, 1988), he charted an intellectual journey that found him, early in his career, establishing radical breaks with Enlightenment and modernist thought, only to appropriate aspects of each into his later work. It is this aspect of Foucault (i.e., his continued intellectual metamorphosis) that has spawned great confusion and criticism, as well as praise and admiration for the full body of his social theory.

195                          Bruce A. Arrigo, Dragan Milovanovic, and Robert C. Schehr

[15]Consider, for example, the domain of penology. Following Foucault's genealogy, the construction of subjugated bodies (i.e., docile bodies), means at each step in the correctional process subjects are placed under a mode of surveillance that is "effective" in its territorialization and regulation (e.g., body cavity searches during initial processing, motion and sound detectors while incarcerated, home detention and electronic monitoring once paroled). For the field of penology, as with other institutional formations in the general culture, the operative mode of social control is directed at promoting increased behavioral transformations through one's unconscious, *though spoken*, internalization of the techniques of control. The result of such peneological practices is a "carceral archipelago;" that is, the ever-expanding reach of state recognized and legitimized modes of social control. Foucault claimed that the inventive modes of punishment initially directed at inmates are also implemented in the culture as a whole. (e.g., the high-tech video surveillance equipment used at shopping malls, banks, and convenience stores; the metal detection devices employed at schools, airports, and courtrooms).

[16]Luce Irigaray, trained to be a psychoanalyst and holding doctorate degrees in linguistics and philosophy, has written extensively on feminism. Although she attended many of Lacan's Seminars in 1974, she was attacked by the Lacanian fashion because of her disagreements and reinterpretations of his psychoanalytic social theory. Feminism has had an uneasy alliance with Lacan: some embracing, some rejecting, some being seduced, some seducing, some seeing a necessity of taking a "tactical position" with his work (e.g., Grosz, 1990). This is apparent with Irigaray's work which draws from many of his key conceptualizations, yet distances itself from its rigid readings. See Irigaray (1985a, 1985b, 1993) for some of the more influential of her works on feminism and psychoanalysis. For an accessible overview of much of Irigaray's work see Whitford (1991).

[17]Kristeva, originally from Bulgaria, arrived in Paris in 1966. She attended Lacan's Seminars and completed and published her dissertation as *Revolution in Poetic Language* (1980; orig, 1974). She has written several Lacanian inspired, though revisionist, works focused on linguistics and psychoanalysis. Her work indicates how women are denied expression (following Lacan, *pas-toute*, not-all) in the dominant patriarchal order, but yet have access to a primordial place, the semiotic chora, which threatens disruptions in the conventional Symbolic Order (Kristeva, 1980, 1986). For an accessible overview of Kristeva's work see, Moi (1986).

[18]Lyotard wrote some 17 books over his lifetime. He passed away in 1998. In his *Peregrinations* (1988a), Lyotard tells us that he had wanted to be a monk, an historian, an artist, and a novelist. Eventually, he was to become a philosopher, but seemingly with these in tow. His first major book was *Discours, Figure* (1971) followed by *Libidinal Economy* (1974). Lyotard saw himself as having written three "real" books: *Discours, Figure, Economie Libidinale and Le Differend* (1988b). Along with *The Postmodern Condition* (1984), our comments on Lyotard are drawn from these seminal texts.

[19]As others have argued, we may also read Lacan prescriptively, offering the possibility of a more liberated form of desire in the idea of *jouissance* of the body, of the Other, an inexpressible and indescribable form of desire (see e.g., Milovanovic 1992, 1997).

[20]COREL sets (constitutive inter-relation sets) are historically constituted constellations of iterable loops demonstrating extreme sensitivity to environmental conditions (Henry and Milovanovic, 1996: 170-180).

[21]We note that our position is consistent with sociolegal scholars such as Sarat and Kearns (1992, 1996), Young and Sarat (1994), Sarat and Felstiner (1995), Ewick and Silbey (1995), and O'Barr (1982). They have shown how the language of law, in different contexts, produces certain effects, including the marginalization of various constituencies where resistance to the cultural power of the law is essential (Merry, 1995). What we suggest, however, is a deeper understanding of the sociological, psychological and symbolic dynamics activated and at work through the selection of words and expressions whose contents represent the perspective of some and silence or dismiss the perspective of others.

[22]For example, several meanings for the sign of mental illness include "sick," "crazy," "psychiatric survivor," "deficient," "mental health systems user," "mad," "troubled," "differently abled." These meanings convey various intents, values, and assumptions about persons identified as psychiatrically disordered; however, only certain values are selected out and are understood to represent the "true" or "real" meaning for the sign of mental illness. These "true" and "real" meanings can be subsequently

Humanity and Society, Volume 24, Number 2, May 2000                    196

linked to the interests of specific collectives invested in the sustained legitimacy of their particular values over and against others (for a detailed exploration of these matters in civil and criminal mental health law see e.g., Arrigo, 1993, 1996c).

[23]The text of executing the mentally ill is repeatedly simulated through conspicuously consumed mass mediated images (e.g., film documentaries chronicling the lives of mentally disordered offenders, news magazines describing the behavior of "crazed" sociopaths, television crime dramas exploring the thought processes of dangerous and psychotic killers). These images are the counterfeit of the real but become more factual than the reality upon which they are based. However, the more-real-than-real representations are themselves illusory. Form and substance, appearance and reality, counterfact and fact collapse and collide through simulations: meaning is conveyed through the pseudo sign values (i.e., simulacra) of the hypertext.

[24]In the *discourse of the master* speech is used (i.e., psycholegal discourse), consciously or unconsciously, in ways that oppress or marginalize individuals or groups (e.g., the psychiatrically disordered). Receivers or listeners of this speech (e.g., mentally ill offenders and/or their defense lawyers) respond by utilizing the same or similar speech responsible for victimization in language. Thus, they reconstitute and re-legitimize the very knowledge that oppresses.

[25]In the *discourse of the hysteric* the repressed subject (i.e., the psychiatrically disordered offender) seeks recognition and legitimacy, through discourse, on his or her own terms. The person offers words and phrases (i.e., replacement values and assumptions) that convey the subject's truth and experience about "mental illness," "execution," "dangerousness," "competency." The other (i.e., the psycholegal system and its agents) is not receptive to these alternative vocabularies of sense making because the established method of communicating permits only certain expressions consistent with the parameters of meaning constituting what is already defined as psychiatric justice.

[26]In the *discourse of the analyst* the despairing subject's truth and experience is validated by another (e.g., a social activist, an insurgent lawyer, a cultural revolutionary, Lacan's analyst) who begins to speak from the perspective of the alienated individual (i.e, the mentally disordered offender). The other attempts to expand and develop the subject's language and knowledge, mindful that "true words" (Freire, 1972) must be spoken. Thus, the other, searches for ways in which the subject's identity can be embodied in words that communicate his or her unique experiences and felt longing.

[27]Despite the obvious conceptual differences in approach to ADR practices as described above, numerous state legislatures have established restorative justice statutes with particular attention to meeting the demands of administering juvenile justice (Levrant, Cullen, Felton and Wozniak 1999). For example, Freivald (1996) identified 24 states that, by the close of 1995, instituted aspects of restorative justice (e.g., Vermont's reparative service boards, victim offender mediation, teen courts) through legislative decree. In addition, there are now more than 1,000 communities operating victim offender mediation programs (Umbreit, Coates, and Roberts 1997), and nearly 10,000 schools conducting teen courts (Kowalski 1998) throughout the United States.

[28]We note that in international conflict mediation, these same signifiers may be found but can more appropriately be recast as "human rights," "equality," "global democratization," and "sovereignty" (Schehr and Milovanovic, 1999).

## CASES CITED

*Ford v. Wainwright*, 477 U.S. 399 (1986).
*R.A.V. v. St. Paul*, 112 S. Ct. 2538 (1992).
*State v. Perry*, 620 SO. 2nd 746 (1992).
*Washington v. Harper*, 494 U.S. 210 (1990).

## REFERENCES

Agger. Ben (1991) "Critical Theory, Post-structuralism, Post-modernism: Their Sociological

197 Bruce A. Arrigo, Dragan Milovanovic, and Robert C. Schehr

Relevance. In W. R. Scott and J. Blake eds., *Annual Review of Sociology.* Palo Alto: Annual Reviews.

Arrigo, Bruce (1993) *Madness, Language, and the Law.* New York: Harrow and Heston.

Arrigo, Bruce (1995a) "(De)constructing Classroom Instruction: Theoretical and Methodological Contributions of the Postmodern Sciences for Crimino-Legal Education." 1 *Social Pathology* 113-148.

Arrigo, Bruce (1995b) "New Directions in Crime, Law, and Social Change: On Psychoanalytic Semiotics, Chaos Theory, and Postmodern Ethics." 33 *Studies in the Social Sciences* 101-129.

Arrigo, Bruce (1995c) "The Peripheral Core of Law and Criminology: On Postmodern Social Theory and Conceptual Integration." 12 *Justice Quarterly* 447-472.

Arrigo, Bruce (1996a) "The Behavior of Law and Psychiatry: Rethinking Knowledge Construction and the Guilty-But-Mentally-Ill Verdict." 23 *Criminal Justice and Behavior* 572-592.

Arrigo, Bruce (1996b) "Desire in the PsychiatricCourtroom: On Lacan and the dialectics of Linguistic Oppression." 16 *Current Perspectives in Social Theory* 159-187.

Arrigo, Bruce (1996c) *The Contours of Psychiatric Justice: A Postmodern Critique of Mental Illness, Criminal Insanity and the Law.* New York/London: Garland.

Arrigo, Bruce (1996d) "Media Madness as Crime in the Making: On O.J. Simpson, Consumerism, and Hyper-reality." In G. Barak, ed., *Representing O.J.: Murder, Criminal Justice, and Mass Culture*, New York: Harrow and Heston.

Arrigo, Bruce (1997a) "Insanity Defense Reform and the Sign of Abolition: Revisiting Montana's Experience." 29 *International Journal for the Semiotics of Law* 121-211.

Arrigo, Bruce (1997b) "Transcarceration: Notes on a Psychoanalytically Informed Theory of Social Practice in the Criminal Justice and Mental Health Systems." 27 *Crime, Law, and Social Change* 31-48.

Arrigo, Bruce (1998) "Reason and Desire in Legal Education: A Psychoanalytic Semiotic Critique." 31 *International Journal for the Semiotics of Law* 3-24.

Arrigo, Bruce (1999) "Martial Metaphors in Medical Justice: Implications for Law, Crime, and Deviance." *Journal of Political and Military Sociology* 27(2): 307-322.

Arrigo, Bruce & Robert Schehr (1998) "Restoring Justice for Juveniles: Toward a Critical Analysis of Victim Offender Mediation." 15 *Justice Quarterly* 629-666.

Arrigo, Bruce & T.R. Young (1998) "Theories of Crime and Crime of Theorists: On the Topological Construction of Criminological Reality." 8 *Theory and Psychology* 219-252.

Arrigo, Bruce & Christopher Williams (1999a) "Law, Ideology, and Critical Inquiry: The Case of Treatment Refusal for Incompetent Prisoners Awaiting Execution." 25 *New England Journal On Criminal and Civil Confinement* 367-412.

Arrigo, Bruce & Christopher Williams (1999b) "The (Im)possibility of Democratic Justice and the 'Gift' of the Majority: On Derrida, Deconstruction, and the Search for Equality." 16 *Journal of Contemporary Criminal Justice.*

Arrigo, Bruce & Christopher Williams (1999c) "Chaos Theory and the Social Control Thesis: A Post-Foucauldian Analysis of Mental Illness and Involuntary Civil Confinement." 26 *Social Justice* 177-207.

Ashe, Marie (1987) "Minds' Opportunity." 38 *Syracuse Law Review* 1129.

Ashe, Marie 1990 "The Doubly-Prized World: Myth, Allegory, and the Feminine." 75 *Cornell Law Review* 644-99.

Baker, P (1993) "Chaos, Order and Sociological Theory." 62 *Sociological Inquiry* 123-149.

Balkin, Jack M. (1987) "Deconstructive Practice and Legal Theory." 96 *Yale Law Journal* 743-786.

Barak, Greg and Stuart Henry (1999) "An Integrative-Constitutive Theory of Crime, Law, and Social Justice." In B. Arrigo, ed., *Social Justice/Criminal Justice: The Maturation of Critical Theory in Law, Crime, and Deviance.* Belmont, CA: West/Wadsworth.

Barak, Gregg. 1988. "Newsmaking Criminology." 5 *Justice Quarterly* 565-87.

Barak, Gregg (1998) *Integrating Criminologies.* Boston: Allyn and Bacon.

Barak, Gregg (1994) (Ed.). *Media, Process, and the Social Construction of Crime: Studies in Newsmaking Criminology.* New York: Garland.

Barthes, Roland. (1964) *On Racine.* New York: Hill and Wang.

Humanity and Society, Volume 24, Number 2, May 2000                198

Barthes, Roland (1967). *System de la Mode*. Paris: Seuil.

Barthes, Roland (1968a). *Writing Degree Zero*. New York: Hill and Wang.

Barthes, Roland (1968b). *Elements of Semiology*. New York: Hill and Wang

Barthes, Roland (1973a). *Mythologies*. England: Paladin.

Barthes, Roland (1973b). *The Pleasure of the Text*. New York: Hill and Wang.

Barthes, Roland (1974) *S/Z*. New York: Hill and Wang.

Barthes, Roland (1988) *The Semiotic Challenge*. New York: Hill and Wang.

Baudrillard, Jean (1968) *Le Systeme des Objets*. Paris: Denoel-Gonthier.

Baudrillard, Jean (1970) *La Societe de Consommation*. Paris: Gallimard.

Baudrillard, Jean (1981) *For a Critique of the Political Economy of the Sign*. St Louis: Telos Press.

Baudrillard, Jean (1983a). *Simulations*. New York: Semiotext(e).

Baudrillard, Jean (1983b). *In the Shadow of the Silent Majorities*. New York: Semiotext(e).

Bell, Vicki (1991) "Beyond the 'Thorny Question': Feminist, Foucault, and the Desexualization of Rape." 19 *International Journal of the Sociology of Law* 83-100.

Bell, Vicki (1993) *Interrogating Incest: Feminism, Foucault, and the Law*. London: Routledge.

Berman, Art (1988) *From the New Criticism To Deconstructionism: The Reception of Structuralism and Post-Structuralism*. Urbana, IL: University of Illinois Press.

Best, Steven (1989) "The Commodification of Reality and the Reality of Commodification: Jean Baudrillard and Postmodernism." 9 *Current Perspectives in Social Theory* 23-51.

Best, Steven & Douglas Kellner (1991) *Postmodern Theory: Critical Interrogations*. New York: Guilford Press.

Bogue, Ronald (1989) *Deleuze and Guattari*. New York: Routledge.

Bracher, Mark (1993) *Lacan, Discourse, and Social Change*. London: Cornell University Press.

Brion, Dennis (1991) "The Chaotic Law of Tort." In Roberta Kevelson, ed., *Peirce and Law*. New York: Peter Lang.

Butler, Judith (1990) *Gender Trouble*. New York: Routledge.

Butler, Judith (1993) *Bodies That Matter*. New York: Routledge.

Butler, Judith (1997a) *Excitable Speech*. New York: Routledge.

Butler, Judith (1997b) *The Psychic Life of Power*. Stanford, California: Stanford University Press.

Butler, Judith (1999) *Subjects of Desire*. New York: Columbia University Press.

Caputo, John, ed ., (1998) *Deconstruction in a Nutshell: A Conversation with Jacques Derrida*. New York: Fordham University Press.

Caudill, David (1997) *Lacan and the Subject of Law*. Atlantic Highland, NJ: Humanities Press.

Cixous, Helene (1985) *Angst*. Jo Levy (trans.). London: John Calder.

Cixous, Helene (1986) *The Newly Born Woman*. Betsy Wing (trans.). Minneapolis, MN: University of Minnesota Press.

Cixous, Helene (1993). *Three Steps on the Ladder of Writing*. Catherine MacGillivray (trans). Minneapolis, MN: University of Minnesota Press.

Cobb, Sara (1997) "The "Domestication of Violence in Mediation." 31 *Law and Society Review* 397-440.

Cohen, Stanley (1979) "The Punitive City: Notes of the Dispersal of Social Control." 3 *Contemporary Crisis* 339-363.

Cohen, Stanley (1988) *Visions of Social Control: Crime, Punishment, and Classification*. Cambridge: Polity Press.

Collins, Barry (199) "Where Have All the Canaries Gone?" 34 *International Journal for the Semiotics of Law*.

Collins, Patricia (1993) "Toward a New Vision: Race, Class, and Gender as Categories of Analysis and Connection." 1 *Race, Sex and Class* 25- 45.

Conklin, William (1998) *The Phenomenology of Modern Legal Discourse*. Aldershot, England: Dartmouth Publishing Company.

Cornell, Drucilla (1991) *Beyond Accommodation: Ethical Feminism, Deconstruction, and the Law*. New York: Routledge.

Cornell, Drucilla (1992) "The Philosophy of the Limit: System Theory and Feminist Legal Reform." In D.Cornell, M. Rosenfeld, and D. Carlson, eds., *Deconstruction and the Possibility of Justice*. New York: Routledge.

199                    Bruce A. Arrigo, Dragan Milovanovic, and Robert C. Schehr

Cornell, Drucilla (1998) *At the Heart of Freedom*. Princeton, N.J.: Princeton University Press.
Cornell, Drucilla., M. Rosenfeld, and D. Carlson, eds., (1992) *Deconstruction and the Possibility of Justice*. New York: Routledge.
Couzens, David H., ed. (1992) *Foucault: A Critical Reader*. New York: Basil Blackwell.
Crenshaw, Kimberle (1989) "Demarginalizing the Intersection of Race and Sex: A Black Feminist Critique of Antidiscrimination Doctrine." *University of Chicago Legal Forum*, 139-167.
Crenshaw, Kimberle (1993) "Beyond Racism and Misogyny: Black Feminism and 2 Live Crew." In Matsuda et al, eds., *Words That Wound*. San Francisco: Westview Press.
Culler, Johnathan (1975) *Structural Poetics*. Ithaca, NY: Cornell University Press.
Culler, Johnathan (1981) *The Pursuit of Signs: Semiotics, Literature, and Deconstruction*. Ithaca, NY: Cornell University Press.
Culler, Johnathan (1982). *On Deconstruction*. Ithaca: Cornell University Press.
Currie, Dawn, Brian MacLean, & Dragan Milovanovic (1991) "Three Traditions of Critical Justice Inquiry: Class Gender and Discourse." In Dawn Currie & Brian MacLean, eds., *Re-Thinking the Administration of Justice*. Halifax, Nova Scotia: Fernwood.
Deleuze, Gilles (1983) *Nietzsche and Philosophy*. New York: Columbia University Press.
Deleuze, Gilles & Felix Guattari (1983) *Anti-Oedipus*. Minneapolis: University of Minnesota Press.
Deleuze, Gilles & Felix Guattari (1986) *Kafka: Toward a Minor Literature*. Minneapolis: University of Minnesota Press.
Deleuze, Gilles & Felix Guattari (1987) *A Thousand Plateaus*. Minneapolis: University of Minnesota Press.
Derrida, Jacques (1973) *Speech and Other Phenomena*. Evanston, IL: Northwestern University Press.
Derrida, Jacques (1976) *Of Grammatology*. Baltimore, MD: Johns Hopkins University Press.
Derrida, Jacques (1978) *Writing and Difference*. Chicago, IL: University of Chicago Press.
Derrida, Jacques (1981) *Positions*. Chicago, IL: University of Chicago Press.
Derrida, Jacques (1992) "Force of Law: The Mystical Foundation of Authority." In D. Cornell, M. Rosenfeld, & D. Carlson, eds., *Deconstruction and the Possibility of Justice*. New York: Routledge.
Derrida, Jacques (1997) "The Villanova Roundtable." In J. Caputo, ed., *Deconstruction in a Nutshell: A Conversation with Jacques Derrida*. New York: Fordham University Press.
Dreyfus, Harold & Paul Rabinow (1982) *Michel Foucault: Beyond Structuralism and Hermeneutics*. Chicago: University of Chicago Press.
Einstadter, Werner & Stuart Henry (1996) *Criminological Theory*. Fort Worth, TX: Harcourt Brace.
Ewick, Patricia & Susan S. Silbey (1995) "Subversive Stories and Hegemonic Tales: Toward a Sociology of Narrative." 29 *Law and society Review* 197-226.
Farnsworth, Margaret (1989) "Theory Integration Versus Model Building." In Stephen Messner, Marvin Krohn, and Allen Liska, eds., *Theoretical Integrations in the Study of Deviance and Crime*. Albany, NY: State University of New York Press.
Ferguson, Margaret & Jennifer Wicke (Eds.) (1994) *Feminism and Postmodernism*. London: Duke University Press.
Ferrell, Jeff, Dragan, Milovanovic, & Steven Lyng (1998) "Base Jumping, Media Practices, and the Elongation of Meaning." Paper presented at the Annual Meeting of the American Society of Criminology, Washington D.C.
Forker, Allison (1997) "Chaos and Modelling Crime." In Dragan Milovanovic, ed., *Chaos, Criminology and Social Justice*. Westport, CT.: Praeger.
Foucault, Michel (1965) *Madness and Civilization*. New York: Vintage.
Foucault, Michel (1972) *Archeology of Knowledge*. New York: Pantheon.
Foucault, Michel (1973) *The Order of Things*. New York: Vintage.
Foucault, Michel (1977) *Discipline and Punish*. New York: Pantheon.
Foucault, Michel (1980) *History of Sexuality, Vol 1: An Introduction*. London: Allen Lane.
Foucault, Michel (1986a) *Use of Pleasure*. New York: Vintage.
Foucault, Michel (1986b) "Of Other Spaces." 16 *Diacritics* 22-27.
Foucault, Michel (1988). *The Care of the Self*. New York: Vintage.
Freire, Paulo (1972) *Pedagogy of the Oppressed*. South Hadley, MA: Herder and Her.
Freivalds, P. (1996) "Balanced and Restorative Justice Project." *Office of Juvenile Justice and*

Humanity and Society, Volume 24, Number 2, May 2000                    200

*Delinquency Fact Sheet* (July).

Fuchs, Stephan & Steven Ward (1994) "What is Deconstruction, and Where and When Does It Take Place: Making Facts in Science, Building Cases in Law." 59 *American Sociological Review*, 481-503.

Galaway, Brian. & J. Hudson (1996) *Restorative Justice: International Perspectives*. Monsey, NY: Criminal Justice Press.

Gane, Michael (1991). *Baudrillard: Critical and Fatal Theory*. New York: Routledge.

Garland, David (1990)*Punishment and Modern Society*. Oxford: Clarendon Press.

Georges-Abeyie, Daniel (1990). "The Myth of a Racist Criminal Justice System?" In Brian MacLean and Dragan Milovanovic, eds.,*Racism, Empiricism and Criminal Justice*, Vancouver: Collective Press.

Gibbons, Don (1994) *Talking About Crime and Criminals*. Englewood Cliffs, NJ: Prentice-Hall

Giroux, H. (1992) *Border Crossings*. New York: Routledge.

Goodrich, Peter (1990) *Languages of Law*. London. Weidenfeld and Nicolson.

Gottdiener, Mark (1995) *Postmodern Semiotics*. Oxford, UK: Blackwell.

Grbich, Judith (1996) "The Taxpayer's Body." In Pheng Cheah, David Fraser and Judith Grbich, eds., *Thinking Through the Body of Law*. New York: New York University Press.

Grosz, Elizabeth (1990) *Jacques Lacan: A Feminist Introduction*. New York: Routledge.

Habermas, Jorgen (1984, 1987) *Theory of Communicative Action, Volumes 1 and 2*. Boston: Beacon press.

Halper, Louise (1995) "Tropes of Anxiety and Desire: Metaphor and Metonymy in the Law of Takings." 8 *Yale Journal of Law and the Humanities* 1-101.

Handler, Joel (1992) "The Presidential Address, 1992 Law and Society: "Post modernism, Protest, and the New Social Movement." 26 *Law and Society Review*, 697-731.

Harris, Angela (1991). "Race and Essentialism in Feminist Legal Theory." In Katharine Bartlett and Rosanne Kennedy, eds., *Feminist Legal Theory*. Oxford: Westview Press.

Harris, M. Kay (1989) "Alternative Visions in the Context of Contemporary Realities." In *New Perspectives on Crime and Justice: Occasional Papers of the MCC Canada Victim Offender Ministries Program and the MCC U.S. Office of Criminal Justice*, Issue 7. Elkhart, IN: Mennonite Central Committee U.S. Office of Criminal Justice.

Hayles, Katherine (1990) *Chaos Bound: Orderly Disorder in Contemporary Literature and Science*. London: Cornell University Press.

Henry, Stuart, & Mark Lanier (1998) "The Prism of Crime: Arguments for an Integrated Definition of Crime." *Justice Quarterly* 609-629.

Henry, Stuart & Dragan Milovanovic (1996) *Constitutive Criminology: Beyond Postmodernism*. London: Sage.

Hooks, Bell (1990) *Yearning: Race, Gender, and Cultural Politics*. Boston: South End Press.

Howe, Adrian (1994) *Punish and Critique: Towards a Feminist analysis of Penality*. London: Routledge.

Hunt, Alan & Gary Wickham (1995) *Foucault and the Law: Towards a Sociology of Law as Governance*. New York: Pluto Press.

Irigaray, Luce (1985) *This Sex Which is Not One*. Ithaca, New York: Cornell University Press.

Irigaray, Luce (1993) *Je, Tu, Nous*. New York: Routledge.

JanMohamed, A.R. (1994) "Some Implications of Paulo Freire's Border Pedagogy. In H. Giroux and P. MacLaren, eds., *Between Borders*. New York: Routledge.

Kairys, David, ed., (1982) *The Politics of Law: A Progressive Critique*. New York: Pantheon Books.

Kelman, Mark (1987) *A Guide to Critical Legal Studies*. Cambridge, Mass: Harvard University Press.

Kellner, Douglas (1989) *Jean Baudrillard: From Marxism to Postmodernism and Beyond*. Cambridge: Polity Press.

Kevelson, Roberta (1988) *The Law as a System of Signs*. New York: Plenum.

Kowalski, K (1998) "Peer Mediation Success Stories: In Nearly 10,000 Schools Nationwide, Peer Mediation Helps Teens Solve Problems Without Violence." 25 *Current Health* 13.

Kristeva, Julia (1980) *Desire in Language* New York: Columbia University Press.

Kristeva, Julia (1986) *Revolution in Poetic Language* New York: Columbia University Press.

Lacan, Jacques (1977) *Ecrits: A Selection* (A. Sheridan Trans.). New York: Norton.

201                          Bruce A. Arrigo, Dragan Milovanovic, and Robert C. Schehr

Lacan, Jacques (1981) *The Four Fundamental Concepts of Psychoanalysis*. New York: Norton.
Lacan, Jacques (1985) *Feminine Sexuality*. New York: W.W. Norton and Pantheon.
Lacan, Jacques (1988) *The Seminars of Jacques Lacan, Book 2: The Ego in Freud's Theory and in the Techniques of Psychoanalysis, 1954-55*. Cambridge: Cambridge University Press.
Lacan, Jacques (1991) *L'envers de la Psychanalyse*. Paris: Editions du Seuil.
Laclau, Ernesto (1996) *Emancipations*. London: Verso.
Laclau, Ernesto & Chantal Mouffe (1985) *Hegemony and Socialist Strategy*. London: Verso.
Lash, Scott & John Urry (1994) *Economies of Signs and Space*. London: Sage
Lawrence, Charles (1987) "The Id, Ego, and Equal Protection: Reckoning with Unconscious Racism." 39 *Stanford Law Review* 317-388.
Legendre, Pierre (1996) "Id Efficeit, Quad Figurat (It is the Symbol Which Produces Effects)." 20 *Legal Studies Forum* 247-263.
Lem, Stanislaw (1981) "Metafantasia." 8 *Science-Fiction Studies* 54-71.
Leverant, S., F. Cullen, B. Fulton, and J. Wozniak (1999) "Reconsidering Restorative Justice: The Corruption of Benevolence Revisited?" 45 *Crime and Delinquency* (1).
Lippens, Ronnie (1995) "Critical Criminologies and the Reconstruction of Utopia." 22 *Social Justice* 32-50.
Lippens, Ronnie (1997) Border-Crossing Criminology. 2 *Theoretical Criminology* 119-151.
Lippens, Ronnie (1998a) "Hypermodernity, Nomadic Subjectivities, and Radical Democracy: Roads Through Ambivalent Clues." 24 *Social Justice* 16-43.
Lippens, Ronnie (1998b) "Hybrid Hopes Ltd.: Reflections on Hybrid Hopes for Rhizologists." 22 *Humanity and Society* 386-410.
Lippens, Ronnie (1998c) "Alternatives to What Kind of Suffering?: Toward a Border-Crossing Criminology."3 *Theoretical Criminology* 311-343.
Lippens, Ronnie (1999) "Into Hybrid Marshlands: Thirdspatial Notes on Postcolonial Theory and Feminist Legal Theory." 34 *International Journal for      the Semiotics of Law* (forthcoming).
Litowitz, Douglas (1997) *Postmodern Philosophy and Law*. Lawrence, Kansas: University Press of Kansas.
Lyotard, Jean-Francois (1971) *Discourse, figure*. Paris: Klincksieck.
Lyotard, Jean-Francois (1974) *Economie Libidinale*. Paris: Minuit.
Lyotard, Jean-Francois (1984) *The Postmodern Condition*. Minneapolis: University of Minnesota Press.
Lyotard, Jean-Francois (1988a) *Perigrinations*. New York: Columbia University Press.
Lyotard, Jean-Francois (1988b) *The Differend*. Minneapolis: University of Minnesota Press.
Martin, Rux (1988) "Truth, Power, Self: An Interview With Michel Foucault." In L. Martin, H. Gutman, & P. Hutton, eds., *Technologies of the Self*. MA: University of Massachusetts Press.
Matsuda, Mari (1990) "Pragmatism Modified and the False Consciousness Problem." 63 *Southern California Law Review* 1763-1782.
Matsuda, Mari (1996) *Where is Your Body*. Boston: Beacon Press.
Matsuda, Mari, Charles Lawrence, Richard Delgado, and Kimberle Crenshaw (1993) *Words That Wound: Critical Race Theory, Assaultive Speech, and the First Amendment*. San Francisco: Westview Press.
Matsuda, Mari & Charles Lawrence (1993) "Epilogue: Burning Crosses and the R.A.V. Case." In Matsuda et al, eds., *Words That Wound*. San Francisco: Westview Press.
Merry Sally Engle (1995) "Resistance and the Cultural Power of Law." 29 *Law and Society Review* 11-26.
Moi, Toril (1985) *Sexual/Textual Politics* London: Methuen.
Moi, Toril (Ed.) (1990) *The Kristeva Reader*. New York: Columbia University Press.
Moi, Toril (1988) *Peregrinations*. New York: Columbia University Press.
Milovanovic, Dragan (1992) *Postmodern Law and Disorder*. Merseyside, UK: Deborah Charles Publications.
Milovanovic, Dragan (1995) "Dueling Paradigms: Modernist versus Postmodernist Thought." 19 *Humanity and Society* 19-44.

Humanity and Society, Volume 24, Number 2, May 2000 202

Milovanovic, Dragan (1996a) "'Rebellious Lawyering.'" 20 *Legal Studies Forum* 295-322.
Milovanovic, Dragan (1996b) "Postmodern Criminology: Mapping the Terrain." 13 *Justice Quarterly* 567-609.
Milovanovic, Dragan (1997) *Postmodern Criminology*. New York: Garland.
Milovanovic, Dragan (1999) "Catastrophe Theory, Discourse, and Conflict Regulation." In Bruce Arrigo, ed., *Social Justice/Criminal Justice*. Belmont, CA: Wadsworth.
Mouffe, Chantal (1992). "Feminism, Citizenship and Radical Democratic Politics." In Judith Butler and Joan Scott, eds., *Feminists Theorize the Political*. New York: Routledge.
Naffine, Ngaire (1996) *Feminism and Criminology*. Philadelphia: Temple University Press.
O'Barr, William M. (1982) *Linguistic Evidence: Language, Power, and Strategy in the Courtroom*. San Diego, CA: Academic Press.
Palmer, B.D (1990) *Descent into Discourse: The Reification of Language and the Writing of Social History*. Philadelphia, PA: Temple University Press.
Pavlich, George (1996). "The Power of Community Mediation: Government and Formation of Self-identity." 30 *Law and Society Review* 30 707-733.
Pavlich, George (1999) "Criticism and Criminology." 3 *Theoretical Criminology* 29-51.
Pfohl, Stephen (1993) "Twilight of the Parasites: Ultramodern Capital and the New World Order." 40 *Social Problems* 125-151.
Poster, Mark, ed., (1988) *Jean Baudrillard: Selected Writings*. Stanford: Stanford University Press.
Price, Mark (1995) "Comparing Victim Offender Mediation Program Models." 6 *Victim Offender Mediation Journal* 1-6.
Quinney, Richard (1977) *Class, State, and Crime*. NY: David Mackay.
Rorty, Richard (1978) "Philosophy as a Kind of Writing: An Essay on Derrida." 10 *New Literary History* 141-157.
Russell, Katheryn (1998). *The Color of Crime*. New York: New York University Press.
Russell, S. (1986) "The Critical Legal Studies Challenge to Contemporary Mainstream Legal Philosophy." 18 *Ottawa Law Review* 1-24.
Salecl, Renata (1994) *The Spoils of Freedom*. New York: Routledge.
Sarat, Austin D. (1993) "Speaking of Death." 27 *Law and Society Review* 19-58.
Sarat, Austin D. & Thomas R. Kearns (1992) *Law's Violence*. Ann Arbor, Michigan: Michigan University Press.
Sarat, Austin D. & Thomas R. Kearns (1996) *The Rhetoric of Law*. Ann Arbor, Michigan: Michigan University Press.
Sarat, Austin D. & William L. Felstiner (1995) *Divorce Lawyers and Their Clients: Power and Meaning in the Legal Process*. New York: Oxford University Press.
Sarup, Michael (1989) *An Introductory Guide to Post-Structuralism and POSTMODERNISM*. Athens, GA: University of Georgia Press.
Schehr, Robert (1996) *Dynamic Utopia*. Westport, CT: Praeger.
Schehr, Robert (1997) "Surfing the Chaotic." In Dragan Milovanovic (ed.) *Chaos, Criminology and Social Justice*. Westport, CT.: Praeger.
Schehr, Robert & Dragan Milovanovic. 1999. "Conflict Mediation and the Postmodern." 25 *Social Justice*.
Scheppele, K. L. (1987) "The Revisioning of Rape Law." 54 *University of Chicago Law Review* 1095-1116.
Schroeder, Jeanne (1995) "The Vestal and the Fasces." 16 *Cardoza Law Review* 805.
Schulman, Caren (1997) "Chaos, Law, and Critical Legal Studies." In Dragan Milovanovic, ed., *Chaos, Criminology and Social Justice*. Westport, CT.: Praeger.
Schwartz, Martin & David O. Friedrichs (1994) "Postmodern Thought and Criminological Discontent: New Metaphors for Understanding Violence." 32 *Criminology* 221-246.
Sellers, Susan (1994) *The Helene Cixous Reader*. New York: Routledge.
Shepherdson, Charles (1996) "The Concept of Race." 1 *Journal for the Psychoanalysis of Culture and Society* 173-178.
Silbey, Susan (1996) "'Let Them Eat Cake': Globalization, Postmodern Colonialism, and the Possibility of Justice." 31 *Law and Society Review* 207-235.
Slaughter, Marty (1995) "Fantasies: Single Mothers and Welfare Reform." 95 *Columbia Law Review*

203                          Bruce A. Arrigo, Dragan Milovanovic, and Robert C. Schehr

301.

Smart, Carol (1989) *Feminism and the Power of the Law*. London/New York: Routledge.

Spivak, G. (1991) "Can the Subaltern Speak" In C. Nelson and L. Grossberg, eds., *Marxism and the Interpretation of Culture*. London: Macmillan.

Stacey, Helen (1996) "Lacan's Split Subjects." 20 *Legal Studies Forum* 277-294.

Stanford Law School (1984) Critical Legal Studies Symposium.36 *Stanford Law Review*, 1-674.

Stanley, Christopher (1996) *Urban Excesses and the Law*. Wharton Street, London: Cavendish Publishing.

Steward, I. (1989) *Does God Play Dice?* New York: Blackwell.

Thorton, M. (1986) "Feminist Jurisprudence: Illusion or Reality?"3 *Australian Journal of Law and Society* 5-29.

Tiefenbrun, Susan (1986) "Legal Semiotics." 5 *Cardozo Arts and Entertainment Law Review* 89-156.

Tushnet, M (1986) "Critical Legal Studies: An Introduction to Its Origins and Underpinnings." 36 *Journal of Legal Education* 505-517.

Umbreit, Mark (1994) *Victim Meets Offender*. Monsey, NY: Criminal Justice Press.

Umbreit, Mark (1995) *Mediating Interpersonal Conflicts*. West Concord, MN: CPI Publishing.

Umbreit, Mark, R. Coates, & A. Roberts (1997) "Cross National Impact of Restorative Justice Through Mediation and Dialogue." 8 *The ICCA Journal of Community Corrections* 46-50.

Unger, Roberto (1986) *The Critical Legal Studies Movement*. Cambridge, Mass: Harvard.University Press.

Unger, Roberto (1987) *False Necessity*. New York: Cambridge University Press.

Velan, Y. (1972). "Barthes." In J. Simon, ed., *Modern French Criticism*. Chicago: University of Chicago Press.

Whitford, Margaret (1991) *Luce Irigaray: Philosophy in the Feminine*. London/New York: Routledge.

Wijeyeratne, Roshan D. (1998) "Deconstruction, Semiotics and Justice." 31 *International Journal for the Semiotics of Law* 105-112.

Williams, Christopher (1998) "Inside the Outside and Outside the Inside: Negative Fusion From the Margins of Humanity." 23 *Humanity and Society* 49-67.

Williams, Christopher & Bruce Arrigo (2000). "Anarchaos and Order: On the Emergence of Social Justice," 4(1) *Theoretical Criminology*.

Williams, Joan (1991). "Deconstructing Gender." In Katharine Bartlett and Rosanne Kennedy, eds., *Feminist Legal Theory*. Oxford: Westview Press.

Willis, S. (1991). *A Primer for Daily Life*. New York: Routledge.

Winick, Bruce(1992) "Competency to be Executed: A Therapeutic Jurisprudence Perspective." 10 *Behavioral Sciences and the Law* 317-338.

Winick, Bruce (1997) *The Right to Refuse Mental Health Treatment*. Washington, DC: American Psychological Association.

Woodhull, Winifred (1988) "Sexuality, Power, and the Question of Rape." In I. Diamond and I. Quinby , ed., *Feminism and Foucault: Reflections on Resistance*. Boston: Northeastern University Press.

Young, Allison (1996) *Imagining Crime*. London: Sage.

Young, Alison & Austin D. Sarat (1994) "Beyond Criticism: Law, Power, and Ethics," 3 *Social and Legal Studies* 323-331.

Young, Iris (1990) *Justice and the Politics of Difference* Princeton, NJ: Princeton University Press.

Young, R. (1995) *Colonial Desire: Hybridity in Theory, Culture, and Race*. London: Routledge.

Young, T.R. (1992) "Chaos Theory and Human Agency." 16 *Humanity and Society* 441-60.

Young, T.R. (1997) "The ABCs of Crime." Dragan Milovanovic, ed.,. *Chaos, Criminology and Social Justice*. Westport, Connecticut: Praeger.

Young, T.R. (1999) "A nonlinear theory of justice: Affirmative moments in postmodern criminology." In B.A., ed., *Social Justice/Criminal Justice: The Maturation of Critical Theory in Law, Crime, and Deviance*. Belmont, CA: West/Wadsworth.

Zehr, Howard (1990) *Changing Lenses*. Scottsdale, PA: Herald Press.

# Part II
# Critical Applications in Law, Crime, Justice and Social Change

# [5]

## NOME LAW: DELEUZE & GUATTARI
## ON THE EMERGENCE OF LAW

JAMIE MURRAY

ABSTRACT. This article orientates Deleuze & Guattari's pragmatic semiotics towards a semiotics of law. This pragmatic semiotics is explored, and directly related to the theory of emergence and complexity that is also a key feature of Deleuze & Guattari's work. It is suggested that the development of these aspects of Deleuze & Guattari's thought in relation to law allows the contours of a noological legal theory to be sketched out. Noology is the study of images of thought, their emergence, their genealogy, and their creation. A first exploration of this noological legal theory is then carried out by the conceptualisation of nome law as the first emergence of law as theorised by Deleuze & Guattari in the plateau "1837: Of the Refrain" from "A Thousand Plateaus". This is a conceptualisation of law's emergence in a far-from-equilibrium palaeolithic hunter-gatherer pack, and contrasts to accounts of law's origin in a founding violence or mythical contract. It is the 'big bang' of legality, and the opening up of a first image of legality, problematic of social organisation, and anthropomorphic knowledge space.

"A musical 'nome' is a little tune, a melodic formula that seeks recognition and remains the bedrock or ground of polyphony (cantus firmus). The nomos as customary, unwritten law is inseparable from a distribution of space, a distribution in space."[1]

## 1. INTRODUCTION

This article turns to the pragmatic semiotics of Deleuze & Guattari in order to orientate it for a semiotics of law. In "A Thousand Plateaus" Deleuze & Guattari develop a semiotic of regimes of signs that draws upon non-linguistic machinic processes and that goes beyond any general semiology. This semiotic is developed with generative, transformational, diagrammatic, and machinic components, and incorporates a conception of social machines. The discussion of this pragmatic semiotics is then set within the theory of emergence and complexity that is also a key feature of Deleuze &

---

[1] Gilles Deleuze and Felix Guattari, *A Thousand Plateaus* (Continuum Press, 1988), p. 312.

Guattari's work. Deleuze & Guattari's ontological modality of the virtual-intensive-actual and their theorisation of processes of terri-torialisation–deterritorialisation imbue their work with a very sophisticated philosophical discussion of order-out-of chaos, emer-gence, self-organisation and complexity. The ramifications of devel-oping Deleuze & Guattari's work in the general field of the semiotics of law lie with these two features of their work. Their pragmatic semiotics leads the semiotic study of law away from linguistics, the signifier, textuality, and deconstruction, towards an expanded material field of forces where meaning and law are effects of emergent and self-organising immanent processes.

With these two aspects of Deleuze & Guattari's work, the article will suggest that it is possible to sketch out not only a Deleuze & Guattari semiotics of law but also a Deleuze & Guattari noological theory of law, of which the semiotics is just a very important part. Noology is the study of images of thought, of their emergence, and of their historical development in social institutions and semiotic regimes. A noological legal theory does this for images of legality. A first exploration of a noological theorisation of law is then put forward in the construction of Deleuze & Guattari's account of the first emergence of legality and the development of the concept of nome law.

In plateaus of "A Thousand Plateaus", particularly "1837: Of the Refrain", Deleuze & Guattari theorise the first opening up of the brain to the virtual, a first opening up of the problem space of social organisation, a first image of legality, and a first social machine. For them this point emerges with a child wandering across a deterritorialised savannah breaking into a first, faltering, little tune: a refrain. The concept nome law theorises this first emergence of an image of legality and of a social machine, and is developed in terms of a pragmatic semiotics of a regime of signs. In this account of law's first emergence and in the concept nome law there is a theorisation of the emergent nature of law in marked contrast to accounts of its origin and nature in a founding violence or mythical contract. Indeed, this emergence of nome law is theor-ised as the 'big bang' of legality: all later legalities are virtually present in nome law, to be explicated by emergent and mutating subsequent social machines. Thus, a noological legal theory of nome law provides a theory of emergent law, and the ontological basis and semiotics for interrogating all other images of legality, their bifurcations from nome law, and their subsequent institutional histories and semiotic developments.

## 2. DELEUZE & GUATTARI'S SEMIOTIC

For Deleuze & Guattari, a semiotic system is approached as a regime of signs and a specific formalisation of expression.[2] Their semiotic, however, is a pragmatic semiotic in which language does not have a universality in itself and in which non-linguistic processes and components play a crucial role. Semiotic systems are understood to be always in reciprocal presupposition with material regimes, and to be part of assemblages. Accordingly, there is a distinct semiotic system for any given assemblage, and there is, therefore, a real diversity of semiotic systems. This insight accounts for the hostility in their semiotic to the semiology of the signifier. The diversity of semiotic systems is theorised in terms of a primitive pre-signifying regime associated with tribal social assemblages, a signifying imperial regime associated with despotic State social machines, a counter-signifying regime linked to nomadic social formations, and a post-signifying semiotic associated with social assemblages of monotheism.[3] These are the four major semiotic regimes for Deleuze & Guattari, but they by no means exhaust the existing diversity of semiotic systems, the emergence of other semiotic regimes, or the complexities of inter-semiotic regime mixtures.

In this way Deleuze & Guattari approach semiotic regimes in terms of social machines. There are social machines such as the tribal social machine, the State social machine, and a monotheistic social machine. Semiotics, as such, becomes inextricably embedded in their broader pragmatic understanding of social formations. Their broad theorisation of social machines turns not only on the analysis of a semiotic regime in association with a material regime, but crucially upon their understanding of processes of emergence and complexity they theorise in terms of machinic processes. In

---

[2] The following discussion draws upon the plateau "587B.C.–A.D.70: On Several Regimes of Signs", *supra* n. 1, pp. 110–148. An excellent introduction to Deleuze & Guattari's understanding and sign, sense and meaning is Brian Massumi, *A User's Guide to Capitalism and Schizophrenia: Deviations from Deleuze & Guattari* (MIT, 1992), pp. 10–46, and generally.

[3] *Supra* n. 1, p. 117/8

social machines, the operator of these machinic processes is termed the abstract machine, and it is the assemblage that is the heterogeneous and intensive consistency of the semiotic regime and material regime as they are machined together by the abstract machine. Thus:

> "It is language that is based on regimes of signs, and regimes of signs on abstract machines, diagrammatic functions, and machinic assemblages that go beyond any system of semiology, linguistics or logic...'Behind' statements and semiotisatons there are only machines, assemblages, and movements of deterritorialisation that cut across the significations of the various systems and elude both the co-ordinates of language and of existence."[4]

Abstract machines are diagrams of machinic operations, and play the 'piloting' role in social machines. They work with unformed matters and non-formal functions, and machine a consistency and consolidation between heterogeneous elements.[5] The abstract machines define the consistency and becomings of the social machine's assemblages, and diagram what the assemblage can be, what it can do, and the transformations it is capable of. An abstract machine is grasped in a proper name in the manner that proper names "designate not persons or subjects but matters and functions".[6]

Assemblages are intensive processes of consistency and consolidation that work less with unformed matters and non-formal functions of abstract emergence as with the forms, substances, matters, contents, and expressions that are drawn from the actual material milieus of their complex self-organisation. Thus, for example, social assemblages have the actual material milieus of the geological earth and the biological environment (in particular, the human cerebral-nervous milieu) with which to draw the heterogeneous materials to intensively give effect to the virtual processes of emergence and self-organisation. These intensive processes of social assemblages draw from matters of expression present in the environment, and use these to intensively re-shape relations between existing forms and substances and so consolidate a new complexity of the semiotic and the material. The assemblage associates the semiotic system of the collective assem-

---

[4] *Supra* n. 1, p. 148.

[5] "What we term machinic is precisely this synthesis of heterogeneities as such." *Supra* n. 1, p. 330.

[6] *Supra* n. 1, p. 142, and "The proper name is a subject of a pure infinite comprehended as such in a field of virtual intensity." *Supra* n. 1, p. 38.

blage of enunciation and the material regime of the machinic assemblage of content. The assemblage of enunciation carries out the intensive processes of extracting language from a smooth flow of matters of expression forming a regime of signs, and co-ordinating how the use of this language can then have a relation upon the material processes that arrange bodies. The assemblage of bodies carries out the intensive processes of arranging the matter-energy flow (movement, food, desire, generation) through bodies and materials.

Thus, with the concepts of social machines, abstract machines, assemblages, and regimes of signs,[7] Deleuze & Guattari's pragmatic semiotic proceeds with generative, transformational, diagrammatic and machinic components:

"Pragmatics as a whole would consist in this: making a *tracing* of the mixed semiotics, under the generative component; making the transformational *map* of the regimes, with their possibilities for translation and creation, for buddings along the line of tracing; making the *diagram* of the abstract machine that are in play in each case, either as potentialities or as effective emergences; outlining the *program* of the assemblages that distribute everything and bring a circulation of movement with alternatives, jumps, mutations."[8]

In conceptualising and theorising any semiotic system, there is the diagrammatic component of conceptualising the abstract machine and naming it, and the machinic component of theorising the assemblage and its collective assemblage of enunciation and its machinic assemblage of bodies. From these, the semiotic analysis then proceeds to understand the generative and transformational components of the regime of signs on the basis of the understanding of the abstract machine and the assemblage.

---

[7] Deleuze & Guattari's work is characterised by a prodigious conceptual creativity and density. For Deleuze & Guattari concept definitions, see Adrian Parr ed. *The Deleuze Dictionary* (Edinburgh University Press, 2005). For readers unfamiliar with Deleuze & Guattari's thought, I can only ask for perseverance with the flow of my argument. The whole article works with these key Deleuze & Guattari concepts, and the understanding will come from seeing how they are used. To echo Massumi's invitation to their thought: "The question is not, Is it true? But, Does it work? What new thoughts does it make possible to think? What new emotions does it make possible to feel? What new sensations and perceptions does it open in the body?" *Supra* n. 2, p. 8.

[8] *Supra* n. 1, p. 146/147.

132                              JAMIE MURRAY

### 3. DELEUZE & GUATTARI'S THEORY OF EMERGENCE

At the risk of blurring the philosophical specificity and complexity of Deleuze's own ontology, the ontology of the virtual that Deleuze & Guattari put forward in *A Thousand Plateaus* can be characterised as a theory of emergence and self-organisation out of chaos.[9] In this ontology being is understood, opposing a chaos/order dichotomy, as a single matter-energy that is just extremely complexified. The extensive existence of a thing is understood as the outcome of processes of emergence and self-organisation that are immanent to this univocal matter-energy. In order to think through these processes of emergence and complexity immanent in being Deleuze & Guattari use the modality of the virtual-intensive-actual. Processes of emergence and self-organisation are theorised in terms of operations in a virtual realm of a manifold of continuous multiplicities, and in terms of syntheses of intensive repetitions of actual bodies. The virtual operations and intensive processes work to deposit the actual as extensive existence and strata. In doing so, the virtual and intensive realms of processes are in reciprical presupposition in an 'edge of chaos' zone where the creative forces of emergence and self-organisation are best tapped and selected: a zone of the eternal return of emergence and complexity in chaosmos. These processes occur in open and dynamic material dissipative systems where flows of matter-energy push the system far-from-equilibrium. In these circumstances the 'edge of chaos' zone is reached, and the dissipative systems begin to demonstrate emergence of order and self-organised complexity out of chaos. For Deleuze & Guattari, the cosmos, nature, and human social organisations are all dissipative systems that demonstrate and tap processes of emergence and complexity.

In this ontology of the virtual it is abstract machines that operate the virtual processes of emergence, and machinic assemblages that operate the intensive processes of self-organisation and complexity. Abstract machines define the patterns and thresholds (attractors and bifurcations) of the complex dynamic material

---

[9] In developing this ontology it appears that Deleuze & Guattari were directly attempting to create an ontology adequate to the physics, mathematics and biology that is now grouped as the scientific paradigm of complexity theory. See Mark Bonta and John Protevi, *Deleuze & Geophilosophy* (Edinburgh University Press, 2004), pp. 3–31. For an excellent introduction to the Deleuzian ontology, relating it to complexity theory, see Manuel Delanda, *Intensive Science & Virtual Philosophy* (Continuum, 2002).

DELEUZE & GUATTARI'S NOME LAW 133

systems that they diagram and arrange. It is in the assemblages that these virtual activities of the abstract machines are developed in intensive complexity as the processes self-organise, bifurcate, and metamorphose as they gradually move away from the far-from-equilibrium 'edge of chaos' and settle into the striations of the actual.

Deleuze & Guattari theorise the relay between the processes of the abstract machines and the processes of the assemblages in terms of territorialisation–deterritorialisation.[10] The crucial idea here, particularly in relation to social machines, is that assemblages necessarily lay down a territory as part of developing a semiotic regime and a material regime. The territory is the intensive and extensive complex structures that the assemblage striates out of the virtual processes of emergence. In any given social machine there will thus be a mode of drawing and constituting a territory in tandem with developing a regime of signs and a material regime of bodies. However, in drawing a territory and semiotic/material regimes out of chaosmos, these stratifications remain in tension with the productive forces of the 'edge of chaos' virtual that continue to break up the stratifications and re-introduce emergence into the complexifications of the actual. This eternal return of emergence is theorised by Deleuze & Guattari as deterritorialisation. Just as a social machine lays down a territory, this territory is simultaneously run through by emergent and metamorphosing deterritorialisation. Indeed, for Deleuze & Guattari, given their understanding of emergence and self-organisation from chaos in dissipative systems, it is deterritorialisation as operated by the abstract machines that provides the transversal consistency to the assemblages of heterogeneous expressions, matters, and territories:

"What holds all the components together are transversals, and the transversal itself is only a component that has taken upon itself the specialised vector of deterritorialisation. In effect, what holds an assemblage together is not the play of framing forms or linear causalities but, actually or potentially, it's most deterritorialised component, a cutting edge of deterritorialisation."[11]

There is an ever-present tension in social machines between the processes of territorialisation and deterritorialisation as they both struggle to take control of the processes of emergence and

---

[10] *Supra* n. 7. Nome law is explicitly an attempt to explore the concepts of territorialisation–deterritorialisation as they are used in *A Thousand Plateaus*, see the discussion in following sections.

[11] *Supra* n. 1, p. 336.

self-organisation. However, it is emergence, as the process of deter-ritorialisation in social machines, that accounts not only for the creation of social machines but also for their continuing existence and the transformations they undergo.

## 4. NOOLOGICAL LEGAL THEORY

A Deleuze & Guattari legal theory, thus, starts with a semiotics of law in a very broad pragmatics that is developed out of an ontology of the virtual that accounts for social organisation through immanent processes of emergence of order from chaosmos. However, to fully develop a Deleuze & Guattari legal theory a further feature of their thought needs to be explored: images of thought.[12]

The virtual, for Deleuze, is also the plane of immanence of thought, and thought also takes place through the tapping of immanent processes of emergence, self-organisation and metamorphosis. As such, the brain and the virtual connect up.[13] The manner in which the brain and the virtual connect up is the image of thought, and this intuition of what it is to think orientates the thinker in the problem space of the virtual that thinking explores. The problem space of the virtual is a continuously respecifying problematics phase space that poses problems to be explored and solved by the emergent and self-organising complexity of abstract machines and assemblages. Abstract machines and assemblages develop as particular consistent solutions to virtual problematics, and their actualisation does not close off the continuing respecification of the virtual problematic.

Every social machine has, at its emergence in the first stirrings of immanent self-organisation of abstract machines in the virtual, a virtual multiplicity – a concept – of what it is to think, an image of thought. It is this image of thought that orientates the assemblage in relation to the virtual as the problem space thinking explores, and directs how that assemblage thinks about the problematic of

---

[12] The concepts of images of thought and noology are pervasive in *A Thousand Plateaus*, but find their most detailed development in Gilles Deleuze, *Difference & Repetition* (Athlone Press, 1994). In particular, Chapter III 'The Image of Thought' pp. 129–167.

[13] See Deleuze & Guattari, *What is Philosophy* (Verso, 1994), "Conclusion: From Chaos to the Brain", pp. 201–218 for a luminescent discussion of the brain, the virtual, and images of thought.

social organisation. Every social assemblage is a dynamic consistency of heterogeneous elements of language, bodies, and territory that is a 'solution' to the open problematic of constituting a social group. The image of thought of the assemblage directs the image of legality that is the assemblage's immanent and self-organising solution to the problem, and forms the basis upon which it develops its institutional structures and legal discourse.

Thus, at the core of what Deleuze & Guattari offer to thinking about social organisation in *A Thousand Plateaus* are theories of anthropomorphic virtual problem space and of images of thought in social machines:

"Noology, which is distinct from ideology, is precisely the study of images of thought, and their historicity."[14]

A noological legal theory would be the study of images of legality, their emergence, their genealogy, and their creation. It would commence by theorising law on a plane of immanence rather than on the plane of transcendence. This would be to virtualise law, and to conceptualise law in the problem space of virtual multiplicities. Through this shift into virtual problem space, law is conceptualised as an open immanent dynamic problematic of social organisation ('The Law' does not exist). Particular legalities emerge as actualised solutions to this open immanent dynamic problematic. A legality is conceptualised as a social machine: an emergent self-organising consistent dynamic complex system. At its virtual emergence, and in its transversal consistency, a legality is formed by a particular abstract machine that operates its array of singularities. This abstract machine is the image of thought and image of legality of that social machine: the diagram of the assemblage. The legality of the social machine is intensively put together in the social machinic assemblage. Legality is constituted through immanent processes of emergence, self-organisation, complexity and metamorphosis. A legality has a semiotic regime, a material regime, a territory, and a transversal of consistency (its image of legality, its abstract machine). The legality, as aspects of its regimes and territory, will also lay down strata on the plane of organisation. This might include norms or institutions. However, for a noology of law the strata on the plane of organisation are precisely what is not of interest (and so radically distinguishes a noology of law from conventional jurisprudence). The noology of law studies the images of legality that

---

[14] *Supra* n. 1, p. 376.

different social machines constitute and enact, their emergence, their intensive genealogy, their mutation into new images of legality and so new social assemblages. It explores their abstract machines, their assemblages, their semiotic regimes, their material regimes, their territories, their relationship to other images of legalities, and their mixtures and transformations. At its limit, a noology of law would also explore the plane of immanence looking for new, as yet unconceptualised and unactualised, images of legality, and to develop new concepts of law.

The following sections start a Deleuze & Guattari noology of law in terms of an account, a theorisation, and the creation of a concept, of the emergence of law.

## 5. REFRAIN AND CHAOSMOS

For Deleuze & Guattari, as they theorise in the plateaus "10,000 B.C.: The Geology of Morals" and "1837: of the Refrain", there is a process by which legalities first emerged on earth.

It could pass for chaos.[15] A sudden effusion and expansion of energy-matter. Non-localisable non-dimensional force, unformed unstable matters, tangled bundles of aberrant lines, flows in all directions, free intensities, nomadic singularities, mad transitory particles.[16] Molecular material blasted through a becoming cosmos. Yet chaos is not without its own directional components.[17] Molecular materials aggregate into matter, and this matter–substance generates emergent forms. Molecules in nuclear fusion, balls of gas, aggregates of rock. A vast number of solar systems. A vast number of galaxies. Dying stars, black holes, comet collisions. One planet with a hardened crust and an atmosphere of nitrogen and oxygen. A cosmos of non-organic life, emerging, expanding, complexifying, collapsing.

"They're alive." Yes, but in a new chaos of teeming organic life. On Earth the directional components of chaos have assembled organic life into organic systems and ecological systems. However, the survival of an organism and its genetic line depends upon the

---

[15] On chaosmic geology and biology see '10,000 B.C.: A Geology of Morals', *Supra* n. 1, pp. 40–76.

[16] *Supra* n. 1, p. 40.

[17] *Supra* n.1, p. 313.

## DELEUZE & GUATTARI'S NOME LAW     137

success with which it occupies its ecological niche. Yet, the ecological systems within which the organisms survive are frequently highly complex and highly volatile dynamic systems, marked by processes of emergence, bifurcation, and catastrophe. Life is lived as chaotic, complex, far-from-equilibrium, between fight or flight. It is a world of organic life that expresses the same processes of emergence, expansion, and complexity as those of the cosmos in an incredible richness and diversity of organic life. However, for a given organism, life is very much a problem of ecological chaos and complexity.

It starts in the middle, between the actual cerebral-nervous system in relation to the local earth environment and the abstract machines in the virtual.[18] The processes are occurring between the virtual abstract machines and the actual biological strata. The abstract machine first composes itself. Among the continuous virtual multiplicities the abstract machine sets up connections, densifications, intensifications, re-enforcement's, injections, intervals, the convergence and divergence of series, the de-limiting of singularities. In the organic milieu of the cerebral-nervous system and the organic milieu of the local earth environment there are vibrations. The milieus are coded blocks of space-time constituted by a periodic repetition of a component. Each milieu therefore has a metered vibration. A chaos of vibrations. However, a milieu vibrates in relation to a neighbouring milieu's vibration. Between these two milieus the periodic vibrations set up a channel of communication, and rhythm emerges between the two vibrations. The communicating rhythm sets up a co-ordination between two heterogeneous space-times. Rhythms between milieus enter into communication with rhythms from other rhythmic milieus. The rhythms densify, intensify, re-inforce each other, inject into each other, pattern intervals, autonomously enchain convergent and divergent series.

Within this chaosmos of rhythms the abstract machine de-limits a singularity as point of virtual attraction, an event of rhythm becoming a matter of expression, the emergence of a proper quality. Between the virtual abstract machine and the actual cerebral-nervous milieu there is a "self-movement of expressive qualities".[19] Through iterations of the same self-organising processes multiple matters of expression emerge, and enter into shifting relations with

---

[18] See 'Of the Refrain', *Supra* n. 1, pp. 310–350.
[19] *Supra* n. 1, p. 317.

each other. A particular matter of expression may enter into a catalysing relation with the self-organising processes. Additional virtual singularities are delimited. A kernel of expressive materials emerges – the refrain:

> "What is primary is the consistency of the refrain, a little tune, either in the form of a mnemonic melody, that has no need to be inscribed locally in a centre, or in the form of a vague motif with no need to be pulsed or stimulated."[20]

In the cerebral-nervous and environmental milieus a rhythmic figure becomes expressive and independent. A virtual multiplicity of attractors becomes sensed: "sensation surges forth from the dark depths of enveloping animality".[21] This intensity may be just a briefest tune repeatedly hummed under the breath to ward off fear in a moment of danger. A self-organising, expressive, repeatable, consistent relation between a few heterogeneous matters of expression, that for a few moments allow the animal to abstract itself from the fully actualised moment, and to establish a calm centre in the midst of chaos. The refrain buys a moment to think abstractly.

In the refrain a point of calm has been drawn from the forces of chaos, and with that a world can be drawn. In the refrain as it emerged in the cerebral-nervous milieu of humans an entire anthropomorphic set of self-organising processes start up, and a human world emerges with its own specific mode of composition. The refrain as an abstract machine is not only realised in expressive matters of voice, but also in expressive matters of marks on the ground and of habitual movement that mark a territory. The refrain develops into song, and into language. The refrain diagrams processes of territorialisation that develop into regimes of social organisation. These processes will be explored in the following sections.

However, the crucial point about the emergence of the refrain from chaos is that it is the threshold and condition for the emergence of thought capable of thinking the virtual to be embodied in an actual brain.[22] Prior to the refrain the virtual processes, whilst operating freely in the virtual, were wholly absorbed in the material processes they organised. The refrain allows a brain to abstract itself from the here and now and think in terms of a dynamic consistency between a number of heterogeneous matters of expression. With the becoming expressive of matters diagrammed in the

---

[20] *Supra* n. 1, p. 332.

[21] See Eric Alliez, *The Signature of the World* (Continuum, 2004), p. 69.

[22] See n. 13, "Conclusion: From Chaos to the Brain".

refrain, the form of expression is now independent of the form of substance. All aspects of the world can be translated into matters of expression, and then related in terms of the self-organising processes that the abstract machines now operate not only in the virtual but also in thought. The chaosmos thinks in us.[23] An intuition drawn form blocks of sensation and intensities emerges and self-organises through the abstract machines and forms a virtual multiplicity and the image of thought. The brain can now enter into an apprenticeship to the virtual processes. The refrain and the image of thought locate the brain in the chaosmos of thought, and establish a *nomos* that orientates the brain on the plane of immanence. The emergence of the image of thought opens up the anthropomorphic knowledge space and the problematic of social organisation. In addressing this problem space of organisation the image of thought forms the image of legality and the problematic of how an individual body is joined to a collective group.

In sum, the refrain plunges the brain into the virtual, and the virtual into the brain, and opens up a knowledge space in which the entire adventure of thought and humans unfolds:

"In this submersion it seems that there is abstracted from chaos the shadow of the 'people to come' in the form that art, but also philosophy and science, summon forth: mass-people, world-people, chaos-people..."[24]

## 6. NOME LAW

"Let us recall Nietzsche's idea of the eternal return as a little ditty, a refrain, but which captures the mute and unthinkable forces of the Cosmos."[25]

With the emergence of the refrain the first anthropomorphic abstract machine and social assemblage also begin to emerge. A nome is a little refrain, a polyvocal signature object, and a territorial distribution. Here nome will be used as the name of the legal multiplicity that is being explored.

Nome law as a concept and framework of law is theorised as an abstract machine, machinic assemblage, and strata. The abstract machine is the refrain. The assemblage is the territorial assemblage, and is the first articulation of language and technology. The strata are minimal since what is striking about this concept of law is that

---

[23] Pierre Levy, *Collective Intelligence* (Plenum Trade, 1997) p. 221.

[24] *Supra* n. 13, "Conclusion: From Chaos to the Brain" at p. 218.

[25] *Supra* n. 1, p. 343.

140                    JAMIE MURRAY

it is an intensive forging of consistency rather than a machine of striation and overcoding. It is the (auto)chthonic law that emerged as de-forrestation created the savannah and steppe, and humans formed hunter-gather packs, walking across these smooth spaces with free hands and supple larynxes. Its development coalesces around a little tune. It is real, immanent, self-organising.

It is inseparable from a distribution in space: a way of distributing things in smooth space.[26] The emergence of a territory is the consistency by which the hunter-gatherer pack distributes itself in space. It is a distribution that not only forms a place of safety from danger, but also an abode, and lines of journey away from that home. Nome law fights back the forces of chaos, and coheres a liveable space of terrestrial forces, and taps directly the cosmic forces of creation.

From the refrain it develops both in song and in the making of a home territory. From that it develops into a collective assemblage of enunciation of language and laws, and into a machinic assemblage of the social organisation of bodies and technology.

This emergent group law establishes a subject group. This is not an homogenous homeostatic subjugated social group, but a far-from-equilibrium heterogeneous dynamic pack. There are subtle group boundaries, and the group is not organised but becoming. In such groups the communication is near instantaneous and correlated at a distance.

Nome law creates the territories distributions in space as lines: lines drawn out musically from the refrain, and lines drawn out rhythmically from walking across smooth space. These lines not only draw out the territory but also traverse it, connecting it to the faraway through lines of flight, and connecting it internally to a sacred intensive natal point that opens up between the earth and the drawing of the territory.

These lines of flight towards the too-far-away, and these lines of flight toward the too-near natal, form the consistency of this legality and its social assemblage in a far-from-equilibrium intensive becoming in which the time remains the time of the intensive becoming of the earth itself.

The time of nome law is a virtual time, Aion, a Dreamtime. The cosmos it draws is molecular and pantheist.[27]

---

[26] "The *nomos* as customary, unwritten law is inseparable from a distribution of space, a distribution in space." *Supra* n. 1, p. 312.

[27] *Supra* n. 1, p. 327.

## 7. NOME LAW: REFRAIN: ABSTRACT MACHINE

The refrain is the abstract machine of nome law. On the plane of consistency the nome law abstract machine composes itself and machines the connections between the continuous multiplicities of the virtual. It intervenes in these multiplicities of unformed matters and non-formal functions and delimits as singularity or array of singularities a self-organising virtual pattern that diagrams a refrain. These are the virtual singularities and attractors that pattern the refrain: the differential relation between two vibrations, the sonorous respiratory and vocal attractors of a fall and a lift. The delimiting of the singularity of the refrain is a virtual event that then enters into a matter of expression that has been able to emerge from the cerebral/environmental milieu of the becoming hunter-gatherers. The refrain is a virtual event that triggers a material process, and connects the brain and the plane of consistency. It makes this connection because from then on the multiplicity of the refrain exists not only on the plane of consistency but also in the brain's neural network.

This refrain abstract machine effects a number of developments. The event of the refrain triggers a symmetry breakage in the virtual and makes time.[28] This is the immemorial time of the eternal becoming beginning, scansioned by the time signature of the refrain. The abstract machine of the refrain makes a new register and complexification of expression. The abstract machine's connecting of the virtual multiplicity has found expression in the embodied thought of a creature that can now express that multiplicity vocally or graphically. The refrain makes language.[29] The refrain makes the territory.[30] The virtual pattern of the refrain can be translated into habitual patterns of behaviour or material objects to directly mark the land of the territory. The calming centre of the refrain extends to make the home.

In this process the abstract machine of the refrain operates in the material processes without itself leaving the plane of consistency.

---

[28] "Time is not an a priori form, rather, the refrain is the a priori form of time, which in each case fabricates different times." *Supra* n. 1, p. 349.

[29] "As matters of expression take on consistency they constitute semiotic systems, but the semiotic components are inseparable from material components and are in exceptionally close contact with molecular levels." *Supra* n. 1, p. 334.

[30] "A refrain is an aggregate of matters of expression that draws a territory and develops into territorial motifs and counterpoints." *Supra* n. 1, p. 326.

Deleuze & Guattari identify a number of different types of abstract machines. Some are wholly caught up within the strata they diagram, such as the geological and biological abstract machines. Others operate on a plane of organisation as they seek to overcode existing assemblages. The key example of this abstract machine is the State. However, the abstract machine of nome law operates on the plane of consistency, and so places the assemblage that it co-ordinates in a very close proximity to the virtual. Nome law is, therefore, in direct contact with absolute cosmic becoming, and the refrain is a kernel of absolute deterritorialisation in the abstract machine.

Thus the nome law abstract machine can be characterised with the formula 'draw a territory and traverse it'. The refrain provides the consistency for the nome law assemblage, but it is precisely a consistency in becomings, mutations, cosmic deterritorialisations. The refrain is a transversal, a process that cuts across everything, connecting the natal through the home to the cosmos and joining everything up on the plane of consistency. The refrain provides consistency to the social assemblage in precisely this transversal consistency. The refrain draws the territory, but then traverses it through elaborating the refrain in song, and traversing it on foot through journeys and migrations, as the very processes of the consistency of the assemblage. The refrain is the set of cutting edges of the abstract machine that enters into the assemblage to draw variations and mutations of it. The refrain, thus, works the territory, diagramming it, providing it with consistency, and incessantly traversing the territory with relative and absolute deterritorialisation. The abstract machine thus prolongs and improvises the kernel of the refrain's multiplicity in converging and diverging virtual series, framing matter and tapping forces.

The refrain is thus a calm centre, a home, and a journey from home; the forces of chaos, the forces of earth, and the forces of the cosmos; the directional components of virtual abstract machines, the dimensional components of the abstract machine's diagrams, and the abstract machine's passages, escapes and metamorphoses. The refrain is itself the performative of nome law.

## 8. Nome Law: Territorial Assemblage

It is in the assemblage that nome law intensively develops, and where the operations of the abstract machine can be seen everywhere. The assemblage is itself the drawing and traversing of the territory.

DELEUZE & GUATTARI'S NOME LAW                 143

The process of intensively developing the refrain is a process of territorialisation. For Deleuze & Guattari the standard way for an assemblage to develop is the procedure to articulate forms and substances, and then to articulate content and expression. This is the double articulation of the assemblage.[31] However, in the territorial assemblage, because there is no overcoding and because of the very close proximity to the plane of consistency in the refrain, the articulations of the assemblage take an intensive and immanent form where there is a co-existence of heterogeneities and a process of self-organisation. This process takes advantage of the aptitude for material of expression to autonomously form themes, and of the molecular imbrication of the semiotic and the material.[32] It is an intensive assemblage in which being, signs, and things exist in a dynamic relation of mutual molecular participation and self-organisation.

The assemblage, thus, articulates a vortex in smooth space, and follows a flow in a haptic vectoral field scattered with singularities. It does not divide or distribute space itself, but distributes in a smooth space.[33] It holds together heterogeneities without them ceasing to be heterogeneous, but whilst enabling emergent systematic effects.

The assemblage articulates this molecular intensive process through a double articulation of refrain and territory. From this there develops a recognisable assemblage of palaeolithic culture: voice and hand; speech and tool; language and technology.[34] The assemblage is not limited to the strata, precisely because of this intensive emergence of a semiotic system and a corporeal regime.[35] However, this means that the territorial assemblage is assembled from two intersecting multiplicities: a sonorous multiplicity of expression, and a material multiplicity of content. These two

---

[31] *Supra* n. 1, "10,000 B.C.: Geology of Morals", pp. 40–76.

[32] "The nomos came to designate the law, but that was originally because it was distribution, a mode of distribution [in smooth space]." *Supra* n. 1, p. 329.

[33] *Supra* n. 1, p. 380.

[34] "But what is not an illusion are the *new distributions* between content and expression: technological content characterised by hand–tool relations, and at a deeper level, tied to a social Machine and formations of power; symbolic expression characterised by face–language relations and, at a deeper level, tied to a semiotic Machine and regime of signs." *Supra* n. 1, p. 63.

[35] "The reason why the assemblage is not confined to the strata is that expression in it becomes a semiotic system, a regime of signs, and content becomes a pragmatic system, actions and passions." *Supra* n. 1, p. 504.

dimensions of the assemblage are independent but in reciprocal presupposition, co-articulated by the abstract machine. The link between the semiotic regime and the social regime is that signs in the semiotic regime can directly trigger material processes and incorporeal transformations.[36]

The assemblage develops both a semiotic regime and a material regime, draws a territory and connects up lines of deterritorialisation. In doing this the assemblage operates molecularly.

The semiotic regim *Supra* e develops out of the refrain.[37] In common with the refrain, the semiotic regime is about extracting a self-organising pattern out of chaos. Here, it is a matter extracting a language from the flow of song and indirect discourse developed out of the refrain. The relations between matters of expression firstly begin to draw a song:

"In effect, expressive qualities or matters of expression enter shifting relations with one another that 'express' the relation of the territory they draw to the interior milieu of impulses and the exterior milieu of circumstances."[38]

In the refrain motifs develop that express relations between various interior milieu impulses, which develop into autonomous rhythmical characters. Also, counterpoints develop in the refrain that express aspects of the exterior milieu of the environment, which develop into melodic landscapes. Thus, the refrain develops to express and explore such things as joy and sadness, sunrise and seasons. From this, anthropomorphically the song can further develop in terms of articulating rhythmical characters as mythic creator figures, and articulating melodic landscapes as particular landscape features. This developed song finds its overall consistency in the refrain of the natal. Thus, the song can explore semiotic consistency and consolidation, mythical origins, map, measure, and explore territory, and mark time. It forms a sonorous mythical haptic cartography.

In this way, the semiotic regime develops out of a complexification of the refrain, and through further consolidations of molecular expressive materials. This emerges to constitute a collective semiotic machine:

---

[36] "There is a new relation between content and expression that was not yet present in the strata: the statements or expressions express incorporeal transformations that are 'attributed' as such (properties) to bodies or contents." *Supra* n. 1, p. 504.

[37] *Supra* n. 1, '1837: Of the Refrain', pp. 317–320.

[38] *Supra* n. 1, p. 317.

DELEUZE & GUATTARI'S NOME LAW 145

"Expression should be understood not simply as face and language, or individual languages, but as a semiotic collective machine that pre-exists them and constitutes a regime of signs."[39]

This semiotic is pre-discursive, a-signifying, polysemic semiotic directly employing intensive singularities in its semiotic fabric:

"It fosters a pluralism or polyvocality of forms of expression that prevents any power take over by the signifier and preserves expressive forms particular to content: thus forms of corporeality, gesturality, rhythm, dance, and rite co-exist heterogeneously with vocal form."[40]

In this semiotic, to state or to invoke the law is to perform the refrain.

The assemblage also develops a material social regime. The refrain is a topological invariant that can be intensively realised in a material regime of bodies just as it is realised in the expressive regime of song/language.[41] The social regime is not merely hand-tool, but the entire technical social machine in which they are taken up.[42]

The initial key function of the material regime is the fabricating of a home. This is consolidated by the assemblage effecting a re-arrangement of functions, and a re-focusing of forces. The functions are re-organised as a new arrangement of the innate and the acquired as integrated into the territory as environmental specialisation. The forces are re-focused in a distinction between the forces of chaos that are kept outside, and the forces of the earth that are now channelled in the pragmatic regime of the territory. This re-focusing of forces leads to the construction within the assemblage of the natal, and to the development of rite, ritual and religion. Collectively, the home, the new arrangement of function and forces, and the emergence of the natal, constitute the basics of the social regime of the territorial assemblage. This assemblage can then extend into organising filiation and alliance, and into developing a general regime of coding and inscription. However, this is

---

[39] *Supra* n. 1, p. 63.

[40] *Supra* n. 1, p. 118.

[41] "One finds these sorts of refrains in Greek Antiquity with the 'nomes' that constituted, in a way, the 'signature tunes', banners and seals for professional associations." Felix Guattari, *Chaosmosis* (Power Publications, 1995), p. 16.

[42] "Content should be understood not simply as the hand and tools but as a technical social machine that pre-exists them and constitutes states of force or formations of power." *Supra* n. 1, p. 61.

already for nome law to start a mutation into the somewhat different assemblage of tribal law.

The operation of the territorial assemblage is territorialisation.[43] Territorialisation is the process of self-organisation in the chaosmos of the milieus of the refrain, the abode, the regime of expression, the regime of content, the forging of the natal, and the constitution of a territory:

"The territory is the product of a territorialisation of milieus and rhythms... Territorialisation is an act of rhythm that has become expressive, or of milieu components that have become qualitative."[44]

The territory in extension is the marks on the earth that draw the territory, the physical structure of the abode, and the local environment in so far as it is structured by the regime of content into feeding grounds, sacred grounds, and through the physical marking of bodies. These are the strata of the territory. There is thus *Supra* a coding of flows and the inscription of the actual territory.

The territory in intension is a creation that differentiates itself from the earth. A consequence of this disjunction between earth and territory is that the point of origin of the territory within the assemblage must necessarily be projected by that assemblage as being outside the assemblage in the forces of the cosmos:

"Although in extension the territory separates the interior forces of the earth from the exterior forces of chaos, the same does not occur in 'intension', in the dimension of depth, where the two types of forces clasp and are wed in a battle whose only criterion and stakes is the earth. There is always a place, a tree, or a grove, in the territory where all the forces come together in hand-to-hand combat of energies."[45]

This re-groups all the forces into forces of the earth at the natal point from which the territory is constituted. The natal places the forces of the earth and the forces of chaos in a fight between good and evil for the very being of the earth. The success of abiding in a territory now depends upon the intensive natal forces of the earth. The natal, in itself, feeds back into the regime of expression where the intensive natal becomes expressed in the refrain, and the natal develops as a focal point for myths, rites and religions.

---

[43] *Supra* n. 1, '1837: Of the Refrain', pp. 314–317.
[44] Supra n. 1, p. 326.
[45] *Supra* n. 1, p. 321.

## DELEUZE & GUATTARI'S NOME LAW                    147

The territorial assemblage, though constituting new semiotic and pragmatic regimes and a territory, is nonetheless simultaneously run through by deterritorialisation. This is because the territory finds its consistency on the plane of immanence and the absolute deterritorialisation that operates on this plane. In the territorial assemblage these lines of deterritorialisation are found in inter-assemblage drift, the ambiguity of the natal, and in the kernel of absolute deterritorialisation that is lodged in the refrain itself.[46]

First, at the level of inter-assemblages, new assemblages develop out of the territorial assemblage:

"The territorial assemblage is inseparable from lines or coefficients of deterritorialisation, passages and relays towards other assemblages."[47]

For example, courtship separates out from the territory, and a mate can be recognised not merely in the territory but individually independent of place. Similarly, autonomous assemblages of group organisation such as kinship and alliance can develop within the territory. Deleuze & Guattari's analysis of these inter-assemblage developments and relations is that a component of the territorial assemblage becomes autonomous in relation to the assemblage through a margin of territorial decoding. The freed component then acts as a component of passage to a new assemblage.[48] This results in the inter-assemblage level being relations of persistent relative movements and relative decodings and transformations towards new assemblages:

"Territory is constantly traversed by movements of deterritorialisation that are relative and may even occur in place, by which one passes from the intra-assemblage to inter-assemblage, without, however, leaving the territory or issuing form the assemblage."[49]

Second, just as with inter-assemblage drift, the consistency of the assemblage in lines of deterritorialisation is again found in the ambiguity of the natal in the territorial assemblage. Hence, the natal operates at different levels: extensively as birthplace abode; intensively as sacred land/creation myths; and virtually as absolute deterritorialisation:

---

[46] *Supra* n. 1, 'Of the Refrain', pp. 324–330.

[47] *Supra* n. 1, p. 333.

[48] "We saw that territory constituted itself on a margin of decoding effecting the milieu; we now see that there is a margin of deterritorialisation effecting the territory itself." *Supra* n. 1, p. 326.

[49] *Supra* n. 1, p. 326.

148                    JAMIE MURRAY

"...a point of convergence of several territories, some earthly, some cosmic, which arrive after long pilgrimages."[50]

The directional elements of chaos enter into the territorial assemblage because that assemblage does not banish the forces of chaos and the cosmos, but re-focuses them in an intensive natal point:

"A world is only constituted on the condition of being inhabited by an umbilical point deconstructive, detotalising, deterritorialising from which a subjective positionality embodies itself...The intense centre is simultaneously inside the territory, and outside several territories that converge on it at the end of an immense pilgrimage (hence the ambiguity of the 'natal')."[51]

The intensive natal plugs and channels the virtual and intensive forces of the plane of consistency directly into the territorial assemblage. The natal is, thus, not only the existential territory of homeland, self-belonging, attachment to clan, but overwhelmingly the natal is the consistency of forces of the earth and an opening into the cosmos and chaosmos.

Third, it is the refrain itself that installs a flight from territory, a deterritorialisation, at the heart of any territory such that the territory is itself held together by a kernel of absolute deterritorialisation:

"Deterritorialisation is absolute when it brings about the creation of a new earth, in other words, when it connects lines of flight, raises them to the power of an abstract vital, or draws a plane of consistency."[52]

In the discussion of Deleuze & Guattari's ontology it was seen that the self-organising processes of an assemblage are theorised in terms of a machinic consistency, and that it is the abstract machine that diagrams this intensive consistency. Thus, for Deleuze & Guattari it is the refrain as abstract machine that provides the consistency of the territorial assemblage:

"Even in a territorial assemblage, it may be the most deterritorialised component, the deterritorialising vector, in other words the refrain, that assumes the consistency of the territory itself."[53]

Territory is thus constituted and finds its consistency on a transversal of music and flight that it opens to a tremendous free

---

[50] *Supra* n. 1, p. 327.

[51] *Supra* n. 1, p. 321.

[52] *Supra* n. 1, p. 510.

[53] *Supra* n. 1, p. 327.

variation and improvisation that is not limited to relative deterrito-rialisation or the exploration of the natal, but directly to absolute deterritorialisation of the cosmos:

"At infinity, these refrains must rejoin the songs of the Molecules, the new born wail-ing of the fundamental Elements...They cease to be terrestrial, becoming cosmic: when the religious Nome blooms and dissolves into a molecular pantheist Cosmos."[54]

Philosophical thought,[55] free music,[56] and revolutionary subject groups[57] continue to explore this blooming and dissolving of nome law, this eternal return.


9. CONCLUSION: NOME LAW & OTHER IMAGES
OF LEGALITIES


What relation does nome law have to other legalities? This ques-tion can be analysed in two sub-question. First, as a question of in-ter-assemblage drift of nome law into other legal assemblages given that the territorial assemblage is defined by becomings into other formations.[58] Second, of the relationship nome law has as first emerging legality to other legalities.

For Deleuze & Guattari one key feature of territorial assem-blages and their tribal complexifications is that they possess sophis-ticated mechanisms of prevention, anticipation, and warding off in relation to transformations to a State legality, to a deterritorialising nomad legality, and to decoding assemblages.[59] There are many transformations territorial assemblages can undergo, but for Deleuze & Guattari these three fates are the ones that nome law most often experiences as the limit of its social formation.[60]

---

[54] *Supra* n. 1, p. 327.

[55] *Supra* n.13, Gilles Deleuze & Felix Guattari, *What is Philosophy* (Verso, 1994).

[56] See Albert Ayler, *Lorrach, Paris 1966* (Hat Hut Records, 2002); Sun Ra and His Solar Myth Arkestra, *Easy Listening For Inter-Galactic Travel* (Evidence Music, 2000).

[57] See Antonio Negri, *Insurgencies* (Minnesota University Press, 1999).

[58] "The territorial assemblage is continually passing into other assemblages." *Supra* n. 1, p. 235.

[59] "Warding off the foundation of a State apparatus, making such a formation impossible, would be the objective of a certain number of primitive social mecha-nisms, even if they are not consciously understood as such." *Supra* n. 1, p. 357.

[60] On State legality, see "Apparatus of Capture", *Supra* n. 1, pp. 351–423; on nomad legality see 'Treatise on Nomadology', *Supra* n. 1, pp. 424–474.

150                          JAMIE MURRAY

For Deleuze & Guattari the State legality is established directly in the milieu of the hunter-gatherers. In a sudden stroke the State abstract machine and assemblage rise up inside the territory and effect an overcoding of that territory in a hierarchical realignment. It is only in this overcoding that State legality takes over the territory for agriculture, re-aligns the semiotic regime on the master signifier, re-channels the social regime of alliance and filiation, and blocks lines of deterritorialisation:

"Primitive people have always existed only as vestiges, already plied by the reversible wave that carries them off (vector of deterritorialisation). What is contingent upon external circumstances is only the place where the [State] apparatus is effected."[61]

In contrast to the deterritorialisation–reterritorialisation of the State, the territorial assemblage also enfolds a mutation along its vectors of deterritorialisation into the nomad assemblage. From within the territorial assemblage a new abstract machine arises that formulates a new concept of time, movement, semiotics, and becomings. There arises a time of intensive vortical becoming itself, a symbiosis with an animal as the motor for accelerated of nomadic lines of flight, a decoded semiotic of numerical relations drawing intensive ordinal series, and the territory is left on a line of flight and a becoming imperceptible.

However, due to nome law's first emergence,[62] Deleuze & Guattari draw the conclusion that all later legalities are virtually diagrammed and intensively present in nome law:

"In a sense, everything we attribute to an age was already present in the preceding age...It has been present 'for all time', but under different perceptual conditions. New conditions were necessary for what was buried or covered, inferred or concluded, presently to rise to the surface, what was composed in an assemblage, what was still only composed, becomes a component of a new assemblage."[63]

And, as such:

"We are compelled to say that there has always been a State, quite perfect, quite complete. The more discoveries archaeologists make, the more empires they discover...It is not adequate to say that the Neolithic or even Palaeolithic State, once it appeared, reacted back on the surrounding world of the hunter-gatherers; it was there already before it appeared, as the actual limit these societies warded off, or

---

[61] *Supra* n. 1, p. 447.

[62] "The territory is the first assemblage, the first thing to constitute an assemblage; the assemblage is fundamentally territorial." *Supra* n. 1, p. 323.

[63] *Supra* n. 1, p. 347.

as the point to which they converged but could not reach without self-destructing."[64]

Even capitalist law is virtually diagrammed and intensely present in nome law:

"In a sense, capitalism has haunted all forms of society, but haunts them in the form of a horrifying nightmare, it is the dread they feel of a flow that would elude their codes."[65]

Thus, as the first emerged abstract machine of legality, nome law has virtually folded up inside it all forms of legalities, and in its intensive emergence all possible states of legality exist in it. The emergence of nome law is the 'big bang' of legality: a virtual and intensive rhizome of primitive societies, State societies, nomad societies, monotheistic societies, capitalist societies, and new earths and new peoples, all in one emergence and becoming. The first image of legality, as well as the first image of thought. The anthropomorphic refrain, as well as the cosmic refrain.

*School of Law*
*Liverpool John Moores University*
*Josephine Butler House*
*1 Myrtle Street*
*Liverpool L7 4DN*
*England*
*E-mail: j.murray1@livjm.ac.uk*

---

[64] *Supra* n. 1, p. 360/431.
[65] *Supra* n. 1, p. 140.

# [6]

# Advancing Science and Research in Criminal Justice/Criminology: Complex Systems Theory and Non-Linear Analyses

*Jeffery T. Walker*

For over a century, criminological research has been able to explain a consistently small amount of the variation in crime. It is plausible that the problem with criminological theory is not in the theory but in the analysis. Complex systems science (CSS) attempts to examine data in a different way – often making the most of error data discarded by linear analyses. This paper addresses the viability of using CSS in criminological research. An example is drawn from social disorganization theory to demonstrate the ability of CSS to explain crime at the neighborhood level. The result is a new theory called Ecodynamics Theory, developed by combining the elements of neighborhood research with complex systems analyses. The implications of this theory to increase the efficacy of criminological research are discussed.

*Keywords* advancing science; complex systems theory; criminal justice; criminology; non-linear analyses; research

Jeffery T. Walker is a professor of Criminal Justice and Criminology in the Department of Criminal Justice at the University of Arkansas, Little Rock, where he has taught since 1990. He has written six books, over 30 journal articles and book chapters, 17 technical reports, and delivered over 70 professional papers and presentations. He has obtained over $9 million in grants from the Department of Justice, National Institute of Drug Abuse, and others. His areas of interest are social/environmental factors of crime and the study of non-linear dynamics as they relate to crime. He is the Immediate Past President of the Academy of Criminal Justice Sciences. Editorial experience includes service as Editor of the *Journal of Criminal Justice Education*, Editor in Chief of *Journal of Critical Criminology*, and Editor of *Crime Patterns and Analysis*. Previous publications include articles in *Justice Quarterly, Journal of Quantitative Criminology*, and *Journal of Criminal Justice Education*, and the books *Leading Cases in Law Enforcement* (6th Edition), *Statistics in Criminal Justice and Criminology: Analysis and Interpretation* (2nd Edition), and *Myths in Crime and Justice*. Correspondence to: Jeffery T. Walker, Department of Criminal Justice, University of Arkansas, Little Rock, Little Rock, AR 72204-1099, USA. E-mail: jtwalker@ualr.edu

556    WALKER

## Introduction

For almost a century, criminal justice/criminology research has been able to explain a consistently small amount of the variation in crime and an even smaller amount of the variation in most actions of the criminal justice system. With recent advances in longitudinal analyses and multilevel modeling, criminology has greatly improved the ability to model criminal behavior, but we are still far short of explanations that can inform policy, reduce crime, or even explain why neighborhoods deteriorate into high-crime areas. Much of the reason for this may be because of the insistence on stodgily following the models of physical science in examining human behavior when we know human behavior is much too complex and variable to neatly conform to the parameters of linear models. Parallel to the inability of science to accurately predict the weather, research in human behavior has fallen far short of the elegant precision of Newtonian mechanics and Leibnizean calculus.

Laub (2006) discussed the scathing findings of the Michael and Adler (1933) report that criminal justice/criminology was unable to properly utilize scientific method to examine issues of crime and justice. After outlining Sutherland's response to this report (1973), Laub proposed a "paradigm for criminology" based on Life-Course Theory. By adopting this paradigm, he argued criminology could move forward as a scientific discipline. I agree with Laub's arguments, but believe he did not go far enough. If criminal justice/criminology is to truly advance in research and analyses, we must look to new methods of examination, not simply attempt to do a minimally better job at the things we have been doing for almost a century.

Criminal justice/criminology also continues to be criticized from within our field for a lack of theoretical base and for rudimentary research and analyses (Savelsberg and Sampson 2002). For example, Sampson (2000) proposed that: "most criminological theory is static in logic and handicapped by a focus on (allegedly) fixed explanatory categories, thereby failing to address the process and dynamics leading to criminal events."

Sampson based this argument on the current methods and analyses in criminology, stating "[t]heories limited to time-stable factors are thus incapable of unpacking the zigzagging and temporally variable patterns of offending." He concluded his argument with a call for a change in the way we examine crime. He stated, "[w]hat is needed is a concerted effort to enhance the science of ecological assessment ('econometrics') by developing systematic procedures for directly measuring social mechanisms in community context, and by developing tools to improve the quality of community-level research."

Savelsberg and Sampson (2002) followed these criticisms with an argument that criminology (and by implication criminal justice) is not a discipline because it does not have an intellectual core. Savelsberg and Sampson (2002) based this conclusion on their argument that "... criminology has a subject matter but no unique methodological commitment or paradigmatic theoretical framework... . There are no common assumptions or guiding insights. There is no intellectual idea that animates criminology." If Savelsberg and Sampson (2002) are right, which I am not convinced they are, we have much work to do in this field to develop theoretical and methodological paradigms to establish ourselves as a separate discipline.

I propose that criminal justice/criminology must move beyond theories based on linear analysis to include theories based on methodologies that are more appropriate for studying complex human behavior. We must put aside strictly linear models in favor of fractal behavior, complex systems, and non-linear analysis. Instead of controlling variables and restricting interaction, we must look at the messy data of everyday life and, in its fullness, richness, and complexity, examine it for the hidden associations buried so deep that our current measures of association could never detect them (Young 1995). No longer must different values of variables or different combinations of variables be used to show variation between the criminal and the non-criminal. We must begin to use methods that allow us to examine complex human behavior in a way that is not constrained by linear models. We must employ a new geometry that allows us to look at changes in time and space. We must use statistical procedures that search large and complex data sets for associations hidden deep in the data. And we must change the way that we think—theoretically, methodologically, and statistically—overcoming our disdain of error in analysis and beginning to examine the very error we have attempted all these years to control. I argue here for the viability of using complex systems science, commonly called chaos theory, in criminal justice and criminology research. An example is drawn from neighborhood-level research to demonstrate the ability of complex systems science to explain crime at the neighborhood level.

The result of this discussion is a new criminological theory or paradigm for examining criminal behavior. I call this Ecodynamics Theory. The rationale for this name comes from the research areas from which it is derived. Following the work of community crime theorists as far back as Shaw and McKay, and more recently in the works of Paul and Pat Brantingham, Marcus Felson, and others in environmental criminology, this theory proposes humans interact in an ecosystem that includes many live and material entities. We must study human behavior within this ecosystem as a whole if we are to truly understand the extent of our topic. This ecosystem is quite complex, however, and not suitable to examination with traditional linear models. We must employ complex systems science, therefore, to begin to truly understand these complex and dynamic systems. Putting these two overarching paradigms together leads us to an ecodynamic examination of crime, communities, and human behavior that changes the way we do theory, methodology, and analysis. The result is Ecodynamics Theory.

## Related Literature

It is not possible within the confines of this discussion to fully present the literature on neighborhoods and crime, ecological theory, or complex systems.

Criminological research on communities spans almost 100 years, and research on complex systems includes literature from almost every field of science (Gleick 1987) and several fields of social science (Goertzel 1994). Literature related to using complex system science to examine criminal behavior is sparse, however (Young 1995, Milovanovic 1997), and using complex systems science to examine crime at the neighborhood level has only been discussed in a few professional conference papers (see Walker 1996, 1997, 2005). To support the discussion at hand, a laconic treatment of these areas must suffice to show how complex systems science can be applied to neighborhood research.

## Neighborhoods and Crime Literature

Analysis of crime related to neighborhoods has a rich history. Even though this line of research can be traced to the 1800s or before, it is generally accepted that examinations of communities and crime solidified with the work of the Chicago School in the 1920s. As one of the most extensive and long-running criminological theories, it has contributed to a variety of methodologies and theoretical perspectives as diverse as geographic information systems and crime mapping, social disorganization, and Routine Activities theory. This literature is too extensive to fully discuss here and is fairly well known, so the comments here will be confined to some of those studies most related to the topic at hand.

The foundation of the study of neighborhoods and crime in the US is the research on social disorganization by Shaw and McKay (1942). Their research in Chicago and eight other cities in the US established the relationship between neighborhood variables, social disorganization, and high levels of crime. Shaw and McKay's study spawned a number of replications and additional research that has spanned to the present. The results of those studies essentially supported the conclusions of Shaw and McKay, though there were differences in specific findings. The variables from this line of research, including homes owned, median rental price, some measure of wealth or social assistance, population turnover, and physical deterioration, have been consistently linked with crime for over 60 years.

More specific to the study of neighborhoods that could easily have been couched in a complex systems paradigm, Schuerman and Kobrin (1986) proposed that neighborhoods pass through a progression of three stages from low, to moderate, to high levels of crime. They termed these stages and the neighborhoods associated with them emerging, transitional, and enduring.

Schuerman and Kobrin (1986) examined the same kinds of variables used in most ecological research, including physical, economic, and population characteristics of the areas. They used cross-lagged regression analysis to identify the temporal relationship between neighborhood characteristics and delinquency. They found that physical deterioration was most highly associated with increases in delinquency in emerging areas. As the neighborhood declined, there were substantial increases in the number of physically deteriorated houses. This produced a sustained migration into and out of the area, creating a substantial change in the population composition. This they considered an area of transition. In enduring crime areas, where the physical condition continued to deteriorate and delinquency rose, the most significant factors shifted to economic characteristics.

The analysis of crime and neighborhood characteristics showed that there was an inconsistent relationship (Schuerman and Kobrin 1986). In early stages of change, structural deterioration in the neighborhood preceded rising crime. As the neighborhood continued to deteriorate and change, however, crime began to precede the onset of further deterioration. This led Schuerman and Kobrin to conclude that "... neighborhood structural components become not causes but consequences, and crime emerges as the dominant force in neighborhood change." In this instance, crime was initially a dependent variable—influenced by the ecological factors. As the neighborhoods moved toward the enduring stage, crime became an independent variable—further propelling the neighborhood toward deterioration. The speed at which change occurred also varied. In emerging neighborhoods, the speed of change in neighborhood characteristics exceeded the rate of change for crime. As crime levels reached the enduring phase, the rates of crime outpaced changes in neighborhood characteristics. These findings of Schuerman and Kobrin will be particularly important in the discussion below. One of the key problems in studying crime at the neighborhood level is that crime is often a dependent variable, independent variable, and confounding variable within very short periods of change in neighborhoods. This created problems for traditional research such as Schuerman and Kobrin, but is addressed relatively easy in complex systems models.

Skogan (1986) also conducted research that could be supportive of using complex systems science in criminological theory. He presented a model demonstrating the recursive relationship between neighborhood characteristics and crime. Skogan found crime appeared to result initially from the onset of increases in ecological factors and later served as a catalyst to increase levels of the ecological variables, further propelling the neighborhood into deeper disorder. This seeming incongruence between recursive and non-recursive models supports the criticism of current criminological theory's inability to properly examine cities that are not stable over time.

Both of these studies and others support an argument that modern cities present a more random pattern of growth that in previous decades. The increasing complexity of cities can be shown in how models of city growth have changed over the years. Park and Burgess (1969) proposed a model of concentric rings where the city grows in circles, with growth rings occurring immediately outside previous rings and only broken up by natural barriers such as rivers or lakes. Hoyt (1939) argued that successive sectors, where a city grows in linear sections with residential areas moving directly behind existing ones, was more appropriate to study change in modern cities. Harris and Ullman (1945) argued that multiple nuclei, essentially smaller models of concentric rings spread throughout a city, were more appropriate. In each of these systems, cities grew predictably and in a contiguous pattern. As cities became more unstable, however, even the patterns proposed to replace concentric rings became unacceptable. Some researchers (Walker 1990) argued that hot spots were a more appropriate pattern for how modern urban cities grow, areas deteriorate, and high-crime areas emerge. This is a pattern that is seemingly more random and may jump around in the urban area. Whatever the paradigm, it is certain that modern cities do not expand or change in well organized patterns.

There have been many objections to the various methods of examining crime at the community level over the years, including the inability to deal with the changing nature of American neighborhoods (Bursik 1988) and using crime as an indicator of social disorganization and as a result of it (Reiss and Tonry 1986). Even research that generally supported Shaw and McKay (Walker 1990) qualified the results due to the change in cities and the fact that the stability found by Shaw and McKay no longer held in modern US cities. Although not as strong of an objection, there is always the question of what combination of neighborhood factors and what levels of change are required to create a situation where a neighborhood moves to higher states of disorder and higher levels of crime.

Many of the objections of neighborhood research, and many expansions of it, have begun to be addressed by a group of researchers examining crime ecology. Researchers dealing with spatio-temporal elements of crime (Brantingham and Brantingham 1981), advancements in Routine Activities Theory (Killias 2006), and the link between plant/animal ecology and criminal ecology (Felson 2006) have made substantial advancements in understanding the complexity of the urban ecosystem. This line of research is promising for increasing the efficacy of criminological research, but it is still hampered by its reliance on traditional methodologies and analysis procedures.

## Complex Systems Science Literature

Even more so than with the literature on crime, the history of scientific knowledge is lengthy. Arguably, it can be divided into three principle eras, however: premodern, modern, and postmodern. From the beginning of time until the 17th century, most knowledge was based in religion, superstition, or myth. Those who were considered most knowledgeable were those who either practiced some kind of religion or were particularly adept at describing their surroundings. Not much in the way of science was undertaken during this time.

In 1620, Francis Bacon published *Novum Organum*, which changed the way humans discovered and verified information. The title translates into the "New Body," and referred to the new body of knowledge, now called modern science, that established empirical observation as the preferred method of acquiring knowledge, displacing inspiration, myth, and religion. This new science placed careful observation and mathematical/empirical support as the bulwark of defensible ideas.

Using a paradigm of experimental methodology and linear analysis, scientists conquered much of the physical sciences. Durkheim brought this Newtonian logic to the social sciences, particularly sociology, in his work on the rules of sociological method. It was to be as simple as extending the methods of the physical sciences to the study of human behavior. It was assumed that, with the right methods, we could ferret out those human characteristics that would allow social scientists to find the same order and consistency in human nature that could be found in physics or astronomy.

Research in the social sciences, including the study of crime, fell far short of the elegant precision of Newtonian laws of motion however. This research did not fit as easily into a linear paradigm where social phenomena followed correlation patterns approaching 1 with unfailing consistency. Although the failure to fit social science and criminological research to a linear paradigm caused some social scientists to conclude that social phenomena were different from the physical sciences, most argued that we have simply not looked hard enough or in the right places for those characteristics that would consistently explain criminal behavior. As T. R. Young (1995) stated:

> We thought, and most who deal in such things still think, if we are smart enough, careful enough and disciplined enough we can tease out the inviolable laws of psyche and society; we can bring the social sciences to the same maturity to which physics and chemistry had come in the two hundred years after Newton.

An exception to the linear scientific method was the work of Poincaré. In his work in astronomy in the 1890s, Poincaré developed an understanding of the nonlinearity of physical systems. This led him to propose that the solar system was unstable.

Despite Poincaré's efforts, Newtonian physics and Euclidean geometry would remain essentially unchallenged until the 1960s. In 1962, an America meteorologist named Edward Lorenz discovered nonlinearity in the dynamics of weather systems. It was Lorenz who determined that not all structures in the physical sciences worked in a purely linear fashion. Lorenz's ideas were accepted with some trepidation within the physical sciences.

At about this same time, the third era of knowledge began to emerge: postmodernism. This paradigm was based primarily on the works of Derrida (1982), Foucault (1965, 1970), Lacan (1977), and Saussure (1966). Although postmodernism did not replace modern scientific thought as happened in changing from the first to the second era, it did signal a change in the philosophy and way of thinking for many people.

Heavy reliance on complicated mathematical models and a departure from traditional methodologies and theoretical designs prevented the spread of complex systems science to the social sciences for many years. It is only in the past 15 years or so that some forward-thinking criminologists began to see the value of a paradigm that was less rigid and allowed for the inconsistencies inherent in human nature. It was against the backdrop of Lorenz's analyses and postmodern thought that complex systems science began to emerge within criminology.

Lorenz's work and those of others related to complex systems science were originally called "chaos theory." This is because they argued that some systems are so complex they look like they are in chaos. Other systems, as will be described below, move from relative order to what could be described as chaos. This became a popular term, showing up in both scientific and lay books, and even making its way into movies. As more people studied chaos theory and began to add to the methods, analyses, and theory, it became more accepted to call it complex systems science or a few similar terms to more accurately describe both the systems under study and the methods used to study the systems.

The use of complex systems science in examining criminal behavior began to take shape in the early 1990s when a small number of researchers in criminal justice and criminology began working with complex systems science in an attempt to adapt its principles for examining crime. Young (1995) was one of the first people to propose using complex systems science in criminal justice and criminology. His work laid the foundation for using complex systems science in examining crime from a postmodern perspective. Others such as Arrigo (1993, 1996), Henry and Milovanovic (1991), and Milovanovic (1992, 1996) continued to develop a postmodern theory of crime using complex systems as the backcloth.

One of the most extensive treatments of complex systems science as it relates to crime is Milovanovic (1997). This book is a collection of essays applying complex systems science to criminology, law, and social justice. The first part of the book is most relevant for the discussion here, as it outlines some of the central concepts of complex systems science as they might be utilized in criminology. Some of Young's early and unpublished thoughts on complex systems and crime can be found in two chapters in this section. Each chapter provides an overview of complex systems science related to postmodernism. Young shows how complex systems science and postmodernism could be used to reconcepualize various forms of violent and non-violent crime. Pepinsky adds to the discussion of violent crime in a shortened version of his "geometry of violence," which uses a complex systems paradigm to discuss this type of behavior. The other two sections of the book deal with postmodern explanations of the application of law and a discussion of using complex systems science through postmodernism to support social change.

Specific to using complex systems science to examine neighborhoods is a series of my previous conference papers. In 1996, I examined the propositions of social disorganization theory from a complex systems science viewpoint and suggested ways the theory could be improved using a complex systems paradigm. I expanded that paper in 1997 and presented a discussion of the foundation of complex systems science principles for use in criminological theory. In 1999, I addressed the data requirements necessary to examine neighborhood characteristics and crime using complex systems science (Walker, 1999). Finally, in 2005, I presented an initial call for using complex systems science in examining cities and neighborhoods. These papers form the foundation of using complex systems science to develop Ecodynamics Theory. The elements of complex systems science needed for the theory are discussed in the next section.

## Description of Complex Systems Science

Complex systems science is a theoretical, methodological, and analytical paradigm that deals with the complex structure of *order* and *disorder* that is exhibited by natural and social systems. The key words here are order and disorder. Both are important in complex systems science as a research paradigm. Both order and disorder are examined through *attractors*, *bifurcations*, and the patterns of attractors and bifurcations drawn in what is called *phase space*. The order of attractors and the likelihood of bifurcation is partially dependent on the *feedback* experienced by the system. It is these concepts that allow the examination of systems that are far too complex for linear analysis.

### Phase Space

Phase space in complex systems theory is a graphical representation of what is occurring in the behavior of a system, in this case human behavior. Think of phase space like a map of a city where a person's movement is plotted. The geographic changes of the person can be plotted on the map to represent movement. Because of the need to also examine time, the map needs to be made 3-D, so geography is plotted on one plane and time on another. The result is something that might resemble a bowl or sphere, and the person's movement over time could be plotted in a continual line that moves horizontally for geographic changes and vertically for time chages. The bowl, which is called a phase-space *basin* in complex systems science, has advantages over strictly two-dimensional space because it allows some variation in time and space, even within a single set of behaviors. Now imagine that each set of behaviors of the person is plotted in separate basins. All activities related to normative behavior (going to school, work, shopping, etc.) are plotted in one basin. All activities related to criminal behavior are plotted in another basin. All activities related to potentially criminal behavior (drinking, gambling, etc.) are plotted in still another basin. The number of basins for a person could be expanded or contracted based on what was being examined. For example, it would be possible to divide the basins of criminal behavior between, say, drug use and burglary; or the number of basins could be increased as a person's criminal activities expanded. Plotting behavior in this way increases the understanding of human behavior and interaction similar to that of Routine Activities Theory or environmental criminology, but it is much more complex. Because of its complexity, it requires analytical methods much stronger than linear analyses.

### Attractors

What is represented in phase-space are attractors. All systems operate in patterns. Even those systems with little or no order have certain points that bind them together. The systems that are most orderly can be represented in linear or curvilinear patterns studied with traditional scientific methods. More complex systems require different and more dialectic methods of representing them. Attractors allow this representation. An attractor is a point or region in a system to which a system factor seems to be attracted or patterned (Briggs and Peat, 1989). For example, a person who is involved in many complex behaviors may wake up at essentially the same time every weekday. The behavior of the individual is very complex and varied; however, it is attracted to a relatively stable point. Using a criminological example, a person may be involved in burglary, drug use, and drug sales, with no observable pattern in his or her actions. If the individual is watched over time, however, a pattern of behavior may be produced that shows the person moving from burglary to get money to buy drugs, to drug use, to sales of the excess drugs bought. The person is, thus, attracted to a relatively stable pattern of what otherwise appears to be random behaviors.

Although there is disagreement concerning how many attractors exist, it is generally accepted that there are four types. They are arranged from systems exhibiting very ordered behavior to systems that are considered in chaos because they have order that is very difficult to detect, and impossible to detect with linear analyses.

The first type of attractor is a point attractor. This is a pattern of behavior that converges in phase-space to one point (see Figure 1). An often quoted example of a point attractor is a pendulum that goes to the same point in an arc at equal intervals and then comes to rest at exactly the same point each time. A point attractor has limited use in understanding human behavior because humans never do the same thing exactly the same way or at the same time; however, a point attractor is exactly what we look for in traditional analyses—a point that is always the same for a given value, a perfect correlation.

A limit attractor represents perhaps a more appropriate pattern for human behavior. This pattern allows unlimited variation between two extremes (Figure 2). An example of this kind of attractor is a thermostat. Temperature is allowed to vary within certain limits. If these limits are not reached, nothing is considered

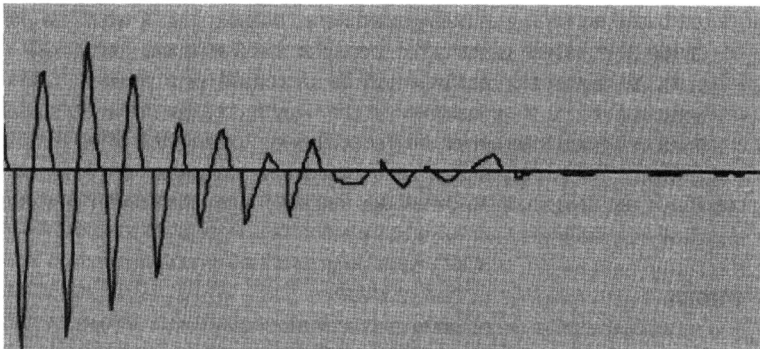

**Figure 1**   Graphical representation of movement in a point attractor.

ADVANCING SCIENCE AND RESEARCH IN CRIMINAL JUSTICE 565

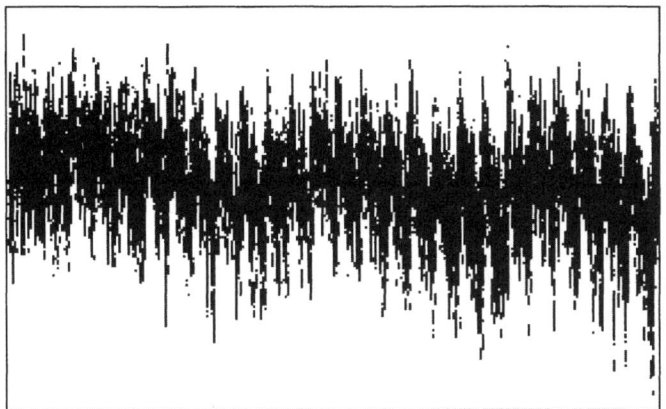

**Figure 2** Graphical representation of movement in a limit attractor.

abnormal, and the heater or air conditioner will not turn on. Only when behavior is outside the limits does the system react. Limit attractors resist change and will work to settle back into their cycle if disturbed. For example, if the temperature moves beyond the limits of the thermostat, it will turn on the heater in an attempt to bring the system back within its boundaries. The system will resist change and recover from perturbations unless the system is disturbed enough to send it into a greater state of variation (Briggs and Peat, 1989, p. 37).

The next level of attractor is a torus attractor. This is the point at which we may truly begin to analyze human behavior. A torus is a pattern that occupies three-dimensional space but that is relatively limited in variation. An example is a marble that is being propelled through a sphere with a lid on it. As that marble moves through the sphere, it is free to move on any side, top or bottom. In fact, it can be said that the marble will probably not take the exact same path twice. As shown in Figure 3, however, if enough rotations of the marble are made and plotted, a pattern of behavior develops. In human behavior, a torus attractor represents a relatively stable pattern where variations in behavior are frequent and unpredictable but still fall within some boundaries of order. The behavior of the person may seem random and unpredictable if followed for only a short period of time; but may begin to show a stable pattern if the person is observed long enough.

The next attractor is a strange attractor. Strange attractors may be of many different types. At the most ordered level, a strange attractor has two outcome basins (two phase space plots of behavior). This type of attractor is often called a butterfly attractor because the pattern of activity in phase space takes on the appearance of a butterfly with its wings spread (see left side of Figure 4). As further bifurcations occur, the attractor may develop 4, 8, 16, 32, or more outcome basins (see right side of Figure 4). Most important for the topic at hand is that a strange attractor represents the point at which a person may move freely between non-criminal and criminal behavior.

566    WALKER

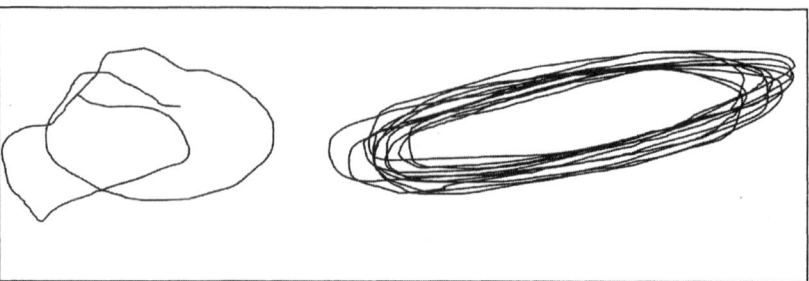

**Figure 3**   Phase space for a torus attractor (two-dimensional only).

In a limit attractor, criminal behavior is an aberration that would cause the system to react to bring the behavior back within limits. For example, a teenager might be caught in some criminal behavior; at which point, the parents step in and make changes to the person's environment to restrict any future criminal behavior. In a strange attractor, however, a person may move freely and randomly between criminal and non-criminal behavior. Additionally, the wings of an attractor do not have to be symmetrical; thus a person could spend more time in criminal behavior, more in non-criminal behavior, or relatively equal time in both. As shown in Figure 5, the time spent in each outcome basin could also vary over time or as conditions change.

## Bifurcations

Complex systems often do not stay in one type of attractor. Frequently, systems exhibit increasingly complex and disordered behavior over time. These systems move from one attractor to another at very specific points as they become more

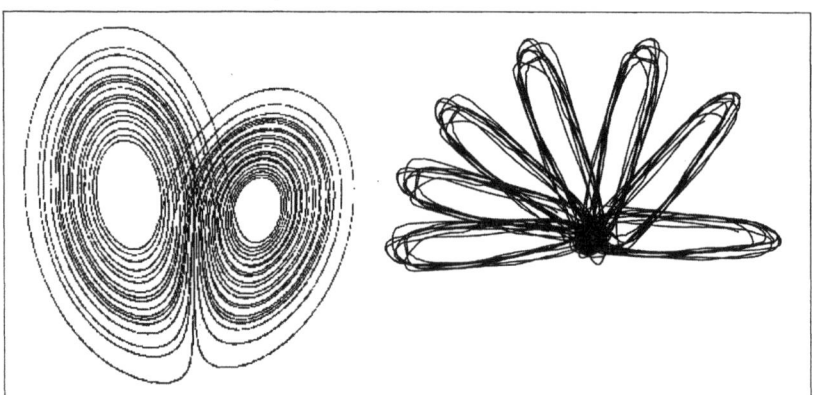

**Figure 4**   Multiple basin strange attractor.

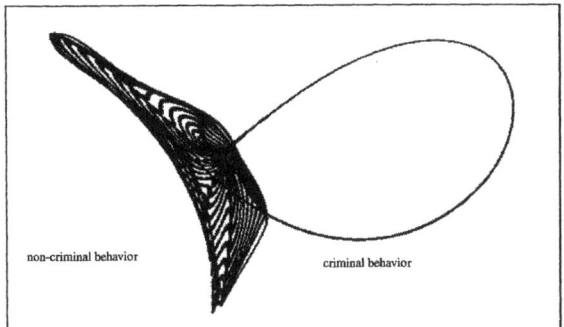

**Figure 5** Strange attractor with differential behaviour patterns.

disordered. The points at which a system moves from one attractor to another are called bifurcations. It is a doubling in the patterns of behavior where the system moves from more to less ordered. For instance, only a slight increase in taxes could cause someone, possibly unconsciously, to begin to consider some form of cheating on his or her taxes; or one additional home going up for sale in a neighborhood could create a perception of "flight" among the residents. The behavior here doubles from a single set of actions (not selling homes) to two sets (selling homes and not selling homes) with potentially equal amounts of behavior. The movement from a point attractor to a strange attractor, and the associated bifurcation points are shown in Figure 6.

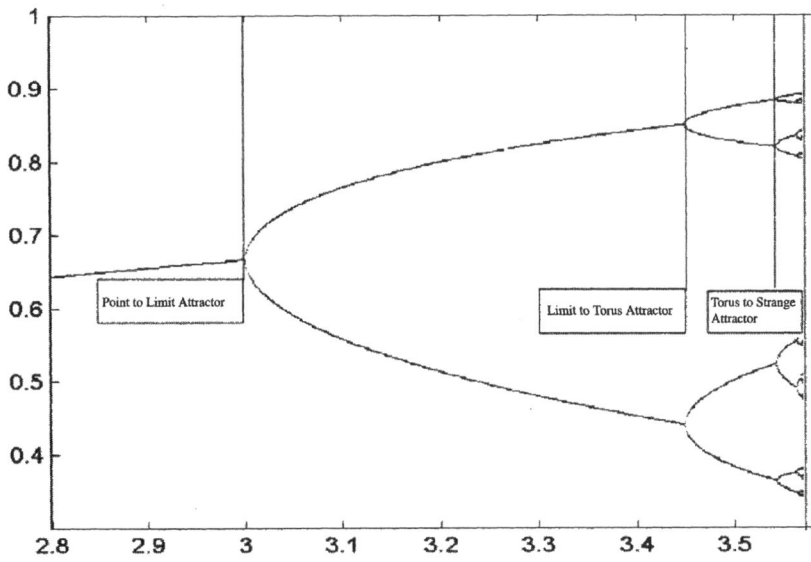

**Figure 6** Bifurcation map.

An important concept associated with bifurcations is that they occur at exact points within a system. These points are called Feigenbaum points or values, after the scientist who discovered them. These bifurcations always occur at exactly the same Feigenbaum value. As illustrated in Figure 7, at a Feigenbaum value of 3.0, the system will bifurcate from a point attractor into a limit attractor. The system will bifurcate to a torus attractor at a Feigenbaum value of 3.4495. After this, the system will bifurcate at increasingly closer values as it moves to systems exhibiting greater amounts of disorder. This process of bifurcation at particular points has been found in many systems from the stock market to the distribution of galaxies in the universe. In fact, in all systems to which Feigenbaum values have been able to be applied, these values hold true (Young, 1995). The value of bifurcations for studying neighborhoods and crime should become evident in the examples below.

## Feedback

The final component of complex systems is feedback. Feedback is an impulse sent to the system from its environment that the system uses to make changes to itself. It is like the feedback in an electric guitar where the sound of the guitar affects the system, which in turn affects the sound of the guitar, which in turn affects the system in a spiraling process of adaptation and change.

There are three types of feedback in complex systems science. These differ by the consequences of the feedback on the system. Some feedback pushes the system to more disorder, some to less disorder, and some depends on the system. It is also possible the feedback has no effect on the system.

First is positive feedback. This tends to push a system toward more unstable states. This is the kind of feedback displayed in the electric guitar where the feedback gets louder and more complex the longer it is allowed to continue. It is also the kind of feedback displayed in the systems discussed by Schuerman and Kobrin (1986) and Skogan (1986). In this research, changes in ecological variables typically preceded changes in crime. At some point, however, crime increased the rate of change in ecological variables. At still other points, crime and ecological variables combined to produce even further changes in themselves. This kind of feedback to the system of the neighborhood served to propel it toward further disorder.

The second type of feedback is negative feedback, which tends to push a system toward a more ordered attractor, continually attempting to reduce variation and instability. An example here was the limit attractor. In that state, any movement outside the boundaries of the attractor was met by the system with attempts to move the system back within the limits and maintain the state of order.

The third type of feedback is non-linear. Non-linear feedback can be either positive or negative, depending on the needs of the system, and tends to maintain the system in the present pattern of stability. Non-linear feedback is like the heart during exercise (Young, 1995). In this example, positive only feedback (promoting change to handle increased levels of activity) would cause the heart to move to a fatally high heartbeat level because it would try to adapt to the level of oxygen needed for the most stressful situations. This would ultimately cause the heart to fail as it continually tried to pump harder and faster to keep up with the demand. Negative only feedback (always attempting to resist change) would prevent the rapid increase of heartbeat to compensate for new energy demands. This would also be a problem because, in response to exercise, the heart would beat slower not faster. This would make increased activity impossible. Nonlinear feedback (positive and negative change at different times) offers a dynamic state with which to respond to such exigencies (increasing the heartbeat in response to exercise but also decreasing the heartbeat to keep from damaging the heart).

Phase space plots, attractors, bifurcations, and feedback mechanisms are far different from the research designs of modern science. This revolutionizes the way criminal behavior is examined. Accepting for the moment that this paradigm of theory, methodology, and analysis is better than previous methods and that it is preferred for building theory in criminology, the discussion now turns to an example of how complex systems science could be used to improve our understanding of neighborhood-level examinations of crime. This discussion represents the initial development of Ecodynamics Theory.

## Ecodynamics Theory in Neighbrood Research: A New Criminological Theory

Combining a complex systems paradigm with the variables that have become relatively standard in research on neighborhoods and crime represents a new way of examining human behavior criminologically. Analyzing neighborhoods in this way may also begin to address the question of what combination of ecological characteristics and at what levels it takes to create a situation where a neighborhood moves toward disorder and high crime. To place neighborhoods within the structure of complex systems, they are described below in terms of attractor states, phase space, bifurcations, and feedback mechanisms.

### Neighborhoods Described as Attractors within Complex Systems

A point attractor essentially cannot exist in neighborhoods and in human behavior. There is never a point that characteristics in a neighborhood are at the same point at exactly the same time each year or where they return to exactly the same point when disturbed. For example, there are virtually no neighborhoods in a given city that have no population turnover in the time between the decennial censuses. Although there may be very little change in a neighborhood population, and it returns to the same number of households, it is unlikely that changes in population in the neighborhood would occur at exactly the same time each year or decade or that the size of a family moving into a neighborhood would exactly match the size of a family moving out. As stated above, it is ironic that point attractors cannot exist in dynamic neighborhoods and human behavior because this is the attractor type sought after in traditional research. The goal of almost all current statistical models is a neighborhood (or person) that does exactly the same thing under the same conditions, and hopefully at the same time. It is no wonder that current criminological analyses struggle; the model sought after does not exist, or exists in such small numbers as to render current statistical analyses ineffective.

A limit attractor describes a neighborhood that is very stable and with little crime exhibited. In this kind of neighborhood, changes occur but they are limited and tend to hover around a given point over time. For example, when interest rates are low, people in a relatively stable neighborhood may take the opportunity to sell their homes and to buy more expensive homes elsewhere. Others will buy the homes vacated in the neighborhood. When interest rates climb again, the population of the neighborhood will return to a point similar to its previous level; probably not the same population, but relatively close in number. Crime in this system will also show low levels and stability. There may be the occasional teenager who commits delinquent activities, but the neighborhood will quickly restabilize after that person leaves, is controlled, or ages out of crime.

If change occurs too rapidly, however, or at high levels, the limits of variability may be broken, and a bifurcation occurs. The system will then change into one where unpredictability is the norm, and behavior is more varied. This is characterized by a torus attractor. While there is constant change in the neighborhood, and variation in key ecological variables, the variation is within some boundaries and represents what one might depict as a fluid neighborhood. For example, there would be some population turnover in the neighborhood as people move in and out. This turnover would be constant and more varied than a limit attractor. The change will not be represented by "social disorganization"; flight; or invasion, dominance, and succession, however. In terms of criminal behavior, there would be some crimes committed by residents but mostly in other parts of the city, or crime might result from a small number of children engaged in a limited amount of crime. While the crime in the neighborhood would be constant and varied, it would not reach levels sufficient to alarm residents and would be relatively stable over time. This is the type of neighborhood Schuerman and Kobrin (1986) would characterize as "emerging crime."

In some neighborhoods, these characteristics may begin to change at increasing rates. The neighborhoods bifurcate into a 2n, butterfly attractor as shown in the left side of Figure 4. At this point, criminal behavior may be as equally a plausible behavior as non-criminal behavior as people begin to move freely between the two phase-space basins. Other characteristics may also take on different outcome basins. For example, population turnover may move from a somewhat stable pattern of in- and out-migration to one exhibiting large changes in number. This is the point that a neighborhood may begin a transition from an emerging crime problem to a more enduring one (Schuerman and Kobrin

1986). People (specifically juveniles) may begin to move from a non-criminal basin of behavior to a criminal basin with increasing frequency. The criminal behavior exhibited by residents may be limited at first as juveniles commit a small number of minor crimes or commit crimes in other parts of the city. This behavior may expand quickly, however, into different outcome basins as the number and types of crimes begins to increase.

If this trend continues, the neighborhood could eventually be said to represent deep chaos. The behavior would be represented by a multiple basin (4n, 8n, or larger) attractor. This is the point Shaw and McKay (1942) called social disorganization and what Schuerman and Kobrin (1986) characterized as "enduring crime." Here, there is seemingly no pattern to behavior, especially criminal behavior. Residents and non-residents alike may move freely between different types of criminal and non-criminal behaviors. The whole system is unstable and, to a large extent, uncontrollable. What once was minor criminal involvement can rapidly turn to many different kinds and levels of criminal behavior as the neighborhood declines and the population becomes more criminally oriented.

Not only is behavior not consistent in this kind of system, change within the system's characteristics can be irrational and unpredictable. In a neighborhood characterized by deep chaos, some people will move to one outcome basin, while others with near identical qualities will move to another outcome basin. Some individuals will be caught and punished, which may cause them to move back to a non-criminal outcome basin; their peers may not get caught or punished and may also return to a non-criminal outcome basin. Others, both caught and not caught, may operate predominately in criminal outcome basins. Others could exist in this environment and not engage in criminal behavior at all. This is the situation often depicted in the media where a young person from a gang-controlled, high-crime neighborhood goes on to become a successful medical doctor. Where the outcome basins meet, which is the attractor, it is impossible to predict what outcome basin a person will move into at any given time.

At this level of complexity and disorder, certain characteristics may feed off of others to produce even greater changes. For example, a particularly heinous crime may produce great fear among residents. That fear may result in an increase in the number of residents who move before selling their house, further increasing disorder in the neighborhood. This, in turn, produces even more dramatic changes in the composition of residents and can greatly increase crime, cascading the neighborhood into more and more outcome basins and levels of complexity and disorder. This will be discussed more fully below in terms of feedback mechanisms.

These differing outcome basins are important for the study of neighborhood change and crime because complex systems science allows the same factors to produce one outcome (non-criminal behavior) at a particular value and a different outcome (criminal behavior) even with the same value. This revolutionizes the way we look at neighborhood change, and is key for the use of Ecodynamics Theory in studying neighborhood change. In traditional analyses, the same combination and level of variables should result in the exact same outcome (a point attractor in complex systems parlance). In complex systems science, no longer must different values of variables or different combinations of variables be used to show variation between neighborhoods. Now, the same variables can be used to describe different outcomes in the same neighborhood; something we could not accomplish with traditional scientific methods.

## Bifurcations: Moving from Order to Disorder

As discussed above in the study of Schuerman and Kobrin (1986) and as described in terms of Ecodynamics Theory, it is easy to see that neighborhoods may move over time from relatively stable and low crime areas to relatively unstable and high crime areas. This phenomenon was shown as far back as Shaw and McKay's (1942) work. It is also easy see points in a neighborhood studied over time that were "critical incidents" in the history of the neighborhood; those instances that pushed the neighborhood to higher levels of crime (Williams 1999). For example, there may be cases where residents are somewhat concerned about the future of the neighborhood. Home owners may begin to move to other parts of the city. Some of them are able to sell their homes quickly, but perhaps some not as quickly. At some point, though, one additional house goes up for sale, which starts a sense of desperation. Many people start putting their homes up for sale. Those who are financially able may even rent their homes. Others may sell to people who rent the homes. This dramatic change in population and in the number of home owners can push the neighborhood to a higher level of disorder and complexity.

These critical incidents represent bifurcation points in neighborhood change. As stated above, bifurcations in complex systems are the points at which a system moves from one attractor to another. It is the one house that causes the rush to sell, or the one additional crime that causes panic among the residents.

According to complex systems science, the first bifurcation may take a long time. A neighborhood may be quite stable for several decades because it is in a good part of the city, the homes are new, many homes are owned, etc. As the neighborhood begins to age and become more disordered, it approaches a Feigenbaum value of 3.0. In the example above, that one extra house going up for sale pushes the system beyond a Feigenbaum value of 3.0 and the system/neighborhood bifurcates and moves to a more complex attractor state. Perhaps more renters move in or people who are more socially unstable (say characterized by crime-prone-aged children) buy the homes. This increases the disorder in the neighborhood and increases the likelihood of crime. Before long, the neighborhood reaches a Feigenbaum value of 3.4495 and bifurcates again to an even more complex attractor. This creates more crime and more disorder, which causes the neighborhood to bifurcate again. The neighborhood continues in this spiral toward disorder at increasing rates. It bifurcates again and again at increasingly smaller time periods as the Feigenbaum values move closer together. This phenomenon can be seen in American cities where a neighborhood will be very stable and desirable for a long time, but, over the course of only 10 or 15 years, may deteriorate rapidly.

Another important concept in bifurcations is that systems, in this case neighborhoods, are the most disordered at bifurcation points. Near a bifurcation point, the system is undergoing a state of flux. It is, in effect, being offered a choice of orders (Briggs and Peat 1989). The system may stay in a more orderly attractor state or move to a more complex attractor state. In points where the neighborhood may be moving to a higher level of disorder, there is often rapid change back and forth. For example, residents may change their minds several times a day about selling their homes. They are confused about what they want to do. In terms of crime, residents may be moving rapidly between criminal behavior and non-criminal behavior; or between different types of crimes. Residents may alternate between being resilient and thinking "everything will be ok" and abject terror of the situation. Interestingly, if the system does make the jump to greater disorder, it often has somewhat of a calming effect. This was shown as far back as Shaw and McKay's (1942) work. They noted that during time of invasion and even dominance, crime was very high, and the neighborhood seemed most disordered. When succession occurred, however, the neighborhood moved back toward a sense of calm, and the crime rate returned to a point very similar to its previous level.

The challenge of criminology is to find these bifurcation points in human behavior or in the dynamics of the neighborhood. If researchers can identify where a neighborhood is in terms of a bifurcation map, changes could possibly be made in the neighborhood (through feedback, see below) that might maintain the stable state. As discussed below, it is easier to maintain a system in its current state than to move it from a less ordered to a more ordered attractor. It would be better, and easier, then, to recognize a potential bifurcation and provide feedback to keep the neighborhood at the current level of order than attempt to return it to a more ordered attractor state once it bifurcates. This is supported by the work of Schuerman and Kobrin (1986) who proposed that neighborhoods with emerging levels of crime are the most likely to be "saved" from moving to high levels of crime. Criminologists have been unable to predict these critical incidents or bifurcation points to this juncture because of the limitations of traditional analyses. Ecodynamics Theory may be used to determine when the conditions are right for a bifurcation to occur and thus might be able to inform policy concerning where government resources would be most helpful.

## Role of Feedback in Ecodynamics Theory

One of the frustrating but ultimately beneficial aspects of a complex systems paradigm is that change, even change in a system characterized by deep chaos, is not absolute. If it was, we could probably predict it using linear methods of analysis. Complex systems science teaches us, however, that some systems can absorb a great deal of change without moving to further disorder. In the discussion above, some neighborhoods may be able to sustain great turnovers in population without moving to a transitional or high crime area. For example, some higher SES neighborhoods that serve as "starter homes" for socially mobile people may experience turnover rates near 100 percent every few years. These areas may not experience increases in crime rates, however, because of their makeup and because the mix of characteristics allow the system to absorb those kinds of changes. Within complex systems science, this relates to feedback mechanisms within the system.

Feedback as it relates to complex systems may also account for the variation in findings that have plagued neighborhood research. For example, Shannon (1982) examined social disorganization characteristics in Racine, Wisconsin in an attempt to show how "large city" characteristics also applied to smaller cities. Shannon found there was not a significant relationship between the amount of change in the characteristics of an area and related changes in the local arrest rates. He concluded from these findings that smaller cities did not follow the same patterns of social disorganization factors as larger cities. Bursik (1988) suggested a possible reason for this is that "local community adaptations to changes in urban dynamics stabilized much earlier in Racine than in larger urban areas." It is equally plausible, though, that Racine as a system experienced negative, or perhaps non-linear, feedback. This would cause the system to absorb changes in the neighborhood characteristics without changing the level of crime.

This phenomenon can also be shown in other neighborhood-based research. In the original work of Shaw and McKay, slight increases or decreases in population produced large changes in the delinquency rate, while large changes in population produced small and inconsistent changes in delinquency. In a replication of Shaw and McKay's research, Walker (1990) found an opposite effect of population. In that study, population changes below the 75th percentile were not significantly associated with delinquency. Population changes in the top 25th percentile, however, were significantly associated with delinquency. The difference in these two studies supports the principle of complex systems science that small changes in certain elements may produce large changes in other elements in some systems, while the same changes or larger in the same factors will not produce any change at all in other systems.

The importance of feedback concerns the proper reaction to changes in neighborhood characteristics related to crime. For example, the reaction of Chicago to the findings of Shaw and McKay's work was the Chicago Area Project that poured money and resources into areas with high crime and disorder. This experiment was largely considered a failure, however. If physical deterioration, poverty, and living conditions are factors that appear related to crime, then why does reducing those factors not reduce crime? The answer may lie in the way the resources are provided to the neighborhood, the timing of those resources, and the state of the system when the resources are provided. Resources, or other crime-prevention efforts, operate as feedback for the system. Some systems are prepared for negative feedback, and such feedback greatly assists in maintaining the order of the system. In other systems, feedback can do more harm than good. If positive feedback is offered to a system, or if the system was not prepared for feedback, it could cause further disorder in the system. If the system was characterized by a limit attractor state and was simply left alone, it would move back within limits of acceptable levels of behavior. In still other systems, the feedback will simply be absorbed with no change to the system.

We must be careful, then, concerning when feedback is offered to the system and in what proportions. Hübler (1992) argued that feedback is only viable for systems below a 4n attractor, and that, in attempting to influence highly complex systems through feedback, the more unstable the system, the gentler the feedback must be. Heavy handed attempts to force the system to remain stable may work for limit or torus attractors, but these tactics could be ineffective or detrimental in systems with greater disorder (Hübler 1992).

For crime control, this means that in the worst neighborhoods in terms of crime and disorder, feedback and attempts to control the system will probably not be of much value. This can be shown in almost any city in the US, where increasing police patrols in high-crime areas often has no effect on the levels of crime. Further, introducing feedback in a system that is not prepared for it, or introducing the wrong type of feedback could cause the system to move to higher levels of disorder. For example, a neighborhood that is close to a bifurcation because of crime could react badly to increased police patrols—in effect, the residents could believe the neighborhood is lost—which could exacerbate the problem and push the neighborhood to a higher level of disorder. Proper timing of the right kind of feedback, however, may be an answer to crime control models. Neighborhoods that are moving from say a torus attractor to one of more disorder might be at the perfect place for feedback. Residents might be getting somewhat fearful for the future of the neighborhood, and the introduction of foot patrols or other crime control measures could be the catalyst that makes residents believe the neighborhood can be saved and make them take actions to maintain order.

## Role of Crime in Ecodynamics Theory

There has always been an underlying tension between crime and research because, even though crime is almost always the dependent variable, in reality it is also an independent variable. This creates real problems for criminology because much of neighborhood research, back to Shaw and McKay (1942), saw crime as the outcome of neighborhood characteristics and disorder, and also the cause of it. Possibly the greatest benefit of adopting an Ecodynamics Theory approach to examine neighborhoods and crime is because of how it allows crime to change roles at different times or within the same system. Crime in Ecodynamics Theory may be a dependent variable and the subject of study; but it may also serve as a cause of additional levels of disorder through feedback as discussed above. Instead of the differing roles of crime (even within the same system) causing problems for the analysis, however, Ecodynamics Theory embraces the nature of crime and uses it to further understand the system.

The reason Ecodynamics Theory can deal effectively with crime in different natures is because it proposes, as discussed above, that the same factors producing non-criminal behavior at one point in the system can produce criminal behavior at other points. This does not mean that the variables interact differently or with other variables. This means that the same variables, even with the same values, can produce non-criminal behavior at one point in the system and criminal behavior at another point. This is because the phase space within Ecodynamics Theory has "enough room" if you will that two objects (characteristics or variables) can occupy the same space at the same time. When this occurs, it is possible for the objects to interact in some systems and not in others. It depends upon the kind of feedback that is being experienced by the system. This may partially account for the many cases where two brothers grow up in the same household under the same conditions, but one becomes a successful businessman and the other goes to prison.

It is the role of feedback that in effect solves the problem of crime being both a dependent and independent variable. Initially in the system, crime is probably a dependent variable. The ecological variables come together in some form that increases the level of crime. Once the system gets sufficiently complex, however, feedback may cause crime to take on different roles, depending on the system and what is happening. For example, in some neighborhoods, crime may continue to be a dependent variable, being influenced by the ecological variables. In other neighborhoods, crime may become an independent variable, increasing the ecological variables rather than the ecological variables increasing crime. The ecological variables and crime may also reach a point where they combine and further influence themselves to push the system/ neighborhood to higher levels of disorder and higher crime.

This is the methodological problem Shaw and McKay (1942) were criticized for, and the situation Schuerman and Kobrin (1986) recognized but could not address with linear analyses and traditional methodology. What makes matters worse for traditional methodologies but not for Ecodynamics Theory is that, in this situation, it is easy to see there is a spiraling nature of the variables. Both crime and the other ecological variables are in a feedback loop where crime is initially influenced by the ecological variables, but then may have an influence on them, eventually reaching a point where crime and the ecological variables come together to increase the disorder of the neighborhood, and that disorder itself increases the level of crime and the ecological variables, which continues to increase the disorder and crime.

This turns our methodological world upside down. We have been taught to look for intervening variables to account for different outcomes in criminological theory. The exact opposite is stressed in Ecodynamics Theory. Here, the same factors may be producing high levels of crime in one neighborhood and low levels in another; and the factors that are dependent at one point in time may be independent at another and may be both within a very small time frame in still another part of the system.

## Limitations of Ecodynamic Theory

Although an argument can be made for an immediate and beneficial use of Ecodynamics Theory in neighborhood research, there are problems inherent in this paradigm, as all other theories. These problems may be overcome to a certain extent in future development of the theory.

The first problem in using Ecodynamics Theory to examine crime lies in its relative infancy of application. To this point, complex systems science has mostly been limited to a mathematical ideal. It has been used to describe the weather, to describe predator prey cycles, and in contrived mathematical experiments, among others. There has been some application of complex systems science, especially in examining characteristics that lend themselves to univariate, mathematical research such as brain waves, heart patterns, and such. There has also been limited research in other areas of psychology and medicine. In those instances where a complex systems paradigm has been used, it has produced results consistent with the mathematical models, so it is reasonable to believe the same will hold true when we begin to test this theory in criminology. There has been very little work, however, in most of the social sciences and especially in criminology, so the methods of conducting research related to social factors such as crime are rudimentary and not well tested.

There is also the problem that research using a complex systems paradigm is very data hungry. The nature of examining patterns where seemingly none exist requires one to collect a large amount of data. It also requires that the data be longitudinal. In the days of limited funds for criminological research, longitudinal studies that are this revolutionary may face difficulty getting funded. This problem, however, may not be as big a detriment for community-level research as it would be for more individual level theories. Much of the research on neighborhoods and cities spans at least two iterations of the decennial census. Although this is still a limited amount of data, it is such that initial assessments of the viability of using Ecodynamics Theory can be tested, at least in terms of the ecological variables associated with the Census. The same cannot be said for crime data; although it is also improving. The kind of crime data needed for these analyses only began to be collected in an electronic format in the 1990s. On its own, this is now probably sufficient to begin to conduct complex systems analyses. We may need a few more years, however, before crime data and neighborhood data reach a point where they are simultaneously sufficient for these kinds of analyses.

The final problem is that Ecodynamics Theory is not a theory of prediction. The nature of change beyond a point attractor prevents us from knowing where the system will be at any given time. Even within ordered systems, such as a limit attractor, we can predict a general pattern of behavior of the system, but cannot predict where a characteristic of the system will be at any given point. For example, research will not be able to predict when a person will commit a crime or who will be criminal—not that we can do that now, but we still cling to the notion of being able to do so with better methods and more data. With a complex systems paradigm, the best that can be accomplished is to identify those factors that most influence the patterns and attractors, and attempt to apply feedback mechanisms that will ensure the greatest possible order in the system. For neighborhood crime control, this means identifying the key parameters that drive neighborhoods to new attractor states; not necessarily eliminating factors of change, but rather working with those factors to maintain a stable state of neighborhood order and crime. This is still a substantial improvement over current criminological theory, but in using Ecodynamics Theory, we must accept from the beginning that it will not be able to identify that one thing in a person that will allow prediction of criminal behavior.

## Conclusion

The purpose of this discussion was to call into question the value of continuing to use traditional methods and analyses to examine complex human behavior and to present a new theoretical and methodological paradigm that, when combined with neighborhood-level analyses, provides a better method for examining neighborhood change and crime. This discussion outlined a theoretical model and research design for the use of complex systems science in the study of neighborhood change, changing crime patterns in cities, and criminological theory. It has attempted to show the benefits of non-linear analysis over linear models in examining these complex systems. In doing so, it has turned traditional statistical procedures around and has turned statistical error upside down.

The result of this discussion is a new criminological theory based on different methods and analyses. Ecodynamics Theory combines the substantial amount of criminological research over six decades, including more recent advancements in environmental criminology, with the methodological and analytical advancements from complex systems science.

I call on criminology and criminal justice researchers to take steps to implement the concepts, methods, and analyses of complex systems science within criminological theory. Even if it is not to advance Ecodynamics Theory, we should begin immediate efforts to identify the key parameters that drive systems to more unstable patterns and begin to understand the changes in systems that influence this change.

Ultimately, I believe this paradigmatic change may move criminology forward from our current state of, essentially, examining different concepts, using slightly different operationalization and propositions, and getting about the same level of explained variance. This may push us to a new level of understanding of the way people, neighborhoods, and cities change over time. We could finally begin to address the concerns of the Michael-Adler report and to use the scientific methods appropriate for studying human behavior—not scientific methods designed for much more ordered systems. It also at least partially addresses Savelsberg and Sampson's (2002) argument that "criminology has a subject matter but no unique methodological commitment or paradigmatic theoretical framework." Use of Ecodynamics Theory as a metatheory for other criminological theories could bind them together sufficiently to represent the paradigmatic theoretical framework Savelsberg and Sampson argue is absent.

I recognize this is a substantial challenge. It may seem I have stated we should completely abandon our previous ways of doing research and our theoretical paradigm and begin anew. That is somewhat overstated in that I argue linear analyses and traditional methods still play a role in research. We must move beyond them, however, if we are to advance our understanding of crime and the role neighborhood change plays in crime. Further, rather than abandoning current criminological theories, I argue changing the paradigm to be consistent with complex systems science would benefit most current theories. Ecodynamics Theory focuses on neighborhoods as the unit of analysis, but the concepts, methods, and analyses are appropriate well beyond neighborhoods. Because of another concept from complex systems science called pattern replication, Ecodynamics could be applied to different geospatial levels, or even to individuals. There are some current theories that may have data sufficient to begin individual-level analyses using complex systems science principles. For example, it might be very fruitful to reexamine some of the data from Life-Course Theory to determine if patterns exist in that data that might be suitable for examination from a complex system paradigm.

I am calling for radical changes in our theories, as well as the methods and analyses of testing the theories, but I argue these will benefit criminology and criminal justice research, and may move us to a more advanced understanding of our field of study. I will end with another quote from Sampson (2000) that I think sums up this discussion.

> To get at the major unanswered questions in the study of crime thus requires a renewed focus on the unfolding of social action, process, and change within both individuals and communities. Such a focus is, of course, foundational to the sociological imagination—Chicago-School style.

## References

Arrigo, B. (1993). Civil commitment, semiotics, and discourse on difference: An historical critique of the sign of paternalism. In R. Kevelson (Ed.), *Flux, illusion, and complexity in law*. New York: Peter King.

Arrigo, B. (1996). *The contours of psychiatric justice: A postmodern critique of mental illness, criminal insanity and the law*. New York: Garland.

Brantingham, P. J., & Brantingham, P. L. (1981). *Environmental criminology*. Prospect Heights, IL: Waveland Press.

Briggs, J., & Peat, F. D. (1989). *Turbulent mirror: An illustrated guide to chaos theory and the science of wholeness*. New York: Harper & Row.

580     WALKER


Bursik, R. J. Jr. (1988). Social disorganization and theories of crime and delinquency: Problems and prospects. *Criminology, 26,* 519-551.

Derrida, J. (1982). *Margins of philosophy,* A. Bass (trans.). Chicago: University of Chicago Press.

Felson, M. (2006). *Crime and nature.* Thousand Oaks, CA: Sage.

Foucault, M. (1965). *Madness and civilization: A history of insanity in the age of reason.* New York: Vintage Books.

Foucault, M. (1970). *The order of things.* London: Tavistock.

Gleick, J. (1987). *Chaos: Making a new science.* New York: Penguin Books.

Goertzel, B. (1994). Chaotic logic: Language, mind and reality from the perspective of complex systems science. Unpublished draft.

Harris, C. D., & Ullman, E. L. (1945). The nature of cities. *Annals, 242,* 7-11.

Henry, S., & Milovanovic, D. (1991). Constitutive criminology. *Criminology, 29,* 293-316.

Hoyt, H. (1939). *The structure and growth of residential neighborhoods in American cities.* Washington, DC: Federal Housing Administration.

Hübler, A. (1992). Modeling and control of complex systems: Paradigms and applications. In L. Sam (Ed.), *Modeling complex phenomena.* New York: Springer.

Killias, M (2006). The opening and closing of breaches: A theory on crime waves, law creation, and crime prevention. *European Journal of Criminology, 3,* 11-31.

Lacan, J. (1977). *Ecrits.* New York: Norton.

Laub, J. H. (2006). Edwin H. Sutherland and the Michael-Adler report: Searching for the soul of criminology seventy years later. *Criminology, 44,* 235-256.

Michael, J., & Adler, M. J. (1933). *Crime, law and social science.* New York: Harcourt, Brace.

Milovanovic, D. (1992). *Postmodern law and disorder: Psychoanalytic semiotics, chaos and juridic exegeses.* Liverpool, UK: Deborah Charles Publications.

Milovanovic, D. (1996). Postmodern criminology: Mapping the terrain. *Justice Quarterly,* 13, 567-610.

Milovanovic, D. (1997). *Chaos, criminology, and social justice: The new orderly (dis)order.* West Port, CT: Praeger.

Park, R. E., & Burgess, E. W. (1969). *Introduction to the science of sociology.* Chicago: University of Chicago Press.

Reiss, A. J. Jr., & Tonry, M. (Eds). (1986). *Communities and crime.* Chicago: The University of Chicago Press.

Sampson, R. J. (2000). Whither the sociological study of crime? *Annual Review of Sociology, 26,* 711-714.

Saussure, F. (1966). *Course in general linguistics,* C. Bally & A. Sechehaye (Eds.). New York: McGraw-Hill.

Savelsberg, J. J., & Sampson, R. J. (2002). Introduction to mutual engagement: Criminology and sociology. *Crime, Law and Social Change, 37,* 99-105.

Schuerman, L., & Kobrin, S. (1986). Community careers in crime. *Communities and crime,* A. J. Reiss Jr. and M. Tonry (Eds.). Chicago: The University of Chicago Press.

Shannon, L. W. (1982). The relationship of juvenile delinquency and adult crime to the changing ecological structure of the city. Iowa City: University of Iowa.

Shaw, C. R., & McKay, H. D. (1942). *Juvenile delinquency and urban areas.* Chicago: The University of Chicago Press.

Skogan, W. (1986). Community careers in crime. *Communities and crime,* eds. A. J. Reiss Jr. and M. Tonry. Chicago: The University of Chicago Press.

Sutherland, E. H. (1932-1933/1973). The Michael-Adler report. In K. Schuessler (Ed.), *Edwin H. Sutherland on analyzing crime.* Chicago: University of Chicago Press.

Walker, J. T. (2005). *Complex systems and criminological theory: Is it time to explore phase space?* Paper presented at the Annual Meeting of the American Society of Criminology, Toronto, Canada.

Walker, J. T. (1990). Human ecology and social disorganization revisit delinquency in Little Rock. In G. Barak (Ed.), *Varieties of criminology*. Westport, CT: Praeger.

Walker, J. T. (1996). *Chaos theory and social disorganization: A new paradigm for neighborhood analysis*. Paper presented at the Annual Meeting of the Academy of Criminal Justice Sciences; Las Vegas, NV.

Walker, J. T. (1997). *Non-linear analysis for neighborhood research: A theoretical model and design*. Paper presented at the Annual Meeting of the Academy of Criminal Justice Sciences; Louisville, KY.

Walker, J. T. (1999). *Nuggets of gold in rivers of numbers: Data requirements for chaos and complexity*. Paper presented at the Annual Meeting of the American Society of Criminology, Toronto, Canada.

Williams, F. P. (1999). *Imagining criminology: An alternative paradigm*. New York: Garland.

Young, T. R. (1995). *Chaos and crime: Explorations in postmodern criminology*. Unpublished manuscript.

# [7]

## The Power of Community Mediation: Government and Formation of Self-Identity

George Pavlich

Recent "alternatives" to law assume diverse forms and include various community mediation programs. Proponents see these programs as a triumph of empowered individuals and communities over the state. By contrast, early critics—in their various ways—view such programs as an expansion and intensification of state control. Against both, and working with "new informalist" insights, this article focuses on the political logic of community mediation practices. Drawing on Foucault, it explores mediation as a governmentalization (cf. expansion) of state dispute resolution which marshals both techniques of discipline and self in an attempt to produce peaceful *individual selves*. A case study is used to analyze community mediation as a confessional institution that deploys sociocultural pressures in search of nondisputing self-identities. The article concludes that the search for fixed notions of individual, self, or even community empowerment may entrench, rather than resist, current forms of regulation in dispute resolution arenas.

These days the phrase "contempt of court" evokes a rather peculiar meaning outside the courtroom. For many critics, from reflexive lawyers to dissatisfied clients, the promise of justice through litigation is an empty one; it is a distant abstraction compromised by the inequities and alienating humdrum of professionalized courtroom practices (see, e.g., Danzig 1973; Sander 1976, 1980; Cook, Roehl, & Sheppard 1980; Arthurs 1980; Salem 1985; Alfini 1986; Blair 1988). Recent bids to reclaim an immediate, popular, and accessible type of justice in our time seem to have evoked earnest searches for "justice without law," for "alternat(iv)e dispute resolution" processes (Auerbach 1983). Here I direct attention to the power relations deployed by those alternative dispute resolution programs that tout mediation as more effective than litigation at settling disputes between people with ongoing relationships in the "community." Such programs as-

The author wishes to thank the editor and two anonymous reviewers of *Law & Society Review* for their helpful comments on a previous version. Address correspondence to George Pavlich, Department of Sociology, University of Auckland, Private Bag 92019, Auckland, New Zealand; e-mail: g.pavlich@auckland.ac.nz.

sume various formats,[1] go under various names (community mediation, neighborhood dispute resolution, informal justice, etc.), and target a range of community disputes (see Wahrhaftig 1982, 1984). These various instances can be placed under the rubric of "community mediation," not to denote a single or homogeneous identity but to highlight a contingently deployed political rationality that lies at the core of such programs.

In an effort to depict this political rationality, the following narrative takes a series of strategic tacks. After briefly depicting a typical model of mediation practice, it moves to an existing debate between advocates and critics on whether community mediation limits or expands the state's control over dispute resolution. I argue that the debate is misconceived because it is founded on narrow and paradoxical precepts, which leads to serious difficulties. In an effort to overcome some of these difficulties, extending insights from more recent "new informalist" critics (see Matthews 1988a), the next section conceives of community mediation as a "governmental" power that deploys techniques of both discipline and self in its quest to recover "nondisputing" selves from the "disputants" who present themselves at mediation sessions (Foucault 1979). Given that the disciplinary techniques of mediation have attracted attention elsewhere (Pavlich 1996; Fitzpatrick 1988; Cameron & Dupuis 1989; Matthews 1988a), I turn in the latter part of the article to a case study to point out how an overlooked element may be developed; namely, how to conceptualize the techniques by which mediation encourages its participants to assume nondisputing self-identities. I shall focus on techniques (or technologies) of self, echoing Foucault's (1979:20) view that the development of these has (along with discipline) entailed a growing "governmentalisation of the State" (see also Foucault 1981a, 1988a). I conclude with brief comments on what my analysis might mean for attempts to nurture an alternative politics of dispute resolution.

An opening caveat is perhaps appropriate to signal the spirit of what follows: Erecting discursive limits is endemic to the "violence" of the written word, to the communicative paths that narratives clear. The path that the ensuing text seeks to clear places limits of its own, but so long as one understands its precepts as tentative enunciations, as attempts to recalculate community justice practices at a particular conjuncture, their Procrustean power is overtly acknowledged. Such enunciations, it should be said, are offered explicitly in the service of a critical ontology of ourselves at a moment in history, focusing on selected calcula-

---

[1] For example, San Fransisco Boards Program (Merry & Milner 1993), community mediation centers (Wahrhaftig 1982), neighborhood mediation (Beer 1986).

tions and practices within contemporary dispute resolution fields.[2] The overall approach takes seriously the contention that

> the political, ethical, social, philosophical problem of our days is not to try to liberate the individual from the state, and from the state's institutions, but to liberate us both from the state and from the type of individualization which is linked to the state. We have to promote new forms of subjectivity through the refusal of this kind of individuality which has been imposed on us for several centuries. (Foucault 1982:216)

It is from such auspices that "I" have lifted "my" figurative—in these days of the word processor—pen.

## A Community Mediation Model

There are several useful references which detail a range of idioms and styles used by mediators in differing contexts (e.g., Bush & Folger 1994; Kolb & Associates 1993; Silbey & Merry 1986; Folberg & Taylor 1984; Goldberg, Green, & Sander 1985; Kressel & Pruitt 1989; Pruitt & Carnevale 1993). Very often, when practitioners reflect on mediation, they refer to a process guided by underlying models of effective dispute resolution. Burdine (1990), for instance, offers a model that is grounded in international research and widely used in British Columbia (Canada). This model underpins the case study that follows, and some indication of its four phases (or stages) seems appropriate. Burdine's first stage requires mediators to set an informal tone (e.g., casual seating patterns) and to explain the process of mediation to participants (e.g., as a voluntary, confidential way of helping people to resolve disputes). The next stage requires disputants to enunciate their respective accounts of the dispute. Parties are required to address one another directly and to speak in "civil" tones, as if to reinforce "normal" patterns of interaction. Here the mediator constantly probes for more detail on, or reiterates (rephrases), salient issues and themes. The third stage tries to establish "common ground" between disputants. What is the conflict "really" about? What is each individual's interest in the dispute? Can these interests be reconciled? If the preceding phases achieve their aims, then the model suggests moving the mediation process into the final stage where specific conditions of settlement are drafted in plain language and signed by the disputants.

Burdine's conception, then, carves the dynamics of mediation into several phases, providing mediators with a practical blueprint for how to create an environment conducive to community dispute resolution. Her view is not an isolated one, and is

---

[2] This clearly echoes the spirit of Foucault's (1984) analysis of critique in his "What Is Enlightenment?" essay.

710    **The Power of Community Mediation**

echoed by many other mediators.[3] For instance, Albie Davis (a prominent community mediator in the United States) offers a comparable synopsis of the process:

> Mediation moves through several natural stages. First, the parties are set at ease, the process is explained, and questions about the process are answered. Then, each party tells his or her "story." Next, the mediators help the parties to define issues, identify interests, and sort them. When issues and interests are clear, the task becomes to draw on the parties' creative talents and develop mutually agreeable options for settlement. In the final stage, an agreement considered satisfactory to the people involved is reached (and often written). (Kolb & Associates 1993:263)

As the numbers of deployed community mediation programs have increased around the globe over the past two decades, many analysts have come to ponder their sociopolitical effects within dispute resolution arenas. In retrospect, one can point to a reasonably clear divide between those who advocate, versus those who oppose, the expansion of community mediation programs.

## Proponents and Critics of Community Mediation

Despite their different visions, most advocates argue that the arrival of mediation programs signals a victory for individual choice in the resolution of community disputes (see Adler, Lovaas, & Milner 1988; Shonholtz 1993). In proponents' formulations, mediation emerges as a means of empowering individual disputants to free themselves from the formal state's tutelage (e.g., Shonholtz 1984, 1988–89; Bush & Folger 1994). It provides, they argue, an opportunity for individuals to reclaim control over conflict resolution by choosing a settlement process that requires—rather than thwarts—their active participation (Wright & Galaway 1989). Furthermore, mediation is touted as a voluntarily chosen (rather than coercively imposed) process that ipso facto entices individuals to abide by the terms of the settlements they have selected (Shonholtz 1988–89). It has the added effect of educating people on how to resolve future disputes without relying on the state's courts in the first instance. As such, it helps individuals to become involved citizens within functioning communities (Kolb 1993:ch. 6; Shonholtz 1984, 1987, 1993; Bush & Folger 1994).

By simultaneously fostering individual participation and restoring peace to conflict-ridden situations, community mediation is said to rebuild and strengthen community ties. Such unfettered community strength, so the narrative goes, is a crucial element of any democracy because the community provides an

---

[3] See also Kolb & Associates (1993), and Bush and Folger's (1994) summaries of the "problem solving" versus the "transformative" approaches to mediation.

arena in which citizens, the "people," operate as free, individual beings. And it is precisely this individual autonomy that constitutes the basis of free, rational political choices deemed vital to a functioning liberal democracy (Shonholtz 1993). Or, to state the case negatively, democracies are significantly weakened if people do not act as free, autonomous beings. So community mediation is implicated in a quest to revitalize communities by nurturing individual freedom. As a prominent advocate puts it, "The promise of community justice is to transform the dormant power and responsibility of citizens and communities into a dynamic form of service and justice" (Shonholtz 1993:237). In this scenario, community mediation offers an alternative to the tutelage of professionalized, formal courtroom justice and promotes a "restorative" justice (Umbreit 1994; Zehr 1986, 1990). That is, with community mediation, "justice is ultimately aimed at the restoration of right relationships more than retribution" (Lederach & Kraybill 1993:375).

Against such elevated visions, early critics of the alternative dispute resolution proposals have argued that far from restricting state control over individual lives, of empowering and liberating individual disputants, community mediation programs actually expand and intensify state control. These programs expand state regulation by increasing the sum total of control sites funded and deployed under the watchful gaze of the state (Cohen 1985, 1988). Community justice augments state control by rendering its regulatory network more dense or by attending to matters that previously had escaped judicial sanction (e.g., how careful the neighbor is not to mow your flowers). Such expansion and intensification of state control is deemed to be particularly insidious because it occurs through "a process that, on the surface, appears to be a process of retraction" (Santos 1982:262; emphasis omitted). As such, community mediation is seen to be an ominous development whose appealing rhetoric of voluntarism and individual empowerment masks an underlying process of greater and more invasive state control.

The critics offered various elaborations of this general theme. For some, mediation is one of many regulatory responses to the crises besetting a specific stage of capitalist development (Abel 1982a, 1982b). In particular, community justice is described as an experiment that promises to alleviate aspects of the state's fiscal and legitimacy crises within the dispute resolution arena: It proposes cost-effective techniques aimed at local conflicts that do not directly involve state agencies. Furthermore, it operates through such legitimating images as individual empowerment, informalism, and popular justice but is really an indirect form of state rule that is masked through the false ideological images er-

712   **The Power of Community Mediation**

ected by advocates (Abel 1982b).[4] Expanding on this notion, Hofrichter (1982, 1987) analyzed "neighbourhood dispute resolution" as part of a capitalist state strategy to maintain (Gramscian) hegemony within civil society. The strategy is driven by an inherent logic of capital accumulation which requires changing "projects" to suppress working-class resistance. Focusing more specifically on one aspect of Hofrichter's eclectic vantage point, Baskin (1988, 1989) and Selva and Böhm (1987) analyzed community mediation as part of an emerging logic of political control, a concomitant process to a "regime of accumulation" that is shifting from Keynesian Fordism to "neo-Fordist" economics. By contrast, Harrington (1982, 1985, 1988) offered a neo-Weberian critique of informal justice as a continued reform of the lower echelons of the court bureaucracy, effectively deploying a new judicial management strategy to manage "minor" disputes. This entails reform by rational, technocratic means that help to consolidate a consensual political ethos. Santos (1982) appeared to incorporate aspects of both neo-Marxist and neo-Weberian approaches to his more explicit analysis of the type of (state) power mustered by community justice.

However varied these critical approaches, all unite behind a chorus that places community mediation as one element of a more general expansion and/or intensification of state control. Of course, brief comments can be highly deceptive, but the above remarks are enough to indicate a clearly drawn battleline between proponents and early critics. Abel (1982a:6) implicitly underscored this by suggesting that the problem of informal justice institutions revolves around a core issue; "the central question must be: Do they expand or reduce state control?" From what has already been said, it should be clear that advocates defended a negative response to the question, while early critics variously but resoundingly replied in the affirmative. Yet there is something troubling about reducing a complex social formation to a clear analytical bifurcation, especially when the latter erects itself around an aporia. To wit, the dichotomy mistakenly presumes it is possible to define "state control" precisely enough to draw comparisons across regulatory sites. Such exactitude is clearly required if one is to make absolute claims about the relative expansion and/or intensification of state control. But is precision of this sort really possible, or even meaningful? Can one distinguish absolutely between one state form and another, and further assume that these forms are sufficiently commensurate to allege reduced, or expanded, or more intensive, state control? These questions point to a fundamental incongruity that lies at the frontiers of the debate, and that leads to various difficulties.

---

4   Other critics criticize the "harmony ideology" implied by the advocates' discourse on community mediation but do not necessarily accept Abel's neo-Marxist underpinnings (see Nader 1988; Tomasic & Feeley 1982).

Most significantly, the bifurcation perpetuates itself in other guises: One is either optimistic about community mediation having the capacity to reduce state control or pessimistically maintains that such mediation inevitably ends up expanding state control. Thus conceived, the debate sustains a simple "for or against" community mediation ethos that has, as one commentator puts it, "precluded the need for a detailed investigation of the political dynamics which were implicated in the expansion of informal justice" (Matthews 1988a:16). If this leads some advocates to naively applaud community mediation as an alternative, popular justice, it has generated amongst critics a definite political apathy, an overwhelming despair that nothing appears to be able to resist the invasive march of a capital-driven, or technocratic (professional), state justice (see Cain 1988:51; Matthews 1988a:17). Yet, and perhaps reflecting the underlying paradox, after detailing hostile critiques of mediation programs, most critics then conclude with surprising allusions to community justice's "progressive" potential.[5] Coming from exegeses that are pessimistic about community mediation achieving any positive political gains, these allusions remain vague, unfounded hopes.

One reason for the latter is as follows: By focusing exclusively on community mediation as a means of expanding state control, the critics' formulations are driven by precepts anchored in the assumption of necessary state expansion. They have, in short, narrowed the debate on community mediation to an exploration of the extent to which it expands and/or intensifies state control. In the process, sustained analyses of community mediation as possibly harboring elements that are not embedded in state control, or functional for the latter, are not placed on critical agendas. And it is this omission that accounts for the dubiousness of the hope echoed by early critics, as well as for the pessimistic political apathy that surrounds their discourses. As a result, if we are to escape the despair that seems to pervade critical thinking, without endorsing the wide-eyed optimism of some advocates, it seems necessary to reconceptualize the very tenets of early debates on community mediation.

Fortunately, there is a lead in this direction, as taken by so-called "new informalist" critics.[6] Although these critics offer diverse visions, most agree that the "for or against" ethos of early debates is misplaced. This is especially so, since they argue that community mediation is neither entirely autonomous from state legality nor completely encompassed by the latter. Fitzpatrick (1988:190-92) summarizes this rather well by suggesting that the

---

[5] Here I refer to the concluding paragraphs of Hofrichter (1987), Baskin (1988), Santos (1982), and Abel (1982b), where the hope for informal justice is expressed. A notable exception is Harrington (1985), who, consistent with her neo-Weberian line, does not hold out any such hopes.

[6] For example, see various contributions to Matthews 1988b.

714    **The Power of Community Mediation**

domains are mutually "constitutive" social fields that affect one another's historical identities. He exploits the notion that, paradoxically, the identity of law relies on the presence of an informal domain, and vice versa. The postulated opposition between them is thus crucial to their continued identities and implies certain things when one is trying to comprehend the current identity of community mediation.

For instance, the opposition suggests, against the advocates, that community mediation is implicated fundamentally in the identity of liberal law; community mediation opposes the law in such a way as to bolster liberal legality (Fitzpatrick 1992a, 1992b, forthcoming). In turn, this implies that, "in the West popular justice, as it is currently understood, is impossible" (Fitzpatrick 1992a:199). However, against the early critics, Fitzpatrick (1988:191) insists that community mediation does not necessarily involve a simple expansion or intensification of state control—it contains an "unembedded" dimension which is the "dark side" of liberal legality. Community mediation cannot be considered as a mere ruse for the expansion of state power but rather deploys techniques of power directly implicated in the very constitution of such "synoptic powers" as state law (ibid., p. 182). Here, Fitzpatrick, echoed by Matthews (1988a), draws on Foucault (1977, 1980) to chart the disciplinary power relations that operate within informal justice and that are not reducible to state models of power. In particular, Fitzpatrick (1988:190) explores in some detail techniques of discipline through which community justice aims to create "a massive non-rebellious normality" by forging normal individuals and situating them in peaceful "communities" (see also Fitpatrick 1992a, 1992b, forthcoming).

This vantage offers a clearer perspective on community mediation's "power." It allows one to focus on community mediation in its own right, without necessarily reducing it to the power of the state (or capital). In turn, this permits a more complex account of contextual political articulations between state and informal modes of dispute resolution, as a preface to any attempts to conceptualize an "alternative" politics of conflict resolution. But as it stands, the variety of power relations deployed by community mediation programs and their articulations with state legal relations are only partially indicated by the techniques of discipline that Fitzpatrick so poignantly analyzes. In this respect, much more can be made of Foucault's work by envisioning community mediation as a contemporary instance of a governmental rationality that involves not only *techniques of discipline* but also *techniques of self.* By thus expanding the analysis, one can isolate another dimension of community mediation's political rationality, beyond the available accounts of community mediation's disciplinary techniques. The chief purchase of such a move is to widen the scope of analysis and to provide more detail on the political rationality of community mediation as currently practiced. In turn, such a detailed "diagnosis" of present practices might eventually be enlisted in the service of attempts to envision the possibilities of an alternative, popular politics of justice beyond the limits of our present.

## Governmental Dispute Resolution Practices

It thus seems entirely appropriate to consider community mediation as part of an emerging political logic constitutively related to, but not entirely reducible to, state power relations. Here, Foucault's work on "government" is particularly poignant as it requires one to conceptualize the rationality of liberal power relations beyond the ambit of formal state power relations (e.g., Foucault 1977, 1978, 1980, 1981b). That is, the political logic of community mediation may be genealogically traced to another model of power. In particular, Foucault draws attention to pastoral government whose logic is conveyed by the image of a shepherd leading a flock, where a concern for the well-being of each entity is seen to affect the welfare of all.[7] Such thinking nurtured a 16th-century discourse on the "art of government" that began to focus political attention on the well-being of individuals as a means of improving the welfare of a population (Raeff 1983; Foucault 1981b, 1980, 1979; see also Foucault 1980; Dean 1994; Burchell 1991, 1993). This art of government was expressly developed outside of, but for the purposes of strengthening the "law and sovereign" model of, the state. Foucault's neologism "governmentality" suggests how this art of government is later developed in modern liberal societies by establishing regulatory environments within which subject "mentalities" are shaped to serve wider political aims (Burchell 1993; Rose 1990, 1992). In these societies, governmentality is deployed within "domains of freedom" beyond state power but which preserve the state's strength and security (Foucault 1981b; Miller & Rose 1990; Donzelot 1991; Burchell 1991; Rose & Miller 1992). These domains have come to embrace a very particular political logic—one directed not at the abstract judicial citizenry of formal state power arrangements but at live individual selves of given collectives (e.g.,

---

7 The latter image connotes a central feature of pastorship: totalities (the flock) are governed by paying detailed attention to singular lives of constituent entities (each sheep). In its ecclesiastical settings, pastorship ties the welfare of the congregation to the well-being of each member within it. The reconciliation between all and each one, *omnes et singulatim*, requires detailed knowledge of individual consciences and the capacity to shape and guide these (see Foucault 1981b, 1982; Gordon 1991; Burchell 1991). As pastorship has expanded into more secular contexts, it has been fundamentally altered—the singular and totalizing objects of its regulation have shifted in various ways. For instance, pastoral government in early modern society focused on life itself, seeking to regulate individual lives as singular elements of a wider population (Pasquino 1978). With the advance of disciplinary power within the modern welfare state, pastoral government comes to regulate "individuals" in a wider "society" (Donzelot 1991).

716    **The Power of Community Mediation**

the population, civil society, the social, community). As such, governmentality concerns itself with the creation of specific individual and self-identities that support a wider totality, and the combination of these serves to strengthen wider state patterns. As Dean (1994:208) puts it, governmentality may then described as, "the articulation of government of the self, others, and the state."

With these remarks in mind, the debate between early critics and advocates can be amended to understand the power of community mediation not simply in terms of state power but as a related political development with a (governmental) political rationality of its own. Community mediation deploys its own techniques of power and so is not simply a way of expanding (or retracting) state power; rather, it extends governmental practices to contemporary dispute resolution arenas. Consequently, it may be that "what is really important for our modern times, that is for our actuality, is not so much the State-domination of society, but the 'governmentalisation' of the State" (Foucault 1979:20). Foucault's reformulation focuses attention on the governmental relations of power through which community mediation practices regulate disputants. But what are the specific techniques of power employed by such governance?

In the context of community mediation, we have already cited research on techniques of discipline directed at creating live individual "disputants" (Fitzpatrick 1988). However, Foucault's later work emphasized another battery of political techniques as central to the art of government:

> If one wants to analyse the genealogy of subjects in Western Civilisation, one has to take into account, not only techniques of domination, but also techniques of self. One has to show the interaction between these types of technique. . . . What we call discipline is something really important. . . . But it is only one aspect of the art of governing people in our societies. (Foucault 1981a:5)

Here he emphasizes the notion that the art of government involves the "contact between technologies of domination of others and those of self" (Foucault 1988:19). As such, the governmental power of community mediation would entail not only discipline but also *techniques of self* geared toward producing nondisputing self-identities. Recognizing the integrity of both techniques in the governmental power of community mediation which seeks the production of nondisputing individual selves that strengthen the (neo-)liberal state, I shall nevertheless focus on the overlooked dimension of techniques of self. Read alongside the studies on community mediation's disciplinary power, the following discussion opens up an analysis of how selves are fashioned through the mediation process. In so doing, it aims to develop further a vision of community mediation as a governmental power within contemporary (postmodern?) dispute resolution arenas.

## Constituting the Self

It is perhaps important to provide some conceptual points of departure for the ensuing analysis of community mediation's techniques of self. To begin with, and tapping into wider discussions in social theory on the relationships between self and society,[8] the "self" is not here recognized as an ontologically fixed entity. Rather, it is seen to be produced by sociohistorical processes that fashion self-identities and impart contingent and dynamic traces. From a general perspective, contemporary selves and their processes of formation are intimately related to significant transformations that have rocked modern, industrial societies (Giddens 1991; Rose 1992). There may well be considerable disagreement on how to conceptualize the scale of these (postindustrial? postproduction? late modern? postmodern?) transformations, but Casey (1995:197) offers a poignant prediction for our times: "Self-constituting processes other than those of work and production will configure selves and collective social life that are qualitatively different from modern industrial configurations" (e.g., see Pavlich 1995; Smart 1992, 1993; Bauman 1992, 1994; Giddens 1990; Beck, Giddens, & Lash 1994). Community mediation is surely one such "self-constituting" process which has, moreover, emerged at a time when greater regulatory focus is being placed on the aspirations of self within neo-liberal, consumer-driven societies (e.g., Rose 1992). In any case, within the narrower confines of particular community mediation sessions, we can readily see the presence of techniques that are specifically directed at producing peaceful, nondisputing self-identities from the disputing selves that arrive before mediators. It is these techniques that we shall here attempt to isolate.

But how are we to approach the ways in which selves are (re-) formed in community mediation sessions. Foucault's (1988a, 1988b, 1985) "ethical" analyses and reflections on technologies of self provide a useful point of departure. He notes that even if subjects are historically placed, they do perform active work on themselves to shape their own self-identities. Thus, for him,

> the subject constitutes himself [*sic*] in an active fashion, by practices of the self, these practices are nevertheless not something that the individual invents by himself. They are patterns that he finds in his culture and which are proposed, suggested and imposed on him by his culture, his society and his social group. (Foucault 1988b:11)

---

[8] See Casey (1995:ch. 3) for a useful synopsis of the area.

718    **The Power of Community Mediation**

From this vantage, techniques of self involve the active participation of historically produced selves, and that participation is mediated by social and cultural spaces where subjects are enticed to develop particular self-identities. That is, the formation of self-identities requires active subjective work that a historically produced self performs on "itself" under the pressures of particular social locations, such as community mediation.

Given these general insights, we might deduce that an analysis of self-forming techniques within community mediation requires one to explore (1) how (by what means?) mediation provides sociocultural pressure on the formation of nondisputing selves; and (2) in view of these pressures, what techniques of self formation disputing selves employ in their attempts to transform their self-identities from "disputing" to "nondisputing" selves. To address these two issues, let us examine a case study of a community mediation session in the Canadian province of British Columbia. Although observation of this case was part of another study with a different emphasis, my report on it provides a glimpse of how particular self-identities were actively sought by mediators.[9] Moreover, unlike prevalent case studies of mediation, this case was not settled, indicating that despite mediation's sociocultural pressure, the disputing selves did not work on themselves in ways that the mediators might have preferred. That the case did not lead to settlement is particularly instructive for the present context because the mediators tried to "pull out all the stops" as they (correctly) perceived that the disputants were not about to reach settlement. In the process, techniques that are usually introduced with great subtlety, or not at all, were more explicitly deployed, and with greater frequency, as the disputants "refused" the settlements on offer. In addition, if nothing else, this case highlights the relatively uncertain outcomes of the regulatory terrain at hand. My description will reflect a sequence roughly comparable to Burdine's (1990) model outlined above, since the mediators of this mediation center were trained using her visions of mediation.

## The Case of the Belatedly Restored Limousine

The community mediation center in question has rented premises in a recently developed shopping plaza. Beyond a reception area is a new large conference room. Here a mediator and co-mediator (a mediator in the final stages of training) are arranging seating around a square table, and have placed a large flip chart at one corner. I am greeted and ushered to a sofa at the far corner of the room, "out of the way," as it were. The

---

9  See Pavlich (1996); this specific case was observed on 26 March 1991 at 2:30 P.M. at a local community mediation center in the Greater Vancouver area.

mediators discuss how they will share their mediation responsibilities and seat themselves with the mediator at the head of the table and the co-mediator to his right-hand side. The mediator warmly receives the first of the disputing parties, Walter, and ushers him to a seat opposite the co-mediator. The other "client," Greg, arrives (in a large limousine) and is seated next to Walter. His expensive suit contrasts markedly with the casual attire of all other people in the room. Both disputants are placed with their backs to the door from which they entered the room (to focus attention within the room, I was later told by the co-mediator). After introductions, the mediator explains, "we are here to try to sort out the problem between you through a process of mediation." He describes the latter as a confidential process to help parties arrive at settlement, requests a $10 fee from both parties, and places 90-minute time limit on the mediation. More specific rules about mediation are raised (listening, no abusive language, etc.) before both parties are asked to read and sign a typed document indicating their agreement to abide by the rules of mediation.

In the next stage of the mediation, Walter narrates that he is a restoration specialist who was approached by Greg to replace the cabinet and panels of an older limousine with rosewood and to install a graphic equalizer system. He had quoted a price ($600) and told Greg that the job would take three to four days to complete. Greg had later delivered the limousine, and Walter commenced work on it. As it happened, Walter could not obtain a supply of Brazilian rosewood and had to delay his work. Greg paid him a little over half of the money owed for the job ($330), and Walter wants payment in full. Prompted by the mediator for his "side of the story," Greg agrees with the substance of Walter's account but adds he was told that it would only take about four days to complete the job. As an owner of a limousine rental company, Greg notes that he had lost some $8,000 while Walter had been "working" on the car. He agreed to pay for all of the materials installed but only one third of Walter's labor costs. At this point the co-mediator interjects, somewhat awkwardly, to compliment Greg for being so honest and to praise Walter for his insightful rendition of events.

The third phase of the mediation sees the two mediators attempting to define the common ground between Walter and Greg. The mediator probes for very specific kinds of information (whether Walter enjoys his work, whether Greg can appreciate Walter's talents at carpentry, etc.). At regular intervals, the mediator sums up discussions with phrases like, "What I am sensing from you, and what you have said . . .," or "What I hear you saying, Walter, is . . .," etc. Humor is often used to break the tension produced by the disputants" argument and counter-argument. After a great deal of negotiation, the mediator offers this summary: "So you both had a concern for . . . you both want good work." Walter agrees, noting, "I am proud of my work," but adds that Greg seems quite unable to appreciate the quality of his work. Greg snaps back: "Walter thinks he is doing me a favor— but he is merely in business." This sets the stage for further confrontations, which the mediator eventually halts by saying that the "main" issue at hand is different perceptions of "time."

Now the mediator feels he is able to clarify the dispute, suggesting that the "common understanding" between Walter and Greg is currently clouded because they are working from different sets of assumptions (adding that this is perfectly "normal"). As he outlines these assumptions, constantly seeking approval from the parties, the co-mediator writes points on the flip chart. Greg is said to view the dispute as a business one, in which Walter's delays have cost Greg money. By contrast, Walter's view is presented as being about not compromising the quality of his craft, even at the expense of breaking his time commitment. The mediator sighs as he says, "You people had different views." He emphasizes that no one is to blame but notes that their differences have resulted in Greg's wasted business time, and Walter's being out of pocket. There is nodding by both parties on this point. The mediator then asks them, "How are you going to solve this? . . . . What are you going to offer the other guy to work this out down the road?"

The questions serve as a precursor for the final phase of the process, which enjoins Greg and Walter to brainstorm possible resolutions—the enjoining is accompanied by the mediator's thinly veiled warning for the participants to take heed of the "risks down the road," including the time and money that will be spent at small claims courts, where a judge's decision will be imposed. He states, "Both you guys are in the same boat," and indicates it is a matter of "communication" to see past their differences and reach an agreement. Greg describes himself as a reasonable and even generous person, given the time his limousine was not in service. He narrates his story using phrases like "Tell me if I am wrong, but . . .," or "To tell the truth . . .," all of which provide rhetorical gestures intimating the truth and reasonableness of his account. He concedes that he is satisfied with Walter's work but cannot overlook his tardiness.

At the mediator's prompting, Walter declares that "I like this guy" but feels he is too "hard-nosed." Ignoring the barb, the mediator compliments him, saying mutual liking and respect are important and wonders if such attitudes might help them to change their assumptions. For example, he asks Walter to consider lowering his price and Greg to consider giving Walter more money. Walter notes that he is "angry" because the amount of time he spent on the project outweighs his quote by far, even though he did "enjoy working on the cabinet." He then notes that time cannot be equated with the quality of his craft. Greg, too, says he will not move but might consider giving Walter other jobs in future as long as it is financially viable to do so. The mediator keeps mentioning the risk of court ("it is a shame to go to courts") and offers more direct comments on the disputants' respective positions. He wonders why they are so recalcitrant, saying "it does not make sense to me." The amount is small and yet nobody seems prepared to "give an inch." He invokes a time constraint ("9 minutes left") and asks what it will be. There is an awkward silence. The mediator implores them to do a "risk analysis" of not settling the dispute, to which Walter responds that going to court might actually be a novel experience and "fun." At that point the mediator (with noticeable displeasure) brings the mediation to an abrupt close, and compliments both parties for their exemplary and fair treatment of each other.

### 1. Community Mediation as Confessional

Let us leave the case here to explore community mediation as a form of government that encourages particular kinds of self-formation. Tackling the first of the previously noted analytical questions, the case study may be used to highlight the sociocultural pressures mediation places on disputing "selves." It shows that community mediation is deployed in a given space (the informal conference room, with seating in particular patterns around a table, with a flip chart, etc.), which will accommodate a process of mediation that is explicitly enunciated by the mediator. As a condition of further participation, disputants must sign an agreement to abide by certain rules; most notably, each is required to offer an account of him or her*self* within a true discourse that details self-interests, what it would take to settle the dispute, and so on. This account should, moreover, be delivered succinctly and without abusive language, name-calling, etc. The discourse is offered for scrutiny by the mediators' probing questions and summaries or the challenges of the other disputant. In such a regulatory environment, the mediators are exposed— often by way of direct probing and rephrasing—to disputants' perceptions of self, self-interest, aspirations, and desired outcomes. As is clear from the case, mediators negotiate discourses of self with the aim of reconciling disputing parties.

These apparently disparate observations situate community mediation as a close relative of an important pastoral technique: confession. Of course, the pattern of mediation (two confessors and two mediators in our case) is somewhat distant from the confession codified in the sacrament of penance by the Latheran Council of 1215 (Foucault 1978:58). Or indeed, mediation's conference room bears little spatial relation to the ecclesiastical confessional boxes of the 16th century (Tambling 1990:9). However,

722    **The Power of Community Mediation**

like its erstwhile incarnations, community mediation invites (requires) "disputants" to confess to local mediators intimate details
of their "transgressions" against community peace. These
mediators shape the narratives produced by confession and try to
nurture nondisputing self-identities. Phrased thus, community
mediation seems to have colonized confession as a way of guiding
disputants' definitions of self (see Miller & Rose 1988; Rose
1990). This is by no means an isolated colonizing practice, and
indeed secular confession is a regular feature of our lives: "one
confesses one's crimes, one's sins, one's thoughts and desires,
one's illnesses and troubles; one goes about telling, with the
greatest precision, whatever is most difficult to tell" (Foucault
1978:59). So commonplace is confession nowadays that we do
not even see it as a form of constraint, as an obligation, or even
as a power. Rather, we seem fixated on telling all, pouring out
the fables that might liberate ourselves from the gnawing suspicion that repressing secrets can lead to events too dark to contemplate. In any case, the desire to participate in mediation implies at least a cathartic willingness to narrate a story of conflict
to a delegated third party.

As such, community mediation can be included as a confessional site that constructs a "ritual of discourse" requiring subjects to disclose the truth about themselves around a given set of
circumstances. Such rituals of discourse involve declarations
made in the presence of

> a partner who is not simply the interlocutor but the authority
> who requires the confession, prescribes and appreciates it, and
> intervenes in order to judge, punish, forgive, console, and rec-
> oncile; . . . a ritual in which the expression alone . . . produces
> intrinsic modifications in the person who articulates it: it exon-
> erates, redeems, and purifies him. (Foucault 1978:61–62)

From this quotation, it is possible to extract three primary ways in
which community mediation embraces a confessional ethos that
pressures disputants as they refashion themselves in the quest to
settle a dispute (see also Hepworth & Turner 1982:6–7).

First, discourses are solicited from participants in the mediation process which requires all parties to declare a version of self
apropos a dispute (what it did or did not do, why it followed a
course of action, what its interests are, the outcomes it desires,
where it is prepared to compromise, etc.). As the case study
shows, the declaration must be detailed, and is spoken out after
the parties have signed a written agreement to follow the rules of
mediation. Selves disclose truths about themselves in a confidential forum where others help to renegotiate interpretations of
self-identity. Visions of self are dialogically shaped by others
within a domain that encourages—or seeks to neutralize—particular exegeses of self, discourses of dispute, and conceptions of
settlement. For example, to focus on one issue, Walter is called

on to account for his actions in the dispute (why he took so long to complete the work) and Greg to explain why he has not paid the account in full. The responses of each help to enunciate specific conceptions of self, or at least annul certain negative definitions. Walter's explanation of difficulties in obtaining wood indicate something beyond his control, negating definitions of, say, a lazy, tardy, self. Likewise, Greg's calculation of paying for all materials and a one-third payment for labor indicate an attempt to define a thoughtful, reasonable self in given sets of circumstances, not, say, a deceptive, or vindictive, self. In each case, definitions of self are narrated, and these come to constitute the building blocks of a negotiated discourse whose aim is to resolve the dispute at hand.

Second, disputants are enticed to confide as fully as possible to delegated local authorities (the mediators). These authorities are more than mere interlocutors; they are leaders of the session and must guide the process of discourse formation with skill and proper training. As the case indicates, the mediators try to extract and fashion particular sorts of confessions by constantly probing for information, rephrasing issues, praising or castigating confessors—all of which are directed at dispute settlement. In the process, mediators reward difficult confessions, acknowledge pent-up emotions, and generally affirm the validity of conceptions of self, especially those that increase the prospects of resolution. So, for example, the co-mediator's praise of Walter's astute depiction of events or Greg's honesty might be read as an affirmation by the co-mediator of two self-identities that are able to agree on the dispute between them—a situation that is promising for later settlement. Similarly, the disputants' mutual liking and respect is emphasized as essential to finding an acceptable resolution. In general, using praise, subtle inflections to indicate unease, probing questions, synopses, and so on, the mediators assert a deliberately understated local authority that "receives" and shapes "confessions" in the direction of dispute settlement.

Finally, as local authorities of mediation, the mediator(s) provide a possible source of exoneration for those who have strayed from a peaceful community life and who voluntarily seek a resolution to conflict. The mediator assumes that conflict is necessarily problematic and thus in need of resolution, but does not blame disputants. They may be in a temporary though unhappy (fallen?) state of conflict, but they can be led back to the fold through mediation's confessional rituals that search for peace. Mediation thus emerges as a form of secular (community?) atonement through which errant self-identities may be redirected toward peace and harmony (Umbreit 1994; Zehr 1990; Wright & Galaway 1989). The case at hand shows how mediators construe themselves as altruistic facilitators, as helpers rather than as judges. They adopt an affirming, supportive, and caring

724    **The Power of Community Mediation**

role that aims to deploy a climate for agreement. When the mediation seems to be faltering, the role of exonerating local authority is placed in question as participants implicitly refuse the mediators' efforts to resolve the dispute. This serves as a point of some frustration for the mediator, who openly declares that the disputants' recalcitrance "does not make sense to me." And in this situation, he makes various coercive, even desperate ("9 minutes left!"), attempts to fashion a settlement. There is in this plight more than a trace of the self-effacing oblate, the pastoral leader, following a duty to counsel the wayward.

To reiterate the theme of this section, community mediation deploys a regulatory environment that shapes disputants' self-reformation through a version of confession that solicits very particular narratives of self from disputants. These narratives are "confessed" to local mediators who encourage self-interpretations that are perceived to open the way for dispute settlement. In the process, mediators aim to "deliver" disputants from conflict through a process whose techniques enjoin the formation of nondisputing self-identities. As the case at hand indicates, mediators are not always successful, but when they are, selves are reconciled and peace is said to be "restored" to communities. Although cursory and even provisional, the above discussion provides a glimpse of the confessional pressures that mediation exerts on disputants; it offers an opening for a discursive space that fruitfully could be elaborated on in future.

## 2. Techniques of Self-Formation

Nevertheless, within the sociocultural pressures of mediation's confessional ethos, participants are enticed to conduct "ethical" work on themselves. More concretely, Walter and Greg are encouraged to reflect on their respective selves in relation to the dispute and to consider modifications to their existing self-identities for the sake of resolving the dispute. The case study evinces how mediators solicit and lead the discourses of self through probing and summation, and how they raise questions of self-reformation (i.e., suggesting what visions of self seem necessary to resolve the dispute). But how are we to analyze the process by which Walter and Greg actively work on themselves, within the confines of a mediation, in search of ways to move from disputing to nondisputing selves? In short, how are we to conceptualize the process of self reformation within the confessional limits of mediation? I suggest, very loosely following Foucault (1985:26–28), that four aspects of self-formative processes may be heuristically distinguished in the context of community mediation.[10]

---

[10] Rose (1990:241) offers a slightly different interpretation of this material as does Dean (1994:197-99).

First, mediation helps to clear the ethical groundwork by requiring subjects to clarify what precise aspects of themselves they
will separate out for active work (Foucault's "ethical substance").
Second, mediators help disputants to narrate how the above aspects of self are set against norms, principles, interests, underlying assumptions, and so on (i.e., a "mode of subjection"). Third,
there are various sorts of tasks that the disputing selves must perform on themselves to modify their disputing self-identities (i.e.,
the "ethical work" required). This work includes all the various
practices of self, the technologies of self-formation, through
which selves create particular self-identities (e.g., listening, talking, confessing, negotiating, reflecting, self-examinations, brain-
storming). These are the various means by which the "new" self
might be "presented," to use Goffman's (1959) parlance. Finally,
subjects of mediation seeking settlement are enticed to specify
the content of their aspirations to nondisputing self-identities
(i.e., the "telos"). That is, what sorts of self-identities should participants aspire toward if they are to achieve dispute settlement?

(Parenthetically, there are two aspects of this telos that ought
to be signaled here as they are only implied by the "unsuccessful"
case described before. On the one hand, the telos of ethical work
is most explicitly addressed by the last stage of mediation, and in
"successful" cases a specific agreement outlines what is required
from each self to settle the dispute. Such injunctions define for
each disputant particular projections of selfhood to which they
must aspire in order to settle a given dispute. On the other hand,
mediation provides a practical conceptualization of how the self
will have to relate to itself to appropriate a style of life, a mode of
being, which will avoid future disputes. It is this dimension of the
telos that leads advocates to view mediation as an educational
process, as a means of imparting a "life skill" to selves, and as a
way of avoiding future conflicts.)

Let us here use Foucault's framework to provide a brief look
at how the techniques of self-formation are used by each disputant in the case study. Walter provides important clues to his self-
identity in the casual manner of his dress and his relaxed disposition. In narrating his story of the dispute, prompted by the mediator, Walter presents himself as a true artisan who sees the quality of his work as central to his very being. He takes pride in his
work and knows that he has high standards of quality. Here is the
ethical substance, that aspect of Walter's overall self-identity that
is deemed to be relevant to the present mediation session. It is
his focus on "quality" without a similar concern for the time he
spends on projects that is deemed to have contributed to the dispute. Undeterred, Walter expressly subjects himself to a norm of
an uncompromising quest for excellence in his craft. He perceives his interest to lie with the preservation of a reputation for
superior work and places rather less emphasis on the punctual

726   **The Power of Community Mediation**

delivery of his products. He also seeks recognition from others (not only in monitory terms) for his careful work. As the mediation unfolds, it becomes clear to him that his very definition of self as a producer of quality restoration is rendered problematic. As the mediator makes clear, his underlying "assumptions" must change in order to resolve the dispute. That is, the kind of ethical work he must perform entails modifying his concept of self as uncompromising artisan, and to accept that he is also—as Greg puts it—"merely in business." The shift would involve a move away from his current identity to one that accepts a role as business contractor. The aspiration of self, the telos, placed before Walter is that of compromising his attachment to an existing self-identity as skilled artisan to become more of a "business professional," all in the interests of settling the dispute. Given his strong commitment to his self-identity, which is repeated throughout the mediation session, Walter is unwilling to accept the aspiration of self on offer or to embark on work required to change his self-identity. Here, he finds the possibility of court action preferable (even holding the promise of "fun"), for it affords him a way of retaining the self-identity that he values.

By contrast, Greg makes bold statements about his self-identity through the manner of his arrival (in a limousine), dress, and reserved, "professional" demeanor. His mediated discourse isolates a particular aspect of self as relevant to the dispute: he is a busy business professional who has to be concerned with "the bottom line," and this translates into a concern with time (he suggests that if he were not, his clients would "give [him] a kick up the bum"). His ability to operate a profitable business successfully, which affords him certain luxuries, emerges as an important part of his self-identity. The values of time and money and the pursuit of profit are norms that Greg uses to justify himself. He also prides himself on being reasonable, "professional," and fair in business, as demonstrated by the gesture of paying Walter for the materials and part of his labor. It is these narrations of self that the mediators describe as establishing a gulf between the disputants. In the process the mediators (and Walter) present Greg with implications of what sorts of ethical work he might be required to entertain; namely, that of problematizing the very identity of business professional as "hard-nosed" and unable to appreciate the finer qualities of skilled artisanship. In turn, this implies an alternative telos of self as someone prepared to acknowledge that equating time with money, and quality with efficient delivery of service, may not always be appropriate. As it turns out, Greg is unwilling to embark on the proposed ethical work, and emphasizes that his main concern is the time that Walter has taken to complete the job. In the process he underscores an allegiance to his original ethical substance and the mode of subjection, indicating an unwillingness to accept the ethical work and telos that the mediation process proposes.

These comments are brief and incomplete, but they do imply at least two useful lines of inquiry for further analyses of self-formation in mediation. First, the approach focuses attention on a neglected area of research into community mediation; namely, how self-formation is guided by the pressures of mediation's confessional ethos. On the one hand, this focus permits close readings of the narratives of self constructed and negotiated in mediation sessions. In turn, this lends itself to future research into the relationships between narratives of self-identity within mediation sessions and wider discourses on group identities within given social formations (e.g., identities around gender, class, race, ethnicity, sexuality, age). For example, to what extent do the techniques of self within a given mediation encourage self-identities that tap into wider group identities? On the other hand, the focus on self-formation within community mediation permits a detailed reading of how particular mediation sessions reach settlements and why others do not. For instance, in the above case, it could be argued that the mediator's summation of the second phase isolates visions of disputing selves (the ethical substance) that are too fundamentally held, and too incommensurable, to fashion reconcilable self-identities. Perhaps an alternative summation might have yielded different results (e.g., a focus on Walter's and Greg's clear desires to get along might have been used as the point of commonality to frame an alternative narrative of the dispute). In any case, the suggested approach opens up a different way of understanding the dynamics of given mediation sessions, and could be developed in much more detail.

Second, the focus on techniques of self elaborates on the governmental rationality of community mediation. The framework draws attention to the techniques by which mediation directs itself not only to the disciplinary creation of individuals but also to the formation of particular kinds of self-identities through confessional pressures. That is, if community mediation provides a panoptic disciplinary gaze over individuals, it also pressures active subjective (ethical) work. If successful, the confessional ethos of community mediation creates nondisputing self-identities who take with them a life skill: the ability to "mediate" their own definitions of self within the "community" to avoid conflicts arising in the future. This conception of community mediation invites analyses that situate mediation sessions within wider (neo-liberal) regulatory environments.

For instance, one might examine how community mediation aligns with other forms of (neo-)liberal governance that work in the "community" and seek to shape particular kinds of self-identities (e.g., community psychology, community health, community corrections). Here, in its prevalent search for settlement and

728    **The Power of Community Mediation**

community peace under the guise of voluntarism and individual empowerment, community mediation seems to echo the promise of achieving ordered security by encouraging very particular practices of freedom and voluntarism. In this way, as Rose puts it, "the objectives of 'liberal' government can be brought into alignment with the selves of 'democratic' citizens" (Rose 1992:147). Yet, the case at hand provides a forceful and sober reminder that the outcome of self-forming practices like mediation is never assured. It reinforces the notion of an open-ended regulatory complex that is in the processes of emerging and shows the constitutive but nonfixed links between "community" and state legal forms. If governmentalized state regulation has the potential to reach far into the aspirations of self, it can do so only by forgoing absolute predictability of outcome. The unpredictability of what may be termed "remote control" (Pavlich 1996) or "governing at a distance" (Miller & Rose 1988) bears directly on the matter at hand, and could profitably be explored in greater depth within the context of understanding the effects of the governmental power of community mediation.

## Concluding Reflections

The discussion here has explored the limitations of early debates on community mediation and taken its cues from the "new informalist" focus on power relations. In particular, it has traced community mediation as a form of governmental power whose political rationality involves deploying techniques of discipline and self in an attempt to reconcile disputing individual selves, and so to preserve notions of a peaceful community. In focusing on techniques of self, the article locates community mediation as a type of secular confession that encourages disputants to seek reformed, nondisputing self-identities. As our case has indicated, the bid for resolution is not always successful, even though a battery of techniques may be employed in context. This highlights the point that the governmentalization of the state involves a series of open-ended, and unpredictable, processes; community mediation is thus never a simple expansion of state control. To glimpse community mediation in operation is not to witness the state operating in Orwellian guises over primordial individuals, or, conversely, to see a domain of individual voluntarism devoid of relations to the state. It is rather to view one example of many governmental practices that aim to nurture and create the very entities on which the modern, liberal (and increasingly postmodern, neo-liberal) state has come to rely: the semblance of a fixed, individual self located within a community. In this sense, the (neo-)liberal state is preserved through a series of governmental practices that for centuries have been colonizing our being, the individuals that we are, and the ideal selves to which we aspire. Our pleasures, our pains, our lives, are "ours" only in a very peculiar sense.

In contrast to early critics, then, the unpredictability of governmental regulation suggests a certain indeterminacy from which it is possible to contemplate an authentically "alternative" politics of disputes. However, and contrary to most community mediation advocates, the search for "empowered" individuals within "communities" is unlikely to offer an alternative to the power relations of existing dispute resolution arenas. So long as community mediation is enlisted in the service of individual dispute settlement, the self-identities it tries to fashion are likely to perpetuate—rather than eradicate—the liberal, governmental power formations that nurture particular conflicts in the first place. Similarly, to the extent that community mediation aims at dispute settlement in the interests of an unspecified "community order," its orientation will always lean toward "restoration" rather than fundamental change. That the "restoration" of supposed community order might too be implicated in the very constitution and recurrence of particular kinds of disputes remains a tale untold by advocates (e.g, sexual harassment cases). But it is here that one glimpses the sutures that bind the government of community mediation to the power of (neo-)liberal legality, hidden under notions of its being an "alternative" to law. In such circumstances, where the identities of law and its informal "opposite" are mutually constituted, it is difficult to contest Fitzpatrick's (1992a) argument that current visions of popular (community) justice are "impossible." It would remove us too far from the previous analysis to suggest that I have provided a comprehensive chart by which to navigate an alternative, popular politics of disputes. What the discussion does suggest, however, is that the quest for "empowered" justice beyond (neo-)liberal patterns of dispute resolution would certainly entail a direct engagement with governmental political rationalities (such as community mediation) that have governmentalized state power. Engagement that transgresses the limits of the present, that glimpses an alternative to current dispute resolution practices, would surely have to redress community mediation's governmental techniques of discipline and self, as well as its search for a "community order." As Foucault succinctly puts it:

> Maybe the target nowadays is not to discover what we are, but to refuse what we are. We have to imagine and build up what we could be to get rid of this kind of political "double bind," which is the simultaneous individualization and totalization of modern power structures. (Foucault 1982:216)

Even if an alternative politics of disputes can only ever be entertained from within specific discursive horizons, focused analyses of the political rationalities that shape us can help to locate the limits of our historically enunciated "being." If anything, the preceding reflections direct the search for alternatives beyond the power of a community "justice" that tries to shackle our very self-aspirations to the yokes of an intangible but consequential community order.

## References

Abel, Richard L. (1982a) "Introduction," in Abel 1982c.

——— (1982b) "The Contradictions of Informal Justice," in Abel 1982c.

———, ed. (1982c) *The Politics of Informal Justice*, vol. 1: *The American Experience.* New York: Academic Press.

Adler, Peter, Karen Lovaas, & Neal Milner (1988) "The Ideologies of Mediation: The Movement's Own Story," 10 *Law & Policy* 317.

Alfini, James J. (1986) "Alternative Dispute Resolution and the Courts: An Introduction," 69 *Judicature* 252.

Arthurs, H. W. (1980) "Alternatives to the Formal Justice System: Reminiscing about the Future," in Canadian Institute for the Administration of Justice, *Cost of Justice.* Toronto: Carswell Co.

Auerbach, Jerold S. (1983) *Justice without Law.* New York: Oxford Univ. Press.

Baskin, Deborah R. (1988) "Community Mediation and the Public/Private Problem," 15 *Social Justice* 98.

——— (1989) "What Is All the Fighting about? Privatism and Neighbor Disputes," 16 *Social Justice* 165.

Bauman, Zygmunt (1992) *Intimations of Postmodernity.* London: Routledge.

——— (1994) "Morality without Ethics," 11 *Theory, Culture & Society* 1.

Beck, Ulrich, Anthony Giddens, & Scott Lash (1994) *Reflexive Modernization: Politics, Tradition and Aesthetics in the Modern Social Order.* Cambridge: Polity Press.

Beer, Jennifer E. (1986) *Peacemaking in Your Neighborhood: Reflections on an Experiment in Community Mediation.* Philadelphia: New Society Publishers.

Blair, Robert A. (1988) "Impetus for the Movement towards Non-court Mechanisms for Dispute Resolution." Presented at Canadian Bar Association's (Ontario) Conference on Alternative Dispute Resolution, Toronto, 3 Oct.

Burchell, Graham (1991) "Peculiar Interests: Civil Society and Governing 'the System of Natural Liberty,'" in Burchell et al. 1991.

Burchell, Graham, Colin Gordon, & Peter Miller, eds. (1991) *The Foucault Effect: Studies in Governmentality.* Chicago: Chicago Univ. Press.

——— (1993) "Liberal Government and Techniques of the Self," 22 *Economy & Society* 267.

Burdine, Marje (1990) *Mediation Skills Manual: "How to Mediate a Dispute."* Vancouver: The Centre for Conflict Resolution Training, Justice Institute of B.C.

Bush, Robert A. Baruch, & Joseph P. Folger (1994) *The Promise of Mediation: Responding to Conflict through Empowerment and Recognition.* San Francisco: Jossey-Bass.

Cain, Maureen (1988) "Beyond Informal Justice," in Matthews 1988b.

Cameron, Jan, & Ann Dupius (1989) *School Mediation in New Zealand: An Assessment of Potential.* Report for the Sociology Department, Univ. of Canterbury.

Casey, Catherine (1995) *Work, Self and Society: After Industrialism.* London: Routledge.

Cohen, Stanley (1985) *Visions of Social Control: Crime, Punishment, and Classification.* Cambridge: Polity Press.

——— (1988) "The Deeper Structures of Law: Or Beware the Rulers Bearing Justice," in S. Cohen, *Against Criminology.* Oxford: Transaction Books.

Cook, Royer F., Janice A. Roehl, & David I. Sheppard (1980) *Neighborhood Justice Centers Field Test: Final Evaluation Report.* Washington: U.S. Department of Justice.

Danzig, Richard (1973) "Towards the Creation of a Complementary, Decentralized System of Criminal Justice," 26 *Stanford Law Rev.* 1.

Dean, Mitchell (1994) *Critical and Effective Histories: Foucault's Methods and Historical Sociology.* London: Routledge.

Donzelot, Jacques (1991) "The Mobilization of Society," in Burchell et al. 1991.

Fitzpatrick, Peter (1988) "The Rise and Rise of Informalism," in Matthews 1988b.

———— (1992a) "The Impossibility of Popular Justice," 1 *Social & Legal Studies* 199.

———— (1992b) *The Mythology of Modern Law.* London: Routledge.

———— (forthcoming) "Relational Power and the Limits of Law," in K. Tuori, Z. Bankowski, & J. Uusitalo, eds., *Law and Power: Critical and Sociol-legal Essays.* Liverpool: Deborah Charles Publications.

Folberg, Jay, & Alison Taylor (1984) *Mediation: A Comprehensive Guide to Resolving Conflicts without Litigation.* San Francisco: Jossey-Bass.

Foucault, Michel (1977) *Discipline and Punish: The Birth of the Prison.* New York: Vintage Books.

———— (1978) *The History of Sexuality,* vol 1: *An Introduction.* New York: Pantheon Books.

———— (1979) "Governmentality," 6 *Ideology & Consciousness* 5.

———— (1980) *Power/Knowledge: Selected Interviews and Other Writings (1972–1977).* Brighton: Harvester Press.

———— (1981a) "Sexuality and Solitude," *London Rev. of Books,* pp. 3, 5–6 (21 May–2 June).

———— (1981b) "Omnes et Singulatim: Towards a Criticism of 'Political Reason,'" in S. McMurrin, ed., 2 *The Tanner Lectures on Human Values.* New York: Cambridge Univ. Press.

———— (1982) "The Subject and Power," in H. L. Dreyfus & P. Rabinow, eds., *Michel Foucault: Beyond Structuralism and Hermeneutics.* Chicago: Univ. of Chicago Press.

———— (1984) "What Is Enlightenment?" in P. Rabinow, ed., *The Foucault Reader.* New York: Pantheon Books.

———— (1985) *The History of Sexuality,* vol. 2: *The Use of Pleasure.* New York: Pantheon Books.

———— (1988a) *Technologies of the Self: A Seminar with Michel Foucault.* Amherst: Univ. of Massachusetts Press.

———— (1988b) "The Ethic of Care for the Self as a Practice of Freedom," in J. Bernauer & D. Rasmussen, eds., *The Final Foucault.* Cambridge, MA: MIT Press.

Giddens, Anthony (1990) *The Consequences of Modernity.* Cambridge: Polity Press.

———— (1991) *Modernity and Self-Identity: Self and Society in the Late Modern Age.* Stanford, CA: Stanford Univ. Press.

Goffman, Erving (1959) *The Presentation of Self in Everyday Life.* New York: Doubleday.

Goldberg, Stephen B., Eric D. Green, & Frank E. A. Sander (1985) *Dispute Resolution.* Boston: Little, Brown & Co.

Gordon, Colin (1991) "Governmental Rationality: An Introduction," in Burchell et al. 1991.

Harrington, Christine B. (1982) "Delegalizing Reform Movements: A Historical Analysis," in Abel 1982b.

———— (1985) *Shadow Justice: The Ideology and Institutionalization of Alternatives to Court.* Westport, CT: Greenwood Press.

———— (1988) "Regulatory Reform: Creating Gaps and Making Markets," 10 *Law & Policy* 293.

**732　The Power of Community Mediation**

Heelas, Paul, & Paul Morris, eds. (1992) *The Values of the Enterprise Culture: The Moral Debate*. London: Routledge.

Hepworth, Mike, & Bryan S. Turner (1982) *Confession: Studies in Deviance and Religion*. London: Routledge & Kegan Paul.

Hofrichter, Richard (1982) "Neighborhood Justice and the Social Control Problems of American Capitalism: A Perspective," in Abel 1982c.

——— (1985) "Rethinking Alternatives to the Courts" (review of Auerbach, *Justice without Law*), 9 *Legal Studies Forum* 89.

——— (1987) *Neighborhood Justice in Capitalist Society: The Expansion of the Informal State*. New York: Greenwood Press.

Kolb, Deborah & Associates (1993) *When Talk Works: Profiles of Mediators*. San Francisco: Jossey-Bass.

Kressel, Kenneth, & Dean G. Pruitt, eds. (1989) *Mediation Research: The Process and Effectiveness of Third-Party Intervention*. San Francisco: Jossey-Bass.

Lederach, John Paul, & Ron Kraybill (1993) "The Paradox of Popular Justice: A Practioner's View," in Merry & Milner 1993.

Matthews, Roger (1988a) "Introduction," in Matthews 1988b.

———, ed. (1988b) *Informal Justice*. London: Sage Publications.

Merry, Sally Engle, & Neal Milner, eds. (1993) *The Possibility of Popular Justice: A Case Study of Community Mediation in the United States*. Ann Arbor: Univ. of Michigan Press.

Miller, Peter, & Nikolas Rose (1988) "The Tavistock Programme: The Government of Subjectivity and Social Life," 22 *Sociology* 171.

——— (1990) "Governing Economic Life," 19 (1) *Economy & Society* 1.

Nader, Laura (1988) "The ADR Explosion—The Implications of Rhetoric in Legal Reform," 8 *Windsor Yearbook of Access to Justice* 269.

Pasquino, Pasquale (1978) "Theatrum Politicum. The Genealogy of Capital—Police and the State of Prosperity," 4 *Ideology & Consciousness* 41.

Pavlich, George C. (1995) "Contemplating a Postmodern Sociology: Genealogy, Limits and Critique," 43 *Sociological Rev.* 548.

——— (1996) *Justice Fragmented: Mediating Community Disputes under Postmodern Conditions*. London: Routledge.

Pruitt, Dean G., & Peter J. Carnevale (1993) *Negotiation in Social Conflict*. Buckingham: Open Univ. Press.

Raeff, Marc (1983) *The Well-ordered Police State: Social and Institutional Change through Law in the Germanies and Russia, 1600–1800*. New Haven, CT: Yale Univ. Press.

Rajchman, John (1991) *Truth and Eros: Foucault, Lacan and the Question of Ethics*. London: Routledge.

Rose, Nikolas (1990) *Governing the Soul: The Shaping of the Private Self*. London: Routledge.

——— (1992) "Governing the Enterprising Self," in Heelas & Morris 1992.

Rose, Nikolas, & Peter Miller (1992) "Political Power beyond the State: Problematics of Government," 43 *British J. of Sociology* 173.

Salem, Richard A. (1985) "The Alternative Dispute Resolution Movement: An Overview," 40 (3) *Arbitration J.* 3.

Sander, Frank E. A. (1976) "Varieties of Dispute Processing," 70 (79) *Federal Rules Decisions* 111.

——— (1980) "Community Justice," 31 (2) *Harvard Law School Bull.* 18.

Santos, Boaventura de Sousa (1982) "Law and Community: The Changing Nature of State Power in Late Capitalism," in Abel 1982c.

Selva, Lance H., & Robert M. Böhm (1987) "A Critical Examination of the Informalism Experiment in the Administration of Justice," 29 *Crime & Social Justice* 43.

Shonholtz, Raymond (1978) "Community Board Program" (Mimeograph, San Francisco).

———— (1984) "Neighbourhood Justice Systems: Work, Structure and Guiding Principles," 5 *Mediation Q.* 3.

———— (1987) "The Citizens' Role in Justice: Building a Primary Justice and Prevention System at the Neighborhood Level,"494 *Annals of the American Academy of Political & Social Science* 42.

———— (1988–89) "Community as Peacemaker: Making Neighborhood Justice Work," 15 *Current Municipal Problems* 291.

———— 1993) "Justice from Another Perspective: The Ideology and Developmental History of the Community Boards Program," in Merry & Milner 1993.

Silbey, Susan S., & Sally Engle Merry (1986) "Mediator Settlement Strategies," 8 *Law & Policy* 7.

Smart, Barry (1992) *Modern Conditions, Postmodern Controversies*. London: Routledge.

———— (1993) *Postmodernity*. London: Routledge.

———— (1995) "The Subject of Responsibility," 21 (4) *Philosophy & Social Criticism* 93.

Tambling, Jeremy (1990) *Confession: Sexuality, Sin, the Subject*. Manchester: Manchester Univ. Press.

Tomasic, Roman, & Malcolm Feeley, eds. (1982) *Neighborhood Justice: Assessment of an Emerging Idea*. New York: Longman.

Umbreit, Mark (1994) *Victim Meets Offender: The Impact of Restorative Justice and Mediation*. Monsey, NY: Criminal Justice Press.

Wahrhaftig, Paul (1982) "An Overview of Community-oriented Citizen Dispute Resolution Programs in the United States," in Abel 1982c.

———— (1984) "Nonprofessional Conflict Resolution," 29 *Villanova Law Rev.* 1463.

Wright, Martin, & Burt Galaway, eds. (1989) *Mediation and Criminal Justice: Victims, Offenders, and Community*. London: Sage Publications.

Zehr, Howard (1986) "Retributive Justice, Restorative Justice," 16 (1) *Peace Section Newsletter* 9.

———— (1990) *Changing Lenses: A New Focus for Crime and Justice*. Scottsdale, PA: Herald Press.

# [8]

## Chaos Theory And Human Agency:
## Humanist Sociology in a Postmodern Era

### T. R. Young
### *Virginia Polytechnic and State University*

### Reflexive Statement

The political agenda which informs this and other work centers around emancipatory uses of postmodern knowledge processes. Postmodern critique questions the grounds for grand unified theory, for sure and certain knowledge as well as for neutrality in the knowledge process (Rosenau 1991). Given the validity of that critique, once again the question of the role for social science in human affairs arises. I want to help fashion a postmodern social science which affirms the possibility of human intervention into the social process but recognizes its politics, its many uncertainties and its limits.

### Human Agency in History

For most of human history, the reach of human agency has been short and feeble. With the advent of hydraulic agricultural societies some 4000 years ago and then industrial capitalism some 400 years ago, human agency has been greatly extended in terms of raw power in many realms of human activity. However, modern science with its penchant for 'totalizing' theory, reduces human agency to compliance with universal laws of nature and society. Much postmodern reflection on human agency accepts the presumptions of modern science about totalizing 'laws' of nature or society and thus, remains pessimist (Rosenau 1992, p.81).

In those postmodern critiques which speak against the possibility of human agency, the data they marshall are convincing. Most human beings were subject to the blind forces of nature: drought, disease, storm, and starvation. For them, life is short, brutal and nasty. Even in the face of the great increase in human agency for those who are captains of industry or leaders of well-armed nations, human agency has been assimilated into elite theory. Some of that elitism focussed upon Natural law as understood by Thomas Aquinas and some focussed upon natural law as understood by Comte, Laplace, Pareto and others. For Aquinas, freedom is collapsed into compliance with divine Law. For Laplace, freedom is encompassed by natural law; in both, structure has precedence over volition.

## Structuralism

Since the publication of *Novum Organum* by Bacon in 1620 and Principia Mathematica by Newton in 1687, there has been a quest for the deep and enduring structures which pre-form natural and social behavior.   In the Enlightenment, the search entailed discovery of universal laws of biology, physiology, psychology and sociology with which to guide public policy.   Rationality and freedom were the icons of modern science but freedom was limited to the use of theory to design society.   Rationality meant that, in order to be a fully active subject, one had to confine one's action to that which was compatible with those natural structures as revealed by universal law.   To act in ways not compatible with natural structures was to be the fool, the idiot or the psychopath; to waste one's time and that of others.

Structuralists see permanent, natural and universal structures everywhere.   Greek and Roman thought began structural analysis with its use of the human body as metaphor for society (Polkenhorne 1983, p.135). Hegel gave structuralism a powerful impetus when he posited and published a coherent map of the structures of history and social life in which a 'Spirit' of orderly Reason emerged to give pattern to art, religion, philosophy and science as well as to mind, soul and society. Movement in history is the movement toward Absolute Spirit by which Hegel meant a state governed by and governing surely and forcibly with knowledge of universal laws of nature and society.   This made a lot of sense given a Newtonian world view and a stratified political economy which privileged people and peoples.   All else was only 'becoming' and could be dismissed as 'imperfection.'

In anthropology, Lévi-Strauss posited deep structures in mind and society which preorganized thought and action.   Wertheimer, in Gestalt theory, posited four grouping structures which organized human perception.   Kant posited 12 natural categories which guided empiric research and did not contaminate pure reason.   Husserl posited deep structures which constituted and preshaped human grasp of natural and social 'facts.'   For Husserl, human beings did have a creative role in the knowledge process but that role was presumed to be based upon such natural and essential structures (eidos) that objective knowledge was possible (Polkenhorne 1983, p.42).   In moral development, six natural stages posited by Kohlberg preempted

## Chaos Theory And Human Agency 443

moral theory. In sociology and in economics, a variety of modernists posited a single set of social functions toward which all structural change was a becoming.

Deep structures, if linear in their geometry, are inimical to human agency. Linearity implies that that which exists in the present fully determines that which shall exist in the future. This is a view which informs much neo-fascist social philosophy in that it tends to privilege the present as necessity and the future as inevitable. Chaos theory, of course, delegitimates that view. There are no inevitabilities in nonlinear dynamics of natural and social systems. Instead what is found are three generic forms of change within which there is more, or less, room for human agency. This essay tells the story of these kinds of change and explores their meaning for a theory of human agency in a time of great uncertainty.

### Fractal Structures: Natural and Analytic

Chaos theory offers a view of 'structure' which reconciles the insistence of reductionists that such totalizing entities do not exist yet accepts the insistence of structuralists that there is a whole from which the behavior of the parts is given both meaning and direction. In Chaos theory, nonlinear dynamics produce natural structures, the fractal geometry of which varies, depending upon their dynamical state; there are five such states discussed below. The geometry of such structures also varies with scale of observation: that which is a solid object from the point of view of a human scale of observation becomes almost completely empty space when viewed at sub-atomic scales. At scales of observation between, there is an interesting self-similarity in structure but there are qualitative differences as well--in the very same object.

In all this Chaos theory grounds a philosophy of science and knowledge very different from that of modern, Newtonian metaphysics and thus renders much of the postmodern critique of modern philosophy of science moot since it decenters modern science and relegates its presumptions to just a small portion of the actually existing natural and social systems. It is not that modern science and its project is to be rejected; only that it is to reserve its claims to those very simple natural and social systems which behave linearly and predictably. There remains much that is valuable in modern science but, as a grounding for a theory of human agency, there is much to criticize. Chaos theory offers a beginning which answers most of the objections of post-structuralism.

*444 Humanity & Society*

## Human Agency In Modern Philosophy

In the Enlightenment version of modernity, in order for human agency to exist, several prerequisites are necessary. For some expressions of the Enlightenment, such as those who follow Nietzsche, only superior individuals have the intelligence and the will to impose their desires on lesser people. For others who follow Hegel, the state is the repository of both Reason and Will. Still others such as Bacon or Comte thought that a collegium of scientists could advise the state. Still others such as Marx thought a far reaching democracy could link reason to otherwise intractable problems of life. More demanding modernist theories of human agency require:

1) an emancipated subject who would have goals above and beyond those activities preprogrammed by genes, or by 'primitive society' or by those mapped by preëxisting norms, laws, customs and morés common to the society in which the person was socialized. To take on preexisting goals is not, in modern understanding of agency, an act of autonomous Will.
2) a knowing subject who would have precise and positive knowledge about the dynamics of that part of the natural and social order s/he wished to shape in their own interest.
3) a creating subject who would be able to provide self with all the tools essential to a task. Use of others as instruments of one's own will is permitted.
4) a rational subject who would have to use instrumental reason with sufficient skill such that the probability with which goals are achieved routinely surpasses chance.
5) A 'principled' subject who would apply scientific or moral principles rigorously and uniformly over the raw material at hand. And finally,
6) a willful subject, some would say ruthless, others would say goal oriented, who would not be deterred by sustained opposition, adversity or defeat.

For many postmodernists, it would be fair of modernists to posit human agency only if the acting person embodied these most stringent standards above. But few can meet these standards.[1] The operative question is whether these standards are fairly set. The argument here is that those who demand these standards for human agency are more interested in control and compliance than in principled behavior founded upon 'rational social philosophy.' As we shall see, Chaos theory instructs us that natural and social systems are

## Chaos Theory And Human Agency 445

stable and survive precisely because they are 'unprincipled,' i.e., they behave nonlinearily. More generally, Chaos theory rejects the clock-like dynamics upon which modern science is based and from which modernist theory of human agency is drawn.

### Post-structuralist Critique

Skeptics in the postmodern camp take their lead from Nietzsche who questioned the facticity of these deep structures. They question the preoccupation of modern science with truth, natural law and objective theory without a human author immersed in a political, constitutive process. For postmodernists, all knowledge about structure is a quest for power more than for truth (Foucault, Derrida). Saussure, in his work on general linguistics, 1915, led critique at the level of thinking and knowing (Polkenhorne 1983, p. 152). Lyotard and Hassan gave the same treatment to the grand narratives of modern science and modern religion. When one deconstructs any such narrative about language, mind, perception or politics, one finds a politics and a poetry which presents itself as universal truth.

### Human Agency In Affirmative Postmodern Thought

Human agency has a more optimistic future in both critical theory and in American social psychology. Predecessors of critical theory in Europe, Vico, Droysen, Windelband, Rickert, Dilthey, Wundt, Husserl, and especially Weber set the human sciences outside the reach of natural law and thus provided space for human action. Marx had insisted that, in capitalism, one could see the possibility of collective human agency; of the end of the 'idiocy' of prehistory. Given good theory and good politics, a universal subject could be brought into being. Critical theorists today argue that there is a shifting and complex connection between economics on the one side and ideological hegemony on the other which, along with other structural constraints such as patriarchy and racism, shapes the possibility of human emancipation (Held 1980).

In America, social psychologists from Mead to Cooley to Blumer saw the possibility of human agency even against the putatively iron laws of nature and society. In their reading of the social process, human agency was not captive to natural law. Rather human beings constructed the social life worlds in which they lived out their lives. Given the human hand in such construction, there are any number of ways to create social realities. Anthropology confirmed the great variety of social forms by reporting data on the 3 to 4000 societies which sentient human beings, collectively, in their wisdom and with their own agency have constructed.

### Postmodern Phenomenology

The postmodern phenomenology offered here differs greatly from Husserlian phenomenology. In it, there are no preëxisting and natural categories which shape thought and action. There are, however, linguistic categories which do preshape thought and action but these do not predate culture nor are they located exclusively in the mind of the single acting individual. Mind, self and society emerge continuously within an ever-changing symbolic envelope. Foucault has laid out, in a wide-ranging series of books, the changing categories with which we grasp the dynamics of madness, crime and human sexuality. Marx has laid out the changing principles with which one can grasp the larger economic factors which preshape thought and action. Gilligan showed the political nature of Kohlberg's rendition of moral development and its preference for linearity. Feminist theologians and others have noted changes in the god concept in religion.

In all this, the human being is very visible as author of the categories of thought and action. In all this, one can see political agendas, legitimated as universal truth, inside the knowledge process. Postmodern phenomenology building upon the work of Husserl, Sussure, Wittgenstein and others offers a much broader field to human agency in the invention of reality and all sciences which purport to describe that reality than do modernist phenomenologists who follow Husserl and assert universal and natural categories of experience or analysis (Young, 1992b). Postmodern phenomenology grounded upon the new sciences of chaos and complexity, offers a view of human agency which concedes that there are 'structures' in the human mind and human culture which preshape thought and action but insist that these structures are themselves historical and ever-changing.

Whatever one's views on human agency, Chaos theory offers insight and guidance into the delicate and shifting relationship between order and disorder in ways not permitted in modern science nor imagined in more traditional knowledge processes. It is in those dynamics that one can find a theory of human agency which is at once, affirmative and realistic. The realm of necessity and the realm of freedom are not mutually exclusive nor does one dominate the other in all dynamical states; they are always found together. There is never a time in a nonlinear system in which there is no order; never a time in a stable system when there is not disorder. Human agency and human determinism dwell in the same theoretical house.

## Chaos And Nonlinear Dynamics

Edward Lorenz, James Yorke, Mitchell Feigenbaum, Stephen Smale, Benoit Mandelbrot and many others developed the theory, math and the sequences of nonlinear dynamics in natural systems (Gleick, 1988). The work of Mandelbrot is central. Mandelbrot worked for the Thomas Watson laboratory of IBM and was charged with solving the problem of interference in electronic transmission of signals. Mandelbrot found that, at all scales of observations, electromagnetic dynamics were fractal rather than integral. From that insight, Mandelbrot (1977) went on to generalize that the ontology of all natural systems was fractal rather than integral.

Given the nonlinear behavior and fractal geometry of almost all natural and social systems, one might first think that, in such an irrational world, human effort and human purpose is pointless. Nothing could be further from the truth. Human agency is possible; the operative question is when and what is possible. It is the changing ratio between order and disorder; between harmony and disharmony; between linearity and nonlinearity which answers such questions. At time, human interests warrant a preference for order but for most human purpose varying degrees of disorder are most helpful.

### Human Action in a NonLinear Social Life-World

In this section, I invite the reader to look at the various dynamic states which social systems can take and to think with me about the degree to which human action and agency is possible within each and between all of them. We will look at the first four dynamical states in some detail and explore the fifth state a bit later. Figure 1 offers two views of four equilibrium regimes. One view is that of the familiar time-series; the second is that of the fractal geometry of systems dynamics in phase-space. It is explication of this fractal geometry which opens up profound implications for the philosophy of science and, in this application, human agency.

The first form in Figure 1 is called a point attractor and the second is called a limit attractor. These two forms describe a dynamics in which there is little space for human agency. There are also two semi-stable attractors; the torus and the butterfly attractor. The latter two are called 'strange' attractors since a system is attracted to a particular region of phase space. These attractors provide space for human agency in ways not possible in those dynamics privileged by Newtonian physics, Aristotelian logic, Euclidean geometry and the linear causality they presume.

*448   Humanity & Society*

## Figure 1:   Four Semi-Stable Attractors: 2 Views

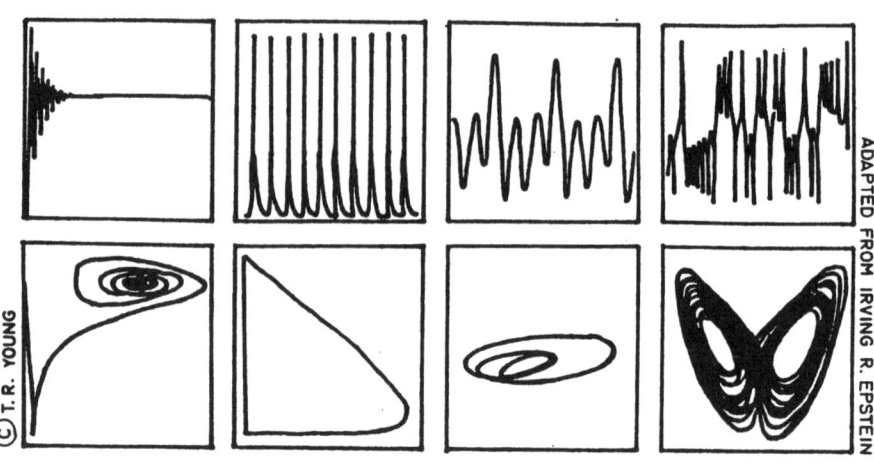

For Box A in Figure 1, the realm of freedom collapses into a single point.  For Box B in Figure 1, the realm of freedom is tightly confined to a single repeating curve.  If one were to base a theory of political agency upon these linear dynamics, one would hold that rational human agency involves the discovery of necessity and compliance to that which is necessary.  However, nonlinear dynamics are far more common and far more open to choice among uncertain futures.  The first such attractor, Box C, is called the torus.  Social dynamics which take the form of a torus have some limited room for human agency.  It is Box D, the butterfly attractor and its close cousins (with 4n, 8n, and 16n outcome basins) in which one finds significant human agency possible.  A fifth kind of dynamics, full chaos, is discussed later since the human agency it offers is qualitatively different.

### First Order Change: The Torus

For all such systems whose key parameters produce a torus, human agency is limited but it is there.  In this first order trans-formation, the regularity found in the point attractor or limit attractor gives way to some uncertainty.  We know that a given system will end up some where within the torus but we do not know just where to find it.

**Figure 2:  The Geometry of a Torus**

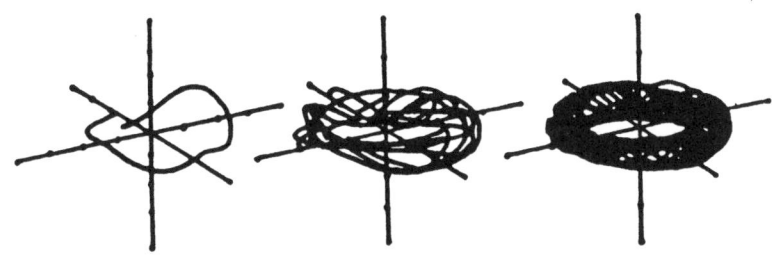

Think of the single line in Figure 2 as the dynamics of a family, a firm, a fellowship or a college class over the course of some given time period, say a year, on any given variable of interest to the researcher. If one is interested in say, number of children, employees, members, or attendance patterns, one would see that such values would stay within given limits over the course of a year but do vary. If a couple needs at least ten children to be certain that five would live to provide social and economic security in old age, human agency is a complex process limited by such exogenous factors as food supply, health care practices, religious values and personal vigor.

If the third set of lines in Figure 2 were, say, a large set of families, firms, fellowships or classes, one might see sufficient pattern to call that behavior a 'structure.' However similar, no iteration of a family or a firm is ever precisely the same as that of another family or firm. Similarity-but-not-sameness is the quintessence of the torus and of first order change.  In any environment in which the key parameters produce a torus, one has latitude to move within the confines of the torus.  Larger freedoms are difficult.  For instance, one does not have the 'freedom' to choose to produce no children else one is bereft in one's old age.  Nor may one choose to have ten healthy children if such numbers exceed the carrying capacity of the political economy at hand.

### Second Order Change

There is one feature of the torus in Figure 2 which does not sit well within the logic of modern science.  It has great import for a theory of human agency.  Modern science does not deal with the changing dynamics found in bifurcated periods or cycles.   If parameters increase linearly, outcomes change linearly.  Not so in Chaos dynamics.  Figure 3 shows a Poincaré section of a torus in which a small change might make a large difference. Figure 4 show that cross section in more detail.

**Figure 3: Section of a Torus**

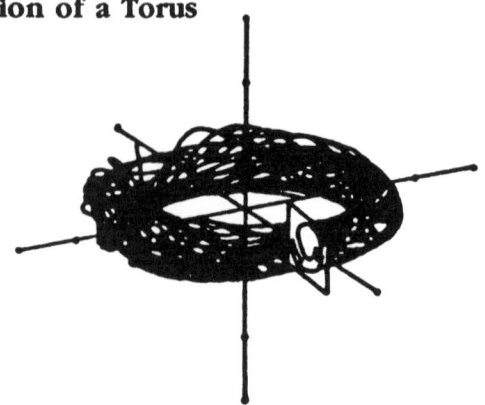

If one looks carefully at the cross section of the torus, Figure 4, one can see two tongues; the first at the extreme left which if expanded more, would expand human agency. This feature of a torus tells us that a new attractor is about to be born. Something is going on with the key parameters in a dynamical field which makes existing ways to do family (or business, religion or education) difficult or undesirable for some portion of the families (or firms, churches or schools) at hand. That tongue alerts us to the nonlinear emergence of, say, new gender relations or new opportunities for business expansion or to imminent sectarian schisms in a fellowship or new programs in a university.

In modern science, there is one and only one outcome basin in an outcome field; all systems of a kind are required to behave alike for a given set of conditions (or at least remain inside the geometry of a torus). All else is random error, faulty research design, inadequate instrumentation or just bad theory. Modern science tolerates variation ('normal' distributions) around a mean but defines such results as producing only 'adequate' theory. Penrose (1989) uses the term, 'superb' for theories which have a precision approaching $10^{14}$. In Chaos theory there can be two or more outcome basins to which similar systems with similar initial conditions can go. The precision with which one can chart those outcomes varies depending upon the complexity of the outcome basin. Weak correlations may be not a product of weak theory or of poor instrumentation but of actual indeterminate dynamics. Moreover, what is a strong correlation in one

## Chaos Theory And Human Agency 451

region of phase-space may be a weak correlation in another for such similarly situated systems.

### Figure 4:  A Poincaré Section of the Torus

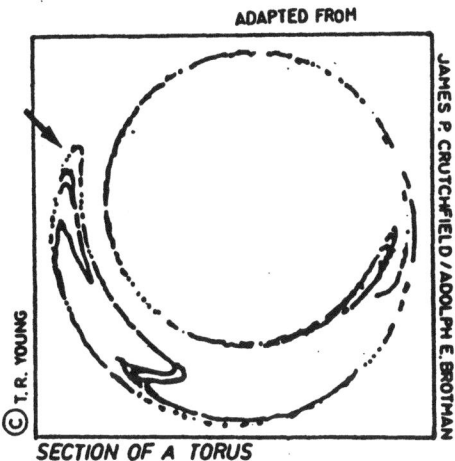

*SECTION OF A TORUS*

Postmodern science grounded upon Chaos theory conceives of structure as a loose and everchanging form, the solidity and reality of which is variable depending upon scale of observation and upon dynamical state.  In that difference is a major insight for a theory of human agency.  Social structures have a fractal value which might be very loose or very tight depending upon the key parameters above.  There is never a time in which causality is so tight in Chaotic regimes that human agency is impossible.  There is always some room for Will and Desire to combine to move to a different region in an outcome basin, even in a torus.

What is process at one scale of observation can be seen as structure at another scale.  It is the pattern of social action which, over countless iterations, produces structure as Figure 2, above suggests.   It is the changing ratio between order and disorder in a given outcome field which is so very different from the ontologies of modern science.  These differences force rethinking of our idea of structure and, indeed, of our philosophies of human agency.  In brief, for any nonlinear system, there is space for human agency.  That space opens up as a torus expands into phase space.  At crucial points, key parameters change and new attractors can be and are invented by human agency.  In their wisdom or folly, human beings act and in that action expand the causal field into two, four, eight or more outcome basins.  In any semi-stable field under stress, a causal basin can explode to fill the space available and thus expand the scope of human agency.

The generic point is that small changes in key parameters can force open a monolithic causal basin to accommodate still more outcome basins thus increasing both the range of choices and the regions of uncertainty in which human agency might play. The term used in Chaos theory to denote such moments at which causal basins expand is bifurcation. The first bifurcation produces a butterfly attractor.

### Butterflies, Bifurcations and Human Agency

Figure 5 presents a different view of the same butterfly attractor shown in Figure 1, above. One will note that, in Figure 5, there is an $2n$ outcome basin rather than the unitary basin in the torus shown in the Poincaré section in Figure 4, above. Near the center of each region of a $2n$ attractor, outcomes are pretty certain and, thus, human agency is limited as it was in the Torus (in fact, a butterfly attractor can be understood to be comprised of two connected tori). At the edge of each causal basin and between the two basins, certainty is lost; a moth or a marriage might end up in either basin or drift endlessly back and forth between two outcome states. To the degree that a family or a firm has control over key parameters, there are quite specific points at which small adjustments can produce large changes. Human agency is greatly expanded given such conditions.

**Figure 5:  A 2n Outcome Basin: The Butterfly Attractor**

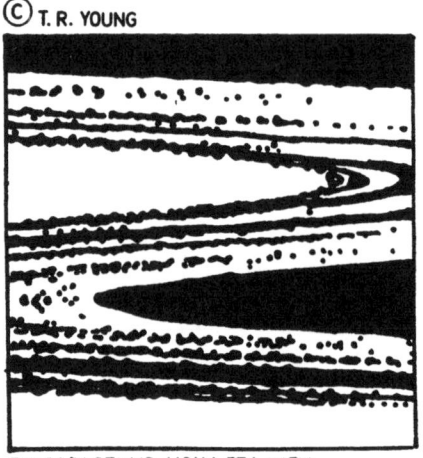

© T. R. YOUNG

ADAPTED FROM JAMES A YORKE

The Butterfly Attractor has, then, at least three major implications for a theory of human agency. In the first instance, there

## Chaos Theory And Human Agency 453

are two options between which, as mentioned, a firm or couple could chose given resources where before there was but one. Today, many couples live childless without social onus or legal sanction and then, after some variable number of years, may separate without legal obligation. The possibility of new forms of intimacy with or without children opens up the realm of freedom, If one were to calculate the portion of phase space in which human agency were possible, one would find that a Butterfly Attractor has more potential available for individual action than does a torus.

A second theoretical point upon which to focus is that there is an area between outcome basins in which dynamics and thus prediction is fractal. There is considerable stability, pattern and predictability for, say, couples which dwell within either basin of a butterfly attractor; for those couples at the margins, they may enter into a fairly stable relationship--or may not. This region of uncertainty is a goodly portion of the total basin of outcomes and greatly expands human choice if not human problems. If certainty is enemy to choice and human agency requires uncertainty, one can determine with considerable precision what ratio exists and thus have a reading on the room for agency.

Loye and Eisler have picked up on still another theoretical point. If one wishes to intervene in near to stable social dynamics (in order to expand or reduce a range of options), one has the benefit of improved forecasting which helps identify points of transition. As they put it (1987, p. 57), Chaos theory can be used to develop 'early warning systems' which can help forestall crises or identify newly emerging routes out of disorder. When human agency requires both pattern and variation, such warnings are most useful.

A fourth point upon which one might focus is that, in such a causal field human agency, hence moral agency, changes its location from the individual acting firm, family or person, in part, to the whole causal basin. Again, Chaos theory offers a most important point for a theory of human agency since some of the parameters which structure the ratio between certainty and uncertainty involves collective agreement as much as individual volition. There are grounds for democratic political theory in this point.

### 2N+ Outcome Fields

If one bifurcation alters the ratio between freedom and necessity, the question becomes what meaning do two, three, four and more bifurcations have for a theory of human agency. The most general point one can make is that, up to a point, an increase in the number of attractors increases potential for human agency. However, there is a caveat: while uncertainty may be essential to agency, several overlapping uncertainties might lead to chaos. For example, a couple might have the resources to handle one uncertainty or perhaps two uncertainties (say about income or about work schedule) in their lives but three or more uncertain parameters (say health, income, or work schedule) could push that couple into a chaotic dynamics.

The realm of human agency grows discontinuously as ever more outcome basins are produced yet there is a very regular procession toward a fully chaotic regime. This procession is very precisely choreographed by the Feigenbaum numbers below. We will find that freedom expands up to a point, often enabling persons sufficient options with which to adjust to the disorder in the larger society then, suddenly, freedom overwhelms human agency...and in the same instant that coherence is lost, qualitatively new forms of order emerge. Those who cry freedom too loudly call forth enough chaos to destroy the delicate balance between creativity and rationality.

### Creation out of Chaos

Figure 6 sets forth the entire series of transformations from order to disorder across the five dynamical states found in Chaos research. At each of four points (identified by 'Feigenbaum numbers'), more bifurcations produce more outcome basins in regular succession--until the fourth bifurcation. It is a remarkable feature of nonlinear dynamics that 2n, 4n, and 8n outcome basins are relatively stable, given nonlinear feedback loops, but with the next small change in a key parameter, full chaos sets in.

**Figure 6: From Order to Chaos to Order**

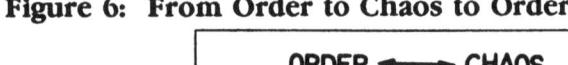
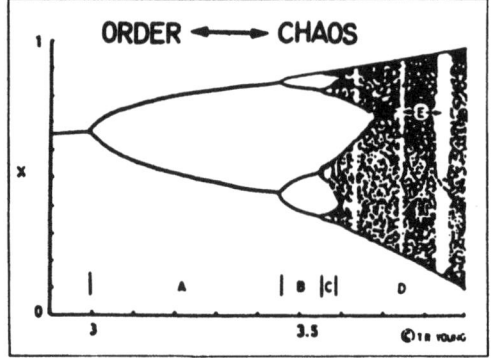

## Chaos Theory And Human Agency 455

One will note that stability and certainty are fairly tight in region A (that of the butterfly attractor), in 2n, 4n, 8n and 16n outcome basins. In Region D, full chaos reigns. One cannot predict the fate of a student, a family, a firm or a society in such a social milieu. However, one will note that, in Region D, there are bars and spots of white (<E>) interspersed in the darker region of fully chaotic dynamics. These white regions are regions of order; entirely new forms of order emerge out of chaos. Chaos is a source of discontinuous change and renewal in both natural and social systems. A fourth source of freedom has to do with the contest between order and disorder in these new regions.

It was Prigogine's explanation of how order emerged out of disorder which won him a Nobel prize in 1977 (Prigogine and Stengers 1984). Prigogine and countless others knew that the basic assumption of thermodynamics was in error; there is no tendency for the universe to disassemble into 'its most probable state' as the second 'Law' demands. More complex forms of organization have developed in both natural and social systems; the question is how? The answer Prigogine gave was that energy dissipated from disintegrating systems can be used to build new systems from the parts discarded. Out of the turbulence of change and disorder come new forms of order.

## Policy Implications

The most encompassing point with which to fashion a theory of human agency and thus a humanist sociology is that transformations from one chaotic regime to another arise from changes in parameters of the whole system. It is bifurcations in key parameters of the whole system which drive it toward an expansion of its outcome field. In studies of weather systems, of gypsy moths, of heart muscles, of DNA or of molecular crystallization, the 'structure' of cells, birds, insects, water or molecules do not change as phase transitions follow upon one another (Holden 1986) but the structures qua patterns of dynamics most certainly do change. One cannot appeal, in the first instance, to the characteristics of the parts with which to explain the changing pattern of the whole. As Briggs and Peat note in their work, Chaos is a science of the whole. In short, one cannot explain transformations in wealth, weather, bankruptcy, biology, economic, medical or marriage forms by appeal to and only to the personal characteristics of the persons affected. Given this insight, the first and most encompassing policy implication is:

*456   Humanity & Society*

I.    Preservation of near-to-stable social dynamics requires identification of key parameters in the whole system at hand and careful modulation of those parameters such that they do not cycle beyond the Feigenbaum point of full chaos.

*Discussion:*  The Feigenbaum numbers suggest that there is some ratio of variety in income, social status or social power which a creative society must exceed and another ratio beyond which a just society (and thus stable) does not exceed.  Chaos theory implies that when effective income inequalities remains but 2, 4, or 8 times that of one sector of the population over another sector, a society can be stable.  If effective income bifurcates beyond 8, 16, and 32 times, the secondary and tertiary needs of the first group tend to drive the economy and to price the poorer group out of the market for primary goods.  In such a case, one can expect human agency of those excluded to create new outcome basins; some of which may be most congenial to the human project and some more hostile.  In like fashion, given a group with 8, 16, or 32 times as much political power as another group, the more powerful group tends to make social policy in public and private sectors which give preference to its own welfare at the expense of minorities.

II.    Nonlinear feedback prevents destabilizing amplification of system periods and cycles.

*Discussion:*  Only Chaos can cope with Chaos.  Conferral of social status may be the most significant stabilizing tactic with which to limit the amplification of deviation in the parameters above.  The essence of social status is that the person to whom it is awarded may participate in the construction of all relevant kinds of social reality and that the person has access to the resources with which to do so apart from merit or income.  One gets what one needs to be a full person irrespective of any linear, quantifiable input the person makes to the occasion at hand.  Market dynamics tend to be rational; hence ultimately destabilizing as wealth and power amplify.  Social justice, in its irrationality, tends to be stabilizing.  Absent status, even social justice programs tend to be cheap, mean-spirited and degrading...this form of social justice amplifies the very bifurcations meant to be constrained by policy.  Absent status, the giving group tends to intrude into the personal life of the recipient group exacerbating resentment and escalating costs.

## Chaos Theory And Human Agency 457

III.   Efficacy of social control institutions as well as the utility of cybernetics varies with equilibrium state.

*Discussion:* Social justice is preferable to criminal justice as a solution to the problem of order.   Pattern and predictability fade as phase transitions cascade toward full chaos.   In social terms, if a system passes the fourth Feigenbaum number, social control tactics fail entirely.   Policies oriented to law and order; recourse to criminal justice, civil suits, monitoring and sanctioning, private security systems and other control systems tend to become ineffective as uncertainties escalate.   Criminal justice tends to be counter-productive on several scores; it tends to increase the amount of pain and resentment in a society and thus encourages conflict.   It tends to be linear while social justice tends to be nonlinear.   Being linear, criminal justice amplifies status inequalities; being nonlinear, social justice tends to damp inequality.

IV.   Small changes in key parameters can prevent large changes later on.

*Discussion:* This point will be very welcome to the ears of those who like minimal intrusion of the state into the economy and private life. Small changes in rental rates, interest rates or tax rates can produce large increases in affordable housing, sustainable agriculture or energy effective transport if made at strategic points.   These strategic points are given by the Feigenbaum numbers; if one wishes to double affordable housing, the Feigenbaum number for the ratio between income and housing costs must be at least 3.0; if one wishes to quadruple affordable housing, the Feigenbaum number is 3.5.   At both these points, a small increase will push the system into the next phase transition while a small decrease in that ratio (by taxation or adjustment in interest rates, for example) will, if Chaos dynamics are instructive, pull it back from the abyss.

V.   Personal freedom on the one hand and social order on the other can be harmonized by some attention to the number of outcome basins offered in any given sector of the social order.

*Discussion:* From the sections above, one can see that differing configurations of outcome basins affect human agency.   There are many important dimensions of personal choice in all near to stable outcome fields; the torus, the butterfly attractor as well as 4n, 8n, and 16n basin fields.   The costs and risks of 32n outcome basins may not be worth the gain in personal freedom for some few persons, given the loss of pattern and coherency for the whole system. Chaos theory thus suggests that social policy can be formed which satisfies our interest in stability and continuity on the one hand together with creativity, spontaneity and flexibility on the other.

VI.     Full Chaos tends to produce new order; not complete disorder.

*Discussion:*   This is that third order change within which human agency is severely limited.   The task for a democratic political philosophy is to invent new forms of politics, new forms of economics, new forms of religion or family and explore their potential for the human project. The events in Eastern Europe lend themselves to this kind of research.

There well may be times and realms of social life in which full chaos is beneficial to the system.   Given unresponsive institutionalization of social practices which amplify inequalities, full blown chaos with its destructive/creative dialectics may serve to unfreeze existing power/class configurations while producing innovations, some of which may be most congenial to the human project. There may be times when revolution is more congenial to the human project than is the slow and gentle evolution of mediated social change.

I would be remiss if I were to fail to point out that it is precisely in such situations one finds both the ugliest as well as the most emancipatory social engagements. This is the time when wisdom and judgment is best deployed and when the ancient teachings of the Buddha, the Christ and Mohammed remain most valuable to the human enterprize.

**Managing Chaos**

There is an emerging literature in both natural and social science about the tactics by which low order chaos can be managed. A. Hübler (1992), of the Beckman Institute at University of Illinois, and Stephen Guastello (1992), Psychology, Marquette University offer papers to that possibility. In brief, one manages chaos by determining its dominant chaotic regime and adding enough matching chaos to maintain the desired balance between order and disorder. There are several advantages to nonlinear regimes for ordinary biological, physiological, psychological and sociological processes. The fact that Chaos can cope with chaos is embedded in all these advantages. In population dynamics, in heartbeat, in thinking and in talking,

## Chaos Theory And Human Agency 459

nonlinearity permits at once of pattern and predictability and, in the same moment, of flexibility and creativity. Without nonlinearity, life would be chancy indeed and communication most primitive.

## Conclusion

As we expand from a knowledge process oriented solely to the linear dynamics of newtonian mechanics, space is opened for reconsideration of the nature of human agency, the concept of deviancy, the utility of stability and the efficacy of authoritarian structures such as bureaucracies and centrally planned economies. Political and ethical implications of Chaos theory await exploration as do its implications for the philosophy of science and the development of the research tools with which to pursue the knowledge process and to evaluate the validity of what we discover.

It is good to keep in mind, in all of this, that the scope of human agency varies with scale; at the scale of direct, real time interpersonal interaction, there is never a time when one cannot change one's own immediate journey through life. One is always responsible for what one does; given 2n+ attractors, one has more choice and becomes more responsible. It is true that there are larger social processes within which one must live and within which one must fit oneself if one is to survive the moment, however variation, change, creativity and surprise are always found in nonlinear social dynamics; the operative questions are how much change and surprise is available and how such whatever agency available contributes to equity and social justice. A central point in this essay is that, at every level of social organization, there is some level of freedom; with that freedom comes responsibility. Unless we develop a politics with which to constrain that science to human values which transcend a given moment or a given class or a given society, human agency might not always be congenial to the human condition.

### REFERENCES

Briggs, John and F. David Peat. 1989. *Turbulent Mirror: An Illustrated Guide to Chaos Theory and the Science of Wholeness.* New York: Harper and Row.

Feigenbaum, Mitchell. 1978. Quantitative Universality for a Class of Nonlinear transformations, in the *Journal of Statistical Physics*, 19:25-52. Cited in Gleick 1987:157.

*460   Humanity & Society*

Gleick, James. 1987. *Chaos: Making a New Science* N.Y.: Penguin Books.

Guastello, Stephen J. 1992. Population Dynamics and Workforce Productivity. Paper presented at The Second Annual Chaos Network Conference, June 10, Santa Cruz.

Held, David. 1980. *Introduction to Critical Theory.* London: Hutchinson University Press.

Hübler, A. 1992. Modelling and Control of Complex Systems: Paradigms and Applications. *Modeling Complex Phenomena.* L. Lam, ed. New York: Springer.

Loye, David and Riane Eisler. 1987. Chaos and Transformation: Implications of Nonequilibrium Theory for Social Science and Society. In *Behavioral Science* 32.

Mandelbrot, Benoit. 1977 [1982]. *The Fractal Geometry of Nature.* New York: Freeman.

Penrose, Roger. 1989. *The Emperor's New Mind.* Oxford: Oxford University Press.

Prigogine, Ilya and Isabelle Stengers. 1984. *Order out of Chaos: Man's New Dialogue with Nature.* New York: Bantam Books.

Polkinghorne, Donald. 1983. *Methodology for the Social Sciences.* Albany: SUNY Press.

Rosenau, Pauline. 1992. *Post-modernism and the Social Sciences.* Princeton: Princeton University Press.

Young, T. R. 1991 Change and Chaos Theory. In the *Social Science Journal* 28:3. Fall.

Young, T. R. 1991 Chaos theory and Symbolic Interaction. In the Journal of *Symbolic Interaction,* 14:3, Fall.

Young, T. R. and L. D. Kiel. 1992a. Chaos Theory and Management Science. Preprint available from the author.

Young, T. R. 1992b Reinventing Sociology. A paper given at the Annual Meetings of the Society for the Study of Social Problems. Pittsburgh. August.

# Part III
# Transformational Analyses
# and Marginalized Identities

# [9]

# From Restoration to Transformation: Victim-Offender Mediation as Transformative Justice

*Robert Carl Schehr*

*In this essay I make the case that victim offender mediation (VOM) adheres to a kind of legal formalism characteristic of relations among lawyers, clients, and the courts. I contend that mediators guide restitution agreements toward activities consistent with dominant cultural interests. Mediators cajole offenders to engage in secondary sector labor market activities, and demonstrate a commitment to dominant cultural norms and values. Having established the system-reproducing aspects of VOM, I conclude by arguing that there is a place for critical application of VOM to perennial social problems in our cities and rural communities. A two-stage process is recommended to achieve this end: (1) offenders must acknowledge harm done to offenders, and (2) offenders must be required to attend critical literacy workshops. It is my belief that when offenders are exposed to the process of uncovering dominant cultural manifestations of power, a truly emancipator praxis unfolds. In this way, mediators are viewed as transformative intellectuals.*

In this article I wish to make the case that victim offender mediation (VOM) adheres to a kind of legal formalism characteristic of relations between lawyers, clients, and the courts. *Legal formalism* is conceptualized here as a system-reproducing steering mechanism (Jessop, 1991; Schehr, 1995; Bertramsen, Thomsen, and Torfing, 1991) employed by the state to assist unstable sectors of society (in this case, criminal justice) toward stasis. I contend that mediators guide restitution agreements toward activities consistent with dominant cultural interests. In doing so, mediators cajole offenders (especially juveniles) in engaging in secondary-sector labor market activities, and they demonstrate

*Note:* Please direct all correspondence to Robert Carl Schehr, Criminal Justice Program, P.O. Box 19243, University of Illinois, Springfield, Ill. 62794

a commitment to dominant cultural norms and values (especially those relating to respect for authority, hard work, property, merit, nationalism, and the like). When this process results in reduced recidivism, VOM has successfully served to promote systemic stability.

Having established the system-reproducing aspects of VOM, I conclude by arguing that there is a place for critical application of VOM to perennial social problems in our cities and rural communities. What it will take to transform the process of VOM—from one imbued with the coercive power of criminal justice authorities to one that empowers offenders beyond the commission of nonnormative and criminal activity—is a two-stage process. I fully acknowledge the responsibility that must be borne by those who have brought fear, intimidation, hardship, injury, or other kinds of interpersonal violation of person or place onto others. However, like most who write in the "restorative justice" literature, I contend that punishment for those who violate standards of normative behavior must not replicate the violence of the initial act. That is, I share with Gilligan (1995) the belief that symbolic manifestations of punishment have real consequences for the perpetuation of cultural violence. If our criminal justice apparatus promotes violent resolutions to nonnormative actions, violence in the culture as a whole will result. In short, responses to nonnormative behavior must acknowledge the harm caused, and restitution must be made. The question that concerns us here is, how can this be accomplished?

I will propose developing a second phase of VOM restitution processes that focuses on critical literacy. Consistent with my belief that the complicated weave that constitutes subjective identity must be addressed if we are to make real changes in our respective communities, requiring young people and adults to attend critical literacy workshops as a component of their restitution agreement promotes the highest ideals of a strong democracy (Barber, 1984). By providing the inducement to attend, VOM facilitators may serve as *transformative intellectuals* (Giroux, 1989)—community activists who recognize the desperate situation of marginalized people and realize that the process of uncovering dominant cultural manifestations of power and domination is truly emancipatory praxis. Moreover, participants in critical literacy workshops are exposed to skills training in the areas of reading comprehension, math, science, geography, history, and the social sciences.

This article is divided into two parts. In the first part, I will discuss the manifestation of legal formalism in VOM sessions and how VOM serves as a system-reproducing steering mechanism for the state. In the second part, I will discuss what I refer to as phase two, a requirement that offenders attend critical literacy workshops. Phase two signifies a commitment to *transformative justice,* an effort to promote a humane alternative to political, economic, and cultural inequity. A commitment to transformative justice stems from considerable sociological and criminological research establishing the links between marginalization and contact with criminal justice authorities (Spector, 1995;

Wright and others, 1999). Following discussion of phase two, I conclude with some general remarks related to possible directions for future inquiry.

## Legal Formalism as a Steering Mechanism

Pursuing attention to VOM through the lens of legal formalism suggests a number of possible considerations. First, since 1994 the American Bar Association has supported the application of VOM in both presentencing diversion and postsentencing conditions of parole. Its support may be based on the perception that VOM signifies a less combative application of legal principles to dispute resolution. The second point relating to the relevance of legal formalism and VOM is the presence of an overt power imbalance, particularly for youthful offenders. The power imbalance appears in many guises. First, there are status differences between the mediator, the "typical victim" of youth crime, and the youthful offender. Second, the power of the mediator as the confidant during the storytelling phases of both the premediation and mediation stages produces power over the offender and the victim. Finally, as I will contend later, the formalistic process of *legalistic storytelling* suggests that to a large degree neither the offender nor the victim will have the time or procedural infrastructure necessary to fully tell his or her story. The emphasis in VOM sessions is on getting to agreement. If there can be no mediated way to resolve differences between offenders and victims, cases are returned to the courts for standard processing.

*Legal formalism* refers to the way in which lawyers are trained, and consequently, the ways in which they translate that training into practice. In general, we can say that this practice of law is "mechanical jurisprudence," producing an "emotional insensitivity and underdevelopment of law students and lawyers" (Delgado, 1997, p. 1113). This is important because reliance on master discourses (Lacan, 1977; Arrigo and Schehr, 1999; Schehr and Milovanovic, 1999) like those practiced in law and mediation suggests the following:

> Doctrinalism is a discourse of power, of mastery. Like positivist thought in early social science, it serves the rise of specialization and meshes well with the profit-making motive already prevalent in capitalist society.

Much like the criticism following from Arrigo and Schehr (1998) and Schehr and Milovanovic (1999), the criticism of law as legal formalism suggests an effort to create an ambiance around legal practice through the application of precedent and analysis of obscure case law, much like that which exists in the natural sciences. Here, the emphasis is on technical precision, the constitution of a scientific approach to the administration of law. The problem, as Delgado (1997) suggests, is that "formalism leaves you with no moral anchor" (13). Schlag makes the point that "legal obsessionism" produces a kind of schizophrenia in practitioners of the law. For example, lawyers are supposed to believe that "racism only exists when it is intended; that everyone knows the law; that all are rational interest calculators and cost avoiders; and that judges are capable of balancing incommensurable values." The result, argues Schlag, is "a mentality prone to coercion, wheedling, needling, harassment, and other rude and crude practices of lawyers" (in Delgado, 1997, p. 1137). Identifying the manifestation of legal formalism in VOM discourse constitutes the remainder of the first part of this article.

VOM constitutes one procedural arm of balanced and restorative justice. Seldom has the question Restored to what? been asked. The answer to this question seems to be contextualized within the communitarian framework (Etzioni, 1995a, 1995b) and emphasizes the need to *heal* victims, offenders, and communities (see Zehr, 1990; Umbreit, 1994; Van Ness and Strong, 1997). Aside from the religious and medical overtones, the more sociologically interesting aspects of VOM emerge from a Durkheimian adherence to solidification of normative practices consistent with dominant cultural interests. Ostensibly, what this produces for victims is a sense of the healing of emotional and psychological damage caused by invasions of private space (objective and subjective). This, supporters of VOM contend, emerges when victims can physically (since most crimes are committed by teens without any adult present) and verbally confront those who have injured them. Procedural emphasis in VOM sessions is on verbally reconstructing the offense. That is, much like the confessional, the situational effect of VOM is to provide a sanctuary setting for the narrative exposition of pain and suffering. Or, put another way, talking can cure. Healing, insofar as it is applied to offenders, is alleged to occur through recognition of harms caused by their actions and any gestures forthcoming to demonstrate a commitment to "pay" for their deviant act. Payment can come in many forms. How "healing" permeates the "community" represents a more ambiguous but nonetheless ideological aspect of VOM, and is consistent with its rhetorical commitment to system maintenance. The community signified in VOM discourse and practice parallels the communitarian explication of community. That is, there seems to be an assumption that a recognizable geographically situated, relatively homogenous body of individuals, values, and interests exists. Healing takes place when young people are held accountable for harms caused and when they are led to understand their place in the broader political, economic, and cultural web of life. To the extent that this occurs, the community has been healed.

I contend in this article that despite rhetorical commitments to healing, the VOM session, influenced by legal formalism, actually imposes greater limits on self-realization (on the part of both the offender and the victim) and community justice than it promotes. The reason for this outcome is twofold: (1) VOM narrative relies too heavily on legal formalism and (2) VOM restitution agreements tend to reproduce existing social relations by returning offenders to their "original state." Commitment to legal formalism and expressions of restoration coexist in political space as steering mechanisms for the reproduction of dominant cultural interests (Offe, 1985; Schehr, 1998; Jessop, 1990; Luhmann, 1986; Bertramsen, Thomsen, and Torfing, 1991; Cohen and Arato,

1992). Much as reliance on *stare decisis* reflects an interest in system maintenance, restorative justice and VOM signify an attempt to return the participants
to their point of origin *(restoration)*. At base, and consistent with legal formalism and restorative justice, VOM signifies a struggle over discursive vehicles
for the perpetuation of dominant cultural norms and values. How does
this work?

As a cousin of legal discourse, VOM serves to promote the status quo by
narrowly channeling narrative constructions of meaning into the same requirements for legal mootness, standing, and relevance to the specific act committed, as is commonplace in courtroom trials. Conducted as they are in a
sanctuary setting, discursive interactions between victims, offenders, and mediators are constituted by the power invested in the "keeper of tales." That is,
mediators serve as secular priests positioned to probe all aspects of one's secrets
and fears. This is especially true during the information-gathering phase of
mediation, where, if the parties are agreeable, mediators conduct in-depth
interviews. The most valuable setting for these interviews is the subject's home.
Here, a wealth of interpretive data unfolds for the mediator. What is interesting is that only between five and ten minutes will be granted to either the victim or the offender, during the actual mediation session, for them to speak to
their concerns. The premediation interview is not performed in all cases but
is clearly advised (Van Ness and Strong, 1997). This strategy is put in place
due to the possibility of one or the other representatives in the dispute changing their stories. It signifies a commitment to quality control. Again, this information-gathering process conducted by victim-offender mediators parallels
encounters with lawyers. Subjects may provide considerable background detail
for their respective attorneys, only to have that information limited by courtroom procedure. Here's how.

The aspects of VOM procedure appropriate to this discussion center
around the actual mediation session itself. While the premediation interviews
are relevant to establishing the role of the mediator as one who "hears confessions," the more formal aspects of VOM procedure—those recognized by supporters as its strength—are precisely where attention to legal formalism can be
drawn. While some variations exist in the way VOM procedures unfold, there
are recognizable patterns that have developed, due in large part to the stan-
dardization of training. The typical VOM procedure is characterized by four
steps: (1) case referral and intake, (2) preparation for mediation, (3) conducting of the mediation session, and (4) mediation follow-up (see Van Ness and
Strong, 1997). It is the actual mediation session that most dramatically demonstrates the influence of legal formalism on VOM. The mediation session will
last approximately one hour and will typically involve the following:

- Introductory statement by mediator
- Storytelling by offender and victim
- Clarification of facts and sharing of information
- Reviewing victim losses and options for compensation

- Developing written restitution agreement
- Closing statement by the mediator

The storytelling phase of the mediation session allows the offender to speak to the details of his or her crime, while the victim has the opportunity to confront the offender, letting the offender know how this event has affected his or her life. This component of the session lasts anywhere from five to ten minutes. The responsibility of the mediator is to explore any unclear aspects of the offender's story (especially since the mediator has, in all likelihood, already spoken to the offender about the story) and to make certain that the exchange between interlocutors remains focused on the issue at hand. The mediator is not to determine guilt. Participation in VOM generally requires the offender to have already admitted responsibility for the crimes committed (either in presentencing interviews or as a component of sentencing once the court determines responsibility). This is a crucial aspect of VOM, in that those standing before the court are faced with the "option" of either taking their chances in juvenile court or admitting their guilt and facing their victim. In short, VOM receives its "willing" participants through coercion.

While not specifically directed at VOM, the views expressed by Leviton and Greenstone (1997) illustrate the restricted and linear emphasis placed on getting to an agreement. They make it very clear that any probing questions, or caucuses to meet with recalcitrant participants, must be solely directed at the issue at hand. Moreover, they are quite clear that the mediator must always remain neutral (change the disputant's perspective; don't try to change his mind). The perspective taken by Leviton and Greenstone is consistent with VOM training and expectations. To be a good mediator, one must be impartial. It is this aspect of mediation that I take up in the next section.

To the extent that in certain instances (for example, first-time nonviolent juvenile and adult offenders) VOM procedure encourages intervention prior to court appearances, mediation signifies a kinder, gentler approach to the administration of justice. It is also true that during the second phase of the VOM process (preparation for mediation), mediators can meet in private with each party to the dispute to establish background information and any details the parties believe to be relevant to the telling of their story. This suggests to the participants that the mediator is someone who cares about their situation and is interested in seeing their concerns taken seriously. Data gathered by Umbreit and Coates (1993) indicate high levels of satisfaction from both the offender and the victim, following participation in VOM. Furthermore, evidence exists that VOM reduces recidivism (Schneider, 1986; Umbreit, 1994; Butts and Snyder, 1991; Nugent and Paddock, 1995) and minimizes victim fear (Umbreit, 1994; Umbreit and Coates, 1993).

Perhaps the most important data emanating from this literature is Umbreit and Coates's evaluation of those aspects of VOM victims and offenders found most important (1993). For victims, the opportunity to hear from the offender was most important; for the offender, the opportunity to apologize to the victim was most relevant. These data seem to suggest the power of communication, the ability to *hear* the other.

However, mediation is effective as an alternative dispute resolution device only to the extent that the victim and the mediator consider the resolution satisfactory. (Because obstruction of the process by the offender would mean that his or her case would be remanded back to the court, this appears to be a less likely scenario.) Because mediation channels communication into areas specifically for redressing harm done, no attention is paid to status, race, ethnicity, class, or gender issues. Even though mediators may possess considerably more information about both the victim and the offender, they are limited by procedure to stick closely to the "facts" of the case as they are presented in the mediation session. This closely parallels the commitment by lawyers adhering to legal formalism to remain closely tied to precedent and case law.

What is true of VOM, and not true of lawyers arguing cases in the courts, is the range of creative possibilities open to mediators who have the power to encourage mediation participants in a specific direction toward resolution of their dispute. However, adherence to legal formalism narrows the range of possibilities by maintaining the adversarial format used in law. It is this aspect of the discourse of mediation that I wish to develop through application of critical literacy. It is not enough for mediators to recognize the participant's experiences with violence, poverty, racism, sexism, and classism; they must be positioned to do something about those experiences. And while restitution agreements may be fashioned in creative ways to teach young people (and adults) how to perform specific work skills or care for others besides themselves, there is nothing in the way of education being offered to teach ways to transform political, economic, and cultural constraints that may have promoted participation in the kind of activity that placed the offenders before the courts in the first place. I suggest that what Delgado (1997) argues should be done with lawyers should also be required of mediators; they must be required to go out into the community and be among those they are serving. Here they will experience for themselves the power of neglect, poverty, and family violence, and the numbing persistence of hopelessness. Without this kind of involvement in the communities they serve, how can mediators come to a truly satisfactory restoration of victim, offender, and community? In effect, all that will come of the mediation session is a restitution agreement that suits the experiences of the mediator and the victim. In other words, what will come of the VOM experience will be the maintenance of social relations of power, inequity, and marginality. And while some offenders will certainly find the restitution agreements valuable in that they may learn a new skill, or they may come to appreciate their responsibility for harm done, what impact will this experience have on the broader political, economic, and cultural conditions of communities and subjects in need? These questions require consideration of a new role for mediators.

## Mediation as the Discourse of Power

Foucault (1978) goes to considerable lengths to emphasize the power inherent in documentation of the personal narrative. For Foucault, subject confessions locate power in the silent interlocutor—the mediator, in our case. Among the factors Foucault names for producing a power imbalance, two are applicable to confessions characteristic of VOM: "clinical codification of the inducement to speak" and "the method of interpretation" (pp. 65–66).

As a first step in the constitution of power, narrative reconstructions of events, feelings, attitudes, thoughts, and actions are listed, organized, and interpreted consistent with scientific principles. This procedural aspect of the confession produces several necessary components of the power relationship, chief among which are (1) the process of inducing a subject's confession through force or coercion and (2) construction of the façade of neutrality through the emphasis on procedural detail. In the first instance, subjects are induced to confess their secrets within the context of coercive power relations. Foucault (1978) suggests that this is done in the presence of one who is not simply a partner in the communicative act but rather "the authority who requires the confession, prescribes and appreciates it, and intervenes in order to judge, punish, forgive, console, and reconcile" (pp. 61–62). Although this process of confessing one's innermost secrets may have profound psychological and emotional efficacy for the subject making the confession, the context within which the confession is given cancels out the perceived benefits. The second significant point concerns the documentation of information. In this instance, the interlocutor receiving the confession conveys the mantle of neutrality by wrapping the confessional material in bureaucratic organizational and scientific/rational signs. In this way, the one receiving the confession can retain the position of ethical neutrality in decisions concerning the "facts of the case"[1] because truth will have been uncovered. The relevance of this process lies in the extent to which the confessor is willing to accept the verdict handed down by the one coercing the confession. To the extent that the veil of objectivity remains in place, the confessor will assume a measure of neutrality in the procedure.

The second aspect of confessions applicable to VOM concerns interpretation of discourse illuminated through confession—what Foucault (1978) referred to as the "hermeneutic function." Documentation of the confessor's story is a necessary precursor to identification of the truth. To that end, it is the responsibility of the authority requesting the confession to decipher the meaning of the confessor's story. In this case, then, the material aspects of the confessor's narrative simply become signs requiring interpretation.

Now consider how Foucault's remarks (1978) are applicable to VOM. Offenders are offered an opportunity to avoid processing through the criminal justice system by taking advantage of VOM. Typically, this also means that no record will be made of their trouble with the law. This is tantamount to coercion, albeit with a velvet glove. Offenders, not victims, are forced to confess their misdeeds. Victims participate in VOM only if they want to. From the start, there is an obvious power imbalance. Moreover, as M. K. Harris (1988) has suggested, the danger also exists for the possibility of a third entity, the community, to get involved in the punishment of offenders. For Harris, there is nothing restorative about adding to the number of interests requiring attention and satisfaction from the offender. (This concern has recently been raised by Levrant, Cullen, Fulton, and Wozniak [1999], who provide a contemporary overview of restorative justice.) So the question remains, can restoration come from coercion? Can offenders and victims find restoration in a system founded on power inequity?

In reference to documentation, the procedural aspects of VOM require considerable note taking during questioning of victims and offenders. Premediation interviews with the parties to the dispute are crucial for gathering data. From these data emerges the formulation of narrative used in the mediation session. It is these data that will provide the guideposts for distinguishing matters of fact from fiction. As the mediation session will be contextualized within recognition of the known facts and subject positions, these data also allow the mediator to retain the perception of neutrality.

VOM training materials strenuously encourage mediators to emphasize to participants that they (the mediators) are not judges. Indeed, offenders must admit guilt as a qualification of participation in the process. It is crucial that mediators remain neutral. And yet it is the responsibility of the mediator to maintain control over the mediation session by focusing attention on the "facts" of the case as they have been suggested by the parties to the dispute (and any available police reports). This places the mediator squarely within the interpretive scheme indicated by Foucault (1978). The mediator must decide, based on previously gathered data, who is more accurately, and perhaps compassionately, telling the truth. In addition, it is the mediator who will help bring the parties to the dispute to a reconciliation agreement. These agreements are filed with the VOM office, but in the case of an offender who violates a restoration agreement, they become the property of the juvenile/adult corrections unit. Guiding the disputants toward a restitution agreement is the responsibility of the mediator.

The state plays a role in legitimating alternative dispute resolution strategies directly by funding research and development efforts, and indirectly through the invocation of legal formalist master narratives associated with intervention strategies like VOM. (Consider, for example, the recent federal restorative justice initiative sponsored by the National Institute of Justice. In addition, Freivalds [1996] indicates that by the end of 1994, twenty-four states had established juvenile justice statutes reflecting restorative justice principles.) As the only institution with the power to legitimate the administration of justice, the state is viewed as occupying the "nodal point bringing about the coherency of a mode of regulation [because it] is the institutional form which condenses the compromises which prevent the different groups making up the national community from destroying one another in an endless struggle" (Lipietz in Bertramsen, Thomsen, and Torfing, 1991, pp. 130–131). In other words, it is in the interest of the state to maintain the preservation of order to allow for economic growth, wealth, and prosperity. The state is constituted by an ensemble of political, economic, and cultural interests who identify at least six specific societal sectors that must be monitored and massaged to maintain behaviors consistent with corporate capitalism's production and distribution initiatives. Delorme (in Betramsen, Thomsen, and Torfing, 1991) identifies these sectors as (1) industry, (2) agriculture, (3) education, (4) finance, (5) the workforce (social security, employment, housing), and (6) the relation between central and local government. Although Delorme's schemata touches nearly every aspect of contemporary corporate capitalist reproduction and regulation, the administration of justice is missing. If we add this aspect of capitalist reproduction to Delorme's account, we can see that the state has at its disposal the opportunity to monitor specific sectors of American society that may indicate dysfunction. Having identified the trouble spot, efforts to remedy the situation are forthcoming and are consistent with preserving dominant cultural capital. This *strategic-relational* process is fluid in that it is based on an evolving relationship between agents of the state and their interpretation and application of state policy. Although master discourses like those constituting VOM are dominant, there is room for mediated interpretations or, as Barthes (1973) would suggest, writerly texts. This opening, or fissure, or bifurcation point (Milovanovic, 1997; Young, 1997; Schehr and Milovanovic, 1999; Arrigo and Schehr, 1999) signifies the possibility for creating a replacement discourse— one that can oppose the discourse of the master in such a way as to fracture consciousness (Schehr, 1995).

While the legal formalist discourse provides limited opportunity for articulation of oppositional rhetoric, VOM can be used as a forceful tool to challenge dominant cultural norms and values. This can only happen, however, to the extent that the VOM process is altered to reflect the needs of those most politically, economically, and culturally disenfranchised—and, not surprisingly, those who are disproportionately under the supervision of criminal justice agencies. That is, I propose a method of VOM articulated as *transformative justice*. In opposition to rhetorical and programmatic efforts directed at restorative justice, a commitment to transformative justice seeks a confluence of sociological and criminological insight into the human costs of political, economic, and cultural marginalization. In practice, transformative justice represents an effort to view an aspect of the criminal justice apparatus—diversion to VOM— as a progressive tool in the administration of justice. *Transformation* refers to potential changes both in the subject and in civil society. Transformation of the subject occurs upon exposure to the deconstruction of dominant cultural power. Recognition of their experiences with cultural capital relative to others induces a kind of critical literacy that holds real potential for social change.

Once people have information concerning their sense of self, place, interests, and the like, the potential for changes within civil society begins to emerge as a real possibility (Brady, 1995; Giroux, 1989; Kumar, 1997; Schehr, 1998; Knoblauch and Brannon, 1993).

## VOM as a Progressive Force for Social Justice

The power of language to heal (Szasz, 1998) and to influence self-perception (Dunn, 1997; Aguinis, Nesler, Hosoda, and Tedeschi, 1994; Berry, Pennbaker, Mueller, and Hiller, 1997; Burgoon, Buller, Floyd, and Grandpre, 1996; Dillard, Huanani Solomon, and Samp, 1996; Drake and Donohue, 1996) is a commonplace assumption in the sociological, psychological, psychoanalytic, and social-psychological traditions. Because narrative expression is at the core of VOM, it stands to reason that this mode of communication can be put to a use that, in its current application, it is not. Simply put, without attention to a reconceptualization of the VOM process, the answer to the question Restoration to what? will continue to mean restoration to dominant cultural values, especially those espoused in the communitarian literature popularized by sociologist Amitai Etzioni (1995a, 1995b). As has been indicated throughout, this is an unacceptable policy from the perspective of crime control, because political, economic, and cultural institutions, associations, and power remain inequitably distributed across the population. Moreover, whether VOM sessions actually "restore" any of the participants remains an open question (Harris, 1988; Levrant, Cullen, Fulton, and Wozniak, 1999; Schehr and Milovanovic, 1999; Arrigo and Schehr, 1998).

In the remainder of this article, I will contend that in order to approach "restoration" of affected subjects and the community, considerably greater attention must be directed at cultivation of just and humane living conditions for each and every member of our society. It is not enough for criminologists, community activists, politicians, and criminal justice officials to simply call for a mode of "reintegrative shaming." (Braithwaite, 1989). Reintegration into what is already an unjust, politicized, and unequal society means reproducing dominant cultural hegemony. I humbly submit that, as criminologists, we have the ethical responsibility to acknowledge and work to eliminate the devastating effects of poverty, ecological decay, and inadequate health delivery. In a related way, we must participate in a concerted effort to confront those aspects of the administration of justice that serve to perpetuate inequity. It is the ability of critical educators to draw associations between positionality and subjectivity and between structural patterns of inequity and oppression that make for a transformative justice. It is appropriate here to suggest that there is no need for stepping gingerly around those who would contend that what is proposed here is intensely political. It is, and it should be! The discourse of meritocracy, rationality (neo-classical-school rhetoric), and utilitarianism continues to pervade American criminal justice, education, and political rhetoric. As it relates to VOM, ideological manifestations of meritocracy, rationality, and utilitarianism can be demonstrated in the kind of activities promoted for creating the restored offender and community (for example, vocational work skills, human relations [caregiving to the elderly or to children], and crime response teams [especially for vandalism]). Although they are clearly an advance over competing calls for more punitive modes of punishment, current VOM activities designed for the restoration of juveniles tend to prepare them for assuming their place in a segmented and stratified workforce. Moreover, attention is directed at correcting aberrant, nonnormative modes of interpersonal interaction. The object is to "return the troubled youth to a state of normalcy"—a normalcy that is defined by dominant cultural norms and values and is codified in law.

What I find most compelling in the activities used by VOM programs is their appropriation of the responsibility for the transmission of cultural capital, which is traditionally the domain of primary and secondary education. It appears as though the criminal justice apparatus has taken responsibility for serving as the final coercive institution capable of producing a law-abiding, work-directed, meritocratic patriot. As previously indicated, this is particularly noticeable in the kinds of activities being required of juvenile offenders. A functionalist emphasis on pragmatism and vocational education signifies an institutional commitment to preparing students for a life of work (consider the Boyer report on high schools, especially its emphasis on technology), while simultaneously inviting them to participate in prevailing civic activities. Knoblauch and Brannon (1993) contend that the "tendency of a functionalist perspective is to accept a given social order, to perceive it as right if not as inevitable, and to insist sincerely on the necessity of 'training' individuals to take useful places in it" (p. 18). If it is indeed the case that the diversion of youth cases through the courts for administration by a VOM program is tantamount to one final stab at functionalist education, then what I propose later on simply redirects the pedagogical emphasis away from class reproduction and toward critical understanding of politics, economics, and culture. To be a transformative option, we must begin to consider ways to infuse aspects of the confession characteristic of VOM, with an emphasis on the multiple ways in which subjects name the world (compare Knoblauch and Brannon, 1993). Young people, especially those in traditionally marginalized groups, should be exposed to piecemeal deconstruction of the modes of class, racial, ethnic, age, and gender discrimination that are characteristic of American society.

To make the case for a progressive application of VOM, I turn for support to the insights offered by proponents of critical literacy (Kumar, 1997; Livingston, 1987; Kozol, 1985; Brady, 1995; Giroux and McLaren, 1989; Knobloch and Brannon, 1993), many of whom have been influenced by Freire's work on liberation pedagogy (1973), especially his emphasis on situated pedagogy. Freire believed that in order to produce real knowledge, knowledge that has meaning and relevance for marginalized people, educators must penetrate the lifeworlds of those they are working with. Insofar as it is possible, teachers must attain a visceral sense of the living conditions experienced by those they teach. Following Foucault, "the intellectual's role is not to elucidate knowledge in abstract symbols, to pose alternative world views, or to express for the masses what they either do not know, or cannot articulate well; rather, it is to 'sap the power, to take the power, it is an activity conducted alongside those who struggle for power and not their illumination from a safe distance'" (in Peters, 1996, p. 57). Foucault envisions a breed of intellectual who illuminates fissures, openings, and smooth as opposed to striated space. This intellectual is attentive to the plight of the marginalized and seeks to promote the confluence of academic insight into the ideological and philosophical constitution of power, with subaltern energy, passion, and insight into the relentless, driving demands of life. I have argued elsewhere (Schehr, 1998) that this is precisely the role sociologists can and should play as humanist intellectuals dedicated to recognizing and facilitating subaltern modes of resistance. The point here is that we have the responsibility as intellectuals committed to transformative justice to actively engage sites of power, oppression, dehumanization, and inequity, in concert with indigenous residents. Attention is directed at local, small, space-bound communities. It is here that we pay attention to speech, especially as it relates to VOM, because "the question 'Who speaks?' is an inherently political one, and 'speaking for' is an act of violence" (Peters, 1996, p. 61). Brady (1995) makes a similar point by arguing that "the issue of who speaks, for whom, under what conditions, and in what manner is intimately tied to a politics of representation that can only be understood by acknowledging how race, class, and gender shape power that legitimates certain forms of authority based on issues of exclusion and marginalization" (p. 30). I cite Brady at length because she encapsulates the position taken by critics of legal formalism discussed earlier in this article. What is eluded to by both Brady and Peters is attention to the structural conditions surrounding cases diverted to VOM (especially coercion), and its confessional aspects (previously discussed). Bruce Arrigo and I have argued elsewhere (Arrigo and Schehr, 1999) that it is conceivable that a VOM confession may produce the opportunity for subjects (both victims and offenders) to recognize and acknowledge elements of desire heretofore unacknowledged that will enhance their capacity to reconcile aspects of the divided subject. Kristeva (1986) points in a similar direction with her attention to cultivation of a "politics of marginality." What she contends, much like Foucault, is that intellectuals can promote a kind of political activism that represents the local citizenry by engaging marginalized groups in a process of discourse analysis. What this accomplishes is a discursive mapping of indigenous identity construction. By communicating with groups using their own stories, folklore, myth, and the like, intellectuals can work to illuminate and exploit possible points of entry in dominant representations of power (political, economic, and cultural) that may have truly transformative results. It is the confessional aspects of VOM, coercion notwithstanding, that enable such an outcome. Moreover, it is adding a second phase to VOM processing, the transformative phase, which truly seeks to encourage promotion of utopian possibility (Wexler, 1992).

## VOM Phase Two: Critical Literacy

With this in mind, I propose the following two-part VOM process for consideration. I first discuss my position on the current status of VOM practice, followed by a more detailed treatment of my proposed addition—a transformative VOM process.

Upon having a case diverted to VOM through the courts, the first phase will consist of contemporary practices, with some modifications. It is understood that the offender has in some way violated, frightened, hurt, or otherwise misused another human being. Physical, psychological, and emotional pain must be recognized and addressed. However, when seeking to arrive at reasonable methods of restitution, mediators must be trained to recognize the cultural capital of the juvenile and adult offenders they meet. To recommend menial work without attention to the fact that offenders typically know the reality of hard work, or, conversely, no work, through their own experiences with work or through the experiences of their parents, relatives, ancestors, or neighbors may induce greater humiliation. This, in turn, according to Katz (1988) and Gilligan (1995), sows the seeds for (re)generation of nonnormative and violent behavior. There are other matters needing attention that may fall within the purview of a restitution agreement, and perhaps paramount among them would be locating and stewarding treatment for psychological, physiological, emotional, and other subjective needs—such as treatment for drug or alcohol abuse, help for victims of abuse, and aggression management. Again, while there will continue to be innovations in the first phase of the VOM process, it is the second phase that will have the greatest impact on young people.

In the second phase of the VOM process—what I have called the transformative justice phase—juveniles will be required to participate in a pedagogical workshop that emphasizes critical literacy. While it may appear odd to consider discussions of pedagogy in an article addressing the administration of justice, it can only be so to the extent that our understanding of pedagogy is limited to conceptualizing education as something that happens in a structured classroom setting. I will make a different though not original claim that pedagogy is not limited to any specific space or content boundaries. Consider the point raised by Zavazadeh and Marton (in Strickland, 1997): "Pedagogy should be understood not commonsensically as classroom practices or instructional methods as such, but as the act of producing and disseminating knowledge in culture, a process of which classroom practices are only one instance. From this position, all discursive practices are pedagogical, in the sense that they propose a theory of reality—a world in which those discourses are true" (p. 168). What Zavazadeh and Marton suggest, then, is rearticulation of the role of the intellectual (consistent with Foucault and Kristeva) as one who possesses the capacity to help direct discursive accounts of discrimination, alienation, violence and aggression, oppression, and inequity toward recognition of possible points of fissure within political, economic, and cultural institutions. The relevance of adopting a pedagogical model to promote deeper comprehension of cultural capital stems from the belief that "education offers one of the few public spaces in which people are engaged with each other in the interactional work of making meaning" (Wexler, 1992, p. 155). To that end, it is conceivable that young people, engaged in the discursive reconstruction of self and group awareness, will come to recognize their collective and subjective strength—what Freire referred to as *conscientization*—the process of attaining political consciousness.

The second phase of the VOM restitution process, then, would include participation in a community-centered program of critical literacy directed at dialogical and situated learning. Workshops can be held in residents' homes (similar to Navajo Peacemaker Court), community centers, churches, schools, or libraries. In short, they should be held anywhere parents and young people can easily assemble. Deciding on a location for the delivery of critical literacy workshops suggests consideration of a politics of space, or what Brady (1995) refers to as "pedagogy of place." Briefly, space matters. Subjects must feel that they can speak freely and openly about their concerns without threat of intimidation or rebuke. Many VOM facilities (particularly those not directly affiliated with the courts) are associated with neighborhood churches, civic and charitable organizations, and the like, which suggests recognition of the importance of claiming a "neutral site" for the determination of restitution. For critical literacy to be effective, we must be sensitive to the ways in which public spaces can be cultivated for the constitution of a critical discourse and activism.

The primary academic emphasis of the workshops would be meeting basic literacy, math, science, and computer skills, with provisions for more intensified learning in each area for those who demonstrate competency. Curricular content would also include information on employee-employer relations and expectations. Emphasis on meeting foundation academic skills training stems from the belief that before social change can occur, stomachs must be filled. For this to happen, young people must have the skills to compete in the labor market. Pedagogy should stress application of methods consistent with recent insight into multiple intelligence (see Armstrong, 1987), especially those characteristic of Montessori. Why? Because among other things, these methods of instruction emerge from a philosophical and political commitment to challenging conventional beliefs about authority, freedom of expression, space and time boundedness, and cognition. Offenders completing participation in the critical literacy program would then have access to a work placement database and support staff provided by regional placement agencies.

Staff members would be trained to teach, using the critical pedagogical perspective, and should ideally come from the communities they service. The critical literacy aspect of VOM would not rely on untrained volunteers. To be effective, resources will have to be dedicated to preparing a core of professional educators to offer the curriculum. The efforts of these core educators would be supplemented with interested community members. I concur with Knoblauch and Brannon (1993) that teachers should include artists, playwrights, musicians, poets, university professors, and primary and secondary school instructors. Giroux (1989) makes the claim that primary and secondary school educators have been spoken to, but not included in, plans for pedagogical change. For phase two to be effective, we must work to rearticulate the role of teachers as "engaged critics and intellectuals in both the classroom and as part of a wider movement for social change" (p. 132). The role of this transformative intellectual is to engage students in contemplation and analysis of relations of power. It means that teachers must become more involved in their communities. It also means that serving as a transformative intellectual "is an ideological referent infused by a passion and commitment [to] justice, joy, and collective struggle" (p. 140). Viewed in this way, there is very little difference between transmission of curricular content in the classroom and commitment to the administration of justice within our respective communities. When we consider VOM, the association between providing the skills necessary to realize strong democracy (Barber, 1984) and reducing nonnormative and criminal behavior seems clear.

While there are many ways to think of critical pedagogy, I accept the following to be characteristics used by most who make use of the concept.

- Accept and promote tolerance of cultural diversity
- Accept and promote tolerance of sex/gender diversity
- Pursue equity with regard to political and economic access
- Expose associations between political, economic, and cultural inequity, poor education, and nonnormative behavior (including violence)
- Promote the value of a politically intelligent and alert citizenry
- Deconstruct interests behind all manifestations of political, economic, and cultural power
- Teach community organizing and political strategy skills
- Draw on student experiences for pedagogical practices
- Promote self-sufficiency in food production, housing construction (especially for rural residents), child care, and the like
- Promote environmental awareness
- Promote nonviolence in all its manifestations
- Promote fairness and equity in the administration of criminal justice

This list of qualities, while clearly not exhaustive, does represent aspects of critical literacy generally accepted by those who practice and write about it. The intent is to develop a curriculum based on the principles previously identified that will be offered to juveniles diverted to VOM for restitution of harms caused. To accept the challenge being proposed here means recognizing the fact that inequitable education continues by design. That is, as Kozol (1985) eloquently states, "illiteracy is not an error." To be willing to teach the principles articulated above is a form of "civil disobedience in pedagogic clothes" (p. 92).

To promote a truly transformative justice, criminologists, sociologists, community activists, and community residents must engage in a process of critical literacy that can begin to name and transform modes of political, economic, and cultural oppression.

## Conclusion

In this article, I have argued that we must make a cognitive and praxis-oriented change from thinking about VOM as a tool for restorative justice to viewing VOM as a mode of social technology that may actually lead to transformative justice. To return (restore) a juvenile or adult to communities and families where class, racial, ethnic, gender, and age discrimination are evident—and have represented normative experiences in the dominant culture—signifies a recipe for perpetuating hopelessness, dehumanization, and the predictable street crimes that so terrify this nation.

Facilitating the illumination of self in relation to political, economic, and cultural institutions is what is being suggested here. The contemporary administration of criminal justice mirrors neo-classical-school rhetoric with regard to responsibility for harms caused, and ways to repay the community. The VOM alternative has arisen as a way to avoid offender absorption in the criminal justice apparatus. VOM, however, serves to reproduce philosophical and ideological commitments to capitalist social relations through its emphasis on functionalist modes of restitution. The humanist alternative to this application of VOM is application of the second-phase proposal. Criminologists, sociologists, and community activists must coalesce around the need to promote transformative justice. In this way, the traditionally marginalized will have the opportunity to begin to critically reflect on who they are, where they are, and why they are where they are. To the extent that this process illuminates the multiple tentacles characteristic of dominant modes of control and oppression, the path toward subject and community transformation will have begun.

## Note

1. College professors know this maneuver all too well. Consider the administration of grades. It is part of collegiate teaching subculture to respond to students who complain about their grades with the statement, "I didn't give you the grade, it is the grade you earned." It is we who have the power of documentation on our side, and we use it to substantiate our position. We also know that this process of documentation requires considerable interpretation, which is never discussed with students!

## References

Aguinis, H., Nesler, H., Hosoda, M., and Tedeschi, J. "The Use of Influence Tactics in Persuasion." *Journal of Social Psychology*, 1994, *134* (4), 429–438.
Armstrong, T. *In Their Own Way.* New York: Putnam, 1987.
Arrigo, B. *Justice at the Margins.* Belmont, Calif.: Wadsworth, 1997.

Arrigo, B., and Schehr, R. "Restoring Justice for Juveniles: Toward a Critical Analysis of Victim Offender Mediation." *Justice Quarterly,* 1999.

Barber, B. *Strong Democracy.* Berkeley: University of California Press, 1984.

Barthes, R. *The Pleasures of the Text.* New York: Hill and Wang, 1973.

Berry, D., Pennbaker, J., Mueller, J., and Hiller, W. "Linguistic Bases of Social Perception." *Personality and Social Psychology,* 1997, 23 (5), 526–538.

Bertramsen, R., Thomsen, J., and Torfing, J. *State, Economy and Society.* London: Unwin Hyman, 1991.

Brady, J. *Schooling Young Children.* New York: State University of New York Press, 1995.

Braithwaite, J. *Crime, Shame, and Reintegration.* New York: Cambridge University Press, 1989.

Burgoon, J., Buller, D., Floyd, K., and Grandpre, J. "Deceptive Realities: Sender, Receiver, and Observer Perspectives in Deceptive Conversations." *Communication Research,* 1996, 23 (6), 724–748.

Butts, J. A., and Snyder, H. N. *Restitution and Juvenile Recidivism.* Pittsburgh, Pa.: National Center for Juvenile Justice, 1991.

Cohen, J., and Arato, R. *Civil Society and Political Theory.* Cambridge, Mass.: MIT Press, 1992.

Delgado, R. "Rodrigo's Thirteenth Chronicle: Legal Formalism and Law's Discontents." *Michigan Law Review,* 1997, 95 (4), 1105–1149.

Dillard, J., Huanani Solomon, D., and Samp, J. "Framing Social Reality: The Relevance of Relational Judgements." *Communication Research,* 1996, 23 (6), 703–723.

Drake, L., and Donohue, W. "Communication Framing Theory in Conflict Resolution." *Communication Research,* 1996, 23 (3), 297–322.

Dunn, R. "Self, Identity, and Difference: Mead and the Poststructuralists." *Sociological Quarterly,* 1997, 38 (4), 687–706.

Etzioni, A. *Rights and the Common Good: The Communitarian Perspective.* New York: St. Martin's Press, 1995a.

Etzioni, A. *New Communitarian Thinking: Persons, Virtues, Institutions, and Communities.* Charlottesville: University Press of Virginia, 1995b.

Foucault, M. *The History of Sexuality: An Introduction.* New York: Random House, 1978.

Freire, P. *Pedagogy of the Oppressed.* New York: Seabury Press, 1973.

Freivalds, P. "Balanced and Restorative Justice Project." Office of Juvenile Justice and Delinquency Prevention Fact Sheet, July 1996.

Gilligan, J. *Violence.* New York: Putnam, 1995.

Giroux, H. "Schooling as a Form of Cultural Politics: Toward a Pedagogy of Difference." In H. Giroux and P. McLaren (eds.) *Critical Pedagogy, the State, and Cultural Struggle.* New York: State University of New York Press, 1989.

Giroux, H., and McLaren, P. *Critical Pedagogy, The State, and Cultural Struggle.* New York: State University of New York Press, 1989.

Harris, M. K. "Alternative Visions in the Context of Contemporary Realities." In *Justice: The Restorative Vision.* Elkart, Ind.: Mennonite Central Committee, 1988.

Jessop, B. *State Theory: Putting Capitalist States in Their Place.* University Park: Pennsylvania State University Press, 1991.

Katz, J. *Seductions of Crime.* New York: Basic Books, 1988.

Knoblauch, C., and Brannon, L. *Critical Teaching and the Idea of Literacy.* Portsmith, N.H.: Reed, 1993.

Kozol, J. *Illiterate America.* New York: Doubleday, 1985.

Kristeva, J. "A New Type of Intellectual: The Dissident." In T. Moi (ed.), *The Kristeva Reader.* Oxford: Blackwell, 1986.

Kumar, A. *Class Issues: Pedagogy, Cultural Studies, and the Public Sphere.* New York: New York University Press, 1997.

Lacan, J. *Ecrits: A Selection.* (A. Sheridan, trans.). New York: Norton, 1977.

Leviton, S., and Greenstone, J. *Elements of Mediation.* Pacific Grove, Calif.: Brooks/Cole, 1997.

*From Restoration to Transformation*     *169*

Levrant, S., Cullen, F., Fulton, B., and Wozniak, J. "Reconsidering Restorative Justice: The Corruption of Benevolence Revisited?" *Crime and Delinquency,* 1999, *45* (1), 3.

Livingston, D. *Critical Pedagogy and Cultural Power.* New York: Bergin & Garvey, 1987.

Luhmann, N. "The Self Reproduction of Law and Its Limits." In G. Teubner (ed.), *Dilemmas of Law in the Welfare State.* Hawthorne, N.Y.: Walter de Gruyter, 1986.

Milovanovic, D. "Catastrophe Theory, Discourse and Conflict Regulation: Generating the Third Way." In B. Arrigo (ed.), *Justice at the Margins.* Belmont, Calif.: Wadsworth, 1997.

Nugent, W. R., and Paddock, J. B. "The Effect of Victim Offender Mediation on Severity of Reoffense." *Mediation Quarterly,* 1995, *4* (12), 357–367.

Offe, C. "New Social Movements: Challenging the Boundaries of Institutional Politics." *Social Research,* 1985, *52* (4), 817–868.

Peters, M. *Poststructuralism, Politics, and Education.* New York: Bergin & Garvey, 1996.

Schehr, R. "Divarications of Employee Drug Testing Through Deconstruction and Discourse Analysis." *Humanity and Society,* 1995, *19* (1), 45–64.

Schehr, R. *Dynamic Utopia: Establishing Intentional Communities as a New Social Movement.* New York: Bergin & Garvey, 1998.

Schehr, R., and Milovanovic, D. "Conflict Mediation and the Postmodern: Chaos, Catastrophe and Psychoanalytic Semiotics." *Social Justice,* 1999, *26* (1), 208–232.

Schneider, A. "Restitution and Recidivism Rates for Juvenile Offenders: Results from Four Experimental Studies." *Criminology,* 1986, *3* (24), 532–552.

Spector, A. "Class Structure and Social Change: The Contradictions of Class Relations in Advanced Capitalist Society." *Sociological Inquiry,* 1995, *65* (34), 329–338.

Strickland, R. "Pedagogy and Public Accountability." In A. Kumar (ed.), *Class Issues.* New York: New York University Press, 1997.

Szasz, T. "The Healing Word: Its Past, Present, and Future." *Journal of Humanistic Psychology,* 1998, *38* (2), 8–21.

Umbreit, M. *Victim Meets Offender.* Monsey, N.Y.: Criminal Justice Press, 1994.

Umbreit, M., and Coates, R. "Cross-Site Analysis of Victim Offender Mediation in Four States." *Crime and Delinquency,* 1993, *39* (4), 565–585.

Van Ness, D., and Strong, K. *Restoring Justice.* Cincinnati, Ohio: Anderson Press, 1997.

Wexler, P. *Becoming Somebody: Toward a Social Psychology of School.* London: Falmer Press, 1992.

Wright, B., and others. "Reconsidering the Relationship Between SES and Delinquency: Causation but Not Correlation." *Criminology,* 1999, *37* (1), 175–194.

Young, T. R. "The ABCs of Crime: Attractors, Bifurcations, and Chaotic Dynamics." In D. Milovanovic (ed.), *Chaos, Criminology and Social Justice.* New York: Praeger, 1997.

Zehr, H. *Changing Lenses.* Scottdale, Pa.: Herald Press, 1990.

*Robert Carl Schehr is associate professor in the criminal justice department at the University of Illinois, Springfield.*

# [10]

# DETERMINATE SENTENCING: A FEMINIST AND POSTMODERN STORY*

## NANCY A. WONDERS
### Northern Arizona University

In this article I employ the concept of storytelling, as developed in feminist and postmodern theory, to explore the assumptions underlying the story about determinate sentencing that has dominated sentencing research and policy since the 1970s. Four analytic tools embedaed in storytelling—a critique of objectivity, a focus on process, an understanding of identity, and a new conceptualization of power—are used to investigate core assumptions that guide determinate sentencing policy. Finally, I offer a new story about sentencing and argue that the incarceration crisis fostered by current sentencing policy is in part a crisis of imagination.

The story about determinate sentencing, as it is currently told, has been written by both liberals and conservatives over the past two decades. Determinate sentencing legislation has taken several forms but typically consists of legislated minimum, maximum, and/ or fixed sentences for some or all offenses.[1] Despite profound differences in the goals that they thought determinate sentencing would achieve, liberals and conservatives hold a common set of assumptions critically important in shaping the narrative about sentencing that currently dominates the political landscape. In this article I examine these assumptions in an effort to tell a new story about determinate sentencing. The story that unfolds here reveals that the understanding of sentencing that has guided reform in the past

---

* Thanks to many supportive colleagues at Northern Arizona University for editorial suggestions and constructive comments: Fred Solop, Raymond Michalowski, Jeff Ferrell, Alison Brown, Alex Alvarez, and Phoebe Stambaugh. This research was funded by an Organized Research grant from Northern Arizona University.

[1] By 1996, according to Tonry (1996:6), "fifteen jurisdictions had adopted sentencing guidelines to limit judicial discretion; more than ten had eliminated parole release; another twenty-five had adopted parole guidelines; many had narrowed the ambit of good time; and all had enacted mandatory minimum sentence legislation (often requiring minimum ten-, twenty-, or thirty-year terms and sometimes mandatory sentences of life-without-possibility-of-parole)." In addition, the federal government and many states have legislated sentencing guidelines; indeed, "twenty-two states had, or were at work on voluntary or presumptive guidelines" (Tonry 1996:29). All of these strategies are part of a nationwide effort to make sure that the length of sentence is "determinate" or certain (rather than "indeterminate" or uncertain).

20 years tends to ignore the complex realities that shape the sentencing process in the United States. The new story I offer suggests that although policy solutions which minimize the complexity of the sentencing process may have some success in reducing sentence disparities between individual offenders, they also have the unfortunate and (un)intended consequence of perpetuating and obscuring systemic discrimination against entire groups of people.

This article begins by describing storytelling as a strategic style of discourse and analysis rooted in feminist and postmodern theory. I explore several concepts embedded in the notion of storytelling; these constitute the analytic tools used to examine the assumptions underlying the old sentencing story. I then briefly describe the old story about determinate sentencing, devoting special attention to the assumptions that provide the foundation for determinate sentencing policy. In the next section I critique the old sentencing story and, in the process, begin to write a new story. In the conclusion I review the assumptions of this new story and address ways that researchers and policy makers can use the story told here to better achieve justice. I call not for an end to determinate sentencing, but for an end to the tale that determinate sentencing is an unqualified step toward justice.

## NEW CONCEPTUAL TOOLS

The emergence of feminist and postmodern theory during the last decade has substantially influenced the work of many disciplines. However, the implications of these theoretical developments for criminological scholarship and criminal justice policy have been underdeveloped.[2] Of course, feminist and postmodern perspectives are quite distinct from one another, and debates and disagreements among scholars working within these perspectives are common (see Hennessy 1993; Lather 1991; Nicholson 1990; Singer 1992). Unfortunately "there is no shorthand way to characterize these differences—nor could such an account be sufficiently totalized so as to do justice to the range of relationships between feminist and postmodern enterprises" (Singer 1992:470). Nevertheless, these perspectives have several conceptual tools in common for analyzing social life.[3] The most important of these, for the purpose

---

[2] Some notable exceptions exist, of course. For example, feminist theory has been addressed by Caufield and Wonders (1993a); Daly and Chesney-Lind (1988), Gelsthorpe and Morris (1990), Messerschmidt (1987), and Simpson (1989); postmodern theory by Arrigo (1995), Michalowski (1993), Pfohl (1993, 1994), and Schwartz and Freidrichs (1994). Some work has drawn self-consciously from both perspectives, such as Ferrell and Sanders (1995) and Howe (1994). See Einstadler and Henry (1995) for an overview of some of these contributions.

[3] Nicholson (1990) makes a similar point, as does Singer (1992).

of this article, is the use of "storytelling" as a metaphor for the social construction of reality.[4] Disch describes the value of storytelling in this way:

> Storytelling both situates our theories in the experiences
> from which they came and engages an audience in a differ-
> ent kind of critical thinking than an argument does. A
> story can represent a dilemma as contingent and unprece-
> dented and position its audience to think from within that
> dilemma. It invites . . . situated critical thinking.
> (1994:110)

For feminists, storytelling is strategically useful because it creates
the possibility of being heard by using a style of speaking and writing that contradicts conventional assumptions. For postmodern
theorists, the narrative form is valued because it undermines
metanarratives or attempts to generate universalized truth claims
about the world (Lyotard 1979). For proponents of both perspectives, storytelling is a methodology for critiquing social theory and
the social world—that is, for critiquing other stories.

In the following section I outline several conceptual tools, explicated by feminist and postmodern theorists, that are embedded in
the notion of storytelling:[5] (1) a critique of objectivity, (2) a focus on
process, (3) an understanding of the construction of identity, and
(4) a new conceptualization of power that focuses on its relationship
to culture and everyday life. These conceptual tools make it possible to *deconstruct* the assumptions that create the foundation for
current sentencing policy and to construct a new story about determinate sentencing.[6]

---

[4] Storytelling as a method of inquiry and analysis is not unique to these theoretical perspectives, nor has it been omitted entirely from other work within criminology. See, for example, Bennett and Feldman (1981) or Gisinan (1982).

[5] I am drawing concepts broadly from postmodernism *and* feminism to weave
my own story. Of course some feminists who are not postmodernists, and some
postmodern theorists who are not feminists, have developed and used the concept of
storytelling in their work. As Singer remarks,

> The thematic and strategic interplay between paradigms, and their opposi-
> tion tends to work against any mechanism of unification. The "and" there-
> fore keeps open a site for strategic engagement. The "and" is a place holder,
> which is to say, it holds a place open, free from being filled substantively or
> prescriptively. The "and" holds/preserves the differences between and
> amongst themselves. (1992:475)

Some theorists unify postmodern and feminist perspectives into a single
"postmodern feminist" perspective (see Yeatman 1994 for a description of
postmodern feminist epistemology). My approach here is relatively consistent with
this emerging perspective, although I do not draw exclusively on "postmodern feminist" thought.

[6] I am referring here to what has been called "social deconstruction" or "social
postmodernism," in which the "ultimate reference is not literary texts but ongoing
social rituals undertaken by human bodies in located historical contexts" (Michalowski 1993:381). *"Social postmodernism* makes the case for a type of social thinking
which integrates deconstruction while simultaneously incorporating some of the analytically synthesizing and expansive political hopes of the modernist tradition of
social theorizing . . . this move might be productive for generating conceptual and
political strategies that can continue to expose inequalities, oppressions, forms of

614    SENTENCING, FEMINIST, POSTMODERN

*Objectivity*

Many feminist and postmodern theorists value storytelling because it implicitly offers a critique of objectivity. In the feminist literature, storytelling is a metaphor for the subjective and transitory nature of all truth (Disch 1994; Ewick and Silbey 1995). Truth, from this view, is never absolute, uncontested, transhistorical, or transcultural. Instead reality is at best a complex composite of different stories being lived and told by different people:

> Gone is the privileged knower . . . both the theorist and her object of knowledge are reconceptualized as historically and culturally variable, as firmly situated within and helping to construct the context of inquiry itself. The truth can thus be little more than a discursive effect produced through local, heterogeneous, and contextual cultural discourses. (Davis and Fisher 1993:7)

Postmodernism, too, has emphasized the value of storytelling and the "subjective" effect of the story, both on the author and especially on the reader (Rosenau 1992). For postmodern theorists, the "text" of reality is not fixed but is subject to the "reader's" interpretations (Hazelrigg 1993). As Michalowski (1993:382) writes, "[E]very text has as many potential meanings as there are decoders/readers, making it al(l)ways impossible to discern either the 'True' meaning intended by the author, or the 'actual' meaning given to it by any reader other than oneself." Thus both postmodern and feminist theorists argue that there is no universal tale to be told about the world. Instead we each fashion themes and plots from some unique mix of biography and history, and use them to develop our own somewhat idiosyncratic narrative.

This critique of objectivity is useful for analyzing sentencing for several reasons. First, the notion that truth is a subjective construction suggests that we ought to be suspicious of claims about "objectivity"—claims that permeate the sentencing literature. Yet from a feminist and postmodern perspective, all such claims are necessarily political and represent attempts by some to have their version of the truth accepted as the "truth" by all. Second, the concept suggests the value of telling different stories about "reality." The sentencing story that supports current determinate sentencing policy, and the key assumptions on which it rests, constitute just

---

social injustice, and sites of conflict and change in societies that mix modern and postmodern features" (Nicholson and Seidman 1995:35; authors' emphasis). Thus, social postmodernism is consistent with affirmative rather than skeptical postmodernism (Rosenau 1992). Some feminists also have highlighted the importance of deconstructive work. Morris and Gelsthorpe (1991), for example, argue that "it is necessary to *deconstruct* criminological frames of reference and to *reconstruct* them. This is the core of the current feminist enterprise: to dismantle or fracture the limits of existing knowledge boundaries and traditional methodologies" (p. 6; authors' emphasis).

one story that might be told. By drawing on feminist and postmodern thought, it is possible to read the extant sentencing research differently and to construct a new and different story. Doing so does not necessarily make the dominant determinate sentencing story "wrong" and other stories, including this one, "right." Instead it implies that we may best understand determinate sentencing by merging, comparing, contrasting, and distinguishing from one another different perspectives—different truths (Minow 1990; Stambaugh 1995).

## Process

A closely related conceptual tool embedded in the notion of storytelling is the idea that reality is always in the process of being written and constructed. The focus on process is particularly important in feminism. As Mies (1991:63) writes, "[W]hile dominant science views things as static, dualistically [sic], ahistorical, mechanical, and additive, feminist science, which has not lost sight of its political goal, strives for a new view of the whole societal constellation in which things appear as historical, contradictory, linked to each other, and capable of being changed." Postmodernism also highlights the dynamic nature of the social world. Postmodern theorists challenge traditional conceptions of causality and linearity, arguing that social reality is indeterminate. Many postmodern theorists recognize that "everything one studies is related to everything else" (Rosenau 1992:112). For postmodern theorists, meaning itself is continuously being constructed and deconstructed; the story about reality is always being written, edited, and rewritten.

In contrast to this processual approach, the dominant story about determinate sentencing relies on a static conception of sentencing. Sentencing historically has been analyzed most often as a single decision point, with little attention to the decisions that precede sentencing and shape how both the offense and the offender are constructed. This fragmented approach inhibits the development of sound solutions to the "sentencing" problem. A focus on process also encourages us to pay attention to the way sentencing reform itself is a process continually shaped by history and by the larger structural context.

## Identity

Storytelling reveals the importance of identity in affecting the way stories are told. In part, the value of telling different stories is in allowing different voices to be heard. Postmodern theorists do not take for granted identity—or categories that serve as surrogates for identity, such as race, class, or gender. These categories, and one's identity, are constantly created and recreated through interaction with others and with the social and physical world (Greenhouse 1995).

> The postmodern subject is not defined either by particular values such as possessive individualism or by class, or by race, ethnicity, or gender. There is no unified essence. Rather, the postmodern subject is a plurality of contingent social, political, and epistemic relations. Moreover, these relations are constantly subject to rearticulation. (Handler 1992:700)

As Winter (1992:794) remarks "[T]he self is no longer a unity or even an entity but a field of social action and contestation."[7]

Feminists have made similar points in their analysis of gender. Many feminists argue that the construction of gender as a meaningful category has varied cross-culturally and historically. People "do gender" differently with different people and in different situations (Butler 1990; Farganis 1994; Martin and Jurik 1996; Thorne 1993; West and Zimmerman 1987). Postmodern feminists in particular "invite the deconstruction of the category woman" and argue that "woman is a fictive device—a device that is socially, historically, and discursively constructed in relationship to other categories (i.e. women/men, white women/black women)" (Davis and Fisher 1993:71).[8] Feminists have extended this analysis to other identity categories as well, such as race and class, arguing that we need to "reconceptualize 'difference' as an ongoing interactional accomplishment" (West and Zimmerman 1995:9). The task, then, is to investigate "those identity categories that are, in fact, the effects of institutions, practices, discourses with multiple and diffuse points of origin" (Butler 1990:xi).

The idea that identity reflects contingent relations which are "constantly subject to rearticulation" is fundamentally a critique of the liberal conception of the "individual," predicated on a belief in a unitary, independent self. Postmodern theorists and many feminist theorists would argue that there is no "true" self, identity, or individual apart from the relations and the situated context in which people exist.

Postmodern and feminist approaches to identity contrast sharply with contemporary research on sentencing. Researchers often look for "race" or "sex" differences, assuming that the meaning of the categories is self-evident and static. The bulk of sentencing

---

[7] Various symbolic interactionists (e.g., Becker and McCall 1990) have made much the same point.

[8] Also see Butler (1990) and Cornell (1992), among others.

research relies on quantitative methodologies that fragment and rigidify the identities of the human beings under study. Such fragmentation and rigidity occur when individuals are represented by discrete variables. Any sense of a living, breathing, whole person is lost when sex, race, class, age, occupation, prior record, and other human histories and characteristics become disembodied and reified variables to be analyzed. The human being fades into the background and becomes a ghost, while dissected parts are brought forward to stand as representatives of the real thing, and are forced to "run" around in regressions until objectified "truth" is found.

The limitations of quantitative approaches to sentencing are especially profound when the primary aim of the research is to uncover discrimination in sentencing. Analysis of "racial" disparity is common; analysis of "sex" discrimination is increasing. Yet recent scholarship by people of color and feminists has drawn our "attention to the interlocking nature of oppression" which "shifts the entire focus of investigation from one aimed at explicating elements of race, gender or class oppression to one whose goal is to determine what the links are among these systems" (Hill Collins 1991:41). Consequently, when researchers say that "race" or some other variable is or is not a significant predictor of sentences when all other variables are controlled, it is not clear what has been said because identity never appears as a single variable, but as a complex and relational set of intersecting categories. The more interesting question is this: When does the particular social characteristic matter—under what circumstances, for whom, and in interaction with what other factors? We must also question the extent to which the categories we create actually represent *discrete* characteristics or features of reality. As I point out shortly, many of the categories researchers employ regularly in sentencing research contain the very biases that scholars intend to uncover by using those variables; thus, for example, the use of variables such as "prior record" may mask prior discrimination within the criminal justice system. Most important, we must explore why some differences make a difference to us at all. As Nicholson (1990:10) puts it, we need to understand that "how we describe the 'differences that make a difference' is itself a political act."

### Power

Finally, the notion of storytelling contains a new conceptualization of power that has implications for understanding crime and justice issues. In general, both feminist and postmodern perspectives highlight the cultural character of power. Instead of trying to pinpoint who has power in society, postmodern and feminist theorists are more likely to analyze relations of domination that develop in particular historical and cultural contexts (Eisenstein 1988; Smart 1989). For these theorists, power is not exercised only by those in the upper echelons of society; instead power is used, abused, and reproduced in everyday life by all of us in our relationships with others (Bordo 1988; Davis and Fisher 1993 Fonow and Cook 1991; Foucault 1978). Foucault refers to this situation as the omnipresence of power:

> The omnipresence of power: not because it has the privilege of consolidating everything under its invincible unity, but because it is produced from one moment to the next, at every point, or rather in every relation from one point to another. Power is everywhere; not because it embraces everything, but because it comes from everywhere . . . power is not an institution, and not a structure; neither is it a certain strength we are endowed with; it is the name that one attributes to a complex strategical situation in a particular society. (1978:93)

Because power is located in everyday actions, situations, and discourses, it is critical to explore "how power is discursively constructed and how politics are about contestations over meaning" (Davis and Fisher 1993:8).[9] Storytelling provides a medium for such exploration; as Disch (1994:8) writes, "[S]torytelling here is credited with bringing insidious power relations to the surface; it does so, however, not by 'telling how it is' to be oppressed, but by charting the repression that undergirds any claim to 'tell how it is,' whether advanced from the center or the margin."

In contrast to this view, sentencing research typically has conceptualized power as the control exercised by one individual, or by the (typically) reified state, over another. Thus, for example, police officers have power over citizens, and judges have power over convicted offenders in the courtroom. Power framed in this way is "top-down" and is visible only because it is overt. The power that matters, however, might reside in small everyday interactions, habits, rituals, and behaviors—actions and resistances—that either limit or expand individuals' opportunities to participate fully in the world. Power, in this sense, is exercised by the probation officer who writes that an individual about to be sentenced has dressed inappropriately for the presentence investigation or evidences a tattoo, but it is also exercised by the individual who may have chosen

---

9 Davis and Fisher (1993), like others (Hall 1986), do not argue that analyzing discourse and meaning is enough. In fact, they argue that "without a structural conception of society it is impossible to assess how strong the power is, the extent of the resistance, or the changing balance between them" (1993:10).

to dress (in)appropriately or who makes sure that tattoos are visibly displayed (Ferrell and Sanders 1995; Miller 1995). As Ewick and Silbey explain:

> The stories and accounts that are told to and by litigants, clients, lawyers and jurors, and other legal actors are not simply reflective of or determined by those dominant meanings and power relations. They are implicated in the very *production* of those meanings and power relations. Through various discursive practices, legal categories, symbols, and authority are organized and maintained across time and space. (1995:211)

In the remainder of this article I use the conceptual developments outlined above—the critical analysis of objectivity, process, identity, and power—to analyze the sentencing story that has dominated sentencing policy for the past 20 years and to construct a new story about determinate sentencing.

## THE OLD STORY: A BRIEF HISTORY AND SOME SHARED ASSUMPTIONS

The development of legislation restricting judges' discretion through determinate sentencing schemes, including sentencing guidelines, constitutes the plot for the old story about sentencing. The emergence of restrictive sentencing practices in the early 1970s resulted from the contradictory interests of two different casts of characters. For liberals, sentencing reform was a plank in the civil rights platform. During the due process revolution fostered by the Warren Court, some liberals called for restrictions on judicial discretion as a way to reduce sentencing discrimination and disparity noted by the American Friends Service Committee, prisoner's rights groups, and others (Greenberg and Humphries 1981; Irwin and Austin 1994; Walker 1980).

In contrast, increasing support for a sentencing policy based on a model of "just deserts" invigorated conservative backing for sentencing reform (Von Hirsch 1976). Partly in response to the apparent rise in crime rates (FBI 1972, 1980, 1991) and to citizens' anxieties about personal safety in the wake of urban unrest, some conservatives called for measures that would "get tough on crime" by ensuring that sentences were both more harsh and more certain (Greenberg and Humphries 1981; Walker 1980). This theme received additional momentum when Robert Martinson's (1974) massive evaluation of correctional programs was interpreted simplistically to suggest that "nothing works"; the study actually indicated that no correctional programs could be shown to work better or worse than any others (Tonry 1995; Walker 1980). The (mis)use

620    SENTENCING, FEMINIST, POSTMODERN

of this study fueled the conservatives' argument for punishment for its own sake.

Although liberals and conservatives hardly agreed about the ends that were to be achieved by sentencing reform, the two camps did agree on the means to achieve their respective goals: limit judicial discretion through determinate sentencing legislation. Determinate sentencing swept the country, and was hailed widely as an important reform and a bold step toward reducing crime and advancing justice. Despite its contradictory political origins, determinate sentencing offered something for everyone. For liberals it promised more equitable treatment for those committing similar offenses, regardless of race or social class, and a reduction in the power of judges and parole boards to discriminate in determining individual destinies. For conservatives it meant the legislation of stiffer sanctions for more people in the belief that lower crime rates would result. In the end, both sides "won" something in the struggle to reform sentencing. Thus, determinate sentencing policies have had the strange but logical consequence of instituting more comparable treatment of overtly similar offenses *and* more severe sentences for offenders.

Though both sides were victorious in the 1970s' political struggle to reform sentencing, by the 1990s it seemed that the majority of citizens, in fact, were the losers. One legacy of determinate sentencing is that "the number of sentenced prisoners in state and federal institutions increased fivefold during the 22-year period between 1972 and 1994" (Kappeler, Blumberg, and Potter 1996).[10] Indeed, the United States now incarcerates a larger percentage of its citizens than any other country in the world (Irwin and Austin 1994). Jails and prisons are crowded beyond capacity, and jurisdictions throughout the nation routinely release prisoners early to make room for the daily influx of new offenders. If this trend continues, current projections suggest that "6 percent of the adult population will be subject to some form of correctional supervision by the year 2000, and 10 percent of American adults will be under correctional control by 2006" (Messner and Rosenfeld 1994:96). The enormous amount of tax money needed to keep thousands of people locked up is rapidly being funneled away from critical social services, education, and the development of a viable economic base

---

[10] Although other factors also have contributed to this trend, I am not alone in suggesting that determinate sentencing has played a major role (also see Heaney 1991; Irwin and Austin 1994).

(Michalowski and Pearson 1988, 1991). Yet "the only reliable, scientific data we have on crime in America tell us that crime is decreasing, has been decreasing, and continues to decrease" (Kappeler et al. 1996).

Equally disturbing is the fact that sentencing inequalities seem to persist. As Irwin and Austin (1994:4) observe, "[T]hose under correctional authority do not represent a cross-section of the nation's population. They tend to be young, African-American and Latino males who are uneducated, without jobs, or, at best, marginally employed in low paying jobs."[11] According to the U.S. Justice Department, 32 percent of black men age 20-29 are under some form of correctional supervision (Mauer and Huling 1995). "African-American men make up less than 7 percent of the U.S. population, yet they comprise almost half of the prison and jail population" (Donziger 1996:102). Other racial and ethnic minority groups remain similarly overrepresented in arrest and incarceration statistics (Donziger 1996). To many citizens, it is far from clear that sentences are more "just" today than they were 20 years ago.

At first glance, it seems surprising that liberals and conservatives believed that such radically different results could be achieved by the same reform strategy. This is understandable, however, if we consider that liberals and conservatives, despite their differences, share a number of assumptions about the sentencing process. These commonalities form the storyline about determinate sentencing which currently shapes public policy. In fact, these assumptions are so pervasive and so much taken for granted that they will seem to most readers to be common sense. According to my reading of the extant sentencing literature, both liberal and conservative support for determinate sentencing schemes are based on the following assumptions:

* Judicial discretion is the source of sentencing disparity.

* To achieve fair sentences, offender characteristics (i.e., extra-legal factors) must be ignored, and "objective" (i.e., legally relevant) criteria must be used.

* Determinate sentencing reduces discrimination based on race, ethnicity, class, and gender, and results in greater "fairness."

These assumptions underlie virtually all determinate sentencing policies developed since the 1970s; in combination they fashion a

---

[11] The differential rate of imprisonment may be due largely to differences in rates of arrest for certain groups in our society, and therefore may not necessarily mean that discrimination in sentencing is occurring. It is also possible, however, that discrimination is deeply implicated in differential rates of arrest or imprisonment (via the legislative process), as I argue shortly. In any event, I think it is appropriate to use imprisonment rates to illustrate why many continue to *perceive* the justice system as unfair and biased.

particular narrative about sentencing. In general this narrative communicates that it is critical to severely limit judicial discretion, if not to eradicate it from the sentencing process, and to develop "objective" criteria to use in sentencing decisions in order to achieve greater fairness.

Although the assumptions that form the text of the old determinate sentencing story may have seemed logical to policy makers and scholars during the 1970s, it is surprising that they have not been revisited during the past 15 years, given the consequences of determinate sentencing for the country. I believe that this revisitation must begin—that analyzing and critiquing the old sentencing story is essential if we are to understand the failure of determinate sentencing to deliver justice or to lower the crime rate, as many had hoped would happen.

In the following section I use the feminist and postmodern conceptual developments described above to analyze the assumptions that underlie determinate sentencing. I also draw on current sentencing research to argue that empirical, positivist science seems to suggest and support many of the theoretical points made by feminist and postmodern theorists. Given my earlier critique of quantitative approaches to sentencing, this approach may seem ironic. Yet I think that if a new story is to be plausible, it must be able to move us from where we now stand. In my view, past and current sentencing research is not so much wrong as partial, incomplete, and therefore potentially distorting. I agree with Mies (1991:67) when she writes that her "criticism of quantifying methods is not directed against every form of statistics but at its claim to have a monopoly on accurately describing the world."[12] The value of revisiting past sentencing research, using postmodern and feminist perspectives, is to reveal the subplots, paradoxes, and ironies that are contained in the old sentencing story. The value is in telling a different tale.

## CRITIQUING THE OLD STORY

*Judicial discretion is the source of sentencing disparity*

Perhaps the most easily identified assumption underlying current sentencing policy is that judges decide sentences. In virtually all determinate sentencing schemes, judges were identified as the

---

[12] Ferrell (1994b) agrees that it can be useful to take advantage of past quantitative research while recognizing that it reflects "imperfect human constructions"; he goes further, however, when he argues that in the use of past methods, we should "turn them on their heads. Where such methodologies once contributed to the epistemic authority of criminology and criminal justice agencies, they now operate so as to unravel such authority" (p. 7).

"problem" with sentencing, whether the objective to be achieved by reducing judicial discretion was greater fairness or greater harshness. Indeed, virtually all determinate sentencing schemes severely limit judicial discretion while almost ignoring other factors that systematically shape sentencing decisions.

Despite researchers' tendency to treat sentencing as a single judicial decision, sentencing, like all social reality, is not a fixed, static point in time but part of a much larger, more complex process.[13] Sentencing takes place in an institutional and relational milieu that shapes how criminal justice workers respond to particular individuals. Individuals are never merely sentenced; first they must be noticed, arrested, charged, prosecuted, and evaluated by probation departments. Each stage of the criminal justice process has implications for subsequent stages, which cannot be ignored. Indeed, it is within this process that individual offense and offender characteristics are made official and are given meaning by workers in the criminal justice system. Put differently, the offender's "identity" is constructed in part by others who process that individual through the system. The meaning given to different offenses and offenders varies by jurisdiction, justice officials' past experience, and institutional constraints; thus meaning is not static, nor does it necessarily depend on the judge, the individual offender, or the "facts" of the case. Prosecutors, probation officers, judges, and others engage in daily rituals and micropractices that define some individuals as "serious criminals" and others as "petty thieves" or "innocent parties."

This point was made as early as 1965, when Sudnow argued that justice officials use stereotypical conceptions of the "normal crime" to interpret the meaning of offenses. A dozen years later, Swigert and Farrell (1977) extended this theme by exploring the ways that justice officials stereotype individual offenders and place them in categories that define both the offender's identity and the way that officials will respond. Minow (1990:23) made a similar point more recently when she contended that we need to shift our focus "from the 'different person' to the social and legal construction of difference."

Understanding that sentencing is part of a larger process reconfigures the way that power is conceived in the courtroom. Judges do not hold all the power, nor did they do so before determinate sentencing. Judges today depend largely on the cumulative perceptions of others who made decisions at earlier points in time. As early as 1977, the publication of *Felony Justice* highlighted the

---

[13] This claim is not new, as I will demonstrate, but its implications have yet to be fully explored.

importance of relationships between various court actors—called "court workgroups"—and sentencing outcomes. In this pathbreaking book, Eisenstein and Jacob (1977:294) contended that "outcomes in the felony disposition process are not the result of singular efforts by judges, prosecutors, or defense councils. Outcomes result from interactions among these courtroom members and others." Similarly, Nardulli (1978) argued that the "courtroom elite"—the judge, the prosecutor, and the defense attorney—have common interests, such as efficiency, which shape courtroom decisions, including sentencing. Offenders who interfere with these goals (by requesting a jury trial, for example) may be penalized by the courtroom elite through the administration of harsher sentences.

These ideas were well received, but not until the 1980s did researchers begin to systematically investigate how relations within the "court workgroup" or "courtroom elite" shape decision making. Scholars who have studied the link between the courtroom elite and criminal sentencing have suggested that discrimination may occur at earlier stages in the criminal justice process, biasing judges toward certain offenders and ultimately leading to sentencing disparity. Research focusing on the influence of particular actors in the system over judicial decision includes analysis of probation officers' and prosecutors' recommendations (Frazier and Bock 1982; Frazier, Bock, and Henretta 1983; Wonders 1990). Some have gone so far as to say that "the single most important predictor of sentencing severity in these data was probation officer recommendations" (Frazier and Bock 1982:269); others claim that "the prosecution's recommendation is more powerful than the probation department's recommendation" (Hagan 1989:115).

Other decisions before sentencing also may influence the ultimate disposition of cases. Certain aspects of court processing may stigmatize an offender before the sentencing decision by shaping perceptions about the dangerousness of the offender and his or her offense. Some research, for example, shows that the inability to obtain pretrial release (Unnever 1982: Wonders 1990) may lead to harsher sentences.[14] Even more important is research linking these pretrial processes to race and sex discrimination (Unnever 1982; Zatz 1984). Some scholars have found that the effect of race

---

[14] Concern about prior court processing is linked closely to the issue of selection bias in sentencing research (Berk 1983; Berk and Ray 1982; Hagan and Zatz) because both contain the implicit argument that one must consider all stages of justice processing in order to assess whether discrimination occurs. The research on prior court processing suggests that failure to consider prior decision making in the criminal justice system may bias results of analysis addressing later decision points.

on sentencing is mediated by bail status. In at least some jurisdictions, black offenders are more likely than white offenders to be denied bail, and the fact that they are in custody at the time of sentencing leads to harsher sentences (Albonetti 1991; LaFree 1985). Similarly, some researchers have found statistically significant relationships between sentencing disparity, the offender's sex, and pretrial release (Kruttschnitt 1984).

This literature suggests that it makes little sense to focus on judicial discretion without addressing discretion that is exercised elsewhere in the system. Indeed, some recent research suggests that determinate sentencing has merely given more discretionary authority to already powerful prosecutors (see Donziger 1996; Tonry 1987). Discretion permeates the criminal justice system; constraining it at one point is likely to heighten the discretionary impact of decisions made at other points (Giset 1994; Tonry 1987). For example, qualitative research by Heaney (1991:163) suggests that under the federal sentencing guidelines, "the role of the prosecutor and the probation officer in the sentencing process has been enhanced and that of the district judge diminished." Focusing on only one part of this discretionary chain obscures the relational manner in which decisions are made.

In general, too little research has explored how everyday decisions within the system, and relationships among people, help to construct the character of "offenders" and shape appropriate sanctions. Sentencing is only one part of the criminal justice process; other stages and other criminal justice actors apparently exert significant influence over the way judges do their jobs. In the end, the meaning attached to characteristics of offenders and offenses is negotiated by a variety of people, who shape the offender's "identity" by documenting their perceptions along the way.[15] As Henry and Milovanovic (1991:229) observe, "[H]uman agents transform events that they see or experiences as micro-events into summary representations, or mind patterns, having achieved the appropriate representation of these events; these are then objectified in coherent narrative constructions."

For the most part, judges depend on others to tell them a story explaining both the offender and the offense. Police officers, prosecutors, defense attorneys, probation officers, and others construct

---

[15] Blumberg (1990) described this well in 1967 when he wrote: "In summary, the accused is confronted by definitions of himself which reflect the various worlds of the agent-mediators—yet are consistent for the most part in their negative evaluation of him [sic]. The agent-mediators have seized upon a wholly unflattering aspect of his biography to reinterpret his entire personality and justify their present attitude and conduct toward him" (p. 483).

individual essays that inevitably foreshadow and form judges' perceptions about both the crime drama and the character before them. Thus judges' apparent nondiscrimination at the point of sentencing may not say much about the level of discrimination within the system, nor about the likelihood that entire groups of people will be defined as "criminals" or "deviants" by those who have the power to define crime. As Coombe writes,

> Legal processes . . . do more than merely reflect or reproduce dominant cultural conceptions of self, personhood, and identity in Western societies. They are, instead, constitutive of subjectivities. By defining and legitimating *particular* representations of how those in different subject positions or social groups experience their selfhood, adjudicative and legislative processes serve to maintain, reproduce and sometimes transform relations of power. (1991:5)

Individuals who participate in the criminal justice system as "offenders" also have opportunities to participate in the construction of their identity, but several constraints limit their freedom to construct themselves as they choose. First, the power of culture and ideology limits individuals' ability to control the meaning that others will make of their (chosen) identities. If individuals choose to wear sagging pants and bandannas as a way of looking hip and participating in a particular subculture, it is not of their choosing that authorities will (re)create cultural meanings which associate that style with trouble. It is clear that some people dress in particular ways as a form of resistance, but the meaning made of that resistance is open to definition and counterdefinition (Ferrell 1994a; Ferrell and Sanders 1995; Miller 1995).

Second, the power of "self-surveillance" limits individual freedom to create identity. Some individuals who appear before a presentence officer know who they are supposed to "be" and adopt behaviors that increase the likelihood that they will be defined in desirable ways. Others, who do not know the cultural script, are disadvantaged because they do not know how to "be" and are penalized in the process of representing themselves (more) honestly (Langston 1995). Beyond the question of whether there is a "true" identity, the "truth" may not set one free.

If we reconceptualize sentencing as a process that reflects a range of relationships, and consider the ways in which this process shapes identities and meanings, it becomes problematic to assume that judicial discretion is the source of disparity in sentencing. This is not to say that discretion within the system is a "good" thing— simply that it is pervasive, and that to pin faulty decision making on judges distracts us from discretion that exists at other locations in the process.

Beyond the types of discretion just considered, the discretion that perhaps ought to concern us most is legislators' discretion to decide who is a "criminal" and who is not. As Seidman (1994:215) writes, "[D]iscourses that carry public authority shape identities and regulate bodies, desires, selves, and whole populations." From the scholarly evidence at hand, we have every reason to believe that the story constructed by legislators about crime is the one that will reinforce cultural myths and beliefs which benefit them as politicians, corporate executives, and professional people, and that will pacify or incapacitate those who might threaten their interests or their understanding of the social world (Caulfield and Wonders 1993b; Humphries 1993; Kappeler Blumberg and Peter 1996; Reiman 1995). Given legislators role in defining crime and their increasing involvement in the development of sentencing policy, it is their discretion that now carries the greatest risk of fostering discrimination in the sentencing process. I believe that it is this discretion scholars and citizens might attend to most productively.

*To achieve fair sentences, offender characteristics (i.e., extralegal factors) must be ignored and "objective" (i.e., legally relevant) criteria must be used*

The old determinate sentencing story reflects a belief that sentencing guidelines or rules must be based on "objective" legal criteria rather than "subjective" social judgments. "Objective" criteria are considered to be unbiased and are believed not to reflect discrimination on the basis of race, sex, class, or other social factors. These criteria, once identified, are written into the law. Thus, they become legally relevant and are thought to legitimately guide sentencing decisions, frequently including deviations from the presumptive sentences set by legislatures under some determinate sentencing schemes.

Although some sentencing scholars have critiqued the distinction between "legal" and "extralegal" criteria (e.g., Hagan and Bumiller 1983), the pervasive use of this distinction among policy makers seems to reflect a genuine belief that some criteria really are more objective than others. On the basis of the feminist and postmodern critique of objectivity, however, such a belief ignores the way that "legally relevant" criteria themselves are social constructions reflecting power relations and particular conceptions of identity and difference.

More than any other criteria, prior record and offense severity consistently have been shown to influence sentencing decisions

(Miethe and Moore 1985; Myers and Talarico 1987; Spohn and Welch 1987; Welch and Spohn 1986). These variables are widely regarded as "legally relevant" because they are considered in virtually all jurisdictions to be legitimate criteria in sentencing decisions. The belief in their legitimacy is so pervasive that sentencing researchers consistently eliminate all the effects of prior record and seriousness before exploring other variables (Chiricos and Crawford 1995). Failure to do so results in claims of shoddy scholarship (see Blumstein et al. 1983). Unfortunately, very little attention has been given to the possibility that both prior record and offense severity actually may conceal discrimination and thus may reproduce systematic bias.

As some scholars have pointed out, we might properly "consider as sociologically problematic the variable seriousness of offense" because "seriousness of offense is not an intrinsic property of behavior" (Inverarity, Lauterdale, and Feld 1983:280). Why some offenses are considered more serious than others may be linked to the kinds of people who commit and are victimized by particular types of offenses. Judgments about the seriousness of a particular offense cannot easily be divorced from knowledge about the offender. For example, the act of throwing a brick through a store window historically has been evaluated as far more serious if committed by an adult than by a juvenile. In the latter case, the act may be viewed as vandalism; in the former, as attempted burglary (if not worse). Similarly, many scholars have highlighted the "administrative segregation" of corporate and white-collar offenses from traditional street crime (Kappeler et al. 1996; Michalowski 1985; Reiman 1995; Sutherland 1945). This distinction seems to be related at least in part to who is doing the offending; clearly it is *not* a function of the actual harm caused, because all measures of corporate and white-collar crime indicate that the harm caused by these offenses far exceeds the harm caused by traditional street crime (Coleman 1985; Michalowski 1985; Reiman 1995).

Another example highlighting the social construction of seriousness is the recent effort to segregate crack offenses from cocaine offenses. In Minnesota and in the federal system, one gram of crack is considered the equivalent of 100 grams of powder cocaine (Shein 1993; Tonry 1995). The view that crack is more serious than powder cocaine, though they are "pharmacologically indistinguishable," is likely related to who uses crack cocaine: "95 percent of federal crack prosecutions are brought against blacks and 40 percent of powder cocaine prosecutions are brought against whites" (Tonry

1995:188). As Uelman (1992:904) observes, "[W]hat this data suggests to me is that the current "drug war" which is filling our prisons at unprecedented rates is a war with serious racial overtones." This perspective is shared by others, including Shein (1993:29), who writes that "the war on drugs is being transformed into a war on the poor and black."[16] I would add that women are increasingly the casualties in this war because "women in prison are substantially more likely than men to be serving a sentence for a drug offense" (Donzinger 1996:151).

Insofar as some crimes are committed disproportionately by African-Americans (e.g., crack possession), by women (e.g., prostitution), by the poor (e.g., petty property crime), or by the wealthy (e.g., white-collar crime), evaluations about their seriousness are inextricably linked to perceptions about who commits such crimes. In addition, to the extent that some crimes disproportionately victimize groups that are already marginalized in society, claims about their seriousness cannot help but be affected by who is harmed (Caulfield and Wonders 1993b; Kleck 1981; Miethe 1987). Yet most research on sentencing does not explore the link between perceptions of seriousness and individual offender or victim characteristics; nor does sentencing policy take these potential sources of bias into account.

Similarly, prior record may hide rather than reveal discrimination in the criminal justice system. Judges use prior record to assess the blameworthiness of individual offenders and the likelihood that offenders will recidivate. Offenders previously convicted and released are often regarded as having been given a "second chance"; recidivism suggests that they did not appreciate this opportunity to reform their behavior, and thus they are viewed as more culpable when caught again. Judges conceive of prior record in extremely static terms; they commonly use counts of prior arrests and convictions to evidence the degree of blameworthiness. This kind of thinking has led to the popular "three strikes and you're out" legislation, which, where implemented, is likely to lead to even greater burgeoning of our prison system (Irwin and Austin 1994).

The treatment of prior record as a legally relevant variable is problematic. Prior record can reflect prior processes of discrimination by the criminal justice system, as well as prior criminal involvement. For example, arrests may be used to deter certain kinds of people (.e.g, suspected drug dealers) from frequenting particular neighborhoods, even though convictions are unlikely (Hagan and Zatz 1985). Research also suggests that some arrests are based on

---

16 Racializing drug use, of course, has a long history as a method of exciting public sentiment in favor of government control of drugs (Donziger 1996).

cultural and stylistic differences between law enforcers and some citizens (Chambliss 1995, Ferrell 1993; Ferrell and Sanders 1995). Ferrell and Sanders (1995:14), for example, argue that "as street cops find fault with sagging pants or shaved heads of gang members, they collectively engage in 'crimes of style'—crimes that reveal the power of shared styles in shaping not only criminal identity, but legal authority and the boundaries of social control." Because some arrests are based on crimes of style or different ways of dressing and acting within certain groups in our society, judges who consider prior *arrest* records "objective" criteria may unintentionally be basing their sentencing decisions on inherently biased measures (Hagan and Bumiller 1983; Hagan and Zatz 1985; Welch, Gruhl, and Spohn 1984).

According to scholars studying selection bias in criminal sentencing research, it also may be problematic to consider prior convictions, because any bias embedded in previous sentencing decisions becomes cumulatively more important when prior convictions are used as a criterion for subsequent sentencing decisions (Farnworth and Horan 1980; Donzinger 1996; Hagan and Parker 1985; LaFree 1980; Myers 1987, 1988; Myers and Talarico 1987; Peterson and Hagan 1984; Zatz 1985; Zatz and Lizotte 1985). Convictions are equally misleading if they are based on biased arrest patterns.

Ultimately this analysis reveals that even the most presumably "objective" criteria are shaped by subjective cultural processes. Legally relevant variables are subjective and biased, as are so-called "extralegal" criteria.[17] The failure to acknowledge this subjectivity allows decision makers to mystify the systematic biases that current criteria perpetuate and to remove the subjective process of defining harmful behavior from public scrutiny. The widespread use of prior record tends to work against the poor because many poor areas are overenforced (Chambliss 1995; Hagan 1994) and because the offenses accessible to the rich do not occur in the public space of the street, where arrest is likely (Reiman 1995).

Some groups also are more likely to face arrest because various forms of expression and stylistic differences are used to provide probable cause for arrest (Ferrell 1993, 1995). For example, many jurisdictions develop typologies of "suspicious persons," "drug courier profiles," or "gang lists" and use them as the basis for stopping and questioning some individuals. These typologies often contain information about the style of car, how a person acts or walks, or even a person's race (Chambliss 1995; Donziger 1996; Heaney

---

[17]  See Ryan and Ferrell (1986) for a similar critique of legal decision making.

1991). The creation and use of the category "suspicious person" ensures that suspicious persons will be found. As Mertz (1995:1248) points out, "[T]he analysis of social identities as heavily . . . contextual, social creations provide[s] a useful counterpoint to the static pre-figured conceptions of individuals and groups in many legal narratives. At the same time, 'fictions' can take on a life of their own; they can have powerful formative effects on the social world even if they lack empirical validity."

It seems self-evident that even without judges' active discrimination against some individuals or groups, the likelihood of conviction is greater when some individuals or groups are more likely than others to be arrested. Despite the structural conditions ensuring that the poorest and most disadvantaged citizens will have longer criminal records, most determinate sentencing schemes require much longer sentences for those with prior convictions. As Heaney writes

> Blacks are over-represented in arrest records for street crimes. The guidelines' mandatory consideration of prior criminal convictions places many minority federal offenders at elevated criminal history categories with higher sentencing ranges. Thus, exercises of legislative and executive discretion may ensure that black offenders, on the average, are subject to more severe guidelines sentences long before such defendants appear in court for sentencing. (1991:206)

Similarly, the unquestioned assumption that the seriousness of an offense should be the basis for sentencing decisions suggests general agreement on which types of crime are most harmful, and implies that the determination of seriousness is not clouded by racial, gender, or class biases or power arrangements in our society. But this assumption is flawed. Indeed, some researchers have found that citizens consider corporate crime to be as serious as traditional street crime (Rossi et al. 1974), but ordinary citizens do not make the law. People who already are privileged have much greater access to decision making and to determinations about the seriousness of crime and the criteria by which people should be sentenced. Therefore, it is not surprising that robbery is considered more serious than violation of regulatory laws when we consider who has the power to decide. Yet the danger lies in believing that definitions of seriousness somehow represent the "truth" about how much society is hurt by each kind of offense. As Michalowski says,

> No judge needs to be particularly hostile to poor defendants for the poor to serve longer and more frequent sentences because they cause someone harm or financial loss than will the corporate violator causing equal or greater injury or loss. That is a form of discrimination that

is built right into the legal system. Sentencing judges in criminal cases seldom have anything but poor and/or non-white defendants before them. (1985:217)

Prior record and the seriousness of the offense are the two axes on which determinate sentencing policies nationwide are based. But prior record and seriousness are also metaphors for the large experiential gap between those who grow up in middle-class neighborhoods and those who spend their lives on inner-city streets. The continued, uncritical use of these criteria perpetuates current power arrangements in our society. Those who are caught and those who commit publicly visible crimes that make middle- and upper-class citizens uncomfortable are sentenced harshly. Legislators give little attention to the fact that some offenses—indeed, many of the most serious offenses—are committed by first-time white-collar offenders in the safety of their offices, or by middle-class wife beaters in the comfort and privacy of their homes. The law could be different—even if it's not.

*Determinate sentencing reduces discrimination based on race, ethnicity, class, and gender, and results in greater "fairness"*

In the Untied States it is widely believed that determinate sentencing reduces discrimination and leads to greater fairness in sentencing. Yet the few studies that have explored the impact of determinate sentencing have been somewhat contradictory.[18] Part of the reason that this belief is so pervasive has to do with the way that "discrimination" and "fairness" are defined by researchers and in our society. Definitions of both discrimination and fairness reflect beliefs about the "individual" that are rooted deeply in liberalism. In this section I employ feminist and postmodern concepts to explore the meaning of these two terms in the context of criminal sentencing.

The "discrimination" that determinate sentencing policy is designed to address is individual discrimination. This kind of discrimination occurs when individual judges differentiate sentences on the basis of race, class, gender, or similar characteristics. Similarly, "fairness" is understood to reflect procedural and substantive outcomes that do not privilege one individual over another. The system is fair if two different individuals who have committed similar offenses are treated similarly. According to this interpretation

---

[18] Some scholars believe that disparity has been reduced (Miethe and Moore 1985); others observe that some disparities continue under determinate sentencing, whether they operate indirectly through features such as case characteristics and presentence outcomes (Miethe and Moore 1985) or through the biases built into the legislation itself (Heaney 1991).

it would be hard to dispute that determinate sentencing has reduced discrimination and has led to greater fairness for individuals who enter the criminal justice system. From another perspective, however, the claim that determinate sentencing is fair, or that it has significantly reduced discrimination, is misleading.

The assumption that discrimination is an activity occurring between two individuals has been criticized widely; more recent literature has focused on the institutional and structural nature of discrimination (Bates Doob 1993; Hacker 1992; West 1993). Institutional discrimination refers to discriminatory practices that are built into significant institutions in our society, such as educational institutions, the state, or the criminal justice system. Structural discrimination occurs when political, economic, or cultural arrangements in a society limit opportunities for some individuals on the basis of their membership in groups (Bates Doob 1993). Institutional and structural discrimination do not require that individuals make bad decisions (though sometimes that happens); instead these types of discrimination are related to the differential effects of situated structural arrangements on some groups and individuals. An example may help to illustrate this point.

Determinate sentencing assumes that discrimination in sentencing is absent because similar offenders are sentenced similarly within the same jurisdiction. Residential patterns, however, reveal tremendous segregation in our society on the basis of race and social class. Even in so-called "integrated" white communities, according to Hacker (1992), African-Americans typically constitute no more than 8 percent of the population (though they are 13 to 14 percent of the U.S. population). The simple coincidence of living in a particular location may shape sentencing outcomes in ways that disproportionately disadvantage some groups and individuals (Myers and Reid 1995).

In fact, some recent research has explored the link between such social structural variables and discrimination in sentencing. This research is important because it illustrates the connections between social location, identity, and privilege. For example, some researchers have investigated the relationship between population size and density, and sentencing disparity (Austin 1981; Hagan 1977; Kempf and Austin 1986; Miethe and Moore 1986; Myers and Talarico 1987; Pope 1976). Virtually all of the research on rural and urban differences finds that urbanization is a significant predictor of sentencing outcomes; most of the recent research concludes that urban courts are more punitive than rural courts (Bridges,

Crutchfield, and Simpson 1987; Kempf and Austin 1986; Miethe and Moore 1985; Myers and Talarico 1987).[19]

Other work exploring the connection between the social structure and sentencing suggests that social inequality within a community shapes sentencing decisions. Although researchers have addressed several types of inequality, two of these are illustrative: income inequality and racial inequality. Some observers argue that the degree of income inequality in a community affects criminal sentencing by increasing the likelihood that formal social control mechanisms will be used to regulate the surplus population (Bridges 1987; Liska and Chamlin 1984; Miethe and Moore 1985; Myers and Talarico 1987). Some also have found that *racial* income inequality leads to harsher sentences; for example, one study revealed a direct relationship between poverty in the minority population and harsher sentences for nonwhites (Bridges et al. 1987), while another found that income inequality affects sentencing indirectly (Myers and Talarico 1987).

The size of the minority population has been identified as another potentially important structural consideration. Two different theories about the relationship between racial composition and sentencing have been offered. First, some researchers argue that social tensions will increase if people feel threatened by those who are different in any way; this situation will lead to discrimination in the courts (Bridges et al. 1987). Second, others argue that a large ethnic minority population may lead to relatively lenient sentencing of ethnic minority offenders because racism and paternalism may cause decision makers to expect more law-abiding behavior from whites and less from minority members (Myers and Talarico 1987). For example, Bridges et al. (1987) found a strong relationship, at the aggregate level, between the size of the minority population and higher imprisonment rates for minority offenders.[20]

Another important feature of the community that may affect sentencing decisions is the nature and extent of the officially defined crime problem. Communities with high crime rates may use

---

[19] Older research by Austin (1981), Hagan (1977), and Pope (1976), however, found that rural courts were more likely than urban courts to discriminate against members of minorities in sentencing. Many methodological problems have been linked to this older research. For example, the failure to include separate measures of bureaucratization in analysis confounds the independent effect of urbanization (Myers and Talarico 1987); also most research dichotomizes counties or cities, designating some as "rural" and others as "urban" (a few also include "suburban") without considering the possible relationship between the degree of urbanization and sentencing disparity (but see Myers and Talarico 1987; Wonders 1990). It is also possible that the contradictory effects of urbanization reflects a historically contingent relationship.

[20] Myers and Talarico (1987), however, suggest that the racial composition of communities has only a limited, and primarily indirect, influence over sentencing.

harsher penalties to "get tough" on crime. Alternatively, a high
crime rate may increase the volume of offenders whom the courts
must process, thus contributing to bureaucratization and consequently reducing sentencing disparity. Indeed, in one of the most
sophisticated quantitative analyses of sentencing to date, Myers
and Talarico found that "high crime rates were consistent and powerful determinants of race and offense differences in sentencing"
(1987:173).[21]

The message of this research is that the larger structural context, including levels of urbanization, inequality, and the crime
rate, seem to influence sentencing decisions.[22] Because some of
this research was based on data collected before determinate sentencing was implemented, it is not clear whether sentencing today
is affected in the same way. Yet the broader implications remain
for other decision makers in the justice system. If we find that race,
class, and sex discrimination occur only in neighborhoods with social inequality or high crime rates, we may need to figure out ways
to influence these processes rather than directing all of our attention toward official discretion. How, for example, might reductions
in inequality shape the discretionary decisions made by justice officials? In addition, if these larger structural forces shaped judicial
discretion before the beginning of determinate sentencing, it seems
likely that legislators and other justice officials now making sentencing decisions are affected similarly by the structural context.
Shifting the decision making to these bodies does not necessarily
change the way that discretion is exercised; it merely changes the
source of the discretion. By defining discrimination solely in individual terms, however, current determinate sentencing policies and
much sentencing research fail to consider these structural factors.
An understanding of sentencing that does not take the structural
context into account overlooks the fact that sentencing occurs in the
wider culture and cannot be separated from it.

Like our understanding of "discrimination," the definition of
"fairness" is culturally contested. Some theorists today argue that
the liberal notion of fairness is a problematic standard in a country
such as ours, which contains profound economic, political, and social inequality (Espeland 1995; Parenti 1995; Young 1990). In general, fairness in the United States means "equality" among

---

21 The importance of using a sophisticated methodology to explore structural-
level variables is revealed by Myers and Talarico's work. In contrast to the finding
reported here, their simpler, additive analysis suggested that crime rates had "little
direct bearing on most decisions, and fostered unexpectedly lenient split sentences"
(Myers and Talarico 1987:81).

22 For a review of other contextual variables, such as unemployment and region of the country, see Chiricos and Crawford (1995).

individuals. The constitutional protection of "legal equality," however, means little to individuals who have experienced economic,
gender, racial, or other inequality throughout their lives (Chambliss and Seidman 1982; Cornell 1992; Parenti 1995; Scott 1990).
As Parenti writes,

> [P]oor and working-class persons, the uneducated, and ra-
> cial minorities are more likely to be arrested, denied bail,
> induced to plead guilty, and do without a pretrial hearing
> or adequate representation. They are less likely to have a
> jury trial if tried; [and are] more likely to be con-
> victed. . .than are mobsters, businesspeople, and upper and
> middle-class Caucasians in general. (1995:129)

Even if such persons are treated "equally" at the point of sentencing
(and quite a bit of research suggests that they are not), can we say
that our system is "fair" in any meaningful way?

> Persons have different standpoints, different places from
> which they actually live and move and think, and justice
> requires not that we detach ourselves from individual par-
> ticularities but that we engage and sympathize with
> them. . . .Postmodernism emphasizes difference as the au-
> thentic characteristic of lived experience and devalues the
> equitable treatment of persons as a false way of taking into
> account what people are really like while masking power
> relations. (Farganis 1994:119-20).[23]

Some recent research suggests that there might be good reasons for applying different sentences to different people who have
committed the same offense (Tonry 1995). Daly (1987, 1989a,
1989b), for example, found that apparent gender diffferences in sentencing were actually the result of judicial efforts to give more lenient sentences to offenders with dependent children. Judges felt
that children should not be made to suffer for their parents' offenses, and believed that the extra cost to the state of caring for
these dependent children, should a custodial parent be incarcerated, warranted more lenient treatment. Bickle and Peterson
(1991) also found that judges took family responsibilities into consideration when sentencing offenders. Others possibly would disa-
gree with these priorities, but I think many would agree that this is
a plausibly different story to tell about sentencing. A similar argument historically has been used to sentence juveniles differently

---

[23] This does not mean that we cannot consider equality to be a valuable goal in
some instances. As Scott (1990) observes, however, it means we must recognize that
"the political notion of equality thus includes, indeed depends on, an acknowledgment of the existence of difference. Demands for equality have rested on implicit
and usually unrecognized arguments from difference; if individuals or groups were
identical or the same there would be no need to ask for equality" (p. 142). Scott adds,
"The only response is a double one: the unmasking of the power relationship constructed by posing equality as the antithesis of difference and the refusal of its consequent dichotomous construction of political choices" (p. 142).

than adults, though this distinction is rapidly disappearing under the push for harsher sentencing practices (Joe 1995). "A politics of difference argues . . . that equality as the participation and inclusion of all groups sometimes requires different treatment for oppressed or disadvantaged groups" (Young 1990:158). In other words, treating people similarly can be just as repressive as treating people differently.

In some ways, the old determinate sentencing story provides a palatable answer to the "problems" of discrimination and fairness because it avoids all the really difficult questions raised by the sentencing process in our country. It is a "feel-good" story that now has predictable conclusions; however, like most feel-good stories, it expresses little concern for developing an understanding of the characters whose lives it supposedly represents. In the United States, determinate sentencing has made it possible to avoid seriously considering whether different offenders convicted of the same offense should be sentenced differently on the basis of particular identities that reflect historically constructed disadvantages: class differences, age differences, gender differences, or other social factors.

This point is especially interesting, given that some European countries have participated in this debate and have decided that some social differences, in fact, are differences that matter. Thus some European countries rely heavily on the use of fines that are graduated according to income (Casale and Hillsman 1986; Tonry 1996). In the Netherlands, for example, "the fine is the legally preferred penalty for every crime"; in Germany "81 percent of all sentenced adult criminals were ordered to pay a fine, including 73 percent of those convicted of crimes of violence. In 1991, 83.3 percent of all sentences were fines" (Tonry 1996:124).[24] In these countries, ability to pay is related directly to the level of the fine in most cases. In the United States, however, legal equality prevails in the face of lived inequality, and there is no active discussion about the fairness of this situation for the majority of citizens.

## A FEMINIST AND POSTMODERN STORY

In the preceding pages I began to write a new story about sentencing. This story emerges from a critique of the assumptions that

---

[24] According to Kappeler, Blumberg, and Potter (1996), "[T]he United States imprisons four times as many people as . . . West Germany and the United Kingdom, seven times as many as Sweden, and eight times as many as the Netherlands" (p. 1975). Perhaps the most important differences between our country and many European countries is that they "have highly developed social safety nets that protect children from poverty. They have severe restrictions on the availability of firearms. They have much shorter prison sentences for nonviolent crimes, and their prisons have a much greater emphasis on rehabilitation" (Donziger 1996:196).

underlie the old sentencing story, but the new story is more than a critique. Embedded in my story is another set of assumptions that form the plot for a different story about sentencing:

* Sentencing must be understood as part of a larger process.
* Decisions made within the criminal justice system are inherently political.
* The existence of "crime" and "criminals" does not precede the criminal justice system; instead, their existence is constructed by decision makers within the system.
* Determinate sentencing is a reflection of power arrangements in our society, as are conceptions of discrimination and fairness.
* Determinate sentencing cannot solve the crime problem, and in fact is likely to exacerbate the problem if current trends continue.

These assumptions, if taken seriously, reveal the old sentencing story as outdated and potentially dangerous. The old story is dangerous because policy makers and scholars believe the myth to be true and use it daily as a basis for decision making about the lives of others. But the new story is still incomplete. What work remains for criminologists to do to if they want a new story to be heard? What text must accompany the assumptions to make the story plausible to the public and to policy makers?

To write the next chapter in the new sentencing story I have begun here, we must continue to look beyond judges to understand discrimination in the justice system. Future scholarly work might do well to explore relationships between decision makers and individuals who come into contact with the justice system, focusing on the micro practices of everyday life and the ways that these practices construct offenders and authorities. The focus should include the police, probation officers, prosecutors, those offering bail money, even the citizens who report crime initially. We should give particular attention to the way that some identities, styles, and personal choices become embedded in the criteria that justice officials use to define and enforce laws, to assess risk, and to mete out punishment.

Even more important is the need to investigate the forces that shape legislators' discretionary decisions, because lawmakers both define what constitutes crime and are increasingly responsible for deciding how to respond to violations of the law. As we try to understand why some problems are defined as crime and some people are defined as criminals, we must explore the structural links between politicians' desire to continue waging a "war" against crime and the "prison-industrial complex" that this war has spawned over the past 20 years. As Donziger (1996:85) states, "[T]he government and private security companies now spend almost as much on crime control each year as the Pentagon spends on national defense." The deepening interdependence between our economy and the imprisonment of large numbers of people poses an ever-growing barrier to the development of alternative crime control policies. At the same time, it is likely that legislators themselves will be challenged to revisit determinate sentencing as the crisis in corrections continues to drain state budgets.

In analyzing how legislators and practitioners define crime and justice, I hope that researchers will give particular attention to the construction of the criteria that are used to distinguish between people. There are no neutral criteria; therefore we must honestly investigate the potential biases in the criteria that are selected, even (and especially) when they seem commonsensical. Determinate sentencing rests on a belief that a rational, objective calculus can be found for justifying sanctions. Yet criteria always contain bias because they inevitably incorporate subjectivity; thus all criteria privilege some persons and repress others. Determinate sentencing reflects power arrangements in our society: not only the great distance between those who have many resources and those who do not, but also the distance between those whose stories are heard and those who are never heard when laws and policies are developed.

Who we are and how we are different matters in profound ways, but how we construct the differences between us matters even more. It is not merely that individual and group identities affect conceptions of crime and justice; conceptions of crime and justice also shape and (re)create individual and group identities. When citizens and politicians clamor for stiffer sentences for those who have committed "serious" offenses, we should be open to the possibility that such calls are really coded expressions of the desire to incapacitate or punish certain kinds of people. The socially constructed nature of prior record also needs greater attention than it has received thus far, and the cultural loading embedded in the notion of prior record ought to be investigated more fully. In my sentencing story, criteria that are based on the degree of harm caused by behaviors are more important than criteria based on the kinds of people who commit the offense, or on the class location of the offense.[25] I do not claim that my criteria are more objective than those now at work, but they pose an alternative to the current system of (in)justice.

---

[25] This point has been made by many others, including Bohm (1993), Michalowski (1985) and Reiman (1995).

640    SENTENCING, FEMINIST, POSTMODERN

Ultimately we need methodologies that capture more precisely the complex, relational, situated aspects of justice processing and the ways in which identity and power reflect and are reflected by those processes. Feminists have suggested greater reliance on qualitative methods including ethnographies, participant observation, life histories, and other forms of participatory research (see, for example, Fonow and Cook 1991; Maynard and Purvis 1994). Postmodern scholars have emphasized the importance of deconstruction as a strategy for revealing taken-for-granted assumptions about the social world. "What allies these particular incursions into the political economy of knowledge is a strategy of disclosing that things are not as they should be by also exposing all the ways in which things are not as we say they are. Both feminist and postmodern writing depends upon relativizing, ironizing, and circumscribing the mechanisms and tactics by which dominant authorities entrench themselves" (Singer 1992:470). Work by Ferrell (1993) and by Carlen (1988) using an ethnographic, case study methodology highlights the importance of taking a different approach when writing stories about crime and justice. If the truth is only partial, there is value in employing diverse methodologies in an effort to supply some of the missing pieces.

Finally, scholars and policy makers must seriously consider the failure of determinate sentencing to solve either the discrimination problem or the crime problem, and must begin to explore other alternatives. Harsh sentencing policies are used increasingly by politicians to cope with the problems associated with decaying inner cities. Stiffer sentencing has become a first-line political response to the social problems associated with large numbers of unemployed and impoverished people, who are (not coincidentally) disproportionately members of racial and ethnic groups with historic legacies of discrimination. But harsh sentencing practices, and especially the widespread use of incarceration, are utter failures as solutions to the plight of inner cities.

Given our current focus on punishment, the prison experience is dehumanizing at best. At its worst (which occurs far too often), it leaves the scars of brutality, sexual violence, and fear (Donziger 1996; Human Rights Watch 1995; Kappeler 1996). Incarcerated individuals are almost always released, and they return to society more alienated than when they entered confinement (Donziger 1996; Irwin and Austin 1994; Kappeler 1996). Those who have been imprisoned come out of prison less able to obtain employment and more hardened to the pain of others.

Determinate sentencing has not solved the crime problem, nor has it significantly reduced the systemic discrimination that permeates our justice system; indeed, it cannot. Sentencing is only one component of a complex process. "Fixing" sentencing is like putting a new carburetor in a car with hundreds of other mechanical problems. The fix actually can make things worse by taking other parts of the system and by creating the illusion that the car is repaired—only to have it explode later on.

Officials and many criminologists claim that our sentencing process is "fair" because legislators develop criteria that are applied systematically to all offenders. They make this claim without questioning the fairness of a system that views discrimination in every other part of the justice system as irrelevant to sentencing decisions, that ignores the way in which decision-making criteria are politically constructed, and that excludes large numbers of people from the debate about what harms should be viewed as most serious. We must begin to consider reductions in economic and social inequality as more effective than extensions of legal equality in solving the discrimination problem.

Although there are some things that we still do not know about crime, we know that "countries with the highest ratio of poverty have the highest rates of crime. The same correlation holds true for cities" (Donziger 1996:28). We must begin to consider mechanisms for responding to street crime that reflect the long-term goal of inclusion in the economy and the social fabric, rather than the short-term expediency of exclusion. It is hard to find justice in a governmental policy which helps to ensure that 32 percent of all black males age 20 to 29 are under the control of the criminal justice system (Mauer and Huling 1995). "Almost three out of four prison admissions today are either African-American or Hispanics" (Donziger 1996:103). We would notice the structural racism if it occurred in countries other than our own; we would call it political crime and demand an end to such abuses of human rights. Other countries have found ways to respond to street crime that do not embrace exclusionary strategies; surely we can do so as well.

What, then, is the value of telling a new story about sentencing? What difference can a different story make? As Disch writes,

> Because it is interpretive (as opposed to definitive), a story can disclose that what counts as a "real" rendering of a political conflict is not simply a matter of truth but also of rhetoric. That is, defining the "way it is" is not simply a task of fact-gathering but an interpretive contest; in turn, it is power, not dispassionate objectivity (which is itself a pose of power), that settles disputes among rival interpretations. (1994:10)

This statement does not make me hopeful that my story will be heard by those who are in positions to affect policy, but it describes accurately why I think it is important to tell a different story. In Ferrell's (1994b:9) words, "[I]n a world where methodologies of objectivity have been shattered, alternative accounts sparkle like bits of broken glass."

Telling a different story may seem to some to be a small contribution, but for those who understand how ideology shapes the choices that we believe are possible, telling a different story is powerful indeed. The crisis that plagues the criminal justice system today is partly a *crisis of imagination*. We know that current criminal justice practices are not working, but it is difficult to even imagine a different way. The value of telling a different tale is in imagining a different way. As Balkin says,

> Deconstruction is not a call for us to forget about moral certainty, but to remember aspects of human life that were pushed into the background by the necessities of the dominant legal conception we call into question. Deconstruction is not a denial of the legitimacy of rules and principles; it is an affirmation of human possibilities that have been overlooked or forgotten in the privileging of particular legal ideas. (1987:763)

In the story I have told here, I have imagined a different kind of justice and have posed a different set of assumptions—and questions—about sentencing. As scholars we know that our research and our quest for knowledge are only as good as the questions we ask. Yet, amazingly, few people seem to suspect that both liberals and conservatives are asking the wrong questions about determinate sentencing. I believe that storytelling and the analytic concepts used by feminist and postmodern scholars provide a strategy for developing new questions about sentencing and new stories about other justice issues. I urge others to consider using the analytic concepts covered here—a critique of objectivity, process, and identity, and a new conceptualization of power—as a way to construct new narratives about crime and justice in the United States. These new narratives are important because the beginning of a story has something to do with how it will end. What you imagine to be possible has something to do with what is ultimately possible. By beginning a new story, I hope to create an opportunity to fashion a different ending. What that ending looks like depends on us all.

# REFERENCE

Albonetti, Celesta A. 1991. "An Integration of Theories to Explain Judicial Discretion." *Social Problems* 38:247-66.

Arrigo, Bruce A. 1995. "The Peripheral Core of Law and Criminology: On Postmodern Social Theory and Conceptual Integration." *Justice Quarterly* 12:447-72.

Austin, Thomas L. 1981. "The Influence of Court Location on Type of Criminal Sentence: The Rural-Urban Factor." *Journal of Criminal Justice* 9:305-16.

Balkin, J.M. 1987. "Deconstructive Practice and Legal Theory." *Yale Law Journal* 96:743-86.

Bates Doob, Christopher. 1993. *Racism: An American Cauldron.* New York: Harper-Collins.

Becker, Howard S. and Michael McCall. 1990. *Symbolic Interaction and Cultural Studies.* Chicago: University of Chicago Press.

Bennett, Lance and Martha S. Feldman. 1981. *Reconstructing Reality in the Courtroom.* New Brunswick, NJ: Rutgers University Press.

Berk, Richard A. 1983. "An Introduction to Sample Selection Bias in Sociological Data." *American Sociological Review* 48:386-98.

Berk, Richard A. and S.A. Ray. 1982. "Selection Bias in Sociological Data." *Social Science Research* 11:352-98.

Bickle, Gayle S. and Ruth D. Peterson. 1991. "The Impact of Gender-Based Family Roles on Criminal Sentencing." *Social Problems* 38:372-94.

Blumberg, Abraham S. 1990. "The Moral Career of an Accused Person." Pp. 480-85 in *Criminal Behavior*, edited by Delos H. Kelly. New York: St. Martin's.

Blumstein, Alfred, Jacqueline Cohen, Susan E. Martin, and Michael H. Tonry. 1983. *Research on Sentencing: The Search for Reform, Vol. 2.* Washington, DC: National Academy Press.

Bohm, Robert M. 1993. "Social Relationships That Arguably Should Be Criminal Although They Are Not: On the Political Economy of Crime." Pp. 3-29 in *Political Crime in Contemporary America: A Critical Approach*, edited by Kenneth D. Tunnell. New York: Garland.

Bordo, Susan. 1988. "Anorexia Nervosa: Psychopathology as the Crystallization of Culture." Pp. 87-117 in *Feminism and Foucault: Reflections on Resistance*, edited by Irene Diamond and Lee Quinby. Boston: Northeastern University Press.

Bridges, George S., Robert D. Crutchfield, and Edith E. Simpson. 1987. "Crime, Social Structure and Criminal Punishment: White and Nonwhite Rates of Imprisonment." *Social Problems* 34:345-61.

Butler, Judith. 1990. *Gender Trouble: Feminism and the Subversion of Identity.* New York: Routledge.

Carlen, Pat. 1988. *Women, Crime and Poverty.* Philadelphia: Open University Press.

Casale, Silvia S.G. and Sally T. Hillsman. 1986. *The Enforcement of Fines as Criminal Sanctions: The English Experience and Its Relevance to American Practice.* Washington, DC: Department of Justice, National Institute of Justice.

Caufield, Susan and Nancy Wonders. 1993a. "Gender and Justice: Feminist Contributions to Criminology." Pp. 213-29 in *Varieties of Criminology: Readings from a Dynamic Discipline*, edited by Gregg Barak. Westport, CT: Praeger.

———. 1993b. "Personal AND Political: Violence against Women and the Role of the State." Pp. 79-100 in *Political Crime in Contemporary America: A Critical Approach*, edited by Kenneth D. Tunnell. New York: Garland.

Chambliss, William. 1995. "Crime Control and Ethnic Minorities." Pp. 235-58 in *Ethnicity, Race and Crime: Perspectives across Time and Place*, edited by Darnell F. Hawkins. Albany: SUNY Press.

Chambliss, William and Robert Seidman. 1982. *Law, Order and Power.* Reading, MA: Addison-Wesley.

Chiricos, Theodore and Charles Crawford. 1995. "Race and Imprisonment: A Contextual Assessment of the Evidence." Pp. 281-309 in *Ethnicity, Race and Crime: Perspectives across Time and Place*, edited by Darnell F. Hawkins. Albany: SUNY Press.

644     SENTENCING, FEMINIST, POSTMODERN

Coleman, James W. 1985. *the Criminal Elite: The Sociology of White Collar Crime.* 2nd ed. New York: St. Martin's.

Coombe, Rosemary. 1991. "Contesting the Self: Negotiating Subjectivities in Nineteenth-Century Ontario Defamation Trials." Pp. 3-40 in *Studies in Law, Politics, and Society,* Vol. 11, Greenwich, Ct: JAI.

Cornell, Drucilla. 1992. "Gender, Sex and Equivalent Rights." Pp. 280-96 in *Feminists Theorize the Political,* edited by Judith Butler and Joan W. Scott. London: Routledge.

Daly, Kathleen. 1987. "Discrimination in the Criminal Courts: Family, Gender, and the Problem of Equal Treatment." *Social Forces* 66:152-75.

————. 1989a. "Neither Conflict nor Labeling nor Paternalism Will Suffice: Intersections of Race, Ethnicity, Gender and Family in Criminal Court Decisions." *Crime and Delinquency* 35:136-68.

————. 1989b. "Rethinking Judicial Paternalism: Gender, Work-Family Relations, and Sentencing." *Gender and Society* 3:9-36.

Daly, Kathleen and Meda Chesney-Lind. 1988. "Feminism and Criminology." *Justice Quarterly* 5:497-538.

Davis, Kathy and Sue Fisher. 1993. "Power and the Female Subject." Pp. 3-20 in *Negotiating at the Margins: The Gendered Discourses of Power,* edited by Sue Fisher and Kathy Davis. New Brunswick, NJ: Rutgers University Press.

Disch, Lisa Jane. 1994. *Hannah Arendt and the Limits of Philosophy.* Ithaca: Cornell University Press.

Donziger, Steven R. 1996. *The Real War on Crime: The Report of the National Criminal Justice Commission.* New York: Harper.

Einstadler, Werner and Stuart Henry. 1995. *Criminological Theory.* Fort Worth: Harcourt Brace.

Eisenstein, James and Herbert Jacob. 1977. *Felony Justice: An Organizational Analysis of Criminal Courts.* Boston: Little, Brown.

Eisenstein, Zillah R. 1988. *the Female Body and the Law.* Berkeley: University of California Press.

Espeland, Wendy. 1995. "Legally Mediated Identity: The National Environmental Policy Act and the Bureaucratic Construction of Interests." *Law and Society Review* 28:1149-79.

Ewick, Patricia and Susan S. Silbey. 1995. "Subversive Stories and Hegemonic Tales: Toward a Sociology of Narrative." *Law and Society Review* 29:197-226.

Farganis, Sandra. 1994. "Postmodernism and Feminism." Pp. 101-26 in *Postmodernism and Social Inquiry,* edited by David R. Dickens and Andrea Fontana. New York: Guilford Press.

Farnworth, Margaret and Patrick M. Horan. 1980. "Separate Justice: An Analysis of Race Differences in Court Processes." *Social Science Research* 9:381-99.

Federal Bureau of Investigation. 1972. *Uniform Crime Reports: 1971.* Washington, DC: U.S. Government Printing Office.

————. 1980. *Uniform Crime Reports: 1979.* Washington, DC: U.S. Government Printing Office.

————. 1991. *Uniform Crime Reports: 1990.* Washington, DC: U.S. Government Printing Office.

Ferrell, Jeff. 1993. *Crimes of Style: Urban Graffiti and the Politics of Criminality.* New York: Garland.

————. 1994a. "Confronting the Agenda of Authority: Critical Criminology, Anarchism, and Urban Graffiti." Pp. 161-78 in *Varieties of Criminology: Readings from a Dynamic Discipline,* edited by Gregg Barak. Westpost, CT: Praeger.

————. 1994b. "(Stumbling toward) a Postmodern Criminology." Presented at the Meetings of the Southwestern Sociological Association, San Antonio.

————. 1995. "Style Matters: Criminal Identity and Social Control." Pp. 169-83 in *Cultural Criminology,* edited by Jeff Ferrell and Clinton Sanders. Boston: Northeastern University Press.

Ferrell, Jeff and Clinton R. Sanders. 1995. *Cultural Criminology.* Boston: Northeastern University Press.

Fonow, Mary Margaret and Judith A. Cook. 1991. "Back to the Future: A Look at the Second Wave of Feminist Epistemology and Methodology." Pp. 1-15 in *Beyond Methodology: Feminist Scholarship as Lived Research,* edited by Mary Margaret Fonow and Judith A. Cook. Bloomington: Indiana University Press.

Foucault, Michel. 1978. *The History of Sexuality,* translated from the French by Robert Hurley. New York: Pantheon.

Frazier, Charles E. and E. Wilbur Bock. 1982. "Effects of Court Officials on Sentence Severity: Do Judges Make a Difference?" *Criminology* 20:257-72.

Frazier, Charles E., E. Wilbur Bock, and John C. Henretta. 1983. "The Role of Probation Officers in Determining Gender Differences in Sentencing Severity." *Sociological Quarterly* 24:305-18.

Gelsthorpe, Loraine and Allison Morris. 1990. *Feminist Perspectives in Criminology.* Philadelphia: Open University Press.

Gilsinan, James. 1982. *Doing Justice.* Englewood Cliffs, NJ: Prentice-Hall.

Greenberg, David F. and Drew Humphries. 1981. "The Cooptation of Fixed Sentencing Reform." Pp. 367-86 in *Crime and Capitalism*, edited by David F. Greenberg. Palo Alto: Mayfield.

Greenhouse, Carol J. 1995. "Constructive Approaches to Law, Culture, and Identity." *Law and Society Review* 28:1231-41.

Griset, Pamela L. 1994. "Determinate Sentencing and the High Cost of Overblown Rhetoric: The New York Experience." *Crime and Delinquency* 40:532-48.

Hacker, Andrew. 1992. *Two Nations: Black and White, Separate, Hostile, Unequal.* New York: Ballantine.

Hagan, John. 1977. "Criminal Justice in Rural and Urban Communities: A Study of The Bureaucratization of Justice." *Social Forces* 55:597-612.

————. 1989. *Structural Criminology.* New Brunswick, NJ: Rutgers University Press.

————. 1994. *Crime and Disrepute.* Thousand Oaks, CA: Pine Forge.

Hagan, John and Kristin Bumiller. 1983. "Making Sense of Sentencing: A Review and Critique of Sentencing Research." Pp. 1-54 in *Research on Sentencing: The Search for Reform*, Vol. 2, edited by Alfred Blumstein, Jacqueline Cohen, Susan E. Martin, and Michael H. Tonry. Washington, DC: National Academy Press.

Hagan, John and Patricia Parker. 1985. "White Collar Crime and Punishment." *American Sociological Review* 50:302-16.

Hagan, John and Marjorie S. Zatz. 1985. "The Social Organization of Criminal Justice Processing Activities." *Social Science Research* 14:103-25.

Hall, Stuart. 1986. "The Problem of Ideology: Marxism without Guarantees." *Journal of Communications Inquiry* 10:28-44.

Handler, Joel F. 1992. "Postmodernism, Protest, and the New Social Movements." *Law and Society Review* 26:697-731.

Hazelrigg, Lawrence. 1986. "Is There a Choice between 'Constructionism' and 'Positivism'?" *Social Problems* 33(6):S1-S13.

Heaney, Gerald W. 1991. "The Reality of Guidelines Sentencing: No End to Disparity." *American Criminal Law Review* 28:161-228.

Hennessy, Rosemary. 1993. *Materialist Feminism and the Politics of Discourse.* New York: Routledge.

Henry, Stuart and Dragan Milovanovic. 1991. "Constitutive Criminology: the Maturation of Critical Theory." *Criminology* 29:293-316.

Hill Collins, Patricia. 1991. "Learning from the Outsider Within: The Sociological Significance of Black Feminist Thought." Pp. 35-59 in *Beyond Methodology: Feminist Scholarship as Lived Research*, edited by Mary Margaret Fonow and Judith Cook. Bloomington: Indiana University Press.

Howe, Adrian. 1994. *Punish and Critique: Towards a Feminist Analysis of Penality.* New York: Routledge.

Human Rights Watch Women's Rights Project: 1995. *The Human Rights Watch Global Report on Women's Human Rights.* New York: Human Rights Watch.

Humphries, Drew. 1993. "Crack Mothers, Drug Wars, and the Politics of Resentment." Pp. 31-48 in *Political Crime in Contemporary America: A Critical Approach*, edited by Kenneth D. Tunnell. New York: Garland.

Inverarity, James M., Pat Lauderdale, and Barry C. Feld. 1983. *Law and Society: Sociological Perspectives on Criminal Law.* Boston: Little, Brown.

Irwin, John and James Austin. 1994. *It's About Time: America's Imprisonment Binge.* Belmont, CA: Wadsworth.

Joe, Karen A. 1995. "The Dynamics of Running Away: Deinstitutionalization Policies and the Police." *Juvenile and Family Court Journal* 46(3):43-55.

Kappeler, Victor E., Mark Blumberg, and Gary W. Potter. 1996. *The Mythology of Crime and Criminal Justice.* 2nd ed. Prospect Heights, IL: Waveland.

Kempf, Kimberly L. and Roy L. Austin. 1986. "Older and More Recent Evidence on Racial Discrimination in Sentencing." *Journal of Quantitative Criminology* 2:29-48.

646    SENTENCING, FEMINIST, POSTMODERN

Kleck, Gary. 1981. "Racial Discrimination in Criminal Sentencing: A Critical Eval-
    uation of the Evidence with Additional Evidence on the Death Penalty." *Ameri-
    can Sociological Review* 46:783-805.
Kruttschnitt, Candace. 1984. "Sex and Criminal Court Dispositions: The Un-
    resolved Controversy." *Journal of Research in Crime and Delinquency* 21:2;13-
    32.
LaFree, Gary D. 1980. "The Effect of Sexual Stratification by Race on Official Reac-
    tions to Rape." *American Sociological Review* 45:842-54.
———. 1985. "Adversarial and Nonadversarial Justice: A Comparison of Guilty
    Pleas and Trials." *Criminology* 23:289-312.
Langston, Donna. 1995. "Tired of Playing Monopoly?" Pp. 100-10 in *Race, Class
    and Gender: An Anthology*, edited by Margaret L. Anderson and Patricia Hill
    Collins. New York: Wadsworth.
Lather, Patti. 1991. *Getting Smart: Feminist Research and Pedagogy With/In the
    Postmodern*. New York: Routledge.
Liska, Allen E. and Mitchell Chamlin. 1984. "Social Structure and Crime Control
    among Macrosocial Units." *American Journal of Sociology* 90:383-95.
Lyotard, Jean-Francois. 1979. *The Postmodern Condition: A Report on Knowledge*,
    translated by Geoff Bennington and Brian Massumi. Minneapolis: University
    of Minnesota Press.
Martin, Susan Ehrlich and Nancy C. Jurik. 1996. *Doing Justice, Doing Gender:
    Women in Law and Criminal Justice Occupations*. London: Sage.
Martinson, Robert. 1974. "What Works—Questions and Answers about Prison Re-
    form." *Public Interest* 35(2):22-54.
Mauer, Marc and Tracy Huling. 1995. *Young Black Americans and the Criminal
    Justice System: Five Years Later*. Washington, DC: The Sentencing Project.
Maynard, Mary and June Purvis. 1994. *Researching Women's Lives from a Feminist
    Perspective*. London: Taylor and Francis.
Mertz, Elizabeth. 1995. "A New Social Constructionism for Sociolegal Studies."
    *Law and Society Review* 28:1243-65.
Messerschmidt, James. 1987. *Capitalism, Patriarchy, and Crime*. Totow, NJ: Ro-
    wand and Littlefield.
Messner, Steven F. and Richard Rosenfeld. 1994. *Crime and the American Dream*.
    Belmont, CA: Wadsworth.
Michalowski, Raymond J. 1985. *Order, Law and Crime*. New York: Random
    House.
———. 1993. "(De)Construction, Postmodernism, and Social Problems: Facts, Fic-
    tion and Fantasies at the 'End of History.'" Pp. 377-401 in *Reconsidering Social
    Constructionism*, edited by James A. Holstein and Gale Miller. New York:
    Aldine.
Michalowski, Raymond J. and Michael Pearson. 1988. "Crime, Fiscal Crisis and
    Decarceration: Financing Corrections at the State Level." Pp. 249-71 in *Trans-
    carceration: Essays in the Sociology of Social Control*, edited by John Lowman.
    Brookfield, VT: Gower.
———. 1991. "You Can Pay Me Now, or You Can Pay Me Later: A Comparison of
    Expenditures for Education and Criminal Corrections in North Carolina."
    *North Carolina Prison News* 1(2):1-5.
Mies, Maria. 1991. "Women's Research or Feminist Research? The Debate Sur-
    rounding Feminist Science and Methodology." Pp. 60-84 in *Beyond Methodol-
    ogy: Feminist Scholarship as Lived Research*, edited by Mary Margaret Fonow
    and Judith A. Cook. Bloomington: Indiana University Press.
Miethe, Terance D. 1987. "Stereotypical Conceptions and Criminal Processing: The
    Case of the Victim-Offender Relationship." *Justice Quarterly* 4:571-93.
———. "Regional Differences in Criminal Processing: The Consequences of Model
    Selection on Conclusions about Differential Treatment." *Sociological Quarterly*
    27:217-37.
Miller, Jody. 1995. "Struggles over the Symbolic: Gang Style and the Meanings of
    Social Control." Pp. 213-34 in *Cultural Criminology*, edited by Jeff Ferrell and
    Clinton Sanders. Boston: Northeastern University Press.
Minow, Martha. 1990. *Making All the Difference: Inclusion, Exclusion, and Ameri-
    can Law*. Ithaca: Cornell University Press.
Morris, Allison and Loraine Gelsthorpe. 1991. "Feminist Perspectives in Criminol-
    ogy: Transforming and Transgressing." *Women and Criminal Justice* 2(2):3-26.

Myers, Laura B. and Sue Titus Reid. 1995. "The Importance of County Context in the Measurement of Sentencing Disparity: The Search for Routinization." *Journal of Criminal Justice* 23:223-41.
———. 1988. "Social Background and the Sentencing Behavior of Judges." *Criminology* 26:649-75.
Myers, Martha A. and Susette Talarico. 1987. *The Social Contexts of Criminal Sentencing*. New York: Springer-Verlag.
Nardulli, Peter F. 178. *The Courtroom Elite: An Organizational Perspective on Criminal Justice*. Cambridge, MA: Ballinger.
Nicholson, Linda. 1990. *Feminism/Postmodernism*. New York: Routledge.
Nicholson, Linda and Steven Seidman. 1995. *Social Postmodernism: Beyond Identity Politics*. Cambridge, UK: Cambridge University Press.
Parenti, Michael. 1995. *Democracy for the Few*. New York: St. Martin's.
Peterson, Ruth D. and John Hagan. 1984. "Changing Conceptions of Race: Towards an Account of Anomalous Findings in Sentencing Research." *American Sociological Review* 49:56-70.
Pfohl, Steven J. 1993. "Revenge of the Parasites: Feeding off the Ruins of Sociological (De)Construction." Pp. 403-40 in *Reconsidering Social Constructionism*, edited by James A. Holstein and Gale Miller. New York: Adeline.
———. 1994. "A Short History of the Parasite Cafe." Pp. 97-103 in *Body Politics: Disease, Desire and the Family*, edited by Michael Ryan and Avery Gordon. Boulder: Westview.
Pope, Carl E. 1976. "The Influence of Social and Legal Factors on Sentencing Dispositions: A Preliminary Analysis of Offender Based Transaction Statistics." *Journal of Criminal Justice* 4:203-21.
Reiman, Jeffrey H. 1995. *The Rich Get Richer and the Poor Get Prison: Ideology, Class, and Criminal Justice*. 4th ed., Boston: Allyn and Bacon.
Ro: enau, Pauline Marie. 1992. *Post-Modernism and the Social Sciences: Insights, Inroads and Intrusions*. Princeton: Princeton University Press.
Rossi, Peter, Emily Waite, Christine Bose, and Richard Berk. 1974. "The Seriousness of Crimes: Normative Structure and Individual Differences." *American Sociological Review* 39:224-37.
Ryan, Kevin and Jeff Ferrell. 1986. "Knowledge, Power, and the Process of Justice." *Crime and Social Justice* 25:178-95.
Schwartz, Martin D. and David O. Friedrichs. 1994. "Postmodern Thought and Criminological Discontent: New Metaphors for Understanding Violence." *Criminology* 32:221-46.
Scott, Joan W. 1990. "Deconstructing Equality-versus-Difference: Or, the Uses of Poststructuralist Theory." Pp. 134-48 in *Conflicts in Feminism*, edited by Marianne Hirsch and Evelyn Fox-Keller. London: Routledge.
Seidman, Steven. 1994. *Contested Knowledge: Social Theory in the Postmodern Era*. Cambridge, MA: Blackwell.
Shein, Marcia G. 1993. "Racial Disparity in 'Crack' Cocaine Sentencing." *Criminal Justice* 8(2):28-62.
Simpson, Sally. 1989. "Feminist Theory, Crime, and Justice." *Criminology* 27:605-31.
Singer, Linda. 1992. "Feminism and Postmodernism." Pp. 464-75 in *Feminists Theorize the Political*, edited by Judith Butler and Joan W. Scott. New York: Routledge.
Smart, Carol. 1989. *Feminism and the Power of Law*. New York: Routledge.
Spohn, Cassia and Susan Welch. 1987. "The Effect of Prior Record in Sentencing Research: An Examination of the Assumption That Any Measure Is Adequate." *Justice Quarterly* 4:285-302.
Stambaugh, Phoebe. 1995. "The Promise of Law: Understanding the Sexual Harassment Complaint Careers of Women." Doctoral dissertation, Arizona State University.
Sudnow, David. 1965. "Normal Crimes: Sociological Features of the Penal Code in a Public Defender Office." *Social Problems* 12:255-76.
Sutherland, Edwin. 1945. *White Collar Crime*. New York: Holt, Rinehart and Winston.
Swigert, Victoria and Ronald Farrell. 1977. "Normal Homicides and the Law." *American Sociological Review* 42:16-32.
Thorne, Barrie. 1993. *Gender Play: Girls and Boys in School*. New Brunswick, NJ: Rutgers University Press.

648     SENTENCING, FEMINIST, POSTMODERN

Tonry, Michael. 1987. *Sentencing Reform Impacts*. Washington, DC: U.S. Department of Justice, National Institute of Justice.
———. 1995. *Malign Neglect: Race, Crime, and Punishment in America*. New York: Oxford University Press.
———. 1996. *Sentencing Matters*. New York: Oxford University Press.
Uelmen, Gerald F. 1992. "Federal Sentencing Guidelines: A Cure Worse Than the Disease." *American Criminal Law Review* 29:899-905.
Unnever, James D. 1982. "Direct and Organizational Discrimination in the Sentencing of Drug Offenders." *Social Problems* 30:212-25.
Von Hirsch, Andrew. 1976. *Doing Justice: The Choice of Punishments: Report of the Committee for the Study of Incarceration*. New York: Hill and Wang.
Walker, Samuel. 1980. *Popular Justice: A History of American Criminal Justice*. New York: Oxford University Press.
Welch, Susan, John Gruhl, and Cassia Spohn. 1984. "Sentencing: The Influence of Alternative Measures of Prior Record." *Criminology* 22:215-27.
Welch, Susan and Cassia Spohn. 1986. "Evaluating the Impact of Prior Record on Judges' Sentencing Decisions: A Seven-City Comparison." *Justice Quarterly* 3:389-407.
West, Candace and Don H. Zimmerman. 1987. "Doing Gender." *Gender and Society* 1:125-51.
———. 1995. "Doing Difference." *Gendera and Society* 9:8-37.
West, Cornel. 1993. *Race Matters*. Boston: Beacon.
Winter, Steven L. 1992. "For What It's Worth." *Law and Society Review* 26:789-818.
Wonders, Nancy. 1990. "Courts in Context: A Sociological Approach to Sentencing Disparity." Doctoral dissertation, Rutgers University.
Yeatman, Anna. 1994. *Postmodern Revisionings of the Political*. New York: Routledge.
Young, Iris Marion. 1990. *Justice and the Politics of Difference*. Princeton: Princeton University Press.
Zatz, Marjorie S. 1984. "Race, Ethnicity and Determinate Sentencing: A New Dimension to an Old Controversy." *Criminology* 22:147-71.
———. 1985. "Pleas, Priors, and Prison: Racial/Ethnic Differences in Sentencing." *Social Science Research* 14:169-93.
Zatz, Marjorie S. and Alan J. Lizotte. 1985. "The Timing of Court Processing: Towards Linking Theory and Method." *Criminology* 23:313-35.

# [11]

## THE ABROGATION OF SUBJECTIVITY IN THE PSYCHIATRIC COURTROOM: TOWARD A PSYCHOANALYTIC SEMIOTIC ANALYSIS

by

### CHRISTOPHER R. WILLIAMS
*California School of Professional Psychology*

*Introduction*

The shared discourse of the psychiatric courtroom (i.e., the predefined, coordinated relations and effects of "clinicolegal" speech) subjects the mental health citizen to a form of linguistic control in which the person's agency disappears. Indeed, the institutions of law and psychiatry embrace each other's discursive reality, and, thus, interpellate individual consumers as "diseased" (or pathologized) subjects in-law. As others have argued, it is in this context that such consumers must defend — often ineffectively — their rights as citizens.[1] This process not only denies or invalidates the existence of the mentally ill as citizens, but re-legitimates the abrogation of their essential being (i.e. their subjectivity or desire) in the courtroom. In short, the clinicolegal apparatus functions as a linguistically violent and coercive mechanism of social control.[2] In the United States, seeking legal redress from institutional confinement all too frequently results, then, in the continued marginalization and alienation of the mentally ill, regardless of courtroom outcomes.

The unconscious dynamics at work in this psycholegal process can

---

1 B. Arrigo, *The Contours of Psychiatric Justice: A Postmodern Critique of Mental Illness, Criminal Insanity, and the Law* (New York: Garland, 1996).

2 E.g. see B. Arrigo, "Transcarceration: Notes on a Psychoanalytically-informed Theory of Social Practice in the Criminal Justice and Mental Health Systems", *Crime, Law, and Social Change: An International Journal* 27/1 (1997), 31-48; B. Arrigo, "Desire in the Psychiatric Courtroom: On Lacan and the Dialectics of Linguistic Oppression", *Current Perspectives in Social Theory* 16 (1996), 159-187; B. Arrigo, "Toward a Theory of Punishment in the Psychiatric Courtroom: On Language, Law, and Lacan", *Journal of Crime and Justice* 19/1 (1996), 15-32.

be elucidated by employing the psychoanalytic semiotic insights of Jacques Lacan. Lacan understood that discourse embodies only certain *forms* of desire. These forms are (re)constituted and privileged given the prevailing system of linguistic coordination. The discourse of the clinicolegal system, then, facilitates important ends. First, knowingly or not, it promotes the "re-legitimation of entrenched ideologies, knowledges and truths".[3] In the context of the overlapping effects of law and psychiatry, as an ossified linguistic coordinate system, only discourse that is consistent with "specialized" knowledge finds expression in the clinicolegal sphere. Thus, by embracing only pre-configured forms of linguistic articulation, this apparatus necessarily legitimates meanings consistent with its own internal system of signs. Second, and consequently, the desiring psychiatric citizen finds nothing but the reaffirmation of her or his own alienation, repression, and despair at the hands of the law.[4]

In this brief review, we demonstrate how the disordered citizen in law experiences psychic alienation and social marginalization from the perspective of Lacan's *desiring subject*. We argue that a Lacanian perspective can further our understanding of the linguistic oppression the mentally ill encounter, given the quashing of their subjectivity in the psychiatric courtroom. We rely on the precedent case of *Boggs* vs. *N.Y. City Health & Hospital Corp.* (1987) to demonstrate, at a provisional and speculative level, the potential utility of Lacanian psychoanalytic semiotics to deepen our regard for this pressing sociolegal concern.

*Subjectivity and Désir*

To grasp the Lacanian notion of the subject one must comprehend his often complex conceptualizations on the nature of intrapsychic and interpersonal communication and desire.[5] This requisite understanding

---

3    B. Arrigo & T.R. Young, "Theories of Crime and Crimes of Theorists: On the Topological Construction of Criminological Reality", *Theory and Psychology* 8/2 (1998), 219-252, at 227.

4    *Ibid.*, B. Arrigo, "Legal Discourse and the Disordered Criminal Defendant: Contributions From Psychoanalytic Semiotics and Chaos Theory", *Legal Studies Forum* 18/1 (1994), 93-112.

5    B. Arrigo, "Insanity Defense Reform and the sign of abolition: Re-visiting Montana's experience", *International Journal for the Semiotics of Law* 10/29 (1997), 191-211, at 201.

entails examining the relationship between language and the unconscious. According to Lacan, the nature of the unconscious presents a structure that resembles the form of a language.[6] The unconscious, designated as the "Other" (*Autre*), is the linguistic cache. Thus, the mobilization of the psychic apparatus, that which produces speech, implicates the unconscious.

Lacan's subject is inherently and inseparably bound to our engagement with discourse. Lacan's perspective on the subject emanates from a restructuring of the Cartesian notion — *cogito ergo sum* — in which the decentered subject ($) is constituted as "I think where I am not, therefore I am where I do not think".[7] Thus, the Cartesian subject (i.e., the unitary "I" ) understood as the rational master of discourse and action, is discarded in favour of an unstable, decentered subject divided by a plethora of discursive signifiers whose language speaks *through* us.[8]

For Lacan, the psychic apparatus is composed of three Orders: the Symbolic, Imaginary, and the Real. The interaction of these three Orders produces the subject's speech. The Symbolic Order is that of language and culture. It is represented by the Other (i.e. the unconscious). Individuals are born into the Symbolic Order. It is the Symbolic Order that establishes our identity within a shared linguistic realm. Thus, entrance into the Symbolic Order supplies us with a means (i.e. language) through which to communicate our desire. The "shared" nature of meaning, however, is privileged over that of individual being. Thus, the subject is represented as the "presence of an absence." The absence is that which fails to be embodied in shared constitutions of meaning; that is, it is the "lack-in-being." Thus, the subject is divided (depicted by Lacan as the divided or slashed subject [$]).

The Imaginary Order is that of images. These images, or imaginary constructions, provide an illusion of completeness.[9] This process can be likened to viewing oneself in the mirror, with others and objects (*objet petit*) that retain the potential for filling in the gaps (i.e. desire) and

6   Jacques Lacan, *Ecrits: A Selection* trld. A. Sheridan (New York: Norton, 1977).

7   *Ibid.*, at 166.

8   *Supra* n.5, at 205; M. Bowie, *Lacan* (Cambridge, MA: Harvard University Press, 1991), 77-78.

9   D. Milovanovic, *A Primer in the Sociology of Law* (Albany, New York: Harrow and Heston, 1994, 2nd ed.), 158.

constituting a unitary subject. While the initial experience follows the mirror stage of development (6-18 months), its outcome produces the possibility for other imaginary constructions that will follow. These imaginary constructions of completeness are harboured by the child throughout her- or his lifetime and are manifested in everyday interactions.[10]

The Real Order is the lived experience of the subject. The subject is forever separated from the Real by her or his initiation into the Symbolic. The Real Order is "forever foreclosed to congruent representation in signifiers".[11] Again, this is the experienced "lack-in-being" that is the product of a linguistic reality that alienates or displaces the subject from the Real, preferring, instead, the divisiveness of "shared" realities.

Thus, for Lacan, the employment of discourse casts one into the sphere of universal meaning. The spoken word necessarily conveys general knowledge and meaning that essentially denies or represses the more personal or intimate dimensions of the subject's being.[12] The meaning communicated in discourse embodies desire, yet the universal nature of such meaning relegates the form of that desire to be consistent with agreed upon linguistic parameters. In other words, the desire that is expressed by shared meaning is necessarily representative of "a sense of identity consistent with only certain points of view that often fail ... to embody a more complete, a more meaningful, regard for the person who speaks".[13] Thus, it stands as a shared "fiction" — a false or incomplete image of reality — known and embodied, however, by a select few.

The psychic apparatus (i.e. the interaction of the three Orders) is mobilized by desire, or the periodic experience of a "lack-in-being".[14] Thus, the Lacanian subject is a *desiring* subject.[15] With this mobilization comes the expression of desire through embodiment in

---

10  Arrigo, *supra* n.5, at 205.

11  Milovanovic, *supra* n.9, at 158.

12  J. Lacan, *The Four Fundamental Concepts of Psychoanalysis* (New York: Norton, 1981); Arrigo, *supra* n.3, at 226.

13  Arrigo, *supra* n.3 at 226; B. Fink, *The Lacanian Subject* (Princeton, NJ: Princeton University Press, 1995).

14  Milovanovic, *supra* n.9, at 159.

15  The desiring subject is depicted in Lacan's Schema L and Graphs of Desire: Lacan, *supra* n.6, at 193-194, 303-316; for a concise overview of Lacan's Schema L, see, e.g., Milovanovic, *supra* n.9, at 158-59.

signifiers. The desiring subject appropriates objects of desire (*objet petit [a]*). The *a*, then, represents the subject's attempt to *suture* or surgically repair the "gaps" in being. Signifiers, or words embodying desire, represent one form of *a*. Put another way, the subject locates a surgical "tool" (e.g., discursive signifiers) that s/he feels will adequately "fill" the experienced "lack" in being as an appropriate embodiment of desire.[16] In this process, however, the subject disappears into the *a* (i.e., the uttered words). The person is now re-presented by signifiers that cannot completely stand for her or his desire (i.e., imbue the experienced "lack") and, thus, the subject remains divided ($) and always in search of identity fulfilment.[17]

*In the Matter of Billie Boggs: The Homeless Mentally Ill and the Semiotics of (In)justice*

The significance of the *Boggs*[18] case lies in its status as a "classic confrontation between the rights of a citizen against governmental authority trying to confront and remedy a pervasive social *problem*[19]" [emphasis added]. The "problem" referred to by the court involved the mentally ill homeless population in the streets of New York and elsewhere. The confrontation and remedy availed by the system

16 Lacan presents this relationship as: $ <> a, where the divided subject ($) "disappears into the signifiers [the objects of desire- a] that represent it in discourse" while the objects of desire provide an illusory (i.e. mirror) basis for the subject's being. Thus, a two-way process is always active in the subject's relation to discourse. Milovanovic, *supra*, n.9, at 160.

17 For more on the interactive effects of being and meaning in the constitution of Lacanian desire see E. Beneveniste, *Problems in General Linguistics* (Coral Gables, Fla: University of Miami Press, 1971); D. Milovanovic, *Postmodern Law and Disorder: Psychoanalytic Semiotics, Chaos Theory, and Juridic Exegeses* (Liverpool, UK: Deborah Charles Publications, 1992).

18 Boggs was a 40 year old woman living on a public sidewalk in New York County. For the past year, this was her bedroom, toilet, and living room. Boggs was identified by authorities as in need of emergency psychiatric services. It was felt that she posed a danger to herself and/or to others. Based on the recommendations of the attending psychiatrist, Billie Boggs was involuntarily confined. For more background on the case see *Boggs* v. *N.Y. City Health and Hospital Corp.*, 132 A.D. 2d 340, 523 N.Y.S. 2d 71 (1987).

19 *Ibid.*, Boggs A.D. 2d at 343.

amounted to involuntary civil confinement for the purposes of "treating" the condition of mental illness and subsequently enabling the patient to achieve a "better style of living".[20] The United States Supreme Court had previously recognized the "massive curtailment of liberty"[21] that accompanies unwanted institutionalization. Indeed, as a previous court opined "the mere presence of mental illness does not disqualify a person from preferring his home to the comforts of an institution".[22] And further, that "a State cannot constitutionally confine without more a non-dangerous individual who is capable of surviving safely in freedom by himself ...".[23] Thus, the issue before the court in *Boggs* was whether the respondents (the hospital) had presented clear and convincing evidence[24] that Ms. Boggs was suffering from mental illness which would have resulted in serious harm to herself if not immediately treated by way of involuntary hospitalization.[25]

We have already made conceptual reference to how the discursive structure of the clinicolegal courtroom is constructed around sense making that fails to embody different ways of knowing and experiencing the world. Subjectivity, as expressed through alternative discourses, is silenced by the psycholegal establishment. Indeed, it is declared non-justiciable speech. This absence of being (Lacan's lack) not only alienates the citizen from him or herself and the rule of law, but reaffirms the power of the established order.[26]

---

20   *Ibid.*, at 340.
21   *Humphrey* v. *Cady*, 405 U.S. 504 (1972), at 509.
22   *O'Connor* v. *Donaldson*, 422 U.S. 563 (1975), at 575.
23   *Ibid.*, at 576.
24   *Addington* v. *Texas*, 441 U.S. 418 (1979), established "clear and convincing" evidence as the standard of proof in matters of civil confinement.
25   *Supra* n.18, at 342.
26   This reaffirmation and reproduction of prevailing ideological notions in law and psychiatry is represented by Lacan's discourse of the master. This discourse essentially directs courtroom proceedings by situating subjects within the system's pre-existing linguistic coordinates. Thus, by turning to the clinicolegal apparatus for legal redress, psychiatric citizens unwittingly endorse those signifiers and sign meanings consistent with that subjectivity reflecting the knowledge and truth claims of the overlapping and interdependent legal and psychiatric communities. For the disordered subject in law, this psycho-semiotic process results in linguistic hegemony and reification. See, e.g., Arrigo, *supra* n.1, at 166-173; *supra* n.3, at 228-

Given our targeted presentation of Lacanian semiosis, *Boggs* is a useful illustration of how abrogation of desire and subjectivity in the psychiatric courtroom occurs.[27] In the pages that remain, we look specifically at the court proceedings to demonstrate how this denial of agency was enacted over and over again. Although our application is limited, we address three noteworthy areas. These include: (1) the role of "expert" knowledge; (2) the determination of mental illness; and (3) the finding of dangerousness.

### The role of "expert" knowledge

The disavowal of Ms. Boggs' desire was fortified by the court's initial qualification that the respective psychiatrists were "experts." This qualification demarcates the inauguration of medical discourse as acceptable and consistent with the *master signifiers*[28] constituting the law.[29] In other words, the acknowledgment of "expert" knowledge is also an acknowledgment of "expert" discourse and, thus, was endorsed by the court absent reconstitution.[30] The court, from the beginning,

---

232.

27  See also B. Arrigo, *Madness, Language, and the Law* (New York: Harrow and Heston, 1993), 108-121, for a postmodern semiotic analysis of the Billie Boggs case.

28  Lacan presents master signifiers (S1) as words or phrases that convey particular meanings. Such words/phrases can be described as illusory ideals or principal beliefs and attitudes which help constitute our identity and regard for others and events. B. Arrigo, "The Behavior of Law and Psychiatry: Rethinking Knowledge Construction and the Guilty-But-Mentally-Ill Verdict" ,*Criminal Justice and Behavior* 23/4 (1996), 572-592, at 582. They appear as universal, i.e. "shared" meanings that represent collective values. In law, master signifiers such as "due process," "fairness," "dangerousness," etc., retain a certain power when employed in discourse. Thus, master signifiers are signifiers that constitute powerful values and subsequently ascribe meaning to a message. Further, master signifiers, as opposed to other challengeable messages, are "accepted as having a value or validity that goes without saying." M. Bracher, *Lacan, Discourse, and Social Change: A Psychoanalytic Cultural Criticism* (Ithaca: Cornell University Press, 1993), 25.

29  Arrigo, *supra* n.27; *supra* n.1.

30  Additionally, we can appreciate the inauguration of the "expert" through Lacan's concept of the "law-of-the-father," or "Name-of-the-Father." Lacan refers here to the assignation of the father's name to a child. In

asserted its authority to validate and privilege specialized (medical) testimony while invalidating all speech that fell outside this signifying sphere. The assumption, then, was that Ms. Boggs was not an "expert" (on her life?) and, thus, was not capable of articulating the "facts" in a manner consistent with accepted courtroom dialogue. This construction of expertise obtained in this case, notwithstanding the psychiatric courtroom's sole purpose was to understand the speech-thought-behaviour of Ms. Boggs. Thus, from the outset, Ms. Boggs' non-clinicolegal subjectivity and desire, as located in and through *her* discourse, was silenced; that is, *her* way of knowing was never deemed relevant in a hearing where *her* liberty was subject to forfeiture. Indeed, as the Appellate Court opined when commenting upon the lower court's assessment of petitioner Boggs' status: "We find the hearing court erred in placing great weight on the demeanour, behaviour and testimony of Ms. Boggs".[31]

*The determination of mental illness*

The extent of Ms. Boggs' mental illness was repeatedly presented by the court as the presence of a thought disorder. This determination was attributable to the testimony of several psychiatrists. More precisely, the identified behaviours (signifiers) in question included : schizophrenia; delusional thinking; loose affect; clanging; ritualistic conduct; possessing private meaning; explosiveness; aggressiveness; violent; threatening; socially isolated; withdrawn; and abnormal. Several of these master signifiers were clinical interpretations (signifieds) of observed behaviour such as throwing and tearing up money, failure to respond directly to questioning, verbal abuse of community mental health staff, avoiding eye contact, and speaking in rhymes. What the court acknowledged as "expert" diagnosis/opinion (i.e. justiciable discourse on mental illness), however, failed to embody the knowledge claims of Ms. Boggs. As a

---

doing so, uncertainty about the identity of the father is foregone. Thus, it is the Law which establishes an identity for the child, much akin to the established courtroom "expert" establishing an identity for the psychiatric citizen. See, e.g., D. Caudill, "'Name-of-the-Father' and the Logic of Psychosis: Lacan's Law and Ours", *Legal Studies Forum*16/4 (1992), 20-41. D. Caudill, *Lacan and the Subject of Law* (Atlantic Highlands, NJ: Humanities Press, 1993), 101-115.

31 *Supra* n.18, at 352.

result, what was "left out" in the courtroom dialogue was Ms. Boggs' understanding of her (mentally ill) condition; that is, her uniquely felt and lived sense of being.

Consider the following passage from Dr. Sabatini, a psychiatrist testifying in favour of Ms. Boggs' continued confinement:

> [Regarding Ms. Boggs tearing up money] ... It's not a general phenomena observed and the indications I got were that there was a meaning to the destruction of this money because it represented, when it was given to her, people saying things about her — negative things about her which had a sexual overtone ... people ... were ... trying to control her sexuality through money. And, I think the destruction of money served to dispel that[32].

The destruction of money was interpreted by the psychiatrist as consistent with a delusional person. Sabatini's speech gave content to the sign of tearing money in a way considered legally acceptable in the psychiatric courtroom. Interestingly, however, at the hearing court, Ms. Boggs offered an alternative explanation for this behaviour. Boggs claimed to destroy money because she found it insulting and degrading when people threw it at her; that is, "given to her in an allegedly offensive manner".[33] Rather than accepting her idiosyncratic response, the Appellate Court declared her speech non-justiciable in the clinicolegal courtroom. The discourse of psychiatry spoke *for* Ms. Boggs and, thus, declared her delusional thinking as indicative of mental illness.

*The finding of dangerousness*

In order for involuntary hospitalization to obtain in the United States, there must also be a finding of dangerousness to self and/or to others beyond a showing of mental illness. In the case of *Boggs*, this matter was addressed, in part, based on perceived suicidality. The clinical description of petitioner Boggs' "suicidal behaviour and thought" appears throughout the appellate transcript. It is worth noting that Ms. Boggs, after having been admitted to the hospital, informed the staff psychiatrist that "she had run into traffic, and that she had a right to do so; she said that if she got hurt, it was nobody's business but her own".[34] Dr. Mahon, Ms. Boggs' treating psychiatrist after confinement,

32   *Ibid.*, at 353.
33   *Ibid.*, at 347.
34   *Ibid.*, at 341.

190          CHRISTOPHER R. WILLIAMS

explained " ... running in front of traffic and saying she has a right to endanger her life is suicidal and as a psychiatrist, I have to call that suicidal behaviour and I have to treat it as a clinician".[35] Interestingly, however, the interpretation offered by Ms. Boggs concerning her own behaviour was never fully acknowledged by the Appellate Court. There is no reported indication in the transcript, aside from the single observation noted, that Ms. Boggs presented any suicidal ideation or maintained any thoughts about intentionally harming herself. Ms. Boggs described that incident as "stepp[ing] between two parked cars and thr[owing] ... slacks [offered to her by Project HELP] into the street."[36] Thus, the signifier "suicidal," as expressed by purported "experts," underscored the court's interpretation of Ms. Boggs' "dangerous" behaviour. Alternative knowledge claims (especially those of petitioner Boggs) never received full articulation and/or validation by the psychiatric court.

A related aspect of Ms. Boggs' "danger to self" finding concerned her inability to recognize her needs (e.g., food, clothing, shelter). Dr. Hess, a psychiatrist with the community mental health organization called Project HELP, concluded that Ms. Boggs, "if left in the street ... would be a danger to herself, since she was incapable of accepting food, clothing, shelter.[37] Similarly, Dr. Mahon diagnosed Ms. Boggs as requiring continued institutionalization because " ... she presently has no capacity to comprehend her need for food, clothing, or shelter, and, in addition, Ms. Boggs cannot comprehend obvious danger.[38] Consider, however, the following:

> ... Ms. Boggs testified that ... she lives ... at that location [the streets], since there is a hot air vent ... [and] she has never been cold; she panhandles for food, and, in that fashion, she makes between $8 and $10 a day; she needs allegedly about $7 a day to buy her food ... she claims she has adequate clothes, and that when she need[s] more she ha[s] "friends" who ... supply them to her; she used profanity in order to make the staff of Project HELP go away; she claims that her umbrella served the purpose of protecting her from the sun[39] ...

Taking her hearing court testimony at face value, Ms. Boggs' incapacity

35   *Ibid.*, at 342.
36   *Ibid.*, at 350..
37   *Ibid.*, at 344.
38   *Ibid.*, at 354.
39   *Ibid.*, at 351.

to comprehend her essential needs is, more apparently, an unwillingness to accept assistance when she regards it as unwanted and intrusive. This aspect of Ms. Boggs' subjectivity manifested itself on numerous instances throughout the hearing court proceedings: Ms. Boggs repeatedly exhibited hostility toward Project HELP staff (this hostility figured prominently into her [re]diagnosis as mentally ill); she threw food that was offered to her by staff members; she threw away warm clothing when offered by staff; her use of profanity served the purpose of making HELP staff go away. In other words, the behaviour interpreted as "dangerous," "delusional," etc., could also be interpreted as merely wanting Project HELP staff to leave her alone. Given that Boggs never engaged in self-injurious behaviour and never injured or threatened anyone else (save Project HELP staff when seeking to invade her privacy), we conclude that the Appellate Court's finding of "danger to self" was a consequence of the mental health profession failing to recognize *her* agency as a choice making homeless person in the streets of New York.

Recalling Lacan's three Orders (Symbolic, Imaginary, Real), we can begin to understand how the subject-in-law is forever separated from the Real. The Symbolic Order, that of language, serves to create a reality — not that of the Real — but a transformation of the Real into social or socially acceptable reality. [40] Thus, in doing so, it "cancels out" the Real — the lived, unadulterated experience of the subject. The Symbolic reality is that which is named by language and, thus, can permeate the discourse of the psychiatric courtroom. That which cannot be said (within the narrowly construed confines of psycholegal discourse) is not part of reality — it does not exist [41]. Thus, in the case of Billie Boggs, her interpellation [42] as a subject-in-law and the consequent discursive implications of such, essentially denied her experience of the Real. The (legal) Order of the Symbolic and the plethora of medical and legal master signifiers that accompanied it, essentially negated Ms. Boggs' lived experience (i.e. *her* subjectivity) in favour of a medicolegal reality (i.e. one which encompassed words/phrases that were consistent

40 B. Fink, *The Lacanian Subject: Between Language and Jouissance* (Princeton, NJ: Princeton University Press, 1995), 56.

41 *Ibid.*, at 25.

42 On the notion of the interpellated subject, see L. Althusser, "Ideology and Ideological State Apparatuses", in *Lenin and Philosophy and Other Essays*, trld. B. Brewster (New York: Monthly Review Press, 1971), 170-177.

with those of the medicolegal community). In short, Ms. Boggs' reality was nullified by a Symbolic reality in which the circumscribed parameters of meaning for the psychiatric courtroom prevailed.

## Conclusion

We examined, on a cursory and suggestive level, the role of desire in the psychiatric courtroom. Employing selected conceptualizations from Lacan's semiosis, we demonstrated how this desire is essentially quashed and silenced by the clinicolegal community. Put another way, given the opinion in *Boggs*, we see how the essential being and way of knowing for diverse mentally ill citizens, are repressed by the psycholegal establishment. Indeed, following *Boggs*, the only knowledge claims embraced by the court were those articulations uttered by experts, and others similarly situated, who spoke the jargon of psychiatric justice. Not only does this decision making deny and invalidate the disparate voices of psychiatric consumers, it limits prospects for developing new and alternative sign meanings in law that more fully represent the experiences of the differently abled and other disenfranchised groups. Thus, regrettably, *Boggs* symbolizes not only the loss of agency for disordered subjects in the clinicolegal system but, more generally, the law's failure to promote emancipatory justice.

# [12]

# Creating the responsible prisoner

Federal admission and orientation packs

MARY BOSWORTH
*University of Oxford, UK*

## Abstract

This article examines official management practices and rhetoric in the US federal prison system as they are set out in admission handbooks that are distributed to inmates on arrival. Using concrete examples from contemporary and historical admission manuals I examine the changing language and style of prison governance. Concentrating in particular on the contemporary documents, I show how many of the ideas articulated in the literature on risk and governmentality form the backdrop of everyday prison life as penal administrators attempt to encourage prisoners to govern themselves. In this endeavour, the handbooks rely on a language of managerialism that presents inmates as just another 'client group' or customer base. This rhetorical shift implicitly denies the particularity of penal institutions, while simultaneously placing all the responsibility on the prisoners for their self-improvement and good order. The handbooks also reveal women's behaviour and sexuality to be more strictly monitored and regulated than that of men, suggesting that, despite the minimal security risk they pose, women are considered in need of greater control.

## Key Words

gender • managerialism • punishment • rehabilitation • risk

'You are expected to be courteous to staff and inmates, conduct yourself as an adult, a gentleman, to respect authority, to obey all institution rules and to completely follow instructions and orders of all staff members who are responsible for your daily supervision' (pp. 6–7 Inmate Handbook, Federal Prison Camp Lompoc, January 2001)

'It is our job to operate an institution in a manner which provides the healthiest setting possible, one which is conducive to your participating in the kinds of activities most likely to benefit you.' (Warden's Welcome, Resident Handbook, FCI Fort Worth, 1971–1975)

Of late, scholars working in criminology, sociology and law have offered a series of interconnected explanations for the current punitive turn in the United States. Invoking, in

PUNISHMENT & SOCIETY 9(1)

various degrees, Foucauldian ideas of governmentality and concepts of risk and actuarial justice, commentators have provided rich, theoretical frameworks for understanding current policy and practice (see, among others, O'Malley, 1992, 1996, 1999, 2004; Feeley and Simon, 1994; Garland, 1996, 2001; Simon, 1997; Hannah-Moffat, 1999, 2005; Rose, 2000; Sparks, 2000; Hudson, 2003). Though little agreement exists among these authors over definitions of risk or the nature of governance strategies, most are agreed that the criminal justice system is more than just a structure for dealing with those who break the law. It is also a primary means of creating accountable and thus governable and obedient citizens.

As risk management practices and their accompanying ideals of responsibility and accountability have gained prominence, these commentators suggest that the role of punishment and, specifically, the role of the prison have shifted. No longer a tool of welfare, nor a means of reform, David Garland (2001: 199) suggests instead that imprisonment now 'serves as an expressive satisfaction of retributive sentiments and an instrumental mechanism for the management of risk and the confinement of danger'. In this view, the future behaviour of offenders is of no particular concern for penal administrators. Instead, the choice of rehabilitation or reform has become the individual prisoner's sole responsibility. The prison is merely expected to provide the arena for such personal decisions while warehousing inmates securely.

In an article published recently in this journal, Kelly Hannah-Moffat (2005: 30) criticized this view both for its pessimism and for the way it fails to see how 'rehabilitation has been revived as a central feature of risk/need analysis and penal control'. Along with Pat O'Malley (2004), Hannah-Moffat argues that ideologies of risk are in fact not necessarily opposed to policy initiatives and practices of rehabilitation at all. Rather, she describes a 'hybridization' of risk/needs assessment in which statistical and actuarial instruments used to measure and change individuals' behaviour behind bars simultaneously reproduce discourses based on dangerousness and risk.

In this article I draw on ideas from both of these approaches to examine official management practices and beliefs in the US federal prison system as they are set out in admission handbooks that are distributed to inmates on arrival.[1] Using concrete examples from contemporary and historical manuals I examine shifts in the language and ideology of governance with a view to mapping how wider expectations about and justifications of punishment are operationalized. Concentrating in particular on those booklets which are currently in circulation, I show how many of the ideas that are central to the literature on risk and governmentality have come to form the backdrop of everyday prison life. Once translated into the mundane and the banal, they have, in turn, become the values inscribed in, and underpinning, the experience of prison itself.

By comparing the 'institutional detail of risk regulation' (Hood et al., 2001: viii) as it appears in these documents, I consider the changing ways in which penal administrators hope to govern prisons. In doing so I reveal how administrators seek to co-opt prisoners themselves into maintaining order and discipline. Reviewing manuals from women and men's prisons I also uncover some of the small-scale ways in which notions of risk and responsibility are gendered in daily prison life. In all periods, women's behaviour and dress tend to be subject to more detailed rules and regulations than those of their male counterparts. This difference, though minor at first glance, reinforces findings from feminist scholars who argue that women behind bars are often subject to stricter rules and regulations despite the relatively low security threat they pose (Howe, 1994; Bosworth, 1999). Such strategies of administration suggest that there is some level of doubt about women's capacity to govern themselves; they need more rules than do men.

Finally, linking and to a large extent obscuring these various manifestations of inequality and injustice in penal institutions is the language of managerialism in which the contemporary handbooks are written. Whereas booklets from the 1960s and 1970s promise individualized care and attention in preparing inmates for release, the recent manuals are characterized by mission statements and promises of inmate satisfaction that seek less to help prisoners realize their potential, but rather to motivate them into becoming willing actors, working towards the goals of the institution and, increasingly, of the wider, globalized, society and marketplace. Such a strategy, I suggest, is not only key to the maintenance of order within the institutions, through the (coerced and more freely given) collaboration of the inmate community, but also to the position of the prison in the broader society.

Prisons, these documents seem to assert, are just like any other institution or corporation. They are rational, reasonable and fair. Yet we must remember that, all too often, this is not true. Representing someone who has had his or her liberty taken away, often for a very long time, as just another client or customer is not a neutral or 'objective' decision. Rather, it is a deliberate and highly effective strategy of governance. This kind of language disguises the workings of power as well as the suffering and frustration that are always present in an institution of confinement. It implies the existence of a kind of social contract between customers and service providers that, in turn, reinforces the logic of inmate responsibility. In doing so, such documents, and the ideas they instil in prisoners and staff alike, make palatable the broader penal institution and help overcome the legitimacy deficit caused by the official rejection of the rehabilitative ideal. As Zygmunt Bauman suggested about a far more horrifying example of society's capacity for brutality in the Holocaust, they point to the worrying ability of 'rational organization' to disguise, or even subsume, profound questions of morality that should detain us all (Bauman, 1989: 212–13).

## FEDERAL PRISONS IN THE 1960s AND 1970s

Individuals convicted of federal offences in the 1960s and 1970s entered a prison system in flux. Though the incarcerated population remained almost static between 1940 and 1980, the number of federal facilities nearly doubled from 24 to 44 over the same period. Many of the new institutions, from Marion Penitentiary at the deepest end of the security spectrum to youth centres and prison camps at the other, experimented with new forms of prison governance and control. Reflecting beliefs that were widely held at the time about the benefits and possibilities of rehabilitation, most of these establishments sought to individualize the care, treatment and punishment of offenders and, at least in the 1960s and 1970s, to involve prisoners directly in their own reform through inmate councils, education, vocational training and therapy.

Unlike the *ad hoc* system of earlier times, where inmates were housed and classified more or less according to the whim of the warden or his deputy (Levinson, 1994), prisoners from the 1960s were acclimatized to their new environment through an initial 'admission and orientation phase' that generally lasted around two weeks. During this

PUNISHMENT & SOCIETY 9(1)

time, individuals were housed separately from the other prisoners and interviewed by staff members in order to determine their housing, work and security classification. As part of this process, institutions developed orientation handbooks in which they set out the basic rules and description of the institution as well as its governing ethos.

Men arriving at Marion Penitentiary in 1969, for example, would be furnished with a 22-page document produced by the inmate resident council and the prison staff that was filled with photographs identifying key members of staff and illustrating inmate activity. Though it contained no formal rules, the booklet presented guidelines and 'procedures . . . geared to assist everyone in their day-to-day living and bring about a smoother operation of the institution' (Marion *Orientation*, 1969: 1). Prisoners were somewhat paternalistically reminded that their 'cooperation and orderly conduct [would] help to maintain the pleasant surroundings that exist' (p. 7). Unlike today, handbooks from this period emphasize the specificity and uniqueness of each institution's regime rather than being concerned with a uniform articulation of Bureau policy. The unfortunately named Federal Youth Center Pleasanton claims, for example, that 'Many innovations and unusual programs have been developed [here]' (p. 1). Likewise, the handbook from Federal Correctional Institution (FCI) Fort Worth takes great pride in the 'experimental' nature of its co-correctional regime while also stressing the twin values of community and care. Prisoners are encouraged at this institution by their Warden 'to be concerned about each other' in favour of 'doing your own time'. 'In any human activity', he reminds them, 'it is important that there be mutual concern' (FCI Fort Worth, *Resident Handbook*, 1971–1975: Warden's Welcome).

At Atlanta Penitentiary, which opened in 1902, the rehabilitative ideal is linked to traditional beliefs about the role of religion in reforming offenders. Though concerned with the individualized needs of its inhabitants, booklets produced in the mid-1960s with titles like *The Way Back* and *Where, When, How, Why?* resonate with earlier reformist ideals of God and charity rather than with the psychology or treatment models which are typically thought to characterize prison regimes of this era (Garland, 1985).[2] Dedicated to 'all those who have covenanted in their hearts that no man ever stands so straight as he who stoops to help another', the former is filled with uplifting stories of convicted criminals who, through hard work and religion, found redemption at Atlanta and returned to 'the sunshine of respectability' (Atlanta, *The Way Back*, 1966: Warden's Welcome, p. 1). The latter explains the system of parole.

These days, at least some of the variety of earlier manuals has been lost as prison admissions have been streamlined and made uniform across the federal system. As part of the arrivals' process that is governed by Federal Bureau of Prison (BOP) Program Statement 5290.14, incoming prisoners must participate in an Admission and Orientation (A&O) programme, attend presentations, participate in tours of the facility and receive written material outlining three interconnected areas: rights and responsibilities, institutional opportunities and the facility's disciplinary system.[3] Prisons typically offer a broad institution-based curriculum and a smaller, unit-based one. Inevitably, of course, institutions do not respond to the programme statement uniformly, and so the A&O lecture programme that accompanies the booklets may last as long as two weeks or be as brief as some hours. Though institutional orientation is meant to occur within four weeks of arrival, many inmates receive admissions information late in their sentences.

## ADMISSION AND ORIENTATION HANDBOOKS

As they were in the 1960s, new inmates are usually given an A&O handbook during their orientation period[4] which is meant to provide them with general information about the institution's programs,

> . . . and the rules and regulations they will encounter during confinement. It is not a specific guide to the detailed policies of the institution or all procedures in effect. . . . Rather, the material in [the] handbook will help new inmates more quickly understand what they will be encountering when they enter prison, and hopefully assist them in their initial adjustment to institution life. (Federal Correctional Institution Tallahassee, 2000: 1)

The A&O booklet, which varies in length but is usually around 70 pages, sets out the rules and regulations of the prison as well as basic guidelines about jobs, education and other opportunities.[5] Although, like their predecessors, such documents retain a flavour of the institution's overall culture, increasingly they have come to resemble one another due to the amount of space dedicated to outlining the 'mandatory national policy' issues as directed by the federal bureau of prisons' Program Statement 5290.14 §9d(1). Some – particularly those for women's institutions – have illustrations, bright covers and are ring-bound in the manner of a short thesis. Most are merely typed, photo-copied and stapled together. Many, though not all, are offered in Spanish. Certain booklets use the first page or two for a welcoming statement from the Warden, while others omit such niceties.

These days, all admissions handbooks contain the same information about the discipline system, listing offences, the punishment they will provoke and the procedures that inmates who violate good order and discipline will undergo. Likewise, each of the contemporary A&O packs lays out the organizational structure of the institution, explaining the unit management system to the incoming prisoner. Regulations and opportunities pertaining to work, visits and education programmes are also always included. These documents, in other words, provide an overview of official BOP policy as well as some concrete examples of the system's managerial ethos and orientation. When read in comparison with one another, they also illuminate the range of local institutional cultures that exist across the large and heterogeneous penal system. When compared across time they provide some rich examples of the shifting nature of penal governance from welfare to control, and, specifically, the changing expectations of, and methods of shaping, prisoner behaviour.[6]

Although the admission documents cannot show us how penal philosophy and policies are actually implemented, they do represent an official articulation of rules, regulations and ethos. To that extent, they provide information about strategies of governance within the federal prison system and, when compared with one another, how these policies and ideologies have changed over time. Not unexpectedly, while the historical brochures are clearly written in the language of rehabilitation and care, the contemporary handbooks focus much more on issues of risk and accountability. Though inmates are still expected to change for the better while incarcerated, far less emphasis is placed on the staff's role in this transformation, as the prisoners are expected to alter themselves. As part of this shift in governance, the more recent documents tend to concentrate on issues of dangerousness and control rather than care. Utilizing an everyday, 'commonsense' language that is unlike the expert knowledge and professionalism that scholars usually attribute to risk

PUNISHMENT & SOCIETY 9(1)

discourses and more akin to the administrative managerialism of the corporate world, they set up an image of the prison as a rational, neutral institution. Yet, though the metaphors of managerialism hold prisoners, like shareholders and employees elsewhere, responsible for their choices, the documents also reveal that the prison administration, like the market, wields ultimate control over people's lives.

## CREATING GOVERNABLE INMATES

In contrast to the punitive sentiments so commonly expressed by the media and in popular discourse that picture criminals as 'animals' or the 'worst of the worst', the contemporary prison handbooks speak of and to individuals capable of exercising reason. Prisoners, it is implied, are able to exercise self-control and obedience. In the 1960s and 1970s by contrast, it was clearly assumed that the staff were pivotal in helping prisoners reach their potential in order to 'benefit in the future' (Marion Orientation, 1969: 1). Thus, whereas the contemporary manuals refer to men and women who already know their rights and responsibilities and, despite the limited options of life behind bars, are expected to take control of their own destinies, many of the earlier manuals spend considerable time on the facilitating role of the prison and its staff. At Pleasanton, for example, the staff:

> . . . hopes to assist all residents in any possible manner. We will operate the facility in a relaxed manner to allow residents to maintain their dignity and self-respect. We hope that our residents are able to take advantage of their environment and atmosphere in order to return to their home communities and accept the responsibilities of mature citizens. (p. 1)

The impact of such a rhetorical shift is manifold. Today's prisoner, who bears a striking resemblance to the traditional liberal man of reason, becomes capable of rational (free) choice (Armstrong, 2003). He is the proto-customer, always assessing his options and then selecting, rationally and soberly, the best among them. Behaviour once thought to reflect socio-economic factors, psychological disturbances and/or opportunities is, in other words, presented these days in the federal handbooks as a simple matter of choice.

Continuing in this vein, the current admissions booklets urge prisoners to be accountable for their conduct, appearance and behaviour in order to learn the most from their sentence and to earn certain rights in prison. Thus, from low security institutions to supermax, the message is the same: prisoners can and must take responsibility for their own lives. At the federal correctional complex (FCC) Coleman (2001: 2), for example, 'All inmates are responsible for their personal conduct', while at the other end of the security spectrum at ADX Florence (2001: 5), '[a]ll inmates have certain rights; such as, the right to be treated humanely. By the same token, inmates are expected to act responsibly'.

In contrast to the earlier documents which emphasize the neediness of the confined, prisoners are informed very early in the contemporary handbooks that it is up to them alone to act responsibly if they are to earn certain rights or privileges. Their 'entitlement' to certain goods and services is, in other words, dependent on the way they behave. Thus, each federal handbook today includes a section labelled 'Inmate rights and responsibilities' (PS 5290.15¶1).[7] This list, which is usually placed near the end of the document, just before the institution's disciplinary procedures, tackles a range of issues, from treating others humanely to gaining access to the courts. In each instance, as in the civil society, a person's 'rights' are presented with a mirror image of his or her duties. Prisoners, in this list, act as citizens. They 'have the right to health care, which includes nutritious meals, proper bedding and clothing and a laundry schedule for cleanliness . . .'. At the same time, however, they must recognize their own responsibility 'not to waste food, to follow the laundry schedule, maintain neat and clean living quarters . . .' etc., etc.

Utilizing this trope of citizenship in prisons, as elsewhere, functions on a number of levels. First, it is an aspirational goal, while, second, it is a means of control. It is, in other words, a strategy of governance. Not only does this kind of language seek to ensure the efficient operation of power within the prison but it helps legitimize the institution by appealing to 'commonsense' ideas and values that appear beyond reproach. Yet, both in the US Federal system and elsewhere, from ethnographic literature and first-hand accounts of life behind bars, we know that prisoners are not always provided with appropriate health care nor with nutritious meals (Bosworth, 2002; Santos, 2004; Frechea, 2005). Indeed, these everyday issues often worsen the 'pains of imprisonment', since prisoners have little control over them. That is to say, though legally prisoners may have the 'right' to such goods and services, they have little means of ensuring their delivery. In contrast, the institution has an array of sanctions it may implement when inmates are found not to have upheld their end of the bargain.

The booklets also speak of reciprocal power-sharing in statements about how prisoners and staff should interact. Unlike traditional sociological studies that represent inmates and guards pitted against one another (Sykes, 1958; DiIulio, 1987), many of the wardens' messages, particularly those drawn from the 1960s and 1970s, depict an ideal environment based on respect and a free exchange of ideas. The Warden at Atlanta (1966: 1), for example, asserts that: 'this booklet is written as a tribute to those men who have found their way back to social sobriety. In reality [it] is a dual tribute: to the men themselves, and to those other men, members of our staff, who counseled [them] while in prison'. In this vision of redemption, where he goes on to 'thank God for each man who has made these pages possible . . . by living the good life', the warden portrays staff and inmates as equals in the pursuit of 'respectability'.

More recently, the Warden at FCI Seagoville (2000: 1), explains that 'only through mutual respect, communication and cooperation can we ensure the institution operates for the positive benefit and to the advantage of all inmates'. Likewise, the warden of FCI Talladega (2001: 1) in Alabama intones: 'Neither I nor my staff believe that we can coerce you to change.' Though such statements appear to present inmates as active participants and an environment in which trust and respect are goals worthy of themselves, closer inspection of the documents reveals that administrators are not really supposing that prisoners can or should act freely. Instead, the current crop of prison handbooks make clear, through constant iterations of the negative sanctions that will ensue, that inmates must bear full responsibility for the decisions they make and must, as a result, be prepared for negative consequences if they choose not to follow prison rules.

In many ways, the federal prison handbooks argue a further-reaching case about behaviour than the earlier documents that championed the rehabilitative ideal, since they seek more complete control. More insidiously, such control is not merely forced

PUNISHMENT & SOCIETY 9(1)

upon the inmates. Rather, in lieu of simple paternalism, or of pure institutional self-interest – although there is some of that as well – they try to co-opt the prisoners into regulating their own behaviour. Through redefining provisions for courses and treatment that were previously central to the rehabilitative model: i.e. in psychology, work and education, as choices that only prisoners can make, the handbooks suggest that is in the prisoners' own self-interest to be law-abiding and obedient. Not only will changes individuals make to their behaviour and value system help them to avoid punishment but, in a shift that resonates with much of the Foucauldian literature on governmentality, acceptance of the need to reform will assist them in constructing a new and better sense of self (Rose, 1989, 2000). In this approach, the language of personal transformation is both absorbed into and helps justify the culture of control as the rhetoric of opportunity and change intertwines with and upholds practices of risk management and prison order.

Formal counselling and psychology services in most federal establishments have been dramatically cut since the demise of the rehabilitative ideal and, to a large extent, have been replaced by so-called 'self-help' courses run by inmates or prison officers known as 'correctional counselors'. Many of these courses, particularly those which are offered at women's institutions like the Federal Medical Centre (FMC) Carswell seek to address issues of 'self-esteem'. More vaguely, at FCI Tallahassee in Florida (2000): 'Unit Counselors and other staff provide a variety of other personal growth groups for inmates working towards self improvement and better coping skills', while prisoners at FCI Talladega are informed most generally of all that they are 'strongly encouraged to take advantage of any program that can lead . . . to a more complete understanding of [themselves] and [their] surrounding environment' (2001: 1). (Re)packaging rehabilitation like this, in which it is presented as a simple matter of self-help or self-esteem, conveniently disregards broader (financial, social, race or gender-based) problems ex-prisoners may encounter in any bid to avoid re-offending (Maruna and Toch, 2001; Petersilia, 2003). Similarly, in those institutions like FCI Waseca and FCI Yazoo City, where the entire enterprise of work and education has been re-labelled under the title 'self-improvement', the utility of many programmes in maintaining institutional order and in contributing real economic benefits is disguised. Presenting personal transformation in this way also overlooks the manner in which the fundamental qualities of liberty and freedom of choice that are necessary for meaningful individual change and development are deeply compromised by imprisonment. Despite the apparent flexibility of the Wardens' introductory comments and the humanity of some of the views expressed in many of the admission books, the power of prison officials is always underlined by their monopoly on force and the power to punish. 'Those who refuse to become responsible, to govern themselves ethically', as Nikolas Rose observes (2000: 202), 'have also refused the offer to become members of our moral community. Hence for them, harsh measures are entirely appropriate'. When the diffuse mode of governance encouraged by the language of 'responsibilization' fails, in other words, the true might of the prison's rigorous and punitive 'moral economy' becomes apparent.

This aspect of prison life – the emphasis on security – is depicted in a number of ways, some more subtle than others, all of which are more emphasized in the contemporary documents than in those from previous decades. Whereas FCI Fort Worth (p. 9) recognizes, for example, that 'it is not realistic to say that no one will ever violate a rule, order, policy statement, etc. . .', it seeks to reassure its readers by noting that 'punishment will not be administered for punishment's sake alone, but in the vein of good treatment'. Indeed, the earlier handbooks overall spend surprisingly little time on matters of discipline and order, in contrast to the contemporary ones that continually remind prisoners of the limits to their freedom by peppering their texts with warnings and admonitions. The precise behaviours singled out for this kind of commentary vary slightly and are often driven by traditional ideas of gender. Yet, in all establishments, the values of prudence, care and docility are encouraged. At Federal Prison Camp (FPC), Lompoc in California, for instance, inmates are warned that 'Smoking, whistling and boisterous conduct are not permitted in the dining hall' (p. 18, *Inmate Handbook*, January 2001). Similarly, at G-Unit of FCI El Reno in Oaklahoma, 'Loud voices, horseplay, etc., shall not be tolerated and is [sic] not permitted in the unit' (Section 4, *Inmate Handbook*, 2000). Singling out these kinds of activities, and referring to them in this particular type of language, reveals the ongoing paternalism of much prison administration. 'Boisterousness' and 'horseplay' after all, are activities usually associated with children rather than serious challenges to the good order and security of an institution.

Most of the current manuals are eventually more explicit about the limits to an inmate's freedom and the negative consequences that failing to change will evoke. The Warden of FCI Miami, for example, first welcomes incoming prisoners in his introduction by promising them 'a wide variety of educational and self improvement opportunities'. He then goes on to remind the new arrival that, 'what you gain during your stay here will depend largely on you'. Such individuals must be self-disciplined, he warns, because though 'Staff will make every effort to meet your basic needs . . . you, on the other hand, will be expected to provide good work habits and a positive attitude'. Lastly, he reminds his inmate readers, 'Violations of institution rules and/or regulations will not be tolerated' (FCI Miami: 2), since all prisoners are subject to formal disciplinary proceedings.

It is in this final area, in contrast to most of the earlier, historical documents from the 1960s and 1970s, that the sovereign power of the prison (Butler, 2004) is unmasked, because each contemporary handbook includes a detailed 'Prohibited Acts and Disciplinary Severity Scale'. Whereas most of the earlier handbooks speak only of vague repercussions for rule-breaking, current manuals provide instead a detailed list dividing offences and sanctions into greatest severity, high severity, moderate severity and low moderate severity derived from the Program Statement 5270.07 on *Inmate Discipline and Special Housing*. According to this list, punishments for the crime of 'killing' range from 'recision' or 'delay' of parole, while someone found guilty of 'interference of a staff member in performance of duties', so long as that interference is of a 'low moderate nature', may be subject only to a warning or reprimand. What this catalogue makes clear is that those behaviours, which are elsewhere presented in the handbooks as personal problems that prisoners must manage for their own good, are in fact subject to strictly graded punishments. Inappropriate appearance, for example, which I shall discuss in more detail below, is an offence of moderate severity. Likewise, prisoners found to have contravened prison rule 330, or 'being unsanitary, failing to keep one's person and one's quarters in accordance with posted standards', may receive any one of a number of sanctions that range from being placed on disciplinary segregation to losing their job.

PUNISHMENT & SOCIETY 9(1)

Each articulation of the power of the prison paradoxically undermines and simultaneously reinforces the broader view presented by these documents that prisoners act rationally, make their own choices and are thus fully responsible for their actions. The threat of sanctions makes it all the more necessary for inmates to monitor their behaviour while simultaneously reminding them that they are constantly under review. As a result, as Hannah-Moffat (2005) observes about the impact of risk/needs assessment practices, alterations to the prisoner's sense of self are meant to create an autonomous responsible subject rather than a dependent one. The new self that is created through counselling and education or through sheer will power is meant to be one who actively supports the same value system as the penal administrators. Given the resonance between many of the key ideas in the prison handbooks and those in documents from other industries, as any quick perusal of corporate or university governance strategies will attest, not only would such a figure be under control while incarcerated but ready for work as well (see, for example, Microsoft, 2005; GlaxoSmithKlein, 2005; Corrections Corporation America, 2005; see also Amoore, 2005).

## GENDER, RISK AND RESPONSIBILITY

A closer examination of the behaviours that institutions tend to police most closely suggests that ideas and practices of governance are shaped by beliefs about gender. This is hardly surprising. Not only have decades of feminist commentators pointed to the exclusion of women from the realm of rationality and the social contract that tends to go with it (Lloyd, 1984; Pateman, 1987), but so, too, have many identified more detailed restrictions of low-level issues in women's prisons (Howe, 1994; Bosworth, 1999). Yet, despite the work of a few notable scholars (Hannah-Moffat, 1999, 2004a, b; Stanko, 1997; Chan and Rigakos, 2002), much of the theoretical literature on risk and governance has paid little attention to socio-economic characteristics or even to specific populations.

Such androcentrism is, ironically, also one of the hallmarks of 'good management' in which practices of governance are typically legitimated by claims that each person is subject to the same rules, regulations and treatment. Usually, a regime (and a business) can be considered 'just' if the institutional processes are fair and the negative sanctions evenly distributed (Tyler, 1990; Sparks et al., 1996; Dolovitch, 2004). Given this tendency to deny or at least overlook crucial differences in the social control of populations, how might we trace some gender differences in the governance of federal prisoners?

For a start, the BOP itself officially acknowledges that female offenders 'have different physical, social and psychological needs' (PS5200.01 ¶1). Indeed, the first paragraph of Program Statement 5200.01 on *The Management of Female Offenders* requires that 'all Bureau policies, programs, and services address and consider the different needs of female offenders'. However, unlike other jurisdictions such as England and Wales, the Bureau does not uniformly include any gender-specific information in its handbooks for women.[8] Nonetheless, it is still possible to distinguish between the information distributed at the women's prisons and that given out at the men's establishments. The differences, however, are subtle. They do not leap off the page but are found in such elements as the document's tone, the order in which the information is presented, and in the extra, often rather esoteric, concerns or aspirations that are specific to the particular institution. In other words, although all facilities seek to regulate behaviour, certain issues are given more weight depending on the sex of the inmate population, while other topics are downplayed or ignored.

Predictably enough, the handbooks reveal institutional(ized) concern over women prisoners' possibly sexualized appearance and behaviour, even though such issues are never addressed in the handbooks for men's prisons. Male prisoners, instead, are warned not to engage in any sexually intimate behaviour with female visitors. At FCI Dublin, for example, the handbook clearly states that sexual relations are not permitted among the (female) inmate population, while in most of the handbooks for men's prisons, the attire of the female visitors is carefully delineated down to the precise length of women's skirts. Such recommendations reflect broader societal views where women everywhere are urged to dress and act soberly both to avoid victimization, and because of an ingrained, but usually unacknowledged fear that women might become uncontrollable (Howe, 1994; Stanko, 1997; Chancer, 2005). Everyday strategies that women are taught and expected to use run the gamut from the clothes we wear to the company we keep. Women's sexuality is usually strictly policed, though when it is 'appropriately' targeted towards a male audience a little more leeway seems to be granted.

In the admission handbook for the women's prison at FCI Dublin (September 2001: 8–9) these three issues: appearance, associates and sexuality are directly linked. Despite the serious problem of forced sex in men's institutions, none of the handbooks from men's prisons refer to sexual relations among inmates other than in the formal statement of bureau policy about sexual assault. In contrast, FCI Dublin states:

> Social interaction between inmates must be non-sexual. All inmates' general conduct and appearance should be appropriate and in good taste at all times. The following basic guidelines apply:
>
> (1) Sexual relationships between inmates are prohibited.
> (2) Inmates should dress in a non-provocative fashion and in compliance with the inmate dress code.
>
> Sitting on the ground with another inmate is permitted in the outside recreation yard only; however, lying down on the ground at any time is prohibited.
>
> Hand holding or other physical contact between inmates is *not allowed*.

FCI Dublin is alone among the recent handbooks in the individualized attention it pays to sexual relations behind bars. It is also singular in the connections it makes and the distinctions it draws between numerous kinds of intimacy: sitting together is allowed but lying down is not – no hand-holding or physical touch at all. Such attention to detail suggests that any close personal relationships between the women are being interpreted as an institutional risk.

In contrast, handbooks from the two historical co-correctional institutions, FCI Fort Worth and the Federal Youth Center Pleasanton, appear not only to encourage interaction between the women and men, but also to condone certain expressions of intimacy. At Fort Worth, for example, though the Warden primly states in his support for the long-term benefits of co-correctional programming that although 'Men and

PUNISHMENT & SOCIETY 9(1)

women need each other . . . there is an important need that men and women have for each other that has no physical contact', the handbook goes on, in words that are repeated more or less verbatim in the Pleasanton handbook to condone physical contact 'which may be described as discreet and momentary hand-holding or arm-in-arm contact while walking, standing, or seated on benches' (FCI Forth Worth, 1971–1975: 9). Without an historical example of a women's only prison to compare, I can only surmise that the difference between this leniency and the rigid denial of any physical contact at FCI Dublin rests on a particular ideology of heterosexism, in which it is not merely women's sexuality per se that must be controlled, but rather certain forms of its expression that might fall outside the purview of men (see, for some discussion of this issue, Thomas and Zaitzow, 2003).

Apparel is another element of governance and risk management given considerable attention in the modern handbooks that is largely overlooked in the historical ones. It is also a further area where the contemporary documents differentiate between the sexes. Though both women and men are advised to present themselves neatly at all times, for women, this tidiness is usually presented as an issue of obedience, whereas for men it is one of responsibility. Reflecting research elsewhere that finds that women in prison are disproportionately subject to disciplinary procedures while incarcerated, usually because of small-scale infractions against prison rules, women at FCI Dublin (p. 8, emphasis in original) are told at length how their uniforms should be worn, and are warned that they will be punished if they fail to adhere to the institution's sartorial guidelines:

> Khaki attire will be worn and the khaki dress will be worn with a khaki shirt underneath. All khaki uniforms will fit comfortably, but neatly. Baggy pants and excessively large shirts are not acceptable. Khaki shirts with tails MUST be tucked in at all times. If voluntary compliance cannot be accomplished, it will become mandatory for all shirts to be tucked with very few exceptions. Incident reports WILL BE written for non-compliance.

In contrast, when discussing the appearance of male inmates, the admission books appear to be most concerned with the impact clothes and cleanliness might have on others. The combined handbook for the male institutions of FCI and FPC Texarkana (2001: 3) stresses 'good old-fashioned' values straight from a guide to grooming and good behaviour:

> The way you look to others, both staff and inmates, will determine how they react to you. It follows that if you are neatly dressed, your hair is combed/trimmed, you are clean, and you have a smile on your face, people will react in a pleasant, positive way toward you. On the other hand, if your clothes are dirty, you need a bath, and your hair is a mess, people will react accordingly.

Here, then, appearance is made the responsibility of the individual, irrespective of financial difficulties some may encounter in paying for hair and sanitary products or in arranging for their clothes to be cleaned. The handbook at FCI Miami (p. 11) speaks of an additional goal to 'making a positive impression on others', informing its readers that appearance can provide 'a feeling of general well-being and personal satisfaction'. Appearance, in these quotes, which is always portrayed as the individual's responsibility, takes on qualities previously accorded to rehabilitation strategies offered by institutions.

Counselling, work and education were once the activities that were promoted in such a way. Now, individuals must seek satisfaction in a pair of clean pants.

Women are not only told that dressing well will be good for them, but they are also given detailed instructions of how not to present themselves. Whereas no similar guidelines exist for men, women at FCI Danbury, for example, are warned against nudity and specific alterations to shorts and t-shirts that could be construed as sexual or provocative. Like FCI Dublin, there is clearly an unexpressed concern to control women's desire. When sunbathing, prisoners are told:

> Shorts and T-shirts will be worn. Shorts may not be rolled up and fashioned into bathing suit bottoms. T-shirts may not be altered or tucked into bras. Sports bras or any revealing clothing may not be worn. Midriff, buttocks or breast areas cannot be exposed. (Handbook, FCI Danbury, 1997: 23)

Rather than regulating men's apparel in this way, men's prisons set out strict and detailed guidelines about the appearance of female visitors. Though the historical booklets for the most part ignore this issue altogether, the 1968 publication 'Facts About Atlanta' includes a brief warning (p. 8). Despite claiming no 'desire to dictate the type of clothing to be worn by female visitors', it goes on to comment that 'glaringly tight clothing, skin-tight leotards, stretch pants, and exceedingly low cut, or backless dresses, are undignified and out of place in the visiting room'. These days, most of the manuals from men's handbooks dispense with notions of dignity, although FCI Estill claims that what is at stake is a matter of 'good taste' (p. 43). Unwilling to leave the matter of decorum open to interpretation, however, this institution provides a long list of examples of the kinds of attire that would be judged unacceptable, including 'sleeveless blouses, shorts/skirts not meeting the knee, absence of undergarments, jeans with holes, see-through clothing, spandex clothes, etc.'. And, indeed, this habit of specifying the precise kinds of clothes that women visitors may not wear is common. Those in charge of the men's federal prison camp FPC Bryan (2001: 34), for example, warn that:

> Halter tops or other clothing of a suggestive or revealing nature will not be permitted in the Visiting Room. Shorts will be allowed. Skirts and dresses must be no shorter than 2″ above the knee.

FCC Beaumont, Low (2000: 14) also seems to assume a predominantly over-sexed female visiting population, reminding the male inhabitants that:

> Visitors wearing revealing clothes (halter tops, transparent or sheer garments, extremely low-cut dresses or blouses, extremely tight jeans or skirts/dresses, skirts or dresses above the knees) will not be permitted to visit. Additionally, visitors will not be permitted to wear thongs, cut-off shorts or tank tops . . .

Only at the end of this list is there any mention of the other security risk posed by visitors who might seek to confuse staff as to their status; 'clothing which resembles the inmate khaki coloured uniform'.

Altogether, the attitude towards women's appearance revealed by these handbooks suggests a very low tolerance of risk. Such intolerance deserves consideration, since its justification is by no means clear. Whereas rules governing the possession of drugs or weapons in the visiting room can easily be explained in terms of institutional safety and order, the implication of the length of a hemline is less apparent. Similarly, while forced sex must always be prevented, the negative effects of hand-holding and other expressions of intimacy are not obvious. Is it female sexuality that must be controlled or the male response to it? How important is the denial of intimate relationships to the everyday running of a prison? Or is it, in fact, the articulation of agency that is the problem?

What is clear is that despite their assertions about the importance of individual rights and responsibilities, prisons do not want inmates to express themselves freely. Even in the most humane of institutions close inmate relationships are routinely monitored, while, in the worst prisons, existing rivalries are manipulated and exacerbated by staff. Such factors form the basis of an unarticulated risk management that has, so far, escaped much attention within the scholarly literature.

## CONCLUSION: GOVERNING THROUGH MANAGEMENT

From whichever period they are derived, the federal admission handbooks are easy to read. Not only are they written in straightforward language, but the values they appeal to – whether they are religion, reform, freedom of choice, responsibility, or account-ability – are widely embraced by the broader society of the time.

All the handbooks appear committed to changing prisoners for the better. Yet the recent ones stand in stark contrast to those shaped by earlier beliefs in rehabilitation. Employing a particular rhetoric and style, they adopt many of the key ideas of adminis-trative managerialism and refer to goals, mission statements, values and rights. In the process, not only do they build a particular notion of inmate responsibility, as discussed in the wider body of literature on risk management, but they also imply that there is nothing significantly unusual or abhorrent about penal institutions. Excerpts from the handbook for the medium security Federal Correctional Complex (FCC) Beaumont (2001: 1), for example, could be drawn from the management dossier of any corpora-tion. FCC Beaumont's mission statement lays claim to a 'philosophical perspective' in which 'The Medium is the Message'. Just like any business plan, the institution's 'core values' are then identified as 'bilateral communicational respect, retention of personal dignity, courteous interpersonal interaction [and] candor at all times'.

Such managerialism affects all areas of prison governance. Rather than strict guardians or disciplinarians, for example, the prison guards at FCC Beaumont sound more like customer service agents. Like decent corporate employees, they are ready to help, and are always fair, courteous and professional in their judgement:

> Medium staff are proficient, will make sound professional decisions, and provide the professional service you are entitled to without delay. When staff deny requests, those decisions will be based in judgment and reasoning, and will be explained to you. Line and supervisory staff will be available, accessible and responsive to your requests for information or assistance, and we encourage you to make use of them to resolve problems.

So, some readers may be thinking, what is wrong with that? And indeed, if federal prison officers are indeed 'available, accessible and responsive', then we should be pleased. However, it is the very familiarity of this kind of language and its accompany-ing presentation of penal power as a mission statement that is troubling, since it all too conveniently disguises the particularity of prisons, placing them instead on par with hospitals, schools, or any private enterprise. It is this language too that masks the near-limitless sovereign power underpinning penal practice by recasting inmates as citizens or consumers with all the 'freedoms' such associations imply.

What might be some reasons for the adoption of this kind of language? Is it simply a craven attempt to disguise power inequalities, or has the shift in rhetoric and practice been inspired by other matters. Broadly speaking, after all, contemporary prisoners do have more rights than their counterparts in the 1960s and (early) 1970s. Notwithstanding the devastating assault on prisoner legal rights throughout the 1990s, inmates today have greater access to the courts and more legal protections than in many earlier times. Even so, there is a severe legitimacy deficit in the contemporary penal enterprise in the United States. Whereas once prisons were justified by their promises of reform through hard work, discipline, counselling and/or religion, these days, we are told, there are no such worthy or forward-looking ideals (Garland, 2001). We are, instead, engaging merely in mass imprisonment. Yet, for all the scholarly conviction that prisons no longer try to 'do' anything to their inmates, it is hard to imagine how those who work or are confined in penal establishments could experience their days behind bars without some sense of their future. A human institution can hardly continue if it has no coherent and morally justifiable purpose. It is not just that it is inefficient to run an institution always by force, but also that to do so would be morally, ethically and practically exhausting.

The issue, then, as many have observed, has become one of persuading individuals to govern themselves. Yet, as Hannah-Moffat (2005) observes, that is not all that is happening behind bars. Rather, certain ideas from rehabilitation, particularly the belief that personal transformation is possible, linger in a slightly new form that upholds broader ideas of risk management and control. Just as law-abiding citizens are encouraged to view themselves as active participants in the making and running of society, so, too, are prisoners. More than this, they must take responsibility for changing their very sense of self. It is this very rhetoric of these booklets which is so effectively borrowed from the corporate world that presents inmates as free, moral, agents, with control over their own actions. In turn, these ideas underpin and, in the process, legitimate, the fundamentally restricted nature of prison life.

Holding inmates responsible for all that may happen to them is, at best, disingenuous, and, at worst, symptomatic of a belief system in which individuals deemed outside the norm are found unworthy of sympathy and become expendable. This is the process labelled by Garland (2001) as a 'criminology of the other', in which greater sanctions are used with ease against entire communities who have been found lacking and judged to be dangerous. What these handbooks suggest is that this punitive shift both occurs through and is upheld by the seemingly objective and banal language of managerialism. That this rhetoric of business and its key ideas also underpin so many other kinds of institution points to a widespread and deeply entrenched way of thinking that characterizes late modern society. In this broader frame of reference, it is not just prisoners, but also the poor, the unemployed, immigrants, those deemed refractory, or anyone else unable to meet the goals of business who become suspect.

Whether in prison or the corporate world, mission statements make palatable and disguise that which is disturbing. For businesses, they provide an opportunity to soften the avarice of capitalism and represent themselves as organizations imbued with 'values'

PUNISHMENT & SOCIETY 9(1)

and virtue. When used by penal administrators, they rhetorically position the prison as more than just a site of punishment and confinement. By presenting the goals of the institution as in the interests of those governed by them they effectively denigrate all alternative viewpoints and behaviour. By employing everyday language and beliefs they co-opt the mainstream. In so doing, the ideology of business administration, in which institutions are driven by a desire for greater economic efficiency rather than loftier goals of justice or morality, resembles other technologies that enabled terrible acts to occur (Bauman, 1989).

## Acknowledgements

I thank Anthony Gerbino, Jonathan Simon and Malcolm Feeley and the anonymous reviewers for their comments on earlier versions of this article. I also acknowledge the assistance of the Federal Bureau of Prisons in providing me with copies of contemporary and historical admissions and orientation materials.

## Notes

1  For felicity of style, I refer to these items interchangeably as 'manuals', 'handbooks', 'orientation packets', 'booklets' and 'documents'. I cite introductory comments that are usually attributed to the warden, as well as specific prison rules and institutional arrangements that are covered. At all times, though they are drawn from different institutions and time periods, I am referring to the same kinds of documents.
2  Atlanta was the second institution built under the so-called Three Prisons Act of 1891 that founded the federal prison system.
3  According to this same Programme Statement, an institution may elect not to collate the information into a booklet form, but merely to hand out separate pieces of information. Whichever option they choose, institutions must provide written materials to supplement the A&O programme.
4  Prisoners may also receive instruction manuals from other divisions within the prison, including work, religion and education.
5  I obtained copies of the booklets for each contemporary US federal prison by filing a Freedom of Information Act (FOIA) request in 2000 while writing a book on the federal prison system (Bosworth, 2002). These items trickled in over the course of about 18 months. Some booklets were sent in electronic format and others were mailed in hard copy. Since I received them, additional institutions have been opened whose manuals are not included in the research for this article. It is also possible that the wording of the A&O packs will have been altered in the intervening period, although typically the texts are not changed much other than in response to new prison regulations or to the arrival of a new warden. To address this concern, however, where possible I indicate the date of the booklet I am using. The historical booklets were obtained in much the same manner, by virtue of a second FOIA request lodged in 2005. Due to time constraints and because I was informed that few manuals from the past had actually been retained by the Bureau of Prisons, I merely requested a selection of handbooks rather than examples from each facility.
6  In my comparison of the documents, I began by carefully studying the current booklets. At first I read merely for 'manifest content', looking for themes to emerge. When it became clear that certain key topics were common across the texts,

including an institutional concern over physical contact and appearance as well as a desire to inculcate the 'values' of accountability, responsibility and respect, I re-read a selection of the booklets. Starting with those from the women's prisons, I looked for key words as well as for general themes related to the topics above. The terms that I searched for included: physical contact; hair; appearance; visitor(s); women/woman; responsibility; respect; clothing and attire. I also examined all wardens' comments. In my analysis of the historical sources I paid greater attention to issues of individualization, treatment and care. Where possible I also looked for discussions of gender.

7  Of the historical manuals, only the undated one from the Federal Youth Center Pleasanton and the mid-1980s one from the Metropolitan Correctional Center (MCC) Miami include a similar list. Both of these handbooks also delineate some offences against prison rules and their consequences.

8  In contrast, the HM Prison Service, for example, has worked with the Prison Reform Trust (2003) in England and Wales to produce a *Prisoners' Information Book Specifically for Women Prisoners and Young Offenders* that addresses pregnancy behind bars, mother and baby units and specific women's health issues.

## References

Amoore, Lucy (2005) 'Risk, reward and discipline at work', *Economy and Society* 33(2): 174–96.

Bauman, Zygmunt (1989) *Modernity and the Holocaust*. Cambridge: Polity Press.

Bosworth, Mary (1999) *Engendering resistance: Agency and power in women's prisons*. Aldershot: Ashgate.

Bosworth, Mary (2002) *The U.S. Federal Prison System*. Thousand Oaks, CA: Sage.

Butler, Judith (2004) *Precarious life: The powers of mourning and violence*. London: Verso.

Chan, Wendy and George Rigakos (2002) 'Risk, and crime and gender', *British Journal of Criminology* 42(4): 743–61.

Chancer, Lynn (2005) *Provoking assaults*. Chicago, IL: University of Chicago Press.

Corrections Corporation America (2005) *The CCA way*. Available at: http://www.correctionscorp.com/guidingFLYER.pdf

DiIulio, John (1987) *Governing prisons*. New York: Free Press.

Dolovitch, Sharon (2004) 'Legitimate punishment in liberal democracy', *Buffalo Criminal Law Review* 307.

Federal Bureau of Prisons (1997) *Management of female offenders*. PS5200.01. Available at: http://www.bop.gov

Federal Bureau of Prisons (2001) *Security designation and custody classification manual*. PS5100.07. Available at: http://www.bop.gov

Federal Bureau of Prisons (2003) *Admission and orientation program*. PS5290.14. Available at: http://www.bop.gov

Federal Bureau of Prisons (2004) *Inmate discipline and special housing*. Program Statement 5270.07. Available at: http://www.bop.gov

Feeley, Malcolm and Jonathan Simon (1994) 'Actuarial justice: The emerging new criminal law', in David Nelken (ed.) *The future of criminology*, pp. 173–201. London: Sage.

Frechea, Tara (2005) 'Health care', in M. Bosworth (ed.) *Encyclopedia of prisons and correctional facilities*, p. 400. Thousand Oaks: Sage.

PUNISHMENT & SOCIETY 9(1)

Garland, David (1985) *Punishment and welfare: A history of penal strategies*. Aldershot: Ashgate.

Garland, David (1996) 'The limits of the sovereign state: strategies of crime control in contemporary society', *British Journal of Criminology* 36(4): 445–71.

Garland, David (2001) *The culture of control: Crime and social order in contemporary society*. New York: Oxford University Press.

GlaxoSmithKlein (2005) *Code of conduct*. Corporate Policy POL-GSK-001 v02. Available at: www.gsk.com/corporate_responsibility/cr_issue/be_code_conduct.htm

Hannah-Moffat, Kelly (1999) 'Moral agent or actuarial subject: Risk and Canadian women's imprisonment', *Theoretical Criminology* 3(1): 71–94.

Hannah-Moffat, Kelly (2004a) 'Gendering risk at what cost: Negotiations of gender and risk in Canadian women's prisons', *Feminism & Psychology* 14(2): 243–9.

Hannah-Moffat, Kelly (2004b) 'Losing ground: Gendered knowledges, parole risk and responsibility', *Social Politics* 11(3): 363–85.

Hannah-Moffat, Kelly (2005) 'Criminogenic needs and the transformative risk subject: Hybridizations of risk/need in penality', *Punishment and Society* 7(1): 29–51.

Hood, C., H. Rothstein and R. Baldwin (2001) *The government of risk: Understanding risk regulation regimes*. Oxford: Oxford University Press.

Howe, Adrien (1994) *Punish and critique*. London: Routledge.

Hudson, Barbara (2003) *Justice in the risk society*. London: Sage.

Levinson, Robert (1994) 'The development of classification and programming', in John Roberts (ed.). *Escaping prison myths: Selected topics in the history of federal corrections*. Washington, DC: American University Press.

Lloyd, Genevieve (1984) *The man of reason: Male and female in Western philosophy*. London: Routledge.

Maruna, Shadd and Hans Toch (2001) *Making good: How ex-convicts reform and rebuild their lives*. American Psychological Association.

Microsoft (2005) *Who we are/missions& values*. Available at: www.members.microsoft.com/careers/mslife/whoweare/mission.mspx.

O'Malley, Pat (1992) 'Risk, power and crime prevention', *Economy and Society* 21(3): 252–75.

O'Malley, Pat (1996) 'Risk and responsibility', in A. Barry, T. Osborne and N. Rose (eds) *Foucault and political reason*, pp. 189–208. London, UCL Press.

O'Malley, Pat (1999) 'Volatile and contradictory punishment', *Theoretical Criminology* 3(2): 175–96.

O'Malley, Pat (2002) 'Globalizing risk? Distinguishing styles of "neo-liberal" criminal justice in Australia and the USA', *Criminal Justice* 2(2): 205–22.

O'Malley, Pat (2004) 'The uncertain promise of risk', *Australian and New Zealand Journal of Criminology* 37(3): 323–43.

Pateman, Carole (1987) *The sexual contract*. Stanford, CA: Stanford University Press.

Petersilia, Joan (2003) *When prisoners come home*. New York: Oxford University Press.

Prison Reform Trust (2003) *Prisoners' information book: Women prisoners and young offenders*. London: Prison Reform Trust.

Rose, Nikolas (1989) *Governing the self: The shaping of the private self*. New York: Routledge.

Rose, Nikolas (2000) 'Government and control', in D. Garland and R. Sparks (eds) *Criminology and social theory*. Oxford: Clarendon Press.

Santos, Michael (2004) *About prison*. Belmont, CA: Wadsworth.

Simon, Jonathan (1997) 'Governing through crime', in Lawrence Friedman and George Fisher (eds) *The crime conundrum: Essays on criminal justice*. Boulder, CO: Westview Press.

Sparks, Richard (2000) 'Perspectives on risk and penal politics', in T. Hope and R. Sparks (eds) *Crime, risk and insecurity: Law and order in everyday life and political discourse*. New York: Routledge.

Sparks, Richard; Anthony Bottoms and Will Hay (1996) *Prisons and the problem of order*. Oxford: Clarendon Press.

Stanko, Elizabeth (1997) 'Safety talk: Conceptualizing women's risk assessment as a "technology of the soul"', *Theoretical Criminology* 1(4): 479–99.

Sykes, Gresham (1958) *The society of captives*. Princeton, NJ: Princeton University Press.

Thomas, Jim and Barbara Zaitzow (eds) (2003) *Women in prison: Gender and social control*. Boulder, CO: Lynne Rienner Publishers.

Tyler, Tom (1990) *Why people obey the law*. New Haven, CT: Yale University Press.

MARY BOSWORTH is University Lecturer in Criminology and Fellow of St Cross College at the University of Oxford. She has published widely on matters of imprisonment and punishment in the US, the UK and France. Her current research examines immigration detention in Britain and America.

# [13]

## AGAINST 'GREEN' CRIMINOLOGY

Mark Halsey*

*This article offers an overview of recent work on environmental crime and regulation. It demonstrated the majority of such scholarship is imbued by quite problematic ideas concerning how best to envisage the nature of environmental harm and the type of regulatory structures which should be promoted to assist in the amelioration of environmental damage. The article concludes with a very brief discussion of the kinds of theoretical tools which might be used in place of orthodox framings of environmental crime and its prevention.*

Let me preface my critique of green criminology with some initial observations about environmental matters. Like previous decades, the first few years of the 21st century have heralded the notion that global depletions of biodiversity, as well as human-induced declinations in air, water and soil quality, are chronic processes rather than fleeting events. These are not, it now seems clear, the result of some inexplicable 'blip' in (supposedly predictable) weather patterns, breeding cycles, market forces or the like. Instead, they are fundamentally linked to the 'normal' operation of various political, cultural and economic practices (United Nations Environment Programme 2002). As a result, and with the possible exception of terrorism and the (in)actions of so-called 'rogue' states, investigating the causes and possible remedies of environmental harm (however defined) are now key priorities for most Western nations.[1] Environmental problems are, in short, recognized to be of a central and serious kind, such that those who trivialize or downplay the fate of the globe are increasingly being asked by governments, by law, by green groups, and by 'average' citizens to justify their (improbable/imprudent) position.

In this context—and as a discipline intimately concerned with the geographies, intensities, frequencies and visibilities of harm—it would be reasonable to assume that the vicissitudes of environmental damage and environmental crime (two very different things) would by now constitute central objects of criminological thought (Cohen 1988). For, make no mistake, environmental harms do markedly impact the capacities of particular populations to actively and benignly engage with the flows of matter–energy conducive to what might be termed 'non-toxic lives'. Sound evidence of this can be found in what remains the most comprehensive study on global ecosystemic health, conducted by some 175 scientists on behalf of the United Nations Development

* PhD, Criminal Justice Program, School of Law, Flinders University of South Australia, Adelaide SA 5001, Australia. E-mail: mark.halsey@flinders.edu.au.

[1] See, e.g. documents emerging from the UN Commission on Sustainable Development, 11th Session, New York, 28 April–9 May 2003. Evidence of further commitment toward resolving particular kinds of environmental damage is (despite the lack of support from countries such as the US and Australia) reflected in the text, 'Kyoto Protocal—Status of Ratification, 10th July 2003' (84 Signatures, 111 Ratifications, Acceptances, Approvals and/or Accessions) (available online at http://unfccc.int/resource/kpstats.pdf).

Programme, the United Nations Environment Programme, the World Bank and the World Resources Institute. The report shows that:

Half of the world's wetlands were lost [during the twentieth century]; Logging and conversion have shrunk the world's forests by as much as half [to around 3 billion hectares]; Some 9 percent of the world's tree species are at risk of extinction; Tropical deforestation may exceed 130,000 square kilometers per year; Fishing fleets are 40 percent larger than the ocean can sustain; Nearly 70 percent of the world's major marine fish stocks are overfished or are being fished at their biological limit; Soil degradation has affected two-thirds of the world's agricultural lands in the last 50 years; Some 30 percent of the world's original forests have been converted to agriculture; Since 1980, the global economy has tripled in size and [the] population has grown by 30 percent to 6 billion people; Dams, diversions or canals fragment almost 60 percent of the world's largest rivers; Twenty percent of the world's freshwater fish are extinct, threatened or endangered. (Media Release, 17 April 2000, Washington, DC, summarizing key trends emerging from *World Resources 2000–2001: People and Ecosystems: The Fraying Web of Life*.)

Despite such disturbing trends—whose 'truth effects' will always be subject to the power of particular discourses to (re)construct the limits of harm—criminological concern for the environment is, quite demonstrably, by far and away the exception to the rule (but see Goff and Geis 1993; Edwards *et al.* 1996; Williams 1996; Beirne 1998; Halsey and White 1998; Pearce and Tombs 1998; A-Khavari *et al.* 1999; Halsey 1997a; 1997b; 1999; Seis 1999; Walters 2004). A key question, therefore, is this: why, at a time when most disciplines (e.g. politics, economics, history, cultural studies) have built or extended their oeuvres to include an analysis of environmental problems, has criminology seen fit *not* to do so? Alternatively, why are there so few criminologists writing about environmental harm/crime, as opposed to the multitude prepared to discuss such issues as illicit drug taking, rape, robbery, homicide and other so-called 'orthodox' crimes?

Such questions stand to generate many important insights about criminology as well as those working within (and beyond) its confines. Elsewhere, I respond to these issues and look specifically at the relationship between criminology, andro/anthropocentrism, and the marginalization of Nature as the other of 'real' criminological work (see Halsey 2005a). For the moment, though, I want to leave these questions at the rhetorical level (as events which cast a shadow over the remainder of this discussion) and move instead toward an equally pressing issue. This has to do with how criminology has talked about environmental crime/harm to date and the problematic dimensions of such discourse.

I want to argue that green criminologists have, with few exceptions, drawn implicitly or explicitly upon one or a combination of five (competing) environmental perspectives— all of which emerge within, and carry with them the kinds of shortcomings associated with, modernist thought.[2] These perspectives are *liberal ecology* (World Commission on Environment and Development 1987; Barbier 1989; Pearce *et al.* 1989; Barde and Pearce 1991; Pearce 1991), *ecomarxism* (Bahro 1984; Castillina 1985; Dunkley 1992; Pepper 1993), *ecofeminism* (Plumwood 1986; Meis and Shiva 1993), *deep ecology* (Leopold 1970; Naess 1973; 1989; Devall and Sessions 1985; Tobias 1985), and *social ecology*

---

[2] Carrington (1994: 263), following the work of Hebdige, has tendered three defining characteristics of modernity: 'its essentializing conception of history, politics, society and the transcendent subject, its teleological search for origins or causes, and its utopian solutions to the problems of modern[ity].'

AGAINST 'GREEN' CRIMINOLOGY

(Bookchin 1986; 1987; Clark 1990; Merchant 1992).[3] My intention is to show that adherence to any of these streams of thought necessarily leads to highly questionable renderings of Nature, society, subjectivity and, concomitantly, of what causes and what might be seen to prevent environmental damage. Green criminology does not, I will argue, possess the lexicon required to move beyond modernist conceptions of harm and reparation. Moreover, I want to suggest that when criminologists engage the term 'green', they necessarily manifest the kind of political baggage which comes with dividing the world into distinct—one might say, polar—domains. Getting better at socio–ecological relations will not, I contend, be simply a matter of siding with the green or red, the anthropocentric or ecocentric, the classical view of offending or the positivist, the constructionist take on 'reality' or the essentialist (Platonic), and so forth. Rather, improved functioning of socio–ecological worlds needs to be tied to ways of thinking–acting which subvert binary modes of thought (i.e. thought which results from the habit of segmenting the world into polar opposites and unified categories).[4] Indeed, I want to suggest that *the term 'green' should be jettisoned from criminological discourse*, primarily because it does not adequately capture the inter-subjective, inter-generational, or inter-ecosystemic processes which combine to produce scenarios of harm. There are particular costs associated with thinking and writing the world in various ways, and green criminology, I will suggest, misunderstands the nature and extent of the task at hand.

## *Review and Critique*

### *The problem of anthropocentrism*

Perhaps the most worrying trend emerging from recent criminological work on environmental issues is that such efforts have generally been of an *un*critical kind. By this I mean that such studies support and adhere to the tenets associated with what I have

---

[3] Under what I term *liberal ecology* (which is, geopolitically, the most dispersed of environmental philosophies), environmental harm tends to be reduced to problems of participatory democracy and unresponsive market mechanisms. In all instances, liberal ecology views as *compatible* both the long-term health of ecosystems *and* the maintenance of the structures inherent to liberal democratic/late-capitalist societies. For *ecomarxists* (who take, as their starting point, the few remarks made by Marx and Engels on the ecologically destructive aspects of industrialism), the primary cause of environmental degradation is capitalism or, indeed, any system based on exponential material growth and antagonistic class relations. The 'solution' to environmental degradation is, therefore, framed in terms of common ownership of the means of production and the application of 'objective' scientific data to environmental problems, like the greenhouse effect, hazardous waste and deforestation. *Ecofeminists* (coming to prominence in the 1970s and beyond in the wake of classic feminist texts by such authors as Marilyn Waring, Simone De Beauvoir, Marilyn French and Gloria Steinem) consider environmental damage to be symptomatic of entrenched patriarchal social relations. In this sense, it is *men* (specifically, the knowledges and practices that they embody and perpetuate), and not just economic *systems* per se (feudalism, capitalism, socialism, anarchism), that are held to be the catalyst of environmental destruction. By excluding women from key debates and issues, men, it is contended, can *only* reinforce androcentrism and its necessary corollary, ecocide. For *deep ecologists*, environmental damage is viewed as the product of widespread ignorance of 'the interconnectedness of all things'—particularly of the individual (or 'small' self) to the world (or 'larger' self). In an attempt to move beyond crude anthropocentric accounts, deep ecology ascribes intrinsic value and indeed moral consideration to ecosystems writ large (called 'biocentric egalitarianism'). Here, indigenous knowledges of various terrains are configured as overarching panaceas to ecological (and social) dilemmas. *Social ecology* conceives environmental problems not only as the logical extension of the domination of women by men, but also of men by men—particularly of those men who hold and wield political and economic power over those who do not. Social ecologists argue that it is possible to read or discern from nature the 'correct' or best way of organizing social relations. Such an idea—echoing the project of Comte—goes hand in hand with the belief that the world has, beneath all its veneers, surfaces, appearances and impressions, an essential and timeless body of signs, waiting to be read and acted on by 'man'. For a detailed account of these perspectives, see Halsey (2005a, forthcoming).

[4] In the final section, I offer a very brief examination of the work of Gilles Deleuze and Felix Guattari as a possible means of reinventing criminological talk about ecological matters.

termed a liberal ecological outlook—an outlook imbued by *anthropocentric* principles and practices. Very briefly, liberal ecology views environmental problems as symptoms of unchecked—but ultimately controllable—market forces. It is no surprise, then, that the solutions to environmental crime (and environmental harm, more generally) have, in the main, been posed in terms of how best to (a) modify (but not radically alter) industrial processes, (b) modify (but not radically alter) environmental law, and (c) modify (but not radically alter) the nature and limits of enforcement (see, e.g. Del Frate and Norberry 1993; Grabosky 1994; Gunningham *et al.* 1995; McDowell 1997; Grabosky and Gant 2000; Davies 2002). A closer analysis of a relevant text will illustrate my concerns.

In a recent piece by the Deputy Commissioner of the Australian Federal Police (AFP), Davies (2002) offers a brief overview of the cost and scope of the illicit trade in wildlife—'said to exceed five million birds, thirty thousand primates and fifteen million furs per year'. He continues, 'The economic value of this trade is estimated at US$1.5 billion and throughout the world over 600 species are threatened by th[e] trade [in wildlife]' (Davies 2002: 20). These are, without doubt, statistics to be deeply troubled by. But equally troubling is the way in which enforcement agencies portray their activities along binary lines. Specifically, the limits of *real* environmental harm equate to all those activities of an ecologically damaging nature *as proscribed by law* (e.g. wildlife smuggling, illegal dumping of chemicals, etc.). For instance, Davies writes that 'Environmental criminals can include the highest level of corporations, organized crime, and as we are now well aware, terrorists' (2002: 21). Here, a definitive line is drawn between the 'inside' and 'outside' of environmental crime, and, more particularly, who counts as 'real' environmental offenders and who do not. On the inside are the illegal activities of individuals and corporations which are capable of being formally construed as 'environmental crime' in a court of law (typically, and most problematically, a court severely limited in power and jurisdiction).[5] On the outside, though, are all those actors and activities which are, for all intents and purposes, 'untouchable'. What these actors do (and do not do) may be intentional, may be harmful, and may lead to long-term deleterious effects on ecosystems, but so long as such acts occupy a sphere beyond that dealt with by enforcement agencies, they do not, indeed cannot, constitute environmental crime.

This is a highly problematic state of affairs because one of the greatest perpetrators of ecological damage is the (post-)modern state (see Goff and Geis 1993; Williams 1996; Halsey 1997b). And yet, the body of this offender will not—indeed, cannot—make it

---

[5] In a three-year period, spanning 1994–6, the Victorian Environment Protection Agency (the primary regulator of a southern Australian State, composed of some 4.5 million people) prosecuted a total of 133 cases, with a conviction rate of 38 per cent. The most common penalty in this period was a fine ($n = 75$) and the average amount imposed was $2,750 (ranging from $40 for littering to $16,000 for breaching air-pollution statutes) (see Environment Protection Authority 1994; 1995; 1996; 1997). This situation continues to reflect national trends up to and including the end of 2002 (see prosecution data, given in the annual reports of each Environment Protection Authority). The fact that so few people receive substantial fines or go to prison for environmental offences surely cannot be an indication that all is well with humanity and various bioregions (i.e. that the harms perpetrated against earth are somehow small, discrete, unintentional or the like). Equally, the fact that the most common type of environmental crime (from an international perspective) likely to result in a prison sentence is 'exceeding bag limits' for various fish species does not mean that the damage 'caused' by such offences is the most serious environmental problem which people the world over consciously or actively perpetuate. Rather, such a circumstance is, critically, an indication of what regulators 'choose' or, more accurately, have the capacity, to name (and, where possible, enforce) as environmental crime. There are many important parallels here with the way in which formal definitions of violence are constructed in a manner to exclude much of what governments, corporations, police and armies do (see Box 1983).

onto Davies' (nor any other liberal ecological) list of environmental criminals, due mainly to the structural constraints which attend a system geared toward exponential profit and commodification of earth. There is a serious problem, therefore, with the way in which enforcement bodies envision, speak about, and frame environmental harm.[6] The most dangerous of these is the belief that the factors which compel people to commit environmental crime are somehow logically separate from those factors and conditions which lead the state to permit environmental damage 'by other means' and at different speeds and scales from moment to moment. Put another way, it is the height of naiveté to believe that capturing environmental criminals means arresting the alliances, personal habits and institutional routines that sanction a more generalized mode of environmental decay.

In addition to the above type of text, there is, of course, a (small) body of criminological writings on environmental harm which is concerned to move beyond the problems harboured by liberal ecology. Indeed, several well known criminological and socio–legal journals have, in recent times, devoted whole issues to addressing themes such as 'The Environment and Social Justice' (Goff and Geis 1993), 'Environmental Victims' (Williams 1996), 'For a Green Criminology' (Beirne 1998), 'Interdisciplinary Perspectives on Environmental Law' (A-Khavari *et al.* 1999), 'Environmental Justice Policy' (Seis 1999) and 'Globalisation and Environmental Harm' (Shank 2002). In addition to these, several books have been published dealing with matters of ecological criminality (e.g. Edwards *et al.* 1996; Pearce and Tombs 1998). Environmental criminological texts situated beyond liberal ecology fall into two broad ecophilosophical schools of thought—*biocentrism* (deep ecology) and *ecocentrism* (ecomarxism, ecofeminism and social ecology) (for a criminologically based outline of the basic principles behind each of these ecophilosophical schools, as well as that of anthropocentrism, see Halsey and White 1998). Although the vast majority of this literature adopts a critically informed position on the structures and processes leading to environmental damage, there are a number of problems associated with such efforts, which need, I think, to be brought to light. As a means of elucidating some of the problems associated with these ecophilosophical schools generally, I will examine the biocentrically informed work of Barnett (1999) and the ecocentrically based work of Benton (1998), as well as that of Lynch and Stretsky (2003).

*The problem of biocentrism*

Barnett's article, 'The Land Ethic and Environmental Crime', attempts to build an 'eco-critical' definition of, and means for dealing with, environmental offences based around the writings of Aldo Leopold—specifically, his 1947 work, *A Sand County*

---

[6] There is, of course, a substantial criminological literature (e.g. Tappan 1947; Sutherland 1949; Schwendinger and Schwendinger 1975) dealing with what should fall within and beyond the criminological gaze. My own view is that criminology should not be constrained by a strictly delimited field of analysis. Indeed, the vitality of the discipline depends on its capacity to subject to critique events and processes which, when viewed through one lens or another, are apt to attract the label 'harm' or a closely associated term. Indeed, a key critical criminological task is to bring to light the factors which function to divide criminal from so-called normal, routine or acceptable practice. This, arguably, is what is so striking about environmental issues and their relation to the criminological purview: namely, that it is very difficult to rename and re-envision much of what we take to be pleasurable, profitable and progressive as one and the same as those events which contribute to the diminution of species and the toxic transformation of the biosphere.

HALSEY

*Almanac.*[7] Specifically, the category 'environmental crime' should be reorganized around Leopold's edict that, '[A] thing is right when it tends to preserve the integrity, stability and beauty of the biotic community. It is wrong when it tends otherwise' (quoted in Barnett 1999: 162). The failure to base definitions of environmental crime around this principle has led, according to Barnett, to a sharp 'divergence between environmental harm in fact and environmental harm as conceived in law' (1999: 182). Further, Barnett explains that Leopold's work is not some romantic call for a 'return to nature', but is, instead, the result of 'good science'. As he writes, 'Leopold's observation of ecosystem dynamics led to *his scientific understanding of sustainability*. He considers the land ethic as science-based in that it aligned ethical demands with *objective need*' (1999: 182, emphasis added). Such an ethic—grounded as it is in science—has, according to Barnett, the capacity to radically transform social relations because 'land owners [would come] to recognise the realities of interdependency and sustainability and accept [ . . . ] self imposed limits on their behaviour' (1999: 182). In addition to Leopold, the work of Edwin Sutherland is invoked by Barnett as a means of illustrating the power of group norms over law in influencing and changing behaviour—the idea being that people learn and internalize environmentally destructive rules and rationales and that they can therefore replace these with rules and rationales of an ecological kind.

From this brief summary, it should be clear that there are a number of problems with Barnett's attempts to reframe matters of environmental harm within a biocentric framework. First, the urge to identify 'right' conduct with everything that tends toward 'integrity, stability and beauty' is a decidedly modernist, not to mention dangerous, idea. For one thing, it ignores the fact that ecosystems do *not* operate around steady-state principles. Instead, the so-called 'integrity' and 'stability' of 'the biotic community' fluctuates in accordance with forces often generated from those biotic communities themselves—storms, drought, fire, volcanic eruptions, and so forth. On a second and related count, it is questionable whether it is possible to logically speak of 'the biotic community' as something existing externally to the happenings of 'humanity'. Perhaps a more productive approach would be to say that there are numerous and heterogeneous interfaces between bodies and practices—some leading to monstrous crossbreeds (e.g. dioxin) and black holes (e.g. nuclear waste repositories) and some drawing lines of deterritorialization (e.g. hemp-based paper mills, nuclear-free zones) (Deleuze & Guattari 1996). Determining whether one is witnessing the former or the latter is an ongoing contestable project that cannot be brought to a halt by some casual and ontologically questionable reference to absolute beauty or integrity.

One might say, therefore, that the concept of 'ecosystemic integrity', along with that of the 'beauty' of biotic environments, are anything but an objective means of positing

---

[7] The use of Leopold's work is, in itself, a problematic move, since it does not sit easily alongside the main tenets of eco-critical criminology (see Seis 1993). One of the key claims of eco-critical criminology is that the human capacity to colonize and dominate most if not all parts of the biosphere *distinguishes* it from *all* other species. Leopold, on the other hand, was firmly of the view that humans are, as he puts it, merely 'plain members' of the biotic community. In short, it is probably not a wise decision to call upon a biocentric theorist to fill out the tenets of an eco-critical criminology, since the latter is somewhat removed from the principle of biospheric egalitarianism (i.e. the belief in the moral equivalence and worth of all species). This said, the point of Barnett's article is to establish a new relationship between (environmental) law and ethics. Indeed, he makes the general point that law necessarily stems from an ethics of one kind or another (1999: 166). This is, of course, a fair enough contention. However, it is also important to know that much law is predicated on *moral*, not ethical, principles (where morality denotes discursive practices of right and wrong, whose form and limits are informed by religious or other transcendental narratives).

a socio–environmental ethic(s). Indeed, what is most apparent is the way in which state departments co-opt the concept of 'ecosystemic integrity' to justify present modes of harvesting and managing all manner of 'resources' (fibres, grains, fruits, flesh, skins, and so forth). The fact, for example, that clearfell logging and the concept of ecological integrity are made to stand as synonymous events in the eyes of most foresters should indicate that what matters in environmental conflict is not the 'harm' attached to a given state of affairs, so much as how various elements (bureaucratic, protest, etc.) bring about particular alignments between expert discourse and the cultural imaginary (see Luke 1997). By taking the concept of 'beauty' as timeless rather than discursively constructed, Barnett is unable to account for the fact that—to continue the example— forest administrators generally view a newly felled coupe as something of great beauty, since it represents the opportunity for 'new' forest structures to emerge (where each stand of trees will be incessantly managed to display the same age, height and density). This, it should be recalled, is the bureaucrat's vision of a forest, exhibiting unsurpassed levels of 'ecological integrity' and 'stability'. One might also draw attention to the way in which 'beauty' has been used to oppress, injure and restrain, not just bodies of Nature, but the bodies of women as well (e.g. the practices of Chinese foot-binding, genital mutilation, and the like). This again shows that of critical importance in environmental matters is an awareness of how words and their associated (assembled) meanings evolve with respect to configurations of power and desire.

A third problem with Barnett's work is its uncritical adherence to the Western scientific method and its ability to know or recognize 'sustainability' in all its guises. Numerous studies have shown that science holds little capacity to name or capture the combination of forces which lead to environmental damage (see Beck 1992; Lash *et al.* 1996). Moreover, where science believes it has adequately categorized Nature, this has most often led not to benign practice, but to a range of unforeseeable deleterious effects (e.g. failure of coupes to regenerate, sedimentation of fresh water streams, declining numbers of arboreal and ground dwelling mammals, etc.). In short, there is ample reason to be highly suspicious of any theory or ethic which tries to derive legitimacy on the basis of its scientificity. Biological science, just like criminology, is a discourse which, while leading to real effects, is constituted and sustained through all manner of rhetorical manoeuvres and assumptions about the limits of knowledge and the operation of power. For this reason alone, science needs always to be subject to critique, not blind acceptance.[8]

A fourth and final problem associated with Barnett's work is his reluctance to think through the criminal-justice-oriented implications of defining environmental crime according to the tenets of the land ethic. As he admits, this approach will see a whole host of acts, presently cast as 'environmental harm in fact' (i.e. harms which fall outside the boundaries drawn by law), come under the rubric of the juridical armature. This, I would suggest, is somewhat antithetical to the project(s) of critical criminology which, as I understand it, advocates for *less*, not more, state intervention in social, economic and ecological life. Moreover, criminologists have shown time and time again that criminalizing a behaviour is a very poor way of reducing its occurrence. Admittedly,

---

[8] This thought, of course, extends to the ecological trends cited at the outset of this discussion. That is, information contained in the World Resources text produces *truth claims* (by injecting a body of data into the body of particular social and political networks) and not *the* Truth about ecosystemic deterioration.

Barnett does invoke Sutherland's work as a means for suggesting that of ultimate importance in ecological matters is that ethics eventually must replace law/juridical coercion. But this does not go very far towards explaining how such an ethic might arise. Indeed, one might question whether it is in fact desirable for all persons to live by the tenets of one edict above all others. One could even say that such a plan harbours the potential for perpetuating a kind of (ecological) fascism. This is something that biocentrists do not seem to want to grasp—that there is strength in diversity of socio-ecological knowledges and practices and that the nature of Nature is not its capacity to foster an equality of relationships or some perfect symbiotic state, but its tendency toward disequilibrium and difference. Given such conditions, it is very hard to see how 'correct action' or 'best practice' could equate to rigidly adhering to the terrains and experiences mapped out by a single edict/principle. Profit, Christ, Progress and Reason have all, at one time or another (and even collectively), been touted as *the* way to a perfected state of affairs. And all, of course, have led to untold violence for countless human and non-human worlds. How logical, therefore, is it to think that the 'new' idols of Integrity, Stability and Beauty will bring an end to such violence?

### The problem of ecocentrism

Perhaps the key criminological statement to emerge around an ecocentric theme in recent times is by Ted Benton (a long-time proponent of ecomarxism), entitled 'Rights and Justice on a Shared Planet: More Rights or New Relations'. This piece—appearing in what has become a key collection in the criminological literature on environmental harm—offers a sophisticated account of environmental protection based on an ecocentric conception of rights and obligations. It discusses and moves beyond both Peter Singer's utilitarian approach and Tom Regan's deontological (consequentialist) stance to the protection of species in order to chart a 'relational' ethical program for combating human-induced environmental decay. Benton sums up his outlook as follows: 'The aim would be to generate harmonious, benevolent and co-operative spirals, as against destructive, competitive and antagonistic ones, through the establishment of new dominant patterns of interaction, experiences and spontaneous sentiments' (1998: 171). He continues:

This alternative would be a many-sided project for social, economic and ecological transformation inspired by spontaneous moral sentiments which flow from anxiety and horror in the face of continuing human destruction of non-human nature, and by the egalitarian co-operative and popular democratic values inherited from earlier anarchist and socialist traditions, and now carried forward by the feminist, peace, green and other progressive social movements. (1998: 171)

To be fair, Benton is quick to admit the utopian nature of his perspective. But such a recognition does not counter other shortcomings harboured by his work. These have mainly to do with the problematic conception of 'human nature', as well as the championing of a *universal* system of human and non-human rights. On the first count, the notion of human nature deployed by Benton is one which claims that there is something that—after all is said and done—gives humanity an *essential* aspect. For Benton, this aspect waxes and wanes between the two poles of innate aggression/competition, as against cooperation/reciprocity. The very fact that he acknowledges these *two* poles should dispel any possibility of a *fixed* human nature. To posit a 'human nature' is to side with the view that humans are essentially and always x *not* y. But in his work, this tension is unresolved and it is this bipolar stance which leads Benton to call *both* for extensive state regulation *and* the maintenance of spaces/opportunities for 'spontaneous moral sentiments' which would somehow 'naturally' lead, as he terms them, to improved socio–ecological relations.

One could say that if there is a human nature, then it would exist always and absolutely, or not at all. Here, Benton—as well as anthropocentric, biocentric and ecocentric theorists generally—runs up against a highly problematic view of the human subject. This problematic revolves around placing the seeds of ecological renewal *either* at the mercy of a benevolent and essentially cooperative subject, waiting to be 'released' from systems/structures of antagonism and repression via sustained periods of mass reflection and rationally planned action, *or* such seeds are given over to the workings of an essentially malevolent and egoistic subject, doomed to entrench structures of ecological collapse. In either case, there is a failure to develop a processual view of subjectivity—one which posits that human nature (just like Nature) is produced and reproduced through the *textual machines*[9] which cut across the *assemblages*[10] (familial, pedagogical, political, leisure) each inhabits from one moment to the next. Criminologically, it is the work of Stuart Henry and Dragon Milovanovic (1996) that has come closest to outlining such a conception. I will say more on this shortly.

On the second count, problems also accompany Benton's appeal to a universal system of rights as the vehicle most capable of protecting human and non-human environments. Again, to be fair, Benton admits that 'rights may be little more than an empty formality, serving merely to legitimate persisting de facto inequalities' (1998: 162). However, he nonetheless goes on to place considerable faith in the 'inherent' emancipative powers common to movements and political creeds which draw/rely heavily upon appeals to universal rights (see Benton 1998: 171). Indeed, the conclusion to his piece—which

---

[9] Deleuze and Guattari (1996) use the term 'machine' (which should *not* be thought of as equating to the mechanical or artificial) to denote the process which brings about and often changes the relationship between words and things. 'Every machine', they write, ' . . . is related to a continual material flow [ . . . ] that it cuts into' (Deleuze and Guattari 1994: 36). These relationships can appear permanent and natural or as contestable and reworkable, depending on the kind of machine operating at any one moment. Machines of axiomisation (e.g. the law machine) will tend toward the former whereas machines of absolute decoding (e.g. the terrorist machine) tend toward the latter. Guattari (1995: 58) writes, 'From now on the machine will be conceived in opposition to structure, the latter being associated with a feeling of eternity and the former with an awareness of finitude, precariousness, destruction and death. Beneath the diversity of beings, no univocal ontological plinth is given, rather there is a plane of machinic interfaces.' Critically, and in contradistinction to structuralist and modernist arguments, there is no single unified subject that commands or sets in train any given machine (entailing that there can be no single cause nor solution to particular kinds of dilemmas). Instead, machines have a thoroughly social dimension to their aspect (everyone or no one is implicated). Poststructuralists argue that the world is best conceived in machinic or textual terms—as replete with formed and unformed things whose meaning is continually negotiated, posited, remade, solidified and put asunder by signs which are '*differential*, not referential' in their performance (Belsey 2002, emphasis added). From a poststructuralist viewpoint, signs do not have lurking within them an essence or an eternal 'expressed'. If this were the case—and this is something which modernity is structurally bound to overlook—then there could be *no* debate over the precise signifi(c)ance of such processes as global warming, habitat fragmentation, bleaching of coral reefs, falling numbers of the Spotted Quoll, and the like. Without machines, though, there would be no such *thing* as greenhouse, habitat, coral, or Spotted Quolls (or Nature, Man, Woman, Species, Environmental Harm, or Law). Instead, and most significantly, there would pass the continual variation and return of the flow of unformed elements, unmarked by anthropomorphisms or distinctions between words and things. All of this is critically important because it enables the texts which write the world (such as government and scientific reports, Acts of Parliament, news headlines, academic theorizing, and so forth) to be understood as machines. And they are machines precisely to the extent that they carve out and bring into relief various kinds of bodies (national parks, industrial zones, endangered species, enforcement personnel, scientists, social dissenters). The point to grasp is that most machines parade their bodies as the natural, immutable and proper state of affairs, where, in fact, such bodies are culturally contingent and politically infused. Ecologically, it is necessary to ascertain whether a text brings about a proliferation of different bodies and potentials or whether it draws a production of the same.

speaks of a time when 'Public regulation would be upholding and protecting what was already favoured and nurtured by every day experience of interaction with humans and other non-human beings and environments'—is laden with all the (problematic) rhetoric of modernity and its inability to resist positing foundations for measuring the moral aptitudes of the universal human subject (1998: 173). As Benton concludes, 'Above all, . . . a strongly institutionalised protection of universal civil liberties would still be required [in Eco-/Utopia?] to offset any tendency for new forms of oppression and exploitation to emerge, or for old ones to reassert themselves' (1998: 173).

This, of course, would present to many as a highly logical and prudent programme. However, I would argue that such a vision is imbued by the modernist dimensions and structures which have helped to create and entrench anti-ecological networks across much of earth. For when, it might be asked, have institutions (which necessarily harbour an abstracted/reified account of 'the individual' and their circumstance(s)) ever been capable of upholding the *rights already extant* in international laws and treaties? Further, what kinds of narratives/voices would such institutions inadvertently marginalize or malign in the quest to uphold the 'Truth' of its socio–ecological vision? In short—and to draw on Foucault's sentiments in the foreword to *Anti-Oedipus*—how would such institutions learn to look for the micro fascist leanings inside each of its structures and programmes? There is, quite demonstrably, an urgent need for the emergence of a very different regulatory terrain—specifically, one which constantly puts asunder the concepts of 'nature', 'sustainability', 'culture', 'economy' and 'humanity', which pervade its aspects. Contrast this against Benton's observation that in the future world, governed by a 'relational' ethical outlook, 'Every imaginable form of human social life . . . will stand in need of regulation' (1998: 172). Here, the world conjured by Orwell in his *1984* seems perilously close—especially if, by 'regulation', Benton means governance of human conduct by 'external powers' (this concept, it should be noted, is never clarified in his work).

Before offering some suggestions of how one might leave the shortcomings of green criminology behind, I want to offer a brief critique of one of the latest pieces to appear in the field. The relevant work here is entitled 'The Meaning of Green: Contrasting Criminological Perspectives' (Lynch and Stretsky 2003)[11] and stands, I would argue, as one of the more thoughtful pieces to appear under the banner of green criminology.[12]

---

[10] Wherever there is an arrangement or ordering of practices and concepts within a defined territory, there is, according to Deleuze and Guattari, the production of an assemblage or body. 'We will call an assemblage every constellation of singularities and traits deducted from the flow—selected, organized, stratified—in such a way as to converge [ . . . ] artificially and naturally; an assemblage, in this sense, is a veritable invention' (1996: 406, emphases removed). On such a count, 'an assemblage [or body] has neither base nor superstructure, neither deep structure nor superficial structure . . . ' (1996: 90). Bodies, in other words, are impermanent—but this certainly does not mean that they are without effects. Instead, each body (the body of a water catchment, the body of a national park, the body of a forest, the body of a law enforcement officer, the body of a protester) can be conceived as a zone of intensity, occupying a space between two poles or 'vectors'. Deleuze and Guattari call these poles the *stratified vector* (or stratum) and *destratified vector* (or substratum). Between these vectors (i.e. throughout a body), there is a constant tension between states of *molarity* (reaction, becoming-the-same), *molecularity* (action, becoming-other) and *supermolecularity* (hyperaction, becoming-immanent). In other words, a body is a conglomeration of volatile forces effected by numerous machines at any one time—a site of rigidities, regularities and blockages (a *territory*) but also a site of experimentation, contingency and possible escapes (a *deterritorialisation*). Bodies, therefore, are always already of the order of micropolitical in(ter)ventions.

[11] Despite stating that their aim is to 'highlight a human-centred orientation' for green criminology (Lynch and Stretsky 2003: 218), I have included this text under ecocentrism because it seeks (a) to move beyond crude market forces as solutions to environmental problems (placing it outside a liberal or anthropocentric framework) and (b) views the human capacity for global ecological destruction as setting this species apart from all others (placing it outside a biocentric stance).

[12] Lynch, it should be noted, was one of the first to raise the possibility of a green criminology (see Lynch 1990).

AGAINST 'GREEN' CRIMINOLOGY

The primary argument put by Lynch and Stretsky is that criminologists have a choice between two competing versions of what it is to be 'green'—the *corporate* perspective and the *environmental justice* view. The former defines environmental crime as events in contravention of the law and tends to disregard the impact of race, gender and power upon the formulation of such definitions (2003: 229–230). The latter, on the other hand, defines 'a green crime [as] an act that 1) may or may not violate existing rules and environmental regulations; 2) has identifiable environmental damage outcomes; and 3) originated in human action' (Lynch and Stretsky 2003: 227). Along with this definition goes the concern to analyse 'how forms of race, class and gender inequities affect the social construction of environmental laws' (2003: 228).

At first glance, this sounds highly promising. However, there are a number of problems that need surveying. First, Lynch and Stretsky do not clarify their position regarding the role of the state and its relationship to strategies of environmental renewal. This is an absolutely critical issue because, as Stanley Cohen reminds us, if more events are formally defined as crime, then the result will be a far wider array of acts (potentially) brought before authorities. The closest Lynch and Stretsky come to clearing up their position is their assertion that the green 'definition focuses attention on acts that, whether or not defined as illegal, *should nonetheless be considered criminal*' (2003: 229, emphasis added). If, on the one hand, they wish to argue—as they seem to do—that the capitalist state is the archetypal example of an institution suffering from chronic regulatory capture (see Paehlke and Torgerson 1990), then they need to explain how such an institution could ever see its way clear to criminalize all those events which, to put it bluntly, make capitalism work. But if, on the other hand, the (future) role of the state is to remain largely unchanged, then (and this brings me to a second point of contention) Lynch and Stretsky need to advance a far more nuanced conception of (socio–cultural) power than they do. Here, it is boldly stated that 'Power [ . . . ] is the key issue that separates the [ . . . ] opposing stances' of the corporate as against the environmental justice version of green criminology (2003: 230).

One of the great weaknesses of Lynch and Stretskys' piece is, I would submit, that they align themselves to a Marxist notion of power—a hydraulic rendering which says that there are people/groups who possess power (in the manner of an object) and those who are devoid of it (for a critique, see Foucault 1977; 1982). Indeed, Lynch and Stretskys' text is imbued by all the traditional dichotomies which flow from such a conception (equality/inequality, powerful/powerless, corporations/citizens, First World/Third World, global/local, to name several).[13] The problem here is that such a view of power—and, specifically, the kind of stochastic modelling of the world it produces—ignores the *micropolitical* and *heterogeneous* practices, thoughts and routines which various persons/groups engage. It is, arguably, through the intra- and inter-subjective modes (doing, thinking, ritualizing) that the reproduction of the discursive frames used to justify, neutralize or normalize (environmental) harm occurs. Lynch and Stretsky are, in one sense, right to point out that the vast bulk of environmental damage stems from privileging 'the *economic sphere* over other social structures and issues' (Lynch and Stretsky 2003: 231, emphasis added). But I want to suggest that structural economic

---

[13] Perhaps the most striking (and damaging) binary in their work is that which attends the statement, '[Beyond all other definitions of environmental crime], [o]nly one viable option remains: the more radical environmental justice definition of green outlined [in our work]' (Lynch and Stretsky 2003: 233). Here, a theoretical fascism has replaced any concern for open-ended exploration of socio–ecological possibilities.

power relies for its efficacy not simply on the relations between government, law and economy, so much as on the *flows of pleasure* which invest the population at any one time. Not only is it profitable to be environmentally destructive (in the sense of mining, manufacturing cars, clearfelling forests), it *feels* good too (in the sense of purchasing a gold necklace, driving on the open road, looking at a table, chair, or house constructed from redwood, mahogany, mountain ash or the like). *Environmental damage is, in short, as much a corporeal (bodily/subjective) event as it is a corporate/state practice* and Lynch and Stretsky fail to address this situation.

A third criticism of Lynch and Stretskys' work concerns their invocation of a dialectical view of society (i.e. one that proclaims the existence of opposites ('Man'/Nature) and that the resolution of opposites is possible and necessary). A green criminology, they argue, must strive for 'the elimination of social and economic inequalities' (2003: 229). Similar to that extolled by Barnett, Benton and others, this conception of the logics of social relations is of the modernist variety. It suggests that it is possible to invent a place and time where all humans can peacefully coexist—and that universal goodwill toward one another will naturally be extended to non-human worlds as well. This, of course, is hubris.[14] To desire an end to 'social and economic inequality' may be politically correct, may make certain people feel good about their regard for others, but it ignores the issue of how one judges (not to mention *who* would judge) where *difference* ends and inequality begins. The point here is that the judgments (laws, discourses, categories) which organize the earth and its inhabitants are viewed as sufficient to their task when they in fact harbour all manner of epistemological dilemmas—such as that concerning language and its (in)ability to adequately name or convey the meaning of events (ecological, cultural, etc.). Here, one runs the very real risk of marginalizing that which gives the world its vitality. These are issues which Lynch and Stretsky neglect to address.

My fourth and final criticism relates to Lynch and Stretskys' deployment of the phrase 'environmental justice'. In this case, they write as if they know—beyond any shadow of doubt—how to recognize this brand of justice (and, presumably, injustice) wherever and whenever it might occur. There is, in other words, an alignment to an Aristotelian view of justice (and, thus, of knowledge about the world). The classically Aristotelian question is of the form: what is x? Here, one either admits of essences and absolutes—that hiding behind appearances and surfaces (of each environmentally harmful event) lies the true or hidden meaning of things, or, one admits that 'truth', just like 'justice' or 'freedom', is discursively produced from moment to moment. Lynch and Stretsky fall foul of the first scenario—which is curious, to say the least. For they correctly state that 'Crimes are constantly made and unmade through acts of social construction and deconstruction' (2003: 228). But, and this is critically important, they do not extend this same constructionist outlook to the concept of environmental justice. It is as if such justice is instinctual, universal, always already 'there', simply waiting to be pronounced. But this, again, is an absurd and dangerous position. What is called 'environmental justice' will be as susceptible to the forces of social, symbolic and rhetorical competition as those impacting the meaning(s) of environmental crime/harm. Justice, to be clear, is never pure or unadulterated. Instead, it arrives through the pronouncements of bodies who are themselves subject to a multitude of

---

[14] Derrida (1992: 28) once remarked, 'Nothing seems to me less outdated than the classical emancipatory ideal' (meaning that there can be no repressed or latent subjectivity, waiting to be released to some ideal state).

genealogical forces—forces which govern what it is logically possible to say about a given (criminal/harmful) event (see Foucault 1991).

*Toward an alternative terrain*

In light of this critique, it is apparent that there are a number of problematic assumptions underpinning recent efforts by criminology to theorize environmental harm. These revolve mainly around: (a) the general reluctance to put into critical relief the concept of environmental damage and the associated (but manifestly distinct) category of environmental crime; (b) the inability to move beyond dialectical models of society and conflict resolution; (c) the unwillingness to do away with modernist accounts of the relationship between 'words' and 'things'; and (d) the incapacity to develop a nuanced account of human/environmental interaction. But, given the ways in which criminology has envisioned Nature throughout its history, these oversights are none too surprising. In highly schematic form, I would say that Nature—as deployed across two centuries of criminological thought from Beccaria to Lombroso, through to Becker and up to Henry and Milovanovic—functions in four main ways. First, in classical criminology, nature appears as the original or primordial sign—as that which can be read, deciphered, and mirrored by humanity in the laws it posits and the conceptions of the body it holds (rational, wilful, responsible, introspective). Here, nature presents as a *mimetic force*—it is something orderly, hierarchical, powerful and thus so should be the key institutions and principles characterizing liberal democracy. Secondly, in positivist criminology, nature presents as that which incites persons toward irrational and problematic conduct. Here, humanity loses the capacity for free and spontaneous action and is subject to the unpredictable conditions and trajectories that nature summons forth *within* the human body. In a sense, nature is cast here as a *dangerous and uncontrollable force.*

Thirdly, in critical criminology (spanning social reactionist perspectives up to and including marxist and early feminist accounts of crime), nature presents as the *external* factor which shapes and influences the capacity for benign or damaging conduct to materialize in a vast range of contexts (peer groups, families, schools, work places, neighbourhoods, states, etc.). In more detailed terms, Nature appears and disappears from the critical criminological scene in line with attempts to come to grips with the thresholds at which consciousness (the transcendental subject) and environment (enunciated not in terms of its ecological dimensions but in terms of *goods* (e.g. alcohol, drugs, guns), *services* (e.g. police, welfare, shelter, hospitals) and *external stimuli* (e.g. media, school curricula, peers, popular culture)) combine to produce scenarios of conflict rather than something other. Within critical criminology, Nature, it could be said, presents as the *recurring yet discursively absent other*—as the force which constitutes the objects of the criminological terrain[15] but which has been simultaneously made, until very recently, to occupy a location at the periphery of criminology's 'real' business.

Fourthly, and finally, there marches the extension of critical criminology informed by a mixture of postmodernist and poststructuralist observations. Here, Nature has yet

---

[15] For example, police vehicles are linked to the production of magnesium and other metals, as much as they are a means of transport or surveillance, and prisons—in so far as they require multiple resources for their construction and day-to-day operation—are as much a drain on the earth's ecology as they are places for incapacitation or rehabilitation.

to be adequately theorized or discussed within criminology (but see Groombridge 1998; Lane 1998; Halsey 1999). However, I would suggest that reference to the work of poststructuralist writers, Gilles Deleuze and Felix Guattari, offers a potentially rich source for thinking through key critical issues associated with nature and its (de)regulation. For it is they (after Thales, Heraclitus, Homer, Anaximander, Cratylus, and, more recently, Nietzsche) who consistently conceive the world (Nature) as *flow* (as that which incessantly returns, despite all attempts to classify, manage and contain portions of the Earth) rather than structure (as that which has a teleology, a definitive inside, an indelible Truth). Such a conception is critical to pulling apart what Deleuze has termed 'the image of thought'[16] (or, better, the image of Nature) which has dominated both criminological work and state policies and practices on environmental issues to date. More than this, the work of Deleuze and Guattari provides a means for keeping pace with the mobility of environmental problems by considering Nature and systems of environmental regulation as always already discursively produced and contested. Significantly, they make no grand claims concerning 'solutions' or the precise conditions for long-term 'ecological sustainability'. Indeed, terms such as these (i.e. solution, sustainability, program) should be subjected to rigorous interrogation and, perhaps, ultimately effaced from the lexicon of environmental struggle. In a sense, it may be better to do to Society and Nature what Nietzsche did to God and Man. And it may be important to do this in order to better know the impact of particular subjectivities (the economic subject, the familial subject, the leisure oriented subject, the technologically embedded subject) on various arrangements of matter–energy (those which invest and make possible assemblages of work, play, education, and so forth). Deleuze and Guattari are invoked here not as environmental saviours, but as thinkers, whose lexicon may produce a new problematic of ecological damage—a problematic which, for instance, brings issues of speed, envisioning, scale and affect[17] to the fore (see Halsey 2005b, forthcoming). The claims, therefore, made by Deleuze and Guattari are decidedly modest. And, in keeping with such modesty, I want now merely to suggest several ideas that it might be useful to keep in mind when addressing problems of Nature (which are, everywhere and always, problems concerning the flows, use and blockages of matter–energy).

First, move beyond Nature toward that which Deleuze and Guattari term the *plane of consistency* (toward the place of 'pure potentials', a place prior to the production of words and things). The plane of consistency presents as an important concept for teasing out the effects of naming, dividing and dichotomizing the cosmos:

The plane of consistency . . . is opposed to the plane of organization and development. Organization and development concern form and substance: at once the development of form and the formation of substance or a subject. But the plane of consistency knows nothing of substance and form: haecceities, which are inscribed on this plane, are precisely modes of individuation proceeding neither by form nor by the subject. The plane consists abstractly, but really, in relations of speed and slowness between unformed elements, and in compositions of corresponding intensive affects. . . . Spinoza,

---

[16] The image of thought—the discursive structuring and limiting of what can be said and done—rigidly marks out the thresholds dividing self from other, inside from outside, the familiar from the unfamiliar, and, importantly, the ecologically significant from the ecologically expendable. On this basis, disengaging the image of thought—or 'the figure in which *doxa* is universalized by being elevated to the rational level'—becomes, for Deleuze and Guattari, the key to rewriting the world, and thereby socio–environmental issues anew (Deleuze 1994: 134).

[17] For a discussion of this concept and its place within Deleuze and Guattari's work, see Massumi (2002).

AGAINST 'GREEN' CRIMINOLOGY

Holderlin, Nietzsche are the surveyors of such a plane of consistency. Never unifications, never totalizations, but rather consistencies or consolidations. (1996: 507)

From this passage, it can be said that Deleuze and Guattari are concerned to show the price paid for blocking/filling out the plane of consistency with particular kinds of bodies—forests, rivers, races, genders, economies, chronologies, legalities, policies. A sustained engagement with Deleuze and Guattari therefore prompts the question: *At what social, cultural and ecological cost do—indeed can—we presently name, divide, and regulate the plane of consistency?* It should not in any way be supposed that the plane of consistency resides as some kind of lost panacea for current ills. For how could, in any case, something be considered 'lost' that is always already there? Rather, the plane of consistency (the plane of supermolecular nature) is that which has the potential to radically problematize present ways of conceiving the society–economy–culture–nature nexus. More than this, it causes each rendering of 'the real' (e.g. forest), 'the proper' (e.g. function), and 'the authentic' (e.g. custodian) to be put asunder. Through its concern to map both the ambiguity of bodies and the (traditionally molar or rigid) responses levied by particular agencies to such ambiguity, Deleuze and Guattari (and, more specifically, their mode of inquiry, called schizoanalysis) stands as a technique for problematizing and perhaps even disengaging the structures of modernity (or the image of (environmental) thought). The key here is to invent concepts which allow one to escape the image of thought which governs what it is possible and not possible to do and say with respect to 'the environment'. In short, conjure an image of the acategorical[18] (of that which eludes description or capture) in order to understand anew the ethical weight which arrives with speaking and naming the limits of environmental harm.

Secondly, think in terms of lines rather than structures. That is, consider the idea that molarity (identity, unity, Truth) equates more often than not to a truncation of the possibilities associated with particular terrains. Conversely, experiment with the Real (the place beyond accepted lexicons and dispositions) in order to maximize the unsaid of each event (in order, that is, to bring to prominence minor or discounted knowledges, viewpoints, experiences) (see Foucault 1980b).

Thirdly, give thought to the juxtaposition of bodies which result from the operation of texts. Indeed, read all events as texts to be pulled this way and that, rather than as objective instruments or data waiting to be acted upon (see Halsey 2001). Here, realize that although there are no limits to the juxtaposition and ordering of bodies, there are, nonetheless, consequences and effects. It is the machines (political, scientific, legal, economic) which portray these consequences and effects as knowable and/or controllable that need to be exposed for what they are—the impossible masquerading as the normal/logical.

Fourthly, put bodies into critical relief (especially so-called 'human' bodies). Conceive bodies (one's own and each others') as projects in the making and as conduits for the flows of commodification which reach across and irrevocably transform the planet.

---

[18] In an erudite review of Deleuze's *Difference and Repetition*, Foucault remarks, 'The most tenacious subjection of difference is undoubtedly that maintained by categories. By showing the number of different ways in which being can express itself, by specifying its forms of attribution, by imposing in a certain way the distribution of existing things, categories create a condition where being maintains its undifferentiated repose at the highest level. Categories organize the play of affirmations and negations, establish the legitimacy of resemblances within representation, and guarantee the objectivity and operation of concepts. They suppress the anarchy of difference, divide differences into zones, delimit their rights, and prescribe their task of specification with respect to individual beings. . . . Difference can only be liberated through the invention of an acategorical thought' (Foucault 1980a: 186)

Think about the body as one's first and last means of resisting the forces establishing a becoming-the-same from one territory to the next. Think, in other words, of the epidermis not as a container, but as a membrane, whose aspects are infused not just by sunlight, sound, water, and so forth, but also by the decisions reached on climate change, corporate investment, trade subsidies, export volumes, the value of the dollar, and the like around the globe. Treat the body as the politico–ecologically interested force par excellence (see Featherstone *et al.* 1991). In terms of instituting meaningful change, put faith in one's own body (which is, in any case, always already, subject to someone else's desires, knowledges, capacities) *before* one puts faith in bodies of laws and regulations.

Fifthly, know that the existence of humans (or various types of subjectivities) will automatically equate to some degree of socio–environmental conflict. What counts is maintaining enough room on the *plane of reference* (filled as it is with subjects, objects and Truth) such that no single solution holds sway for any length of time. To run contrary to this would be to invite the forces of fascism into the discourse(s) of environmental harm and its possible renewal. These forces, are, of course, omnipresent. But the *proliferation and diversification of environmental strategies* may help to limit their impact on day-to-day struggles. As Guattari writes, 'Rather than looking for a stupefying and infantilising consensus, it will be a question in the future of cultivating a dissensus and the singular production of existence' (2000: 50). In simpler terms, 'We must ward off, by every means possible, the entropic rise of a dominant subjectivity' (Guattari 2000: 68).

A sixth and final (although there can be no final) point for criminologists to keep in mind when dealing with the problematics of Nature would be to know that one is never totally removed from 'the action'. *Mapping the limits of environmental harm and legal intervention always already has an ethical and social dimension to its aspects.* This is why it is not enough to merely become acquainted with the machines plugged into one's own body. Instead, it is equally vital to develop a knowledge of how and where to plug one's body into the machine or machines deemed capable of delivering the desired socio–ecological effect(s).[19]

In order to avoid the charge of epiphenomenalism, I think it important to draw attention to the kind of criminological work which resonates with what I have been advocating to date. I mentioned earlier that Henry and Milovanovic (1996) are two seminal authors, concerned to advance a criminological perspective which eschews modernist as well as (some kinds of) postmodernist constraints (see also Nelken 1994; Young 1996; Pavlich 1999; 2000; 2001). Central to their work has been the formulation of a *constitutive* definition of crime—a definition that enables commentators to conceive of crime as having corporeal effects without having to rely upon notions of 'human nature' or the 'universal subject' nor upon linear conceptions of cause and effect. Although, at times, their articulation of such a definition seems imbued by an anthropocentric outlook,[20] and, further, although the very positing of a definition is, in many

---

[19] Indeed, this is the task I set myself in *Becoming Contested: Deleuze and the Lexicon of Ecological Struggle* (Halsey 2005a, forthcoming), where I apply the tenor of the six aforementioned suggestions to a key site of environmental struggle and regulation. In such a forum, I put, as it were, *my* criminological machine to work within the 'real' world(s) of environmental damage, protest, and state intervention.

[20] For instance, at one point, these authors remark, '[C]rime is the expression of some agency's energy to make a difference on others and it is the exclusion of those others who in the instant are rendered powerless to maintain or express their *humanity*' (Henry and Milovanovic 1996: 116, emphasis added).

senses, a decidedly modernist trait (embodying the will to represent or contain events), there remains, I believe, something useful in such an attempt. In specific terms, Henry and Milovanovic assert:

Crimes [ . . . ] are nothing less than moments in the expression of power, such that those who are subjected to them are denied their own contribution to the encounter and often to future encounters, are denied their worth, are simultaneously reduced and repressed in one or several ways. Crime [ . . . ] is the power to deny others their ability to make a difference. It is the ultimate form of reification in which those subject to the power of another agency suffer the pain of being denied their own humanity, the power to make a difference. . . . (1996: 116)

Clearly, it is necessary to view 'others' as having to include non-human as well as human bodies. It is also necessary to envisage 'the power to make a difference' as denoting the literally infinite array of colours, smells, sounds, as well as geological/ botanical/hydrological flows and coagulations of particular regions, which, if allowed to emerge, might meaningfully impact social, legal, political and aesthetic relations. Here, the major strength of Henry and Milovanovics' work is that they are sensitive to the fluid nature of the concept 'harm', as well as to who or what is capable of being harmed from one moment (or politico–historical juncture) to the next. As they write, 'We need to define crime and its harm in terms of specific, but historically contingent, victim categories, but *to be aware of the emerging social constructions whose relations of power are relations of harm*' (1996: 119). In this sense, the problem is not crime, but the limits placed upon who and what can count as criminal subjects and/or criminal objects. More than this, *the problem is how to think beyond crime as a useful category of thought.*

A further strength of constitutive criminology is its understanding of the role of language in framing and producing harm—that words are, to greater or lesser degree, violent events.

The call for universality in discourse (as in Habermas' call for a search for consensus in 'ideal speech situations') is a form of harm: it makes common that which is irregular, it homogenizes the heterogeneous. As an alternative to the legalistic definition of crime, our postmodernist definition of crime focuses on harm inflicted *in all its guises* and would certainly include the ' "violence of language" [ . . . ], particularly how the disenfranchised, disempowered, and marginalized have been denied expressive forms for their desires and yearnings . . . ' (Henry and Milovanovic 1996: 118).

What matters here is not the 'truth' or 'falsity' of Henry and Milovanovic's conception of crime, so much as *how it might be put to work.* That is, what counts is the fact that such a definition may open up new discursive and *extra*-discursive pathways where other definitions have fallen short. As a means of teasing small-scale/local revolutions from overarching (seemingly fixed) situations or states of affairs, a definition of crime that puts the emphasis on inter-relatedness over and above segmentation would seem to be a good starting point. The utility of a definition of environmental crime will be the degree to which it elicits new types of existential territories, makes possible new modes of envisioning the human/earth nexus, invites a reconceptualization of the relationship between speed and damage, and, following Spinoza, asks of bodies what each can *do* rather than what each *is* (i.e. what manner of becomings are sustained or curtailed by particular decisions to use or regulate earth).

849

Another sign of a good definition[21] of environmental crime would be its ability to chart *multiple ethical paths* and programmes without, at the same time, falling into a hyper-relativism. Following Nietzsche, it is crucial to consider the value of current values, which means, in effect, to consider which kind of body modernity has most often aligned itself with—the body of the herd, the same, and the representative? Or the body ceaselessly transforming, reaching, and creating 'beyond itself'? A crucial part of enacting a *transvaluation of all values* (Nietzsche 1968) is to see to it that one does not remain overtly and purely nihilistic—something which Henry and Milovanovic go to great lengths to reiterate.[22] Significantly, the process of de(con)struction[23] always already has an ethic or a trajectory residing within its parameters. The challenge is to discern the limits of the process of reconstruction, the limits of affirmation—the limits, in other words, of the new alignments between bodies and words that (might) emerge from critique. But, just as it is important to be affirmative, it is equally important to be aware of the logic underpinning affirmation. For, to chart a definition of crime or harm is to side with a *particular logic of accusation* (Pavlich 2000). And, to do this is to bring (back) into play at least some of the dualisms so common to the criminological terrain (harm/benign, cause/effect, culpability/incapacity, etc.). This, in turn, often leads to the appearance of bodies whose task it is to judge the moment when one side of the binary should divorce from the other. But, in a constitutive world, it will be necessary to focus not on 'environment' versus 'jobs', 'protesters' versus 'administrators', 'crime' versus 'law', or 'harm' versus 'integrity', but on the molarized structures which force particular assemblages of enunciation (such as courts, science, politics) to view these aspects as discrete points on a plane of reference rather than as becomings or intimations of the possible on the plane of consistency. And what of the role of commentary in a constitutive environment? Simply, *the task of the critic will be to draw attention to the possible by showing the contingent dimensions of the actual.*[24] More than this, the challenge is one of nurturing assemblages (academic and countless others) willing to throw the transformative weight of the acategorical behind socio–ecological struggles.

References

A-Khavari, A., England, P. and Godden, L., eds (1999), 'Interdisciplinary Perspectives on Environmental Law', *Griffith Law Review*, Special Issue, 8/2.

Bahro, R. (1984), *From Red to Green*. London: Verso.

Barbier, E. (1989), 'The Contribution of Environmental and Resource Economics to an Economics of Sustainable Development', *Development and Change*, 20: 429–59.

Barnett, H. (1999), 'The Land Ethic and Environmental Crime', *Criminal Justice Policy Review*, 10/2: 161–92.

Barde, J. and Pearce, D., eds (1991), *Valuing the Environment*. London: Earthscan.

[21] Of course, the plane of consistency knows nothing of definitions and perhaps, in an 'ideal' world, it would be best to be rid of them. But, as a means of marking out the vicissitudes of various problems—indeed, what counts *as* 'a problem'—definitions would seem to be an indispensable aspect of current states of affairs.

[22] This is evident in their efforts to chart the distinction between a nihilist and an *affirmative* postmodern stance.

[23] I am using this term in the Derridean sense. Pavlich (2001: 162) gives voice to this by observing that 'Deconstruction . . . is concerned with experiences that dissociate, open, welcome and include; it is not concerned with attempts to gather, entrench, defend or exclude by defining the present in absolute ways'.

[24] In the words of one writer, each 'becomes the watch, the witness, who flags multiple shifting dangers that attach to social formations' (Pavlich 2001: 163).

AGAINST 'GREEN' CRIMINOLOGY

BECK, U. (1992), *Risk Society*. London: Sage.
BEIRNE, P. (1998), 'For a Green Criminology', *Theoretical Criminology*, Special Issue, 2/2.
BELSEY, C. (2002), *Poststructuralism: A Very Short Introduction*. Oxford: Oxford University Press.
BENTON, T. (1998), 'Rights and Justice on a Shared Planet: More Rights or New Relations', *Theoretical Criminology*, 2/2: 149–76.
BOOKCHIN, M. (1986), *The Modern Crisis*. Philadelphia: New Society Publishers.
—— (1987), 'Social Ecology versus "Deep Ecology": A Challenge for the Ecology Movement', *The Raven Anarchist Quarterly*, 1/3: 219–50.
BOX, S. (1983), *Power, Crime and Mystification*. London: Tavistock.
CARRINGTON, K. (1994), 'Postmodernism and Feminist Criminologies: Disconnecting Discourses?', *International Journal of the Sociology of Law*, 22: 261–77.
CASTILLINA, L. (1985), 'Why 'Red' Must be 'Green' Too', in M. Nikolic, ed., *Socialism on the Threshold of the Twenty-first Century*. London: Verso.
CLARK, J., ed. (1990), *Renewing the Earth: The Promise of Social Ecology*. London: Merlin Press.
COHEN, S. (1988), *Against Criminology*. New Brunswick: Transaction Books.
DAVIES, J. (2002), 'To Fight Environmental Crime, Together, and Win', *The Journal of the Australian Federal Police: Platypus Magazine*, 74: 20–8.
DELEUZE, G. (1994), *Difference and Repetition*. New York: Columbia University Press.
DELEUZE, G. and GUATTARI, F. (1994) *Anti-Oedipus*. Minneapolis: University of Minnesota Press.
DELEUZE, G. and GUATTARI, F. (1996), *A Thousand Plateaus*. Minneapolis: University of Minnesota Press.
DEL FRATE, A. A. and NORBERRY, J., eds (1993), *Environmental Crime, Sanctioning Strategies and Sustainable Development*. Rome/Canberra: UNICRI/AIC.
DERRIDA, J. (1992), 'Force of Law: The 'Mystical Foundation of Authority'', in G. Carlson, D. Cornell and M. Rosenfeld, eds, *Deconstruction and the Possibility of Justice*. New York: Routledge.
DEVALL, B. and SESSIONS, G. (1985), *Deep Ecology: Living as if Nature Mattered*. Salt Lake City: Gibbs Smith.
DUNKLEY, G. (1992), *The Greening of the Red: Sustainability, Socialism and the Environmental Crisis*. Leichardt: Pluto Press.
EDWARDS, S., EDWARDS, T. and FIELDS, C., eds (1996), *Environmental Crime and Criminality: Theoretical and Practical Issues*. New York: Garland Publishing.
ENVIRONMENT PROTECTION AUTHORITY (1994), *Environment Protection Authority Annual Report 93/94*. Melbourne: EPA.
—— (1995), *Environment Protection Authority Annual Report 94/95*. Melbourne: EPA.
—— (1996), *Environment Protection Authority Annual Report 95/96*. Melbourne: EPA.
—— (1997), *Environment Protection Authority Annual Report 96/97*. Melbourne: EPA.
FEATHERSTONE, M., HEPWORTH, M. and TURNER, B., eds (1991), *The Body: Social Process and Cultural Theory*. London: Sage.
FOUCAULT, M. (1977), *Discipline and Punish*. Ringwood: Penguin.
—— (1980a), *Language, Counter-Memory, Practice: Selected Essays and Interviews by Michel Foucault*. New York: Cornell University Press. Edited by Donald F. Bouchard.
—— (1980b), *Power/Knowledge: Selected Interviews and Other Writings 1972–1977*. New York: Pantheon Books. Edited by Colin Gordon.
—— (1982), 'Afterword: The Subject and Power', in H. L. Dreyfus and P. Rabinow, eds, *Michel Foucault: Beyond Structuralism and Hermeneutics*. Chicago: University of Chicago Press.

HALSEY

—— (1991), 'Nietzsche, Genealogy, History', in P. Rabinow, ed., *The Foucault Reader*. London: Penguin.

GOFF, C. and GEIS, G., eds (1993), 'The Environment and Social Justice', *The Journal of Human Justice*, 5/1.

GRABOSKY, P. (1994), 'Green Markets: Environmental Regulation by the Private Sector', *Law and Policy*, 16/4: 420–48.

GRABOSKY, P. and GANT, F. (2000) *Improving Environmental Performance, Preventing Environmental Crime*, Research and Public Policy Series, 27, Canberra: AIC.

GROOMBRIDGE, N. (1998), 'Masculinities and Crimes Against the Environment', *Theoretical Criminology*, 2/2: 249–68.

GUATTARI, F. (1995), *Chaosmosis: An Ethico-Aesthetic Paradigm*. Sydney: Power Publications.

GUATTARI, F. (2000), *The Three Ecologies*. London: Athlone Press.

GUNNINGHAM, N., NORBERRY, J. and MCKILLOP, S., eds (1995), *Environmental Crime*. Conference Proceedings Series, 26, Canberra: AIC.

HALSEY, M. (1997a), 'Environmental Crime: Towards an Eco-Human Rights Approach', *Current Issues in Criminal Justice*, 8/3: 217–42.

—— (1997b), 'The Wood for the Paper: Old-growth forest, Hemp and Environmental Harm', *Australian and New Zealand Journal of Criminology*, 30/2: 121–48.

—— (1999), 'Environmental Discontinuities: The Production and Regulation of an Eco-experience', *Criminal Justice Policy Review*, 10/2: 213–55.

—— (2001), 'An Aesthetic of Prevention', *Criminal Justice*, 1/4: 385–420.

—— (2005a, forthcoming), *Becoming Contested: Deleuze and the Lexicon of Ecological Struggle*. London: Ashgate.

—— (2005b, forthcoming), 'Environmental Visions: Deleuze and the Modalities of Nature', *Ethics and the Environment*, Special Issue, Ethics of Seeing: Consuming Environments.

HALSEY, M. and WHITE, R. (1998), 'Crime, Ecophilosophy and Environmental Harm', *Theoretical Criminology*, 2/3: 345–72.

HENRY, S. and MILOVANOVIC, D. (1996), *Constitutive Criminology: Beyond Postmodernism*. London: Sage.

LANE, P. (1998), 'Ecofeminism Meets Criminology', *Theoretical Criminology*, 2/2: 235–48.

LASH, S., SZERSZYNSKI, B. and WYNNE, B., eds (1996), *Risk, Environment and Modernity*. London: Sage.

LEOPOLD, A. (1970), *A Sand County Almanac*. New York: Ballantine Books.

LUKE, T. (1997), *Ecocritique*. Minneapolis: University of Minesota Press.

LYNCH, M. (1990), 'The Greening of Criminology: A Perspective for the 1990s', *The Critical Criminologist*, 2: 11–12.

LYNCH, M. and STRETSKY, P. (2003), 'The Meaning of Green: Contrasting Criminological Perspectives', *Theoretical Criminology*, 7/2: 217–38.

MASSUMI, B. (2002), *Parables for the Virtual*. London: Duke University Press.

MCDOWELL, D. (1997), *Wildlife Crime Policy and the Law: An Australian Study*. Canberra: AGPS.

MEIS, M. and SHIVA, V. (1993), *Ecofeminism*. Melbourne: Spinifex.

MERCHANT, C. (1992), *Radical Ecology: The Search for a Liveable World*. New York: Routledge.

NAESS, A. (1973), 'The Shallow and the Deep, Long-Range Ecology Movement: A Summary', *Inquiry*, 16: 95–100.

—— (1989), *Ecology, Community, and Lifestyle*. Cambridge: Cambridge University Press.

NELKEN, D., ed (1994), *The Futures of Criminology*. London: Sage.

NIETZSCHE, F. (1968), *The Will to Power*. New York: Vintage Books.

AGAINST 'GREEN' CRIMINOLOGY

PAEHLKE, R. and TORGERSON, D., eds (1990), *Managing Leviathan: Environmental Politics and the Administrative State.* London: Belhaven.

PAVLICH, G. (1999), 'Criticism and Criminology: In Search of Legitimacy', *Theoretical Criminology*, 3/1: 29–51.

—— (2000), 'Forget Crime: Accusation, Governance and Criminology', *Australian and New Zealand Journal of Criminology*, 33/2: 136–52.

—— (2001), 'Critical Genres and Radical Criminology in Britain', *British Journal of Criminology*, 41/1: 150–67.

PEARCE, F. and TOMBS, S. (1998), *Toxic Capitalism: Corporate Crime and the Chemical Industry.* Brookfield, VT: Ashgate.

PEARCE, D., MARKANDYA, A. and BARBIER, E. (1989), *Blueprint for a Green Economy.* London: Earthscan.

PEARCE, D., ed. (1991), *Blueprint 2: Greening the World Economy.* London: Earthscan.

PEPPER, D. (1993), *Eco-Socialism: From Deep Ecology to Social Justice.* New York: Routledge.

PLUMWOOD, V. (1986), 'Eco-Feminism: An Overview and Discussion of Positions and Arguments', *Australasian Journal of Philosophy*, (supplement) 64: 120–38.

SCHWENDINGER, H. and SCHWENDINGER, J. (1975), 'Defenders of Order or Guardians of Human Rights?', in I. Taylor, P. Walton and J. Young, eds, *Critical Criminology.* London: Routledge and Kegan Paul.

SEIS, M. (1993), 'Ecological Blunders in US Clean Air Legislation', *Journal of Human Justice*, 5/1: 58–81.

SEIS, M., ed. (1999), *Criminal Justice Policy Review*, Special Issue on Environmental Justice Policy, 10/2.

SHANK, G., ed. (2002), *Social Justice*, Special Issue: Globalisation and Environmental Harm, 29: 1/2.

SUTHERLAND, E. (1949), *White Collar Crime.* New York: Dryden Press.

TAPPAN, P. (1947), 'Who is the Criminal?', *American Sociological Review*, 12: 96–102.

TOBIAS, M., ed. (1985), *Deep Ecology.* San Diego: Avant Books.

UNITED NATIONS ENVIRONMENT PROGRAMME (2002), *Global Environment Outlook 3: Past Present and Future Perspectives.* Nairobi: UNEP.

WALTERS, R. (2004) 'Criminology and Genetically Modified Food', *British Journal of Criminology*, 44/2: 151–67.

WILLIAMS, C., ed. (1996), *Social Justice*, special issue on Environmental Victims, 23/4.

WORLD COMMISSION ON ENVIRONMENT AND DEVELOPMENT (1987), *Our Common Future.* Oxford: Oxford University Press.

YOUNG, A. (1996), *Imagining Crime.* London: Sage.

# Part IV
# International, Transnational
# and Post-National Directions

# [14]

## "Let Them Eat Cake": Globalization, Postmodern Colonialism, and the Possibilities of Justice

Susan S. Silbey

This essay presents three accounts or narratives of globalization. Each narrative describes the triumph of a central character or institution (science, markets, law) against its challenges or enemies (ignorance, regulated or planned economies, human caprice and unreason). The stories convey moral tales about what justice might look like and how social relations might be justly organized and governed. I argue that under the dominant accounts of globalization, the dynamics of power are obscured so that social relations seem to be produced by invisible or natural forces. When the operation of power is masked, I argue, justice, and efforts to confine and regulate power, is made less probable. Law and society scholarship can contribute to a critique of globalization by continuing to identify the ways in which law and power are mutually implicated and embedded in social relations. Rather than describe current forms of international social exchange as globalization, a seemingly neutral terms, the essay urges scholars to identify the role of power by naming global social exchanges as "postmodern colonialism."

## Introduction: "Let them eat cake!"

In 1995, France Telecom announced that it was beginning a process of restructuring and privatization. This announcement followed a decade during which the state telecommunications

This article was originally delivered as the Presidential Address at the annual meeting of the Law and Society Association in Glasgow, Scotland, on 13 July 1996. The research and writing were undertaken during a sabbatical leave from Wellesley College, supported in part by Wellesley College and by a fellowship from the American Association of University Women. I also relied on stimulating conversations with colleagues at the Rockefeller Study Center, Villa Serbelloni, Bellagio, Italy, and the Maison des Sciences de l'Homme and Maison Suger, Paris, France. Although I am responsible for the limitations of this essay, I am particularly grateful for the help provided by generous friends and colleagues who tried to educate me and protect me from my own errors: Patricia Ewick, Austin Sarat, Joel Handler, Felice Levine, Kristin Bumiller, Bryant Garth, David Kennedy, Harrison White, Stewart Macaulay, Kim Scheppele, Chantal Kourilsky, Magali Larson, Gabor Halmi, Martin Chanock, Robert Paarlberg, Rodney Morrison, Agnes Simonyi, Andre Jean Arnaud, Yves Dezalay, Maurice Aymard, Ramon Grossfogl, Ulrich Wegenroth, Wilhelm Streeck, and Hans Georg Brose. Finally, I thank my research assistant Bethany Hoffman without whom I could not have done this work while traveling so far from home. Address monopoly pushed a backward and inept telephone system to a position of international leadership (in basic and applied research, advanced computer networking, and reliable universal service) that made it the envy of other public and private corporations. Despite this remarkable accomplishment, over the next five years, France Telecom will privatize pieces of itself by exchanging capital shares with other telecommunications enterprises. Not unexpectedly, angry consumers and employees have been protesting against the plan. In October 1995 there was what Telecom employees called a warning strike, and again in April 1996 employees organized job actions in which more than 75% of the work force participated. Consumers and employees complain that calling within Paris, within Grenoble, Marseilles, Lyon, and other places in France is going to cost more under the proposed restructuring plan. In response to the mounting protests and job actions, Michel Bon, the newly appointed chairman of France Telecom, is reported to have agreed that indeed local calls will cost more. However, those calling New York would benefit, as international rates will be reduced in the face of global market competition. Bon implied that because they could obtain a better rate, they ought to call New York.[1]

History records that in 1789, a little more than 200 years earlier, French citizens were also mobilized, at that time protesting not telephone charges or reduced social security but severe bread shortages. Marie Antoinette, Queen to Louis XVI, took notice of the complaints and advised that if bread were not available, they ought to eat cake.[2]

Although more than 200 years separate these moments of protest, the official French responses are the same: let them eat cake and let them call New York. Despite the consistency in the French state's responses to citizen grievances, however, I suspect the consequences will not be similar. This is not solely because bread was more essential and necessary to 18th-century French citizens than the telephone is in the late 20th century, nor solely because contemporary French democracy is more legitimate and secure than the 800-year-old monarchy had been, nor finally because the French have exhausted their capacity for rebellion. Rather, I suggest that at least part of the difference in the popular expression of grievances lies in an absence in the late modern era of imagined alternatives and commonplace narratives of social organization, law, and the possibilities of justice through law.

correspondence to Susan S. Silbey, Department of Sociology, Wellesley College, 106 Central Street, Wellesley, MA 02181-8256 (e-mail: ssilbey@wellesley.edu).

[1] *Europe 1* (television) 11 April 1996, 18h49. Interview with Michel Bon, president of France Telecom.

[2] More accurately, the Queen is reported to have recommended that the French citizens eat brioche.

In 1789, law appeared to play a minimal role in constituting the organization of everyday life. Although starving citizens ultimately held the King responsible, it was not because they envisioned the French law as being significantly involved in bread making. In 1996, however, the development of telecommunications, the provision of telephone service, and the restructuring of these technologies is all too apparently a process organized through law and legal techniques.

Thus, as citizens protest against what they experience as social threats, 18th- and 20th-century French men and women can imagine very different alternatives and remedies to their situations. Eighteenth-century French citizens struggled for what they saw as the universal rights of man as a general solution to their problems. The rule of law looked better than the rule of kings. Twentieth-century French citizens facing increased telephone costs have difficulty making similar claims and imagining similar alternatives. The situations and the threats—of rising costs, unemployment, and diminishing social security—that contemporary French men and women daily experience, comment on, and protest against emerge not from the absence of the rule of law but in the face of its very powerful presence.

We live, we are told, in a new world order, a new—perhaps as some claim radically new—organization of time, space, people, and things. While it is clear that law occupies a prominent place in the global society—because most of the global exchange of persons, capital, and culture is managed through legal forms—it is not clear where the place of justice is in this new world order.[3] Although justice seems to serve as a standard to which law is held accountable, it is an elusive and slippery gauge against which law and power are measured and tested. In this contingent, ever moving, and asymptotic relationship, justice can both challenge and underwrite legal power (Young & Sarat 1994). While law may be understood to vary with human capacity and social organization, justice is often believed, David Garland (1990) suggests, to lie "beyond culture and outside of history; a kind of absolute truth which is unaffected by change or by convention" (p. 205).

In this world of global markets, hyperspace, and virtual reality, is it possible that justice can claim a position as a transcendent unchanging standard as it has at other times and places? Or, perhaps—as much law and society scholarship has told us— justice is not eternal and universal but is a culturally and historically constructed ideal whose values and approximate performance simultaneously shape and are shaped by local and variable social organization. Which story of justice—the popular invoca-

---

3 The relationship between law and justice is tenuous at the best of times. One is reminded of a comment Justice Holmes is alleged to have made to a young attorney arguing before the Supreme Court. "Young man," the great justice is reputed to have said, "never forget that this is not a court of justice, it is a court of law."

tion of an absolute value or the sociolegal account of local and situationally constructed rationality—applies to the new world order? Under globalization, what is the place of justice, and where is the space to make claims of justice?

I wonder whether these changes in social organization, the kinds and methods of exchange, and the legal regimes that help organize and facilitate this exchange require students of law and society to reinvent our skills and competencies. Or is it possible that much of what we have learned through the 70 or more years of empirical studies of law has provided us with the tools to describe and critically analyze the new world order.

For sociolegal scholars, I suggest, globalization is not really a new notion; instead, it is a rather familiar, banal story, many of whose elements and narrative structure have been explored and documented in the myriad volumes of law and society research. Like new Tide®, globalization is an updated, smartly packaged, reengineered version of an old product. Rather than soap powder, here we have the elements of free market capitalism and its representative—liberal legalism—recycled for new markets—particularly for all those places on the globe where the earlier model failed to establish a secure market niche. Lest the metaphoric association with soap powder appear merely playful, we need only recall that globalization on the ground is experienced as soap powder, and beef, and cars, and as computers, movies, and CDs—that is, compact disks and those all-important certificates of deposit.[4] Whether globalization is about justice, however, may be another story.

In my analysis, global justice is an oxymoron, more or less. But that "more or less" is the heart of the matter, and exactly the matter that is made less possible, if not impossible, in the emerging global economy and society. "More or less" conveys colloquially what sociolegal scholarship has taught us about the relationships between law and justice: it is never one thing but always several; never the same everywhere but always variable; never exactly what it claims to be but also not irrelevant that it makes these claims. Although justice is presumed to be transcendent and ahistorical, notions of justice have, in fact, varied with varying social and legal orders.[5] Although human experiences of law and justice are variable, each of the differing stories told about

---

  [4] There is a third "cd" known in physics and chemistry as circular dichroism that is also part of global exchanges. This term describes the capacity of physical systems to respond to light by turning either to the right or to the left. It is an ancillary property of the right- and left-handedness of molecular structures and is often used as a means of identifying the "handedness" of molecules. Knowing the "handedness" of molecules is essential for the creation of new products that circulate in the global economy. For example, the thalidomide disaster of the 1950s (in which a drug taken by pregnant women caused deformation in the limbs of the fetuses) was a result of not separating out the left-handed molecules. Only the right-handed molecules were safe for human consumption.

  [5] The historically observed changes in notions of justice are "understood to be accounted for by changes in power—who has it, how it is exercised, against whom, and for

law and justice claims to describe a single uniform phenomenon, erasing the plurality and heterogeneity that may be a source of the depth and durability of legal institutions.

The term "globalization" signals several ongoing complex transformations. Anthony Giddens (1990:64) defines it as "the intensification of worldwide social relations which link distant localities in such a way that local happenings are shaped by events occurring many miles away and vice versa." Globalization or what some call global formation (Chase-Dunn 1991) or others call global culture (Appadurai 1990) is not just a process, however; it is also a story. To be more precise, there are several stories. The different accounts have different authors, purposes, and audiences. Each story of globalization, like all narratives, is structured through an opposition of forces representing good and evil, human agency and historic fate, desire and the law (White 1987; Ewick & Silbey 1995). As narrative accounts of the triumph of a central character against its enemies, the stories of globalization convey moral lessons. The stories of globalization not only describe how social relations are organized globally; they also construct ethical claims about the way the world should be organized and how social relations should be governed. Each globalization narrative reveals a particular construction of justice and its possibilities.

In the remainder of these comments, I use the language of narrative as a heuristic device for analytically distinguishing alternative models of globalization. I first present the two most common and popular accounts, and then I offer a sociolegal narrative. With these synopses, I do two things: display alternative conceptions of justice and suggest how the skills and competencies of sociolegal scholars may be relevant. I suggest that although sociolegal scholarship has the capacity to challenge the dominant narratives of globalization, we cannot rest content with what we have thus far produced.

## Globalization I: A Narrative in Which Reason Triumphs over Nature

My first narrative of globalization describes a world engirded by a finely wrought network of cables, satellites, air and sea lanes, as well as old familiar land routes, transporting information, things, and people from one place to any other place on the globe in anywhere from a minute to a day. This story describes a world in which the boundaries that once had been created by time and space have been eroded by developments in communication and transportation. It is a story of the triumph of reason

---

what purposes. These changes merely [are believed to] represent better or worse approximations of those transcendent values of justice" (Ewick 1997).

over nature. It is the conventional history of the Enlightenment in which the unique capacities of human reason try to trap and harness nature by its own laws. This is the chronicle of a 300-year struggle "to develop objective science, universal morality and law, and autonomous art according to their inner logic" (Habermas 1983:9).

Two of the principal characters, science and technology, eventually tame both the enormous powers of nature and the arbitrary powers of human beings as well. The narrative is told through metaphors of motion, light, and progress. What had appeared to be random and arbitrary activity and the whims of God and nature—lots of motion but little light or progress—human reason reveals to be highly organized networks and structures governed by predictable laws and procedures. Using these precious discoveries, the globalization version of the Enlightenment narrative describes how humans slowly accumulate the knowledge and ability to produce ever increasingly rational forms of social organization and technological innovation, in the end overcoming ignorance, superstition, myth, religion, and scarcity to create relative abundance, human freedom and worldwide mobility.

The story moves through different settings in which the relationships between freedom and mobility are emplotted. Some Enlightenment accounts emphasize the international coordination of scientific research to control disease, prolong lifetimes, and improve conditions of everyday life. Others focus on the transnational flow of people, goods, and capital which creates a global division of labor with an equally global diffusion of material and cultural goods. Goods produced with Korean or Chilean labor from materials mined in Zaire or grown in India are sold in the shops on the Faubourg St. Honore, Rodeo Drive, or the Ginza. People born and raised in Mexico, Guatemala, Turkey, Greece, Algeria, or Ethiopia travel north to find work to sustain families left behind. At the same time, rap music from American urban ghettos is played in the shops in Paris and on the streets in Budapest, portable telephones manufactured in Finland adorn the hips of stock brokers and manual laborers from Santiago to Sidney, from Cancun to Cape Town, and television stations around the globe fill their schedules with the likes of *Melrose Place, Beverly Hills 90210,* and *Miami Vice* while the office workers from Moscow to Buenos Aires munch on Big Macs and fries.[6]

At the same time as we see how local sites become linked in the global circulation of people, signs, and material goods, the Enlightenment narrative describes how being connected reshapes the parts now joined. While some people and phenomena

---

6 Legal and illegal markets circulate proscribed drugs, currencies, and people as well. The trade in women, for example, is as domestic workers and sex workers. See Heyzer, Lycklama à Nijeholt, & Weerakoon (1994).

are ripped from spatial and territorial moorings, others—for example, social groups based on ethnic, linguistic, or religious practices—become "reterritorialized," making claims to specific pieces of geography with newly recognized boundaries as the ground of their participation in the new world order. While some localities experience marked increases in standards of living (measured in terms of reduced infant mortality, longevity, education, and calories consumed), other people experience an equally marked decline in the material, psychological, and sociological conditions of everyday life. In these Enlightenment accounts, the new world order is linked internally by its globally exchanged and shared culture and externally through its collective scientific exploration beyond this globe.

This Enlightenment parable conveys its justice claims by demonstrating how those without reason, those still subject to superstition, myth, and religion, fall by the wayside. Because globalization seems inevitable and necessary in the Enlightenment narrative, "those who embrace it seem modern, reasonable, realistic, and pragmatic while those who do not seem nostalgic, rigid, and radical" (Kennedy 1994:4).

## Globalization II: A Narrative in Which Desire Triumphs over Law

There is, however, a second narrative of globalization. This second story appropriates pieces of the Enlightenment tale to its own purposes, and lately seems to be told more often and with greater authority.[7]

Rather than being a portrayal of the success of science and technology, this second globalization narrative is a story of the historic struggle and triumph of the market economy. It is an account of how the market—against the powerful opposing forces of centralized planning and socialized ownership, as well as technological backwardness—establishes itself worldwide after being confined within national and regional boundaries. It is a story of how people with energy and imagination live freely and efficiently ever after, relying solely on price signals to decide, in the canonical phrase, "who gets what, when, how" (Lasswell 1936). In some versions, the rapid expansion of global markets is attributed primarily to the independent success of its ally technology, while in other versions globalization succeeds because of the failures of its enemies. In this latter account, the collapse of planned economies is validation of the superiority of markets and thus evidence of the "justness" of globalization's triumph. In this tale, the creation of global markets not only improves effi-

---

[7] The Enlightenment tale has clear counternarratives (e.g., feminism, environmentalism, holistic medicine) that the market narrative currently lacks.

ciency and controls costs; it also creates justice by empowering consumers and overthrowing unresponsive bureaucracies that have outlived whatever useful purposes they may at one time have served.

The narrative of desire triumphant describes how worldwide sourcing, flexible production, low-cost transportation, and communication meet in three major scenes of action: Western Europe with its trading partners in Central and Eastern Europe and northern Africa; Japan and the little tigers with their partners in Asia; and North America—Canada and the United States with its engagements in Latin America. Just as the boundaries between time, space, people, and things are erased in the Enlightenment tale, the market narrative of globalization describes how the traditional distinctions among market tools—between banking, brokerage, business, housing, and consumer credit—are loosened. New financial instruments are created as well as markets in these inventions, new markets in commodities, stocks in commodities, funds that collect stocks in commodities, as well as markets in currencies and debts. Time future is discounted into time present in such fantastic and baffling ways that few people claim to understand the way it all works.

> An English buyer can get a Japanese mortgage, an American can tap his New York bank account through a cash machine in Hong Kong and a Japanese investor can buy shares in a London based Scandinavian bank whose stock is denominated in sterling, dollars, Deutsche marks and Swiss francs. (From *Financial Times* (London), 1987, quoted in Harvey 1990:161)

> This bewildering world of high finance encloses an equally bewildering variety of cross-cutting activities, in which banks borrow massively short-term from other banks, insurance companies and pension funds assemble such vast pools of investment funds as to function as dominant market makers, while industrial, merchant, and landed capital become so integrated into financial operations and structures that it becomes increasingly difficult to tell where commercial and industrial interests begin and strictly financial interests end. (Harvey 1990:161)

In this labyrinth of creative accounting and innovative financial services—what Robert Reich (1983) has called "paper entrepreneurialism"—capital is also mobile, residing nowhere more than in cyberspace. Ever liquid, flowing from one merger to another acquisition, the capital that fuels the global circulation of goods, services, and people is faceless and rootless, free of the solid ground in which humans, despite their successful electronic and space explorations, must be born, spend most of their days, and die.

In this market account, we can identify episodes of dispersion and integration. Global dispersion is typified by the creation of new producers and sites of production within nations and transnationally. So we see large and small companies increasing their subcontracting, and doing so with several geographically distant subcontractors for the same product. We see industrial homework spreading into the hinterlands of remote parts of the world at the same time as highly skilled cognitive (mind-work) laborers and professionals move their work from office to home, sometimes also at great distances from the centers of control and management. This diffusion of worldwide outsourcing—fueled by low transportation costs and computerized communication linkages—creates flexible production and higher profits for corporate managers and owners while relegating labor and suppliers to hyper-competition and increasingly insecure income.

The scientific accomplishments highlighted in the Enlightenment tale become the technical means through which the market can be efficiently globalized. The territorial dispersion is accompanied, however, by a parallel concentration of centralized control to manage and finance the dispersed production. The remotest site of individual production is tied by centralized management through a closely linked chain of financial and design control located primarily in the global cities—such as New York, London, and Tokyo. But these cities, Saskia Sassen (1991:5) claims, are not merely control sites. They are centers of independent production as well. They produce the "specialized services needed by complex organizations for running spatially dispersed networks of factories, offices, and service outlets." They also produce the "financial innovations and the making of markets . . . central to the internationalization and expansion of the financial industry" (ibid.).[8]

Like the first story, this second narrative also communicates clear moral lessons, the most important of which is that private property rights are paramount and should be inviolable. The major actors or characters in this story are private persons. This means that states should cease engaging in economic activity and state-owned productive enterprises should be privatized. In this political and moral economy, national borders should cease being barriers to trade; all national economies should be open to trade. Exchanges and engagements in this moral universe are marked solely by market prices (which are the means of rewarding good action and punishing bad). Public regulation of private enterprise, as an alternative to price regulation, should cease. As a corollary to the dominant role of prices as the major form of communicating participation in the market economy, domestic prices should conform to international prices and monetary policies should be directed to the maintenance of price and

---

8 In Sassen's telling of the tale, these cities are the scenes in which concentrated low-skill, low-wage, infinitely replaceable "throwaway" labor provides the support services in the restaurants, luxury hotels, hand laundries, gourmet shops, and child care facilities demanded by managers in the centers of financial and managerial control.

balance of payments stability. These are the universal constants—
the morality—of market economies.

Although markets depend on law to provide a stable normative environment, ensuring security of property and contracts,
the market narrative insists that law do no more. Beyond the as-
surance of mutual trust and normative order, the market demands that the rest of economic affairs remain entirely matters
of market (i.e., price) decisions rather than consequences of
political organization or legal reason. In other words, the market
urges law to police a fixed boundary between the public and the
private, between economics and politics. Even though national
legal orders have, for more than a hundred years, created various
adjustments to counteract market instabilities and imperfect
competition, a key feature of this globalization story is the fury of
its critique of legal intervention. And although the shift from national to global regimes brings in new levels of legal regulation—
international economic law and international public law—it
turns out that these international legal regimes merely recreate
the public private divide. Historical experience notwithstanding,
this globalization narrative insists that the private law regime of
property and contracts, at both the national and the international levels, is an apolitical realm, merely supportive of private
initiative and decisions, immune from public or political contestations and without redistributive consequences (Kennedy
1994).[9]

Whether the story is told on the front pages of newspapers or
the back pages of academic journals, whether the story is told to
applaud what is happening, to voice criticism, or to express fear,
the understanding of justice and morality is consistent. Globalization is not a matter of where government and law shall issue, nor
a matter of shifting jurisdiction from the nation state to the
globe. Instead, this narrative of globalization offers a change in
*how* collective life will be governed. It signals a movement from
politics, in the Aristotelian sense—of debates about how we shall
live together—to economics, that is, how our individual desires
can be unconsciously coordinated through prices. This narrative,
as a conventional account of the market, demands very little
from collective human action or conscious human design, only

---

[9] Despite globalizers' claims, however, the international legal regime "contains just
the combination of hyper-formality (standard terms, absolute property rights) and 'reasonableness' or 'comity,' even policy, of conflicting rights and clashing institutional pre-
rogatives, which opens domestic private law to the politics of adjudication" (Kennedy
1994:14). Transposing these legal forms to global markets will likely also open international economic regulation to similar discursive and interpretive (i.e., political) practices.
Rather than keeping politics outside of the market, legal regulation brings politics to the
center.

that all things—land, labor, and resources—be available for exchange through commodification and pricing.[10]

In the Enlightenment narrative, reason occupied a central role as the force for taming unruly nature. In the market narrative, desire triumphs over both law and reason. Reason is relegated to a subordinate role as a technically useful instrument for calculating costs and benefits of alternative means for satisfying wants and desires. Law is relegated to an equally subordinate role as a background figure providing context but little determinative action. By subordinating reason and law to desire, the market narrative is a parable about lowering expectations about what collectivities can or should do. It thus asks us to limit our conceptions of justice to a contentless efficiency (Bittner 1983) and to forgo aspirations for equality or quality of social life. As several marketeers recently suggested, we need "to focus . . . on measures that enlarge the scope for wage differentials [inequality] without making it socially unacceptable" (Kosai, Lawrence, & Thygesen 1996).

## Interpreting the Globalization Narratives: Postmodern Colonialism

We could argue, and I expect we will, about whether I have correctly characterized or wrongly caricatured these accounts of globalization. Suffice it to emphasize that both stories can be and are the subject of diverse interpretations.

### Diverse Interpretations

For example, there are some commentators who see in the Enlightenment narrative the possibility of a new democratic transformation. Some stress that the circulation of capital and culture is—as the phrase suggests—a circulation, not solely a movement from the center to the peripheries. By dissolving political, temporal, and spatial boundaries, the technological revolutions underwriting this transnational exchange create capacity for movement in all directions and with less capital investment than was heretofore possible. From this perspective, globalization enables more diverse participation and more sources of influence—what we might consider a form of enfranchisement—throughout the world system (Santos 1995). Those at the geographical peripheries of the world system welcome the chance to be regular and possibly influential members of the virtual global community. In the global networks of communication and ex-

---

[10] As we know, "in a market system, everything has a price—each commodity and each service. Even the different kinds of human labor have prices. . . . We each receive income for what we sell, and we use this income to buy what we want" (Samuelson & Nordhaus 1983:43). See also Polanyi 1944.

change, human creativity can be unleashed from traditional cultural and material constraints to find new forms of expression in what now seems like an unbounded space of possible interactions and connections. Here, observers point to the importance of human rights discourse in shaping an actual, not merely a virtual, community, and the empirically documentable changes that discourse has wrought in heretofore authoritarian regimes (Woodiwiss 1994). Similarly, some commentators note the growing significance of environmental concerns in mobilizing social movements across traditional political, racial, and gender boundaries. For optimistic observers, the market poses an opportunity and challenge.

Other interpreters, however, claim that the Enlightenment narrative is a saga of disenchantment (Weber 1978). Noting the immediacy with which persons, goods, information, and technologies move across vast distances, and the expanding breadth and accelerating pace of consumption, these observers emphasize how the loss of sacred illusions has left a corrosive absence at the center of human life where "all that is solid melts into air" (Marx & Engels 1848 [1993:12].[11] Critics notice the bombardment by stimuli, the neurological overloads, and the homogenizing consequences of the escalating circulation of signs and symbols removed from local experiences and interpretive frameworks (Simmel 1971 [1903]; Berman 1988; Postman 1986, 1993). They point to isomorphisms, convergences, and hybridizations that create a sense of pervasive sameness across heretofore diverse cultures.

I share some of these more critical and pessimistic interpretations. Nonetheless, because I retain a commitment to portions of the Enlightenment story, I like to believe it is an unfinished story; the denouement remains uncertain. I am also firmly attached to some of the critical values of Enlightenment science: the insistence on public methods of research, publicly displayed, with empirically demonstrable criteria of validity, and faith in the pragmatic reason of common people. But (and this is a big but), I am

---

11 The paragraph in *The Communist Manifesto* reads:

The bourgeoisie cannot exist without constantly revolutionizing the instruments of production, and thereby the relations of production, and with them the whole relations of society. Conservation of the old modes of production in unaltered form was, on the contrary, the first condition of existence for all earlier industrial classes. Constant revolutionizing of production, uninterrupted disturbance of all social conditions, everlasting uncertainty and agitation distinguish the bourgeois epoch from all earlier ones. All fixed, fast frozen relations, with their train of ancient and venerable prejudices and opinions, are swept away, all new-formed ones become antiquated before they can ossify. All that is solid melts into air, all that is holy is profaned, and man is at last compelled to face with sober senses his real conditions of life and his relations with his kind. (Marx & Engels 1993 [1848]:12)

The continual innovation in productive techniques has led to the instability Marx and Engels describe; whether it has produced the popular self-reflection they predicted is, however, less clear.

less sanguine about the ability of reason and science to resist the seductions of the market and desire.

### Postmodern Colonialism

Thus, for the present, I regard globalization as a form of postmodern colonialism where the worldwide distribution and consumption of cultural products removed from the contexts of their production and interpretation is organized through legal devices to constitute a form of domination.[12] I offer two examples of postmodern colonialism, conjunctures of unexpected combinations that defy spatial, temporal, and cultural distances. For example, I saw a man riding a bicycle along the trolley tracks of Milan. He was dressed not in an Armani or Versace costume common enough in this city but in a laborer's jacket and pants. He was peddling quickly and expertly, overtaking Ferrari and Ford, while talking feverishly into his portable telephone. Two months earlier, while accompanying my husband to a scientific conference, I had observed a four-year-old Japanese boy unwrapping a package of blow-up water wings and swimming goggles at the hotel's pool. The little boy was excitedly pestering his rather reserved mother to get into the swimming pool with him so that he could demonstrate his effectiveness with these technological marvels. The background sounds were provided by a group of German and French scientists sitting in the jacuzzi energetically debating a problem in quantum mechanics. All of this going on in four languages, and watched over by the American sociologist. I thought of the miles and centuries and animosities that had brought this particular group to this place in Australia, so untroubled in their familiarity and pleasure. I also believed that few observing the scene could imagine that the little boy's vigorous desires and appeals to his mother were other than market creations.

In postmodern colonialism, control of land or political organization or nation-states is less important than power over consciousness and consumption, which are much more efficient forms of domination. Moreover, this is neither a necessary nor a particularly benign development in social relations; nor is it the consequence of some natural law of human evolution writ in our genes several million years ago. Globalization, or what I am calling postmodern colonialism, is an achievement of advanced capitalism and technological innovation seeking a world free from restraints on the opportunity to invent and to invest. It is a world in which size and scale in terms of numbers of persons (who can produce), and in numbers of outlets (to disseminate and place

---

[12] This description of postmodern colonialism first appeared in the *Law & Society Newsletter*, November 1995 and May 1996.

the products), and capital (to purchase both labor and land) determine the capacity to saturate local cultures.

Significantly, this is not something occurring outside the law or without the active collaboration of law and legal scholars. Keeping in mind the conventional analyses of colonialism as a form of domination perpetrated by more powerful nations on those believed by the colonizers to be at the peripheries of the world system, we might also recall the active role that law played in that history of organized domination. Although the last several centuries of European imperialism have been transformed in this century by successful liberation movements, it seems that we are witnessing a new form of domination that may be more insidious and difficult to dislodge. My worries, of course, are not meant to overstate the success of Western penetration, to ignore the role of Asian capitalism, or to underestimate the resistances to colonialism. I mean to highlight, however, some worrisome features of globalization.

First, we have what Jürgen Habermas (1992) refers to as the colonization of the life world. This refers to the proliferation of media produced, marketed, and disseminated messages that become the images and symbolic resources of ordinary people, although these images and messages are independent of, and often at odds with, people's daily lived experiences. People live in worlds in which their emotions, desires, and rationalities may be produced independently of their experience. There is an active ongoing struggle to retain access to and hold onto locally produced and experienced physical, emotional, and cognitive interactions. Instead, what is local is supplanted by what is global; what is emotive, physical, and interactive is replaced by what is remote, mediated, commodified, manufactured, and produced for purchase and consumption globally. What distinguishes this postmodern colonialism from more traditional forms of colonialism and capitalism is that the production and distribution is driven by and about signs, symbols, and communication as much or more than it is about things, or what Marx called the forces of production. Significantly, the signs or messages circulate independently of what they supposedly represent, and thus have an independent effect on action and experience. The truth value of representations or images is somewhat irrelevant to their power. Moreover, the production of the images and messages is a self-conscious activity of particular profit-driven occupations and professions.

Law is a part of this symbolic communicative aspect of postmodern colonialism because the medium that colonizes consciousness is itself saturated with legal images and issues. The globally exchanged culture is typified by televised images of American law. Like everything else, law has become entertainment. American television—which is broadcast all around the world—is bathed in law. Fictional trials, real trials, news of trials, analyses of trials, not to mention crimes and legislation, all are represented without serious distinction between what is supposed to have actually happened to living, breathing human beings and what is merely a product of someone's imagination. American television drama, preoccupied with law and crime, is a major staple of global television entertainment; half-hour situation comedies that rely on local knowledge for their humor are rarely exported. The life and death drama, the sexual subplots, and struggles for power that characterize television "drama" are apparently understandable despite the enormous variation in local cultures. This is one way in which American law circulates around the globe; both the practices and ideals of law, the history and the fictions, become part of the engagements between social movements and corporate capital in diverse corners of the globe.

The second, perhaps more important, aspect of this postmodern colonialism that is energized by law refers to the explicit selling—rather than implicit representations—of American law around the world, especially but not exclusively in Eastern Europe. Sociolegal scholars have long understood and written about the ways in which liberal law provided the "infrastructure" for capitalist investment and development. Contemporary "wanna be" capitalists also know that they need that law to create the market economies that are supposed to be the vehicle for modernization and democratization, wealth and power. We also know that the International Monetary Fund and the World Bank demand efforts at democratization and formal appearances of the rule of law as conditions for their aid. How are needy nations and "wanna be" capitalists going to democratize and institutionalize the rule of law? Well, we have Western lawyers, experts, and good samaritans ready to provide the means. Without buying the property of other nations, without occupying the territory, and even without investing its own capital in the economic and social development of other nations, the West is able to shape the culture and economies by offering the legal forms through which social exchange takes place.

I have two concrete examples of the gift of Western law to add to my collection of postmodern moments. Shortly after the demise of the Soviet Union, I encountered a group of American college students, none with legal training, translating the Uniform Commercial Code (UCC) into Ukrainian. They had been enthusiastic students of Soviet culture and were now working at a new economic institute engaged in the task of bringing the market to the Ukraine. The history of trade practices and cultural norms that had been so much a part of Karl Llewellyn and Soia Mentschikoff's ambitions for (and the history of the development of) the UCC was unknown and unimportant to the new capitalists. The Ukrainians needed a code, and they took the most obvious and perhaps accessible one they could find. How, I wondered, were the courts in Ukraine going to refer to conventional practices of the trade—which is a crucial aspect of the UCC—when disputes arose? Was it really possible to just move a code developed—after so much struggle and caselaw—somewhere else and expect that the organizing functions would work the same? Everything I have ever learned in sociology and law encouraged me to believe that this was folly, which would not work as sold or expected. Nonetheless it was a folly in which some careers at home and in Ukraine were going to be made with rapid success.

Just recently, I encountered a similar but considerably less naive example in which American charitable foundations—for example, Ford, Rockefeller, Kellogg, MacArthur—are training people in Third World countries to set up "foundation-like" organizations. Although these Third World organizations will not have the capital endowments that are the lifeblood of American foundations, this activity is seen by the mentoring foundations as a means of teaching about charity, the responsibilities of capital, and a healthy division between public and private spheres in developing economies.

I am not suggesting that Western law might not in some circumstances be useful to a wide range of nations and peoples, or that human rights and environmental movements have not produced some noticeable goods for humanity. Rather, I am concerned about the consequences of marketing specific legal devices as if they were one of those dresses that fit all sizes. I am worried about how local justice can be achieved within a supposedly universal, all-purpose, one-size-fits-all law.

Describing globalization as a kind of colonial domination may overstate the case. It seems to overlook the amount of variation and invention in the local uses of what otherwise might appear to be uniform products. These local practices have the capacity to transform what might superficially seem like cultural imperialism into expressions of individual identity, local innovation, and possibly cultural and political resistance (Cushman 1995). But, I wonder, how much local innovation needs to exist before it is not plausible to say that local cultures are being colonized by global market forces? If all social structures involve not only repetition and reproduction but also appropriation, invention, and innovation (which I believe they do), how can I claim that the contemporary patterns of cultural transmission are a form of colonization? How can I ignore variation (and the power of any cultural product or social process certainly varies) and offer a characterization of popular culture and law that seems to ignore that variation and local agency?

Although I admit that there are lots of local inventions and innovations displacing global forces, I suggest that there is nothing like an equal exchange taking place. It is this inequality in effects that is sufficient, I want to argue, to ground an interpretation of globalization as a form of domination, like colonialism. The global transmission of standardized products and signs—facilitated, organized, and protected through increasingly standard legal forms and processes—is much more effective in structuring local social exchanges and imposing meaning on local cultures than are local innovations able to appropriate and reconstruct the mediums of global exchange.

As an illustration of unequal exchange and cultural construction that might be characterized as postmodern colonialism, let me offer an example from the work of Rick Fantasia (1995), who has been studying fast food and the spread of MacDonald's in France. MacDonald's now has at least 323 restaurants in France, the single largest number of restaurants belonging to one company. There are a number of other fast-food establishments in France, some of American origin such as Burger King, and others with American-sounding names but with French ownership, such as Quick. Just about every MacDonald's restaurant— whether in Paris or in Lille, or in Bayreuth, Milan, Moscow, Tokyo, Sydney, or Chicago—looks just like every other MacDonald's, serving the same food, in similar packages, in physical spaces that are nearly alike, and with common production, organization, and management techniques.

However, Fantasia (1995) writes in a recent essay in *Theory and Society*, that it would be wrong to think that the marketing of hamburgers, milk shakes, french fries, and soft drinks is only about what is constant: nourishment and food consumption. That which appears uniform and can, in fact, be accurately described by standardized measures is anything but invariable. Rather, it is very possible to argue, and easy to demonstrate, that eating hamburgers has quite variable meanings, and in particular that MacDonald's has a very different cultural meaning in France than it does in the United States. In France, for example, a meal at MacDonald's is seen by French youth as a space of freedom from conventional norms, stuffy restaurants, and French cultural pretensions with regard to food. MacDonald's is seen as a distinctly American place, with an exotic atmosphere of loud music, bright lights, and funny colors and costumes (the servers' uniforms). In France, unlike the situation in the United States, MacDonald's has a very small working-class market. Adolescent and student consumers are supplemented by a large contingent of middle-level managers and white-collar employees who make up more than 50% of MacDonald's French consumers. Moreover, the French people do not purchase from and eat at MacDonald's as Americans do; for example, the cash register does not signify the head of a line for ordering food in France as it does in the United States. In France, large crowds of people hover around the counter, vying for a server's attention. It is clear, in other words, that eating at MacDonald's does not constitute the same cultural practice in France as it does in the United States, or in Boston as it might in Sheridan, Wyoming. Thus one might read in the consumption of MacDonald's hamburgers examples of local innovation and invention that might seem to challenge a claim that MacDonald's is an example of postmodern colonialism.

Nonetheless, it would be a second mistake to assume that because MacDonald's can have this variable cultural meaning that there are no more general and structural consequences for social relations, and for law, in the global distribution of fast food. In fact, several consequences mark the exchanges taking place in and through MacDonald's as quite unequal, and the disparity is so large, I contend, that it justifies the claim that the spread of MacDonald's is part of a new form of colonialism. At the level of cultural symbols already discussed, I note that while eating hamburgers has a distinctly different meaning in France than it has in the United States, I also note that it is hamburgers, and not crocque monsieur, on which French office workers and youth are writing their local scripts. A critic would respond by noting that quiche has become equally common in the United States, so common that quiche can be the subject of popular humor (remember "Real men don't eat quiche"?). I agree but note a significant difference, a difference that leads me to other important aspects of inequality. On one hand, the importation of hamburgers into France and other countries is the result of a centralized integrated effort by one or two organizations' rationalized marketing processes. On the other hand, the importation and adoption of quiche in the United States is the result of dispersed discoveries and adaptations—from Julia Child's successful television shows generating an entirely new interest in food to the training of chefs in a myriad of competing culinary institutes—which have in the end produced a uniquely American (and I might add less gendered) cuisine. The difference between a bottom-up adoption and amendment of a cultural product and the rationalized production and distribution of an absolutely uniform product for global consumption is the significant difference and a source of inequality.

The success of MacDonald's and the spread of global markets is the result of systematic intentional rationalization at just about every level of action. It is also integrated through highly centralized corporate hierarchies. It is this centralized and integrated rationalization that constitutes and colonizes everyday life around the globe and is the source of increasing inequality. What MacDonald's has created never existed before in France: a family restaurant and possibilities of eating out for masses of French people for whom eating in a restaurant had been a rare occasion. But MacDonald's achieved this through a work process that is a quintessential example of the deskilling and reengineering that is also systematically lowering wages and incomes. An increasing share of food consumption in France (and elsewhere) takes place through a production and distribution system that is organized into programmed and computerized systems, involving low-skill, low-paid, part-time labor. The product is designed and distributed in consistent standardized processes and legal forms (that secure material and economic capital) with the most variable and transient human labor.

These processes are part of a global transfer of income and intellectual capital that has increased the divide between the haves and the have nots. For example, although recent investment in the U.S. and global markets is growing, and productivity is rising markedly, wages and real incomes for more than 80% of U.S. workers has steadily fallen. This situation is repeated in France, Belgium, Germany, Canada, and the United Kingdom. Government statistics claim that the weekly earnings of 80% of the American work force fell 18% between 1973 and 1995. The income of the executives and high-level managers (the other nearly 20%) rose between 19% and 66%. Moreover, during this same period employees' share of companies' increased income has also fallen. During the 1980s, labor earned 52% of income; in 1993, labor was taking 38%. The share paid out to capital investment remained at a constant 28%.[13] While the same has happened in most of the industrialized world, it cannot be interpreted as a simple transfer from more to less industrialized nations.

More to the point, the processes of restructuring and reengineering that are bringing about this increased productivity and reduced real wages (as measured by most economic indicators) is being exported around the globe in order to create similar increases in productivity. The policies and techniques that have stimulated this new productivity in the United States and Japan, for example, are being aggressively promoted and sold as models for other nations to adopt. Thus, while there is a transfer of production and managerial technique (and with it an apparent increase in income for previously less industrialized nations), the new technologies will put a ceiling on the rates of growth (in workers' real incomes) in those developing economies. A downward shift in wages accompanies the restructuring for greater productivity. Two recent studies have tracked these changes globally, estimating that within the United States alone between 75%

---

[13] These numbers come from "The Best of Times—The Worse of Times," remarks by Lawrence B. Lindsay, a governor of the Federal Reserve Bank to the Baltimore Chapter of the Commercial Finance Association, 7 March 1994, quoted in Head 1996.

and 80% of the largest companies have begun reengineering their work forces and that these efforts are increasing in the United States as well as elsewhere (Hammer & Champy 1993; Hammer & Stanton 1995; Champy 1995).

Restructuring and reengineering involve the computerized redesign of manufacturing and white-collar work to use the simplest most interchangeable parts and persons; they purposively displace the need for abundant human labor and capital. (They also rely on highly paid consultants who help train managers to do the hard work of firing workers.) The newly designed and computer-aided manufacturing and office work require little education or training. The examples are abundant. Nissan and Honda claim, for example, that they give very little emphasis to the educational and vocational qualifications of their prospective employees whether hiring in Germany, the United States, or Japan. Manual "dexterity, enthusiasm, and an ability to fit into the team" are much more important than calculation, interpretive, or other cognitive skills, they claim (Head 1996:48). Manpower International claims that it can provide the computer skills necessary to do most of the newly designed white-collar work with two months' training and through its pool of ever temporary help. And MacDonald's prides itself on its ability to train its restaurant workers in 20 minutes—through videotaped instructions—for any job required to staff a MacDonald's restaurant.

Not only are we seeing a transfer of income from workers to upper-level managers and investors, but consistent with this division of income we are witnessing an accelerated division of intellectual labor. The new systems that organize work and production are designed by highly educated, technically trained specialists. Such skills are difficult to acquire, take many years of preparation, and thus command these noticeably higher salaries. And yet the increases in productivity have been already achieved without any reforms in public education. In other words, the increased productivity requires the talents of few and not the education of many.

Thus, what the global economy of lean production gives us is a highly stratified work force with millions of people constituting the interchangeable parts in the rationalized production designed by the precious intellectual labor of a few. Although most people use, rely on, work their individual imaginations responding to and adapting these standardized products and services, they are—by these very same processes—put at an increasing remove from the material substance of their daily lives (the design and control of these systems of production, distribution, and consumption). Although the beneficiaries are no longer nation-states, and may be less territorially confined, I think it not unreasonable to characterize these global processes as a new form of colonialism.

Importantly, as sociolegal scholars we need to remember that the global dispersal of production, distribution, and consumption is taking place with the active participation of legal actors and legal forms. These processes of global marketing and restructuring are constructed, and can only be constructed, with the collaboration of law. A final example from MacDonald's provides an apt illustration of how the law plays a crucial role integrating and rationalizing this new colonialism. In 1972 MacDonald's opened its first outlet in Paris, which Fantasia reports became the first fast-food establishment in the country. In the first 10 years, from 1972 to 1982, the local franchiser holding the rights to develop in France opened 12 outlets. In the next 15 years, more than 310 more outlets were opened. It is not irrelevant that the rapid expansion of MacDonald's in France took place following a legal suit in which the parent corporation claimed that the local franchise was mismanaging the French outlets. Only after this successful litigation did MacDonald's regain control of the franchises in France and set to work on its expansion.

## Burying Power and Injustice

I have been arguing that despite claims of increased openness, exchange, and participation, globalization has increased the divide between the rich and the poor. At the same time, it has concentrated in relatively fewer hands ever greater wealth and power over larger numbers of persons: that is the critical distinguishing variable, the increasing number of persons subject to concentrations of power. The current economic data are quite explicit on this point, and even those commentators who advocate free markets agree that inequality is increasing.

The problem, however, is more than simply the fact of inequality or of concentrations of power. The possibilities of justice are eroded under globalization primarily because that greater power has been made less visible (Ewick forthcoming). Both the Enlightenment narrative and the market narrative bury the injustices of globalization. In the first story in which reason and science triumph, globalization is driven by what seems like inevitable progress: invention capturing nature—time and space—through transportation and communication. In the second story, globalization is not inevitable but nonetheless also disguised by the operation of the unconscious and invisible hand of the market. By concealing the social organizations of science and of markets, these globalization narratives substitute abstract logic for sociology. By cloaking social organization in inevitable progress and unconscious markets, the globalization narratives return us to a world governed by mysteries rather than by humans. And in this move—deftly obscured in the suppressed sociology—the conventional narratives of globalization erode the possibilities of justice.

For there can be no justice—defined or sought—without power. "Notions of justice," Ewick (forthcoming) writes, "are defined by the power against which they are poised." Indeed, it is the experience and imagination of power unchecked that has underwritten the historic debates and struggles that have occupied not only legal scholars but all human groups as far as we know about how to constitute a just society. The major social movements that have characterized modern history—beginning with the early peasant revolts, the liberal revolutions, and the socialist movements of more modern times—have each represented transformations in just these understandings of how human agency and power shapes the world (Turner 1969).

When human life and social conditions were understood to be beyond the power of the powerful, misfortune was not something for which power was held responsible. On the other hand, when power is held responsible, the situation is understood not as misfortune but as injustice. And the victims of injustice do not petition for charity; instead they claim rights to a remedy. In effect, modern social movements brought transformations in the understandings of the capacities and responsibilities of power. To the extent, however, that the world is understood to operate by inevitability for which no human power is responsible, there is no room for right or injustice, only inefficiency or charity.[14] By disguising power within the invisible hand of the market or inevitable progress, the dominant narratives of globalization deny the existence of a recognizable and powerful other from whom one can demand justice.

## The Sociolegal Narrative: Law Triumphs but Is Not Enough

Although the Enlightenment and market narratives are commonplace and conventional tales, they succeed in part because they are banal. They draw on commonplace understandings of the world; their familiarity enhances their power because the unstated implications are unquestioned, their assumptions and elisions unrecognized. Conveying moral accounts of how the world works, these narratives warn about what happens to those who do not go along with the moral instruction: those who are not reasonable, instrumentally efficient, or do not participate in the

---

[14] Human rights provides a counterexample. Without doubt, human rights discourse makes explicit justice claims. I suggest, however, that human rights discourse is a prominent but weak counterexample because the meaning of those rights is energetically contested, and when proponents of human rights make claims to economic rights and improvement, there is much less consensus and support.

global market. The popularity of these globalization narratives also stifles alternative accounts.[15]

Thus, we observe what every parent knows: It makes a difference what stories we tell ourselves. But if it is the case, as Patty Ewick and I have recently tried to show, that narratives can be both hegemonic and subversive, perhaps it is possible to construct a counternarrative, a subversive story.[16] More directly for the interests of the Law and Society Association, I wonder if is it possible to construct a sociolegal narrative of globalization that remains attentive to power and thus accounts for the possibilities of injustice, and justice.

If these globalization narratives become legitimate and commonplace—hegemonic—by effacing the social organization of power and injustice, sociolegal scholarship can contribute a subversive story by revealing how law contributes to the social organization of power, specifically by tracing the ways in which law's power underwrites globalization. If narratives can be hegemonic by suppressing their sociology within abstract logics, then I like to believe that sociolegal research has already contributed to a counternarrative through its empirical accounts of the social construction and organization of law.

To the extent that we can forge a narrative out of sociolegal scholarship, it is a story not of the triumph of reason as the Enlightenment tale provides, nor a story entirely of individual choice and desire surpassing reason and social organization as the marketeer's narrative suggests. Rather, framed in this idiom, the sociolegal narrative is an account of the triumph of law.[17]

If I read the literature correctly, and judge from the papers presented at annual meetings, sociolegal scholarship has discovered law everywhere, not only in courtrooms, prisons, and law offices but in hospitals, bedrooms, schoolrooms, in theaters and films and novels, and certainly on the streets and in police stations and paddy wagons. And there are even times when the sociolegal scholar maps the places where law ought to be but is not. For sociolegal scholarship, then, "the law is all over" (Sarat 1990). Thus, portrayed as a narrative with a structure of struggle and opposition emplotting a moral tale, the sociolegal account is

---

[15] Together the commonplace narratives of cumulative progress and individual choice, of rational invention and unconscious markets, contain sufficient breadth, variation, and contradiction—what some refer to as polyvocality or heteroglossia—so that together they are effectively protected from critique. Globalization is discursively constituted through these variations and contradictions. In other words, most of the discursive terrain is occupied, and it is difficult to find alternatives to these dominant narratives within familiar symbols and logics.

[16] See Ewick & Silbey 1995 for an elaborated account of what constitutes a hegemonic as against a subversive narrative.

[17] A "law-first" paradigm constructs law as the central character of sociolegal scholarship. Even those works that abandon the law-first paradigm as a research strategy nonetheless attempt in the end to tell a story about law (e.g., Sarat & Felstiner 1995; Merry 1990; Greenhouse, Yngvesson, & Engel 1995).

a story of how the law triumphs over desire. Whether law triumphs over reason is less certain, however, for in different genres and paradigms of sociolegal scholarship, reason may be the devil or the heroine of the plot.

By relying on this fundamental insight of sociolegal scholarship—that law is where it does not appear to be—sociolegal scholarship has the capacity to track the social organization of power in the abundant sites and social spaces now described by "globalization." Moreover, studying the social organization of law is a particularly good way to study the exercise of power under globalization: first, because so many of these new forms of interaction and exchange are organized through law; and, second, because to some extent, we have already been there.

The subject under the lens of sociolegal scholarship—liberal legalism—is structurally homologous with the contemporary accounts of globalization. Indeed, the narratives of globalization reproduce large pieces of liberal legalism's accounts of itself. Each relies on methodological individualism. They share a conception of the world—markets, science, and liberal law—as the cumulative outcome of individual will and agency. The narratives of the market and of liberal legalism also share the conceptual logic of the commodity form (Balbus 1977).

Not only is there a noticeable structural homology between the narratives of globalization and liberal legalism, but the gap between law on the books and law in action revealed in much sociolegal scholarship can also be observed in the accounts and practices of globalization. Not only do we observe a consistent contradiction—a gap between ideal and reality—but the same gap is produced: abstract formal equality and substantive concrete/experiential inequality.

In accounting for this gap, sociolegal research has been able to depict how power is instantiated in all sorts of social relations and to demonstrate not only that social organization matters but how it matters. In just about every piece of empirical research on law, the insight is repeated. In historical studies of litigation, in studies of policing, in studies of the legal profession and delivery of legal services, in reports on access to law, in histories of how particular legal doctrines and offices developed, in studies of court cultures and judicial biographies, in studies of the effectiveness of legal regulation and crime control, and in studies of legal consciousness as well, research has shown how organization, social networks, and local cultures shape law. This research has also demonstrated how law is recursively implicated in the construction of social worlds—of organizations, social networks, and local cultures—and thus how law contributes both to the distribution of social resources and the understandings of the worlds so constituted.

Thus, by reading the pages of *Law & Society Review, Law and Social Inquiry, Law and Policy, Social and Legal Studies, Droit et Société,* the *International Journal of the Sociology of Law, Law and Human Behavior,* or the host of other journals that represent our enterprise, it is possible to find accounts of the organization of power through law. These accounts describe how in doing legal work, legal actors and officials respond to particular situations and demands for service rather than to general prescriptions or recipes of the task. Although law claims a general rationality, it is no different from most other work and, rather than operating on the basis of invariant general principles, proceeds on a case-by-case basis. This is certainly evident in the production of law through litigation and in the creation of precedent through decision in individual cases; it is true of law enforcement as well. Moreover, most lay participants also operate on a reactive, situationally specific rationality. And even in those instances of social movement litigation by labor unions, the civil rights movement, or the recent women's movement for pay equity (McCann 1994), movements' strategies relied on this understanding that long-term changes would depend on the ability to aggregate the outcomes of individual cases.

Because legal action is not rule bound but situationally responsive, it involves extralegal decisions and actions; thus, all legal actors operate with discretion. Documenting the constraints and capacities of legal discretion has occupied several generations of law and society scholarship and provides a store of transferrable wisdom about how inevitable discretion is invoked, confined, and yet ever elastic. In exercising this inevitable discretion, legal actors respond to situations and cases on the basis of typifications developed not from the criteria of law or policy but from the normal and recurrent features of social interactions. These "folk" categories are used to typify the variations in social experiences, in an office, agency, or professional workload and to channel appropriate or useful responses. These typifications function as conceptual efficiency devices.

By relying on ordinary social logics, local cultural categories, and norms, legal action both reflects and reproduces other features and institutions of social life. On the one hand, as a tool for handling situations and solving problems, law is available at a cost, a cost distributed differentially according to social class, status, and organizational position and capacity. On the other hand, law is not merely a resource or tool but a set of conceptual categories and schema that provide parts of the language and concepts we use for both constructing and interpreting social interaction. These ideological or interpretive aspects of law are also differentially distributed.

Finally, by documenting how law both helps to constitute social interaction and is itself constructed by social action, sociolegal scholarship has been able to demonstrate the ways in which law is internal to the market, something marketeers fail to notice or seek to ignore by insisting that law is external. Among such research is the extensive work done early in this association's history on public regulation of business and markets and on administrative law. Similarly, the classic works on contracts—their history, use, and nonuse—and family law have revealed the perpetual struggles to establish a public private divide that is naturalized in some of the globalization narratives.

The stunning tradition of research has consistently challenged the law's claims to autonomy as it has simultaneously challenged the market's claims of autonomy and supremacy. More recent work on scientific disputes and on the use of scientific evidence in legal cases has similarly questioned the claims of science to disinterested truth telling and logic divorced from social organization. In its efforts to map the life of the law—that which has been experience as well as logic—sociolegal scholars have ended up modeling the intersections of semiautonomous social fields.[18] Thus, if sociolegal research can be described as a narrative of the triumph of law, it is important to remember that the law triumphs only by its ubiquity, not by its omnipotence. And when it comes to power and justice, the clear and unambiguous lesson of the sociolegal story is that law is not enough.

## Conclusion: The Possibilities of Justice

Being able to recognize what might at first seem new and even strange—globalization—in what is familiar—liberal legalism—is not sufficient to produce a counterhegemonic narrative. We cannot rest content with some notion that we have been here before. If the dominant narratives of globalization make questions and claims of justice less possible by masking the operation of power through invisible hands and inevitable change, we must expose and track the power that nonetheless operates below the surface of prices and progress.

We need a sociology of globalization. This is the challenge for sociolegal scholarship. We need to pay attention to variables and variations we may have observed insufficiently in the past but which now seem to shape both law and globalization. For example, we need to attend more directly and more energetically to issues of scale and complexity. In the new world order, vast temporal, spatial, and cultural distances are bridged; social organizations based on similarity and proximity have been transformed into functionally interdependent connections among very different and very distant people. Not only has the qualitative sub-

---

18  Sociolegal scholars create as well as map semiautonomous fields. This is, after all, a multi- or interdisciplinary association.

stance of interactions changed but at the same time the quantity and pace of social interactions have increased geometrically. The everyday lives of the majority of people in most social classes all over the globe are constituted by more encounters, of shorter duration, over greater distances than ever before. We need to consider how matters of time, space, and complexity, how issues of volume as well as content, help frame legality and globalization.

Let me be explicit. I am not suggesting that we pursue social theory because of a scholastic desire for knowledge for knowledge's sake nor as a justification for occupation. I suggest that we pursue sociology more seriously because without that theoretically informed analysis of the social organization of power and law, without analysis that begins with the elemental dimensions of social interaction, critical questions of justice cannot be answered. In my view, sociological inquiry is the minimal prerequisite for engaged action on behalf of justice.

If we take social theory more seriously, we cannot exempt our own role in the social organization of power and our complicity in the globalization narratives. Stories are not only read or told, they are made. By entitling our narratives "globalization" rather than "capitalism," "late capitalism," or "postmodern colonialism," we camouflage the organization of power and thus misrepresent the targets of, and impede the struggles for, justice.

I conclude by revisiting the stories of French government responses to protest and grievance with which I began. Marie Antoinette and Michael Bon were separated by more than 200 years, the guillotine, and the demise of French monarchy. They are also distinguished by their varying acknowledgment of the claims of justice, social organization, and power. Marie Antoinette's remark mocked the French peasants; she didn't really expect them to eat cake in lieu of bread. Her sarcasm grew out of and expressed a consciousness of power, inequality, and entitlement. It was, moreover, unconcerned with the demands for justice. By contrast, Michael Bon was not being cynically dismissive. He really believes in global markets and really offers New York as an alternative to Grenoble, Paris, and Lyon. He truly regards cheaper calls to New York as compensation for local networks, obligations, and attachments. He imagines cross-global connections adequate and sufficient to sustain emotional and social life; he values what is distant more than what is near. He thus helps to erode the boundaries whose absence he also bemoans. Where Marie Antoinette was aware of the distance between herself and her subjects, Michel Bon is oblivious to the power of France Telecom and the way it shapes the lives of ordinary people. In contemporary France, power has become so disguised that it is unrecognizable even to itself. Michel Bon can see French citizens only as consumers in a market, and in that blindness he undermines the possibilities of justice.

## References

Appadurai, Arjun (1990) "Disjuncture and Difference in the Global and Cultural Economy," 2 *Public Culture* 1–24.

Balbus, Isaac C. (1977) "Commodity Form and Legal Form: An Essay on the Relative Autonomy of the Law," 11 *Law & Society Rev.* 571–88.

Berman, Marshall (1988) *All That Is Solid Melts into Air: The Experience of Modernity.* New York: Penguin.

Bittner, Egon (1983) "Technique and the Conduct of Life," 30 *Social Problems* 249–61.

Champy, James (1995) *Reengineering Management: The Mandate for New Leadership.* New York: Harper Collins.

Chase-Dunn, Christopher (1991) *Globalization: Structures of the World Economy.* Cambridge, Eng.: Polity Press.

Cushman, Thomas (1995) *Notes from Underground: Rock Music Counterculture in Russia.* Albany: State Univ. of New York Press.

Ewick, Patricia (forthcoming) "Punishment, Power and Justice," in B. Garth & A. Sarat, eds., *Power and Justice in Law and Society Research.* Evanston, IL: Northwestern Univ. Press.

Ewick, Patricia, & Susan S. Silbey (1995) "Subversive Stories and Hegemonic Tales: Toward a Sociology of Narrative," 29 *Law & Society Rev.* 197–226.

Fantasia, Rick (1995) "Fast Food in France," 24 *Theory & Society* 201–43.

Garland, David (1990) *Punishment and Modern Society: A Study in Social Theory.* Chicago: Univ. of Chicago Press.

Giddens, Anthony (1990) *The Consequences of Modernity.* Stanford, CA: Stanford Univ. Press.

Greenhouse, Carol J., Barbara Yngvesson, & David M. Engel (1994) *Law and Community in Three American Towns.* Ithaca, NY: Cornell Univ. Press.

Habermas, Jürgen (1983) "Modernity: An Incomplete Project" in H. Foster, ed., *The Anti-aesthetic: Essays on Post Modern Culture.* Port Townsend, WA.

——— (1992) *The Structural Transformation of the Public Sphere,* trans. T. Burger. Cambridge, MA: MIT Press.

Hammer, Michael, & James Champy (1993) *Reengineering the Corporation: A Manifesto for Business Revolution.* New York: Harper Collins.

Hammer, Michael, & Steven A. Stanton (1995) *The Reengineering Revolution: A Handbook.* New York: Harper Collins.

Harvey, David (1990) *The Condition of Postmodernity.* Cambridge, Eng.: Basil Blackwell.

Head, Simon (1996) "The Ruthless Economy," *New York Rev. of Books,* pp. 47–52 (29 Feb.).

Heyzer, Noeleen, Geertje Lycklama à Nijeholt, & Nedra Weerakoon, eds. (1994) *The Trade in Domestic Workers: Causes, Mechanisms and Consequences of International Migration.* Atlantic Highlands, NJ: Zed Books.

Kennedy, David (1994) "Receiving the International," 10 *Connecticut J. of International Law* 1–26.

Kosai, Yutaka, Robert Z. Lawrence, & Niels Thygesen (1996) "Don't Give Up on Global Trade," *International Herald Tribune,* 30 April, p. 2.

Lasswell, Harold D. (1936) *Politics: Who Gets What, When, How.* New York: McGraw-Hill.

Marx. Karl, & Frederick Engels (1993 [1848]) *The Communist Manifesto.* New York: International Publishers.

McCann, Michael W. (1994) *Rights at Work: Pay Equity Reform and the Politics of Legal Mobilization.* Chicago: Univ. of Chicago Press.

Merry, Sally Engle (1990) *Getting Justice and Getting Even: Legal Consciousness among Working-Class Americans.* Chicago: Univ. of Chicago Press.

Polanyi, Karl (1944) *The Great Transformation: The Political and Economic Origins of Our Time.* Boston: Beacon Press.

Postman, Neil (1986) *Amusing Ourselves to Death: Public Discourse in the Age of Show Business.* New York: Penguin.

———— (1993) *Technopoly: The Surrender of Culture to Technology.* New York: Vintage.

Reich, Robert (1983) *The Next American Frontier.* New York: Times Books.

Ropke, Wilhelm (1955) "Economic Order and International Law," in *Recueil des Cours 1954, Academie de Droit International.* Leyden, The Netherlands: Sijthoff.

Samuelson, Paul A., & William D. Nordhaus (1983) *Economics.* New York: McGraw Hill.

Santos, Boaventura de Sousa (1995) *Toward a New Common Sense: Law, Science and Politics in the Paradigmatic Transition.* New York: Routledge.

Sarat, Austin D. (1990) "'. . . The Law Is All Over': Power, Resistance and the Legal Consciousness of the Welfare Poor," 2 *Yale J. of Law & the Humanities* 343–79.

Sarat, Austin D., & William L. F. Felstiner (1995) *Divorce Lawyers and Their Clients: Power and Meaning in the Legal Process.* New York: Oxford Univ. Press.

Sassen, Saskia (1991) *The Global City: New York, London, Tokyo.* Princeton, NJ: Princeton Univ. Press.

Simmel, Georg (1971 [1903]) "The Metropolis and Mental Life," in D. Levine, ed., *On Individuality and Social Forms.* Chicago: Univ. of Chicago Press.

Turner, Ralph H. (1969) "The Theme of Contemporary Social Movements," 20 *British J. of Sociology* 300–315.

Weber, Max (1978) *Economy and Society: An Outline of Interpretive Sociology,* ed. G. Roth & C. Wittich. Berkeley: Univ. of California Press.

White, Hayden V. (1987) *The Content of the Form: Narrative Discourse and Historical Representation.* Baltimore: John Hopkins Univ. Press.

Woodiwiss, Anthony (1994) "Human Rights and Pacific Capitalism: Towards a New Mode of Governance?" Presented at American Sociological Association annual meeting, Los Angeles.

Young, Alison, & Austin Sarat (1994) "Beyond Criticism: Law, Power and Ethics," 3 *Social & Legal Studies* 323–31.

# [15]

# Alternatives to what kind of suffering?

## Towards a border-crossing criminology

RONNIE LIPPENS
*Ghent University, Belgium*

Abstract _____

This article seeks to imagine a renewed common ground for critical criminologies. In this article, the quest of imagination is developed as an answer to the question: 'On *what kind of suffering* should critical criminologies/ists be concentrating their attention?'. Looking for answers to that question, the paper explores the broad contours of our contemporary era, which is read as a 'hypermodern' zone of strategized ambivalence, or ambivalent strategics. This hypermodern zone, which has seeped into the very capillaries of everyday life, is also the zone which (re)produces contingent logics of incoherence/coherence within politics of identity/difference; it is the zone of hyperflexibility, and of hyperreflexivity, of ambivalent social fragmentation/contraction, and of ambivalent communities, of ambivalent de(re)centring identities, of contingent locations of multiple, multivocal and often incoherent and contradictory voices of oppression/liberation. Answering the question: 'Alternatives to what kind of suffering?', then, must take this hypermodern ambivalence into account. One way of doing so, as is argued here, is in and through a discursive praxis of 'border-crossing', during which critical criminologists will find a renewed common ground only (paradoxically) while dissolving or evaporating into a radical democratic politics.

Key Words _____

ambivalence • border-crossing • critical criminologies • hypermodernity • radical democracy

## 1. Into the maelstrom

There has been much talk during the past few decades about the so-called crisis in critical criminology. Remember, for example, the 1980 publication, edited by James Inciardi, that treated the 'coming crises' of radical criminology. Though this volume was not so much a discussion among 'critical criminologists' (it criticized radical criminology largely from more or less conservative angles), its date of publication is significant: the book was published at the onset of what we will call the 'hypermodern' move of the contemporary era.

It seems that now, after almost two decades of 'crisis talk', the heroic winds which bore 'critical criminology'—the 'outlaw' criminology or the 'counter culture' of mainstream criminology of the 1960s and 1970s—have died down. They have stranded on a set of discourses, each of which has, mostly during the 1980s, tried to hold a separate stand on a few basic assumptions and aspirations, clutching desperately to an essentialized identity politic, whether *'classist'* (or 'Marxist', or 'left realist'), *'feminist'*, *'ethnicist'*, *'communitarianist'*, *'victimist'* (following Rorty, 1989, for example), or other.[1] In the 1990s, however, it looks as if the decentring process of critical criminology, branching out into separate tracks, has proliferated even further and has, so to speak, melted down into a sea of voices in which it is hard, by now, to distinguish those voices that are still thriving on the heroic spirit of the old days. By now it looks as if that spirit, the spirit of 'emancipation', has dissolved—better still, has *evaporated* into the contemporary unlimited and unlimiting stream of voices.

In the process of dissolving, the 'crisis' of critical criminology has evaporated as well. There is, apparently, no more crisis in critical criminology; there is only a sea of shaky ambivalence left (see also Morrison, 1995). There is only that bleak and rather undifferentiated zone of ambivalence which forms and reproduces the contemporary discursive streams of voices of suppression/liberation. The old discursive contractions/contraptions which, in the 1980s, looked as if they, each of them separately, held the promise of being able to fulfil the old aspirations of 'freedom', of 'emancipation', and of real and definite 'liberation', have been confronted, through contemporary blunt ambivalence, with their own limits. The self-assured and even harsh sounds which used to be uttered once from the trenches—from the separate bunkers of essentialism, from the nicely built positions of a splintered and frozen identity politic have, by now, lost quite some volume. They have, to a large extent, dissolved into that one terrible question: whither critical criminology? Although efforts have been made recently to answer this impossible question (some pointing at the necessity of reconstructing a new core (Schwartz, 1997) for critical criminology, others suggesting quite the opposite (that is, to deconstruct whatever kind of core being constructed; e.g. Ericson and Carrière, 1994; see also Friedrichs, 1996), this way of talking critical criminology seems not to be the most fruitful one any more. This way of talking critical criminology is, indeed, losing touch with contemporary experience, which is already nestling in hypermodern everyday life.

## 2. What kind of suffering?

That is why, in this article, we will try to answer this question by rephrasing it, and by gradually concentrating on a more down-to-earth one, a question which starts from the ambivalence of contemporary experience, and not from the discursive contractions/contraptions critical criminologists have been inventing and cherishing 'all those years' (to paraphrase Fish, 1989). This is, of course, not to deny that the contractions/contraptions constructed by critical criminologists are themselves part and parcel of that ambivalent zone of human experience. In fact, quite the opposite assumption sustains our reformulation; it is precisely *because* there are reasons to assume that the discursive constructions of critical criminologists are fully embedded in everyday ambivalent experience that we will leave aside the 'whither critical criminology?' question and concentrate on another one.

Contemporary ambivalence leaves us with the question as to *what kind of suffering* we would need to pay attention to. Which voices are the ones we should be listening to? What kind of discursive constructions would be helpful for us in order to be able to hear, to listen and to attend to those voices? Or, to use another language, in and through what kind of 'replacement discourse' (see, of course, Henry and Milovanovic, 1996) can we imagine grappling with contemporary suffering? It is these questions which we will attempt to address in the following pages. These questions refer to the deeply ambivalent and contradictory experiences which affect people in various contexts, in everyday praxis, in the midst of a seemingly unstoppable and ever-proliferating stream of metaphors and signs with which these experiences are being (re)constructed, or simply given a name. The answer to these questions will show us some possible openings as to what critical criminology, or better: critical criminologies/ists, could be hoping for. At least, this belief is the hope of this essay.

## 3. The (inevitably shaky) gist (of the argument)

This is how we will proceed. In the next section, we will try to sketch the broad contours of what we consider to be the significance of the signifier 'critical' in 'critical criminology' (see also Thomas and O'Maolchatha, 1989). To us, this signifier has always had some Blochian connotations; it has always, and inevitably, been filled with splinters of the 'principle of hope' (Bloch, 1959); it has always been the location where 'suffering' has been fixed and found, and where 'liberation' has utopistically, and inevitably, been roaming (both of these moments are inextricably intertwined). Now, where critical criminology is concerned, this Blochian and inevitably hopeful 'critical' flow of discursively constructed locations of 'suffering' (and thus, of liberation, and vice versa) has, up until the end of the 1970s, been able to keep a rather centred social and cultural momentum. From the 1980s onwards, however, when it became clear that no centre seemed to hold any more, that is, during an era of culturalized *strategics* in which criticism assumed and reproduced specific exclusive identities, and *imagined communities*, this centred momentum splintered into separate discursive tracks, each of them pinpointing specific, and mostly exclusive, locations of suffering and fixing specific and often defensive contractions/ contraptions of hope. In the 1990s, then, also a 'postmodern' or decentring flow of consciousness has reached the surface of contemporary experience, and has probably even percolated into the ways of everyday life. 'Suffering' and 'hope', then, under contemporary *hypermodern* conditions, have melted down into a deeply felt cultural space of mostly contingent de(re)centring, of often contingent fragmentation/contraction, of proliferating incoherent coherences and of coherent incoherences. These signifiers, 'suffering', and 'hope' have become unfixed, ambivalent, multi-layered, shaky, full of *rhizomic* energies (*pace* Deleuze and Guattari, 1976) and (most of the time) they are free-floating signifiers, forged and broken into a myriad stream of de(re)centring subject positions and communities. These signifiers are roaming, then, kaleidoscopically spangled with the fragmented colours of unfixed and unfixing fractured experiences (e.g. see Bauman, 1995a), in the spaces/places of hypermodernity, *the gist of which* cannot be grasped any more in or through the old contractions/ contraptions of critical criminology, nor by its old *stories* (e.g. Caplan, 1991), or in other words, by its *univocal* logics (of coherence) and aspirations. We are in need, then, of a renewed Blochianism, one that tries to grasp hypermodern experience; one that will hope to start from the unfixed, unfixing, refixing and unfixable experience of hypermodernity. In other words, we are in need of a language which will try to fill an inevitable Blochianism of hope and suffering with *ambivalence*; a language which will show no trace of fear of ambivalence; a discursive location where it will be felt that ambivalence can only be eradicated (though always *illusorily*) through exclusion and through destruction of all and every Other and, eventually, of Oneself (Bauman, 1991; see also, from geography, Sibley, 1995).

We will start developing the contours of such a language in section 5. In that section, we will first try to explain what 'hypermodernity' means to us. This section has three purposes. First of all, it will shed some light on the cultural context within which the aforementioned (discursive) process of fragmentation and contraction, of *decentring* and *recentring*, of *'coherenciation'* and *'incoherenciation'* has occurred. Secondly, it will try to outline the ambivalence of the contemporary era (of hypermodernity), and as such, it will describe some characteristics of the contemporary discursive field of voices; of voices of oppression and liberation, of suffering and hope.

And lastly, this section will try to gather some conclusions as to what kinds of suffering critical criminologists are forced to grapple with in ambivalent hypermodernity. It is here, in this section, that we will look for clues to possible answers to the question which is the focus of this (hypermodern) paper: 'Alternatives to what kind of suffering?'.

Section 6 draws some conclusions for critical criminology. We will argue for a *border-crossing* criminology. That is, we will try to open a discursive future for critical criminology as one that is sensitive to the ambivalent, as one in which communities will not be fixed; as one in which neither identity nor difference will be frozen into exclusive bunkers; as one, finally, in which a radical democratic politics can be imagined in and through a cultural praxis of border-crossing.

The final conclusion draws together the main lines of argument, while pointing at the same time to some 'hypermodern' problems for a border-crossing criminology.

## 4. Blochian beginnings

Some time ago, after having read a text which tried neatly to explain where crime came from, and what should be done about it, one of our students complained, muttering about the neatness of it all.

> Why should the world be represented in a square? Why is it that apparently nobody seems to try to picture the world, for instance, as a formless blob? That, anyway, would be more plausible, more 'realist', than a rattling contraption which is not even close to representing the fluidity of our everyday floating and slippery experience. Could this type of reasoning be typical for a Western standard of control and power, directed towards the 'squaring' of people, and towards the arrogant social play of chess?[2]

We will not enter the discussion here—again, after all those years—of whether left realism (still) has something to offer to a hypermodern critical criminology. But this student's remark is, nevertheless, important here. This remark, one will probably have felt already, touches, even in those very few lines, all of the themes hypermodern academia is wrestling with. These lines are a revolt, bubbling straight out of hypermodern experience, against the terror of universalist arrogance of those who pretend to have found the one big square to squeeze all possible representations and aspirations into. These lines are, however, also part of the search for possible ways towards a better world, and are, in that sense, as we all are, stumbling helplessly, in an uncertain, square-shaped no man's land between the mud of our limited experience, our *local knowledges*, the obstinate ambivalence of everything social—always slipping through our clumsy fingers, which are always busy making social *sutures*—(*pace* Laclau and Mouffe, 1985), and the ever-fleeing, allegedly universal horizon of all (wo)man's salvation. And this square stumbling, head over heels, is what critical criminology has been doing all the way.

Critical criminology has always been looking for suffering, has always been building promising squares and cubes, offering hope to the distressed, making hopeful promises, explaining found disasters and located suffering, only to explain, shortly afterwards, its own drawbacks and failures when confronting 'found' suffering, stumbling and mumbling. But always continuing, never being tired, always hopeful, and trying again. This is, to us, what the word *critical* is still doing in critical criminology, after 'all those years' of disaster and suffering. It is this mark of sustained hope for a better world that has, up to now, been inspiring critical criminology, and *should be* inspiring our works, our representations, for and in the times to come. We should go on looking for suffering, that is for sure, and looking for alternatives to this suffering, that is obvious. With the spirit of Enlightenment in the back, if you wish (that is: with the hope of human liberation), but with a sensitive recognition of the multiform Other (the Other is everywhere, and has more than a thousand faces), forcing us into reflexive caution as to the ways of our Enlightened tumbling and stumbling. This probably sounds rather trivial. But again, it should be, because if critical criminology has ever meant anything, it has been rooting, all those years, in this vague, but *hopelessly* inevitable modern *hope*. Indeed, critical criminology, in all its diverging and converging tracks, in all its glittering fountains, even in its most scientistic corners, has always and inevitably been rooted in that which Ernst Bloch (1959) once described as *the principle of hope*, that pulse of modernity, which is brewed, forged and broken again in that hazy zone of the *'not-yet-conscious'* between past, present and future. It has been rooting inevitably in that ambiguous zone of promise, possibility and peril, where dark pictures of suffering and sparkling visions of liberation (of Utopia) are made out of experience— experience which is itself made out of the stream of effects, and which is again the nurturing well of the modern *pulse* of hope. Critical criminology has always been there, *rhizomically* enmeshed in that stream of voices of suffering and of liberation.

None of critical criminology's old univocal, coherent representations, none of its solid *stories*, none of its nicely carved squares and cubes, seem to get any more hold of today's fluid ambivalence and contingency, in and through which the cultural *rhizome* has—as we all start to feel—been cut loose and is driven towards everyday life and cultural consciousness. In the early days of critical criminology, when pragmatism reigned in criminology's academia, and even some time afterwards, when workerist/ classist and feminist contractions/contraptions and flows were inundating this original pragmatist discourse, everything within criminology seemed very well, very neat. This was the case when critical criminology was forging itself in and through a centred coherence (criticizing the cultural dynamics and effects of a perceived centre of State, Structure and System, hoping and striving for an alleged pure authenticity) as well as when critical criminology (especially during the 1980s) diverged gradually into separating discursive tracks, each, under swelling conditions of hypermodern strategics, de(of)fensively looking for (and finding) coherent suffering, and solid promises of liberation. Although stories and ambitions were slowly bubbling up everywhere within this critical criminology, very few people within critical criminology really bothered about that. For there seemed to be enough of everything for everyone: the world, that is, the Western world of relative certainty and steady-paced predictability, would care for everything, and would, in the end, care for each and every individual. It would even care for those who, for instance in Western critical criminology's academia, backed-up as it was by Keynes(ianism), were kicking, with all kinds of boots (pragmatist whether radical), Keynes' rock-like vehicle. As in social life, that bright and glittering café of everyday experience, the people who dwelled in the different chambers of critical criminology's academia also seemed to know exactly where one was to search for human suffering, and above all, they knew exactly which alternatives were to be aspired to and which solutions ought to be brought in. Under the reign of Keynes, every story on suffering and on liberation, every square and cube of critical criminology, could cherish a few illusions of universality—all and everything Other being pushed out of sight/site (see also, e.g. Encinoza and del Olmo, 1981; Sumner, 1982). In short, as in other Western spaces/places, everyone in there *knew* exactly which boundaries should be drawn, and which constructions were to be built.

Now, we feel that these partial constructions did not 'really' fit, but in those days, that did not seem to matter much. Each of the cherished stories, each of the Truths of Suffering and of Liberation felt as a rather reliable construction, evoking and mobilizing preferred '*imagined communities*'. (Anderson, 1991)[3] of suffering and liberation (e.g. the Working Class, Woman, the post-colonial Subaltern, etc.), all of which would allegedly hold the clue to and the promise of universal liberation. Under contemporary conditions of rather contingent fragmentation and restructuring (fuelled by global capital flexibility, and with post-Keynesian consumerism catalyzing globally flexible competition), things are changing. Now, when boundaries are blurring everywhere, when centres are crumbling gradually, and when hypermodern experience is dedifferentiating into a diffuse fluid stream of social anxieties, uncertainties, risks and delights to be experienced from ever-changing and always deconstructing and reconstructing subject positions, to be managed strategically and reflexively, things are indeed on the move. In this hypermodern whirlpool, it is not very easy any more to find clear-cut and one-dimensional suffering, and to get some instant alternatives (as it was in the old days of Keynesian alleged certainty). Now is a time when there seems to be no ultimate deliverance any more at the end of arrogant roads on which travellers forget the multiform discursive layers that mediate, represent and reproduce human inter-dependent and 'interconnected' experience.

## 5. Hypermodernity: hyperreflexivity and hyperflexibility

### 5.1. Hypermodernity

This section deals first with what we have labelled 'hypermodernity'. We use this signifier, 'hypermodernity', instead of, say, 'postmodernity'[4] or 'high modernity'[5] because the prefix 'hyper' is probably better for conveying the strategic dimension of contemporary modernity. It is precisely this strategic dimension of the contemporary which is producing extreme levels of reflexivity and flexibility. These, in turn, (re)produce a process of socio-cultural hyperdifferentiation (see also Crook et al., 1992), and, as such, feedback into contemporary *strategization*.

This is, to us, hypermodernity. It is the contemporary zone of unavoidable ambivalence, of contingency, of the accumulated historical logics of hope and exhaustion. It is the contemporary, which, as world-system theorists would say, has entered a contingent zone of transition, a 'chaotic' era (Amin, 1991) of ambivalent *un*fixation and *re*fixation, of fragmentation and reconcentration, of *de*centring and *re*centring, of *de*construction and *re*construction (e.g. Hopkins and Wallerstein, 1996). In this section we will try to sketch, very roughly, the contours of the ambivalent contemporary, of hypermodernity, because it is there, in that turbid zone, the question of this paper is drifting and floating in numerous contexts; it is there, in that hypermodern zone of cloudy ambivalence, in this world in which everywhere people are looking for 'a centre that holds' (Bauman, 1995b), that answers to our questions are proliferating, deconstructing in one moment, and reconstructing in another, clustering and fixing in one moment, diverging and splintering in another.

### 5.2. Hypermodern strategics: everyday life and JIT-culture

For over two decades now, centred/ordered Fordist production and Keynesian regulation have been gradually erased. Fordist productivity hit the limits of consumption at the beginning of the seventies while, at the same time, core consumer markets were gradually flooded with goods from the few regions (e.g. the *dragon* states in Asia) that succeeded in linking a politics of austerity to increasing industrial production and very competitive prices on the world market. Delocalization of labour-intensive production away from the Western core increased, and technological competition exploded, and created, in all kinds of spin-offs, the conditions for a flexible mode of production and consumption, in turn feeding on a growing culture of elite-mimicking life-style and JIT-life (JIT: Just in Time). Moreover, with the abandonment, in 1971 and 1973, of the Bretton Woods agreement on fixed rates of currency exchange, an almost endless space of JIT-money opened up and has been filled at a dazzling pace (see e.g. Axford, 1995). While the risks of direct investments were rising, this space for JIT-money was rapidly filled with staggering volumes of speculative transactions, unbounded, and whirling freely through a thoroughly globalized financial hyperspace. In this hyperspace, economic means are prevented from crystallizing into productive investments, while huge profits are made and lost in a sea of panic, leaving state structures and economic policy as mere shadows of the illusions that once used to be alive.

This is, to a large extent, the new, hypermodern, enterprise culture.[6] It is an almost unlimited stream of converging and conflicting strategies, of obsessive 'time-space compression' (Harvey, 1989),[7] of contradictory regulations, of exclusions and controls, of flexible laws and flexible transgressions, of *rhizomichaotically* flourishing desire(s)/control(s) or regulation(s) (see also Stanley, 1996). It is the rush and the terror of hypermodern JIT-life. It is part and parcel of a more general strategic mood of risk calculation and risk management into which the global core has been sliding. It is the experience of hypermodern worries and fears. It is the experience of hypermodern desires and delights. It is the mark of an era that has wrenched itself free from stable certainties. It is the swing of New Times (e.g. Hall, 1989) in which Capital has freed itself from Labour and its divisive containment within State boundaries; New Times in which the State gradually loses its function as the site of the organization of production and reproduction. The State has, under hypermodern conditions, become only one of the slowly unfixing and fragmenting locations where flexible games of regulation and control are being played, where flexible strategies of holding, saving and abandoning are being implemented with unforeseeable and often even unknown consequences (e.g. Lash and Urry, 1994).

According to some of the leading world-system theorists, the global capitalist economy has, since about 1970, entered a phase of transition, the outcome of which cannot be predicted at all. The historical game of periodic capitalist reproduction through expanding successive global waves of (semi-)proletarization and commodification, resulting almost invariably in one-way exploitation and surplus drainage (remember dependency theory, e.g. Frank, 1967), is not possible any more in a thoroughly proletarized and hyper-commodified global landscape. Capitalist accumulation nowadays has to reproduce itself through unfixed strategies of flexible investments, speculations, exclusions, inclusions, transgressions and regulations. This is probably why the contemporary global economy is considered to have entered a chaotic phase (Amin, 1991), while its production and reproduction, while the process of surplus drainage, can no longer be represented using more or less stable *laws/Laws*, as they were before (see e.g. from world-systems theory: Wallerstein, 1991). With the crumbling of all kinds of stabilizing sites of regulatory organization (such as the nation-state) and with no sites *(sights)* of order and stability in sight *(site)*, the world is to be considered as the contingent und unexpected outcome of an almost unlimited and ever-proliferating bulk of flexible strategies, fragmented micro-politics and local struggles, these, in turn, reproducing options for flexible accumulation, *hit and run* consumption, self-styling sub(ob)jectivization(s) and the *rhizomic* mobilization of exploding, unbounded cultural energies (Jameson, 1991). This new global condition of strategic reflexivity and localized struggles seems to have already percolated into everyday life—especially in those Western social democracies where state structures are fragmenting and falling apart. When securities formerly taken for granted melt as snow, strategic reflexivity invades all the corners of social life; the latter, in turn, reproducing multiple sites of often unintendedly produced risks and risk perception (Beck, 1992). And this happens very easily in the more or less atomized social arenas (atomized already during Keynes' reassuring experiment) where diverging and everproliferating wants and needs, ever-expanding desires, ever-expanding Rights and Laws, ever-expanding transgressions, have been flourishing, *all those post-war years.*

Now is a contemporary in which ambivalence bubbles straight into the reflexive corners of everyday consciousness; it is an era marked by profound uncertainties and by proliferating streams of voices that will speak ever more reflexively, strategically, begging and threatening, controlling and evading. Old and allegedly indestructable *imagined communities*, old centres of power and old beacons of reference are crumbling, are being torn apart and reconstructed into a myriad other ones, largely unpredictably. Old and seemingly stable identities are being deconstructed and reconstructed into other ones, largely unpredictably. Individual selves are being splintered and are splintering themselves reflexively, looking for fitting positions and locations, trying them out, abandoning them in dissatisfaction, reaching out for alternative identities. Individuals are using and reproducing discourses, deconstructing other discourses while doing so, and then, again, throwing away the previously chosen discourses only to pick out another one, or articulating a specific set from the ever-multiplying hypermodern discursive stream. This hypermodern 'habit' of *hopping* between self-chosen or constructed identities, or of *JIT-ing* identities, of *consuming* identities (e.g. Mackay, 1997), is what makes things unpredictable. One can never know which identities will be chosen, today, by whom, which discourses will be latched on to, for what kind of purposes. This is one stream of hypermodern flux (see also Calhoun, 1994, 1995) which has probably percolated into everyday life and experience.

But there is another flux, a quite contradictory one, to be found in the *accumulated heap* of strategized hypermodernity; a flux of *contraction*, fixing meaning, concentrating imaginative energies within sharply bordered and, thus, exclusive, communities. This hypermodern stream of defensive contraction has also been taking root deeply in everyday life and experience. Both of these everyday hypermodern streams, JIT-ing flux and contracting and defensive fixation, reflect, one could say, the whirls of contemporary global capital, clustering energies into defensive communities in one place, while shattering them in other places, forging coherence while excluding all and everything Other outside the bunkers and fortresses Mike Davis (1990)—amongst others—has been describing only in their rudest forms. Generating centrifugal dynamics in one place, while concentrating flux in another place. This can be taking place at the same time and at one and the same place. In hypermodernity, decentring into contracting parts is a well-known phenomenon. There is, in hypermodernity, certainly a contractive, even a pre-modern, move towards recentring fixation. There is, indeed, a moment which gathers and concentrates discursive energies within attempts to block time. It is precisely the dialectic between the (modern) moment of time-deferment, the (postmodern) moment of time-consumption, and the (pre-modern) moment of time-fixation, which is at the *accumulated* core of hypermodern strategics and hypermodern ambivalence (see also Heelas, 1996).

### 5.3. Ambivalence

Again, all this makes hypermodernity into a flow of ambivalence. A flow which can no longer be stopped through modern 'governmentality', or through practices of obsessive ordering, and legitimated through and within (universalist) rationalism (Bauman, 1991). Ambivalence is surfacing in all those spheres and contexts which have lost their allegedly timeless stabilities and certainties, and have, since, fallen prey to unlimited deconstructions and reconstructions, to reflexive flexibility. Fixed meaning is losing its hold. Whenever meaning is concentrated, whenever centres are built, whenever *communities* are *imagined*, when boundaries are drawn, whenever inclusions are proposed or practised (whenever exclusions are proposed and practised), they all seem to be of an ephemeral and fragile nature. Just as the multi-central whirling of global capital, and the centrifugal de(re)nationalizations of the contemporary, are not very stable, nor fixed, everyday life and experience thrive on proliferating fears and anxieties, flowing in and between melancholically constructed clusters of imagined and illusory straws of certainty. Straws that, moreover, more and more, seem to have unexpected consequences and unwanted effects. Ambivalence, then, pours out of the permanent constructions and deconstructions of these straws of salvation. Ambivalence is what issues from the distress caused when grasping for a construction, for an inclusion, while, at the same time, inevitably, deconstructing and excluding everything Other. Ambivalence is what is to be found in the rebounds of the straws of salvation, of the cherished inclusions, creating, in this way, inevitably, Others. Others, excluded, but in turn, and inevitably, part of the interconnectedness and interdependency of hypermodernity, in such a way as to offer new chances for the ways of global capital. Other(s) which will be preparing, inevitably, a blow to the excluders. It is ambivalence which emerges when boundaries are drawn to favour an *imagined community* while Other(s) are excluded, when, that is, we forget that the Other(s) make(s) us what we believe we are; when we forget that it is us who make the Other, and, in turn, again ourselves. This is, in sum, hypermodernity: hyperreflexivity, hyperflexibility, and no clear way out, no centre, no fixed straw of hope in sight/site.[8]

Ours is a contemporary which can be represented as a seamless skein[9] of highly interconnected forms of oppression, exploitation and exclusion. Of suffering, say. And, precisely because of this deeply rooted interconnectedness, alternatives cannot be represented in rigid ways, forcing one-dimensional solutions, vehemently protecting our own imaginary communities, ignoring oppression and exclusion *within* and *without*, as seems to happen now at a fast competitive pace. How are we, in today's formidable mess of proliferating ambivalent exclusive/inclusive censures,[10] to choose and pick the ones that are helpful in constructing such an articulatory politics of 'liberation'? It is to that question that we will turn in the following pages.

## 6. Border-crossing criminology

### 6.1. Speech, suffering and ambivalence

What has been developed above may seem all very abstract and not very close to the matters we are concerned with here, namely, the search for answers to the question: 'Alternatives to what kind of suffering?' What has been described is the hypermodern zone where multiple streams of suffering voices are being (re)produced. It is in this ambivalent zone where answers to this question are flowing and proliferating. It is there, in that zone of ambivalence, where alternatives will have to be anchored in uncertain and troubled waters. This is the zone where progressive aspirations to change things for the better will have to be articulated. This is the zone which has generated mostly defensive contractions, generalized competition, possessive inclusions and a myriad of exclusions. This is the zone which has known, up to now, very little solidarity with the competitive Other, and has had little attention to the 'needs and rights of distant strangers' (Corbridge, 1994). How can we distribute progressive attention and reach for alternatives, without reproducing at the same time multiple forms of suffering? This is a rather fundamental question which has, under reflexive hypermodern conditions, reached the contingent discursive space that was vacated by the disappearance of the Absolute Truths of Once-and-for-All Universalism.

Some will keep on assuming that there *has to be* (imperative!) some space/place somewhere, present or imagined, but nevertheless specific, charged with immanent meaning, which simply cannot be avoided and which would be the space/place for progressives (or critical criminologists) to meet and change things for the better. This assumption is still deeply entrenched, even in the midst of hypermodern ambivalence, and after decades of fragmenting/contracting politics of identity/difference. We would rather assume that imagining a common space/place inevitably boils down to imagining ever-fluctuating gains and losses. Imagining a common space/place inevitably implies imagining differences to be respected and equalities to be striven for. Imagining a common space/place is a praxis and a matter of never-ending negotiation and contestation. It has become more and more clear that whatever space/place is being referred to in speech or praxis it will inevitably be an imagined space, full of inclusions, full of exclusions. In every imagined space/place, difference is rubbed out *within*, as well as unity with the Other, with everything *outside* the boundaries of the imagined space/place (see also Abel, 1994).

There is—to us—no universalist guarantee to be invoked, no simple Truth to be established when speaking or practising. Speech and praxis refer to *imagined communities*, and will inevitably have consequences of both including and excluding. Inclusions, by repressing or by excluding difference *within*, and exclusions of those Others whose equality is denied and whose difference is emphasized. Now this is inevitable, as previously stated, because a space/place of unquestioned unity, a real universal space of *total community*, is not (yet) of this world. Moreover, it is precisely this kind of assumption and/or aspiration which has, *all those years*, produced multiple terrors. This has to be borne in mind when there is talk of alternatives. Trapped in ambivalence, without the old comforts of the illusions of universalism, carved up through a myriad of contextualities and an almost unlimited reservoir of textualities, we can only try to include the Other(s) and hope that, by these inclusions, we will keep from excluding other Others as much as possible. It is this ambivalence that will have to be dealt with in all those spaces/places between the ordered Other and an Othered order. In those spaces/places that open themselves when we construct and order Others, and when we deconstruct Ourselves looking for Others.

Does all this imply that we should wallow in a kind of detached, or worse, disinterested relativism? No. But it could lead to the conclusion that producing alternatives to suffering will have to be thought of more and more as a kind of active search for Others. Reflecting deeply on every Other, on everything Other we exclude (*within* and *outside*) each time when we say 'We' or 'Us' or 'Them'. We will have to develop an attitude of eccentricity when talking and practising global capital's distribution (see Abu-Lughod, 1995). Or, using yet another language, *crossing borders* of self-centredness, crossing borders of imagined Truths, crossing borders of the imagined 'Us' and 'Them' (Giroux, 1992). Crossing the borders of the here and now of our limited and limiting localities, trying to get some sense out of all the *heterotopias* that are pushed aside by whatever is being said and done. Resisting frozen/fixed representations (hooks, 1994) and evoking Others, that is; freeing textual outlaws and voicing outlaw cultures (Young, 1996). This is not relativism. It is an affirmative decision to direct global capital's distribution towards everything and everyone Other, towards everything and everyone forgotten or repressed whenever there is talk of 'We' and 'Us' (see also Fraser, 1995).

Does all this imply that there should be no more talks of 'We' and 'Us' any more? Does this imply that we should stop using 'We', 'Us', and 'Them'? No. Simply because the Other can only be known (and this may sound as a paradox) through the discursive construction of our 'We' and our 'Us' communities. The Other is everything and everyone excluded from these communities. But will that incessant cycle of de(re)construction not lead to the endless reproduction of the centrifugal dynamic of hypermodern fragmentation? No, this reproduction is more likely to occur where hypermodernity's centrifugal energies are used to build and proliferate imaginary shelters, concrete bunkers and flexibly guarded fortresses. This would reproduce the opportunities for and the ways of hypermodern global capital. A progressive strategy would precisely need to counter this centrifugal and fragmenting flow, and this can be done by incessantly looking for Others. Now, who then are these Others to be looked for and to be respected, if they can only be found while de(re)constructing the 'We's and 'Us'es of our fluid imagined communities? They are those whose difference is to be respected; they are those whose inequalities are to be lessened and whose 'capabilities' (*pace* Sen, 1992) are to be equalized with those of 'Our' communities. The Other is where suffering is not heard through the noise of the hypermodern whirlpool. The Others are they who possibly have even lost their voice, or have forgotten they are exploited and/or excluded, or have—desperately—settled down into resignation. They are (again paradoxically) those Universal Others who are Othered through our Universal and/or Fixed speech and practice (see also Leonard, 1997: 30).

Now this may resemble very much Zygmunt Bauman's call for a 'postmodern' Being-for-the-Other morality which, he *hopes*, could be forged out of ambivalent interdependent contextualities (Bauman, 1992: 200–210. 1993, 1995a). Bauman's call goes beyond a mere multiculturalist Being-with-the-Other morality and, as such, inclines towards a Levinasian position of an unconditional morality for the Other. Bauman, however, stops at this moment of hope. According to Bauman, every search for the fixation of conditions which would provide an environment in which a Being-for-the-Other morality could thrive, risks producing multiple exclusions. A Being-for-the-Other morality can only be unconditional. Though there may be arguments (such as Bauman's) for an unconditional morality for/towards inevitable Other(s), this morality will only be with us in and through language, and will, as such, need certain metaphors which will be able to grasp the multiple ambivalences and contextualities people find themselves in. We will try to expand on that thought.

### 6.2. Searching for new metaphors

It seems, then, that we are in need of other tools when we will try to represent the contemporary hypermodern experience. This is an experience which is forged of and which reproduces an accumulated variety of different cultural logics (whether they be called *pre-modern*, *modern*, and *postmodern*, or Otherwise), and which fills an ever-expanding cultural space of kaleidoscopic hybrids. We are in need of Other(ed) metaphors by which we would be able to answer the burning question 'alternatives to what kind of suffering?'—a question which is still valid, even after a decade (the 1970s) full of a centred (yes, centred, but also *decentring*) *authentistic* universalism, after the 1980s' stream of *recentring* (yes, *recentring*, but also *decentring*) contractions/contraptions, and after the 1990s bewildering fountain of de(re)centring splinters of culturalized and culturalizing *postmodern* Capital (see on this especially Jameson, 1991). We are in need, one could say, of a new language which grapples with hypermodern ambivalence, which avoids universalist arrogance, but one which avoids equally a detached, 'postmodern' playfulness. This language should, then, be able to express sensitiveness to contemporary ambivalence, and would, as such, embody a reflexive refusal to pretend having access to the Ultimate suffering, and having Knowledge of the Ultimate key to Liberation. This language would hesitate to believe that there are specific, authentic, vernacular spaces/places of oppression/suppression, of suffering, and of resistance or of liberation. We are imagining a language here, that would fear the arrogance of an extreme identity politic as much as a radicalized politics of difference (see Young, 1990)—a language that would, in other words, try to skate reflexively and carefully on the ambivalent ice between the dangers of coherent stories of universalism, even those that are couched in a *civilized* ethics of communication (Habermas, 1984, 1988), and the dangers of stories of incoherence and of radical, localized *incommensurabilities* (remember—already—Lyotard, 1986). This language would talk of the heterotopic zone (Foucault would have said)[11] left out of a mechanics of solids, but which is equally left out of a 'mécanique des fluides' (*pace* Irigaray, 1977). This new, 'hypermodern' language would try, then, to connect to a still Enlightened intentional drive, or rather: a 'weak messianic force',[12] towards an open future in which things could possibly be better. In that sense, it would still be an utopian, or utopistic language (see also Lippens, 1995) with a deep sense of ambivalent contextualities. The most eloquent of contemporary theorists/critics of *the postmodern*, Zygmunt Bauman (1992), would be talking of a language that is inscribed in an ethics of 'deconstruction of immortality', that is, a language that takes the ambivalent contextualities and contextual ambivalence which make up our present into account; deconstructing, then, the modernist zeal for the Absolute, for immortality; refusing to contract into a pre-modern (fascist-like) traditional past or to refer to a distant future, to a rigid Utopia which would only be reachable via tracks of universalist arrogance. Bauman's time is the present: it is *now* that the voices of the Other are to be listened to; it is now that Utopia has to be practised in unlimited contextualities, using the energies of faint promises which slumber in multiple and ambivalent discursive spaces, mobilizing energies from unlimited life strategies of Others.

In the following pages we will try to develop a language which we think could offer some possible ways to answer the question as to what kind of suffering needs critical, progressive—inevitably Blochian, though no longer univocally Marxist—attention (of criminologists), and as to what kind of alternatives can be deployed within and from hypermodern conditions. We will hopefully be able to demonstrate that, while broadly outlining the metaphorical texture of that hypermodern language, we will have left the old essentializing discourses (of critical criminology) behind. In other words, we will have *crossed borders.*

### 6.3. *Walking borders, crossing boundaries*

What we have tried to show earlier is that under hypermodern, '*strategized*' conditions of flexible and reflexive decentring of subjectivity, of flexible and reflexive de(re)contruction of identity/difference, and of '*community*', we have lost our illusions that human suffering can be divided into clear-cut localities. We have lost our illusions that the flow of their representations can be stopped and fixed onto the Absolute, and that their remedies (their '*alternatives*') can be assumed to be dwelling in specific, neatly delimited, Certain corners. This has probably never been the case. Any fixation of representations, any clustering of discursive energies into an alleged Absolute, have always been the result of historical fluxes, and have always been forced out of energies of whatever (whatever Other) had been pushed aside. The anti-colonial rage, *tangible* and *muscular* even (remember Fanon, 1967), as it burst out of a long history of deep-seated oppression/suppression, out of a silenced history, into the flexible history of post-colonial hypermodernity, could, for example, be read as a sign of this motion of exclusion. These anti-colonial energies are, then, to be considered as the concentrated product of concentrated, fixed representations, of closed and excluding discursive constructions and practices. In this intense and muscular rage—in that brief and fragile moment—the alleged Absolute and Certain fixations of 'Western' *orientalist* imperialist discourse (remember Said, 1995), were reversed. That brief moment of reversal, so to speak, blasted into the discursive open what had been silenced and neglected, *all those years.*

What is being said here refers to what Chantal Mouffe—following a Derridian road—has called the 'constitutive outside' which is silenced in any speech which assumes identity and difference, that assumes 'community'. It is that unlimited zone which falls outside the tracks covered by speech; it is the zone of neglect; but nevertheless, it is the zone which gathers the conditions for the speech-tracks to form; it is what constitutes the representations uttered; it is the 'constitutive exterior' (Mouffe, 1994). There is always a 'constitutive exterior'. Speech can never cover the social, speech can never represent the social Absolutely nor Universally; speech *always* silences identity and difference; speech *always* assumes 'community' *repressively*; speech can never represent Total 'community' (there is always difference *within*, and identity with the exterior, silenced in the practice of speech), there is no Absolute community of Total identity; the social cannot be sutured once and for all; there is always an excess of meaning, which is an excess of the 'impossibility of society' (see on these matters, of course, again Laclau and Mouffe, 1985; Laclau, 1990, 1994, and, from Derridian inspiration, Corlett 1989). We have tried to show that under hypermodern conditions any fixation of representations, any blockage of an excess of meaning, can only be done (as it always has been the case) at the cost of silencing Other voices. It can only be done by expelling everything that could possibly bind us to equality, anything that possibly could situate us into respected differences, out of the essentialized discursive (*and thus* also political) space/place that is being carved out in the act of fixation. This has, indeed, always been the case. Under hypermodern conditions of radicalized strategics, under conditions of social fragmentation/contraction and of de(re)centring subjectivities, under conditions of flexible reflexiveness (or reflexive flexibilities, for that matter), under conditions also of deep inter-connectedness and interdependency, things become rather complicated, and, to say the least, openly ambivalent (see, recently Kirby, 1996, on the inevitable shakyness of ever-ambivalent, 'indifferent' borders of subjectiv-ities). Each and every time 'identity' and 'difference' ('community') are assumed or discursively practised, ambivalence is being evoked, because these assumptions and discursive practice arise from flexible, reflexive, fragmented and decentred ambivalence. Each and every time 'identity' and 'difference' ('community') are assumed or discursively practised, this hyper-modern zone of ambivalence is likely to be reproduced. In other words, it has, indeed, become very unclear how to distinguish decentred and frag-mented voices—all of them uttering suffering—and how to replace them with 'alternatives', in the absence of clear-cut social containers of coherent subjectivity, of identity and difference (see also Levitas, 1995).

Now, this has some major implications for critical criminologies. First of all for critical criminologies as a set of critical discourses, as a bundle of proliferating assumptions as to the nature of suffering and its remedies. Flexible and reflexive hypermodernity, this zone of transition and ambi-valence, has some implications for critical criminologies which assume and (re)produce essentialized discursive constructions, which continue to fix and block an excess of meaning within specific discursive boundaries, and which continue (separately) to coagulate specific locations of suffering and specific roads to 'liberation', inevitably blocking off others (Others), *and thus*, themselves. What has been described, above, as hypermodernity, will, however, also have major implications for critical criminologies as a set or bundle of discourses which proliferate under the signifier 'criminology', discourses which, in other words, assume there is something 'crimino-logical' to talk about.

The way critical criminologies/ists have been carving out specific dis-cursive tracks, has, under hypermodern conditions, become untenable. The way critical criminologies/ists have been assuming and constructing imagined communities, believing in the One Truth and the Certainty of the cherished road towards Universal deliverance, is, by now, losing touch with hypermodern ambivalent experience. This kind of criminology, thriving on essentialized discursive constructions and barrelled, contained, exclusive hopes, is now, under hypermodern conditions of interdependency, gradually getting bogged down in the (re)production of its own impasses and impossibilities. At a time when ambivalence has fully reached the whirling discursive surfaces of hypermodernity, that is, now, when alleged safeties can no longer be (re)produced within discursively constructed clear-cut borders, this kind of critical criminology is losing much of its original *prophetic* force.[13] Though there are, of course, within hypermodernity, attempts being made to fix meaning, to produce essentialized Truths, to enforce safeties-by-exclusion. However, now the steady illusions of allegedly coherent subjectivities and communities are collapsing or are obviously in need of reconstruction, now that boundaries are blurring, any sharp and steady answers to the simple question as to what kind of suffering is in need of attention from progressives, and what kind of alternatives are worthy of progressive politics, are losing much of their once-promising critical edge (see also, from geography, the collection in Pile and Keith, 1997).

This cannot be done by trying to forge a new essential discursive space out of the various essentialized tracks of hope that have formed themselves out of hypermodern strategics. That would imply another essentialization; one that would be made out of all other essences, of all other Truths, Certainties and unshakeable foundations. It is unlikely that such a new essence, built with the bricks and mortar of Truth and self-centredness, will be able to cluster various and often diverging answers to our question (see also Sumner, 1997). Producing this allegedly essential progressive space would inevitably entail an explicit rejection or exclusion of all Other voices. This exclusion would, in turn, undermine the progressive ambitions which would have been fixed in the newly essentialized discursive space. Moreover, this essentializing strategy would be very unlikely to succeed in grappling with the ever-proliferating de(re)constructions of subjectivity, of identity/difference, of 'community', which are roaming in and out of hypermodern strategics.

This is why we will argue here for another road towards an answer to our question on suffering and alternatives. In this article, we propose to follow a road that takes contemporary fluidities, hyperreflexivity and hyperflexibility into account. This road will try to connect with the multiple and multi-layered energies which are permanently (re)produced in an ever-ambivalent and contingent discursive hypermodern. Hypermodernity does not scare us. It is in hypermodernity that we will look for energies and resources for imagining and practising alternatives to the conditions which (re)produce voices of suffering.

Now, which discursive tools can be imagined and used to build this hypermodern progressive road? We can think of two. The answer to our original question could be read as one of *radical democracy*. In and through the language and practise of radical democracy, hypermodern progressiveness should stand a better chance of success in addressing the multiple fragmenting and decentring voices of ambivalent suffering. The imagination and the practice of a radical democratic (discursive) space (so we will argue in the following pages) can be conceived of as imagining and practising *border-crossing*. This kind of *border-crossing radical democracy* skates cautiously in between the dangerous Truth of a *radical* democratic politic (that is, a politic still in search of the Absolute, Essential Root of all Evil, and the Absolute, Essential Root of all Liberation), and the dangerous Truth of a radical *democratic* politic (that is, a politic that assumes and enforces the Essential search of Incommensurabilities). It is to the development of these discursive tools that we will turn now.

### 6.4. Border-crossing as/is the production of radical democratic space

The road of border-crossing and radical democracy is not paved with essential Truths, nor with the hard and unbreakable stones of allegedly coherent, centered communities of liberation.[14] The road of border-crossing and radical democracy is, on the contrary, an uneasy road of permanent de(re)construction, of unlimited connections, of multiple layers, of innumerable detours. It is, in Gilles Deleuze's words, a *rhizomic* spread of interconnections in the ambivalent zone of hypermodernity; it is an impossible and enigmatic texture of constructions, deconstructions and reconstructions in the ambivalent and contingent zone which holds all those Other voices whenever there is self-centred and self-assured speech and practice. It is a winding road in the zone of Others, the uncertain road in the *heterotopic* zone (to use Foucault's words again) in between the essential Truths of Total Communities.

This is, then, what is being argued here. Critical criminologies would probably gain a new, hypermodern momentum, and a new, hypermodern 'prophetic' force, by abandoning the old essentialized Truths, and by connecting with the (re)production of radical democracy through walking the borderless road of border-crossing. Walking this borderless road is, in itself, already practising radical democracy. For radical democracy *is* what is being (re)produced by walking this road. This road, as shall be shown later on, is a road on which travellers are prepared to question and deconstruct own experiences, and are willing to walk the borders of their own *texts*. On this road travellers are permanently exploring the heterotopic margins of essentializing speech and practice, that is, fixative discursivity. They do this because they assume that it is there, in that marginal zone, that the conditions for their own discursive positions are being produced. These hypermodern border-crossing travellers, crossing the discursive borders of their subjectivities, are practising a kind of hypermodern cautious morality which is filled with a sense of *rhizomic* interconnectedness and interdependency. These hypermodern travellers are those who feel that We are the Other(s), and They are what We say and do. These travellers on the difficult road of hypermodernity feel that We are what We discursively exclude from this 'We' (and this is what We do every time We speak and practise) and that the Other(s) is/are Those who are not included in Our discursive space. 'We' can, then, only *be* through The Other(s). Our text, in other words, can only carve out a discursive space through all that it has pushed outside its margins; our text can only exist through its multiple margins, that is, the multiple texts of multiple Other(s). Travelling on this hypermodern de(re)constructive road of radical democracy is a never-ending search for Other voices, excluded in and through our speech and practice. Crossing each and every discursive border is then what travelling on this road is supposed to entail: it is to connect incessantly with all Other 'outside'. Travellers on this road of border-crossing believe that it will be these incessant connections that will enable Other voices to reclaim discursive space/place, and, thus, enable Ourselves to speak and practise, that is, to make use of that space of radical democracy to build and reshape 'Ourselves'. And this is, indeed a never-ending story: the Absolute *is* never, it is always to come. As Jacques Derrida has argued recently: 'Justice' is never, justice is always to come, it is always 'à venir', it is always 'avenir'. 'Justice' stops whenever it is assumed to be Here, already, among us. Justice leaves this world whenever voices are blocked, and when meaning is fixed in the Absolute. Paraphrasing Derrida (especially Derrida, 1994: 60), we could say that radical democracy *is* never (among us), it is always to come, it is expelled each and every time its arrival is celebrated.[15] Each and every time when borders are being drawn definitively, when border-crossing stops, when ambivalence is assumed to have been defeated in and through an Ultimate and obsessive bout of gardening that is alleged to have exterminated all the weeds of ambivalence (remember Bauman, 1989).[16]

### 6.5. Debunking bunkers

Understood in this way, border-crossing criminology has become weary of all those stories of liberation which have been cherished as bunkers of Truth and Liberation *all those years*. Border-crossing criminology is an incessant effort to debunk the language of binary oppositions in which logics of exclusion are frozen. In the bunkers of binary discursivity, the flow of possibilities is being coagulated into a limited and limiting discursive space that is filled completely with a fixed discourse on a single polarity between an *imagined community* and the 'outside'; between the 'Us' and 'Them'. Examples of such binary language and logic can be found in all those discourses in which the social is being represented as 'structured' in a binary polarization; e.g. man/woman (or, masculinities/femininities), capital/labour, white/coloured, West/East, Europe/Orient, etc. This list can go on forever: criminal/non-criminal, also belongs on it. This kind of discourse assumes coherence within both of the poles (differences are repressed and silenced), while it fails to grasp, at the same time, the unlimited connections of equality/identity which can be represented, in Other spaces, between the assumed poles.

In those discursive spaces, there is no room for other (Other) representations of suffering and alternatives. Endless differences and equalities, infinite possibilities are (b)locked in those bunkers of self-assured Truths. Border-crossing criminology will, on the contrary, try to free as much of these locked-up possibilities in an ongoing border-crossing discursive practice, that is, in a reflexive, permanent cycle of de(re)construction of subjectivity, with an ever-proliferating sensitivity to contextualities and ambivalence.

This is a border-crossing practice that will be able to use hypermodern energies of reflexive flexibility (or flexible reflexivity) in order to free those repressed and silenced voices and thereby to fulfil the thin promise of an ever-elusive radical democratic space. Border-crossing criminology thus tries to make use of the new possibilities of de(re)fixating hypermodernity. Border-crossers will make use, indeed, of the hypermodern loss of the old illusions of coherent subjectivities, in order to debunk the defensive contractions/contraptions or the arrogant Truths that keep on whirling as exclusive 'safe havens' in the midst of hypermodern contingencies. Border-crossing criminologists will imagine and practise the vast space of possibilities that opens up as soon as ambivalent energies are freed from within the discursive bunkers in which they have been frozen. This is hypermodern border-crossing: it is evoking the promise of radical democracy *in and through* the discursive practice of deconstructing Truths and allowing Other voices to fill the space that opens up after deconstruction; and again; and again . . .

Radical democracy (grappling with ambivalent human suffering) is to be found and (re)produced 'outside' the bunkers of binary foundations and unshakeable Truths. And it is precisely hypermodern energies of defixation which *can* be mobilized for such border-crossing moves. At a time when, *again*, 'all that is solid melts into air',[17] there is some slight hope that things can become for the better, far away from exclusive Truths and foundations. It is this hypermodern moment—as a source of dislocations—that also can be read as the promise of radical democracy.

### 6.6. From feminist criminology to border-crossing criminology

Feminism, in its amazing diversity, with its enormous flexibility, has already been deconstructing whatever kind of boundary critical criminology has ever drawn or dreamt of. Feminisms have vehemently been deconstructing every discursive border. The borders which are often assumed between a politics of formal rights and a politics of substantial recognition, the borders between a politics of the personal (of the private) and a politics of the political (the public), the borders between a politics of identity and the politics of difference, and so on—all have been dissolved in the subtle but pervasive net of feminist deconstruction. If there would ever be a 'real' postmodern flow, it will probably resemble very much contemporary feminism as a multipled location of hypermodern responsiveness—a responsiveness that bursts in and out of feminist diversity itself. This makes feminism extremely critical to its own discursive production and praxis.

Feminisms have practised border-crossing *avant la lettre*. More correctly, some feminisms have, not all of them. There are feminists who keep on representing the social (suffering and alternatives, that is) strictly within binary discourses. Some feminists refuse explicitly or implicitly to read radical democracy as a condition for their own cherished Truths and ambitions to become 'true'. The world, according to 'binary' feminists, can be represented using a binary, and thus, an exclusive—or 'masculine'— language and logic. Feminist preoccupations can, according to this kind of reasoning, be met by concentrating on the universality of 'gender' differentiation. However, this type of feminism, which seems to have 'forgotten' that suffering flows in and out of unlimited contextualities, and can be represented in numerous voices, using an infinite range of languages, has been severely criticized. First of all by feminists who claim that 'feminism' can only have sense in a radical democratic perspective and in radical democratic practice (Mouffe, 1995; see also the collection in Butler and Scott, 1992). 'Binary' feminism cannot even ground itself: it excludes other (Other) representations of suffering and alternatives from its nicely carved out discursive space of liberation; it represses equalities (with the 'outside') and differences (within), and it assumes a coherent subjectivity and a fixed 'community' instead of actively producing them by way of allowing Other representations of it onto multiple discursive surfaces. This process of assuming a coherent standpoint which is then placed at the centre of discourses on liberation, will not help 'feminism' further. Paradoxically, 'feminism' can only force itself towards 'liberation' when 'it' allows all Other voices of suffering and liberation to fill a radical democratic space. That is, when 'it' respects unlimited differences 'within' and equalities 'outside', or in other words, when 'it' deconstructs the concrete bunkers of rigid, essentialized and impermeable standpoints. Though feminists are still making considerable efforts to defend coherent *standpoint* feminisms (e.g. Lovibond, 1996, and from *criminological* corners, to a certain extent, Cain, 1995), there seems to be a shift in 'feminism' towards a more decentred feminism, such as Chantal Mouffe's. Clearly, the old *strategic*, binary kind of feminism has transcended itself, along with that collection of discourses once called critical criminology (e.g. Smart, 1990; Young, 1996; Naffine, 1997). Not only has feminism succeeded in deconstructing its own former *imagined communities*, it is constantly reaching for more openness, flowing in and out of other discursive structures, always trying to articulate sources of hope (e.g. hooks, 1994).

This type of decentred feminism tries to connect with a radical democratic politics; 'knowing' that the deconstruction of discursively constructed essences is the very condition of radical democracy, *and thus*, also of 'feminism'. 'Feminism', in this radical democratic vision, is a bundle of multiple struggles in various contexts in which the signifier 'Woman' (and 'Man') is used in relations of oppression/suppression; 'feminism' is the ever-proliferating set of deconstructions of these discursively constructed oppressions/suppressions in an unlimited stream of Other struggles; 'feminism' is the complex set of deconstructions of Other essences within 'feminist' discourse and struggle. 'Feminism', then, *is* radical democracy.

What has been described here can, of course, also be said with regard to all those Other struggles that, each of them separately, thrive on essentialized constructions, unshakeable foundations, privileged representations of suffering and alternatives, and allegedly coherent subjectivities. But the credit for having broken through the discursive limitations within these essentializing discourses, which implicitly block or freeze energies of liberation, goes to feminism, at least to those who have taken to the border-crossing paths of radical democracy. 'Border-crossing' has thus—*avant la lettre*—emerged from feminism. Substantial efforts have been made by women of 'ethnic minorities' who experience, in their everyday life, very sharply the multiple and ambivalent contextualities life is made of. This move has largely been absent in other discourses that have concentrated on other privileged representations of suffering and alternatives.[18]

This 'feminist' border-crossing move has transcended sterile discussions on essentialized (though ever-imagined) communities of suffering and of liberation; these border-crossing feminists have refused to fix meaning and transformative possibilities into specific privileged discourses; moreover, border-crossing feminists have crossed also the borders of 'criminological' discourse (for an overview, see Cain, 1990; Smart, 1990; Naffine, 1997). They have—simply, but effectively—transcended the profound binarisms criminological discourse has been (re)producing, *all those years*. According to border-crossing feminists, there is no reason to assume these discursive boundaries, these binary logics and languages, to be of another kind. There is no reason to spare these boundaries from de(re)construction. There is no reason, then, to save them from the promise of radical democracy. Following border-crossing feminists, we can only hope for a shady glimpse of a radical democratic space when we are prepared to cross whatever border is being constructed; to cross whatever border is blocking hope; to cross whatever border is expelling alternatives and other representations (Other voices) to the margins of the privileged discourse. This move has, indeed, been inspired by feminist criminologists who have 'known', *all those years*, the repressive limitations of *binarist* criminology, which keeps focusing its *masculine* 'scientific' view on specific discursively constructed borders, ignoring the vast Other plains of life, of transgressions and regulations (see also Howe, 1994). It is from feminist discourse, which has always taken into account the complexities and ambivalence of everyday contextualities, that this discursive move has originated (for a precursor move, see Pfohl and Gordon, 1986).

## 7. Conclusion

In this article we have tried to concentrate on the question 'Alternatives to what kind of suffering?'. This question is one that has been at the centre of various discourses that have, the past few decades, become known as 'critical criminology'. The answers to that question have often resulted in answers that were constructed around specific privileged (imagined) communities, based on essentialized Truths and unshakeable foundations. These answers, we have argued, have lost much of their critical edge under hypermodern conditions of reflexive and flexible strategics. Now, in a hypermodern space of ambivalent fragmentation/fixation and of decentring/recentring subjectivity, answers to this question will have to take account of the multiple contextualities that make up contemporary, fractured life. Now, when ambivalence has fully reached the vast and infinite discursive surface, we are in need of new answers; answers, that is, that will be sensitive to the ambivalence that has become a part of hypermodern (everyday) experience.

In this article, we have argued for an answer that will try to mobilize hypermodern energies of dislocation in order to debunk privileged discursively (re)produced Truths and foundations that, inevitably, block out the voices and the hopes of multiple Others. Our answer lies in a radical democratic politic that tries to fertilize the Othered margins of essentializing discourse. The radical democratic space which is assumed here is produced in and through border-crossing speech and praxis, in and through border-crossing discursivity. Our answer to the question that has been the central focus of this essay can be read as a plea for a border-crossing criminology, precursors of which can be found in the writings of some feminist criminologists.

Border-crossing criminology is a permanent process of de(re)construction of discursively constructed, essentialized borders. Border-crossing criminology is a reflexive and flexible (hypermodern) praxis: it evokes infinite Other voices of oppression/suppression, even those that are—inevitably—being silenced in and through specific border-crossing discursive moves. Border-crossing criminology fully subscribes to a radical democratic politics, and this is why it understands that 'suffering' and 'alternatives' can only reach the discursive surface when privileged discourses on fixed (but nevertheless always imagined) communities are being deconstructed and when silenced equalities and differences are 'freed' from the fetters of exclusive discourses of Truth and essential foundations. Border-crossing criminology tries to grapple with hypermodern ambivalence and contextualities, using the energies that are being released in the hypermodern process of decentring subjectivity. Skating reflexively on the thin, dangerous and always deeply ambivalent ice between the universalist and terrorist 'Truths' of reductionism, and the terrorism of those who thrive on a rhetoric of assumed complete and unfixated openness of the possibilities allegedly to be found in our neo-tribal era (on *neo-tribes*, see Maffesoli, 1996).

Border-crossing criminology, while practising radical democracy, will also be crossing the discursive borders of 'criminological' discourse. It will follow, as some feminists have done before, various ways of transcending the specific boundaries criminology has, for all too long, been drawing around specific flows of life, casting the latter in binarist logic and language. Border-crossing criminology will, then, criticize criminology's inclination to focus on specific (though always discursively constructed) borders, while ignoring the vast plain of social, always multiple, *rhizomic* experience. According to border-crossing criminologists, this immense plain of transgressive regulations and of regulatory transgressions is where radical democracy has to be produced. That vast plain is life, or, in other words, the ambivalent network of specific voices of suffering. These voices are inextricably woven into an almost unlimited spectrum of exclusion and inclusion (of inclusive exclusions and of exclusive inclusions), of equaliza- tion and differentiation (of equalizing differentiations and of differentiating equalizations), of discursively constructed borders and discursively con- structed border-crossings, of discursive spaces/places assumed and experi- enced to be central, and discursive spaces/places assumed and experienced to be at the margins (Shields, 1991), of chosen destructions and of ever destructive choices (see also Van Hoorebeeck, 1997).

In all that, a remarkable shift in emancipatory vision is to be noticed. While in the old days of certainty, deconstruction and reconstruction seemed to be practiced from specific, cherised loci, nowadays deconstruc- tion and reconstruction should be practiced in locating all these founda- tionalist stories that are affirming their own right, and are ignoring the vast complexity, ambivalence, interconnectedness and interdependence of humanity. We should be doing this de(re)constructive work, knowing, feeling 'single-track' solutions to be already terrorist. We should be sub- scribing, in other words, to a *politics of location* (e.g. Kaplan, 1994 referring to Adrienne Rich) that will hover incessantly over the belief that every location, every speech emerging from ambivalent and multiple loca- tions, that every sight/site, that every bit of coherence forged out in- coherences, that every flow of incoherence drawn from fixed coherences, holds promises for respect as well as dangers leading to repression of all and everything Other. Hovering over the hope of respectful recognition of identity/difference which inevitably hides in ambivalence. Hovering, finally, over the belief that all our stories of suffering and liberation can always be read as chaotic *dissipative structures*, forged out of ambivalent rhizomics, ready for unlimited multiple evaporations (see the collection in Hayles, 1991).

This praxis of articulation is a deeply paradoxical praxis. But then, this can not surprise us. Emancipatory praxis has always been paradoxical, only able to realize its hopes and pre-conditions by constructing them, discursively, practically, in the emancipatory process itself. In that sense, we would agree with the following phrase which Zygmunt Bauman, in a more Enlightened mood, once wrote: 'the liberation of man [sic] can be promoted only in conditions of liberty' (Bauman, 1976: 112). This is not very much, but it is all (of ambivalence) we have got.

## Notes

This essay is also based on some material drawn from three talks; one on 'alternatives to what kind of suffering?' (Saarbrücken, Germany, November 1995), one on 'hypermodern social policy and the global Other' (Manchester, September 1996), and finally a talk on 'hypermodern ambivalence and radical democracy' (Maastricht, the Netherlands, June 1997). This paper has benefitted from comments given on the occasion of these presentations and on other occasions, by Alessandro Baratta, René van Swaaningen, George Gilligan, Ian Taylor, Fritz Sack, Nigel South, Jock Young, Christopher Stanley, Bart Van Hoorebeeck, Koen Raes, Ruddy Doom, Hans Hofman and Claudius Messner.

1. We will not go into this 1980s proliferation of contracting voices here. There is only room to acknowledge this contracting proliferation of critical criminologists' voices into defensive tracks, each of them evoking as well as mobilizing assumed identities/differences, in other words, evoking and mobilizing around *imagined communities*. We will come back to this later. However, for a more detailed analysis of the *status questionis* of critical criminology at the end of the 1980s, see, among others: Cain, 1990; Cardarelli and Hicks, 1993; de Haan, 1990; MacLean and Milovanovic, 1991; Thomas and O'Maolchatha, 1989.
2. Words of Mohammed Najib Chakouh, student at Ghent University.
3. Anderson (1991) was concentrating on nationalism. According to Anderson, every imaginary space which supercedes local space is to be read as an evocation of a discursively constructed *imagined community*. In this paper, Anderson's term 'imagined community' is used in myriad other ways. Wherever boundaries are discursively being drawn, this means, whenever there is inclusion and exclusion, or identity and difference, *communities* are being *assumed*, that is, *imagined*. This means that every 'community' is an imagined community. There is no community with a 'real' ontological unity (see also Corlett, 1989), because every community—always an *imagined community*—can be deconstructed, and, under hypermodern conditions, will be deconstructed in an (almost) unbounded way. We do assume here, then, that imagined communities are discursive constructions which assume fixed identities within the boundaries of the so-called 'community' and fixed differences with regard to the 'outside' of the alleged 'community'. We are applying, then, Anderson's term onto whatever kind of dicourse that evokes and/or assumes 'communities'; this goes, of course, for nationalist discourses, but also for ethnicist discourses,

classist discourses, gendered discourses, etc. See also Wallerstein and Balibar (1991).

4. We are thus not referring to the contemporary as the zone of total hypertextual dedifferentiation, that is, a kind of Baudrillardian zone of deterritorialized, hyperspaced, flows of signs–as–commodities–as–signs. (For a recently published outline of 'Baudrillardian' postmodernity, see e.g. Baudrillard's recent collection, 1994.)

5. See, of course, A. Giddens (1990). Giddens' well-known attempt to signify the contemporary as an extremely radicalized self-reflexive modernity is very similar to what we call 'hypermodernity' here. There are, however, some specific signifieds we would like to subsume under the signifier 'hypermodernity'. The prefix 'hyper' would, in a sense, refer to the contingency and ambivalence both of which (re)produce a radicalized reflexivity and flexibility, which, in turn, would be (re)producing contemporary contingency and ambivalence.

6. This is not to say, of course, that contemporary globalization would be 'financial' globalization. See on this the seminal paper by A. Appadurai, 'Disjuncture and difference in the global cultural economy' (1990). Appadurai considers globalizing tendencies *in finanscapes, ethnoscapes, technoscapes, mediascapes, and ideoscapes*. The language is Appadurai's. It is these globalizing 'scapes' that produce fluidity and (de)centring at one place, while concentrating and (re)centring energies in another place (and, under *hypermodern* conditions, often *in the same* place).

7. For a critique of Harvey's univocal, *masculine* Marxism, see Morris (1992).

8. This is probably why a discourse of security has, during the last few decades, been able to catch the multiple uncertainties, the deep contingency of hypermodern everyday life and experience. This is probably why the open language of security and risk has been able to clot the contemporary, while, at the same time, reproducing the proliferating dynamic of fragmentation and decentring.

9. '*A seamless skein*' is taken from Wallerstein's 'Unthinking social science' (1991). Wallerstein used the metaphor in a somewhat different context, when referring to the modern blurring of the boundaries between economy, politics and society-culture, that awful 'holy trinity' that 'has no intellectual heuristic value today. It probably never did, but it certainly does no longer' (Wallerstein, 1991: 265).

10. On (social) censures, see Sumner (1979, 1990).

11. On Foucault's 'Des espaces autres' (written originally in 1968, published as 'Of other spaces' in 1986), see the recently published 'genealogical' evocation by Daniel Defert (1997) of Foucault's use of the concept 'heterotopic zone'/'heterotopia' in the *rhizomic* Documenta X collection.

12. The phrase is Derrida's, and is drawn from his 'Spectres de Marx' (1993). The book can be read as Derrida's deconstruction of (anti-Marxist) deconstructions of Marx. Derrida argues that a 'weak messianic force' is what can be retained from Marx's ghost. Though Derrida rejects

Marx(ism) as a totalizing discursive construction, he acknowledges that Marxist discourse is impregnated with various 'spectres of Marx', spectres of Marxism, which are—as all ghosts or spectres are—with us to stay; dead but immortal, undestructible, full of hopes and desires, full of dreams of liberation; but most of all they are spectres amongst an unlimited company of others, of Others.

13. The term is from the Afro-American theologist, Cornel West. West argues for a 'prophetic criticism' or a 'prophetic pragmatism' which is still inscribed in an enlightened activism, filled with utopistic experimentalism, as it was in the 1960s and 1970s, but which is, at the same time, sensitive to contemporary ambivalence and flexibilities, and which shuns monistic pronouncements (West, 1995).

14. In that sense, we are sympathetic to other proposals that have criticized essentializing or recentring criminology (e.g. Ericson and Carrière, 1994; Friedrichs, 1996). However, we see no point in assuming Total fragmentation and decentring (such assumption would imply in itself an abject foundationalism). This is why our conception of a border-crossing criminology tries to forge paths in between discourses on decentring and *recentring* discourses.

15. Interesting critical remarks on the problematic justice in Derrida's Justice are to be read in Wolcher (1996).

16. Bauman's Levinasian move towards an *Othered morality* (instead of an *Ordered Modernity*), is indeed what can be read in the lines we have written above. Other sources of inspiration can be found in Derridian deconstructionism. However, these sources of inspiration are very close to each other (see Critchley, 1992).

17. The phrase is, of course, from the 'Communist Manifesto' (1848) by Marx and Engels, in which they wrote on the constant need for capital to revolutionize the forces of production. Marshall Berman (1983) has taken this phrase as the title of his book on the modern experience; an experience, that is, of infinite change and detraditionalization.

18. E.g. those who still speak a classist binarist language, assuming the signifier 'working class' would still—even under hypermodern conditions of globalized strategics—refer to a fixed essence. See on this Pakulski and Waters (1996).

## References

Abel, Richard (1994) *Speech and Respect.* London: Stevens & Sons/Maxwell.

Abu-Lughod, Janet (1995) 'The World-System Perspective in the Construction of Economic History', *History and Theory* 34: 86–98.

Amin, Samir (1991) *L'Empire du Chaos.* Paris: l'Harmattan.

Anderson, Benedict (1991) *Imagined Communities. Reflections on the Origin and Spread of Nationalism.* London: Verso.

Appadurai, Arjun (1990) 'Disjuncture and Difference in the Global Cultural

Economy', in Mike Featherstone (ed.) *Global Culture*, pp. 295–310. London: Sage.

Axford, Barry (1995) *The Global System. Economics, Politics, and Culture.* Cambridge: Polity Press.

Baudrillard, Jean (1994) *The Illusion of the End.* Cambridge: Polity Press.

Bauman, Zygmunt (1976) *Towards a Critical Sociology. An Essay on Commonsense and Emancipation.* London: Routledge and Kegan Paul.

Bauman, Zygmunt (1989) *Modernity and the Holocaust.* Cambridge: Polity Press.

Bauman, Zygmunt (1991) *Modernity and Ambivalence.* Ithaca: Cornell University Press.

Bauman, Zygmunt (1992) *Mortality, Immortality, and Other Life Strategies.* Cambridge: Polity Press.

Bauman, Zygmunt (1993) *Postmodern Ethics.* Oxford: Blackwell.

Bauman, Zygmunt (1995a) *Life in Fragments. Essays in Postmodern Morality.* Oxford: Blackwell.

Bauman, Zygmunt (1995b) 'Searching for a Centre that Holds', in Mike Featherstone et al. (eds) *Global Modernities*, pp. 140–54. London: Sage.

Beck, Ulrich (1992) *Risk Society. Towards a New Modernity.* London: Sage.

Berman, Marshall (1983) *All that is Solid Melts into Air. The Experience of Modernity.* London: Verso.

Bloch, Ernst (1959) *Das Prinzip Hoffnung.* Frankfurt am Main: Suhrkamp Verlag. (transl. Neville Plaice, Stephen Plaice, and Paul Knight, 1986; Basil Blackwell Ltd.)

Butler, Judith and Joan Scott (eds) (1992) *Feminists Theorize the Political.* London: Routledge.

Cain, Maureen (1990) 'Towards Transgression: New Directions in Feminist Criminology', *International Journal of the Sociology of Law* 18: 1–18.

Cain, Maureen (1995) 'Horatio's Mistake: Notes on Some Spaces in an Old Text', *Journal of Law and Society* 22(1): 68–77.

Calhoun, Craig (1994) 'Social Theory and the Politics of Identity', in: Craig Calhoun (ed.) *Social Theory and the Politics of Identity*, pp. 232–63. Oxford: Blackwell.

Calhoun, Craig (1995) *Critical Social Theory. Culture, History, and the Challenge of Difference.* Oxford: Blackwell.

Caplan, Paul (1991) 'Critical Criminology: Trust Me, I'm Telling You Stories', *Law and Critique* II(2): 191–205.

Cardarelli, Albert P. and Stephen C. Hicks (1993) 'Radicalism in Law and Criminology: a Retrospective View of Critical Legal Studies and Radical Criminology', *The Journal of Criminal Law and Criminology* 84(3): 501–53.

Corbridge, Stuart (1994) 'Post-Marxism and Post-Colonialism. The Needs and Rights of Distant Strangers', in David Booth (ed.) *Rethinking Social Development*, pp. 90–117. Harlow: Longman.

Corlett, William (1989) *Community without Unity. A Politics of Derridian Extravagance.* Durham: Duke University Press.

Critchley, Simon (1992) *The Ethics of Deconstruction: Derrida and Levinas.* Oxford: Blackwell.

Crook, Stephen et al. (1992) *Postmodernization. Change in Advanced Society.* London: Sage.

Davis, Mike (1990) *City of Quartz. Excavating the Future in Los Angeles.* London: Verso.

Defert, Daniel (1997) 'Foucault, Space, and the Architects', in Françoise Joly et al. (eds) *Po/e/li/tics-Documenta X*, pp. 274–83. Ostfildern-Ruit (Germany): Cantz.

de Haan, Willem (1990) *The Politics of Redress. Crime, Punishment, and Penal Abolition.* London: Unwin Hyman.

Deleuze, Gilles and Felix Guattari (1976) *Rhizome: Introduction.* Paris: Les Editions du Minuit.

Derrida, Jacques (1993) *Spectres de Marx. L'Etat de la Dette, le Travail du Deuil, et la Nouvelle Internationale.* Paris: Galilée.

Derrida, Jacques (1994) *Force de Loi. Le Fondement Mystique de l'Authorité.* Paris: Galilée.

Encinoza, Argenis Rieira and Rosa del Olmo (1981) 'The View from Latin America—Against Transnational Criminology: a Call for Democratic International Cooperation', *Crime and Social Justice* 15 (Summer): 61–70.

Ericson, Richard and Kevin Carrière (1994) 'The Fragmentation of Criminology', in David Nelken (ed.) *The Futures of Criminology*, pp. 89–110. London: Sage.

Fanon, Franz (1967) *The Wretched of the Earth.* Harmondsworth: Penguin.

Fish, Stanley (1989) 'Still Wrong After all those Years', in Stanley Fish *Doing what Comes Naturally. Change, Rhetoric, and the Practise of Theory in Literary and Legal Studies*, pp. 356–71. Durham: Duke University Press.

Foucault, Michel (1986) 'Of Other Spaces', *Diacritics* 16(1): 22–7.

Frank, Andre Gunder (1967) *Capitalism and Underdevelopment in Latin America. Historical Studies of Chile and Brasil.* New York: Monthly Review Press.

Fraser, Nancy (1995) 'From Redistribution to Recognition? Dilemmas of Justice in a "Post-Socialist" Age', *New Left Review* 212: 68–93.

Friedrichs, David (1996) 'Critical Criminology: Strength in Diversity for these Times', *Critical Criminology* 1: 121–8.

Giddens, Anthony (1990) *The Consequences of Modernity.* Cambridge: Polity Press.

Giroux, Henry (1992) *Border Crossings: Cultural Workers and the Politics of Education.* New York: Routledge.

Habermas, Jürgen (1984, 1988) *The Theory of Communicative Action. Vols I and II.* Boston: Beacon.

Hall, Stuart (1989) *New Times: the Changing Face of Politics in the 90s.* London: Verso.

Harvey, David (1989) *The Condition of Postmodernity. An Inquiry into the Origins of Cultural Change.* Oxford: Blackwell.

Hayles, N. Katherine (ed.) (1991) *Chaos and Order. Complex Dynamics in Literature and Science*. *Chicago*: University of Chicago Press.

Heelas, Paul et al. (eds) (1996) Detraditionalization. Critical Reflections on Authority and Identity. Oxford: Blackwell.

Henry, Stuart and Dragan Milovanovic (1996) *Constitutive Criminology. Beyond Postmodernism*. London: Sage.

hooks, bell (1994) *Outlaw Culture. Resisting Representations*. London: Routledge.

Hopkins, Terence and Immanuel Wallerstein (eds) (1996) *The Age of Transition. Trajectory of the World-System (1945–2025)*. London: Zed Books.

Howe, Adrian (1994) *Punish and Critique. Towards a Feminist Analysis of Penality*. London: Routledge.

Inciardi, James (ed.) (1980) *Radical Criminology: the Coming Crises*. Beverly Hills: Sage.

Irigaray, Luce (1977) 'La 'Mécanique' des Fluides' in Luce Irigaray *Ce Sexe Qui n'en est pas Un*, pp. 103–16. Paris: Les Editions du Minuit.

Jameson, Fredric (1991) *Postmodernism, or the Cultural Logic of Late Capitalism*. London: Verso.

Kaplan, Caren (1994) 'The Politics of Location as Transnational Feminist Critical Practice' in Inderpal Grewal and Caren Kaplan (eds) *Scattered Hegemonies. Postmodernity and Transnational Feminist Practices*, pp. 137–56. Minneapolis: University of Minnesota Press.

Kirby, Kathleen (1996) *Indifferent Boundaries. Spatial Concepts of Human Subjectivity*. New York: The Guildford Press.

Laclau, Ernesto (1990) *New Reflections on the Revolution of our Time*. London: Verso.

Laclau, Ernesto (ed.) (1994) *The Making of Political Identities*. London: Verso.

Laclau, Ernesto and Chantal Mouffe (1985) *Hegemony and Socialist Strategy. Towards a Radical Democratic Politics*. London: Verso.

Lash, Scott and John Urry (1994) *Economies of Signs and Space*. London: Sage.

Leonard, Peter (1997) *Postmodern Welfare: Reconstructing an Emancipatory Project*. London: Sage.

Levitas, Ruth (1995) 'We: Problems of Identity, Solidarity and Difference', *History of the Human Sciences* 3: 89–105.

Lippens, Ronnie (1995) 'Critical Criminologies and the Reconstruction of Utopia', *Social Justice* 22(1): 32–50

Lovibond, Sabina (1996) 'Meaning what We Say: Feminist Ethics and the Critique of Humanism', *New Left Review* 220: 98–115.

Lyotard, Jean François (1986) *Le Postmoderne Expliqué aux Enfants*. Paris: Galilée.

Mackay, Hugh (ed.) (1997) *Consumption and Everyday Life*. London: Sage/ The Open University.

MacLean, Brian and Dragan Milovanovic (eds) (1991) *New Directions in Critical Criminology*. Vancouver: The Collective Press.

342    *Theoretical Criminology 2(3)*

Maffesoli, Michel (1996) *The Time of the Tribes. The Decline of Individualism in Mass Society*. London: Sage.

Morris, Meaghan (1992) 'The Man in the Mirror', *Theory, Culture & Society* 9: 253–79.

Morrison, Wayne (1995) *Theoretical Criminology: from Modernity to Post-Modernism*. London: Cavendish Publishing.

Mouffe, Chantal (1994) 'For a Politics of Nomadic Identity', in George Robertson et al. (eds) *Travellers' Tales. Narratives of Home and Displacement*, pp. 105–13. London: Routledge.

Mouffe, Chantal (1995) 'Feminism, Citizenship, and Radical Democratic Politics', in Linda Nicholson and Steven Seidman (eds) *Social Postmodernism. Beyond Identity Politics*, pp. 315–31. Cambridge: Cambridge University Press.

Naffine, Ngaire (1997) *Feminism and Criminology*. Cambridge: Polity Press.

Pakulski, Jan and Malcolm Waters (1996) *The Death of Class*. London: Sage.

Pfohl, Stephen and Avery Gordon (1986) 'Criminological Displacements: a Sociological Deconstruction', *Social Problems* 6: 94–113.

Pile, Steve and Michael Keith (eds) (1997) *Geographies of Resistance*. London: Routledge.

Rorty, Richard (1989) *Contingency, Irony, Solidarity*. Cambridge: Cambridge University Press.

Said, Edward (1995) *Orientalism. Western Conceptions of the Orient* (2nd edition). London: Penguin Books. (1st edition: 1978)

Schwartz, Martin (1997) 'Does Critical Criminology Have a Core? Or Just Splinters?', *Critical Criminologist*: http://sun.soci.niu.edu/~critcrim/CC/cc.html.

Sen, Amartya (1992) *Inequality Reexamined*. New York: Russell Sage Foundation.

Shields, Rob (1991) *Places at the Margin. Alternative Geographies of Modernity*. London: Routledge.

Sibley, David (1995) *Geographies of Exclusion. Society and Difference in the West*. London: Routledge.

Smart, Carol (1990) 'Feminist Approaches to Criminology, or Postmodern Woman Meets Atavistic Man', in Loraine Gelsthorpe and Allison Morris (eds) *Feminist Perspectives in Criminology*, pp. 70–84. Milton Keynes: Open University Press.

Stanley, Christopher (1996) *Urban Excess and the Law. Capital, Culture, and Desire*. London: Cavendish Publishing.

Sumner, Colin (1979) *Reading Ideologies. An Investigation into the Marxist Theory of Ideology and Law*. London: Academic Press.

Sumner, Colin (ed.) (1982) *Crime, Justice and Underdevelopment*. London: Heinemann.

Sumner, Colin (1990) 'Rethinking Deviance: towards a Sociology of Censure', in Colin Sumner (ed.) *Censure, Politics, and Criminal Justice*, pp. 15–41. Milton Keynes: Open University Press.

Sumner, Colin (1997) 'The Decline of Social Control and the Rise of Vocabularies of Struggle', in Roberto Bergalli and Colin Sumner (eds) *Social Control and Political Order. European Perspectives at the End of the Century*, pp. 131–50. London: Sage.

Thomas, Jim and Aogan O'Maolchatha (1989) 'Reassessing the Critical Metaphor', *Justice Quarterly* 6: 143–72.

Van Hoorebeeck, Bart (1997) 'Prospects for Reconstructing Aetiology', *Theoretical Criminology* 1(4): 529–46.

Wallerstein, Immanuel (1991) *Unthinking Social Science. The Limits of Nineteenth-Century Paradigms*. Cambridge: Polity Press.

Wallerstein, Immanuel and Etienne Balibar (1991) *Race, Nation, Class: Ambiguous Identities*. London: Verso.

West, Cornel (1995) 'Prophetic Pragmatism: Cultural Criticism and Political Engagement', in Russell B. Goodman (ed.) *Pragmatism: A Contemporary Reader*, pp. 209–33. London: Routledge.

Wolcher, Louis (1996) 'The Man in a Room: Remarks on Derrida's Force of Law', *Law and Critique* 7(1): 35–46.

Young, Alison (1996) *Imagining Crime. Textual Outlaws and Criminal Conversations*. London: Sage.

Young, Iris Marion (1990) *Justice and the Politics of Difference*. Princeton: Princeton University Press.

RONNIE LIPPENS is a Researcher in Criminology at Ghent University, Belgium (Department of Criminal Law and Criminology). He has written—mostly in Belgian and in Dutch journals—on critical criminology, on *hypermodernity*, and on radical democracy.
[email: ronny.lippens@rug.ac.be]

# [16]

# Doing newsmaking criminology from within the academy

GREGG BARAK

*Eastern Michigan University, USA*

## Abstract

Newsmaking criminology refers to the conscious efforts and
activities of criminologists to interpret, influence or shape the
representation of 'newsworthy' items about crime and justice. In this
reflexive and evaluative thought piece, I critically assess the value of
this criminological intervention from the vantage point of the
person who coined the term and first introduced it some 20 years
ago. I conclude that newsmaking criminology as a perspective on
the theory, practice and study of mass communications as well as on
the representations of crime and justice, is still an invaluable
approach for understanding as fundamental to the larger
criminological enterprise in general and to administrative
criminology in particular, the joint roles that each plays as part of
neoliberal-bourgeois statecraft.

## Key Words

expert commentary • frames of discourse • mass communications •
newsmaking criminology • news media • social constructionism

Twenty years ago next year, in a *Justice Quarterly* article, using the insights
of Stan Cohen, Jock Young, Stuart Hall, Tony Jefferson and others, and in
accordance with a Gramscian approach to hegemony and class struggle, I
introduced the concept and practice of 'newsmaking criminology' (Barak,
1988). This referred to the processes whereby criminologists use mass communication for the purposes of interpreting, informing and altering the
images of crime and justice, crime and punishment, and criminals and victims (Barak, 2001: 190). More specifically, newsmaking criminology refers
to the conscious efforts and activities of criminologists to interpret, influence

or shape the representation of 'newsworthy' items about crime and justice. Furthermore, a newsmaking criminology attempts to demystify images of crime and punishment by locating the mass-media portrayals of incidences of 'serious' crimes in the context of all illegal and harmful activities. It strives to affect public attitudes, thoughts and discourses about crime and justice so as to facilitate a public policy of 'crime control' based on structural and historical analyses of institutional development; allows criminologists to come forth with their knowledge and to establish themselves as credible voices in the mass-mediated arena of policy formation; and asks of criminologists that they develop popularly based languages and technically based skills of communication for the purposes of participating in the mass-consumed ideology of crime and justice (Barak, 1988: 566).

A little background history is in order here. In 1987, when I wrote the article that would appear in *Justice Quarterly* the next year, the USA was in the midst of the 'cocaine wars' on many of its urban streets and moving into its peak years, 1988 to 1991, for drug-related killings. These were the beginning years of the golden era of crime coverage in local television news when if 'it bleeds, it leads'. At the time, what was particularly striking to me across the media- and politically dominated discussions of crime, violence and justice on mass-mediated television was the scarcity of social and behavioral scientists in general and the conspicuous absence of criminologists in particular; this was no less true of prime time, cable or public access television. This situation has not substantively changed in 20 years.

This is unlike other disciplinary areas of expertise wherein mass-mediated public discussions do occur. Take politics, about which audiences hear from political scientists; economics, about which audiences hear from economists; or the weather, about which audiences hear from meteorologists. However, when it comes to public discussions about crime and justice, audiences do not generally hear from criminologists. This is not to say that there are not a handful of criminologists in the States who 'pop up' consistently. Probably the two most recognizable criminologists in the USA are James Alan Fox and Alfred Blumstein. Even when these parties appear, however, they rarely if ever drive the story. On the contrary, they are usually being 'used' as criminological props to give some credence or legitimacy to an already decided upon news 'peg'. Moreover, seldom are any of these criminologists seen on any of the television news programming and talk show formats, whether we're talking *CNN*, *NSMBC*, cable, *Court TV*, public access or prime time magazine news where substantive exchanges take place. In other words, the appearances of most 'newsmaking criminologists' rarely ever get beyond the 'soundbite' effect. This is not very efficacious newsmaking if one desires to influence policies on crime and crime control in a progressive direction.

Typically, what was the case 20 years ago is essentially the case today: when public discussions about crime and justice occur, the mass media primarily rely on agents of the State, from law enforcement and prosecution through adjudication and sentencing to punishment and incarceration; on attorneys, judges and chiefs of police; and, last but not least, on various politicos whether they be office-holders or seekers. Hence, when I introduced 'newsmaking criminology' it was a call for criminologists both to become 'public intellectuals' and to 'take sides' in the Howard Becker tradition, and to do 'newspaper sociology' in the Alvin Gouldner tradition.

In short, newsmaking criminology was and is still a 'call for action', which asks criminologists to eschew notions of alleged value neutrality and 'objectivity'. I have always thought that this was (and is) a very tall order in the context of the political economy of mass media. In other words, I have never envisioned nor do I now that newsmaking criminology will be easy to actualize, especially within the context of contemporary capitalism and neo-liberalism.

However, slowly but surely, there has been a rising knowledge base and lessons learned about working with the news media. For example, understanding the motivations of journalists in general and of crime and criminal justice reporters in particular is fundamental to successful newsmaking as a criminologist. Even more important is the ability of newsmaking criminologists to develop their own journalistic sources, connections and associations with people who are in the business of reporting on crime and justice news. There are reciprocal and trusting relationships that need to be nurtured here. Newsmaking criminology, in other words, cannot be left to chance; it is not about responding to a phone call or an email from a local or national reporter 'out of the blue'. Rather it is about developing enduring mutually based conversations, if at all possible, with journalists who are involved with mediating crime and justice stories on a regular basis.

Some of the information, method and analysis associated with newsmaking criminology have been elaborated in academic publications. One book notable in this regard was authored by James Alan Fox (a leading newsmaking criminologist himself) and Jack Levin (1993), and I organized another edited volume about newmaking criminology entitled *Media, Process, and the Social Construction of Crime: Studies in Newsmaking Criminology* (1994). A contributor to the latter volume, Stuart Henry (1994), elaborated on four styles of newsmaking criminology he believed might be helpful for better understanding—and actualizing—criminologists' influence in varied media. According to Henry, criminologists can appear in newsmaking venues as 'experts', 'journalists', 'subjects' and/or as 'educative provocateurs'. In the same reader, Cecil Greek asked whether or not newsmaking criminology was even possible, speculating:

> that trying to use the media to bring the findings of criminological research to a larger audience and enlighten the public is a more difficult task than originally envisioned. It requires an understanding of how the media operate, knowledge of how to communicate successfully in a variety of formats and circumstances, and advance preparation.
>
> (1994: 280)

Greek is essentially correct. Based on my own experience, and the efforts of colleagues, I have observed that doing 'newsmaking criminology' is challenging indeed—sometimes succeeding and often not. In retrospect, it strikes me that success, when it comes, usually does so because the newsmaking criminologist has a thorough appreciation of the particular format, frame and genre of specific media. One needs to endeavor, as precisely as possible, to use an appropriate discourse or style of newsmaking that accords with specific modes and venues of journalism. This is one way of maximizing the chances that criminologists who wish to enter the public sphere of media may be able—at least sometimes—to influence how crime and justice, law and order, are portrayed (Barak, 2007a: 101). In other words, the time has come to develop more culturally and materially nuanced accounts of the representations of law and order, or of crime and justice, if criminologists are to have an effect.

This is not a particularly new argument. However, in an age of globalization and satellite communication, it has become an increasingly significant one as the blending of genres and frames starts to appear as though a cultural hybridization of materiality and hyperreality (Arrigo, 1996). With the exception of Simon Cottle (2006: 44) and his colleagues who have developed, for example, a 'communicative architecture of televised news', students of media and crime and/or justice have generally paid scant attention to 'exactly how mediatization is enacted in and through the media's available communicative forms'. As a result, many 'newsmaking criminologists' have gone about the practice of newsmaking by trial and error, or by hit and miss; again, though exceptions exist, they have not tended to develop a systematic appreciation for how the media works very differently depending on the genres and frames of newsmaking in play. Thus, while doing newsmaking criminology 'successfully' is undoubtedly difficult, scholars need to tailor their discourses appropriately according to frame and genre. We need to improve the likelihood of productively using the media (rather than the media using criminologists), and the chances of getting major points and policy recommendations across. Simultaneously, we need to avoid engaging in newsmaking situations that are not conducive to criminological intervention, progressive or otherwise, in the first place.

I begin this article by briefly summarizing the communicative frames identified by Cottle in the context of doing television news journalism. Next I look back retrospectively on how I employed some of these and other frames in the context of doing newsmaking criminology as a radio news/journalist on a twice a week, Tuesday and Friday mornings, 'talk' show based in Ann Arbor, Michigan, that for nine months covered 'live' the O.J. Simpson criminal trial. Finally, I reflect on newsmaking criminology in relation to both my O.J. experience and more generally speaking.

## The architecture of televised news: Cottle's theoretical framework

In the business of television news/journalism, Cottle identifies a number of conventionally communicative frames oriented toward either 'conflict' or 'consensus'. Narrative frames of social conflict include *dominant, contest, contention, campaigning* and *exposés/investigations*. Narrative frames of social consensus include *community service, collective interests, cultural interests, cultural recognition* and *mythic tales*. While each of the former frames routinely structures the communication of conflicts in different ways, they all do so in terms of propositions, claims, counter-claims and arguments. By contrast, the consensual frames revolve around 'cultural displays' rather than 'analytic deliberations'. Unlike the conflict-driven and analytical frames grounded in 'rationalism' and 'objectivism', the consensus frames tend to work as 'expressive' or 'emotional' modes of communication, moving from the semiotic to the symbolic and mythic.

*Reflection: ideally, newsmaking criminologists should prefer working in conflict rather than in consensus-driven media or news frames.* Cottle contends that in addition to the conflicting and consensus frames, there are also two archetypal news frames: reporting and reportage. Consistent with the daily production cycles of television news, the classic or stock reporting frame functions in terms of information conveyance and surveillance of current events. This mode of communication delivers the cold hard facts; at best, these thin news accounts of events are typically without context, background, explanation or competing definitions. As Cottle explains, reporting frames privilege 'an epiphenomenal and disaggregated view of reality in which violent events and reactions, rather than underlying conditions, possible causes, or motivations, become the focal point' (2006: 25).

The reportage frame, by contrast, 'represents a relatively elaborative and often powerful frame for the exploration of conflicts and their origins, dynamics, and impact' (Cottle, 2006: 34). This frame serves to provide the means for generating a deeper understanding, as it allows for 'thicker' rather than 'thinner' news reports. Reportage frames, given their affinity with documentary modes (Nichols, 1991), and unlike reporting frames, provide rich descriptions of reality, invariably moving the story treatment from 'what is' to 'what ought to be'. The point is that by employing film, video and other visuals as well as testimonies, for example, reportage frames position themselves as well as viewers in the place or virtual space of 'bearing witness', moving beyond the more dualistic frames of fact and fiction, and entering into the emotional realms of human identification (see also Nassar, 2005). *Reflection: although newsmaking criminologists might intrinsically prefer working in reportage rather than reporting frames, it is more complicated because each of these archetypal frames can variously draw upon both analytic/propositional (conflict) and aesthetic/expressive (consensus) modes of communication.*

Similarly, as David Altheide (1987) pointed out 20 years ago in his comparative study of formats and symbols in the TV coverage of terrorism in the USA and the UK, there are basic distinctions between 'event-type' frames associated with regular evening news broadcasts and the 'topic-type' frames associated with interviews and documentary presentations. The former frames tend to focus on visuals such as, for example, the aftermath, and tactics of terrorism; the latter frames are more likely to include materials about purposes, goals and rationales. But here again, as Altheide (2006), Cottle (2006) and Kavoori and Fraley (2006) have all demonstrated, whether we are talking about the news coverage of terrorism in the Middle East, Southeast Asia, Europe or North America, in the contemporary world of globalism a mixture of event and topic as well as other frames for representing 'terrorism' or 'counterterrorism' can be discerned.

## From theory to practice: newsmaking criminology through the O.J. Simpson trial

The fundamental distinction between the architecture of radio news and that of televised news is, of course, the former's lack of visuals. However, in the context of a mass-mediated visual culture of consumption, radio news or commentaries (especially traditional talk show formats) are supplemented by a plethora of circulating montages of ever-ready or accessible images of 'law and order' in general, and of event-based topical news stories in particular. *Reflection: these mass-mediated collective narratives on crime and justice can be and should be used or incorporated wherever possible by newsmaking criminologists.*

In my radio coverage of the O.J. Simpson criminal trial from opening arguments to the 'not guilty' verdict, I tried to draw on widely circulating images. I endeavored to rely predominantly on frames of conflict and topic-type, but I ended up utilizing consensus and event-type frames of discourse as well. The radio coverage of the trial, over a period of nine months, was also conducive to both reporting and reportage types of framing. Ultimately, it was the ability to employ reportage-type journalism that made for a successful newsmaking criminological experience; in general, I believe radio formats provide excellent opportunities for newsmaking interventions.

### Expert commentary and newsmaking criminology

In high-profile criminal trials, a cottage industry of medial trial experts has emerged. Greta Van Susteren, Leslie Abramson, Gerry Spence and Nancy Grace, to name only a few, have become familiar faces as armchair analysts on the network and prime time news shows. Some of these parties went on to have their own televised shows, whether on network stations like *CNN* or cable stations like *Court TV*. There is absolutely no reason why criminologists, or others for that matter, cannot join the ranks of these commentators, whether on prime time or public access.

For example, from 1987 to 1995, criminologist Ronald Kramer from Western Michigan University hosted and co-produced *WMU Forum*, a monthly Kalamazoo public access cable television program. Over an 8-year period, 85 programs were produced and broadcast. Among the topics Kramer covered were violence against women, prison overcrowding, solid waste management, crime victims, corporate crime, parental consent and abortion laws, psychological aspects of rape, the Israeli–Palestinian conflict and Michael Harrington and democratic socialism. As Kramer describes it on his online vita from 2004, this 'half-hour program explored important social issues and current events, drawing on the Western Michigan University faculty, students, staff, and occasional guests to provide their insights and expertise' (2004: 5). Of course, this monthly program provided Kramer and company with perhaps the ideal newsmaking forum for producing critical and progressive intervention on behalf of such topical areas as human rights and social justice for all.

Similarly, when it came to the high-profile case of O.J. Simpson, it was my contention that newsmaking criminologists could both provide blow-by-blow legal descriptions required by media coverage (i.e. reporting) and, even more importantly, vitally omitted criminological contexts (i.e. reportage) that are far broader in scope than the information supplied by lawyers alone. Not limited to merely an informed discussion of the substantive and procedural aspects of criminal law, newsmaking criminologists were far more apt to discuss the disposition of crime and criminals, as well as punishment and its relationship to institutionalized patterns of class, race and gender discrimination in the USA (Barak, 1996: 114–15).

In the remainder of this section, I would like to describe how this newsmaking opportunity came about so as to contextualize the O.J. program that aired live twice weekly at 6.40 a.m. for approximately 6–7 minutes as a part of the regular daily *Morning Show* on 107.1 FM 'Kool' radio in Ann Arbor, Michigan. During the pretrial hearings and in anticipation of the upcoming criminal trial of O.J., I wrote a couple of op-ed pieces on domestic violence and criminal justice that were featured prominently in the *Ann Arbor News*. Then, one week before the Simpson trial was set to begin, a press release on Barak's expertise about crime, justice and the media was sent to print and electronic news sources from the Office of Public Information at Eastern Michigan University. The release included copies of the two op-ed pieces and some provocative quotations from me about O.J. and the upcoming trial, the future of domestic violence and the criminal law in the context of 'multiculturalism' and diversity. As a result, I was immediately contacted by radio stations in the area and did three broadcast interviews on the upcoming trial, two live and one taped, that were played about six times in the greater metropolitan Detroit.

One of the first live interviews I did was with the city of Ann Arbor's only 'oldies but goodies' FM station at the time, the *Morning Show* that aired 6.00 a.m. to 10.00 a.m. Monday through Friday. At the time, Lucy Ann Lance and Dean Erskin, who had a large and loyal following, hosted the show. Demographically aimed at the Baby Boomers, the *Morning Show* not only played 'oldies but goodies' music (mostly from the 1960s and 1970s era of hard and soft rock) but also aired news, weather and traffic reports, and local community service and public announcements as well. Fortunately for me, prior to the joint interview by Lance and Erskin, I had been a regular listener, waking and driving to work in the mornings with 107.1 music and the voices of Lucy Ann and Dean in my head.

I knew something about the co-hosts of the *Morning Show*. Lucy Ann and Dean were there to have a good time and to make themselves and their audiences laugh, but they also expressed a serious side or political consciousness appropriate for the Ann Arbor community. In other words, they were also about sharing their points of view on public issues and current events. I also believed that I knew something about their 'sensibilities' or 'mind sets' at the time (Barak, 1996), which helped me to feel an instant rapport had been established between us. After the first interview, they invited me back twice more to discuss the O.J. case, once before the actual trial began and one day after the trial had started. After the third interview, we then entered an agreement that I would provide live O.J. trial 'commentary' on their radio program two mornings a week for the duration of the criminal trial.

Typically, a couple of minutes before I was to go on the air, Lucy Ann and/or Dean and I would confer over the phone about the trial 'events' that had occurred since the previous show. Together, at least initially, we would more or less carve out the parameters as well as the issues to be addressed on that day's show. Within the framework of our pre-show discussion, Lucy Ann or Dean would return from a commercial break, set the stage for me by highlighting the O.J. 'news of the hour' with some kind of segue such as what does 'our very own expert and professor' have to say about this? At the beginning of the trial, I often engaged the co-hosts in a question/answer format augmented by a playful back and forth bantering between the three of us. From the middle of the trial until the jury verdict, I also sometimes filled the time with more and more commentary as my co-hosts were getting 'bored' by the repetition and length of the trial as it dragged on.

Thus in a very short period of time—that is, less than a month—I had gone from 'outside expert' to 107.1's O.J. expert that you 'can hear live on the Lucy Ann Lance and Dean Erskin *Morning Show* twice weekly every Tuesday and Friday at 6.40 a.m.' as the commercial promos plugged their listening audiences several times a week. In terms of Henry's classification of newsmaking interventions, I was no longer the criminologist as 'expert' or the criminologist as 'educative provocateur', but I had actually become the criminologist as 'journalist'. In fact, as the co-hosts literally tired of the O.J. trial about six months into it, our pre-broadcast conferences became a conduit to provide them with virtually all of their opening remarks and with the questions I would be asked during a given program. This allowed me to guide story lines and to introduce, for example, studies on jurors, domestic violence, mass media, gender, victimization, race and the administration of justice and class justice.

In a nutshell, the 'power of the narrative' became mine to construct over a fairly long period of 'mediated dialogue'. This power of the narrative generally has as much to do with what one omits from the conversations, chooses not to discuss or reinforce, or sets out to demystify or deconstruct, as it does with what one is actually trying to construct or establish as a 'new' foundation for contemplating if not confronting, in this case, 'criminal justice in America'. At the same time, this particular radio format demanded that I juggle other 'mediated balls' as well.

In other words, keeping in mind that the format of the *Morning Show* was essentially one of infotainment, combining both news and entertainment, I did not ever fully remove myself from being a criminologist 'as subject' or 'of interest' to Lucy Ann and Dean who always seemed to enjoy my 'radical' take on things. I also had interjected a third personality into the show's radio format as I was expected to mesh with Lucy Ann and Dean's personas. At the same time, I was granted my own biases and points of view; though I was journalistically expected not to take sides in the case but to be objectively reporting at the very same time that I was constructing a very different take on law and order, and on crime and justice, than most of my other expert legal counterparts. In short, as a newsmaking criminologist, I had become a journalist and disc jockey rolled into one.

## Mainstream and progressive newsmaking: themes or frames of discourse

My handwritten notes and commentaries on the Simpson criminal trial that I prepared before each show comprise about 150 legal size pages in length. Moreover, more than 10 hours of taped radio broadcasts were made from 'my' show. What follows is not meant to be an exhaustive analysis based on these retrospective 'data' but an indication of newsmaking possibilities that arose through the use of both reporting and reportage on the Simpson trial. Nor do I mean to suggest that these two different types of legal representation or narrative construction are mutually exclusive (Barak, 2004). On the contrary, to varying degrees, both the lawyer-legal analysts and the social science-criminologists engaged in overlapping narratives.

For instance, from the time of closing arguments through and beyond the unexpected and sudden jury verdict of not guilty (as it turned out, a long and drawn out process in the Simpson case), 'discourses' of mainstream and marginal contents came to overlap as broad discussions ensued about socially topical issues like law enforcement and racism, class and the administration of justice, and gender inequality and domestic violence (Barak, 1996: 118–19). What I am calling 'mainstream' commentaries were framed primarily by legal considerations while the progressive or 'marginal' commentaries were framed by both legal and social considerations. In terms of the potential for social change, the mainstream newsmakers' discourse tended to emphasize procedural legal reforms and substantive details about the law. In contrast, 'marginal' discourses (my own included) tended to focus more on issues of race and class discrimination, raising issues that suggested not only that legal procedures but the larger society required deep re-examination as well.

More specifically, the mainstream themes presented on most radio and television shows and read in newspapers and magazines (other than in alternative news venues) usually concerned issues of the criminal 'law in action'. Attorneys who had once practiced or were currently practicing defense and/or prosecution work typically articulated these themes for mass consumption. For the most part, these criminal legal 'experts' limited their remarks to assessing how well the judge, the defense, the prosecution and the witnesses performed their duties on any given day. Moreover, legal commentators often found themselves responding to questions about the usual or unusual character of an approach the prosecution or defense team had taken on a given day. These legal pundits relied heavily on cases from their own trial experiences or on other cases that they were aware of in order to establish some kind of context for their take on the O.J. trial. Indeed, as I wrote at the time, much of their time consisted of supplying endless criticisms and praises for the way the attorneys on either side of the issue had performed with respect to opening arguments, direct arguments, cross-examinations, re-directs and closing argument (Barak, 1996: 118).

By the second or third month of O.J. coverage, though, this kind of 'legal scoring' had become rather tired and redundant for both the legal pundits and the consuming public. In other words, the legal commentators and the listeners could only stomach so many times remarks like 'each day is like a little battle, some days the prosecution wins, some days the defense wins' or 'the judge has to take more control of the trial and get tougher with the attorneys on both sides'. Increasingly, even the mainstream attorneys ventured outside the legal arena to discuss such topics as race, racism and the wider administration of criminal justice, the strengths and the weaknesses of the jury system or the relationship between domestic violence and gendered homicide.

Nevertheless, in general, mainstream legal commentaries were defensive of the criminal law and the administration of justice. After all, most of these experts were or had been working attorneys within the system. Not surprisingly, then, most of their commentary revolved around the 'performances' of the various legal actors on any given day; their critiques were primarily of individual execution rather than the system or administration of justice as a whole. Even when these legal analysts broached issues of race, gender or class, rarely if ever did any of them address the differential impact of institutionalized racism, sexism or classism associated with the administration of criminal justice in the USA. By comparison, of course, my agenda as a news-making criminologist was different. I was less concerned about getting to the verdict of the O.J. Simpson case than about using the case as a pedagogical tool for examining the relations between class, race, gender and crime, on the one hand, and the social realities of justice in the USA, on the other (Barak et al., 2007). Moreover, as a 'social critic' more generally, I had no desire or interest to defend the administration of criminal justice as was often the case with legal pundits who seemed obsessed by the purported legal exceptionality of the Simpson trial. Rather, armed with a more complex understanding of the history of crime and punishment in the USA, I was in a better position to offer critical analyses and explanations of the relationship between high- and low-profile criminal cases (Barak, 1996: 119–20).

In short, as a progressive newsmaking criminologist, my discussions were largely concerned with demystifying crime and justice in the USA. For most of the nine months, I was busy trying to connect 'crime and justice' with larger arrangements of social, political and economic inequality. I was also trying to make sense of the disparate attitudes and behaviors that were manifesting themselves across society both during the trial and after the jury's verdict acquitted 'O.J.' of the double murders of Nicole Brown Simpson and Ronald Goldman.

## Concluding reflections on newsmaking criminology

Twenty years later, I still believe that it is important that, as criminologists, our voices be heard among all the other sounds and images associated with crime and justice, especially if these voices are resonating alternative rather than conventional themes. Do not misunderstand me: I am not trying to be some kind of criminological snob here. Rather, I do believe that as a 'collective body of knowledge or expertise', criminology does not get the 'respect it deserves' (at least not in the USA). In the cultural and mass-mediated age of *CSI*-like televised programming and serial-type killers, one might have thought that there would have been some sort of transference or spill over to criminologists. However, the presence of criminologists in the public domain did not significantly change or grow before, during or after the height of the 'CSI effect' (Shelton et al., 2007).

Moreover, when it comes to alternative themes or progressive newsmaking criminology I have not meant to imply that other commentators—legalistic, journalistic or politico—are not capable of tackling the same kinds of questions, issues or problems that policy-oriented criminologists, newsmaking or not, address. However, there are differences between what 'critical' and 'non-critical' criminologists know, let alone between what criminologists in general know and what criminal lawyers and laypersons know about crime and justice or law and order. As Freda Adler (1994) noted at the annual meetings of a mid-1990s New Jersey Association of Criminal Justice Educators: 'Everyone has an opinion about crime, if not their own, then it is one or the other of the positions constantly espoused by the media. These opinions are not the product of deep thought and reflection.' I would echo that the same is true of the viewpoints on crime and justice held by most legalistic and journalistic commentators who have not been trained in one of the formal disciplines that traditionally study matters of 'crime and punishment'.

Comparatively, the views of newsmaking criminologists who study crime and justice as well as media and culture are based on 'reflection, insight and the analysis of factual complexities which are unknown to the general public' (Adler, 1994). These complexities pertain not only to the administration of justice in relation to class, race and gender, but also to the relations between crime, criminals and crime control, and to the historical interaction of all of these constituencies in the social construction of 'crime', 'law', 'order' and

'justice'. Armed with a knowledge of these intricacies, newsmaking criminologists find themselves in an especially unique position to analyze and
explain the nature of the relationship between high- and low-profile criminal cases and the practices of criminal justice in everyday life.

In terms of this high-profile criminal trial with a mixture of news and
entertainment values, the context of a radio infotainment show worked
rather successfully as a newsmaking criminology medium. The format of
the *Morning Show* program afforded me the combination of the frames of
both reporting and reportage, which in turn, allowed me to 'spin' my criminological take on the *People versus O.J. Simpson* to tens of thousands of
listeners twice weekly. What is more, radio is a 'user-friendly' medium compared to television. Primarily because success on the radio requires basically
the exclusivity of a palatable voice and the ability to ad-lib without the
complication of TV's prerequisite audience approval of the visual presentation of self, I was able to intervene in the public presentation of the O.J.
Simpson trial from the comfort and privacy of my own home, sitting at the
kitchen table, surrounded by my yellow legal pads, jokes and marked-up
newspapers spread all about.

Three more reflections on this unique newsmaking radio experience and
its relation to newsmaking criminology and then on to some of the larger
theoretical concerns or implications. First, from the perspective of newsmaking, it is important to realize that I was not just another sound bite heard
occasionally in the context of all the other sound bites and noise. Quite the
contrary. By the time of the criminal jury's verdict, my recurrent voice on
O.J. had been constructing an analysis of crime and justice for almost 10
consecutive months against a backdrop of an ongoing public discussion of
some 16 months in duration, or since the double homicide occurred in June
of 1994. In short, I had developed my own audience and following that was
both about immediacy and a continuing long-range listening relationship.
Moreover, over the duration of the trial and the *Morning Show*'s coverage
of O.J., as mentioned earlier, I had become an 'insider'. In other words, my
answers and comments were less about reacting to or confronting the newsmaking process, than they were about collaborating with 'my' co-hosts to
produce a show with high ratings. What was particularly satisfying was
that I was not only able to forge an analysis of crime and justice that converged around the intersections of class, race and gender, but I was also able
to anticipate from the trial's very beginning the types of underlying social
and cultural tensions that would inevitably surface during the course of the
trial, regardless of the outcome.

Second, as a newsmaking criminologist I was sharing the knowledge
bases of criminology, media studies and the social and behavioral sciences
more generally. Because of the uniqueness of the reporting/reportage and
event/topical modes of newsmaking, I was able, when the mood struck or
the situation called for, to introduce a wide range of relevant studies on jury
behavior, domestic violence and even mass-media theory. From time to
time, I also incorporated lessons in history, philosophy and economics

when I felt it germane to the discussions as 'I' defined them implicitly and explicitly in relation to social justice. Suffice it to say, this radio format provided me ample opportunities to influence people's views, if not so much their images, of crime and justice or of law and order as these swirled around the Simpson spectacle.

Third, as already emphasized in my capacity as co-newsmaker with Lucy Ann Lance and Dean Erskin, I was able to interact with the media not in a reactionary or confrontational way but as a partner in the newsmaking process. This 'consultative' experience replicates other positive experiences that I as well as other newsmaking criminologists have found working within a variety of news media venues. When this occurs, newsmaking criminologists have the opportunity to ply the trade of proactive newsmaking where they can find the relative freedom to use their discourse choices and to frame crime and justice through the lens of alternative voices and/or progressive politics.

Opportunities such as covering the O.J. criminal trial rarely, if ever, come along. I subsequently tried to interest the *Morning Show* in doing a follow-up program covering the civil trial. Despite our previous high ratings, I was told that people were tired of O.J. I, too, was tired of O.J., but I guess never too tired to 'exploit' the opportunity to do newsmaking criminology with a substantive consequence. So, if one is engaging in newsmaking criminology, one more reflective bit of advice: regardless of the media whenever a 'good' newsmaking situation presents itself, be prepared to seize that moment, for it may not come again.

Finally, in 2007, what do I think about newsmaking criminology and its value as a tool for influencing pubic policy on crime and justice? As I have viewed the relationship between newsmaking criminology and public policy formation for more than two decades now, it has always been a tenuous or indirect one at best. Nevertheless, newsmaking criminology as a perspective on the theory, practice and study of mass communications and the representation or social construction of crime and justice, is still an invaluable approach for grasping as fundamental to the larger criminological enterprise in general and to administrative criminology in particular, their joint roles or 'function' in 'playing out' as part and parcel of neoliberal-bourgeois statecraft. At the same time, newsmaking criminology holds out the possibility of contributing to the development of a progressive politics on law and order, and crime and justice. As I envision the relative influence of newsmaking criminology in the future, it will most likely occur in one of the 'newer' rather than 'older' forms of mass communications.

Again, I am talking about websites, blogs and podcasts as the preferred newsmaking criminological media of tomorrow. In fact, from an email exchange that I received on 5 December 2006 from Paul Leighton, a US scholar who considers himself a 'critical criminologist' on the future of newsmaking criminology, Leighton wrote, and I quote with hispermission:

The next generation of newsmaking criminologists will be the persons who understand mobile computing. They will be able to send text messages on breaking topics and engage viewers through video downloaded to cell phones. In between will be the YouTube commentators who achieve followings through viral videos (forwarded by viewers, rather than distribution via an 'old' media outlet) and blog posts distributed through social networking sites like dig and reddit.

Interestingly, there have been relatively few criminologists who have developed substantive websites on crime and justice that can be used by students, academics, journalists, researchers, consumers, workers, citizens, lobbyists, advocates and others. Those academicians who have developed such websites find that their 'readership' can quickly move into the tens of thousands annually. That has been my experience at www.greggbarak.com. In criminology, probably the most visited websites of substance are Leighton's www.stopviolence.com and www.paulsjusticepage.com: together they receive about a million page requests per year.

One need not be a Webmaster (or even a 'criminologist' if you ignore what I stated at the beginning of this section) to do newsmaking criminology on the World Wide Web. All one has to do is write an 'op-ed' or commentary piece on virtually any crime- and justice-related topic and send it off to a blog, an online newsletter or listserve. Before one knows it, his or her revolutionary ideas will be circulating in cyberspace competing head-to-head so to speak with the world of bourgeois domination. For example, one highly recommended electronic newsletter, published daily, is www.countercurrents.org. A sampling from 1 December 2006 included Phil Rockstroh's *Wal Mart Nihilism Versus the Punk Rock Of Blogging* that began:

> The Holiday Season has arrived, unfolding before us, like a cheap vinyl wallet, here in The United States of American Express. The days spill forth, their hours comprised of shopping and shooting sprees, of retail and retaliation. Jingle bells and the crackle of gunfire. This is the way an empire falls, with armies of confused killers abroad and legions of killer clowns at home.
>
> (p. 1)

The point is that the era of the 'citizen-journalist' has already arrived vis-a-vis the blogosphere. There is absolutely nothing stopping newsmaking criminologists from doing the same. Anyone today can 'speak truth to power' and can 'be heard' doing so.

On the other hand, theoretically, this is not to say that I do not for a minute recognize the power and influence of the monopolies of the National Entertainment State, including mega-corporate conglomerates the likes of General Electric, Disney/Cap Cities, Westinghouse and AOL/Time Warner, that not only serve as advertising conduits for the stimulation of mass consumption of goods and services, but also for the marketing of particular life styles and values; not to mention the virtual colonizing of American culture in the process, complete with its views on law and order, crime and justice, human rights, the United Nations, terrorism, AIDS and so on and so forth. But the blog allows the blogger to once again 'speak truth to power' and to challenge conventional wisdom and ideology at the same time.

In the context of the dialectics of mass communications and bourgeois capitalism (Schiller, 1973, 1976) and in terms of a fully extended analysis of media, intellectuals and crime, let us now return to Gramsci's approach to hegemony that assumes that the prevailing orders of political economy depend on both the passive and active content of the governed, and on the collective will of the people in which various groups within society unite and struggle. In other words, hegemony includes not only the dominating classes' worldviews but also the worldviews of the masses. In the everyday social construction of the 'wired' electronic age of information and instant message, the role of mass communications is thus central to the contradictory relations of hegemonic domination.

In the postmodern age of ideology and technology, mass communications about crime and justice or law and order, whether as literature, audio, video or cyber messaging, are all integral to accumulation, legitimation and repression in capitalist society (Gouldner, 1976; Mosco, 1986). Dialectically, of course, mass communications represent an essential framework for social and political struggle. Regarding its crucial application, mass communications have been used increasingly by the State to manage and mitigate the consequences of the widening conflicts and contradictions of monopoly and multinational global capitalism. For example, 'disinformation' campaigns are an obvious illustration of the way in which state-mediated conceptions of official reality are used to misrepresent reality. In the area of crime and crime control, for example, there are the police wires or news dispatches that are released daily, and the semi-annually released reports in the States by the FBI that officially track and disseminate the magnitudes and rates of street but not suite crime (Barak, 2007b).

In opposition to this kind of political and cultural hegemony are myriad various struggles involving the poor and the working classes, women, people of color, homosexuals and other powerless groups, opponents of domestic violence, nuclear energy and environmental destruction, and those who support a variety of peacemaking projects in general and in relationship to restorative justice, punishment, incarceration and community re-emergence in particular. Linking up with these social movements and other concerned citizens whether in street or virtual reality today becomes one means in which newsmaking criminologists can ply their trade, as it were. Working with those involved in the 'struggles for justice' allows newsmaking criminologists to help shape the 'progressive' discourse, language and representation of crime and justice, and ultimately the policies that are adopted and acquiesced to by societies in their 'fights' against crime and injustice.

## References

Adler, F. (1994) Speech given at the annual meetings of the New Jersey Association of Criminal Justice Educators, April.

Altheide, D. (1987) 'Format and Symbols in TV Coverage of Terrorism in the United States and Great Britain', *International Studies Quarterly* 31(2): 161–76.

Altheide, D. (2006) *Terrorism and the Politics of Fear.* Lanham, MD: Rowman & Littlefield.

Arrigo, B. (1996) 'Media Madness as Crime in the Making: On O.J. Simpson, Consumerism, and Hyperreality', in G. Barak (ed.) *Representing O.J.: Murder, Criminal Justice and Mass Culture*, pp. 123–35. Guilderland, NY: Harrow & Heston.

Barak, G. (1988) 'Newsmaking Criminology: Reflections on the Media, Intellectuals, and Crime', *Justice Quarterly* 5(4): 565–87.

Barak, G. (ed.) (1994) *Media, Process, and the Social Construction of Crime: Studies in Newsmaking Criminology.* New York: Garland.

Barak, G. (1996) 'Media, Discourse, and the O.J. Simpson Trial: An Ethnographic Portrait', in G. Barak (ed.) *Representing O.J.: Murder, Criminal Justice and Mass Culture*, pp. 104–22. Guilderland, NY: Harrow & Heston.

Barak, G. (2001) 'Newsmaking Criminology', in E. McLaughlin and J. Muncie (eds) *The Sage Dictionary of Criminology*, pp. 190–1. London: Sage.

Barak, G. (2004) 'Representing O.J.: The Trial of the Twentieth Century', in F. Bailey and S. Chermak (eds) *Famous American Crimes and Trials*, vol. 5: 1981–2000, pp. 189–208. Westport, CT: Praeger.

Barak, G. (2007a) 'Mediatizing Law and Order: Applying Cottle's Architecture of Communicative Frames to the Social Construction of Crime and Justice', *Crime, Media, Culture* 3(1): 101–9.

Barak, G. (2007b) *Violence, Conflict, and World Order: Critical Conversations on State-Sanctioned Justice.* Lanham, MD: Rowman & Littlefield.

Barak, G., P. Leighton and J. Flavin (2007) *Class, Race, Gender, and Crime: The Social Realities of Justice in America* (2nd edn). Lanham, MD: Rowman & Littlefield.

Cottle, S. (2006) 'Mediatizing the Global War on Terror: Television's Public Eye', in A.P. Kavoori and T. Fraley (eds) *Media, Terrorism, and Theory: A Reader*, pp. 19–48. Lanham, MD: Rowman & Littlefield.

Fox, J.A. and J. Levin (1993) *How to Work with the Media.* Newbury Park, CA: Sage.

Gouldner, A. (1976) *The Dialectic of Ideology and Technology: The Origins, Grammar, and the Future of Ideology.* New York: Seabury.

Greek, C. (1994) 'Becoming a Media Criminologist: Is "Newsmaking Criminology" Possible?', in G. Barak (ed.) *Media, Process, and the Social Construction of Crime: Studies in Newsmaking Criminology*, pp. 265–86. New York: Garland.

Henry, S. (1994) 'Newsmaking Criminology as Replacement Discourse', in G. Barak (ed.) *Media, Process, and the Social Construction of Crime: Studies in Newsmaking Criminology*, pp. 287–318. New York: Garland.

Kavoori, A. and T. Fraley (eds) (2006) *Media, Terrorism, and Theory: A Reader*. Lanham, MD: Rowman & Littlefield.

Kramer, R.C. (2004) Online Vita. www.google.com (retrieved 11 November).

Mosco, J. (1986) 'Marxism and Communications Research in North America', in B. Ollman and E. Vernoff (eds) *The Left Academy: Marxist Scholarship on American Campuses*, vol. 3, pp. 237–62. New York: Praeger.

Nassar, J. (2005) *Globalization and Terrorism: The Migration of Dreams and Nightmares*. Lanham, MD: Rowman & Littlefield.

Nichols, B. (1991) *Representing Reality Issues: Issues in and Concepts in Documentary*. Bloomington, IN: University of Indiana Press.

Schiller, H. (1973) *The Mind Managers*. Boston, MA: Beacon.

Schiller, H. (1976) *Communication and Cultural Domination*. White Plains, NY: International Arts and Sciences Press.

Shelton, D., Y. Kim and G. Barak (2007, forthcoming) 'A Study of Juror Expectations and Demands Concerning Scientific Evidence: Does the "CSI effect" Exist?', *Vanderbilt Journal of Entertainment & Technology Law* 9(2).

GREGG BARAK is Professor of Criminology & Criminal Justice and Grievance Officer for the AAUP at Eastern Michigan University. His most recent book is *Violence, Conflict, and World Order: Critical Conversations on State-Sanctioned Justice*, published by Rowman & Littlefield, 2007.

# Part V
# Postmodern and Post-Structural Criminology and its Interlocutors

# [17]

## Postmodernism, Protest, and the New Social Movements

Joel F. Handler

**M**y subject is postmodern politics and law, protest from below, and the "new" social movements. The question I am concerned with is the value of postmodernism for transformative politics.

Scholars concerned with the struggles of subordinate groups have long emphasized protest from below. Accounts of the resistance of blacks and poor people became prominent in the 1960s. This tradition, joined by feminists, gays and lesbians, as well as others, continued in the 1980s. The new social movements are, roughly, environmental, antinuclear, peace, feminist, and gay and lesbian. Whether these broad movements are "new" or variations of older movements is much debated. For our purposes, they are included here insofar as they are antimaterialist, antistatist, antibureaucratic; they seek to cross traditional class lines in favor of humanistic, interpersonal, and communitarian values.

There have always been protest movements and struggle on the part of oppressed peoples. What has this to do with postmodernism? And what does postmodernism have to do with politics and law? The major theme in postmodernism that I emphasize is subversion, the commitment to undermine dominant discourse. The subversion theme—variously described as deconstruction, radical indeterminacy, anti-essentialism, or antifoundationalism—whether in art, architecture, literature, or philosophy—seeks to demonstrate the inherent instability of seemingly hegemonic structures, that power is diffused throughout society, and that there are multiple possibilities for

This essay is an expanded version of my presidential address, Law & Society Association Annual Meeting, 27–31 May 1992, Philadelphia, Pa. I wish to thank William Forbath, Austin Sarat, Susan Silbey, Lucie White, and the UCLA Faculty Colloquium.

resistance by oppressed people. The postmodern conception of subversion is a key part of the explanations and ideological commitments of contemporary theorists of protest from below and the new social movements.

I first describe postmodernism's theory of subversion in the broader culture. The starting point is deconstruction. Deconstruction, developed first in literary theory, then applied in art, architecture, and philosophy, seeks to destabilize dominant or privileged interpretations. Then I discuss deconstruction or subversion in postmodern political and legal theory. The goal, say postmodern political theorists, is radical, plural democracy. A major criticism of postmodern politics is that deconstruction amounts to relativism or radical indeterminacy, which, at best, results in passive, status quo politics and, at worst, fails to defend against fascism and terrorism. Postmodern political theorists rely on American pragmatism to meet the challenge of relativism.

Postmodernism, naturally, covers a large territory. To try to assess what postmodern politics means, I look at scholars of protest from below in the 1960s and compare their work to contemporary stories of protest from below that I think are in the postmodern tradition. While both sets of scholars are concerned with the struggles of oppressed peoples, they tell very different stories. The commonality of struggle and social vision of the 1960s disappears in the contemporary message. There are some exceptions, and I use some contemporary feminist and minority scholars to contrast the structuralist tradition. I then look at the new social movements and review the reasons for their lack of success. The key, I argue, to the distinctiveness of postmodern politics lies in deconstruction. My thesis is that deconstruction, as a form of politics, is ultimately disabling. In the final section, I speculate on the reasons for the attractiveness of deconstruction politics.

The grand theories of the Left have collapsed. The humane side of the Enlightenment is under attack. However, I question the value of postmodernism as transformative politics.

## I. Postmodern Theory

### Deconstruction as Subversion

The postmodern concept of subversion developed first in language and literary theory, art, and architecture and then spread into politics and law. Deconstruction, which may be considered the parent of postmodernism, starts with Wittgenstein's proposition that there is no logical correspondence between language and the "objective" world. There are no clearcut logical explanatory concepts; rather, there are many uses or "grammars" or "enabling conventions as diverse in nature as the jobs that they are required to do." If one accepts this idea—that while one cannot dispense with language, there is no necessary, logical connection between the use of language and what it purports to describe—then it follows that there is no self-authenticating truth or method or reason that is independent of language. As applied to literature, there is no one *authentic* reading or meaning of a given text; as applied to philosophy, claims of pure reason are likewise subject to rhetorical questioning—to *deconstruction* (Norris 1991:18–21, 129).

Nevertheless, we do read, interpret, and make claims about the world. What "grammar" are we using? Here enters the second idea, which is probably the foundation concept of deconstruction: It is Derrida's critique of identity—that every "identity" necessarily suppresses an alternative identity. When we define something—anything—we are necessarily excluding or "repressing" something else. Thus, all meaning has a "surplus," that which is repressed along with that which is articulated. All meaning, then, is always deferred; there is never a conceptual closure because language can never offer a *"total and immediate* access to the thoughts that occasioned its utterance" (ibid., pp. 46, 64).

But why is this "deconstruction"? Deconstruction "is a matter of taking a repressed or subjugated theme . . . , pursuing its various textual ramifications and showing how these subvert the very order that strives to hold them in check" (ibid., p. 39).

However, even though identity represses an alternative meaning, what if the articulated interpretation is *privileged*, that is, apparently (normatively) preferred or dominant or totalizing? Postmodernists deny that either the dominant or the suppressed meaning *ought* to be privileged. The very point of deconstruction, it is insisted, is to deny, to subvert, privileged discourses. "Deconstruction tears a text apart, reveals its contradictions and assumptions; its intent, however, is not to improve, revise, or offer a better version of the text" (Rosenau 1992:xi). In postmodern art, popular forms are freely mixed with "fine" art as a method of internal critique, to *decanonize* fine art (Wicke 1991). However, while the suppressed or alternative meaning (popular art) subverts or reorders the dominant priorities, it is also in complicity with the dominant form by taking advantage of it (Deutsche 1991:21; Thomas 1991:4).

In architecture, postmodernists rebelled against modernism. Modernism was obsessed with form; a form, moreover, dictated by function. Postmodernists viewed the relationship of function to form as a "tragic" or false "necessity"—another key idea—that unnecessarily limits, confines, and distorts the fullness of human experience. However, postmodern architecture does not totally reject modern architecture; that would also be a futile attempt at a privileged, totalizing meaning. Rather, postmodern architecture challenges the modern tradition by using that tradition and simultaneously questioning it. Perhaps the most famous example is Philip Johnson's AT&T building. The repressed meaning—in this case, the decorative pediment—sits on top of the classic modernist, sleek skyscraper in "ironic juxtaposition." Ironic juxtaposition is used by postmodernists to clarify simultaneously both the meaning and the suppressed meaning of the modernist form (Boyle 1991).

### Postmodern Politics

Derrida's critique of identity describes the organization of society itself. The constitution of a social identity is an act of power. Accordingly, postmodernists consider foundationalism or essentialism—whether liberal capitalism or Marxism—a fundamental obstacle to the deepening and extension of democracy throughout civil society (Laclau & Mouffe 1985:19; Thomas 1991). In contrast, deconstruction refers back to the contingency, the contextual determinant of all meaning.

The rejection of foundationalist theories is based on two key ideas: the decentered subject and a reconceptualization of the theory of hegemony (Hunt 1990). The postmodern subject is not defined either by particular values such as possessive individualism or by class, or by race, ethnicity, or gender. There is no unified essence. Rather, the postmodern subject is a plurality of contingent social, political, and epistemic relations. Moreover, these relations are constantly subject to rearticulation. Because there are no a priori relations based on hegemonic practices, agents are only contingently allied in more or less stable arrangements (Deutsche 1991:21; Laclau & Mouffe 1985:27, 28; Thomas 1991:2, 4).

Hegemonic structures—that is, the processes of mobilizing consent—are also contingent. Social relations are constructed and transformed through discourse and articulation that are never complete, never totalizing, even if not contested. In contrast to the Frankfurt school, the postmoderns believe that hegemony is never stable. People are never merely passively subordinated, never totally manipulated. Opposition is always possible within alternative practices, structures, and spaces (Deutsche 1991:20; Grossberg 1988:52–53; Laclau & Mouffe 1985:30).

Postmodernists think that the potential for subversive struggle today is especially propitious because of the discrediting of Marxism, the instabilities of late capitalism, and the contradictions of the bureaucratic welfare state. Interpersonal relations have been commodified and bureaucratized. Postmodernists see these negative effects as a source of resistance and freedom (Laclau & Mouffe 1985:36, 37).

Change will be brought about through small-scale transformation. By increasing the plasticity of social structures, the state itself will be converted from a source of stability to a source of change (Boyle 1985). Change will be in the democratic direction. Equality and rights discourse play a fundamental role in reconstructing collective identities. When people accept the legitimacy of the principal of equality in one sphere, they will attempt to extend it other spheres (Laclau & Mouffe 1985:39). In this way, the contradictions and instabilities of late capitalism can be subverted from within (Thomas 1991:2). Subversion from "within" usually means from "below." "Below" could encompass geographically situated communities, such as factories, offices, neighborhoods or "intentional" communities (Aronowitz 1988:47).

The theoretical elements of postmodern philosophy link together to form the basis for a postmodern political theory: through deconstruction, hegemonic structures are destabilized, making resistance always possible. The ideology of equality transforms subordinate relations into oppression and then resistance. However, while subversive groups need a conception of the social order, postmodernists, in contrast to foundationalists, insist that this conception must always be unstable, contested, and open. The task is to "institutionalize *discursive discontinuity*" (Laclau & Mouffe 1985:30).

What, then, is the project? The goals of postmodern politics are stated in terms of a *radical* and *plural* democracy. The contemporary state, reflecting the logic of modernity, is characterized by extreme centralizing tendencies; it is colonizing, totalizing, bureaucratic. In contrast, the postmodern state is minimalist because radical democracy depends on the proliferation of public spaces where social agents become increasingly capable of self-management (Aronowitz 1988:45). The postmodern goals are extensive citizen participation in free democratic egalitarian societies.

A *democratic plurality* follows from the concept of radical contingency. Rather than privileged positions, there is only a discontinuous series of social formations. Struggle can arise out of a variety of practices from a variety of political spaces. This will be a *radical* pluralism because there are no *necessary* connections between various interests; there is no unitary subject and therefore no common or totalizing discourse (e.g., class). Rather, the links between the various interests have to be articulated from moment to moment (Laclau & Mouffe 1985:22; Thomas 1991:5). Postmodern politics would not permit domination between groups. Rather, there has to be a "democratic equivalence" in that demands must be articulated in a new "common-

702    **Postmodernism, Protest, and the New Social Movements**

sense" equivalence of competing demands. The articulation of different demands according to democratic equivalences means not merely establishing alliances but actually modifying the very identity of these forces. The ethical principle of defending individual liberty thus becomes more important than ever, but liberty is not bourgeois, possessive individualism. Rather, postmodernists see individual liberty and rights as relational, as collectively exercised, which means recognizing the rights of others (Mouffe 1988:45).

Critics of this political vision of postmodernists have argued that without foundationalism, moral judgments cannot be made, and progressive politics becomes impossible. Instead of extending democracy, postmodernism's radical pluralism amounts to unbridled relativism; politics becomes either passive or regressive or provides no defense against fascism and terrorism (Harvey 1989). While many postmoderns admit that deconstruction does not *necessarily* lead to beneficent outcomes, two strategies are used to avoid the harmful turn. One is to adhere to the humanist values of the Enlightenment without embracing the transcendental part.[1] The other is embracing the American pragmatism of James and Dewey.[2]

*Pragmatism*

Pragmatism is attractive to postmodernists for a number of reasons. It rejects foundationalism; all knowledge, including science, is historical, contextual, language-dependent, and therefore radically contingent (Grey 1989; West 1989:192). The test of knowledge is efficacy, whether it *works* according to

---

[1] "Postmodernity does not imply a *change* in the values of the Enlightenment modernity but rather a particular weakening of their absolutist character" (Laclau 1988).

This is where postmodernists differ with Habermas (1987). Habermas's project is to preserve and enhance progress toward the liberal, humanistic values of liberty, autonomy, respect, dignity, justice. The quarrel is not with this part of his conceptualization. The quarrel comes, rather, on Habermas's transcendental or foundational views. Habermas argues that through rational discourse (the ideal speech situation), rational agreement (reason) can be reached that transcends, both in time and space, the immediate interests of the participants. And it is only through reason that the liberal, humane values can be saved from the forces of darkness. Postmoderns reject the notion that any politics can generate another meta-narrative. Consensus is always temporary, merely a phase in the discourse. The legitimacy that Habermas thinks can be achieved through consensus that will emerge from discussion "does violence to the heterogeneity of language games"; it is a "coercive code" (Hassan 1987:199, 222; Deutsche 1991:21).

[2] Ihab Hassan (1987) in *The Postmodern Turn* quotes William James:

"No one of us ought to issue vetoes to the other, nor should we bandy words of abuse. We ought, on the contrary, delicately and profoundly to respect one another's mental freedom: then only shall we bring about the intellectual republic; then only shall we have that spirit of inner tolerance without which all our outer tolerance is soulless, and which is empiricism's glory; then only shall we live and let live, in speculative as well as in practical things."

Hassan (p. 187) comments on this passage: "How far, beyond this, does any postmodern pluralist go?"

human goals and aspirations. Inquiry is practical in two senses. First, thinking is always contextual and situated; it is always embodied in habits, in practices of perceiving and conceiving. And because of the crucial importance of language, these habits are collectively developed. Pragmatists reject methodological individualism (Grey 1989).[3] Second, thinking is instrumental, adaptive, functional, problem-solving (West 1989:5).

Significant among pragmatism's attractions is its normative, progressive cast.[4] Pragmatists believe in the uniqueness of individuals, collective democracy, and the possibility in goodness and greatness through the application of human intelligence (Grey 1989; West 1989; Westbrook 1991). The pragmatists are concerned about the relationship between knowledge, power, and economic organization and the ways in which discourses, whether in science, politics, or ethics, are linked to structures of domination (Grey 1989). Dewey's emphasis on the role of critical intelligence was inseparable from his promotion of creative democracy (Putnam 1991; Westbrook 1991). He believed that social conflict could be resolved through consensus and that creative democracy could be furthered by education and discussion. His vision was a radical democracy in which self-creation and communal participation could flourish in diversity and plurality (West 1989:103). The renaissance and contemporary reinterpretation of American pragmatism to fulfill progressive, emancipatory, democratic goals is well illustrated in Cornel West's (p. 223) "prophetic pragmatism" which emphasizes the central role of human agency.

Pragmatists deny that antifoundationalism necessarily means relativism. Hypotheses, systematic thought, evidence, and inference are taken seriously. "All the major pragmatist figures accepted and asserted the importance of general principles and systematic thought; they insisted only that the test of abstractions must be their usefulness for action and concrete inquiry" (Grey 1989:824). On the other hand, they would not privilege any procedure as having access to truth or reality, including science. While truth is contingent and subject to revision, the "best available truths are warranted and acceptable" (West 1989:67).[5]

---

3 Wrote Dewey: "Of all affairs, communication is the most wonderful . . . and that the fruit of communication should be participation, sharing. . . . Shared experience is the greatest of human goods" (quoted in Westbrook 1991:337, 365; see also Menand 1992).

4 There is dispute with this proposition (e.g., Baker 1991, Fish 1991, Menand 1992, Rorty 1992, Singer 1990).

5 Minow and Spelman (1990) argue that there is a false distinction between abstraction and context. Abstractions, or any theoretical statement, are born in context. There is " 'no view from nowhere' " (ibid., p. 1627, quoting Nagel). The very process of categorization, of selecting some facts and not others, involves choices, values, judgments, preconceptions, and moral positions. These categories can be generalized. In other words, just as abstract theories are rooted in particular contexts, so, too, contex-

**704    Postmodernism, Protest, and the New Social Movements**

Postmodernists use pragmatism to deny that contingency is the equivalent of indeterminacy. Just because a *"rational"* motive for a decision cannot be established does not mean a decision is not *"reasonable"* (Laclau & Mouffe 1985:35). How does one decide what is "reasonable"? The process is essentially open. Consensus is reached by discursive and argumentative practices. Judgment avoids the false dilemmas between universal criteria and arbitrariness. Reasonable opinions can be formed within a given tradition. Liberal democracy is the main tradition in our societies (ibid., p. 39; Mouffe 1988:42). Postmodernism, by tolerating alternative contingent rationalities, only appears irrationalist by comparison to a universal rationality that purports to legitimize "truths."

But what kind of politics do pragmatists offer? The experimental attitude of pragmatism means questioning the existing structures of power, gender, race, ethnicity, and nationality. It is a *critical* rather than a passive or complacent posture (Grey 1989:814; Minow & Spelman 1990:1647–51; Singer 1989). It means questioning the views of the most powerful, those who have silently structured the agenda and the terms of the debate. Critical contemporary pragmatists would apply the same stance to what they see as a danger of pragmatism. By emphasizing "common sense," pragmatism runs the temptation of accepting the status quo (Singer 1989, 1990; Radin 1990; West 1989). What is called for is the recognition that there are multiple, even conflicting, points of view or common senses. When pragmatists (or anyone else, for that matter) ask whether a particular practice works, "we must ask ourselves, 'works *for whom?*' Who benefits and who loses from existing political, economic, and legal structures?" (Singer 1990:1841). "Pragmatism is a form of cultural criticism and locates politics in the everyday experience of ordinary people" (West 1989:213).

The attractiveness of pragmatism for postmodern politics is apparent—the rejection of meta-narratives or foundationalism, its focus on language, power, and context, its experimentalism, and its progressivism. However, postmodernism is selective in its use of pragmatism. What it chooses to emphasize and what it chooses to ignore will be discussed in the sections on protest from below and the new social movements.

*Postmodern Law*

The failure of contemporary bureaucratic capitalism translates into the "legitimation crisis" in postmodern law. It is ar-

tual observations are expressive of more general values. These more general values can then be applied to the *universe* of other particular cases that are similar. Thus, "contextualism," while eschewing the ideal of generality, does embody the idea of universality (p. 1646). We make "situated judgments based on the values accepted by particular communities" (Singer 1990:1822).

gued that the modern regulatory state has become dysfunctional either by "colonizing other life-worlds" (Habermas 1987) or because it has inappropriately interfered with the functioning of other subsystems (Luhmann 1985; Teubner 1986). The result has been inefficiencies in managing economic and social problems and the distortion of human relations (A. Scott 1990:70–75).

The postmodern alternative combines legal pluralism with postmodern conceptions of the diffusion of power. The state is not the only source of rules of law. People operate in several spheres simultaneously—in the market, at work, in the family, as consumers; hence, there is an uneven and unstable, nonsynchronic mixing of types of rules, some of which may be empowering, others oppressive. However, state law, while not exclusive, "is still a decisive political factor," dominating and exploitive (Santos 1990; Hunt 1990:315; Hutchinson 1989: 568).

Santos (1990) argues that the modern idea of global rationality has disintegrated into a multitude of uncontrollable, irrational mini-rationalities. What is needed is to reinvent these mini-rationalities so that they form a new totality. The postmodern struggle of mini-rationalities will be different from that of modernity because of the nature of postmodern knowledge. Postmodern knowledge is "situational, empathetic and participatory rather than objectively distanced"; it is "local, but being local, it is also total." Postmodern critical theory is different from modern critical theory in that it arises out of "emancipatory everyday practices." Politics and law in the postmodern transition is "the emergence of a new legal minimalism and of micro-revolutionary practices." Because we are in an increasingly complex network of subjectivities, a proliferation of political and legal "interpretive communities" will emerge out of the struggle against the "monopolies of interpretation." These postmodern communities, based on a new political common sense (local knowledge), represent the only way of defending the accomplishments of modernity—a fairer distribution of economic resources and a significant democratization of the political system. The political agenda will emphasize postmaterialist goods (e.g., ecology and peace) and participatory democracy to prevent the demise of representative democracy. As the domination of bureaucratic capitalism is exposed, victimized groups will be empowered. Law will be decanonized as it proves ineffective, opening a "gap in social imagination." Social change will come about as "autonomous subjectivities . . . free themselves from the prejudices of legal fetishism."

706     **Postmodernism, Protest, and the New Social Movements**

*Feminism*

The ideals as well as the tensions in postmodernism can be illustrated in selected aspects of feminist and race theories.

There is, by now, a wide range of feminist theory and jurisprudence. Women's rights feminists would be analogous to the liberal legal conception. Communitarian feminists, who hold that women are ontologically different from men because they are epistemologically and morally connected to life from the very beginning, have been criticized as essentialist (Radin 1990:1707 n.20).[6]

The postmodern conception of feminism argues that there is no such thing as a generic "woman" (Spelman 1988). Such talk masks the heterogeneity of women and perpetuates the privileged position and domination of white middle-class feminists. There is a difference between sex and gender, and it is an error to focus on gender in isolation from identity. Identity is constructed by race, ethnicity, class, community, nation; it is both multiple and unstable.

Margaret Radin (1990) draws the connections between contemporary pragmatism and her view of feminism. She argues that the feminist commitment to learning through consciousness raising—its "concrete methodology"—is squarely in the pragmatist tradition. For pragmatists, "for consciousness to exist at all, there must be shared meaning arising out of shared interactions with the world. . . . Dewey's treatment is suffused with the interrelationship of communication, meaning, and shared group experience" (p. 1708). Further, argues Radin, it is the methodology of consciousness raising that supplies the distinctive critical dimension of feminism to pragmatism, because there cannot be communication where there is oppression (p. 1708).

On the other hand, some prominent feminists question the value of postmodern politics for feminism. While Nancy Fraser and Linda Nicholson (1988) applaud the critique of foundationalism and essentialism, they find the postmodern conception of social criticism to be "anemic." Rather than speaking of an "overarching theory of justice," postmodernist theorists (e.g., Lyotard) speak of a " 'justice of multiplicities' " (p. 87, quoting Lyotard). Because Lyotard rejects the idea of a common consciousness or social identity, "he rules out the sort of critical social theory that employs general categories like gender, race, and class" as being too reductive (pp. 88–89). Instead, there are "smallish, localized narrative[s]." Thus, ac-

---

6 On the other hand, communitarian feminists move toward the postmodern conception of identity by emphasizing the constitutive and transformative nature of the social bond. Identity is not a priori to context. Those who are part of the social bond constitute and transform one another (Radin 1991).

cording to postmodernists, there "are no large scale, systemic problems that resist local, ad hoc, ameliorative initiatives" (p. 89).

Fraser and Nicholson say that one cannot grasp the full dimensions of the subordination of women without

> large narratives about changes in social organization and ideology, empirical and social-theoretical analyses of macrostructures and institutions, interactionist analyses of the micropolitics of everyday life, critical-hermeneutical and institutional analyses of cultural production, historically and culturally specific sociologies of gender. . . . The list could go on. (Pp. 90–91)

Many of these approaches are essential to feminist criticism, but they do not mean a return to foundationalism. They call for a more "robust" theories of social criticism that would be more useful for contemporary feminist political practice (p. 100).

*Critical Race Theory*

The questions Fraser and Nicholson (1988) raise about the usefulness of postmodern political theory for feminists have been a major concern of critical race theorists. As with feminist theory, there is a large scholarly literature dealing with race and ethnicity. There are important postmodern influences in critical race theory. Nevertheless, at least in the area of law and politics, race theorists, while avoiding essentialism, such as biology, are quite firm about rejecting deconstructive politics (for literary theory, see Fuss 1989).

At the 1987 Critical Legal Studies Conference, minority scholars presented their critique of deconstruction politics. The conference took place during the "trashing" period of Critical Legal Studies, when the regime of civil rights was subject to a withering deconstructive attack. CLSers argued that rights were malleable and manipulative, that in practice they served to isolate and marginalize rather than empower and connect people, and that progressive people should emphasize needs, informality, and connectedness rather than rights. CLSers (with some notable exceptions) avoided constructive programs, arguing instead that the repressive structures of liberal capitalism first had to be exposed and dismantled before progressive constructive work could begin (Dalton 1987).

As I recall, virtually all minority scholars raised serious criticims of the CLS position. Patricia Williams (1991) said that whites misunderstood the African-American experience. Although blacks have no illusions about the efficacy of rights, most blacks have not turned away from the pursuit of the rights " 'governing narrative' or metalanguage about the significance of rights which is quite different for whites and blacks." For

708    **Postmodernism, Protest, and the New Social Movements**

blacks, the assertion of rights "affords at least a modicum of protection." "To say that blacks never fully believed in rights is true. Yet it is also true that blacks believed in them so much and so hard that we gave them life where there was none before. . . . This was the resurrection of life from ashes four hundred years old" (p. 163). This was the product of a "whole nation and the kindling of several generations" (p. 163). "The concept of rights, both positive and negative, is the marker of our citizenship, our relation to others" (p. 164). Instead of deconstructing the "myth of rights," Williams sees such deconstruction as threatening blacks' fragile empowerment. Therefore, "rights rhetoric has been and continues to be an effective form of discourse for blacks." Although rights can be isolating or disabling for whites, for blacks "the experience of rights-assertion has been one of both solidarity and freedom, of empowerment of an internal and very personal sort; it has been a process of finding the self." These differences between blacks and whites, says Williams, "are differences rooted firmly in race, and in the unconsciousness of racism." She calls the difference between the radical left and the "historically oppressed" an "essential difference." "Whites . . . must learn to appreciate the communion of blacks in more than body, as more than the perpetually neotenized, mothering non-mother. They must recognize us as kin."

In the postmodern tradition, Williams acknowledges the richness of ethnic and political diversity; nevertheless, "I do believe . . . that the simple matter of the color of one's skin so profoundly affects the way one is treated, so radically shapes what one is allowed to think and feel about this society, that the decision to generalize from this devision is valid." "[T]he term 'black' . . . accentuate[s] the unshaded monolithism of color itself as a social force."

Harlon Dalton (1987) expressed similar themes. One of the central differences that people of color have with Critical Legal Studies is "rooted in biography, in specific history." CLSers, he points out, were organized by white males out of their experience of the 1960s. "And by the term 'white male,' I mean to capture the social meaning that attaches to being part of the master race, and that flow from being one of those for whose benefit patriarchy exists." Further, CLSers are members of the white intellectual elites; their world is books and ideas. He contrast these CLSers with the "biography of the black, brown, red, and yellow."

> No matter how smart or bookish we were, we could not retreat from the sights, sounds, and smells of the communities from which we came. We learned from life as well as from books. We learned about injustice, social cruelty, political hy-

pocrisy and sanctioned terrorism from the mouths of our mothers and fathers and from our very own experiences. We learned that "our fate and that of all persons of similar hue were inseparably intertwined. That fundamental connectedness, together with our distinctive subcultures, nourished and sustained us, created in us an unshakeable sense of community." "A thorough-going familiarity with Foucault, Derrida, Habermas and Gramsci will not save us from the 'the fishy stare on the bus.' "

Dalton says that it is this difference between the "classic CLSers" and "us pretenders" that helps explain why CLS "patriarchs (again, with notable exceptions)" feel no need to articulate specific programs, whereas people of color continue the search, and why the deconstructive critique of rights is "oblivious to, and potentially disruptive of, the interests of people of color."

For Dalton, a key difference between people of color and whites is the role of community. Community is a source of strength, a resource for people of color. It is also a source of racial oppression. But for people of color there is no choice. "We can't choose to be part of the community; we can't choose not to be part of the community."

Williams emphasizes the importance of rights for people of color and Dalton the need for programs to deal with the immediate as well as long-range problems.[7] These authors (as well as many others) are clearly aware of postmodern intellectual developments. They are sensitive to context, the diversity of influences, the multidimensionality of experience.[8] As we shall see, they use narrative. However, their basic methodology and policy prescriptions are distinctly nonpostmodern. In terms like those of Fraser and Nicholson, they deny that the experience of people of color can be understood without discussing the large narratives of societal racism in its full historical, ubiquitous,

---

[7] Not surprisingly, contemporary race scholarship pursues both of these lines. While space does not permit a full survey, two prominent examples are Kimberlé Crenshaw's (1989) work on discrimination law and Chuck Lawrence's (1987, 1990) and Mari Matsuda's (1989) work on hate speech. Crenshaw argues that black women are burdened by both race and patriarchy, which is not taken account of in either antidiscrimination doctrine, feminist theory, or antiracist policies. Although she talks about the multidimensionality of black women's experiences, she considers black women as a group sharing a common experience of both race and gender discrimination that is not sufficiently understood or recognized. Black women face a "distinct set of issues" (p. 159). "Black women, like Black men, live in a community that has been defined and subordinated by color and culture" (p. 162).

Lawrence (1990) and Matsuda (1989), in arguing for the regulation of hate speech, stress the power and the uniqueness of the injury that people of color suffer, and argue that this amounts to a denial of equality.

[8] Matsuda (1989:2323–24) calls the contemporary critical race theory "outsider jurisprudence." It is the "new jurisprudence of people of color. . . . [It] is a methodology grounded in the particulars of their social reality and experience. This method is consciously both historical and revisionist, attempting to know history from the bottom."

710    **Postmodernism, Protest, and the New Social Movements**

structural manifestations. They speak of the deeply rooted, profound common experiences of people of color. And they propose broadly based, state-enforced remedies (e.g., Delgado et al. 1985).

## II. Protest from Below

I illustrate the tensions with postmodern politics by turning first to stories of protest from below and then to accounts of the new social movements. Here I compare contemporary stories of protest from below with works written in a more structuralist tradition. Authors tell stories to make a point. In so doing, they write both *for* and *against* something; they suggest that prior interpretations are wrong or misleading or incomplete. Both sets of authors write about the struggles of oppressed people, but, as we shall see, they tell very different stories. By comparing the two sets of authors, I hope to illustrate what is distinctive about postmodern politics. I think that this will shed light on the problems of the new social movements and on the transformative potential of postmodern politics.

### Stories Predating Postmodernism

The 1950s and 1960s were a period of protest and social movements. The rise of African nation states and Pan-Africanism had a deep influence on African-American consciousness. There were tremendous black migrations. Along with the rise of black electoral politics, there were increases in poverty and crime, the urban riots of the 1960s, and rising welfare rolls. The country experienced a legal rights revolution on behalf of minorities, the poor, women, children, and the disabled.

Two major issues of that era were the identity of African-Americans and the role of protest. At the risk of oversimplification, I suggest that the dominant approach of the civil rights struggle has been integration and assimilation. At the same time, African-Americans have always fought to preserve and enhance of their separate identity. The tensions and ambiguities of African-American aspirations and politics were reflected in the differing leadership roles of Martin Luther King, Jr., and Malcolm X. This was the general context within which Eugene Genovese (1972), Carol Stack (1974), and Piven and Cloward (1977) wrote.

Historical scholarship on American slavery had developed two lines of argument—the Southern apologists and the liberal, integrationists who believed in the basic irrelevance of race (Oliver 1976). Both lines of thought were unsatisfactory to Genovese (1972). He sought to establish that African-Americans, despite the horrors of slavery, were able to preserve and forge their own identity in opposition to the slaveholders.

Genovese's basic argument is that the hegemonic system of the slaveholders was not that complete. It allowed some space, however fragmentary and minute, for resistance. In a variety of ways, the slaves were able to reinterpret the masters' code to assert their identity, to counterpoise themselves as autonomous human beings. They could shirk, manage, or otherwise negate, however minor, the work. There were ways of learning to read, to visit, to take care of one another.

The slaves did more than resist. They laid the foundations of a collective identity. The slaves managed to adapt Christianity into their own version of black Christianity. Christian love and human dignity, individual moral worth, spiritual freedom and equality, and a sense of community all denied the slaveholder code. The intense struggle for literacy was based, for the most part, on religion. The African-American religion laid the foundation for building a "nation within a nation," the creation of a "protonational black consciousness," a collective identity and pride (p. 168).

In addition, the slaves developed their own language. Pidgin or "Black English" was their unique form of communication, separate from that of the master. The slave language was more than a tool of resistance; it built bonds of identity, constructed their community. Then, there was the pull of the family. The slaves, against great odds, built powerful norms of family life and struggled to maintain their families.

In one sense, Genovese's account adumbrates postmodernism's version of protest from below. Despite the efforts of the slaveholders, oppression was never complete; the hegemonic system, manifesting the dialectic of accommodation and resistance, reflected deep contradictions. In these spaces, the slaves were able to develop a sense of moral worth by asserting their rights, thus rejecting slavery itself (p. 658). On the other hand, Genovese's analysis is decidedly unpostmodern. Despite the great variety among the slaves as well as free African-Americans, he emphasizes commonalities—particularly the development of religion and language. The emphasis on building a nation within a nation contrasts with the postmodern view that the subject is composed of many influences that are in flux and that alliances are always temporary. Genovese's message is different: African-Americans created a unique community of shared experiences, forged out of a great struggle. African-Americans have a common identity; they are a "nation within a nation."

Carol Stack (1974), in her study of African-Americans in a Midwest city in the 1960s, was writing against the culture of poverty literature, which characterized changes in the African-

712     **Postmodernism, Protest, and the New Social Movements**

American family as the generational transmission of "maladaptive" values and behaviors. Stack's argument is that, in contrast, this was a highly adaptive community struggling to survive in an extremely hostile environment. She found an extensive network of cooperation and mutual aid as strategies for coping with severe poverty that constituted an underlying element of black identity in the community.

Piven and Cloward (1977) looked at more overt, direct conflicts between oppressed people and the state. Protest movements emerge when there is a transformation of both consciousness and behavior, when people believe that they have been wronged and develop a sense of efficacy. Defiance is acted out collectively rather than individually. Piven and Cloward's major example is the poor people's movement of the 1960s. The National Welfare Rights Organization (NWRO) developed out of the activities of the War on Poverty's neighborhood service centers: groups of African-American welfare recipients meeting in the centers, helping each other, working with the activist workers and professionals, strategizing, and engaging in direct action. Although NWRO attracted civil rights activists, professionals, religious leaders, and middle-class organizers, its core strength and driving energy came from African-American welfare recipients; this was a poor minority women's campaign (Katz 1986:253).

**Stories in the Postmodern Era**

Accounts of protest from below written during the postmodern period tell a different story.

Linda Gordon (1988, 1990), on the basis of her study of family violence in Boston, 1870–1960, says that urban poor mothers were not always victims of social control; they often used social control agencies to defend children's rights, especially against abusive husbands and fathers. Clients were active bargainers in complex negotiations. Of course, in seeking agency help, the women paid a price; they did not necessarily get what they needed but rather what the professionals interpreted as their needs. But the important point is that the actual policies were "the results of contestation, not only between organized political forces but also between individuals at the level of 'social work' encounters" (Gordon 1990:5).

Lucie White (1990) tells the story of Mrs. G., her client, a welfare recipient, in a small North Carolina town. Mrs. G. received a lump sum payment as a result of a personal injury. Her caseworker told her that she could spend the money without any deductions from her welfare check. Later, the welfare department decided that this advice was in error. The lump sum was to be counted against the welfare grant, and thus Mrs. G.

had received overpayments. The department sent her a routine overpayment notice instructing her to come to the department to sign a repayment contract with the county fraud investigator. Mrs. G. was quite upset. White, on the basis of her experience in such matters, advised Mrs. G. that she did not have to attend the meeting or sign the contract. Nevertheless, Mrs. G. did both. It was decided that Mrs. G. could still appeal. White outlined two choices for her. She could claim estoppel on the part of the department; this would require her to challenge her caseworker. Or she could claim "necessities"—overpayments would not be charged if in fact the client spent the money on necessary items. This story would require Mrs. G. to beg for mercy.

At the hearing, Mrs. G., to White's surprise, refused to confront her caseworker. She did describe the necessities that she used the money for, but, without warning, she defiantly said that she spent some of the money for Sunday shoes so that her children could attend church. The county won. On appeal, without explanation, the state reversed and Mrs. G. was not charged with overpayments.

White interprets these events as resistance from below. Why? Even though Mrs. G. knew that her only means of protection was in "speaking female . . . to reflect what she senses that the Other—'the Man'—wanted her to say," nevertheless, Mrs. G. stepped "out of the role of the supplicant. . . . She demanded *meaningful* participation in the hearing and the right to define her needs." White's interpretation: "Although dominant groups may control the *social institutions* that regulate these languages, those groups cannot control the *capacity* of subordinated peoples to speak" (p. 50). Yet, White acknowledges that Mrs. G. remained an impoverished African-American woman on welfare—"poor, dependent, despised" (p. 52).

White concludes by exploring the possibilities of supporting "such fragile moments of dignity." She asks, can we create "post-bureaucratic institution[s]"? "Can we reimagine the economy as a network of face-to-face deliberations, among citizens, about the production and allocation of social wealth?" White is cautious. She warns about "ideological suppositions" in deciding the future and "misguided leaps." For a postmodern, she says, "rather, the relocation of bureaucratized governance in participatory institutions must proceed cautiously, experimentally, guided by local knowledge rather than grand design. . . . [T]he shape of post-bureaucratic institutions will come . . . from the diverse, localized institution-building activities that poor Black single women with children—citizens—undertake for themselves, on their own ground" (pp. 57–58).

Ewick and Silbey (1992) tell a similar story. Millie Simpson

**714    Postmodernism, Protest, and the New Social Movements**

(a pseudonym), a middle-aged African-American woman who worked as a maid, was erroneously charged with a traffic crime. Simpson goes to court; there are the usual bureaucratic mystifications; the public defender shows up too late; she is fined, temporarily loses her license, and is ordered to perform 15 hours of community service. It turns out that the church that was selected (at her suggestion) was, unbeknownst to the court, the church where she was already doing volunteer work. Shortly thereafter, her employer learned of her misfortune. The family lawyer was able to get the case reopened, the misunderstanding was cleared up, the fine was repaid, and the case was dismissed.

Ewick and Silbey are concerned with legal consciousness— the "ways in which the law is experienced and understood by ordinary citizens as they choose to invoke the law, to avoid it, or to resist it" (p. 11). In the postmodern tradition, they argue, legal consciousness is local, contextual, contingent, and contradictory.

In Simpson's story, there is acquiescence, resistance, and contestation. Legal consciousness varies accordingly. During the first period—acquiescence—there is compliance with the state and more or less passive mystification about the process. During the last period—contestation—there is withdrawal; Simpson was barely a subject as elites decided her fate. The authors emphasize the resistance. In arranging for the community service, Simpson "successfully insinuated her life into the space of the law and . . . reversed for a moment the trajectory of power" (p. 26). "Thus, with her ruse, she succeeded, where earlier she had failed, to infiltrate the dominant text" (p. 27).

The authors admit that in one sense not much changed— the laws and the sentencing practices remained intact. Yet, the act of resistance was "not inconsequential." Why? Simpson took "immense pleasure"; she was "triumphant in her private victory won within the cracks of the institution." It is a mistake, say the authors, to dismiss these victories as trivial and without political significance. They still may have "transformative potential," which "may prefigure more formidable and strategic challenges to power" (p. 33).

Austin Sarat (1990) explores the varieties of legal consciousness of the welfare poor. "While the welfare poor are surrounded and entrapped by legal rules as well as by officials and institutions which claim authority to say what the law is and what the rules mean," there are ways in which those at the bottom were able to find spaces and opportunities to resist. Some used legal services lawyers. In going to legal services, some felt "no more in control of their own destiny than when dealing with the welfare bureaucracy." Many suffered additional humiliations and burdens at another public office. But "they went

because they have exhausted other possibilities and were at the
" 'end.' " Consciousness and senses of efficacy varied. Some
pleaded; others tried to " 'work the angles' " or " 'beat the system at its own game' " (p. 373). Nevertheless, "because the
welfare poor are in positions of continuing dependency, they
must engage in an uphill struggle to make their voices heard
and their understandings of right and justice part of the legal
order." They are not "paralyzed"; "they struggle to resist the
official definition of their subjectivity," but they also have "little
hope of success" (pp. 377–79).

All the authors—two decades ago and now—celebrate the
acts of resistance by the most marginalized people in society.
Yet, one cannot help but be struck by the difference in tone.
The authors of the 1960s and 1970s speak of solidarity and
struggle with an optimism reflecting the dreams of that era. In
contrast, Gordon (1988) says, "Most of this book is sad. Most
of the individual stories had bad endings." Gordon and White
(1990) speak vaguely of common concerns of the poor, of women, and of people of color. Sarat (1990) is pessimistic about
the welfare poor; it is an "uphill struggle to make their voices
heard"; they have "little hope of success." And Ewick and
Silbey (1992) only hint that these acts may be important for
social change.

The stories that Genovese, Stack, and Piven and Cloward
choose to tell are about groups, communities, and movements.
While considerable attention is paid to context and individual
self-identity, the stories are about *collective* identity and *collective*
strength.

In contrast, the heroes of the contemporary authors are isolated. Interactions are hierarchical rather than lateral. This is
ironic, and puzzling. Pragmatism interpreted the importance of
language and identity as a *collective* act; it rejected methodological individualism. Emancipatory democracy is based on communication. Radin (1991), in her interpretation of feminism
and pragmatism, emphasizes the "shared group experience."
Yet, in the stories told by the contemporary authors, commonalities are in the minds of the narrator only.

Nancy Fraser (1989), who questions the rejection of large
narratives, tells different stories, stories of groups and social
movements. Her examples include the political struggle to
transform wife beating into wife battery, the resistance of black
pregnant teenagers to white, therapeutic family planning counseling norms, and the welfare rights campaigns of the 1960s.
Fraser emphasizes collective efforts. The feminist insistence on
the new term "wife battery" invoked not only the criminal law
but also the claim that this was a systemic, pervasive public
problem reflecting societal female subordination. Activists engaged in consciousness raising, establishing shelters, and coun-

seling; bonds were forged, contributing to political identification (Fraser 1989:213–14).

In the family planning counseling example, the African-Americans were able to resist what they perceived as white, middle-class norms. They resented the therapeutic approach, the social worker's seemingly nondirectiveness and moral neutrality, and what they regarded as her overly personal questions when they could not ask her questions in return. They were able to resist through open challenges, humor, and "quasi-deliberately" misunderstanding the social worker's questions. The African-American women were able to use those aspects of a health service program that they considered appropriate to their needs as they defined them while avoiding other aspects. The black teenage response is not so much a rejection of conventional morality as an example of adaptation to the stress of extreme poverty. Without meaningful prospects of marriage or steady employment until they reach their mid-20s, young African-American women have their children early, use mothers and other kin for child care while many complete their education, and then they enter the labor market when child care costs are much reduced. Much as Stack (1974) had found in the 1970s, they opted for an "alternative life course" (Testa 1992).

**Stories from Minority Scholars**

Among contemporary African-American stories of struggle, two of the most prominent are Derrick Bell's chronicles (1987, 1992) and Patricia Williams's *Alchemy of Race and Rights* (1991).

Bell tells a series of metaphorical tales covering major legal-political battles for civil rights (1987). He starts with the framing of the Constitution and proceeds through several issues of the civil rights campaigns (e.g., voting rights, education, reparations, employment) and moves into issues facing the black community (male-female relationships, self-help). He questions the use of conventional legal strategies. In some respects, Bell reflects postmodernism: his exposition is narrative. He uses allegory, fantasy, methaphor, and irony, rather than legal abstraction. He presents multiple paths to the truth. He is an astute observer of the varieties of white cultural and political power as manifested in the subtle, informal processes of everyday life. He emphasizes the experience of the law rather than doctrine. The malleability of doctrine and ideology is a key element in Bell's interpretation of black history as well as in his program for the future. In urging the Third Way, in which blacks continue to seek a just society despite their repeated setbacks, he makes the telling point that just as blacks were able to use the Christian Bible for their salvation, so, too, they eventually will be able to use the values in the Constitution for their continued struggle.

However, while these are postmodern elements, Bell's stories in his first collection *And We Are not Saved* are about the *collective* struggles of blacks. While recognizing differences among blacks, his emphasis is on the commonality of black identity. Bell continues these themes in his latest collection, *Faces at the Bottom of the Well* (1992) with even more allegorical stories. Despite the failures and defeats, the tone is optimistic. Again, the emphasis is on commonalities—history, identity, struggle, and hope for freedom. In the search for Afrolantica, "black people . . . did not rely on one leader or seek deliverance through one organization. Rather, they worked together in communities" (p. 44). The failed search did not lead to despair. Instead, "the miracle of Afrolantica was replaced by a greater miracle. Blacks discovered that they themselves actually possessed the qualities of liberation they had hoped to realize on their new homeland. . . . Feeling this was . . . a liberation— not of place, but of mind" (pp. 45–46). Bell's concluding chapter, called "Beyond Despair," calls for "an unremitting struggle that leaves no room for giving up. We are all part of that history, and it is still unfolding" (p. 200).

Patricia Williams (1991) also uses postmodern techniques—narrative, the multiple uses of language, the layering juxtaposition of tales in irony, paradox, parable, and contradiction—"that forces the reader both to participate in the construction of meaning and to be conscious of that process" (pp. 7–8). Her themes are power relations, domination and submission, deference. Her stories, though, are about being black, being black in contemporary America. Significantly, Williams begins with her great-great-grandmother—her sale as an 11-year-old, her rape by the slave owner (a "self-centered child molester") and the birth of Williams's great-grandmother, and continues with the careers of her children and their children as they struggled to survive. Her stories often start with individuals—for example, a white teenage clerk in a fancy retail store who, after looking Williams over, refused to press the buzzer to admit her, and her feelings of alienation as a black female law professor—but they are about the common experience of racism—blacks humiliated in stores, in restaurants, by the police, physically attacked and murdered by whites when they dare to venture into white neighborhoods (Howard Beach), the stereotypical justification for violence (Bernard Goetz, Eleanor Bumpers), the suffering of racial indignities of everyday life. Williams believes that skin color so profoundly affects people's lives that generalizations are valid.

The other minority scholars—Dalton (1987), Delgado et al. (1985), Lawrence (1987, 1990), Matsuda (1989), Torres

718    **Postmodernism, Protest, and the New Social Movements**

(1991), and many others—also use narrative to illustrate the pain of discrimination. But they emphasize the themes found in the authors predating the postmodern era—commonality, the struggle to resist and survive as a people, the bonds of solidarity. While the stories themselves are often about individuals suffering from specific acts of discrimination, their most significant point is to deny individualism. Acts of racism are not individual aberrations; rather, they are manifestations of our society's major structural characteristics. The victims of racism are more than individuals. As Dalton says, they are inextricably rooted in their communities, which are sources of oppression and a source of strength.

Regina Austin develops these themes in a remarkable statement on the centrality of community for African-Americans (1992a, 1992b). Without romanticizing, Austin looks at the varieties and range of black lawbreaking not only in terms of struggle and resistance ("oppressed people need to know when to obey the law and when to ignore it"; 1992b:1799) but also in terms of solidarity and identification. She urges the creation of bridges between straight people and street people to foster an understanding of an "appropriate balance of the modes and mores of each" (ibid.). Austin talks about the sharing of benefits and earnings from the informal economy in much the same terms as did Stack (1974)—both in economic and social importance. Austin's politics of identification is founded on the understanding that "blacks from different classes have talents and strengths to contribute to 'a revitalized black community' " and requires "a legal agenda tied to a politics of identification" that would "make the legal system more sensitive to the social connection that links 'the community' and its lawbreakers and affects black assessments of black criminality" (p. 1815). Austin recognizes the great variety of blacks and that differences of gender, class, geography, and politics keep blacks apart. Nevertheless, "to be a part of a real black community requires that one go Home every once in a while and interact with the folks" (p. 1817).

In trying to define what a critical social agenda would like, Fraser and Nicholson (1988) and the minority scholars look to larger stories both to describe the plight of oppressed peoples and to frame an agenda for struggle. This brings us to the new social movements. They, too, emphasize solidarity and the common struggle. At the same time, they are infused with the values of postmodern politics—antifoundationalism, antimaterialism, antibureaucracy, antistatism. They reject bourgeois hegemony. They emphasize grass-roots democracy, experimentation, and social change at the local level. To what extent are the new social movements vehicles for transformative politics?

## III. The New Social Movements

The origins of the "new" social movements are said to arise from the student movement of the 1960s, which spread from Berkeley to Paris and Berlin. It marked the beginning of a broader wave of social protest—environmental, feminist, gay and lesbian, consumer, antinuclear, and peacegroups—and change that affected virtually all advanced industrial democracies (Tarrow 1989).

The new social movements can be considered the archetypical form of postmodern politics—grass roots, protest from below, solidarity, collective identity, affective processes—all in the struggle against the established order outside the "normal" channels (A. Scott 1990; Tarrow 1989).

These movements advocate a new form of citizen politics based on direct action, participatory decisionmaking, decentralized structures, and opposition to bureaucracy. They advocate greater attention to the cultural and quality-of-life issues rather than material well-being. They advocate greater opportunities to participate in the decisions affecting one's life, whether through direct democracy or increased reliance on self-help groups and cooperative styles of social organization. They appeal to value- and issue-based cleavages instead of group-based or interest group issues. While the new movements envision a better society for all, there is no inclination to withdraw into a spiritual refuge. They are determined to fight for a better world here. While the humanistic component is not new—there have been repeated criticisms of modernization—the willingness to challenge the existing order in practical ways claiming to represent the interests of the population at large sets them apart from historical predecessors (Dalton et al. 1990; Offe 1990).

On the other hand, there is no grandiose plan for a better society. These movements critique modernity's institutionalized patterns of rationality. They reject both the liberal and the Marxist traditions. Their concept of the future society is largely negatively defined. They know what they do not want, but they are unsure and inconsistent about what they want in operational detail. While they oppose modernity, they do not advocate a return to an idealized version of traditional institutions such as the family, religious values, or the nation. They are clearly different from "reactionary" forms of social protest; instead, they represent a universal critique of modernity and modernization by challenging institutionalized patterns of technical, economic, political, and cultural rationality. These movements are also distinguished from both the liberal and Marxist traditions because of their lack of a comprehensive vision or institutional theory for a new society. The "enemy" is

720    **Postmodernism, Protest, and the New Social Movements**

not a social class but rather a kind of dominant rationality. Because of the absence of strict doctrine, these movements have been called "post-ideological" which is probably the most significant reason why they deserve to be called "new" (Kuechler & Dalton 1990; Offe 1990).[9]

Although these "post-ideological" characteristics are distinctive, Claus Offe (1990) believes that they make it extremely difficult for new social movements to develop the necessary institutional forms to achieve their demands. Because of the lack of a comprehensive vision or institutional design for a new society, the new social movements are incapable of using the language of the liberal and the socialist traditions. The scattered set of issues, complaints, and demands do not constitute a unified force or vision. Rather than a social class or other essentialist category, the "enemy" is a more abstract kind of dominant rationality. There is no notion of a universal class which, by establishing its own institutions, would perform a civilizing and liberating mission for society. There is no comprehensive design of a just order as the necessary and desirable outcome of revolutionary or reformist change. Under such conditions, the absence of a basic and global "alternative" is not just a matter of the failure of intellectual imagination and political vision;, it is, rather, a result of substantive difficulties that do not easily lead to feasible and attractive transformative strategies.

Drawing on the experience of the Green Party in Germany, Offe (1990) describes the dilemmas that social movements face when the initial burst of enthusiasm begins to fade. The use of the political institutions of liberal representative democracy appeared rational. In 1989, the pragmatists gained control and led the Greens into a formal coalition with the Social Democrats in Berlin. Despite a great many conditions—all of which were quickly abandoned—designed to make the Green parliamentary members unlike regular members—all of which were quickly abandoned—Green members quickly and effectively substituted all the essential elements of the parliamentary discourse for much of the discourse of anti-institutional movement politics and gradually abandoned their original promise to be a party of a "new type." While it is claimed that the Greens are the only movement party that has gained a "significant success," they have not produced any significant restructuring of German politics. Rather, the requirements of coalition politics have resulted in splits within the Greens of suicidal proportions (pp. 248–49).

Offe's point is that the transformation of the movement happened because of the deliberate rejection of a global revo-

---

[9] There is a dispute about whether these social movements are "new" or how "new" they are (A. Scott 1990; Tarrow 1990).

lutionary critique. There was no vision of alternative relations of production or political authority. In these circumstances, accommodation with the political institutions of liberal democracy appears pragmatically attractive because there hardly seems anything else. Faced with these dilemmas, movements often act in uneasy coalitions with traditional parties. The outcome is often, at best, reform—partial, disappointing, incremental (Tarrow 1990:267–68).

Carl Boggs (1986) offers a similar analysis concerning the "new populism" in the United States. The focus of these movements is on the local level—neighborhoods, local communities, local governments—to begin the process of popular involvement in the workplace, the community, and the political system. The populists today consider themselves the heirs of the 1960s. But rather than continuing the traditional struggle of labor and capital, they anticipate social change through a broad citizens' movement—a grass-roots revolt—opposing elite domination. Such a movement would fill the void left by the erosion of corporate liberalism and the marginalization of the Marxist left.

New social movements have won important local victories. As Boggs (1986) tells us, in Santa Monica, California, a broad-based tenants' organization, SMRR, elected the mayor and the majority of the city council. In addition to rent control, SMRR favored "human-scale" development in a city long dominated by conservative, development interests. To encourage and maintain grass-roots democracy, SMRR proposed a network of neighborhood councils. In its initial year, there was a great deal of enthusiasm and a flurry of reforms. The city council did enact and implement a radical rent-control law, imposed limits on high-rise developments and condominium conversion, and set up a task force to propose a variety of projects, including setting up neighborhood councils. But none of these projects materialized because, beyond the issue of tenants' rights, the new populist agenda lacked coherence. Instead of a comprehensive theory or program, there were only visionary statements. Once the rent-control struggle was won, popular interest faded, forward motion slowed, and within three years, SMRR, including the mayor, lost power.

Boggs attributes the decline of the Santa Monica populists to the failure to resolve three dilemmas of democratic reform: (1) politics, (2) the bureaucracy, and (3) the workplace. There is a disjuncture between the populists' view of postmodern issues and their theory of structural reform. The new populists see the full range of power and domination—in the economy, the community, and the family as well as the state—and therefore correctly conclude that all these structures must be democratized, but they lack strategies for pursuing these goals. Thus far, populists have only engaged in traditional politics—courting elites, building alliances, and working with or around bureaucracies. Instead of seeking to undermine the existing institutions, the populists collaborate. Access and influence inevitably mean integration rather than opposition (Boggs 1986:148).

Similar dilemmas apply to the bureaucracy and the workplace. In the absence of concrete democratic alternatives, the promise of nonbureaucratic social arrangements remains unfilled. In the absence of alternatives to the control of wage labor by capital, cooperatives and worker-owned firms will always be marginal. There is nothing to distinguish the present-day community-based efforts from those that have either failed in the past or have been coopted. So far, the new populists not only have not offered an alternative politics, but because they participate in traditional pluralists rules, they might actually contribute to the status quo (ibid., p. 153).

In Boggs's opinion, the Santa Monica experience (as well as other examples he discusses) demonstrates that "economic democracy" and "citizen empowerment" require more than social engineering and legislative reform; rather, to transform society, what is needed are reconstituted beliefs, values, and lifestyles. It is not enough merely to challenge bourgeois hegemony; the Left must create a counter- or alternative hegemony; otherwise, there will always be assimilation and cooptation. He is contemptuous of a popular version of the new populism "neither left nor right." The use of this "meaningless slogan" avoids the issues of capital accumulation and political power and "looks to an illusory solution attached to the limited reality of small-scale communities." The new populism seeks to avoid the dilemmas international issues pose by pursuing an essentially localist strategy. But even local power cannot be confronted without a comprehensive political and economic plan.

## IV. Conclusion

The contemporary stories are not happy. Yet, it may be too early to tell. This century is ending in a period of great uncertainty. Since the past is still very much a part of us, efforts at significant social change are bound to be fragile and often doomed. The bonds of liberal capitalism, the state, racism, and patriarchy will not be brushed aside quickly.

In addition, it is in the nature of transitions that the future is cloudy. It is not clear where society is going, which directions will emerge. Postmodernists are the first to admit that future can hold despotism as well as freedom. There seem to be very strong countermovements—ecology, feminism, perhaps peace.

On the other hand, the course of American racism, homophobia, and now worldwide ethnic killing is, to say the least, sobering.

But do the problems of postmodernism go deeper? Is postmodern politics a reliable guide for transformative politics?

Both Offe (1990) and Boggs (1986) argue that the dilemmas of the new social movements stem from the core beliefs of antistatism, antibureaucracy, and antipower as well as their rejection of large-scale social theories. Yet, these beliefs are regarded as fundamental to the postmodern project. Ernesto Laclau and Chantal Mouffe—considered by many to be among the more prominent of the postmodern political theorists (Thomas 1991)—reject the possibility that a coherent politics can be based either on class or social movements (Laclau & Mouffe 1985). They reject capitalism because of the inherent coercive relations between capital and labor. They reject socialism on the grounds that it is essentially teleological. Instead, there are varieties of social conflicts, none more valid than any other; there is no way to predetermine the outcome of these struggles (A. Scott 1990). Consider Rosenau's (1992:144) description of "affirmative post-modernists" (as compared to "skeptical post-modernists"):

> They . . . agree on several politically relevant dimensions: a rejection of modern science, a questioning of the modern idea of progress, a refusal to affiliate with any traditional, institutionalized political movements that have what they consider a "totalizing ideology" and an abandonment of logocentric foundational projects with comprehensive solutions—be they liberal, centrist, or conservative. . . . They are "post-proletarian, post-industrial, post-socialist, post-Marxist, and post distributional."

Laclau and Mouffe's notion of "radical, plural democracy," like Habermas's (1987) ideal speech situation, is purely formal; it says nothing about the positive outcomes of the historical struggle. For Laclau and Mouffe, this vagueness is precisely the attraction (A. Scott 1990). Instead, they propose "discourse theory." But discourse theory is not really theory. Rather, it is a method or process for raising questions and criticizing the presumptions of theory. It is a "kind of anti-theory theory" (A. Scott 1990:103–5; Rosenau 1992:176).

Discourse theory brings us to the starting point—the importance of deconstruction to postmodern politics. Allan Hutchinson (1988:288), in his book on deconstruction politics, states the point well: Language is an act of power, a form of social action. "To acquire and exercise a language is to engage in the most profound of political acts; to name the world is to control it." It is through democratic dialogue that the powerless become engaged. Democratic dialogue denies closure.

### 724    Postmodernism, Protest, and the New Social Movements

Thus, "democracy is the appropriate institutional complement to deconstruction." Just as deconstruction subverts the oppressive culture of rationality, democracy is "antithetical to traditional styles of political theory and practice" (p. 290). The two go together.

Postmodern politics is the politics of discourse. The actors are detached from institutional constraints. Anti-institutionalism is a necessary condition of postmodern political theory. However, without a positive theory of institutions, postmodernism cannot come to grips with institutionally based power. And that, according to Offe and Boggs, is the more fundamental problem.

Consider again the stories of protest from below and the new social movements. What do they tell us about the postmodern account of struggle and the production of knowledge? The contemporary stories are about *individuals*, in the most marginalized spaces, engaging in very small acts of defiance, and, for the most part, very little if anything happens. The authors, at best, are extremely reluctant to draw common connections, to talk about the possibilities of collective action in any concrete manner, or even to suggest middle-level reforms, let alone reforms at a more societal level. The contemporary stories are stories of resistance, but they are also stories of despair (Rosenau 1992:11). When we turn to the new social movements, we find the Greens riven and the Santa Monica coalition defunct.

What accounts, then, for the difference between the stories written today and those of two decades ago? Why the attraction of discourse theory or deconstruction politics?

It is always hazardous to try to "account" for the emergence of large, cultural influences, but let me suggest two reasons. One is the collapse of European socialism, and the other is the intellectual impasse of modernity.

Space does not permit a detailed discussion, but consider three examples. In Sweden, social democracy presented a viable alternative to neoliberalism—a high standard of living, a liberal community, and an unemployment rate of less than 2%. But this was a corporatist state—the antithesis of postmodernism: top-down, bureaucratic, technical, rational, planned. The Swedish way is now being abandoned, by the Social Democrats as well as the conservatives, in favor of liberal capitalism (Pontusson in press). "The age of collectivism is at an end now," says the new Swedish prime minister (Fisher 1992).

Another example, of course, is France. The right turn by the Socialists in the early 1980s is familiar. Recently, in a desperate effort to save the Socialist party, French President Mitterand appointed as prime minister a lifelong Socialist, who as finance minister enjoyed such enormous respect in the financial community that the Paris Bourse jumped (Riding 1992).

Then, there is England. Despite Labour's right turn, its continental model of social democracy was obsolete. For the first time since the French Revolution there is no plausible social vision on the left (Jenkins 1992). In the United States, there is Bill Clinton and, for a moment, Ross Perot.

In short, since the late 1970s, the Western alternative vision of society—whether socialist or social welfare corporatist—has disappeared, leaving the field to liberal capitalism.

The connection between the collapse of the Left and the attraction of deconstruction politics came to mind when I read Susan Handelman's arresting book, *The Slayers of Moses: The Emergence of Rabbinic Interpretation in Modern Literary Theory* (1982). Her argument is that the theory and practice of postmodern literary theory has "striking and profound *structural* affinities" with the Rabbinic interpretive tradition of the Talmud (p. xv; emphasis original). Although the Jewish concentration on the Torah had a long development, starting with the destruction of the First Temple (586 B.C.), it became coextensive with Judaism after the destruction of the Second Temple, when the Jewish state ceased to exist in antiquity and Judaism was no longer a national religion in any physical sense. "After 135, [The Torah's] rule became complete because there was nothing else left" (Johnson 1987:147).

One doesn't want to press the analogy too far, but it is curious that the rise of deconstruction, as a broad cultural movement, coincided with the death of Marx and the rise of Thatcher and Reagan. Is there a parallel in the turn to the text?[10]

The analogy breaks down because Rabbinic Judaism, even though interpreting the text, does have a coherent vision, which brings me to my second suggestion—the intellectual impasse of modernity.

Anthony Giddens (1990) argues that the rise of antifounda-

---

[10] Writes Handelman (1982:39): "[A]ll aspects of existence can be seen as ramifications of and connected to the Torah. Nothing is allowed to be 'irrelevant' or outside its scope. (As Derrida or Barthes would say: 'There is nothing outside the Text.')." Cf. "The Rabbis' interpretation subtly takes primacy over the text in a way unprecedented in the history of religion: human interpretation becomes divine" (p. 42).

Handelman says further (p. 49):

> The text [of the Torah] which gives rise to the interpretation is so intertwined with the interpretation that one cannot really separate the description of the process, the rules which govern the process, from the process itself. . . . There is, then, no ultimate outside point of view. The text continues to develop each time it is studied, with each new interpretation, for the interpretation is an uncovering of what was latent in the text, and thus only an extension of it; the text is a self-regenerating process.

For a different account of the rise of deconstruction, see Post 1992 and perhaps Pecora 1992.

tionalism is not postmodernism but actually the fulfillment of modernity. The distinguishing epistemological characteristic of modernity is reflexivity. All knowledge claims are, in principle, revisable. Reason is no longer certain. Doubt has been institutionalized. Modernity is endlessly open. There is no stable social world to know. We are left with questions where once there appeared to be answers. Yet, modernity has not brought us peace; the 20th century is the century of war. We have lost our belief in "progress." We have lost our faith in knowledge.

Reflexivity is the hallmark of postmodernism. Postmodern intellectuals and academics focus on language. They believe in the inherent power of language—"to name the world is to control it," they say. But at the same time, language is inherently malleable. How can you control the world if your construction is unstable?

The struggle is about power and politics. Yet, the postmodernists' conception of language sets up the opposition between discourse and action. We are warned against "ideological suppositions" and "misguided leaps." "Post-modernism," says Rosenau, "questions causality, determinism, egalitarianism, humanism, liberal democracy, necessity, objectivity, rationality, responsibility, and truth. . . . [It] makes any belief in the idea of progress or faith in the future seem questionable" (1992:ix, 5). Reflexivity becomes disabling.

The results of deconstruction politics are serious. Postmodernism celebrates its lack of global vision. The postmodernists defend their position with the claim, "But there *are* no Grand Narratives." However, the opposition is not playing that game. It has belief systems, meta-narratives that allow theories of power, of action.

When we look around, everyone else is operating *as if* there were Grand Narratives. In the West, we see the ideological and political sweep of liberal capitalism. Much of the world adheres to religious fundamentalism. Major economic powers are communal, authoritarian societies. We see the rise of ethnic nationalism.

Without going into the details of the causes of these changes, I do want to mention two seemingly inevitable consequences. In Western Europe and the United States, a permanent large class of unemployed and only marginally employed citizens has developed. This has particularly serious consequences for the young, for women, for the disabled, for those of color, and for other ethnics who are considered strangers. People who cannot establish a meaningful connection to the labor market not only suffer from grinding poverty but are also excluded from the community (Dahrendorf 1988). Nevertheless, this development is met with equanimity—the "price one has to pay" in a world market. I regard this as a major tragedy. These are the marginalized people.

What is the response of the new social movements? To quote Rosenau:

> Post-modern social movements are not interested in speaking for the working class, which they consider reactionary or obsolete. The politics of redistribution is not part of their program. Nor do they struggle for the social benefits that were central to the old left, such as welfare or unemployment insurance. Such assistance, these post-modernists contend, just creates problems. They look to new forms of politics that go beyond emancipation because the "enemies," if they exist at all, are no longer the bourgeoisie or the boss so much as the bureaucracy, centralized government, and "democratically" elected representatives. (Rosenau 1992:146; citations omitted)[11]

The second consequence is institutionalized or structural racism. The Rodney King verdict and the Los Angeles riots only exposed what has been endemic for centuries, as the critical race scholars have reminded us. Yet, the individualistic Grand Narrative of liberal capitalism continues to mask the institutionalized basis of racism.

It seems to me that if postmodernism is to seriously challenge the ideological hegemony of liberal capitalism, it must come up with an alternative vision, a vision of the economy and of the polity that will complement its vision of community. Allan Hutchinson calls his postmodern book *Dwelling on the Threshold* (1988). That concedes the field.

James Scott (1990), in his book on protest from below, starts with an Ethiopian proverb: "When the great lord passes, the wise peasant bows deeply and silently farts." Progressive forces need trumpets, not farts. They have to act *as if* the walls will come tumbling down. Postmoderns are willing to *believe* in the humane side of the Enlightenment. Whether they admit it or not, this is a meta-narrative—a construction of human nature that transcends context.[12] They now must believe in a

---

[11] The one major exception is Roberto Unger (1987), who sets forth a comprehensive set of policies in *Politics: A Work in Constructive Social Theory*. What is curious— but also proves my point—is that with the exception of a few Critical Legal Studies scholars, this work of Unger is virtually ignored—not even cited, let alone seriously discussed—by the major scholars of postmodern political theory.

[12] The "distinctive appeal of American pragmatism . . . is its unashamedly moral emphasis and its unequivocally ameliorative impulse; . . . [it is motivated] by a moral faith in the possibility that goodness and greatness will emerge in the future owing to human creative powers" through the application of a critical intelligence" (West 1989:4, 5). West quotes (p. 227) Raymond Williams (1966):

> The real key, to the modern separation of tragedy from "mere suffering," is the separation of ethical control and, more critically, human agency, from our understanding of social and political life. . . . To see no ethical content or human agency in such events, or to say that we cannot connect them with general meanings, and especially with permanent and universal meanings, is

728     **Postmodernism, Protest, and the New Social Movements**

political economy. The enemies of the poor and those who suffer discrimination do not rely on localized knowledge in minirationalities.

## References

Aronowitz, Stanley (1988) "Postmodernism and Politics," in Ross 1988.
Austin, Regina (1992a) "Black Women, Sisterhood, and the Difference/Deviance Divide," 26 *New England Law Rev.* 877.
—— (1992b) " 'The Black Community,' Its Lawbreakers, and a Politics of Identification," 65 *Southern California Law Rev.* 1769.
Baker, Lynn (1991) " 'Just Do It': Pragmatism and Progressive Social Change," in Brint & Weaver 1991:99–120.
Bell, Derrick (1987) *And We Are not Saved: The Elusive Quest for Racial Justice.* New York: Basic Books.
—— (1992) *Faces at the Bottom of the Well: The Permanence of Racism.* New York: Basic Books.
Boggs, Carl (1986) *Social Movements and Political Power: Emerging Forms of Radicalism in the West.* Philadelphia: Temple Univ. Press.
Boyle, James (1985) "Modernist Social Theory: Roberto Unger's Passion" (Book Review), 98 *Harvard Law Rev.* 1066.
—— (1991) "Is Subjectivity Possible? The Postmodern Subject in Legal Theory," 62 *Univ. of Colorado Law Rev.* 489.
Brint, Michael, & William Weaver, eds. (1991) *Pragmatism in Law & Society.* Boulder, CO: Westview Press.
Crenshaw, Kimberlé (1989) "Demarginalizing the Intersection of Race and Sex: A Black Feminist Critique of Antidiscrimination Doctrine, Feminist Theory and Antiracist Politics," 1989 *Univ. of Chicago Legal Forum* 139.
Dahrendorf, Ralph (1988) *The Modern Social Conflict.* New York: Weidenfeld & Nicolson.
Dalton, Harlon (1987) "The Clouded Prism," 22 *Harvard Civil Rights–Civil Liberties Law Rev.* 435.
Dalton, Russell J., & Manfred Kuechler, eds. (1990) *Challenging the Political Order: New Social and Political Movements in Western Democracies.* Oxford: Polity Press.
Dalton, Russell, Manfred Kuechler, & Wilhelm Burkin (1990) "The Challenge of New Movements," in Dalton & Kuechler 1990:3–20.
Delgado, Richard, Chris Dunn, Pamela Brown, Helena Lee & David Hubbert (1985) "Fairness and Formality: Minimizing the Risk of Prejudice in Alternative Dispute Resolution," 1985 *Wisconsin Law Rev.* 1359.
Deutsche, R. (1991) "Boys Town," 9 *Society & Space* 5.
Ewick, Patricia, & Susan Silbey (1992) "Conformity, Contestation, and Resistance: An Account of Legal Consciousness," 26 *New England Law Rev.* 73.
Fish, Stanley (1991) "Almost Pragmatism: The Jurisprudence of Richard Posner, Richard Rorty, and Ronald Dworkin," in Brint & Weaver 1991:47–83.
Fisher, Marc (1992) "Sweden's Socialist Utopia Gets a Conservative Jolt," *Washington Post*, p. A13 (30 May).
Fraser, Nancy (1989) *Unruly Practices: Power, Discourse, and Gender in Contemporary Social Theory.* Minneapolis: Univ. of Minnesota Press.
—— (1990) "Struggle over Needs: Outline of a Socialist-Feminist Critical Theory of Late-Capitalist Political Cultures," in Gordon 1990a.

to admit a strange and particular bankruptcy, which no rhetoric of tragedy can finally hide.

Fraser, Nancy, & Linda Nicholson (1988) "Social Criticism without Philosophy: An Encounter between Feminism and Postmodernism," in Ross 1988.
Fuss, Diana (1989) " 'Race' under 'Erasure'? Poststructuralist Afro-American Literary Theory," ch. 5 in *Essentially Speaking*. New York: Routledge.
Genovese, Eugene (1972) *Roll, Jordan, Roll: The World the Slaves Made*. New York: Vintage.
Giddens, Anthony (1990) *The Consequences of Modernity*. Stanford, CA: Stanford Univ. Press.
Gordon, Linda (1988) *Heroes of Their Own Lives: The Politics and History of Family Violence, Boston, 1880–1960*. New York: Viking.
———, ed. (1990a) *Women, the State, and Welfare*. Madison: Univ. of Wisconsin Press.
——— (1990b) "Family Violence, Feminism, and Social Control," in Gordon 1990a.
Grey, Thomas (1989) "Holmes and Legal Pragmatism," 41 *Stanford Law Rev.* 787.
Grossberg, Lawrence (1988) "Putting the Pop Back into Postmodernism," in Ross 1988.
Habermas, Jurgen (1984) *The Theory of Communicative Action:* Vol. 2, *Lifeworld and Systems: A Critique of Functionalist Reason*, trans. T. McCarthy. Boston: Beacon Press.
Handelman, Susan (1982) *The Slayers of Moses: The Emergence of Rabbinic Interpretation in Modern Literary Theory*. Albany: State Univ. of New York Press.
Harvey, David (1989) *The Conditions of Postmodernity*. Cambridge, MA: Blackwell.
Hassan, Ihab (1987) *The Postmodern Turn: Essays in Postmodern Theory and Culture*. Columbus: Ohio State Press.
Hunt, Alan (1990) "Rights and Social Movements: Counter-hegemonic Strategies," 17 *J. of Law & Society* 309.
Hutchinson, Allan C. (1988) *Dwelling on the Threshold*. Toronto: Carswell.
——— (1989) Book Review: "The Three 'Rs': Reading/Rorty/Radically," 103 *Harvard Law Rev.* 555.
Jenkins, Peter (1992) "Goodbye to All That," *New York Review of Books*, pp. 16–17 (14 May).
Johnson, Paul (1987) *A History of the Jews*. New York: Harper & Row.
Kaplan, E. Ann, ed. (1988) *Postmodernism and Its Discontents* New York: Verso.
Katz, Michael (1986) *In the Shadow of the Poorhouse*. New York: Basic Books.
Kuechler, Manfred, & Russell Dalton (1990) "New Social Movements and the Political Order: Inducing Change for Long-Term Stability?" in Dalton & Kuechler 1990:277–300.
Laclau, Ernesto (1988) "Politics and the Limits of Modernity," in Ross 1988.
——— (1990) *New Reflections on the Revolution of Our Time*. New York: Verso.
Laclau, Ernesto, & Chantal Mouffe (1985) *Hegemony & Socialist Strategy: Towards a Radical Democratic Politics*. New York: Verso.
Lawrence, Charles R., III (1987) "The Id, the Ego and Equal Protection: Reckoning with Unconscious Racism," 39 *Stanford Law Rev.* 317.
——— (1990) "If He Hollers Let Him Go: Regulating Racist Speech on Campus," 1990 *Duke Law J.* 431.
Luhmann, Niklas (1986) "The Self-Reproduction of Law and Its Limits," in Teubner (1986a).
Matsuda, Mari (1989) "Public Response to Racist Speech: Considering the Victim's Story," 87 *Michigan Law Rev.* 2320.
Menand, Louis (1992) "The Real John Dewey," *New York Rev. of Books*, pp. 50–55 (25 June).
Minow, Martha, & Elizabeth Spelman (1990) "In Context," 63 *Southern California Law Rev.* 1597.

730    **Postmodernism, Protest, and the New Social Movements**

**Mouffe, Chantal** (1988) "Radical Democracy: Modern or Postmodern?" in Ross 1988.

**Norris, Christopher** (1991) *Deconstruction: Theory and Practice.* Rev. ed. New York: Methuen.

**Offe, Claus** (1990) "Reflections on the Institutional Self-Transformation of Movement Politics: A Tentative Stage Model," in Dalton & Kuechler 1990:232–50.

**Oliver, Melvin L.** (1976) Book Review, No. 28 *Telos* 215.

**Pecora, Vincent** (1992) "What Was Deconstruction?" 1 (No. 3) *Contention* 59.

**Piven, Frances, & Richard Cloward** (1977) *Poor People's Movements: Why They Succeed, How They Fail.* New York: Pantheon.

**Pontusson, Jonas** (1992) "At the End of the Third Reich: Swedish Social Democracy in Crisis," 20 *Politics & Society* 305.

**Post, Robert** (1992) "Postmodern Temptations," 4 *Yale J. of Law & the Humanities* 391.

**Putnam, Hilary** (1991) "A Reconsideration of Deweyan Democracy," in Brint & Weaver 1991:217–43.

**Radin, Margaret** (1991) "The Pragmatist and the Feminist," 63 *Southern California Law Rev.* 1699.

**Riding, Alan** (1992) "Mitterrand Names an Old Ally as New French Prime Minister," *New York Times*, p. A6 (3 April).

**Rorty, Richard** (1989) *Contingency, Irony, and Solidarity.* New York: Cambridge Univ. Press.

——— (1992) "What Can You Expect from Anti-foundationalist Philosophers? A Reply to Lynn Baker," 78 *Virginia Law Rev.* 719.

**Rosenau, Pauline** (1992) *Post-Modernism and the Social Sciences.* Princeton, NJ: Princeton Univ. Press.

**Ross, Andrew, ed.** (1988) *Universal Abandon? The Politics of Postmodernism.* Minneapolis: Univ. of Minnesota Press.

**Santos, Boaventura da Sousa** (1991) "The PostModern Transition: Law and Politics," in Sarat & Kearns 1991:79–118.

**Sarat, Austin** (1990) " '. . . The Law Is All Over': Power, Resistance and the Legal Consciousness of the Welfare Poor," 2 *Yale J. of Law & Humanities* 343.

**Sarat, Austin, & Thomas Kearns, eds.** (1991) *The Fate of Law.* Ann Arbor: Univ. of Michigan Press.

**Scott, Alan** (1990) *Ideology and the New Social Movements.* Boston: Unwin Hyman.

**Scott, James** (1990) *Domination and the Arts of Resistance: Hidden Transcripts.* New Haven, CT: Yale Univ. Press.

**Singer, Joseph** (1989) Book Review: "Should Lawyers Care about Philosophy?" 1989 *Duke Law J.* 1752.

——— (1990) "Property and Coercion in Federal Indian Law: The Conflict between Critical and Complacent Pragmatism," 63 *Southern California Law Rev.* 1821.

**Spelman, Elizabeth** (1988) *Inessential Woman: Problems of Exclusion in Feminist Thought.* Boston: Beacon Press.

**Stack, Carol** (1974) *All Our Kin: Strategies for Survival in a Black Community.* New York: Harper Torchbook.

**Tarrow, Sidney** (1989) *Struggle, Politics, and Reform: Collective Action, Social Movements, and Cycles of Protest.* Ithaca, NY: Center for International Studies, Cornell Univ.

——— (1990) "The Phantom at the Opera: Political Parties and Social Movements of the 1960s and 1970s in Italy," in Dalton & Kuechler 1990:251–73.

**Testa, Mark** (1992) "Racial Variation in the Early Life Course of Adolescent

Welfare Mothers," in M. Rosenheim & M. Testa, eds., *Early Parenthood and Coming of Age in the 1990's*. New Brunswick, NJ: Rutgers Univ. Press.

Teubner, Gunther, ed. (1986a) *Dilemmas of Law in the Welfare State*. Berlin: Walter de Gruyter.

—— (1986b) "After Legal Instrumentalism? Strategic Models of Post-regulatory Law," in Teubner 1986a.

Thomas, Richard (1991) "Milton and Mass Culture: Toward a Postmodernist Theory of Tolerance," 62 *Univ. of Colorado Law Rev.* 525.

Torres, Gerald (1991) "Critical Race Theory: The Decline of the Universalist Ideal and the Hope of Plural Justice—Some Observations of an Emerging Phenomenon," 75 *Minnesota Law Rev.* 993.

Unger, Roberto (1987) *Politics: A Work in Constructive Social Theory*. Cambridge: Cambridge Univ. Press.

West, Cornel (1989) *The American Evasion of Philosophy*. Madison: Univ. of Wisconsin Press.

Westbrook, Robert Brett (1991) *John Dewey and American Democracy*. Ithaca, NY: Cornell Univ. Press.

White, Lucie E. (1990) "Subordination, Rhetorical Survival Skills, and Sunday Shoes: Notes on the Hearing of Mrs. G.," 38 *Buffalo Law Rev.* 1.

Wicke, Jennifer (1991) "Postmodern Identity and the Legal Subject," 62 *Univ. of Colorado Law Rev.* 455.

Williams, Patricia (1987) "Alchemical Notes: Reconstructed Ideals from Deconstructed Rights," 22 *Harvard Civil Rights–Civil Liberties Law Rev.* 401.

—— (1991) *The Alchemy of Race and Rights*. Cambridge, MA: Harvard Univ. Press.

Williams, Raymond (1966) *Modern Tragedy*. Stanford, CA: Stanford Univ. Press.

# [18]

# POSTMODERN THOUGHT AND CRIMINOLOGICAL DISCONTENT: NEW METAPHORS FOR UNDERSTANDING VIOLENCE*

MARTIN D. SCHWARTZ
Ohio University

DAVID O. FRIEDRICHS
University of Scranton

*Although postmodern theory has virtually exploded throughout the social sciences, thus far it has only begun to touch criminology. This piece identifies some of the principal themes associated with postmodern thought, reasons for the current interest in it, and its potential relevance for criminology. There are many postmodernisms, but special attention is paid here to the popular models borrowed from literary and linguistic analysis. Violence is used as a concrete example to explore these issues. The postmodern critique is a challenge not only to the philosophical underpinnings of traditional and empirical criminology, but also to the basic premises of both mainstream and progressive social policy responses to criminal violence.*

Frustration with the past and anxiety about the future have recently spawned a prodigious outburst of social science commentary characterized as postmodern (e.g., Bauman, 1991; Crook et al., 1992; Doherty et al., 1992; Rosenau, 1992; B. Smart, 1993; Turner, 1990; Woodiwiss, 1990). Yet criminology generally has not been affected in an important way by postmodern theory. Even critical criminologists, who are increasingly aware of postmodern thought, for the most part have not incorporated it into their writings (Matthews and Young, 1992). In this paper we explore some of the tensions and intersections between postmodernism and criminology. To move from the completely theoretical toward the concrete, we pay special attention to the implications for formulating responses to various forms of violence.

Further, although we argue that postmodern thought has relevance for criminology generally, it is linked most closely to critical criminology and

---

* An earlier version of this paper was presented at the annual meeting of the Society for the Study of Social Problems, held in Pittsburgh in August 1992. We thank Jody Miller, Leon Anderson, Dragan Milovanovic, Robert Shelly, and several anonymous reviewers for their helpful comments on earlier drafts. Research was supported in part by a University of Scranton faculty research grant.

222      SCHWARTZ AND FRIEDRICHS

should be viewed in that context. This perspective arose in the late 1980s as the principal successor to a tradition (never an entirely unified enterprise) often known as radical criminology (Inciardi, 1980; Lynch and Groves, 1989). Critical criminology, an umbrella designation for a series of evolving, emerging perspectives such as feminism, left realism, and peacemaking (Schwartz, 1989), or a metaphor that allows an alternative discourse (Thomas and O'Maolchatha, 1989),[1] is characterized particularly by an argument that it is impossible to separate values from the research agenda, and by a need to advance a progressive agenda favoring disprivileged peoples. Of the various perspectives that make up critical criminology, however, postmodern thought is perhaps the least developed and least understood.

Without losing sight of the many criticisms of postmodernist theory to be made here, including the suggestion that much of what has been published is only a pretentious intellectual fad, we argue that postmodernist theory offers the following for criminology:

(1) A method that can reveal starkly how knowledge is constituted, and can uncover pretensions and contradictions of traditional scholarship in the field. This method further provides an alternative to linear analysis;

(2) A highlighting of the significance of language and signs in the realm of crime and criminal justice;

(3) A source of metaphors and concepts (e.g., "hyperreality") that capture elements of an emerging reality, and the new context and set of conditions in which crime occurs.

## THE POSTMODERNIST CONCEPTUAL CHALLENGE

According to many observers, we have already entered a postmodern world and need to change our social analyses to recognize that fact; that is, to develop a postmodern perspective. Unfortunately, there seems to be an almost infinite number of postmodern perspectives.[2] In any event, it may well be a fundamental contradiction to attempt any coherent definition[3] of

---

     1. Thomas and O'Maolchatha (1989) have provided the most comprehensive and most careful analysis of what a critical criminology is, and who its major proponents are. They should be consulted on any issue on that school of thought.

     2. As a young PhD remarked to us when we noted that he had been studying with some of America's premier postmodernists and asked for his definition of postmodernism, "If you ask a question like that, then you don't understand what postmodernism is." This may sound pompous (and no doubt was), but actually it is a very good answer.

     3. This is not to suggest that such an introduction has not been attempted. A rapidly growing literature provides explications of postmodernist thought. Two of the most helpful are Rosenau (1992) and Sarup (1989). Some other recent books of special relevance to the themes discussed in this piece (there are many more) include Bauman

## POSTMODERN THOUGHT 223

postmodernism if indeed it can be characterized only as a somewhat loose collection of themes and tendencies (Dews, 1987) or as amorphous and politically volatile (Huyssen, 1986). It will not clear up any confusion to point out that the term *postmodern* is commonly used to refer to different things. In particular, it has been invoked to refer to a specific historical period representing a fundamental break with modernity, to post-1960 movements in the fine arts and architecture, and to a collection of contemporary social theories associated most closely with French writers such as Baudrillard and Lyotard (Dowd, 1991; Haldane, 1992; B. Smart, 1993). More recently it has been used to discuss alternatives to a general linear model of social relations, such as chaos theory (Baker, 1993; Young, 1992). All of these dimensions are related but are hardly synonymous.

In this paper we are concerned with interpretations of contemporary society and social theories inspired by French writers including not only Baudrillard and Lyotard, but also Derrida, DeLeuze, Foucault, Barthes, Lacan, Bataille, Kristeva, and others.[4] Rather than attempting to explain the complex work of each of these writers, we will try to identify some common themes inspired by their works which have some relevance to criminology. Later we will focus on a few authors who have brought these themes into criminology and sociolegal thought. We will highlight some of the ideas of Baudrillard, who in sociology has generally been considered one of the most important postmodern theorists.[5] He argues that new technologies have become the guiding forces which shape the world. A number of major breaks have been made from the modern to the postmodern: from representation to simulation, from reproduction to replication, from sex to genetic engineering, and from mind to artificial intelligence (Haraway, 1990). Modernity is based on a belief that people can control objects, nature, and each other; Baudrillard, however, finds that objects now have more and more control over us.

For those who can grope their way through the fog of a semiotic theory

---

(1991), Boyne (1990), Callinicos (1989), Carty (1990), Conner (1989), Denzin (1991), Frug (1992), Gane (1991), Giddens (1990), Harvey (1989), Jameson (1991), Lash (1990), Nicholson (1989), Rose (1991), Seidman and Wagner (1992), B. Smart (1993), Turner (1990), and Woodiwiss (1990).

4. Some scholars would argue that all of these theorists represent the field of poststructuralism, which is only a part of postmodernism (B. Smart, 1993), or that some represent a literary tradition while others represent a social science tradition (Michalowski, 1993). As seen above, however, boundary lines are notoriously difficult to draw.

5. Amazingly, Baudrillard himself has claimed "I have nothing to do with postmodernism," and has attacked or has been hostile to much that is associated with postmodernist thought (Gane, 1991:46). It is appropriately "ironic" that someone who specifically disassociates himself from postmodernism is widely cited as one of its leading exponents.

224          SCHWARTZ AND FRIEDRICHS

based on Saussure, Baudrillard (1983) argues further that commodities in a consumer society acquire use values so that we consume them for their *signs* and statements rather than for the exchange value of their utility. When the simulations constructed for us by technology (mostly television) conceal that the real no longer exists, when we cannot tell the difference between simulations and reality, we have entered *hyperreality*. Our primary experience now is to live and respond to simulations (Glassner, 1992). Accordingly Willis (1991:162) asserts, "We have no way to experience or conceptualize relationships between people except as these are defined by the exchange of commodities."

The postmodern critique challenges the system of values and priorities that sustain contemporary life. It contends that modernity is no longer liberating, but rather has become a force for subjugation, oppression, and repression; this contention applies to social science itself, which is a product of modernity (Graham, 1992). Postmodernists are disillusioned with liberal notions of progress and radical expectations of emancipation (Kellner, 1990). Certainly there are points in favor of this argument. The forces of modernism (e.g., industrialism) have extended and amplified the scope of violence in the world. Even worse, according to the postmodern critique, the major form of response to this violence is through rational organizations (e.g., the court system and the regulatory bureaucracies), with great reliance on specialists and experts. Such a response simply reproduces domination, the critique suggests, in perhaps new but no less pernicious forms.

Criminology has long concerned itself with accurately representing the "truth" about violence, but postmodernist thought challenges any attempt to develop "totalizing" theories that reveal the fundamental "truth" about violence and "explain" it (Currie and Kline, 1991). Truth claims are a "form of terrorism," modern truth is "fragmentary, discontinuous, and changing," theory "conceals, distorts and obfuscates," and human experience must be understood in terms of inconsistencies and contradictions (Rosenau, 1992:78–82). Not only can concepts such as "violence against women" never be understood "coherently"; we should not even attempt such an understanding.

Rather, postmodern thought tends to reverse the approach taken by criminology: violence is regarded as a form of "representation" (Armstrong and Tennenhouse, 1989). From a postmodern perspective, language is used in different historical contexts to "represent" very different acts as violent; thus representation itself is a form of violence because of its capacity to empower some entities and to cast others into subjugation. A challenge for postmodern analysis is to "deconstruct" a modernist rhetoric in which ruling ideas increasingly have become a form of violence in their own right (Michalowski, 1993).

## POSTMODERN THOUGHT     225

Both Foucault and Derrida, as premier figures here, have promoted the notion of a rhetoric of violence, or "the violence of the letter." Foucault's (1977) proposition as advanced in *Discipline and Punish*, that criminology is a discourse/practice which in some sense creates the category of criminality,[6] can be extended to the notion of all violence as a product of discourse: "From . . . an order of language which speaks violence—names certain behaviors as violent, but not others, and constructs objects and subjects of violence, and hence violence as a social fact—it is easy to slide into the reverse notion of a language which, itself, produces violence" (de Lauretis, 1989:240). The purpose of the postmodernist endeavor is to explore how images and meanings pertaining to such violence are constituted, giving privilege to the experience and perspective of the victimized over the victimizers, and attending to the marginal rather than the "representative" cases. Sociological and criminological scholarship, in the postmodernist view, has failed to provide us with a penetrating understanding of how ordinary people experience a postmodern world dominated increasingly by a media-generated "virtual" reality (Denzin, 1986; Pfohl, 1992). The guiding premise here is that a postmodernist approach enables us to comprehend at a more appropriate level our knowledge of a dynamic and complex human environment. It looks to different layers of "texts,"[7] which are interrelated with each other as the locus of social reality, and discounts the notion of some separate, "factual" reality.

Postmodernism addresses some of the enduring fundamental questions—on such matters as causality, determinism, egalitarianism, humanism, liberal democracy, necessity, objectivity and subjectivity, responsibility, rationality, and truth—and rejects most if not all of the conventional epistemological assumptions pertaining to these questions.

Further, one of the most important aspects of postmodernism in social sciences is an attack on all aspects of positivism. Postmodernism calls on empirically oriented social scientists to be reflexive and to confront "the ways in which their own analytical and literary practices encode and conceal value positions that need to be brought to light" (Agger, 1991:121). Conventional positivist sociology is regarded as biased in a fundamental way, and as engaged in a distorted misrepresentation of social reality. Of

---

6. Of the postmodernist thinkers, Foucault, especially his *Discipline and Punish*, probably has attracted the most attention from criminologists. For some recent examples of discussion of Foucault's work for criminological concerns, see Forsythe (1990) on penal practice, V. Bell (1991) on sexual assault, and Hunt (1992) on law. We regard Foucault, however, as a somewhat special case in postmodernist tradition, and we have chosen to focus on other strands as more central to contemporary postmodernist thought.

7. Everything in life can be considered a text in postmodernist thought, including people, events, or even writings.

226              SCHWARTZ AND FRIEDRICHS

course, much of the postmodernist critique simply reiterates a number of existing critiques. Yet it often goes further, taking the critique to its most extreme form. An example of the difference begins with a celebrated critique from within sociology, Mills's (1959) *The Sociological Imagination*. Here Mills not only uses the term *postmodern* but also attacks the emergence of a new form of militarily guided economic rationality. Denzin (1990), however, argues that Mills *imposes* his interpretation on ordinary people, viewing them as "the other," whose lives could be described and explained objectively. Such a virtuoso reading of a social text by a theorist, according to Denzin (1990:13), no longer works in late capitalist, postmodern society because there is no longer a fixed reality that can be mapped by a theory or a method: "Our theoretical signifiers have lost their signified referents. They now refer to other texts, which in turn refer to yet others . . ."

Similarly, although it can be argued that postmodernist interpretations continue along a path already laid out within criminology by social constructionists, the difference lies in the tremendous distance traveled down that path by postmodernists. Social constructionist critiques of science tend to ascribe intentions to those engaged in the practice of science. Woolgar and Pawluch (1985) demonstrate some of the conundrums that arise in relativist (e.g., definitional) approaches to social problems; these approaches, perhaps inevitably, incorporate some objectivist presuppositions or assumptions. Yet Hazelrigg (1986) showed that Woolgar and Pawluch hardly escape the problem of nonobjective interpretation, of which they accuse social constructionists. The important difference, as stated above, is that social constructionist critiques of science tend to ascribe intentions to those engaged in the practice of science, whereas the postmodern critique does not necessarily make such ascriptions. Pfohl (1985:230), responding to Woolgar and Pawluch's criticism of his study of child abuse on precisely these grounds, contends:

> The aim of my work was not *constructive*—to uncover the true story of child abuse and to show how this truth was obscured at earlier points in history. Rather, it was *deconstructive*—to displace the truth of a dominant story about the humanitarian march of therapeutic intervention.

Thus if both social constructionism and postmodern thought embrace a relativistic approach to the interpretation of social phenomena, the latter takes this relativism a step further, focusing not on how meaning is constructed and imposed, but rather, as Pfohl (1985:230) suggests, on the "ceaseless repetition of an indeterminant act of differentiation between colliding practices." In this view *all* knowledge, including that of the social observer, is indeterminant and artifactual.

## POSTMODERN THOUGHT     227

Unfortunately the problem still remains: whether the discourse now being recommended advances our understanding of real people's suffering, or whether it is a form of rhetoric that is becoming increasingly irrelevant (Tong, 1989). Rosenau (1992:111) points out:

> Critics argue that debate over issues such as the existence of an independent reality are of interest only to post-modernists (and other intellectuals) who, insulated from reality, never personally experience the violence, terror, and degradation prevalent in modern society.

Here in a nutshell is one of the strongest reservations about the postmodernist enterprise, one with potent relevance to our concern with violence.[8]

## THE POSTMODERNIST SEMANTIC CHALLENGE

Postmodernist thought is focused intensely on the central role of language in human experience; it is somewhat infamous for its own tendency to invoke a specialized jargon, to invent and discard terms, and to "play" with words (Rosenau, 1992). This postmodernist approach may sensitize us to the importance of language in creating our understanding of violence in all its many guises. Not only can the power of the word be exposed as creating domination; in addition, one means of resistance for those who are oppressed is to recapture the meaning of words (Freire, 1970) or at least to bring "into awareness suppressed, alternate meanings which are subversive to the established order" (Currie and Kline, 1991:15). The problem is that these arguments have not been convincing to many students of violence (to say nothing of its victims). Those who do not agree with postmodernists tend to locate their core experience outside the realm of language, and to find that "word games" tend to trivialize or diminish their view of the nature of violence. Even those postmodernists who are not playing "games" may, at times, be accused of substituting an increasingly abstract study of language for a focus on what modernists might call empirical reality.[9]

Beyond the issue of word play, however, remains the problem of the prose too often preferred by postmodernists. There is no virtue, they

---

8. Critical and Marxist criminologists hardly have been immune from similar attacks. Boehringer et al. (1983), for example, chastised the left for preaching irrelevant theory to the masses, suggesting that "the customary working class victim is understandably unimpressed by heady talk of the socialist millennium and this fact has played into the hands of the Right."

9. Palmer (1990:199), for example, cuts right to the chase: "Much writing that appears under the designer label of poststructuralism/postmodernism is, quite bluntly, *crap*, a kind of academic wordplaying with no possible link to anything but the pseudo-intellectualized ghettoes of the most self-promotionally avant-garde enclaves of that bastion of protectionism, the University." (author's emphasis).

228            SCHWARTZ AND FRIEDRICHS

argue, in catering to the lowest common denominator in understanding. Among the arguments in favor of a dense and abstruse postmodernist style, (1) it is more responsive to the complexity of what is being addressed, or, alternatively, (2) it is a worthy enterprise to be deliberately playful because this enables readers to assume the central and appropriate role of making their own sense of the writing. The idea of the latter is to release the subject from the prison of language, to provide the opportunity to construct or read the text differently as a method of discovery. Thus the question: Is postmodernist work gratuitously obscure, incoherent, and undisciplined? Alternatively, is the obstacle the fact that the rest of us are unable to liberate ourselves from the constraints of interpreting the world in the familiar idiom of rational, contemporary social science? If we reoriented ourselves, would we find modes and styles of understanding that are ultimately more valid and more revealing in a changing, endlessly complex world?

The dilemma is not that it is impossible to decipher what Lacan or Derrida are saying. Rather, it is the difficulty of imagining how a body of work will ever attain broad influence when the "style" of writing—in the work of postmodernism's major figures (Derrida, Lacan, Lyotard, Baudrillard) and those directly influenced by those figures—is so dense and so obscure that it is largely inaccessible to all but the exceptionally dedicated or the masochistic (Michalowski, 1993), and ultimately to the "inner circle" of self-identified students of this body of work (Ritzer, 1990).[10] Although feminist postmodernism can be regarded as a different field, these criticisms apply there as well. Tong (1989:231) recently noted the complaint that "postmodernist feminists apparently delight in their opacity, viewing clarity as one of the seven deadly sins of the phallologocentric order."

All of this raises some basic questions about the nature of intellectual influence and intellectual elitism. A paradox is involved in the postmodernist insistence on not "privileging" the voices of the powerful over the voices of the powerless (including the victims of violence) but then writing and speaking in a form and style largely inaccessible to the powerless as well as to most of those in a position to act on their behalf. At some sociology and criminology conferences it has become common to see panelists at a session on postmodernism carefully excluding from the discussion anyone who is not a member of a clique well versed in a special

---

10.  Even when it is reaching out to broaden its influence, the self-characterization of the project is frequently obscure, as exemplified by Pfohl's introduction in a preconference program (1992:34): "If postmodernism is about anything it is about the materiality of language as a dynamic force in the ritual social transformation of an indeterminate range of human possibilities into the restricted moral economy of a given order of things in time."

vocabulary, delivering papers that criticize modernists for excluding the voices of the oppressed from their narratives.[11] At the same time, the decision by some postmodernists (e.g., Baudrillard, not Foucault) to focus on the mundane (e.g., shopping malls) also may raise questions about their relevance for criminologists, who tend to favor topics such as conflict and violence. The focus by some key postmodernists on surfaces, imagery, and the mundane rather than on violence and suffering can be viewed as representing a highly privileged position. In a world filled with extraordinary starvation and bloodshed on mass scale, and with malnutrition and terrible suffering on the individual scale, finding the superficial images portrayed in suburban shopping malls to be the most relevant objects of study is a powerful statement. This is not to say that these objects are not worthy of study; the question is whether one claims that they are the most important objects of study.

Despite our reservations about such stylistic obfuscation, we are open to the argument that the substance of postmodernist themes can be separated from the style in which they are originally formulated (undoubtedly this possibility is not universally acceptable). Here we will attempt some small conceptualization of this sort.

## POSTMODERNIST POSSIBILITIES FOR UNDERSTANDING VIOLENCE

Postmodernism promotes a greater sensitivity to the "intertextuality" of different forms of violence. This key term refers to the idea that there is a complex and infinite set of interwoven relationships, "an endless conversation between the texts with no prospect of ever arriving at or being halted at an agreed point" (Bauman, 1990:42). Absolute intertextuality assumes that everything is related to everything else. Because postmodernists already have rejected the concept of "truth" waiting to be discovered, the concept of intertextuality redefines knowledge generally not as enquiry, but rather as "conversation" (Graham, 1992).

This is one of the areas in which some fruitful cross-fertilization can take place, perhaps at the margins of both criminology and postmodernism. Here it is possible to raise questions about connections between (for example) corporate violence and violence against women (Messerschmidt, 1993). There has been little investigation of the interaction between corporatism and patriarchism in generating the "texts" of both types of violence. One can ask, however, how male attitudes in the corporate context and in regard to women are related, and whether victimization by corporate violence affects domestic violence. Some recent scholarship (e.g.,

---

11. It has been suggested that a postmodernist bumper sticker might read "Be Tolerant or Die" (Jamieson, 1991:581).

230          SCHWARTZ AND FRIEDRICHS

DeKeseredy and Hinch, 1991; Gerber and Weeks, 1992) suggests how corporations engage in domestic violence against women. "Institutionalized" sexual harassment, on the other hand, may be conceived of as a form of violence against women in a corporate context.

Still, postmodernism refutes any "necessary" reading of the "texts" on violence. It raises the possibility that criminologists impose "truths" on readers in inherently authoritarian ways. It also at least suggests—very controversially—that the pain and suffering associated with violence reside principally in the domination of a particular meaning of such violence. Do policies intended to challenge and "punish" violence "reproduce" the structures of dominance? Do they lead to the diffusion of violence in new forms? Stanley Fish (1989), one of the most prominent theorists of postmodernism, argues that there is no difference between being forced into an act by a gunman and being forced by law.

Indeed, some of this dispute concerns which approach is more elitist. Earlier we discussed whether the *language* of postmodernism fostered elitism. Here we debate whether it is elitist to presume that we, as researchers and theoreticians, can explain something of how the world operates. Are we imposing our categories of explanation on the oppressed peoples of the world with our analyses, silencing their voices in favor of our own? Certainly it is not hard to find examples of this tendency within criminology. Just as one example (not chosen because it is the most problematic), when we label sex trade workers as oppressed, do we simply add another layer to their oppression by labeling them as helpless women when they might not view themselves as such (Assiter, 1993; L. Bell, 1987; Jenness, 1993; McClintock, 1993)?[12] At the same time, the postmodern tendency toward nihilism in denying the legitimacy of all categories (racism, sexism, classism, rape, robbery) can be viewed, despite claims to the contrary, as providing a justification for a lack of political action (Matthews and Young, 1992; Schwartz, 1989). Throughout all of this discussion, the question endures: What should be the primary mission of scholars and academics?[13]

---

12. On the other hand, if we follow Lather's (1991) advice to engage only in fully collaborative research, do we work with women who claim to be victimized by men who read pornography? Or do we collaborate with women who make pornography and claim it is not at all harmful?

13. Twitchell (1992:269) sets forth the basic argument for a return to the principles of modernity:

> The purposeful obscurity of much contemporary criticism may well prove salutary, may well turn us from the ditzy theories du jour we have hidden behind and return us to what the preprofessional generation (roughly 1890 to 1930) of modern academic gatekeepers did: explain the world around them to the world around them.

Even more cynically, Schlag (1991) suggests that the primary influence of

## POSTMODERN THOUGHT          231

A key point is that postmodernism suggests it is more liberating to empower "victims" (an imposed category?) of violence (an imposed category?) to reconstitute the meaning of the violence they experience than to impose on them a critical interpretation (e.g., "knowledge," "truth," "social policy") of this violence (Lather, 1991; Rosenau, 1992). Exposing the ultimate subjectivity of truth is regarded as intrinsically desirable. Of course, critical and progressive sociological and criminological analysis traditionally has championed the oppressed, including at least some classes of victims. The postmodernist criticism, however, is that progressive analysis presumes to speak for the oppressed rather than allowing the oppressed to speak for themselves. Denzin's (1990:4) attack on Mills is that "nowhere in the pages of his work(s) do these little people and their personal troubles speak. Mills speaks for them; or he quotes others who have written about them." At the same time, it is possible that the postmodern approach—which includes the rejection of all metanarratives—is vulnerable to the similar claim (whatever its stated intentions) that it is removed even farther from the reality experienced by ordinary people than is Mills's allegedly patronizing approach.

## POSTMODERN THEORISTS

Criminology may be the social science discipline affected least by postmodernism, although postmodernist thought has been far more conspicuous in the related field of sociolegal scholarship.

Meanwhile, the few criminologists who have embraced postmodern thought have taken quite different approaches. Dragan Milovanovic is the most energetic promoter of this perspective directly within criminology (e.g., 1986, 1988, 1989, 1991, 1992). Stuart Henry and Milovanovic (1991) have developed a "constitutive criminology" to integrate elements of postmodernist thought with a more traditional criminological project. They are concerned especially with highlighting the role of ideology, discursive practices, symbols, and sense data in the production of meaning in the realm of crime. We must understand, in their view, how those who engage in crime, who seek to control it, and who study it "co-produce" its meaning. Henry and Milovanovic argue (1993:1–2):

> Crime then is the power to deny others. It is the ultimate form of reification in which those subject to the power of another suffer the pain of being denied their own humanity, the power to make a difference.

Others have attempted to apply a semiotical analysis to criminological

postmodernist theory among U.S. academics so far has not been to transform political reality, but to get people tenure.

232          SCHWARTZ AND FRIEDRICHS

phenomena. Peter Manning (1988), for example, finds concepts generated from semiotics useful in his analysis of the handling of 911 calls, with special emphasis on the coding of calls and the transmission of their meaning. For Manning (1991), critical semiotics has many potential applications in criminology for the study of signs that are commodified and circulated within the justice system; distorted communication is an important consequence.

Stephen Pfohl offers a different approach—an authentically heretical approach—to the creation of a postmodernist criminology. He would have us abandon not only conventional methodology but also conventional modes of communication among scholars. According to Pfohl, an emerging postmodernist era calls for new, multimedia modes of communication and for the juxtaposition of direct observation, literary allusions, textual analysis, epiphanies, parenthetical observations, visual images, transcriptions of dialogue, and so forth (Pfohl, 1993; Pfohl and Gordon, 1986). For Pfohl, the objective of criminology should be to produce a "different knowledge" that exposes the nature of subjectivity and marginalization in a postmodern (or ultramodern) social environment where power and knowledge generate new forms of violence.

Law and society scholars thus far have been more attentive to postmodernist concerns than have criminologists. Language, signs, and discourse generally play a central role in the legal realm, and some scholars view postmodernist analysis as especially appropriate. Rosemary Coombe (1989), for example, draws on postmodernist thought in her effort to develop a theory of practice that integrates structuralist with subjectivist strands of critical legal theory. She is concerned primarily with exploring how "practices reproduce and change symbolic systems of power and domination and how these same systems construct the agents who realize and transform them" (1989:121). Other sociolegal scholars who have been inspired by postmodernist work include Susan Silbey and colleagues (Ewick and Silbey, 1992; Silbey and Sarat, 1988), who have explored how localized discourses have contributed to general institutional production and to the multiple and contingent character of legal consciousness. Jonathan Simon and colleagues (Feeley and Simon, 1992; Simon, 1988, 1993a, 1993b) have examined the emergence of postmodern modes of social control and penal practice, with a shift from individuals to categories, from society to subdivisions, and from normalization to prevention.

Perhaps the best-known sociolegal scholar to adopt an appreciative attitude toward postmodern theorists' insights is Alan Hunt (1990, 1991, 1992, 1993), although at the same time he argues that this critique goes too far. Hunt regards as valuable the postmodernist challenge to the rationalist legacy of the Enlightenment in legal and criminological scholarship, but also considers it one-dimensional and overstated. He views the postmodernist critique of political metanarratives as provocative but ultimately insensitive to the dependence of local politics on larger institutional arrangements as well as vulnerable to nihilism.

## POSTMODERNISM AND THE SOCIAL POLICY DILEMMA

In the preceding sections we attempted to identify some of the ways in which postmodern thought raises questions about the intellectual underpinnings of an enterprise such as criminology. Here we shift to a different type of concern: Does postmodern thought have anything to contribute to some of the current debates among criminologists on state intervention in response to various forms of violence?

The major social policy question is what to do about violence, assuming we have agreed that violence exists and is not the imposition of a category by criminologists on innocent people. As we have seen, postmodernism asks criminologists to consider whether various calls for the fundamental transformation of social policies, and of the structures that create oppression, are illusionary as to what can be accomplished, or ultimately reproduce an unequal distribution of power.

It is difficult to see whether this question inherently represents the left or supports the status quo (Agger, 1991). At least one strand of postmodernism has sunk so deeply into its epistemological relativism that it denies the legitimacy of any political view because any such views necessarily imply a foundational basis (Rosenau, 1992). Radical postmodernists who hold this view may urge withdrawal from political participation on the grounds that the struggle for social change is meaningless and that individual human beings are powerless to influence government and society (Jacoby, 1987; Palmer, 1990).

This withdrawal is not frustrating to the person sitting in a rustic but luxurious lodge on a $2,500 five-day New Age retreat, or at a $375 entrepreneurial seminar on Postfeminist Male Parenting. The survivors of violence, however, and the frontline workers who deal with these survivors, have found it very easy for the past two decades to feel that criminologists, in the evocative Texas phrase, are "all hat and no cattle." These workers and survivors understandably may regard some postmodern thought as an effete mockery of their efforts and their suffering. Certainly some postmodernist theorists have a strong political agenda, as contradictory as this sounds (see Lather, 1991 for an example). As Malcolm Bradbury (1988:4) points out, however, earlier theorists were strong on plight and anguish, but altogether too much postmodernism, "in keeping with the times, is clean absurdism or cool philosophy; it is laid back, requires no weighty black gear, and goes very well with Perrier water and skiing."

## THREE CONCRETE EXAMPLES

### RESPONDING TO VIOLENCE AGAINST WOMEN

The problem of whether to attempt reform by engaging the state has been debated most heavily within feminist theory, especially as it involves the problem of battered women. Many feminist authors and criminologists, for example, believe that it is essential for the state to step in and deal with men who commit violence against women by arresting them and sending them to prison for long terms (e.g., Box-Grainger, 1986; Edwards, 1989; Gregory, 1986). Many feminist theorists have argued that to work with the criminal justice system is to risk being coopted by it (C. Smart, 1989), but some analysts believe that the risk of not using the state is more serious than the risk of using it (Dobash and Dobash, 1992). Far more than in most countries, the U.S. battered women's movement has succeeded in making changes in criminal justice system practice. Police departments across North America have moved to a pro-arrest or mandatory arrest policy, and quite a broad variety of other changes such as protection orders, streamlined prosecution, and increased use of jail are being implemented widely (Hirschel et al., 1992), even though there is little or no "objective" evidence that these policies will have the desired effect (Sherman, 1992).

On the other hand, many feminist theorists have argued for an emancipatory agenda that incorporates postmodernist thought with a praxis (e.g., Lather, 1991). This agenda would include allowing women to define what is best for themselves, the ways in which they want help, and what they think will help them. Such an empowering of women may have some theoretical advantages, but at times (such as in battering) it may simultaneously be fairly meaningless. This position may assume a degree of agency that battered women lack when they are living in frightful circumstances with all of their energies focused on getting out alive and protecting their children (Horley, 1991). It is admirable to be antihegemonic, but we may need to take some time out from congratulating ourselves to wonder how much responsibility we are placing on women in crisis to solve their own problems.

Thus there is a dilemma in assessing the value of postmodern analysis. Postmodern thought at least can help us appreciate both the limitations and the dangers involved in state intervention. This appreciation, however, provides an unsatisfactory basis for attending to the extraordinary vulnerability and powerlessness of many abused women. We are persuaded much more strongly by authors such as Dobash and Dobash

(1992), who argue that an appreciation of these dangers mainly should be put to use in a modernist project to improve the interventionist role of the state in relation to women's struggles.

## RESPONDING TO CORPORATE CRIME

The question of how to respond to corporate violence presents criminologists with some conundrums. Our understanding of violence has an important political component, and violence has implicit and explicit political consequences (Friedrichs, 1981). Corporate violence—e.g., polluting the environment, dangerous working conditions, unsafe products—is primarily a consequence (with the specific harm unintended) of efforts to enhance corporate profit making; yet it may be far more pervasive and more harmful than conventional forms of violence. The purely radical strain of critical criminology obviously views corporate violence as an absolutely inevitable feature of a modern capitalist society, which cannot be obliterated or even diminished significantly without a revolutionary, structural transformation of the political economy (Lynch and Groves, 1989). Furthermore, the state is viewed as an important source of violence, and is connected closely with corporations in some of the most substantial forms of violence. In this view, state-based reform efforts directed at corporate violence are regarded largely as a means of enhancing the legitimacy of the political economy without substantially reducing corporate violence.

Most criminologists, however (including critical criminologists), concede that revolution is hardly imminent in the United States or other developed Western nations. Even most critical criminologists do not regard revolution as the necessary solution to oppressive social conditions. As a parallel to the feminist response, some criminologists favor strong state intervention against corporate violence (e.g., Pearce and Tombs, 1992; Snider, 1990); others favor alternative tactics that avoid reliance on the state and emphasize community-rooted solutions (e.g., Pepinsky and Jesilow, 1984). All camps, however, are likely to be united in skepticism toward a postmodern perspective that at least implicitly grants the victims of corporate violence—citizens, workers, and customers—the prerogative of assigning it their own meaning. The problem of "agency" may be even more difficult in this area than with battered women because victims of corporate violence often are not even aware of their victimization in the short run.

Some unfulfilled promise for future collaboration at the margins of criminology and postmodernism would seem to exist in the development of many new forms of crime, or "techno-crimes" (Bequai, 1987), which are emerging in the "age of information." These crimes involve computers, telecommunications, and other aspects of high technology. The analyses

236        SCHWARTZ AND FRIEDRICHS

of postmodern approaches to the understanding of crimes that occur in a symbolic universe, and often in the realm of the "hyperreal," would seem to have some potential for criminology.

ANALYZING "STREET" CRIME

Conventional forms of criminal violence are viewed widely today as becoming more pervasive and more vicious, with ever-younger juveniles involved. Perhaps because of the considerable frustration with the limitations of mainstream approaches to understanding such violence, the publication of Jack Katz's (1988) highly original *Seductions of Crime: Moral and Sensual Attractions in Doing Evil* attracted much attention. Although Katz does not consciously adopt a postmodernist perspective, his approach has distinctive postmodernist elements. Specifically, he draws on the Nietzschean notion of a need to create ourselves within the chaotic void of contemporary existence, and repudiates a positivist approach to science in favor of a reading of multiple "texts." He directs special attention to the centrality of language and symbolism while challenging conventional boundaries between crime and resistance (Ferrell, 1992). Katz takes seriously the texts of popular culture; finally, his approach is at least implicitly consistent with the postmodernist skepticism toward rational policy-making responses to crime. Altogether Katz's approach to understanding conventional criminal violence, with an emphasis on foreground as opposed to background factors, is quite consistent with some basic premises of the postmodern approach, and demonstrates how postmodern ideas could influence criminological theorizing.

Although both Katz and postmodern writers have been criticized severely for neglecting or dismissing background factors relevant to understanding crime, they counterbalance excessively structuralist explanations by attending to how causes of crime are "constructed" or "constituted" by an individual adapting to an unstable, complex social environment. For example, Katz (1991:416) observes that reducing the availability of guns might reduce the number of fatalities from crimes of passion,

> [b]ut guns remain symbols that are embraced with uniquely profound passions in America. The key research question about guns and American violence is not how much or whether removing guns will reduce crime, but why guns have acquired such strong moral and sensual meanings in the United States.

## CONCLUSION: POSTMODERNISM AND POLICY

Here we have concerned ourselves partially with the concrete example of violence as an important criminological concern. Drawing insights from postmodernist thought to contribute to the development of policy responses to violence is a difficult proposition. The more extreme version of postmodernism questions the possibility of changing society; it compels us to consider whether the commonplace calls for reform (e.g., regulating and controlling corporations) are a self-indulgent fantasy and illusion, and largely meaningless. This is not the call, more familiar in Marxist literature (e.g., Collins, 1982; Lynch and Groves, 1989), to ignore reform in favor of revolution; if anything, the postmodernist skepticism applies even more fully to calls for revolutionary transformation (e.g., Fish, 1989). We can only engage in personal, local efforts of "resistance." Postmodernism also challenges faith in "expertise" and rational organizations, and calls for a shift of focus to the ordinary, "local," daily experience of violence rather than its broad and large-scale dimensions. Postmodernism challenges tendencies to produce categories, and at least implicitly rejects conflating very different forms or dimensions of violence in order to advance broad propositions.

Thus postmodernism does not provide any practical guidance on policy (Dews, 1987; Matthews and Young, 1992). At most it offers a basis for exposing possible pretenses and illusions in the pursuit of a just policy. This theorizing can be defended as deeply political in that it destroys hegemonic discourses and creates a space to construct a new politics (Michalowski, 1993). Further, at least one major strand of postmodernist thought seems to promote empowerment of victims, enabling them to engage more fully in a process of reconstituting the meaning of violence. Yet at the same time, others seem to echo the romantic early days of radical criminology in regarding terrorism, violence, and insurrection as laudatory efforts to deny legitimacy to the state (Rosenau, 1992). The victims of terrorism, one presumes, are not the ones who are empowered here. Overall an approach that argues against direct action in favor of semantic groundwork opens itself, at the least, to criticism as idealistic and as utterly insensitive to the direct, concrete experience and needs of victims and survivors. According to Matthews and Young (1992:13) it ultimately becomes "a conservative stance, which is unable to offer any directions for social change."

Still, Baudrillard is correct in many ways about the effect of media imagery. Indeed, for close to 24 years it has been a standard and central theme of criminology that the public's attitude toward crime is shaped by the media. Baudrillard, however, has failed to analyze the idea that the media are a battleground which need not be won automatically by the forces of corporate capitalism. Perhaps the most potent critique of Baudrillard is that his theory depends on a stronger break with modernity than in fact has occurred; he "confuses *tendencies* of contemporary society with a *finalized state* of affairs" (Best, 1989:48; author's emphasis).

There are important implications to the argument that society today

238          SCHWARTZ AND FRIEDRICHS

might be described more accurately as being in a state of modernity while showing signs or tendencies in the direction that Baudrillard describes. It means that although it is possible to create a hyperreality to which most people react, it is also possible (although very difficult) to create a counter-hyperreality. Loseke (1992), for example, describes in detail the process by which women in the battered women's movement have created the image of the "battered woman." This image actually may fit the lived realities of few of the women who show up at the doors of shelter houses, but it dovetails into other U.S. ideologies that we use to choose which victims should be denied or awarded aid. In other words, just as we have constructed the concept of "battered woman" as a wife and mother severely abused, morally pure, and not complicit in her plight, grassroots claims makers rooted firmly in the project of modernity are able to create other definitions and realities. Postmodernists have claimed that this can be done only outside modernity.

Beyond the fact that we are not living in the seamless and completed postmodern society described by Baudrillard, in many ways the current condition of postmodernism *depends* on modernity for its vitality; the attack on modernity is the primary project of postmodernist theory. At the same time, of course, the essential justification of modernity—the opposition to the forces of feudalism—is long dead. Thus Ferraris (1992:25) argues that modernity similarly needs postmodernism: "What could Habermas write without Derrida?"

Postmodernism serves to remind modernity of the reason for modernity's existence. It is not to serve progress in the sense of carrying the technical hyperreality of the postmodern world ever faster and ever closer. It is not to extend domination. The reminder delivered by postmodernism is that "progress" and domination are exactly the ends now being served by modern solutions. The key point of modernity is that it believes in human agency and reason: that we can, through our will and our hard work, change society for the better. Postmodernism has reminded modernity that too often it has failed in this task (Freire and Giroux, 1989); even if it has not failed, "the truth is that a [modernist criminology] has never been fully implemented" (Matthews and Young, 1992).

The various criticisms of postmodernist thought, especially as applied to criminological concerns, inevitably raise the question "Why bother with it at all?" We have been persuaded that exposure to this literature in fact is worthwhile and stimulating. First, it sensitizes us to certain ephemeral, fragmentary, and chaotic emergent tendencies in contemporary society, although we need not accept the claim that contemporary society as a whole is more postmodern than modern. Second, it exposes some of the pretenses of both mainstream and critical forms of criminological analysis, although we need not embrace deconstructive analysis in its totality.

## POSTMODERN THOUGHT 239

Finally, it provides us with some striking concepts (e.g., hyperreality), metaphors, and analytical tools (e.g., semiotics), which at least potentially enable us to achieve a richer understanding of contemporary social and criminological phenomena, although we need not adopt these concepts, metaphors, and analytical tools uncritically.

The task for criminology is to renew a sense of urgency that we can change the direction of the world, and to energize people into working toward that goal. It is impossible in a short paper to specify all of the directions in which we would move to accomplish this goal, but we must read Baudrillard as the parable Charles Dickens found in the Ghost of Christmas Future. If we ignore the postmodernists' warning, our future may be the seamless technological hyperreality that Baudrillard describes.

## REFERENCES

Agger, Ben
   1991   Critical theory, poststructuralism, post-modernism: Their sociological
         relevance. In W. Richard Scott and Judith Blake (eds.), Annual Review
         of Sociology. Palo Alto: Annual Reviews.

Armstrong, Nancy and Leonard Tennenhouse, eds.
   1989   The Violence of Representation: Literature and the History of Violence.
         London: Routledge.

Assiter, Alison
   1993   Essentially sex: A new look. In Alison Assiter and Avedon Carol (eds.),
         Bad Girls and Dirty Pictures: The Challenge to Reclaim Feminism.
         London: Pluto.

Baker, Patrick
   1993   Chaos, order, and sociological theory. Sociological Inquiry 63:123–149.

Baudrillard, Jean
   1983   In the Shadow of the Silent Majorities. New York: Semiotext(e).

Bauman, Zygmunt
   1990   Philosophical affinities of postmodern sociology. Sociological Review
         38:411–444.
   1991   Intimations of Postmodernity. New York: Routledge.

Bell, Laurie
   1987   Good Girls, Bad Girls: Sex Trade Workers and Feminists Face to Face.
         Toronto: Women's Press.

Bell, Vikki
   1991   Beyond the "thorny question": Feminism, Foucault, and the desexualiza-
         tion of rape. International Journal of the Sociology of Law 19:83–100.

Bequai, August
   1987   Techno-Crimes. Lexington, Mass.: Lexington Books.

240        SCHWARTZ AND FRIEDRICHS

Best, Steven
    1989    The commodification of reality and the reality of commodification: Jean
            Baudrillard and post-modernism. Current Perspectives in Social Theory
            9:23–51.

Boehringer, Gill, Dave Brown, Brendan Edgeworth, Russell Hogg, and Ian Ramsey
    1983    "Law and Order" for progressives? An Australian response. Crime and
            Social Justice 19:2–12.

Box-Grainger, Jill
    1986    Sentencing rapists. In Roger Matthews and Jock Young (eds.), Con-
            fronting Crime. Beverly Hills: Sage.

Boyne, Roy
    1990    Foucault and Derrida: The Other Side of Reason. Winchester, Mass.:
            Unwin and Hyman.

Bradbury, Malcolm
    1988    My Strange Quest for Mensonge. London: Penguin.

Callinicos, Alex
    1989    Against Postmodernism: A Marxist Critique. New York: St. Martin's.

Carty, Anthony (ed.)
    1990    Post-Modern Law. Edinburgh: Edinburgh University Press.

Collins, Hugh
    1982    Marxism and Law. Oxford: Clarendon.

Conner, Steven
    1989    Postmodernist Culture: An Introduction to Theories of the Contempo-
            rary. Cambridge, Mass.: Blackwell.

Coombe, Rosemary J.
    1989    Room for maneuver: Toward a theory of practice in critical legal studies.
            Law & Social Inquiry 14:69–121.

Crook, Stephen, Jan Pakulski, and Malcolm Waters
    1992    Postmodernization: Change in Advanced Society. London: Sage.

Currie, Dawn H. and Marlee Kline
    1991    Challenging privilege: Women, knowledge and feminist struggles. Journal
            of Human Justice 2:1–36.

DeKeseredy, Walter S. and Ronald Hinch
    1991    Woman Abuse: Sociological Perspectives. Toronto: Thompson.

Denzin, Norman K.
    1986    Postmodern social theory. Sociological Theory 4:194–204.
    1990    Presidential address on the sociological imagination revisited. Sociological
            Quarterly 31:1–22.
    1991    Images of Postmodern Society: Social Theory and Contemporary Cinema.
            Newbury Park: Sage.

Dews, Peter
    1987    Logic of Disintegration: Poststructuralist Thought and the Claims of
            Critical Theory. New York: Verso.

Dobash, R. Emerson and Russell P. Dobash
    1992    Women, Violence and Social Change. London: Routledge.

# POSTMODERN THOUGHT 241·

Doherty, Joe, Elspeth Graham, and Mo Malek
1992    Postmodernism and the Social Sciences. New York: St. Martin's.

Dowd, James J.
1991    Social psychology in a postmodern age: A discipline without a subject. American Sociologist 22:188–209.

Edwards, Susan S.M.
1989    Policing "Domestic" Violence: Women, the Law and the State. London: Sage.

Ewick, Patricia and Susan Silbey
1992    Conformity, contestation and resistance: An account of legal consciousness. New England Law Review 26:731–749.

Feeley, Malcolm M. and Jonathan Simon
1992    The new penology: Notes on the emerging strategy of corrections and its implications. Criminology 30:449–474.

Ferraris, Maurizio
1992    Postmodernism and the deconstruction of modernism. In Marco Diani (ed.), The Immaterial Society: Design, Culture, and Technology in the Postmodern World. Englewood Cliffs, N.J.: Prentice-Hall.

Ferrell, Jeff
1992    Making sense of crime: A review essay on Jack Katz's Seductions of Crime. Social Justice 19:110–123.

Fish, Stanley
1989    Doing What Comes Naturally: Change, Rhetoric, and the Practice of Theory in Literary and Legal Studies. Durham: Duke University Press.

Forsythe, Bill
1990    Foucault's carceral and Ignatieff's Pentonville-English prisons and the revisionist analysis of control and penality. Policing and Society 1:141–158.

Foucault, Michel
1977    Discipline and Punish: The Birth of the Prison. New York: Pantheon.

Freire, Paulo
1970    Pedagogy of the Oppressed, Myra Bergman Ramos (trans.) New York: Herder and Herder.

Freire, Paulo and Henry A. Giroux
1989    Pedagogy, popular culture, and public life: An introduction. In Henry Giroux, Roger I. Simon, and contributors, Popular Culture, Schooling, and Everyday Life. Granby, Mass.: Bergin and Garvey.

Friedrichs, David O.
1981    Violence and the politics of crime. Social Research 48:135–156.

Frug, Mary Joe
1992    Postmodern Legal Feminism. New York: Routledge.

Gane, Mike
1991    Baudrillard: Critical and Fatal Theory. New York: Routledge.

Gerber, Jurg and Susan L. Weeks
1992    Women as victims of corporate crime: A call for research on a neglected topic. Deviant Behavior 13:325–347.

242          SCHWARTZ AND FRIEDRICHS

Giddens, Anthony
    1990     Consequences of Modernity. Stanford: Stanford University Press.

Glassner Barry
    1992     Bodies: Overcoming the Tyranny of Perfection. Los Angeles: Lowell
             House.

Graham, Elspeth
    1992     Postmodernism and paradox. In Joe Doherty, Elspeth Graham and Mo
             Malek (eds.), Postmodernism and the Social Sciences. New York: St.
             Martin's.

Gregory, Jeanne
    1986     Sex, class and crime: Toward a non-sexist criminology. In Roger
             Matthews and Jock Young (eds.), Confronting Crime. Beverly Hills:
             Sage.

Haldane, John
    1992     Cultural theory, philosophy and the study of human affairs: Hot heads
             and cold feet! In Joe Doherty, Elspeth Graham and Mo Malek (eds.),
             Postmodernism and the Social Sciences. New York: St. Martin's.

Haraway, Donna
    1990     A manifesto for cyborgs: Science, technology, and socialist feminism in
             the 1980s. In Linda J. Nicholson (ed.), Feminism/ Postmodernism. New
             York: Routledge.

Harvey, David
    1989     The Condition of Postmodernity: An Enquiry into the Origins of Cultural
             Change. Cambridge, Mass.: Blackwell.

Hazelrigg, Lawrence
    1986     Is there a choice between "constructionism" and "objectivism"? Social
             Problems 33:510–513.

Henry, Stuart and Dragan Milovanovic
    1991     Constitutive criminology: The maturation of critical theory. Criminology
             29:293–316.
    1993     Back to basics: A postmodern redefinition of crime. The Critical
             Criminologist 5:1–2, 12.

Hirschel, J. David, Ira W. Hutchison, Charles W. Dean, and Anne-Marie Mills
    1992     Review essay on the law enforcement response to spouse abuse: Past,
             present, and future. Justice Quarterly 9:247–283.

Horley, Sandra
    1991     The Charm Syndrome. London: Papermac.

Hunt, Alan
    1990     The big fear: Law confronts postmodernism. McGill Law Journal
             35:507–540.
    1991     Postmodernism and critical criminology. In Brian D. MacLean and
             Dragan Milovanovic (eds.), New Directions in Critical Criminology.
             Vancouver, B.C.: Collective Press.
    1992     Foucault's expulsion of law: Toward a retrieval. Law and Social Inquiry
             17:1–38.
    1993     Explorations in Law and Society: Toward a Constitutive Theory of Law.
             London: Routledge.

# POSTMODERN THOUGHT 243

Huyssen, Andreas
  1986   Mass culture as woman: Modernism's other. In Tania Modleski (ed.), Studies in Entertainment: Critical Approaches to mass Culture. Bloomington: Indiana University Press.

Inciardi, James A. (ed.)
  1980   Radical Criminology: The Coming Crises. Beverly Hills: Sage.

Jacoby, Russell
  1987   The Last Intellectuals: American Culture in the Age of Academe. New York: Basic Books.

Jameson, Fredric
  1991   Postmodernism: Or, The Cultural Logic of Late Capitalism. Durham, N.C.: Duke University Press.

Jamieson, Dale
  1991   The poverty of postmodernist theory. University of Colorado Law Review 62:577–595.

Jenness, Valerie
  1993   Making It Work: The Prostitutes' Rights Movement in Perspective. New York: Aldine De Gruyter.

Katz, Jack
  1988   Seductions of Crime: Moral and Sensual Attractions of Doing Evil. New York: Basic Books.
  1991   Criminals' passions and the progressive's dilemma. In Alan Wolfe (ed.), America at Century's End. Berkeley: University of California Press.

Kellner, Douglas
  1990   The postmodern turn: Positions, problems and prospects. In George Ritzer (ed.), Frontiers of Social Theory: The New Synthesis. New York: Columbia University Press.

Lash, Scott
  1990   Sociology of Postmodernism. New York: Routledge.

Lather, Patti
  1991   Getting Smart. London: Routledge.

Lauretis, Teresa de
  1989   The violence of rhetoric: Considerations on representation and gender. In Nancy Armstrong and Leonard Tennenhouse (eds.), The Violence of Representation: Literature and the History of Violence. London: Routledge.

Loseke, Donileen R.
  1992   The Battered Women and Shelters: The Social Construction of Wife Abuse. Albany: State University of New York Press.

Lynch, Michael J. and W. Byron Groves
  1989   A Primer in Radical Criminology. 2nd ed. New York: Harrow and Heston.

Manning, Peter K.
  1988   Symbolic Communication: Signifying Calls and the Police Response. Cambridge, Mass.: MIT Press.

244        SCHWARTZ AND FRIEDRICHS

1991    Critical Semiotics. In Brian D. MacLean and Dragan Milovanovic (eds.), New Directions in Critical Criminology. Vancouver, B.C.: Collective Press.

Matthews, Roger and Jock Young
1992    Reflections on realism. In Jock Young and Roger Matthews (eds.), Rethinking Criminology: The Realist Debate. London: Sage.

McClintock, Anne
1993    Gonad the barbarian and the Venus flytrap: Portraying the female and male orgasm. In Lynne Segal and Mary McIntosh (eds.), Sex Exposed. New Brunswick: Rutgers University Press.

Messerschmidt, James W.
1993    Masculinities and Crime. Lanham, Md.: Rowman and Littlefield.

Michalowski, Raymond J.
1993    (De)construction, postmodernism, and social problems: Facts, fiction, and fantasies at the "end of history." In James A. Holstein and Gale Miller (eds.), Reconsidering Social Constructionism: Debates in Social Problems Theory. New York: Aldine De Gruyter.

Mills, C. Wright
1959    The Sociological Imagination. New York: Oxford University Press.

Milovanovic, Dragan
1986    Juridico-linguistic communicative markets: Toward a semiotic analysis. Contemporary Crises 10:281–304.
1988    Primer in the Sociology of Law. Albany: Harrow and Heston.
1989    Critical criminology and the challenge of post modernism. The Critical Criminologist 1:9–10, 17.
1991    Images of unity and disunity in the juridic subject and the movement to the peacemaking community. In Harold Pepinsky and Richard Quinney (eds.), Criminology as Peacemaking. Bloomington: Indiana University Press.
1992    Postmodern Law and Disorder: Psychoanalytic Semiotics, Chaos and Juridic Exegeses. Liverpool: Deborah Charles.

Nicholson, Linda (ed.)
1989    Feminism/Postmodernism. New York: Routledge.

Palmer, Bryan D.
1990    Descent into Discourse: The Reification of Language and the Writing of Social History. Philadelphia: Temple University Press.

Pearce, Frank and Steve Tombs
1992    Realism and corporate crime. In Roger Matthews and Jock Young (eds.), Issues in Realist Criminology. London: Sage.

Pepinsky, Harold E. and Paul Jesilow
1984    Myths That Cause Crime. Cabin John, Md.: Seven Locks Press.

Pfohl, Stephen
1985    Toward a sociological deconstruction of social problems. Social Problems 32:228–231.
1992    Postmodernity as a social problem: Race, class, gender and the new social order. Preliminary program: Annual meeting of the Society for the Study of Social Problems.

1993 Twilight of the parasites: Ultramodern capital and the new world order. Social Problems 40:125–151.

Pfohl, Stephen and Avery Gordon
1986 Criminological displacements: A sociological deconstruction. Social Problems 33:94–113.

Ritzer, George
1990 Frontiers of Social Theory: The New Syntheses. New York: Columbia University Press.

Rose, Margaret
1991 The Post-Modern and the Post-Industrial. Cambridge: Cambridge University Press.

Rosenau, Pauline Marie
1992 Post-Modernism and the Social Sciences: Insights, Inroads, and Intrusions. Princeton: Princeton University Press.

Sarup, Madan
1989 An Introductory Guide to Post-Structuralism and Postmodernism. Athens: University of Georgia Press.

Schlag, Pierre
1991 Introduction: Postmodernism and law: A symposium. University of Colorado Law Review 62:439–454.

Schwartz, Martin D.
1989 The undercutting edge in critical criminology. The Critical Criminologist 1:1–5.

Seidman, Steven and David Wagner (eds.)
1992 Postmodernism and Social Theory. Cambridge, Mass.: Blackwell.

Sherman, Lawrence W.
1992 Policing Domestic Violence. New York: Free Press.

Silbey, Susan and Austin Sarat
1988 Dispute processing in law and legal scholarship: From institutional critique to a reconstruction of the juridical subject. Denver Law Review 66:437–498.

Simon, Jonathan
1988 The ideological effect of actuarial practices. Law & Society Review 22:771–800.
1993a From confinement to waste management: The post-modernization of social control. Focus on Law Studies 8:4, 6–7.
1993b Poor Discipline: Parole and the Social Control of the Underclass, 1890–1990. Chicago: University of Chicago Press.

Smart, Barry
1993 Postmodernity. London: Routledge.

Smart, Carol
1989 Feminism and the Power of Law. London: Routledge.

Snider, Laureen
1990 Cooperative Models and Corporate Crime: Panacea or Cop-Out? Crime and Delinquency 36:373–390.

246          SCHWARTZ AND FRIEDRICHS

Thomas, Jim and Aogan O'Maolchatha
     1989     Reassessing the critical metaphor: An optimistic revisionist view. Justice Quarterly 6:143–172.

Tong, Rosemary
     1989     Feminist Thought. Boulder: Westview.

Turner, Bryan S. (ed.)
     1990     Theories of Modernity and Postmodernity. Newbury Park: Sage.

Twitchell, James B.
     1992     Carnival Culture: The Trashing of Taste in America. New York: Columbia University Press.

Willis, Susan
     1991     A Primer for Daily Life. London: Routledge.

Woodiwiss, Anthony
     1990     Social Theory after Postmodernism: Rethinking Production, Law and Class. Winchester, Mass.: Unwin and Hyman.

Woolgar, Steve and Dorothy Pawluch
     1985     Ontological gerrymandering: The anatomy of social problems explanations. Social Problems 32:214–227.

Young, T.R.
     1992     Chaos theory and human agency: Humanist sociology in a postmodern era. Humanity & Society 16:441–460.

Martin D. Schwartz is chair of the Department of Sociology and Anthropology at Ohio University, and a former president of the Association for Humanist Sociology. The author of some 50 research articles, chapters, and edited works, he has published mainly in the area of violence against women. Currently he is interested in the intersection of criminology with culture, and is working on a text in criminology and a book on male peer support for violence against women.

David O. Friedrichs is Professor of Sociology and Criminal Justice at the University of Scranton, and a former editor of the *Legal Studies Forum*. He has published some 50 articles and essays on such topics as legitimation of legal order, radical criminology, victimology, violence, and narrative jurisprudence. Currently he is working on a book on white-collar crime.

# Name Index

Abel, Richard 199, 200 , 401
Abraham, F. 33, 54, 59, 60, 75
Abraham, R. 33
Abramson, Leslie 428
Abu-Lughod, Janet 401
Aczel, A. xxii
Adler, Freda 433
Adler, M.J. 168, 190, 198
Adorno, Theodor W. 43
Agger, Ben 105, 483, 491
Aguinis, H. 255
A-Khavari, A. 336, 339
Albonetti, Celesta A. 279
Alfini, James J. 195
Altheide, David 427, 428
Althusser, L. 37
Amin, Samir 396, 397
Anaximander 348
Anderson, Benedict 395
Appadurai, Arjun 363
Arato, R. 248
Armstrong, Lucy 320
Armstrong, Nancy 482
Armstrong, T. 259
Aronowitz, Stanley 447
Arrigo, Bruce A. xiii, xvi, xvii, xxi, xxii, 27–52,
        54, 79, 87, 97–138, 174, 247, 254, 255,
        257, 426
Artaud, Antonin 109
Arthurs, H.W. 195
Ashe, Marie 110
Assiter, Alison 488
Auerbach, Jerold S. 195
Austin, James 273–5
Austin, Regina 464
Austin, Roy L. 287
Austin, Thomas L. 283, 287, 288, 294
Axford, Barry 397

Baack, D. xx, 73
Bacon, Francis 172, 224, 226
Bahro, R. 336
Baker, Patrick 54, 126, 481

Balbus, Isaac C. 382
Balkin, J.M. 67, 104, 105, 114, 118, 296
Bannister, Shelley 7, 87
Barak, Gregg 18, 43, 86, 102, 114, 115, 423–39
Baratta, Alessandro 414
Barber, B. 246, 260
Barbier, E. 336
Barde, J. 336
Barnett, H. 339–42, 346
Barr, S. 82
Barthes, Roland xi, xvii, 32, 41, 97, 98, 99–100
        passim, 109, 117, 122, 124, 125, 254, 481
Baskin, Deborah R. 200
Bataille, Georges 481
Bates Doob, Christopher 287
Baudrillard, Jean xiii, xvi, xvii, 76, 97, 98, 101–2
        passim, 111, 118, 120, 481, 482, 486,
        487, 495–7
Bauman, Zygmunt 205, 317, 330, 392, 396, 399,
        402, 403, 408, 414, 479, 487
Beach, Howard 463
Beccaria, Cesare 347
Beck, Ulrich 205, 341, 398
Becker, Howard 425
Becker, Peter 347
Beirne, P. 336, 339
Bell, Derrick 462, 463
Bell, L. 488
Bell, Vicki 107
Benson, R.W. 30, 39, 42
Benton, Ted 342–4, 346
Bentz, Malhotra 34
Bequai, August 493
Berger, J. 44
Bergson, H. xxii
Berman, Art 100
Berman, Marshall 370
Bernard, T. 44
Berry, D. 255
Bertramsen, R. 245, 248, 254
Best, Steven 101, 103, 106, 107, 495
Bickle, Gayle S. 290
Bittner, Egon 369

Black, Donald J. 13
Blair, Robert A. 195
Bloch, Ernst 391, 394
Blumberg, Abraham S. 274, 281
Blumer, Herbert 227
Blumstein, Alfred 282, 424
Bock, E. Wilbur 278
Boggs, Billie 307–14 *passim*
Boggs, Carl 467, 468–70
Bogue, Ronald 111, 112
Bohm, Bob 11, 18, 33, 70
Böhm, Robert M. 200
Bon, Michel 360, 385
Bookchin, M. 337
Bordo, Susan 272
Bosworth, Mary xx, 315–33
Bourdieu, Pierre 8, 13
Box-Graininger, Jill 492
Boyle, James 42, 446, 447
Bracher, Mark 99
Bradbury, Malcolm 491
Brady, J. 255–7, 259
Braithwaite, J. 255
Brannon, L. 255, 256, 260
Brantingham, Pat 169, 172
Brantingham, Paul 169, 172
Bridges, George S. 287, 288
Briggs, J. xv, 33, 56, 57, 74, 176, 177, 185, 237
Brigham, John 14
Brion, D. 33, 34, 110
Brown, L. 34
Buddha 240
Buller, D. 255
Bumiller, Kristin 281, 284
Bumpers, Eleanor 463
Burchell, Graham 203
Burdine, Marje 197, 206
Burgess, E.W. 171
Burgoon, J. 255
Bursik, R.J., Jr. 172, 186
Bush, Robert A. Baruch 197, 198
Butler, Judith 85, 86, 91, 99, 108, 110–3, 115, 120, 121, 123, 270, 323, 410
Butts, J.A. 250
Butz, M. 33, 59

Cain, Maureen 35, 119, 201, 410, 411
Calhoun, Craig 398
Cameron, Jan 196
Caplan, Paul 392

Caputo, John 106
Carlen, Pat 294
Carlson, D. 106
Carnevale, Peter J. 197
Carrière, Kevin 390
Casale, Silvia S.G. 291
Casey, Catherine 205
Casti, J. 73, 78
Castillina, L. 336
Caudill, David 99
Caulfield, Susan 281, 283
Chambliss, William 284, 290
Chamlin, Mitchell 288
Champy, James 378
Chan, Wendy 324
Chancer, Lynn 325
Chase-Dunn, Christopher 363
Chesney-Lind, Meda 12, 35
Child, Julia 376
Chiricos, Theodore 282
Cicourel, Aaron 9, 11
Cislo, A. 59
Cixous, H. xvii,43, 115
Clark, J. 337
Clinton, Bill 471
Cloward, Richard 456, 458, 461
Coates, R. 250
Cobb, Sara 108, 124
Cohen, J. 248
Cohen, Stanley 9, 15, 18, 27, 28, 108, 123, 199, 335, 345, 423
Cohn-Vossen, S. 82
Coleman, James W. 282
Collins, Hugh 495
Collins, R. 44, 65, 119, 124
Colvin, M. 44
Comer, D. 54, 59
Comte, Auguste 224, 226
Conklin, William 110
Cook, Judith A. 272, 294
Cook, Royer F. 195
Cooley, Charles H. 227
Coombe, Rosmary J. 4–6, 280, 490
Corbridge, Stuart 400
Corlett, William 405
Cornell, Drucilla xvi, 28, 35, 41, 99, 106, 108, 109, 111, 112, 114, 115, 122, 123, 290
Cottle, Simon 426–8
Couzens, David H. 106
Cratylus 348

Crawford, Charles 282
Crenshaw, K.W. 63, 65, 119, 120, 121
Cressey, Donald 60, 68–70
Crook, Stephen 479
Crutchfield, Robert D. 288
Cullen, J.B. 73, 123, 253, 255
Culler, Jonathan 100
Cunningham, W.J. 57
Currie, Dawn 35, 101, 482, 485
Cushman, Thomas 374

Dahrendorf, Ralph 472
Dalton, Harlon 454, 455, 463, 465
Dalton, Russell 453, 466
Daly, Kathleen 12, 35, 290
Danzig, Richard 195
Darwin, Charles 42
Davies, J. 338, 339
Davis, Albie 198
Davis, Kathy 268, 270, 272
Davis, Mike 399
Day, D. 59, 73
Dean, Mitchell 203, 204
DeKeseredy, Walter S. 488
DeLanda, M xxi
Deleuze, Gilles xv, xvi, xvii, xviii, xxi, xxii, 33,
    38, 40, 42, 63, 64, 70, 97, 98, 100, 102–4
    *passim*, 111–3, 117, 118, 122, 124, 125,
    141–3, 145–50, 156, 157, 161–4, 340,
    348, 349, 392, 407, 481
Del Frate, A.A. 338
Delgado, R. 247, 248, 251, 456, 463
Del Olmo, Rosa 395
Delorme, André 254
Denzin, Norman K. 483, 484, 489
Derrida, Jaques xiii, xvi, xvii, xxi, xxii, 9, 67,
    97, 98, 104–6 *passim*, 111, 113–5, 117,
    124–6, 173, 227, 408, 445, 446, 455, 481,
    483, 486, 496
Descartes, René 36, 37
Deutsche, R. 445, 446
Devall, B. 336
Dewey, John 448, 449
Dews, P. 38, 41, 481
Dickens, Charles 497
Dillard, J. 255
Dilthey, Wilhelm 227
Dilulio, John 321
Disch, Lisa Jane 267, 268, 272, 295
Dobash, R. Emerson 492

Dobash, Russell P. 492
Doherty, Joe 479
Dolovitch, Sharon 324
Donohue, W. 255
Donzelot, Jaques 203
Donziger, Steven R. 275, 279, 283, 284, 292,
    294, 295
Doom, Ruddy 414
Dor, J. 55
Dowd, James J. 481
Drake, L. 255
Dreyfus, Harold 106, 107
Droysen, Johann Gustav 227
Dunkley, G. 336
Dunn, R. 255
Dupuis, Ann 196
Durkheim, Emile 32, 172
Dworkin, R. 32, 42
Dyer-Witheford, N. xxii

Edwards, Susan M. 336, 339, 492
Einstadter, Werner 15, 30, 114
Einstein, Albert xxiii, 110
Eisenstein, Jacob 278
Eisenstein, Zillah R. 272
Eisler, Riane 54, 235
Elliot, D. 44
Encinoza, Argenis Rieira 395
Engels, Friedrich 370
Ericson, Richard 390
Erskin, Dean 429–31, 435
Espeland, Wendy 289
Etzioni, Amitai 248, 255
Ewick, Patricia 122, 268, 273, 363, 379–1,
    459–61, 490

Fan, K. 82
Fanon, Franz 404
Fantasia, Rick 375, 379
Farganis, Sandra 270, 290
Farnworth, Margaret 114, 284
Farrell, Ronald 277
Featherstone, M. 350
Feeley, Malcolm 316, 330, 490
Feigenbaum, Mitchell 33, 180, 229, 236, 238,
    239
Feld, Barry C. 282
Felson, Marcus 169
Ferraris, Maurizio 496

Ferrell, Jeff 54, 66, 72, 73, 76, 81, 102, 273, 280, 284, 294, 296, 494
Fink, B. 87, 88
Fish, Stanley 391, 488, 495
Fisher, Marc 470
Fisher, Sue 268, 270, 272
Fitzpatrick, Peter 9, 13, 17, 196, 201, 202, 204, 217
Floyd, K. 255
Folberg, Jay 197
Folger, Joseph P. 197, 198
Fonow, Mary Margaret 272, 294
Forker, A. 59, 110
Foucault, Michel xiii, xvi, xvii, xxi, xxii, 9, 11, 17, 39, 41, 97, 98, 106–7 *passim*, 113, 115, 118, 124, 173, 196, 197, 202–5, 209, 210, 212, 213, 217, 227, 251, 253, 257, 258, 345, 347, 349, 403, 407, 455, 481, 483, 487
Fox, James Alan 424, 425
Fraley, T. 428
Frame, M. 57, 64
Frank, Andre Gunder 397
Frank, J. 38
Fraser, Nancy 402, 452, 453, 455, 461, 462, 464
Frazier, Charles E. 278
Frechea, Tara 321
Frechet, M. 82
Freire, R. 46, 99, 111, 126, 256, 259, 485, 496
Freivalds, P. 253
Freud, Sigmund 37, 89, 103, 106, 109
Friedrichs, David O. xxi, 4, 27, 28, 31, 106, 390, 479–504
Fromm, E. xiii
Fuchs, Stephan 106
Fulton, B. 123, 253, 255
Fuss, Diana 453

Galaway, Brian 123, 198, 211
Gane, Michael 101
Gant, F. 338
Garland, David 107, 316, 318, 329, 361
Geis, G. 336, 338, 339
Gelsthorpe, L. 35
Genovese, Eugene 456, 457, 461
Georges-Abeyie, Daniel 122
Gerber, Jurg 488
Gerbino, Anthony 330
Gibbons, Don 114
Giddens, Anthony xv, 5, 6, 32, 205, 363, 471

Gilligan, Carol 35, 246, 258
Gilligan, George 414
Giroux, H. 72, 104, 113, 114, 246, 255, 256, 260 401, 496
Glassner, Barry 482
Gleick, J. 33, 170, 229
Gödel, K. 33, 54, 110
Goertzel, B. 170
Goetz, Bernard 463
Goff, C. 336, 338, 339
Goffman, Erving 7, 10, 213
Goldberg, Stephen B. 197
Goldman, Ronald 433
Goodrich, P. 28, 99
Gordon, Avery 411
Gordon, Linda 458, 461, 490
Gouldner, A. 437
Gottdiener, Mark 102
Gottfredson, M. 32
Gouldner, Alvin 425
Grabosky, P. 338
Grace, Nancy 428
Graham, Elspeth 482, 487
Gramsci, Antonio 437, 455
Grandpre, J. 255
Granon-Lafont, J. 81, 83, 87–9
Grbich, Judith 108
Green, Eric D. 197
Greenberg, David 4, 273
Greenhouse, Carol J. 270
Greenstone, J. 250
Gregersen, H. 54, 66–70
Gregory, Jeanne 492
Grey, Thomas 448–50
Griset, Pamela 279
Groombridge, N. 348
Grossberg, Lawrence 446
Grosz, Elizabeth 108
Groves, W. Byron 480, 493, 495
Gruhl, John 284
Guastello, Stephen 240
Guattari, Felix xv, xvi, xvii, xviii, xxi, xxii, 33, 38, 40, 63, 64, 71, 97, 98, 100, 102–4 *passim*, 117, 118, 122, 124–6, 141–3, 145–50, 156, 157, 161–4, 340, 348–50, 392
Gunningham, N. 338

Habermas, Jürgen 16, 39, 41, 42, 110, 351, 364, 372, 403, 451, 455, 469, 496

Hacker, Andrew 287
Hagan, John 278, 281, 283, 284, 287
Haldane, John 481
Hall, Stuart 397, 423
Halleck, S. 84
Halper, Louise 99
Halsey, Mark xx, 335–55
Hammer, Michael 378
Handelman, Susan 471
Handler, Joel F. xxi, 28, 270, 443–77
Hanmer, T.J. 35
Hannah-Moffat, Kelly 316, 324, 329
Haraway, Donna 481
Hardt, M xxi
Harrington, Christine 13, 200
Harrington, Michael 429
Harris, Angela 119, 120, 123
Harris, C.D. 171
Harris, M.K. 253, 255
Hart, H.L.A. 42
Harvey, David 366, 397, 448
Hassan, Ihab 227
Hayles, N. Katherine 33, 114, 413
Hazelrigg, Lawrence 268, 484
Head, Simon 378
Heaney, Gerald W. 279, 284, 285
Heelas, Paul 399
Hegel, Georg Wilhelm Friedrich xiii, 7, 42, 103,
    111, 112, 224, 226
Heidegger, Martin 106
Heisenberg, Werner 33
Held, B. 85
Held, David 227
Hennessy, Rosemary 266
Henretta, John C. 278
Henry, Stuart xv, xvii, xxii, 4, 7, 8, 13, 17, 30, 40,
    42, 43, 59, 63, 65, 66, 87, 90, 100, 102,
    110, 113–5, 121, 122, 174, 279, 343, 347,
    350–2, 391, 425, 489
Hepworth, Mike 210
Heraclitus 348
Hilbert, D. 82
Hill Collins, Patricia 271
Hiller, W. 255
Hillsman, Sally T. 291
Hinch, Ronald 488
Hirschel, J. David 492
Hirschi, T. 32, 44
Hoebel, A. 38
Hofman, Hans 414

Hofrichter, Richard 200
Hölderlin, Friedrich 349
Holmes, O.W. 38
Homer 348
Hood, C. 316
Hopkins, Terence 396
Horan, Patrick M. 284
Horley, Sandra 492
Hosoda, M. 255
Howe, Adrien 91, 107, 114, 317, 324, 325, 411
Hoyt, H. 171
Huanani Solomon, D. 255
Hübler, A. 187, 240
Hudson, Barbara 316
Hudson, J. 123
Huling, Tracy 275, 295
Humphries, Drew 273, 281
Hunt, Alan 4, 13, 28, 40, 107, 446, 451, 490
Husserl, Edmund 224, 227, 228
Hutchinson, Allan C. 451, 469, 473
Huyssen, Andreas 481

Inciardi, James 390, 480
Inverarity, James M. 282
Irigaray, Luce xvii, 34, 36, 37, 41, 97, 98, 108
    *passim*, 113, 115, 122, 125, 403
Irwin, John 273–5, 283, 294

Jacob, Herbert 278
Jacoby, Russell 491
Jackson, Bernard 15, 87
James, William 448
Jameson, Fredric 398, 403
JanMohamed, A.R. 113
Jefferson, Tony 6, 423
Jenkins, Peter 471
Jenness, Valerie 488
Jesilow, Paul 493
Jessop, Bob 11, 245, 248
Jesus Christ 240
Joe, Karen A. 291
Johnson, Philip 446, 471
Jordan, Michael 80
Joyce, James 89, 109
Jung, Carl xxiii
Jurgens, H. 57
Jurik, Nancy C. 270

Kafka, Franz 103
Kairys, David 105

Kant, Immanuel 224
Kaplan, Caren 413
Kaplan, M. 54
Kaplan, N. 54
Kappeler, Victor E. 274, 275, 281, 282, 294
Katz, Jack 54, 66, 72, 73, 76–8, 81, 84, 86, 258,
     458, 494
Kavoori, A. 428
Keith, Michael 406
Kellner, Douglas 101–3, 106, 107, 482
Kelman, M. 39, 106
Kempf, Kimberly L. 287, 288
Kennedy, David 365, 368
Kevelson, Roberta 119
Keynes, John Maynard 395, 398
Killias, M. 172
King, Martin Luther Jr. 456
King, Rodney 34, 121, 473
Kirby, Kathleen 405
Klare, Karl 13
Kleck, Gary 283
Kline, Marlee 482, 485
Klockars, Carl 4
Knoblauch, C. 255, 256, 260
Knorr-Cetina, Karen 9, 11
Kobrin, S. 170, 171, 180, 182–5, 188
Kohlberg, Lawrence 224, 228
Kolb, Deborah 197, 198
Kosai, Yutaka 369
Kozol, J. 256, 260
Kramer, Ronald 428, 429
Kraybill, Ron 199
Kressel, Kenneth 197
Kristeva, Julia xvi, xvii, xxii, 34, 41, 97, 98,
     109–10 *passim*, 113, 115, 126, 257, 258,
     481
Krohn, M.D. 44
Kruttschnitt, Candace 279
Kuechler, Manfred 466
Kumar, A. 255, 256

Lacan, Jacques xii, xiii, xv, xvi. xvii, xviii, xxi,
     9, 10, 31, 36, 37, 38, 41, 54, 55, 65, 69,
     79–84, 86–91, 97, 98–9 *passim*, 103,
     108, 109, 112, 115, 118, 122–6, 173, 247,
     304–6, 308, 313, 314, 481, 486
Laclau, E. 91, 99, 114, 120, 393, 405, 446, 447,
     450, 469
LaFree, Gary D. 279
Lahey, K. 36

Lance, Lucy Ann 429–31, 435
Lane, P. 348
Langston, Donna 280
Lanier, Mark 114
Laplace, Pierre-Simon 224
Lash, Scott 114, 205, 341, 397
Laswell, Harold D. 365
Lather, Patti 266, 489, 491, 492
Laub, J.H. 168
Lauderdale, Pat 282
Lauretis, Teresa de 483
Lawrence, Charles 120–2, 463
Lawrence, Robert Z. 369
Lecercle, J.J. 39, 40
Lederach, John Paul 199
Lee, J.S. 38, 80
Legendre, Pierre 99
Leifer, R. 59
Leighton, Paul 435, 436
Lem, Stanislaw 114
Leonard, Peter 402
Leopold, Aldo 336, 339, 340
Levin, Jack 425
Levinson, Robert 317
Levinas, E. xvi, xxii
Levitas, Ruth 405
Leviton, S. 250
Lévi-Strauss, Claude 224
Levrant, Sharon 123, 253, 255
Lipietz, A. 254
Lippens, Ronnie xx, 104, 113, 389–421, 403
Liska, Allen E. 44, 288
Litowitz, Douglas 107
Livingston, D. 256
Lizotte, Alan J. 284
Llewllyn, Karl 38, 373
Lloyd, Genevieve 324
Lombroso, Cesare 347
Lorenz, Edward 173, 174, 229
Loseke, Donileen R. 496
Louis XVI 360
Lovaas, Karen 198
Lovibond, Sabina 410
Loye, David 54, 235
Luhmann, Niklas 10, 32, 42, 44, 248, 451
Luke, T. 341
Lyng, S. 54, 72, 76, 102
Lynch, Michael J. 339, 344–6, 480, 493, 495
Lyons, N.P. 35

,yotard, Jean Francois xvii, xxii, 31, 41, 54, 73, 97, 98, 110–11 *passim*, 117, 118, 125, 227, 267, 403, 452, 481, 486

MacKay, Hugh 398
MacKinnon, Catherine 35, 112
MacLean, B. 28, 101
MacMillan, I. 59, 60, 73
Maffesoli, Michel 413
Malcolm X 456
Mallarme, Stephane 109
Mandel, D. 59
Mandelbrot, Benoit 33, 54, 66, 229
Manning, Peter 9, 10, 12, 15, 16, 18, 28, 490
Marie Antoinette 360, 385
Marino, G. 33
Martin, Susan Ehrlich 270
Martinson, Robert 273
Maruno, Shadd 322
Marx, Gary 14
Marx, Karl 7, 41, 81, 89, 101, 102, 106, 226–8, 370, 372, 471
Matsuda, Mari 72, 85, 91, 114, 119–22, 463
Matthews, Roger 196, 201, 202, 479, 488, 495, 496
Matza, D. 54, 59, 60, 62–4, 72, 78, 81, 84, 86
Mauer, Marc 275, 295
Maynard, Mary 294
McCann, Michael W. 383
McClintock, Anne 488
McDermott, M.J. 41
McDowell, D. 338
McKay, H.D. 169, 170, 172, 183–8
McLachlan, N.W. 57
McLaren, P. 112, 256
McRobie, A. 75, 76
Mead, George Herbert 227
Meis, M. 336
Mentschikoff, Soia 373
Merchant, C. 337
Merry, Sally 13, 197
Merton, Robert K. 32
Mertz, Elizabeth 285
Messerschmidt, James W. 487
Messner, Claudius 414
Messner, Steven F. 44, 274
Michael, J. 168, 190
Michalowski, Raymond J. xxi, xxii, 275, 282, 285, 482, 486, 495
Mies, Maria 269, 276

Miethe, Terance D. 282, 283, 287, 288
Miller, Peter 203, 210, 216, 280
Mills, C. Wright 484, 489
Milner, Neal 198
Milovanovic, Dragan xiii, xv, xvi, xvii, xxii, 3–29, 31, 33, 38, 40, 42, 43, 46, 53–138, 170, 174, 247, 254, 255, 279, 343, 347, 350–2, 391, 489
Minow, Martha 269, 277, 450
Mohammed 240
Moi, Toril 110
Montessori, Maria 259
Moore, Charles A. 282, 287, 288
Morris, A. 35
Morrissey, Elizabeth R. 11
Mosco, J. 437
Mouffe, Chantal 91, 99, 112, 120, 393, 404, 405, 410, 446, 447, 450, 469
Mueller, J. 83, 255
Murphy, H. 73
Mugford, S. 54, 66, 72, 73, 76, 78, 81, 84
Murray, Jamie xviii, 141–65
Myers, Laura B. 287–9

Naess, A. 336
Naffine, Ngaire 108, 410, 411
Nardulli, Peter F. 278
Nasio, J.-D. 55, 83, 84
Nassar, J. 427
Negri, A. xxi
Nelken, David 18, 350
Nesler, H. 255
Nettler, G. 32
Newton, Isaac 224
Nichols, B. 427
Nicholson, Linda 266, 271, 452, 453, 455, 464
Nietzsche, Friedrich xiii, xxii, xxiii, 7, 42, 86, 106, 113, 153, 226, 348, 349, 352
Norberry, J. 338
Norris, Christopher 445

Offe, C. 248, 465, 466, 469, 470
Oliva, T. 59, 73
Oliver, Melvin L. 456
O'Malley, P. 54, 66, 72, 73, 76, 78, 81, 84, 316
O'Maolchatha, Aogan 3, 391, 480
Orwell, George 344

Paehlke, R. 345
Palmer, Bryan D. 28, 102, 491

Parenti, Michael 289, 290
Pareto, Vilfredo 224
Park, R.E. 171
Parsons, Talcott 32
Pateman, Carole 324
Pauly, J. 44
Pavlich, George xviii, 108, 110, 124, 125,
    195–21, 350, 352
Pawluch, Dorothy 484
Peak, D. 57, 64
Pearce, Frank 336, 339, 493
Pearson, F.S. 44
Pearson, Michael 275
Peat, F.D. xv, 33, 56, 57, 70, 74, 176, 177, 185,
    237
Pecheux, M. 43
Peitgen, H.O. 57, 70
Peller, G. 39
Pennbaker, J. 255
Penrose, Roger 232
Pepinsky, Harold 18, 43, 174, 493
Pepper, D. 336
Peters, M. 73, 257
Petersilia, Joan 322
Peterson, Ruth D. 290
Perot, Ross 471
Pfohl, Stephen 102, 411, 483, 484, 490
Pickover, C. 66
Pile, Steve 406
Piven, Frances 456, 458, 461
Plumwood, V. 336
Poincaré, Henri xiii, 173, 231, 234
Polkinghorne, Donald 224, 227
Pontusson, Jonas 470
Pope, Carl E. 287
Porter, E. 33
Poster, Mark 101, 102
Postman, Neil 370
Posner, R.A. 32
Potter, Gary W. 274, 281
Pound, R. 38
Price, Mark 125
Prigogine, I. xv, 33, 62, 237
Pruitt, Dean G. 197
Purvis, June 294
Putnam, Hilary 449

Quinney, Richard 18, 43, 110

Rabinow, Paul 106, 107

Radin, Margaret 450, 452, 461
Raeff, Marc 203
Raes, Koen 414
Ragland, E. 89, 90
Ragland-Sullivan, E. 37, 89, 90
Reagan, Ronald 471
Regan, Tom 342
Regnault, F. 83
Reich, Robert 366
Reid, Sue Titus 287
Reiman, Jeffrey H. 281, 282, 284
Reiss, A.J., Jr. 172
Rich, Adrienne 413
Richardson, W. 83
Rickert, M. 227
Riding, Alan 471
Rigakos, George 324
Ritzer, G. 28, 486
Rockstroh, Phil 436
Roehl, Janice A. 195
Rorty, Richard 105, 390
Rose, Nikolas 203, 205, 210, 216, 316, 322
Rosenau, P.A. 28, 223, 268, 269, 445, 469, 470,
    473, 479, 485, 489, 491, 495
Rosenfeld, M. 106, 274
Rossi, Peter 285
Rossi-Landi, F. 81
Rumble, W., Jr. 38
Russell, Katheryn 121, 122
Russell, S. 106

Sack, Fritz 414
Said, Edward 404
Sailer, L. 54, 66–70
Salecl, R. 78, 84, 99, 124
Salem, Richard A. 195
Samp, J. 255
Sampson, R.J. 168, 169
Sander, Frank E.A. 195, 197
Sanders, Clinton R. 273, 280, 284
Santos, Boaventura de Sousa 199, 200, 369, 451
Santos, Michael 321
Sarat, Austin D. 120, 361, 381, 460, 461, 490
Sarup, M. 41, 105
Sassen, Saskia 367
Saupe, D. 57
de Saussure, Ferdinand 173, 227, 228, 482
Savelsberg, J.J. 168, 169
Schehr, Robert C. xvi, xvii, xix, xxi, 97–138,
    245–63

Scheppele, K.L. 106
Schiller, H. 437
Schneider, A. 250
Schroeder, Jeanne xxii, 99
Schuerman, L. 170, 171, 180, 182–5, 188
Schulman, C. 59, 110
Schutz, Alfred 10
Schwartz, Martin D. xx, 3, 27, 28, 31, 72, 106, 390, 479–504
Schwendinger, H. 61
Schwendinger, J. 61
Scott, A. 451, 465, 469
Scott, James 473
Scott, Joan W. 290, 410
Seidman, Steven 281, 290
Seis, M. 336, 339
Sellers, S. 37
Selva, Lance 11, 200
Serres, M. 33, 40
Sessions, G. 336
Shank, G. 339
Shannon, L.W. 186
Shaw, C. 33
Shaw, C.R. 169, 170, 172, 183–8
Shein, Marcia G. 282, 283
Shelton, D. 433
Shepherdson, Charles 120
Sheppard, David I. 195
Sherman, Lawrence W. 492
Shields, Rob 413
Shiva, V. 336
Shonholtz, Raymond 198, 199
Silbey, Susan xx, 120, 122, 197, 268, 273, 359–87, 392, 459–61, 490
Silverman, K. 90
Simmel, Georg 370
Simon, Jonathan 316, 330, 490
Simpson, Edith E. 288
Simpson, Millie 459, 460
Simpson, Nicole Brown 433
Simpson, O.J. 87, 101, 102, 426, 428–34
Sinanoglu, O. 66
Singer, Joseph 450
Singer, Linda 266, 294
Singer, Peter 342
Skogan, W. 171, 180
Skriabine, P. 88, 89
Slaughter, Marty 99
Smale, Stephen 229
Smart, Barry 205, 479, 481

Smart, Carol 28, 35, 36, 272, 410, 411, 492
Smith, C. 54, 59
Snider, Laureen 493
Snyder, H.N. 250
South, Nigel 414
Sparks, Richard 316, 324
Spector, A. 246
Spelman, Elizabeth 450, 452
Spence, Gerry 428
Spinoza xxii, 348
Spivak, G. 108, 111, 112, 123, 125
Spohn, Cassia 284
Stacey, Helen 99
Stack, Carol 456–8, 461, 462, 464
Stambaugh, Phoebe 269
Stanko, Elizabeth 324, 325
Stanley, Christopher 397, 414
Stanton, Steven A. 378
Stengers, Isabelle xv, 33, 63, 237
Stewart, I. 33, 110
Stinchcombe, A. 44
Stretsky, P. 339, 344–6
Strickland, R. 258
Strong, K. 248, 249
Stuart, Henry 3–26
Sudnow, David 9, 277
Sumner, Colin 395, 406
Surette, R. 86
Sutherland, E.H. 168, 282, 340, 342
Swigert, Victoria 277
Sykes, Gresham 321
Szasz, T. 255

Talarico, Susette 287–9
Tambling, Jeremy 209
Tarrow, Sidney 465, 467
Taylor, Alison 197
Taylor, Ian 414
Tedeschi, J. 255
Tennenhouse, Leonard 482
Testa, Mark 462
Teubner, G. 28, 32, 451
Thales 348
Thatcher, Margaret 471
Thom, Rene 73
Thomas Aquinas 223
Thomas, Jim 3, 6, 9, 10, 15, 18, 87, 326, 391, 480
Thomas, Richard 445–7, 469
Thompson, M. 76
Thomsen, J. 245, 248, 254

Thorne, Barrie 270
Thorton, M. 107
Thygesen, Niels 369
Tiefenbrun, Susan 100
Tobias, M. 336
Toch, Hans 322
Tombs, Steve 336, 339, 493
Tong, Rosemary 485, 486
Tonry, M. 172, 273, 279, 282, 290, 291
Torfing, J. 245, 248, 254
Torgerson, D. 345
Torres, Gerald 463
Turner, Bryan S. 210, 479
Turner, Ralph H. 380
Tushnet, M. 105
Tyler, Tom 324

Uelmen, Gerald F. 283
Ullman, E.L. 171
Umbreit, Mark 123, 199, 211, 248, 250
Unger, R. 46, 106, 123
Unnever, James D. 278
Urry, John 114, 397

Van Hoorebeeck, Bart 413, 414
Van Ness, D. 248, 249
Van Susteren, Greta 428
van Swaaningen, René 414
Vappereau, J.-M. 83
Velan, Y. 100
Vico, Giambattista 227
Von Hirsch, Andrew 273

Wagner, D. 44
Wahrhaftig, Paul 196
Walker, Jeffery T. xviii, 167–93
Walker, Samuel 273
Wallerstein, Immanuel 396, 397
Walters, R. 336
Ward, Steven 106
Weber, Max 32, 42, 370
Weeks, J. 82
Weeks, Susan L. 488
Weiner, N.A. 44
Weiss, Bob 14
Welch, Susan 284

Wertheimer, Max 224
West, Candace 270
West, Cornel 287, 448–50
Westbrook, Robert Brett 449
Wexler, P. 258, 259
White, Hayden V. 363
White, Lucie E. 458, 461
White, R. 336, 339
Wicke, Jennifer 445
Wijeyeratne, Roshan D. 106
Williams, Christopher R. xix, 303–14, 336, 338, 339
Williams, Joan 104, 106, 110, 114, 119, 120, 184
Williams, Patricia 453–5, 462, 463
Williamson, J. 90
Willis, Paul 11, 102
Willis, Susan 482
Windelband, Wilhelm 227
Winick, Bruce 116
Winter, Steven L. 270
Wittgenstein, L. 31, 228, 444
Wolf, F.A. 33
Wolinksky, S.H. 33
Wonders, Nancy A. xix, 265–302
Woodhall, Winifred 107
Woodiwiss, Anthony 370, 479
Woolgar, Steve 484
Wozniak, J. 123, 253, 255
Wright, B. 247
Wright, Martin 198, 211
Wundt, Wilhelm 227

Yngvesson, Barbara 13, 91
Yorke, James 229
Young, Jock 414, 423, 479, 488, 495, 496
Young, Alison 361
Young, Iris Marion 401, 403, 410
Young, T.R. xviii, 33, 56, 59, 99, 104, 107, 110, 112, 115, 169, 170, 173, 174, 180, 223–42, 254, 289, 290, 350, 481

Zaitzow, Barbara 326
Zatz, Marjorie S. 278, 283, 284
Zeeman, E.C. 73, 75, 90
Zehr, Howard 199, 211, 248
Zimmerman, Don H. 270